D1519079

Chrysler LH-series Automotive Repair Manual

by Mike Stubblefield and John H Haynes

Member of the Guild of Motoring Writers

Models covered:

Chrysler New Yorker, LHS and Concorde,
Dodge Intrepid and Eagle Vision
1993 through 1997

(3A2 - 25025)

ABCDE
FGHIJ
KLMNO
PQ

Haynes Publishing Group
Sparkford Nr Yeovil
Somerset BA22 7JJ England

Haynes North America, Inc
861 Lawrence Drive
Newbury Park
California 91320 USA

Acknowledgements

Technical writers who contributed to this project include Rob Maddox, Jay Storer and Larry Warren.

A book in the Haynes Automotive Repair Manual Series

Printed in the U.S.A.

ISBN 1 56392 316 5

Library of Congress Catalog Card Number 98-70963

While every attempt is made to ensure that the information in this manual is correct, no liability can be accepted by the authors or publishers for loss, damage or injury caused by any errors in, or omissions from, the information given.

96-320

Contents

Haynes mechanic, author and photographer with 1995 Dodge Intrepid

About this manual

Its purpose

The purpose of this manual is to help you get the best value from your vehicle. It can do so in several ways. It can help you decide what work must be done, even if you choose to have it done by a dealer service department or a repair shop; it provides information and procedures for routine maintenance and servicing; and it offers diagnostic and repair procedures to follow when trouble occurs.

We hope you use the manual to tackle the work yourself. For many simpler jobs, doing it yourself may be quicker than arranging an appointment to get the vehicle into a shop and making the trips to leave it and pick it up. More importantly, a lot of money can be saved by avoiding the expense the shop must pass on to you to cover its labor and overhead costs. An added benefit is the sense of satisfaction and accomplishment that you feel after doing the job yourself.

Using the manual

The manual is divided into Chapters. Each Chapter is divided into numbered Sections, which are headed in bold type between horizontal lines. Each Section consists of consecutively numbered paragraphs.

At the beginning of each numbered Section you will be referred to any illustrations which apply to the procedures in that Section. The reference numbers used in illustration captions pinpoint the pertinent Section and the Step within that Section. That is, illustration 3.2 means the illustration refers to Section 3 and Step (or paragraph) 2 within that Section.

Procedures, once described in the text, are not normally repeated. When it's necessary to refer to another Chapter, the reference will be given as Chapter and Section number. Cross references given without use of the word "Chapter" apply to Sections and/or paragraphs in the same Chapter. For example, "see Section 8" means in the same Chapter.

References to the left or right side of the vehicle assume you are sitting in the driver's seat, facing forward.

Even though we have prepared this manual with extreme care, neither the publisher nor the author can accept responsibility for any errors in, or omissions from, the information given.

NOTE

A **Note** provides information necessary to properly complete a procedure or information which will make the procedure easier to understand.

CAUTION

A **Caution** provides a special procedure or special steps which must be taken while completing the procedure where the Caution is found. Not heeding a Caution can result in damage to the assembly being worked on.

WARNING

A **Warning** provides a special procedure or special steps which must be taken while completing the procedure where the Warning is found. Not heeding a Warning can result in personal injury.

Introduction to the Chrysler LH models

The Chrysler LH models are available only in the four-door sedan body style. They feature longitudinally mounted V6 engines, equipped with electronic multi-port fuel injection. The engine drives the front wheels through a four-speed automatic transaxle via independent driveaxles.

The fully-independent front suspension consists of coil spring/strut units, lower control arms with tension struts and a stabilizer bar. The independent rear suspension uses coil spring/strut units and spindle/hub units located by trailing arms and lateral links.

The power-assisted rack-and-pinion steering unit is mounted behind the engine.

Front brakes are discs; the rears are either drum or optional disc-type. Power assist is standard.

Vehicle identification numbers

Vehicle identification numbers

Modifications are a continuing and unpublicized process in vehicle manufacturing. Since spare parts manuals and lists are compiled on a numerical basis, the individual vehicle numbers are essential to correctly identify the component required.

Vehicle Identification Number (VIN)

The Vehicle Identification Number (VIN), which appears on the Vehicle Certificate of Title and Registration, is also embossed on a gray plate located on the upper left (driver's side) corner of the dashboard, near the windshield (see illustration). The VIN tells you when and where a vehicle was manufactured, its country of origin, make, type, passenger safety system, line, series, body style, engine and assembly plant.

Body Code Plate

The body code plate, which is located in the engine compartment, provides more specific information about the vehicle - type of engine, transaxle, paint, etc. - to which it's attached (see illustration).

The Vehicle Identification Number (VIN) is stamped into a metal plate fastened to the dashboard on the driver's side - it's visible through the windshield

Engine Identification Number (EIN)

The Engine Identification Number (EIN) is stamped into the rear of the engine block just below the cylinder head (see illustration).

Transaxle Identification Number (TIN)

The Transaxle Identification Number (TIN) is located on a sticker on top of the left end of transaxle housing (see illustration).

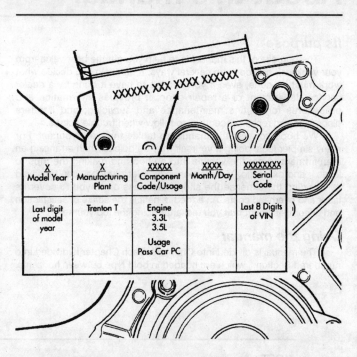

X Model Year	X Manufacturing Plant	XXXXX Component Code/Usage	XXXX Month/Day	XXXXXXX Serial Code
Last digit of model year	Trenton T	Engine 3.3L 3.5L Usage Pass Car PC		Last 8 Digits of VIN

Engine Identification Number is located on the engine block, just below the cylinder head

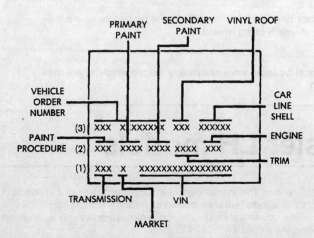

The Body Code Plate is located in the engine compartment - it provides information about the type of engine, transaxle, paint, etc.

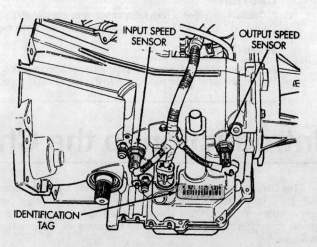

The automatic transaxle identification number is located on a sticker at the left (driver's) end of the transaxle

Buying parts

Replacement parts are available from many sources, which generally fall into one of two categories - authorized dealer parts departments and independent retail auto parts stores. Our advice concerning these parts is as follows:

Retail auto parts stores: Good auto parts stores will stock frequently needed components which wear out relatively fast, such as clutch components, exhaust systems, brake parts, tune-up parts, etc. These stores often supply new or reconditioned parts on an exchange basis, which can save a considerable amount of money. Discount auto parts stores are often very good places to buy materials and parts needed for general vehicle maintenance such as oil, grease, filters, spark plugs, belts, touch-up paint, bulbs, etc. They also usually sell

tools and general accessories, have convenient hours, charge lower prices and can often be found not far from home.

Authorized dealer parts department: This is the best source for parts which are unique to the vehicle and not generally available elsewhere (such as major engine parts, transmission parts, trim pieces, etc.).

Warranty information: If the vehicle is still covered under warranty, be sure that any replacement parts purchased - regardless of the source - do not invalidate the warranty!

To be sure of obtaining the correct parts, have engine and chassis numbers available and, if possible, take the old parts along for positive identification.

Maintenance techniques, tools and working facilities

Maintenance techniques

There are a number of techniques involved in maintenance and repair that will be referred to throughout this manual. Application of these techniques will enable the home mechanic to be more efficient, better organized and capable of performing the various tasks properly, which will ensure that the repair job is thorough and complete.

Fasteners

Fasteners are nuts, bolts, studs and screws used to hold two or more parts together. There are a few things to keep in mind when working with fasteners. Almost all of them use a locking device of some type, either a lockwasher, locknut, locking tab or thread adhesive. All threaded fasteners should be clean and straight, with undamaged threads and undamaged corners on the hex head where the wrench fits. Develop the habit of replacing all damaged nuts and bolts with new ones. Special locknuts with nylon or fiber inserts can only be

used once. If they are removed, they lose their locking ability and must be replaced with new ones.

Rusted nuts and bolts should be treated with a penetrating fluid to ease removal and prevent breakage. Some mechanics use turpentine in a spout-type oil can, which works quite well. After applying the rust penetrant, let it work for a few minutes before trying to loosen the nut or bolt. Badly rusted fasteners may have to be chiseled or sawed off or removed with a special nut breaker, available at tool stores.

If a bolt or stud breaks off in an assembly, it can be drilled and removed with a special tool commonly available for this purpose. Most automotive machine shops can perform this task, as well as other repair procedures, such as the repair of threaded holes that have been stripped out.

Flat washers and lockwashers, when removed from an assembly, should always be replaced exactly as removed. Replace any damaged washers with new ones. Never use a lockwasher on any soft metal surface (such as aluminum), thin sheet metal or plastic.

Fastener sizes

For a number of reasons, automobile manufacturers are making wider and wider use of metric fasteners. Therefore, it is important to be able to tell the difference between standard (sometimes called U.S. or SAE) and metric hardware, since they cannot be interchanged.

All bolts, whether standard or metric, are sized according to diameter, thread pitch and length. For example, a standard 1/2 - 13 x 1 bolt is 1/2 inch in diameter, has 13 threads per inch and is 1 inch long. An M12 - 1.75 x 25 metric bolt is 12 mm in diameter, has a thread pitch of 1.75 mm (the distance between threads) and is 25 mm long. The two bolts are nearly identical, and easily confused, but they are not interchangeable.

In addition to the differences in diameter, thread pitch and length, metric and standard bolts can also be distinguished by examining the bolt heads. To begin with, the distance across the flats on a standard bolt head is measured in inches, while the same dimension on a metric bolt is sized in millimeters (the same is true for nuts). As a result, a standard wrench should not be used on a metric bolt and a metric wrench should not be used on a standard bolt. Also, most standard bolts have slashes radiating out from the center of the head to denote the grade or strength of the bolt, which is an indication of the amount of torque that can be applied to it. The greater the number of slashes, the greater the strength of the bolt. Grades 0 through 5 are commonly used on automobiles. Metric bolts have a property class (grade) number, rather than a slash, molded into their heads to indicate bolt strength. In this case, the higher the number, the stronger the bolt. Property class numbers 8.8, 9.8 and 10.9 are commonly used on automobiles.

Strength markings can also be used to distinguish standard hex nuts from metric hex nuts. Many standard nuts have dots stamped into one side, while metric nuts are marked with a number. The greater the number of dots, or the higher the number, the greater the strength of the nut.

Metric studs are also marked on their ends according to property class (grade). Larger studs are numbered (the same as metric bolts), while smaller studs carry a geometric code to denote grade.

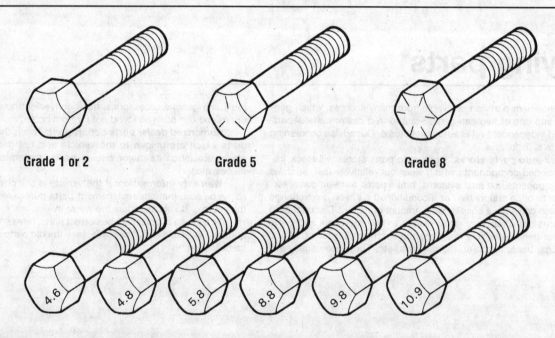

Bolt strength markings (top - standard/SAE/USS; bottom - metric)

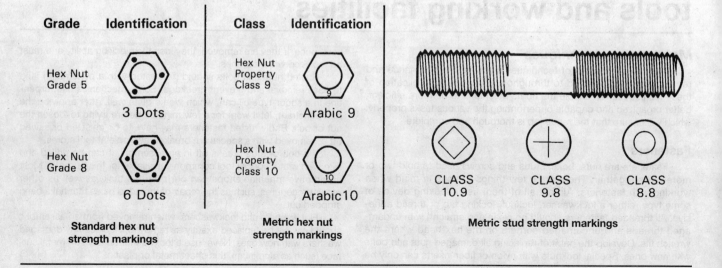

Standard hex nut strength markings

Metric hex nut strength markings

Metric stud strength markings

It should be noted that many fasteners, especially Grades 0 through 2, have no distinguishing marks on them. When such is the case, the only way to determine whether it is standard or metric is to measure the thread pitch or compare it to a known fastener of the same size.

Standard fasteners are often referred to as SAE, as opposed to metric. However, it should be noted that SAE technically refers to a non-metric fine thread fastener only. Coarse thread non-metric fasteners are referred to as USS sizes.

Since fasteners of the same size (both standard and metric) may have different strength ratings, be sure to reinstall any bolts, studs or nuts removed from your vehicle in their original locations. Also, when replacing a fastener with a new one, make sure that the new one has a strength rating equal to or greater than the original.

Tightening sequences and procedures

Most threaded fasteners should be tightened to a specific torque value (torque is the twisting force applied to a threaded component such as a nut or bolt). Overtightening the fastener can weaken it and cause it to break, while undertightening can cause it to eventually come loose. Bolts, screws and studs, depending on the material they are made of and their thread diameters, have specific torque values, many of which are noted in the Specifications at the beginning of each Chapter. Be sure to follow the torque recommendations closely. For fasteners not assigned a specific torque, a general torque value chart is presented here as a guide. These torque values are for dry (unlubricated) fasteners threaded into steel or cast iron (not aluminum). As was previously mentioned, the size and grade of a fastener determine the amount of torque that can safely be applied to it. The figures listed

Metric thread sizes	Ft-lbs	Nm
M-6	6 to 9	9 to 12
M-8	14 to 21	19 to 28
M-10	28 to 40	38 to 54
M-12	50 to 71	68 to 96
M-14	80 to 140	109 to 154

Pipe thread sizes		
1/8	5 to 8	7 to 10
1/4	12 to 18	17 to 24
3/8	22 to 33	30 to 44
1/2	25 to 35	34 to 47

U.S. thread sizes		
1/4 - 20	6 to 9	9 to 12
5/16 - 18	12 to 18	17 to 24
5/16 - 24	14 to 20	19 to 27
3/8 - 16	22 to 32	30 to 43
3/8 - 24	27 to 38	37 to 51
7/16 - 14	40 to 55	55 to 74
7/16 - 20	40 to 60	55 to 81
1/2 - 13	55 to 80	75 to 108

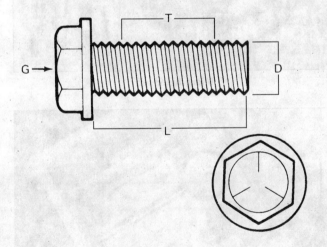

Standard (SAE and USS) bolt dimensions/grade marks

G   *Grade marks (bolt strength)*
L   *Length (in inches)*
T   *Thread pitch (number of threads per inch)*
D   *Nominal diameter (in inches)*

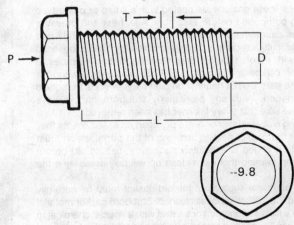

Metric bolt dimensions/grade marks

P   *Property class (bolt strength)*
L   *Length (in millimeters)*
T   *Thread pitch (distance between threads in millimeters)*
D   *Diameter*

here are approximate for Grade 2 and Grade 3 fasteners. Higher grades can tolerate higher torque values.

Fasteners laid out in a pattern, such as cylinder head bolts, oil pan bolts, differential cover bolts, etc., must be loosened or tightened in sequence to avoid warping the component. This sequence will normally be shown in the appropriate Chapter. If a specific pattern is not given, the following procedures can be used to prevent warping.

Initially, the bolts or nuts should be assembled finger-tight only. Next, they should be tightened one full turn each, in a criss-cross or diagonal pattern. After each one has been tightened one full turn, return to the first one and tighten them all one-half turn, following the same pattern. Finally, tighten each of them one-quarter turn at a time until each fastener has been tightened to the proper torque. To loosen and remove the fasteners, the procedure would be reversed.

Component disassembly

Component disassembly should be done with care and purpose to help ensure that the parts go back together properly. Always keep track of the sequence in which parts are removed. Make note of special characteristics or marks on parts that can be installed more than one way, such as a grooved thrust washer on a shaft. It is a good idea to lay the disassembled parts out on a clean surface in the order that they were removed. It may also be helpful to make sketches or take instant photos of components before removal.

When removing fasteners from a component, keep track of their locations. Sometimes threading a bolt back in a part, or putting the washers and nut back on a stud, can prevent mix-ups later. If nuts and bolts cannot be returned to their original locations, they should be kept in a compartmented box or a series of small boxes. A cupcake or muffin tin is ideal for this purpose, since each cavity can hold the bolts and nuts from a particular area (i.e. oil pan bolts, valve cover bolts, engine mount bolts, etc.). A pan of this type is especially helpful when working on assemblies with very small parts, such as the carburetor, alternator, valve train or interior dash and trim pieces. The cavities can be marked with paint or tape to identify the contents.

Whenever wiring looms, harnesses or connectors are separated, it is a good idea to identify the two halves with numbered pieces of masking tape so they can be easily reconnected.

Gasket sealing surfaces

Throughout any vehicle, gaskets are used to seal the mating surfaces between two parts and keep lubricants, fluids, vacuum or pressure contained in an assembly.

Many times these gaskets are coated with a liquid or paste-type gasket sealing compound before assembly. Age, heat and pressure can sometimes cause the two parts to stick together so tightly that they are very difficult to separate. Often, the assembly can be loosened by striking it with a soft-face hammer near the mating surfaces. A regular hammer can be used if a block of wood is placed between the hammer and the part. Do not hammer on cast parts or parts that could be easily damaged. With any particularly stubborn part, always recheck to make sure that every fastener has been removed.

Avoid using a screwdriver or bar to pry apart an assembly, as they can easily mar the gasket sealing surfaces of the parts, which must remain smooth. If prying is absolutely necessary, use an old broom handle, but keep in mind that extra clean up will be necessary if the wood splinters.

After the parts are separated, the old gasket must be carefully scraped off and the gasket surfaces cleaned. Stubborn gasket material can be soaked with rust penetrant or treated with a special chemical to soften it so it can be easily scraped off. A scraper can be fashioned from a piece of copper tubing by flattening and sharpening one end. Copper is recommended because it is usually softer than the surfaces to be scraped, which reduces the chance of gouging the part. Some gaskets can be removed with a wire brush, but regardless of the method used, the mating surfaces must be left clean and smooth. If for some reason the gasket surface is gouged, then a gasket sealer thick enough to fill scratches will have to be used during reassembly of the components. For most applications, a non-drying (or semi-drying) gasket sealer should be used.

Hose removal tips

Warning: *If the vehicle is equipped with air conditioning, do not disconnect any of the A/C hoses without first having the system depressurized by a dealer service department or a service station.*

Hose removal precautions closely parallel gasket removal precautions. Avoid scratching or gouging the surface that the hose mates against or the connection may leak. This is especially true for radiator hoses. Because of various chemical reactions, the rubber in hoses can bond itself to the metal spigot that the hose fits over. To remove a hose, first loosen the hose clamps that secure it to the spigot. Then, with slip-joint pliers, grab the hose at the clamp and rotate it around the spigot. Work it back and forth until it is completely free, then pull it off. Silicone or other lubricants will ease removal if they can be applied between the hose and the outside of the spigot. Apply the same lubricant to the inside of the hose and the outside of the spigot to simplify installation.

As a last resort (and if the hose is to be replaced with a new one anyway), the rubber can be slit with a knife and the hose peeled from the spigot. If this must be done, be careful that the metal connection is not damaged.

If a hose clamp is broken or damaged, do not reuse it. Wire-type clamps usually weaken with age, so it is a good idea to replace them with screw-type clamps whenever a hose is removed.

Tools

A selection of good tools is a basic requirement for anyone who plans to maintain and repair his or her own vehicle. For the owner who has few tools, the initial investment might seem high, but when compared to the spiraling costs of professional auto maintenance and repair, it is a wise one.

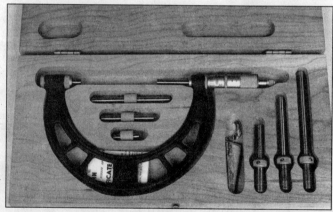

Micrometer set

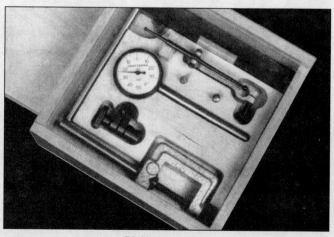

Dial indicator set

Dial caliper

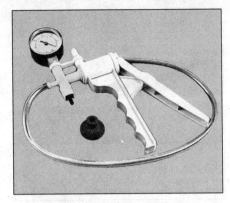

Hand-operated vacuum pump

Timing light

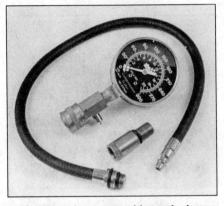

Compression gauge with spark plug hole adapter

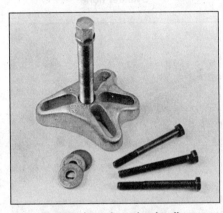

Damper/steering wheel puller

General purpose puller

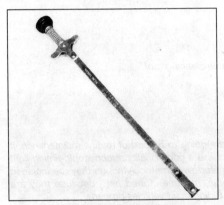

Hydraulic lifter removal tool

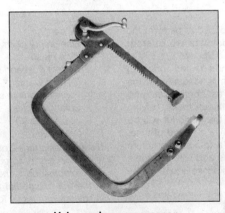

Valve spring compressor

Valve spring compressor

Ridge reamer

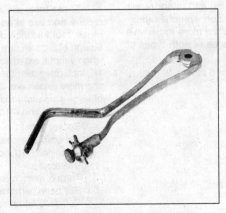

Piston ring groove cleaning tool

Ring removal/installation tool

Ring compressor

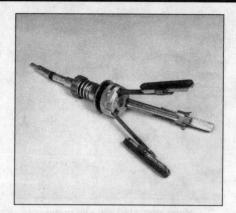
Cylinder hone

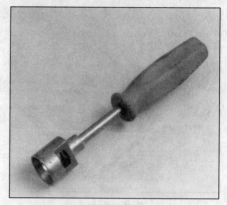
Brake hold-down spring tool

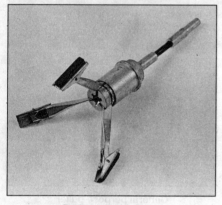
Brake cylinder hone

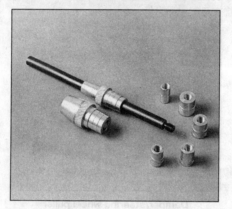
Clutch plate alignment tool

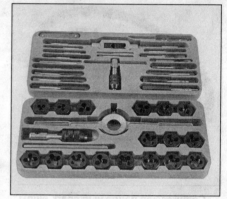
Tap and die set

To help the owner decide which tools are needed to perform the tasks detailed in this manual, the following tool lists are offered: *Maintenance and minor repair, Repair/overhaul* and *Special.*

The newcomer to practical mechanics should start off with the *maintenance and minor repair* tool kit, which is adequate for the simpler jobs performed on a vehicle. Then, as confidence and experience grow, the owner can tackle more difficult tasks, buying additional tools as they are needed. Eventually the basic kit will be expanded into the *repair and overhaul* tool set. Over a period of time, the experienced do-it-yourselfer will assemble a tool set complete enough for most repair and overhaul procedures and will add tools from the special category when it is felt that the expense is justified by the frequency of use.

Maintenance and minor repair tool kit

The tools in this list should be considered the minimum required for performance of routine maintenance, servicing and minor repair work. We recommend the purchase of combination wrenches (box-end and open-end combined in one wrench). While more expensive than open end wrenches, they offer the advantages of both types of wrench.

Combination wrench set (1/4-inch to 1 inch or 6 mm to 19 mm)
Adjustable wrench, 8 inch
Spark plug wrench with rubber insert
Spark plug gap adjusting tool
Feeler gauge set
Brake bleeder wrench
Standard screwdriver (5/16-inch x 6 inch)
Phillips screwdriver (No. 2 x 6 inch)
Combination pliers - 6 inch
Hacksaw and assortment of blades
Tire pressure gauge
Grease gun

Oil can
Fine emery cloth
Wire brush
Battery post and cable cleaning tool
Oil filter wrench
Funnel (medium size)
Safety goggles
Jackstands (2)
Drain pan

Note: *If basic tune-ups are going to be part of routine maintenance, it will be necessary to purchase a good quality stroboscopic timing light and combination tachometer/dwell meter. Although they are included in the list of special tools, it is mentioned here because they are absolutely necessary for tuning most vehicles properly.*

Repair and overhaul tool set

These tools are essential for anyone who plans to perform major repairs and are in addition to those in the maintenance and minor repair tool kit. Included is a comprehensive set of sockets which, though expensive, are invaluable because of their versatility, especially when various extensions and drives are available. We recommend the 1/2-inch drive over the 3/8-inch drive. Although the larger drive is bulky and more expensive, it has the capacity of accepting a very wide range of large sockets. Ideally, however, the mechanic should have a 3/8-inch drive set and a 1/2-inch drive set.

Socket set(s)
Reversible ratchet
Extension - 10 inch
Universal joint
Torque wrench (same size drive as sockets)
Ball peen hammer - 8 ounce
Soft-face hammer (plastic/rubber)
Standard screwdriver (1/4-inch x 6 inch)

Standard screwdriver (stubby - 5/16-inch)
Phillips screwdriver (No. 3 x 8 inch)
Phillips screwdriver (stubby - No. 2)
Pliers - vise grip
Pliers - lineman's
Pliers - needle nose
Pliers - snap-ring (internal and external)
Cold chisel - 1/2-inch
Scribe
Scraper (made from flattened copper tubing)
Centerpunch
Pin punches (1/16, 1/8, 3/16-inch)
Steel rule/straightedge - 12 inch
Allen wrench set (1/8 to 3/8-inch or 4 mm to 10 mm)
A selection of files
Wire brush (large)
Jackstands (second set)
Jack (scissor or hydraulic type)

Note: *Another tool which is often useful is an electric drill with a chuck capacity of 3/8-inch and a set of good quality drill bits.*

Special tools

The tools in this list include those which are not used regularly, are expensive to buy, or which need to be used in accordance with their manufacturer's instructions. Unless these tools will be used frequently, it is not very economical to purchase many of them. A consideration would be to split the cost and use between yourself and a friend or friends. In addition, most of these tools can be obtained from a tool rental shop on a temporary basis.

This list primarily contains only those tools and instruments widely available to the public, and not those special tools produced by the vehicle manufacturer for distribution to dealer service departments. Occasionally, references to the manufacturer's special tools are included in the text of this manual. Generally, an alternative method of doing the job without the special tool is offered. However, sometimes there is no alternative to their use. Where this is the case, and the tool cannot be purchased or borrowed, the work should be turned over to the dealer service department or an automotive repair shop.

Valve spring compressor
Piston ring groove cleaning tool
Piston ring compressor
Piston ring installation tool
Cylinder compression gauge
Cylinder ridge reamer
Cylinder surfacing hone
Cylinder bore gauge
Micrometers and/or dial calipers
Hydraulic lifter removal tool
Balljoint separator
Universal-type puller
Impact screwdriver
Dial indicator set
Stroboscopic timing light (inductive pick-up)
Hand operated vacuum/pressure pump
Tachometer/dwell meter
Universal electrical multimeter
Cable hoist
Brake spring removal and installation tools
Floor jack

Buying tools

For the do-it-yourselfer who is just starting to get involved in vehicle maintenance and repair, there are a number of options available when purchasing tools. If maintenance and minor repair is the extent of the work to be done, the purchase of individual tools is satisfactory. If, on the other hand, extensive work is planned, it would be a good idea to purchase a modest tool set from one of the large retail chain stores. A set can usually be bought at a substantial savings over the individual tool prices, and they often come with a tool box. As additional tools are needed, add-on sets, individual tools and a larger tool box can be purchased to expand the tool selection. Building a tool set gradually allows the cost of the tools to be spread over a longer period of time and gives the mechanic the freedom to choose only those tools that will actually be used.

Tool stores will often be the only source of some of the special tools that are needed, but regardless of where tools are bought, try to avoid cheap ones, especially when buying screwdrivers and sockets, because they won't last very long. The expense involved in replacing cheap tools will eventually be greater than the initial cost of quality tools.

Care and maintenance of tools

Good tools are expensive, so it makes sense to treat them with respect. Keep them clean and in usable condition and store them properly when not in use. Always wipe off any dirt, grease or metal chips before putting them away. Never leave tools lying around in the work area. Upon completion of a job, always check closely under the hood for tools that may have been left there so they won't get lost during a test drive.

Some tools, such as screwdrivers, pliers, wrenches and sockets, can be hung on a panel mounted on the garage or workshop wall, while others should be kept in a tool box or tray. Measuring instruments, gauges, meters, etc. must be carefully stored where they cannot be damaged by weather or impact from other tools.

When tools are used with care and stored properly, they will last a very long time. Even with the best of care, though, tools will wear out if used frequently. When a tool is damaged or worn out, replace it. Subsequent jobs will be safer and more enjoyable if you do.

Working facilities

Not to be overlooked when discussing tools is the workshop. If anything more than routine maintenance is to be carried out, some sort of suitable work area is essential.

It is understood, and appreciated, that many home mechanics do not have a good workshop or garage available, and end up removing an engine or doing major repairs outside. It is recommended, however, that the overhaul or repair be completed under the cover of a roof.

A clean, flat workbench or table of comfortable working height is an absolute necessity. The workbench should be equipped with a vise that has a jaw opening of at least four inches.

As mentioned previously, some clean, dry storage space is also required for tools, as well as the lubricants, fluids, cleaning solvents, etc. which soon become necessary.

Sometimes waste oil and fluids, drained from the engine or cooling system during normal maintenance or repairs, present a disposal problem. To avoid pouring them on the ground or into a sewage system, pour the used fluids into large containers, seal them with caps and take them to an authorized disposal site or recycling center. Plastic jugs, such as old antifreeze containers, are ideal for this purpose.

Always keep a supply of old newspapers and clean rags available. Old towels are excellent for mopping up spills. Many mechanics use rolls of paper towels for most work because they are readily available and disposable. To help keep the area under the vehicle clean, a large cardboard box can be cut open and flattened to protect the garage or shop floor.

Whenever working over a painted surface, such as when leaning over a fender to service something under the hood, always cover it with an old blanket or bedspread to protect the finish. Vinyl covered pads, made especially for this purpose, are available at auto parts stores.

Jacking and towing

Jacking

The jack supplied with the vehicle should be used only for raising the vehicle when changing a tire or placing jackstands under the frame. **Warning:** *Never work under the vehicle or start the engine when this jack is being used as the only means of support.*

The vehicle should be on level ground with the wheels blocked and the transaxle in Park (automatic). If a tire is being changed, loosen the lug nuts one-half turn and leave them in place until the wheel is raised off the ground. Make sure no one is in the vehicle as it's being raised off the ground.

Place the jack under the side of the vehicle at the jacking point nearest the wheel to be changed **(see illustrations)**. **Caution:** *Never place the jack under the rear trailing arms or lateral links.* If you're using a floor jack, place it beneath the crossmember at the front or rear. Operate the jack with a slow, smooth motion until the wheel is raised off the ground. If you're using jackstands, position them beneath the support points along the front or rear side sills. Remove the lug nuts, pull off the wheel, install the spare and thread the lug nuts back on with

the beveled sides facing in. Tighten them snugly, but wait until the vehicle is lowered to tighten them completely.

Lower the vehicle, remove the jack and tighten the lug nuts (if loosened or removed) in a criss-cross pattern. If possible, tighten them with a torque wrench (see Chapter 1 for the torque figures). If you don't have access to a torque wrench, have the nuts checked by a service station or repair shop as soon as possible. Retighten the lug nuts after 500 miles.

If the vehicle is equipped with a temporary spare tire, remember that it is intended only for temporary use until the regular tire can be repaired. Do not exceed the maximum speed that the tire is rated for.

Towing

The vehicle must be either towed with the front (drive) wheels off the ground or carried on a flatbed truck to prevent damage to the transaxle. A wheel lift is recommended.

While towing, the parking brake must be released and the transaxle must be in Neutral. The steering must be unlocked (ignition switch in the OFF position). Don't exceed 50 mph (35 mph on rough roads).

Safety is a major consideration while towing and all applicable state and local laws must be obeyed. A safety chain system must be used at all times. Remember that power steering and power brakes will not work with the engine off.

Use only the indicated lifting points when jacking up the vehicle

Make sure the jack saddle is properly positioned

Booster battery (jump) starting

Observe these precautions when using a booster battery to start a vehicle:

a) *Before connecting the booster battery, make sure the ignition switch is in the Off position.*
b) *Turn off the lights, heater and other electrical loads.*
c) *Your eyes should be shielded. Safety goggles are a good idea.*
d) *Make sure the booster battery is the same voltage as the dead one in the vehicle.*
e) *The two vehicles MUST NOT TOUCH each other!*
f) *Make sure the transaxle is in Neutral (manual) or Park (automatic).*
g) *If the booster battery is not a maintenance-free type, remove the vent caps and lay a cloth over the vent holes.*

Connect the red jumper cable to the positive (+) terminals of each battery **(see illustration).**

Connect one end of the black jumper cable to the negative (-) terminal of the booster battery. The other end of this cable should be connected to a good ground on the vehicle to be started, such as a bolt or bracket on the body.

Start the engine using the booster battery, then, with the engine running at idle speed, disconnect the jumper cables in the reverse order of connection.

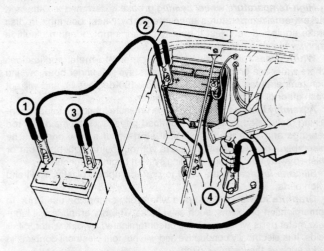

Make the booster battery cable connections in the numerical order shown (note that the negative cable of the booster battery is NOT attached to the negative terminal of the dead battery)

Automotive chemicals and lubricants

A number of automotive chemicals and lubricants are available for use during vehicle maintenance and repair. They include a wide variety of products ranging from cleaning solvents and degreasers to lubricants and protective sprays for rubber, plastic and vinyl.

Cleaners

Carburetor cleaner and choke cleaner is a strong solvent for gum, varnish and carbon. Most carburetor cleaners leave a dry-type lubricant film which will not harden or gum up. Because of this film it is not recommended for use on electrical components.

Brake system cleaner is used to remove grease and brake fluid from the brake system, where clean surfaces are absolutely necessary. It leaves no residue and often eliminates brake squeal caused by contaminants.

Electrical cleaner removes oxidation, corrosion and carbon deposits from electrical contacts, restoring full current flow. It can also be used to clean spark plugs, carburetor jets, voltage regulators and other parts where an oil-free surface is desired.

Demoisturants remove water and moisture from electrical components such as alternators, voltage regulators, electrical connectors and fuse blocks. They are non-conductive, non-corrosive and non-flammable.

Degreasers are heavy-duty solvents used to remove grease from the outside of the engine and from chassis components. They can be sprayed or brushed on and, depending on the type, are rinsed off either with water or solvent.

Lubricants

Motor oil is the lubricant formulated for use in engines. It normally contains a wide variety of additives to prevent corrosion and reduce foaming and wear. Motor oil comes in various weights (viscosity ratings) from 5 to 80. The recommended weight of the oil depends on the season, temperature and the demands on the engine. Light oil is used in cold climates and under light load conditions. Heavy oil is used in hot climates and where high loads are encountered. Multi-viscosity oils are designed to have characteristics of both light and heavy oils and are available in a number of weights from 5W-20 to 20W-50.

Gear oil is designed to be used in differentials, manual transmissions and other areas where high-temperature lubrication is required.

Chassis and wheel bearing grease is a heavy grease used where increased loads and friction are encountered, such as for wheel bearings, balljoints, tie-rod ends and universal joints.

High-temperature wheel bearing grease is designed to withstand the extreme temperatures encountered by wheel bearings in disc brake equipped vehicles. It usually contains molybdenum disulfide (moly), which is a dry-type lubricant.

White grease is a heavy grease for metal-to-metal applications where water is a problem. White grease stays soft under both low and high temperatures (usually from -100 to +190-degrees F), and will not wash off or dilute in the presence of water.

Assembly lube is a special extreme pressure lubricant, usually containing moly, used to lubricate high-load parts (such as main and rod bearings and cam lobes) for initial start-up of a new engine. The assembly lube lubricates the parts without being squeezed out or washed away until the engine oiling system begins to function.

Silicone lubricants are used to protect rubber, plastic, vinyl and nylon parts.

Graphite lubricants are used where oils cannot be used due to contamination problems, such as in locks. The dry graphite will lubricate metal parts while remaining uncontaminated by dirt, water, oil or acids. It is electrically conductive and will not foul electrical contacts in locks such as the ignition switch.

Moly penetrants loosen and lubricate frozen, rusted and corroded fasteners and prevent future rusting or freezing.

Heat-sink grease is a special electrically non-conductive grease that is used for mounting electronic ignition modules where it is essential that heat is transferred away from the module.

Sealants

RTV sealant is one of the most widely used gasket compounds. Made from silicone, RTV is air curing, it seals, bonds, waterproofs, fills surface irregularities, remains flexible, doesn't shrink, is relatively easy to remove, and is used as a supplementary sealer with almost all low and medium temperature gaskets.

Anaerobic sealant is much like RTV in that it can be used either to seal gaskets or to form gaskets by itself. It remains flexible, is solvent resistant and fills surface imperfections. The difference between an anaerobic sealant and an RTV-type sealant is in the curing. RTV cures when exposed to air, while an anaerobic sealant cures only in the absence of air. This means that an anaerobic sealant cures only after the assembly of parts, sealing them together.

Thread and pipe sealant is used for sealing hydraulic and pneumatic fittings and vacuum lines. It is usually made from a Teflon compound, and comes in a spray, a paint-on liquid and as a wrap-around tape.

Chemicals

Anti-seize compound prevents seizing, galling, cold welding, rust and corrosion in fasteners. High-temperature anti-seize, usually made with copper and graphite lubricants, is used for exhaust system and exhaust manifold bolts.

Anaerobic locking compounds are used to keep fasteners from vibrating or working loose and cure only after installation, in the absence of air. Medium strength locking compound is used for small nuts, bolts and screws that may be removed later. High-strength locking compound is for large nuts, bolts and studs which aren't removed on a regular basis.

Oil additives range from viscosity index improvers to chemical treatments that claim to reduce internal engine friction. It should be noted that most oil manufacturers caution against using additives with their oils.

Gas additives perform several functions, depending on their chemical makeup. They usually contain solvents that help dissolve gum and varnish that build up on carburetor, fuel injection and intake parts. They also serve to break down carbon deposits that form on the inside surfaces of the combustion chambers. Some additives contain upper cylinder lubricants for valves and piston rings, and others contain chemicals to remove condensation from the gas tank.

Miscellaneous

Brake fluid is specially formulated hydraulic fluid that can withstand the heat and pressure encountered in brake systems. Care must be taken so this fluid does not come in contact with painted surfaces or plastics. An opened container should always be resealed to prevent contamination by water or dirt.

Weatherstrip adhesive is used to bond weatherstripping around doors, windows and trunk lids. It is sometimes used to attach trim pieces.

Undercoating is a petroleum-based, tar-like substance that is designed to protect metal surfaces on the underside of the vehicle from corrosion. It also acts as a sound-deadening agent by insulating the bottom of the vehicle.

Waxes and polishes are used to help protect painted and plated surfaces from the weather. Different types of paint may require the use of different types of wax and polish. Some polishes utilize a chemical or abrasive cleaner to help remove the top layer of oxidized (dull) paint on older vehicles. In recent years many non-wax polishes that contain a wide variety of chemicals such as polymers and silicones have been introduced. These non-wax polishes are usually easier to apply and last longer than conventional waxes and polishes.

Conversion factors

Length (distance)

Inches (in)	X	25.4	= Millimetres (mm)	X 0.0394	= Inches (in)
Feet (ft)	X	0.305	= Metres (m)	X 3.281	= Feet (ft)
Miles	X	1.609	= Kilometres (km)	X 0.621	= Miles

Volume (capacity)

Cubic inches (cu in; in^3)	X	16.387	= Cubic centimetres (cc; cm^3)	X 0.061	= Cubic inches (cu in; in^3)
Imperial pints (Imp pt)	X	0.568	= Litres (l)	X 1.76	= Imperial pints (Imp pt)
Imperial quarts (Imp qt)	X	1.137	= Litres (l)	X 0.88	= Imperial quarts (Imp qt)
Imperial quarts (Imp qt)	X	1.201	= US quarts (US qt)	X 0.833	= Imperial quarts (Imp qt)
US quarts (US qt)	X	0.946	= Litres (l)	X 1.057	= US quarts (US qt)
Imperial gallons (Imp gal)	X	4.546	= Litres (l)	X 0.22	= Imperial gallons (Imp gal)
Imperial gallons (Imp gal)	X	1.201	= US gallons (US gal)	X 0.833	= Imperial gallons (Imp gal)
US gallons (US gal)	X	3.785	= Litres (l)	X 0.264	= US gallons (US gal)

Mass (weight)

Ounces (oz)	X	28.35	= Grams (g)	X 0.035	= Ounces (oz)
Pounds (lb)	X	0.454	= Kilograms (kg)	X 2.205	= Pounds (lb)

Force

Ounces-force (ozf; oz)	X	0.278	= Newtons (N)	X 3.6	= Ounces-force (ozf; oz)
Pounds-force (lbf; lb)	X	4.448	= Newtons (N)	X 0.225	= Pounds-force (lbf; lb)
Newtons (N)	X	0.1	= Kilograms-force (kgf; kg)	X 9.81	= Newtons (N)

Pressure

Pounds-force per square inch (psi; lbf/in^2; lb/in^2)	X	0.070	= Kilograms-force per square centimetre (kgf/cm^2; kg/cm^2)	X 14.223	= Pounds-force per square inch (psi; lbf/in^2; lb/in^2)
Pounds-force per square inch (psi; lbf/in^2; lb/in^2)	X	0.068	= Atmospheres (atm)	X 14.696	= Pounds-force per square inch (psi; lbf/in^2; lb/in^2)
Pounds-force per square inch (psi; lbf/in^2; lb/in^2)	X	0.069	= Bars	X 14.5	= Pounds-force per square inch (psi; lbf/in^2; lb/in^2)
Pounds-force per square inch (psi; lbf/in^2; lb/in^2)	X	6.895	= Kilopascals (kPa)	X 0.145	= Pounds-force per square inch (psi; lbf/in^2; lb/in^2)
Kilopascals (kPa)	X	0.01	= Kilograms-force per square centimetre (kgf/cm^2; kg/cm^2)	X 98.1	= Kilopascals (kPa)

Torque (moment of force)

Pounds-force inches (lbf in; lb in)	X	1.152	= Kilograms-force centimetre (kgf cm; kg cm)	X 0.868	= Pounds-force inches (lbf in; lb in)
Pounds-force inches (lbf in; lb in)	X	0.113	= Newton metres (Nm)	X 8.85	= Pounds-force inches (lbf in; lb in)
Pounds-force inches (lbf in; lb in)	X	0.083	= Pounds-force feet (lbf ft; lb ft)	X 12	= Pounds-force inches (lbf in; lb in)
Pounds-force feet (lbf ft; lb ft)	X	0.138	= Kilograms-force metres (kgf m; kg m)	X 7.233	= Pounds-force feet (lbf ft; lb ft)
Pounds-force feet (lbf ft; lb ft)	X	1.356	= Newton metres (Nm)	X 0.738	= Pounds-force feet (lbf ft; lb ft)
Newton metres (Nm)	X	0.102	= Kilograms-force metres (kgf m; kg m)	X 9.804	= Newton metres (Nm)

Power

Horsepower (hp)	X	745.7	= Watts (W)	X 0.0013	= Horsepower (hp)

Velocity (speed)

Miles per hour (miles/hr; mph)	X	1.609	= Kilometres per hour (km/hr; kph)	X 0.621	= Miles per hour (miles/hr; mph)

Fuel consumption*

Miles per gallon, Imperial (mpg)	X	0.354	= Kilometres per litre (km/l)	X 2.825	= Miles per gallon, Imperial (mpg)
Miles per gallon, US (mpg)	X	0.425	= Kilometres per litre (km/l)	X 2.352	= Miles per gallon, US (mpg)

Temperature

Degrees Fahrenheit = (°C x 1.8) + 32   Degrees Celsius (Degrees Centigrade; °C) = (°F - 32) x 0.56

*It is common practice to convert from miles per gallon (mpg) to litres/100 kilometres (l/100km),
where mpg (Imperial) x l/100 km = 282 and mpg (US) x l/100 km = 235

Safety first!

Regardless of how enthusiastic you may be about getting on with the job at hand, take the time to ensure that your safety is not jeopardized. A moment's lack of attention can result in an accident, as can failure to observe certain simple safety precautions. The possibility of an accident will always exist, and the following points should not be considered a comprehensive list of all dangers. Rather, they are intended to make you aware of the risks and to encourage a safety conscious approach to all work you carry out on your vehicle.

Essential DOs and DON'Ts

DON'T rely on a jack when working under the vehicle. Always use approved jackstands to support the weight of the vehicle and place them under the recommended lift or support points.

DON'T attempt to loosen extremely tight fasteners (i.e. wheel lug nuts) while the vehicle is on a jack - it may fall.

DON'T start the engine without first making sure that the transmission is in Neutral (or Park where applicable) and the parking brake is set.

DON'T remove the radiator cap from a hot cooling system - let it cool or cover it with a cloth and release the pressure gradually.

DON'T attempt to drain the engine oil until you are sure it has cooled to the point that it will not burn you.

DON'T touch any part of the engine or exhaust system until it has cooled sufficiently to avoid burns.

DON'T siphon toxic liquids such as gasoline, antifreeze and brake fluid by mouth, or allow them to remain on your skin.

DON'T inhale brake lining dust - it is potentially hazardous (see *Asbestos* below).

DON'T allow spilled oil or grease to remain on the floor - wipe it up before someone slips on it.

DON'T use loose fitting wrenches or other tools which may slip and cause injury.

DON'T push on wrenches when loosening or tightening nuts or bolts. Always try to pull the wrench toward you. If the situation calls for pushing the wrench away, push with an open hand to avoid scraped knuckles if the wrench should slip.

DON'T attempt to lift a heavy component alone - get someone to help you.

DON'T rush or take unsafe shortcuts to finish a job.

DON'T allow children or animals in or around the vehicle while you are working on it.

DO wear eye protection when using power tools such as a drill, sander, bench grinder, etc. and when working under a vehicle.

DO keep loose clothing and long hair well out of the way of moving parts.

DO make sure that any hoist used has a safe working load rating adequate for the job.

DO get someone to check on you periodically when working alone on a vehicle.

DO carry out work in a logical sequence and make sure that everything is correctly assembled and tightened.

DO keep chemicals and fluids tightly capped and out of the reach of children and pets.

DO remember that your vehicle's safety affects that of yourself and others. If in doubt on any point, get professional advice.

Asbestos

Certain friction, insulating, sealing, and other products - such as brake linings, brake bands, clutch linings, torque converters, gaskets, etc. - contain asbestos. Extreme care must be taken to avoid inhalation of dust from such products, since it is hazardous to health. If in doubt, assume that they do contain asbestos.

Fire

Remember at all times that gasoline is highly flammable. Never smoke or have any kind of open flame around when working on a vehicle. But the risk does not end there. A spark caused by an electrical short circuit, by two metal surfaces contacting each other, or even by static electricity built up in your body under certain conditions, can ignite gasoline vapors, which in a confined space are highly explosive. Do not, under any circumstances, use gasoline for cleaning parts. Use an approved safety solvent.

Always disconnect the battery ground (-) cable at the battery before working on any part of the fuel system or electrical system. Never risk spilling fuel on a hot engine or exhaust component. It is strongly recommended that a fire extinguisher suitable for use on fuel and electrical fires be kept handy in the garage or workshop at all times. Never try to extinguish a fuel or electrical fire with water.

Fumes

Certain fumes are highly toxic and can quickly cause unconsciousness and even death if inhaled to any extent. Gasoline vapor falls into this category, as do the vapors from some cleaning solvents. Any draining or pouring of such volatile fluids should be done in a well ventilated area.

When using cleaning fluids and solvents, read the instructions on the container carefully. Never use materials from unmarked containers.

Never run the engine in an enclosed space, such as a garage. Exhaust fumes contain carbon monoxide, which is extremely poisonous. If you need to run the engine, always do so in the open air, or at least have the rear of the vehicle outside the work area.

If you are fortunate enough to have the use of an inspection pit, never drain or pour gasoline and never run the engine while the vehicle is over the pit. The fumes, being heavier than air, will concentrate in the pit with possibly lethal results.

The battery

Never create a spark or allow a bare light bulb near a battery. They normally give off a certain amount of hydrogen gas, which is highly explosive.

Always disconnect the battery ground (-) cable at the battery before working on the fuel or electrical systems.

If possible, loosen the filler caps or cover when charging the battery from an external source (this does not apply to sealed or maintenance-free batteries). Do not charge at an excessive rate or the battery may burst.

Take care when adding water to a non maintenance-free battery and when carrying a battery. The electrolyte, even when diluted, is very corrosive and should not be allowed to contact clothing or skin.

Always wear eye protection when cleaning the battery to prevent the caustic deposits from entering your eyes.

Household current

When using an electric power tool, inspection light, etc., which operates on household current, always make sure that the tool is correctly connected to its plug and that, where necessary, it is properly grounded. Do not use such items in damp conditions and, again, do not create a spark or apply excessive heat in the vicinity of fuel or fuel vapor.

Secondary ignition system voltage

A severe electric shock can result from touching certain parts of the ignition system (such as the spark plug wires) when the engine is running or being cranked, particularly if components are damp or the insulation is defective. In the case of an electronic ignition system, the secondary system voltage is much higher and could prove fatal.

Troubleshooting

Contents

This section provides an easy reference guide to the more common problems which may occur during the operation of your vehicle. These problems and their possible causes are grouped under headings denoting various components or systems, such as Engine, Cooling system, etc. They also refer you to the chapter and/or section which deals with the problem.

Remember that successful troubleshooting is not a mysterious black art practiced only by professional mechanics. It is simply the result of the right knowledge combined with an intelligent, systematic approach to the problem. Always work by a process of elimination, starting with the simplest solution and working through to the most complex - and never overlook the obvious. Anyone can run the gas tank dry or leave the lights on overnight, so don't assume that you are exempt from such oversights.

Finally, always establish a clear idea of why a problem has occurred and take steps to ensure that it doesn't happen again. If the electrical system fails because of a poor connection, check the other connections in the system to make sure that they don't fail as well. If a particular fuse continues to blow, find out why - don't just replace one fuse after another. Remember, failure of a small component can often be indicative of potential failure or incorrect functioning of a more important component or system.

Engine

1   Engine will not rotate when attempting to start

1   Battery terminal connections loose or corroded (Chapter 1).
2   Battery discharged or faulty (Chapter 1).
3   Automatic transaxle not completely engaged in Park (Chapter 7).
4   Broken, loose or disconnected wiring in the starting circuit (Chapters 5 and 12).
5   Starter motor pinion jammed in flywheel ring gear (Chapter 5).
6   Starter solenoid faulty (Chapter 5).
7   Starter motor faulty (Chapter 5).
8   Ignition switch faulty (Chapter 12).
9   Starter pinion or flywheel teeth worn or broken (Chapter 5).
10   Engine seized

2   Engine rotates but will not start

1   Fuel tank empty.
2   Battery discharged (engine rotates slowly) (Chapter 5).
3   Battery terminal connections loose or corroded (Chapter 1).
4   Leaking fuel injector(s), fuel pump, pressure regulator, etc. (Chapter 4).
5   Fuel not reaching fuel injection system (Chapter 4).
6   Ignition components damp or damaged (Chapter 5).
7   Worn, faulty or incorrectly gapped spark plugs (Chapter 1).
8   Broken, loose or disconnected wiring in the starting circuit (Chapter 5).
9   Broken, loose or disconnected wires at the ignition coil or faulty coil (Chapter 5).

3   Engine hard to start when cold

1   Battery discharged or low (Chapter 1).
2   Malfunctioning fuel system (Chapter 4).
3   Fuel injector(s) leaking (Chapter 4).

4   Engine hard to start when hot

1   Air filter clogged (Chapter 1).
2   Fuel not reaching the fuel injection system (Chapter 4).
3   Corroded battery connections, especially ground (Chapter 1).

5   Starter motor noisy or excessively rough in engagement

1   Pinion or flywheel gear teeth worn or broken (Chapter 5).
2   Starter motor mounting bolts loose or missing (Chapter 5).

6   Engine starts but stops immediately

1   Loose or faulty electrical connections at distributor, coil or alternator (Chapter 5).
2   Insufficient fuel reaching the fuel injector(s) (Chapters 1 and 4).
3   Vacuum leak at the gasket between the intake plenum/fuel injection throttle body (Chapters 1 and 4).

7   Oil puddle under engine

1   Oil pan gasket and/or oil pan drain bolt washer leaking (Chapter 2).
2   Oil pressure sending unit leaking (Chapter 2).
3   Valve covers leaking (Chapter 2).
4   Engine oil seals leaking (Chapter 2).
5   Oil pump housing leaking (Chapter 2).

8   Engine lopes while idling or idles erratically

1   Vacuum leakage (Chapters 2 and 4).
2   Leaking EGR valve (Chapter 6).
3   Air filter clogged (Chapter 1).
4   Fuel pump not delivering sufficient fuel to the fuel injection system (Chapter 4).
5   Leaking head gasket (Chapter 2).
6   Timing belt and/or pulleys worn (Chapter 2).
7   Camshaft lobes worn (Chapter 2).

9   Engine misses at idle speed

1   Spark plugs worn or not gapped properly (Chapter 1).
2   Faulty spark plug wires (Chapter 1).
3   Vacuum leaks (Chapter 1).
4   Uneven or low compression (Chapter 2).

10   Engine misses throughout driving speed range

1   Fuel filter clogged and/or impurities in the fuel system (Chapter 1).
2   Low fuel output at the injector(s) (Chapter 4).
3   Faulty or incorrectly gapped spark plugs (Chapter 1).
4   Incorrect ignition timing (Chapter 5).
5   Leaking spark plug wires (Chapters 1 or 5).
6   Faulty emission system components (Chapter 6).
7   Low or uneven cylinder compression pressures (Chapter 2).
8   Weak or faulty ignition system (Chapter 5).
9   Vacuum leak at the fuel injection throttle body, intake manifold, or vacuum hoses (Chapter 4).

11   Engine stumbles on acceleration

1   Spark plugs fouled (Chapter 1)
2   Fuel filter clogged (Chapter 1)
3   Check injector driver circuit (Chapter 4) and injector resistance
4   Throttle Position Sensor (TPS) binding or sticking (Chapter 6)
5   EVAP system leaking or malfunctioning (Chapter 6)
6   Alternator output low or excessive (Chapter 5)

12   Engine surges while holding accelerator steady

1   Intake air leak (Chapter 4)
2   Fuel pump faulty (Chapter 4)
3   Malfunctioning TCC system (Chapter 6)
4   Loose fuel injector wire harness connectors (Chapter 4)
5   Contaminated or defective oxygen sensors (Chapter 6)
6   Fuel system rich or lean (Chapters 4 and 6)

13   Engine stalls

1   Accelerator cable linkage binding or sticking (Chapter 4)
2   Idle air control system malfunctioning (Chapter 4)
3   Fuel filter clogged and/or water and impurities in the fuel system (Chapters 1 and 4)

4   MAP sensor or circuit defective (Chapter 6)
5   EGR valve stuck open (Chapter 6)
6   Check cylinder compression (Chapter 2C)

14 Engine lacks power

1   Incorrect ignition timing
2   Faulty or incorrectly gapped spark plugs (Chapter 1)
3   Faulty coils (Chapter 5)
4   Rear brakes binding (Chapter 9)
5   Automatic transmission fluid level incorrect (Chapter 1 and 7)
6   Fuel filter clogged and/or impurities in the fuel system (Chapters 1 and 4)

15 Engine backfires

1   Emission control system not functioning properly (Chapter 6)
2   Ignition timing incorrect (Chapter 5)
3   Faulty secondary ignition system; cracked spark plug insulator, faulty plug wires, distributor cap and/or rotor (Chapters 1 and 5)
4   Fuel injection system malfunction (Chapter 4)
5   Vacuum leak at fuel injectors, intake manifold or vacuum hoses (Chapter 4)
6   EGR stuck open all the time (Chapter 6)

16 Pinging or knocking engine sounds during acceleration or uphill

1   Incorrect grade (octane) of fuel
2   Fuel injection system faulty (Chapter 4)
3   Improper or damaged spark plugs or wires (Chapter 1)
4   Faulty or incorrect thermostat (Chapter 3)
5   Low coolant levels (Chapter 1)
6   Knock sensor system faulty (Chapter 6)
7   Vacuum leak (Chapter 2C and 4)
8   EGR system not functioning properly (Chapter 6)

17 Engine runs with oil pressure light on

1   Low oil level (Chapter 1).
2   Short in wiring circuit (Chapter 12).
3   Faulty oil pressure sender (Chapter 2).
4   Worn engine bearings and/or oil pump (Chapter 2).

18 Engine diesels (continues to run) after switching off

Excessive engine operating temperature (Chapter 3).

Engine electrical system

19 Battery will not hold a charge

1   Alternator drivebelt defective or not adjusted properly (Chapter 1).
2   Battery electrolyte level low (Chapter 1).
3   Battery terminals loose or corroded (Chapter 1).
4   Alternator not charging properly (Chapter 5).
5   Loose, broken or faulty wiring in the charging circuit (Chapter 5).
6   Short in vehicle wiring (Chapter 12).
7   Internally defective battery (Chapters 1 and 5).

20 Alternator light fails to go out

1   Faulty alternator or charging circuit (Chapter 5).
2   Alternator drivebelt defective or out of adjustment (Chapter 1).
3   Alternator voltage regulator inoperative (Chapter 5).

21 Alternator light fails to come on when key is turned on

1   Warning light bulb defective (Chapter 12).
2   Fault in the printed circuit, dash wiring or bulb holder (Chapter 12).

Fuel system

22 Excessive fuel consumption

1   Dirty or clogged air filter element (Chapter 1).
2   Incorrectly set ignition timing (Chapter 1).
3   Emissions system not functioning properly (Chapter 6).
4   Fuel injection system malfunction (Chapter 4).
5   Low tire pressure or incorrect tire size (Chapter 1).

23 Fuel leakage and/or fuel odor

1   Leaking fuel feed or return line (Chapters 1 and 4).
2   Tank overfilled.
3   Evaporative canister filter clogged (Chapters 1 and 6).
4   Fuel injection system malfunction (Chapter 4).

Cooling system

24 Overheating

1   Insufficient coolant in system (Chapter 1).
2   Water pump drivebelt defective or out of adjustment (Chapter 1).
3   Radiator core blocked or grille restricted (Chapter 3).
4   Thermostat faulty (Chapter 3).
5   Electric coolant fan blades broken or cracked (Chapter 3).
6   Radiator cap not maintaining proper pressure (Chapter 3).

25 Overcooling

1   Faulty thermostat (Chapter 3).
2   Inaccurate temperature gauge sending unit (Chapter 3)

26 External coolant leakage

1   Deteriorated/damaged hoses; loose clamps (Chapters 1 and 3).
2   Water pump seal defective (Chapter 3).
3   Leakage from radiator core or coolant reservoir bottle (Chapter 3).
4   Engine drain or water jacket core plugs leaking (Chapter 2).

27 Internal coolant leakage

1   Leaking cylinder head gasket (Chapter 2).
2   Cracked cylinder bore or cylinder head (Chapter 2).

28 Coolant loss

1   Too much coolant in system (Chapter 1).
2   Coolant boiling away because of overheating (Chapter 3).
3   Internal or external leakage (Chapter 3).
4   Faulty radiator cap (Chapter 3).

29 Poor coolant circulation

1   Inoperative water pump (Chapter 3).
2   Restriction in cooling system (Chapters 1 and 3).
3   Water pump drivebelt defective/out of adjustment (Chapter 1).
4   Thermostat sticking (Chapter 3).

Automatic transaxle

Note: *Due to the complexity of the automatic transaxle, it is difficult for the home mechanic to properly diagnose and service this component. For problems other than the following, the vehicle should be taken to a dealer or transmission shop.*

30 Fluid leakage

1   Automatic transmission fluid is a deep red color. Fluid leaks should not be confused with engine oil, which can easily be blown onto the transaxle by air flow.
2   To pinpoint a leak, first remove all built-up dirt and grime from the transaxle housing with degreasing agents and/or steam cleaning. Then drive the vehicle at low speeds so air flow will not blow the leak far from its source. Raise the vehicle and determine where the leak is coming from. Common areas of leakage are:
   a) *Pan (Chapters 1 and 7)*
   b) *Dipstick tube (Chapters 1 and 7)*
   c) *Transaxle oil lines (Chapters 3 and 7)*
   d) *Speed sensor (Chapter 7)*

31 Transaxle fluid brown or has a burned smell

Transaxle fluid burned (Chapter 1).

32 General shift mechanism problems

1   Chapter 7, Part B, deals with checking and adjusting the shift linkage on automatic transaxles. Common problems which may be attributed to poorly adjusted linkage are:
   a) *Engine starting in gears other than Park or Neutral.*
   b) *Indicator on shifter pointing to a gear other than the one actually being used.*
   c) *Vehicle moves when in Park.*
2   Refer to Chapter 7B for the shift linkage adjustment procedure.

33 Transaxle will not downshift with accelerator pedal pressed to the floor

Fault in the transaxle electronic controls.

34 Engine will start in gears other than Park or Neutral

Shift linkage out of adjustment (Chapter 7B).

35 Transaxle slips, shifts roughly, is noisy or has no drive in forward or reverse gears

There are many probable causes for the above problems, but the home mechanic should be concerned with only one possibility - fluid level. Before taking the vehicle to a repair shop, check the level and condition of the fluid as described in Chapter 1. Correct the fluid level as necessary or change the fluid and filter if needed. If the problem persists, have a professional diagnose the cause.

Driveaxles

36 Clicking noise in turns

Worn or damaged outboard CV joint (Chapter 8).

37 Shudder or vibration during acceleration

1   Excessive toe-in (Chapter 10).
2   Worn or damaged inboard or outboard CV joints (Chapter 8).
3   Sticking or worn inboard CV joint assembly (Chapter 8).

38 Vibration at highway speeds

1   Out-of-balance front wheels and/or tires (Chapters 1 and 10).
2   Out-of-round front tires (Chapters 1 and 10).
3   Worn CV joint(s) (Chapter 8).

Brakes

Note: *Before assuming that a brake problem exists, make sure that:*
   a) *The tires are in good condition and properly inflated (Chapter 1).*
   b) *The front end alignment is correct (Chapter 10).*
   c) *The vehicle is not loaded with weight in an unequal manner.*

39 Vehicle pulls to one side during braking

1   Incorrect tire pressures (Chapter 1).
2   Front end out of line (have the front end aligned).
3   Front or rear tires not matched to one another.
4   Restricted brake lines or hoses (Chapter 9).
5   Malfunctioning caliper or drum brake assembly (Chapter 9).
6   Loose suspension parts (Chapter 10).
7   Loose calipers (Chapter 9).
8   Excessive wear of brake shoe or pad material or disc/drum on one side (Chapter 9).

40 Noise (high-pitched squeal when the brakes are applied)

1   Front disc brake pads worn out. The noise comes from the wear sensor rubbing against the disc (does not apply to all vehicles). Replace pads with new ones immediately (Chapter 9).
2   Incorrectly installed new pads (many require an anti-squeal compound on the backing plates).

41 Brake roughness or chatter (pedal pulsates)

1   Excessive lateral runout of brake disc (Chapter 9).
2   Brake drum out-of-round (Chapter 9).

3 Uneven pad wear (Chapter 9).
4 Defective disc (Chapter 9).

42 Excessive brake pedal effort required to stop vehicle

1 Malfunctioning power brake booster (Chapter 9).
2 Partial system failure (Chapter 9).
3 Excessively worn pads or shoes (Chapter 9).
4 Piston in caliper or wheel cylinder stuck or sluggish (Chapter 9).
5 Brake pads or shoes contaminated with oil or grease (Chapter 9).
6 New pads or shoes installed and not yet seated. It will take a while for the new material to seat against the disc or drum.

43 Excessive brake pedal travel

1 Partial brake system failure (Chapter 9).
2 Insufficient fluid in master cylinder (Chapters 1 and 9).
3 Air trapped in system (Chapters 1 and 9).

44 Dragging brakes

1 Incorrect adjustment of brake light switch (Chapter 9).
2 Master cylinder pistons not returning correctly (Chapter 9).
3 Restricted brake lines or hoses (Chapters 1 and 9).
4 Incorrect parking brake adjustment (Chapter 9).
5 Caliper piston sticking (Chapter 9).

45 Grabbing or uneven braking action

1 Malfunction of proportioning valve (Chapter 9).
2 Malfunction of power brake booster unit (Chapter 9).
3 Binding brake pedal mechanism (Chapter 9).
4 Brake fluid, grease or oil on brake pads or shoes (Chapter 9).

46 Brake pedal feels spongy when depressed

1 Air in hydraulic lines (Chapter 9).
2 Master cylinder mounting bolts loose (Chapter 9).
3 Master cylinder defective (Chapter 9).

47 Brake pedal travels to the floor with little resistance

1 Little or no fluid in the master cylinder reservoir caused by leaking caliper or wheel cylinder piston(s) (Chapter 9).
2 Loose, damaged or disconnected brake lines (Chapter 9).

48 Parking brake does not hold

Parking brake linkage improperly adjusted (Chapters 1 and 9).

Suspension and steering systems

Note: *Before attempting to diagnose the suspension and steering systems, perform the following preliminary checks:*

a) Tires for wrong pressure and uneven wear.
b) Steering universal joints from the column to the steering gear for loose connectors or wear.
c) Front and rear suspension and the steering gear assembly for loose or damaged parts.
d) Out-of-round or out-of-balance tires, bent rims and loose and/or rough wheel bearings.

49 Vehicle pulls to one side

1 Mismatched or uneven tires (Chapter 10).
2 Broken or sagging springs (Chapter 10).
3 Wheels in need of alignment (Chapter 10).
4 Front brake dragging (Chapter 9).

50 Abnormal or excessive tire wear

1 Wheel alignment (Chapter 10).
2 Sagging or broken springs (Chapter 10).
3 Tire out of balance (Chapter 10).
4 Worn strut damper (Chapter 10).
5 Overloaded vehicle.
6 Tires not rotated regularly.
7 Tire pressure not correct (Chapter 1).

51 Wheel makes a thumping noise

1 Blister or bump on tire (Chapter 10).
2 Improper strut damper action (Chapter 10).

52 Shimmy, shake or vibration

1 Tire or wheel out-of-balance or out-of-round (Chapter 10).
2 Loose or worn wheel bearings (Chapters 1, 8 and 10).
3 Worn tie-rod ends (Chapter 10).
4 Worn lower balljoints (Chapters 1 and 10).
5 Excessive wheel runout (Chapter 10).
6 Blister or bump on tire (Chapter 10).
7 Steering gear mounting bolts loose (Chapter 10).

53 Hard steering

1 Lack of lubrication at balljoints, tie-rod ends and steering gear assembly (Chapter 10).
2 Front wheel alignment (Chapter 10).
3 Low tire pressure(s) (Chapters 1 and 10).
4 Power steering fluid low (Chapter 1).
5 Power steering pump or steering gear defective (Chapter 10).

54 Poor returnability of steering to center

1 Lack of lubrication at balljoints and tie-rod ends (Chapter 10).
2 Binding in balljoints (Chapter 10).
3 Binding in steering column (Chapter 10).
4 Lack of lubricant in steering gear assembly (Chapter 10).
5 Front wheels in need of alignment or front suspension components bentChapter 10).

55 Abnormal noise at the front end

1 Lack of lubrication at balljoints and tie-rod ends (Chapters 1 and 10).

2   Damaged strut mounting (Chapter 10).
3   Worn control arm bushings or tie-rod ends (Chapter 10).
4   Loose stabilizer bar (Chapter 10).
5   Loose wheel nuts (Chapters 1 and 10).
6   Loose suspension bolts (Chapter 10).

56   Wander or poor steering stability

1   Mismatched or uneven tires (Chapter 10).
2   Lack of lubrication at balljoints and tie-rod ends (Chapters 1 and 10).
3   Worn strut assemblies (Chapter 10).
4   Loose stabilizer bar (Chapter 10).
5   Broken or sagging springs (Chapter 10).
6   Wheel alignment (Chapter 10).

57   Erratic steering when braking

1   Wheel bearings worn (Chapter 10).
2   Broken or sagging springs (Chapter 10).
3   Leaking wheel cylinder or caliper (Chapter 9).
4   Warped brake discs (Chapter 9).

58   Excessive pitching and/or rolling around corners or during braking

1   Loose stabilizer bar (Chapter 10).
2   Worn strut dampers or mountings (Chapter 10).
3   Broken or sagging springs (Chapter 10).
4   Overloaded vehicle.

59   Suspension bottoms

1   Overloaded vehicle.
2   Worn strut dampers (Chapter 10).
3   Incorrect, broken or sagging springs (Chapter 10).

60   Cupped tires

1   Front wheel or rear wheel alignment (Chapter 10).

2   Worn strut dampers (Chapter 10).
3   Wheel bearings worn (Chapter 10).
4   Excessive tire or wheel runout (Chapter 10).
5   Worn balljoints (Chapter 10).

61   Excessive tire wear on outside edge

1   Inflation pressures incorrect (Chapter 1).
2   Excessive speed in turns.
3   Front end alignment incorrect (excessive toe-in). Have professionally aligned.
4   Suspension arm bent or twisted (Chapter 10).

62   Excessive tire wear on inside edge

1   Inflation pressures incorrect (Chapter 1).
2   Front end alignment incorrect (toe-out). Have professionally aligned.
3   Loose or damaged steering components (Chapter 10).

63   Tire tread worn in one place

1   Tires out of balance.
2   Damaged or buckled wheel. Inspect and replace if necessary.
3   Defective tire (Chapter 1).

64   Excessive play or looseness in steering system

1   Wheel bearing(s) worn (Chapter 10).
2   Tie-rod end loose (Chapter 10).
3   Steering gear loose (Chapter 10).
4   Worn or loose steering intermediate shaft (Chapter 10).

65   Rattling or clicking noise in steering gear

1   Insufficient or improper lubricant in steering gear assembly (Chapter 10).
2   Steering gear attachment loose (Chapter 10).

Chapter 1
Tune-up and routine maintenance

Contents

Specifications

Recommended lubricants and fluids

Engine oil

Type
  Gasoline engine .... API SG or SG/CD multigrade and fuel efficient oil
  Flexible fuel engine .... Mopar Flexible Fuel engine oil meeting Chrysler Standard MS-9214

Viscosity
  Gasoline engine .... See accompanying chart
  Flexible fuel engine .... SAE 10W30

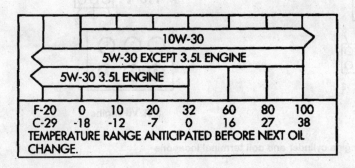

10W-30
5W-30 EXCEPT 3.5L ENGINE
5W-30 3.5L ENGINE

F-20	0	10	20	32	60	80	100
C-29	-18	-12	-7	0	16	27	38

TEMPERATURE RANGE ANTICIPATED BEFORE NEXT OIL CHANGE.

Engine oil viscosity chart - For best fuel economy and cold starting, select the lowest SAE viscosity grade for the expected temperature range

Recommended lubricants and fluids (continued)

Automatic transaxle fluid	DEXRON II
Differential oil	SAE 80W90 gear oil
Power steering fluid	Chrysler power steering fluid or equivalent
Brake fluid	DOT 3 brake fluid
Engine coolant	50/50 mixture of ethylene glycol-based antifreeze and water
Parking brake mechanism grease	White lithium-based grease NLGI no. 2
Chassis lubrication grease	NLGI no. 2 EP grease
Hood, door and trunk/liftgate hinge lubricant	Engine oil
Door hinge and check spring grease..	NLGI no. 2 multi-purpose grease
Key lock cylinder lubricant..	Graphite spray
Hood latch assembly lubricant	Mopar Lubriplate or equivalent
Door latch striker lubricant	Mopar Door Ease no. 3744859 or equivalent

Capacities*

Engine oil (including filter)	
3.5L engine...	5.5 qts
3.3L engine...	5.0 qts
Automatic transaxle	
From dry (including torque converter).....................................	9.9 qts
Fluid and filter change...	4 qts
Cooling system	
3.5L engine...	12 qts
3.3L engine...	10 qts

All capacities approximate. Add as necessary to bring to appropriate level.

Brakes

Disc brake pad wear limit (including metal shoe)	5/16 inch
Drum brake shoe wear limit...	1/16 inch

Ignition system

Spark plug type	
1993	
3.5L..	Champion RN12LYC5, or equivalent
3.3L..	Champion RN14MC5, or equivalent
1994	
3.5L..	Champion RN12LYC5, or equivalent
3.3L gasoline..	Champion RN14MC5, or equivalent
3.3L flexible fuel	Champion RN12MC4, or equivalent
1995	
3.5L..	Champion RC14E5, or equivalent
3.3L gasoline..	Champion RN14MC5, or equivalent
3.3L flexible fuel	Champion RN12MC4, or equivalent
1996 and later	
3.5L..	Champion RN12LYC, or equivalent
3.3L..	Champion RN14MC5, or equivalent

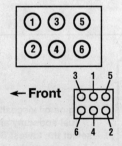

3.3L V6 engine

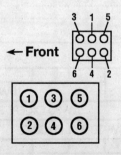

3.5L V6 engine

Engine cylinder and coil terminal locations

Spark plug gap
  1993
    3.5L .... 0.048 to 0.053 inch
    3.3L .... 0.048 to 0.053 inch
  1994
    3.5L .... 0.048 to 0.053 inch
    3.3L gasoline .... 0.048 to 0.053 inch
    3.3L flexible fuel .... 0.043 to 0.048 inch
  1995
    3.5L .... 0.048 to 0.053 inch
    3.3L gasoline .... 0.048 to 0.053 inch
    3.3L flexible fuel .... 0.043 to 0.048 inch
  1996 and later
    3.5L .... 0.030 inch
    3.3L .... 0.048 to 0.053 inch
Spark plug wire resistance
  Minimum .... 3000 ohms per foot
  Maximum .... 12,000 ohms per foot
Firing order 1-2-3-4-5-6

Torque specifications   **Ft-lbs** (unless otherwise indicated)
Spark plugs 20
Wheel lug nuts 95
Automatic transaxle
  Pan bolts 15
  Filter-to-valve body screws .... 40 in-lbs
Differential
  Fill plug 35
  Drain plug .... 60 in-lbs

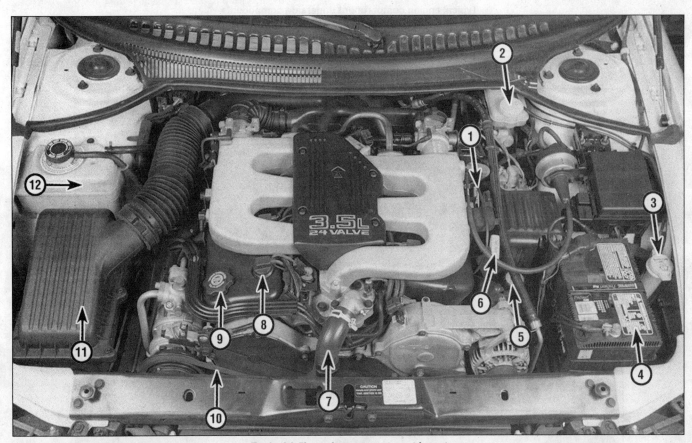

Typical 3.5L engine compartment layout

1 *Automatic transaxle dipstick*	5 *Power steering fluid reservoir*	9 *Engine oil filler cap*
2 *Brake master cylinder reservoir*	6 *Engine oil dipstick*	10 *Drivebelt*
3 *Windshield washer fluid reservoir*	7 *Upper radiator hose*	11 *Air filter housing*
4 *Battery*	8 *Spark plug boot*	12 *Engine coolant reservoir*

Typical engine compartment underside components

1	Evaporative system canister	5	Inner CV joint boot	9	Differential oil drain plug
2	Front brake caliper	6	Exhaust system	10	Outer CV joint boot
3	Lower radiator hose	7	Engine oil drain plug		
4	Spring and shock absorber strut	8	Automatic transaxle		

Typical rear underside components

1	Resonator/tailpipe	4	Shock and spring assembly	7	Parking brake cable
2	Fuel tank	5	Fuel filter	8	Rear sway bar
3	Fuel filler hose	6	Muffler	9	Rear disc brake

1 Chrysler LH model maintenance schedule

The following maintenance intervals are based on the assumption that the vehicle owner will be doing the maintenance or service work, as opposed to having a dealer service department do the work. Although the time/mileage intervals are loosely based on factory recommendations, most have been shortened to ensure, for example, that such items as lubricants and fluids are checked/changed at intervals that promote maximum engine/driveline service life. Also, subject to the preference of the individual owner interested in keeping his or her vehicle in peak condition at all times, and with the vehicle's ultimate resale in mind, many of the maintenance procedures may be performed more often than recommended in the following schedule. We encourage such owner initiative.

When the vehicle is new it should be serviced initially by a factory authorized dealer service department to protect the factory warranty. In many cases the initial maintenance check is done at no cost to the owner (check with your dealer service department for more information).

Every 250 miles or weekly, whichever comes first

Check the engine oil level; add oil as necessary (see Section 4)
Check the engine coolant level; add coolant as necessary (see Section 4)
Check the windshield washer fluid level (see Section 4)
Check the battery electrolyte level (see Section 4)
Check the brake fluid level (see Section 4)
Check the tires and tire pressures (see Section 5)
Check the automatic transaxle fluid level (see Section 6)
Check the power steering fluid level (see Section 7)
Check the operation of all lights
Check the horn operation

Every 3000 miles or 3 months, whichever comes first

Change the engine oil and filter (see Section 8)*

Every 7,500 miles or 6 months, whichever comes first

Check and clean the battery (see Section 9)
Check the cooling system hoses and connections for leaks and damage (see Section 10)
Check the condition of all vacuum hoses and connections (see Section 11)
Check the wiper blade condition (see Section 12)
Rotate the tires (see Section 13)
Check for freeplay in the steering linkage and balljoints (see Section 14)
Check the exhaust pipes and hangers (see Section 15)

Every 15,000 miles or 12 months, whichever comes first

Check the differential lubricant level (see Section 16)
Lubricate the front suspension steering balljoints (see Section 17)*
Check the brakes (see Section 18)*

Check the fuel system hoses and connections for leaks and damage (see Section 19)
Check the drivebelts (see Section 20)

Every 30,000 miles or 24 months, whichever comes first

Replace the air filter element (see Section 21)*
Change the automatic transaxle fluid and filter (see Section 22)*
Check the driveaxle boots (see Section 23)*
Replace the differential lubricant (see Section 24)
Drain and replace the engine coolant (see Section 25)
Check and replace if necessary, the PCV valve (see Section 26)
Check the fuel evaporative emission system hoses (see Section 27)
Replace the spark plugs (see Section 28)
Check the condition of the primary ignition wires and spark plug wires (see Section 29)
Check the operation of the seat belts (see Section 30)

Every 60,000 miles or 48 months, whichever comes first

Replace the fuel filter (see Section 31)

Every 105,000 miles or 84 months, whichever comes first

Replace the timing belt (3.5L engines only) (see Chapter 2B)
* This item is affected by "severe" operating conditions as described below. If the vehicle in question is operated under "severe" conditions, perform all maintenance procedures marked with an asterisk (*) at the following intervals:
Consider the conditions "severe" if most driving is done . . .
In dusty areas
Towing a trailer
Idling for extended periods and/or low-speed operation
When outside temperatures remain below freezing and most trips are less than four miles
In heavy city traffic where outside temperatures regularly reach 90-degrees F or higher

Every 2,000 miles

Change the engine oil and filter

Every 9,000 miles

Check the driveaxle, suspension and steering boots
Check the brakes
Lubricate the tie-rod ends

Every 15,000 miles

Replace the air filter element
Change the automatic transaxle fluid and filter

1

2   Introduction

This Chapter is designed to help the home mechanic maintain the Chrysler LH models with the goals of maximum performance, economy, safety and reliability in mind.

Included is a master maintenance schedule, followed by procedures dealing specifically with each item on the schedule. Visual checks, adjustments, component replacement and other helpful items are included. Refer to the accompanying illustrations of the engine compartment and the underside of the vehicle for the locations of various components.

Adhering to the mileage/time maintenance schedule and following the step-by-step procedures, which is simply a preventive maintenance program, will result in maximum reliability and vehicle service life. Keep in mind that it's a comprehensive program - maintaining some items but not others at the specified intervals will not produce the same results.

As you service the vehicle, you'll discover that many of the procedures can - and should - be grouped together because of the nature of the particular procedure you're performing or because of the close proximity of two otherwise unrelated components to one another.

For example, if the vehicle is raised, you should inspect the exhaust, suspension, steering and fuel systems while you're under the vehicle. When you're rotating the tires, it makes good sense to check the brakes, since the wheels are already removed. Finally, let's suppose you have to borrow or rent a torque wrench. Even if you only need it to tighten the spark plugs, you might as well check the torque of as many critical fasteners as time allows.

The first step in this maintenance program is to prepare yourself before the actual work begins. Read through all the procedures you're planning to do, then gather up all the parts and tools needed. If it looks like you might run into problems during a particular job, seek advice from a mechanic or an experienced do-it-yourselfer.

3   Tune-up general information

The term "tune-up" is used in this manual to represent a combination of individual operations rather than one specific procedure.

If, from the time the vehicle is new, the routine maintenance schedule is followed closely and frequent checks are made of fluid levels and high wear items, as suggested throughout this manual, the engine will be kept in relatively good running condition and the need for additional work will be minimized.

More likely than not, however, there will be times when the engine is running poorly due to lack of regular maintenance. This is even more likely if a used vehicle, which hasn't received regular and frequent maintenance checks, is purchased. In such cases, an engine tune-up will be needed outside of the regular routine maintenance intervals.

The first step in any tune-up or diagnostic procedure to help correct a poor running engine is a cylinder compression check. A compression check (see Chapter 2, Part C) will help determine the condition of internal engine components and should be used as a guide for tune-up and repair procedures. For instance, if a compression check indicates serious internal engine wear, a conventional tune-up will not improve the performance of the engine and would be a waste of time and money. Because of its importance, the compression check should be done by someone with the right equipment and the knowledge to use it properly.

The following procedures are those most often needed to bring a generally poor running engine back into a proper state of tune:

Minor tune-up

Check all engine related fluids (see Section 4)
Clean, inspect and test the battery (see Section 9)
Replace the spark plugs (see Section 28)
Inspect the spark plug wires (see Section 29)
Check and adjust the drivebelts (see Section 20)
Check the air filter (see Section 21)
Check the PCV valve (see Section 26)
Check all underhood hoses (see Section 11)
Service the cooling system (see Section 25)

Major tune-up

All items listed under Minor tune-up plus . . .
Replace the air filter (see Section 21)
Check the fuel system (see Section 19)
Replace the fuel filter (see Section 31)
Check the charging system (see Chapter 5)

4   Fluid level checks (every 250 miles or weekly)

Note: *The following are fluid level checks to be done on a 250 mile or weekly basis. Additional fluid level checks can be found in specific maintenance procedures which follow. Regardless of the intervals, develop the habit of checking under the vehicle periodically for evidence of fluid leaks.*

1   Fluids are an essential part of the lubrication, cooling, brake and window washer systems. Because the fluids gradually become depleted and/or contaminated during normal operation of the vehicle, they must be replenished periodically. See *Recommended lubricants and fluids* at the beginning of this Chapter before adding fluid to any of the following components. **Note:** *The vehicle must be on level ground when fluid levels are checked.*

Engine oil

Refer to illustrations 4.4a, 4.4b and 4.5
2   The engine oil level is checked with a dipstick which is located at

4.4a The engine oil dipstick is located at the front left (driver's side) of the engine

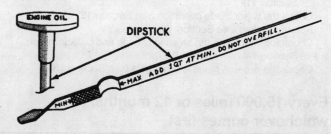

4.4b The oil level should be between the MIN and MAX marks on the dipstick - if it isn't, add enough oil to bring the level up to or near the MAX mark (it takes one quart to raise the level from the MIN to MAX mark)

4.5 Turn the oil filler cap counterclockwise to remove it

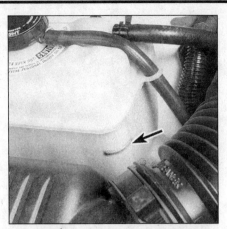

4.8 Make sure the coolant level in the reservoir is at or near the MAX mark - if it's below the MIN mark, add more coolant mixture or water

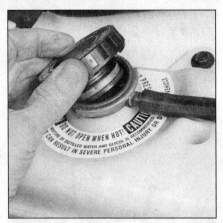

4.11 Remove the cap to add more coolant to the reservoir

the front left (driver's) side of the engine. The dipstick extends through a tube and into the oil pan at the bottom of the engine.

3   The oil level should be checked before the vehicle has been driven, or about 15 minutes after the engine has been shut off. If the oil is checked immediately after driving the vehicle, some of the oil will remain in the upper engine components, resulting in an inaccurate reading on the dipstick.

4   Pull the dipstick out of the tube **(see illustration)** and wipe all the oil off the end with a clean rag or paper towel. Insert the clean dipstick all the way back into the tube, then pull it out again. Note the oil level at the end of the dipstick. Add oil as necessary to keep the level at the Max mark **(see illustration)**.

5   Oil is added to the engine after removing a cap located on the valve cover **(see illustration)**. The cap will be marked "Engine oil" or something similar. A funnel may help reduce spills as the oil is poured in.

6   Don't allow the level to drop below the Min mark or engine damage may occur. On the other hand, don't overfill the engine by adding too much oil - it may result in oil fouled spark plugs, oil leaks or seal failures.

7   Checking the oil level is an important preventive maintenance step. A consistently low oil level indicates oil leakage through damaged seals, defective gaskets or past worn rings or valve guides. If the oil looks milky in color or has water droplets in it, the block may be cracked. The engine should be checked immediately. The condition of the oil should also be checked. Each time you check the oil level, slide your thumb and index finger up the dipstick before wiping off the oil. If you see small dirt or metal particles clinging to the dipstick, the oil should be changed (see Section 8).

Engine coolant

Refer to illustrations 4.8 and 4.11

Warning: *Do not allow antifreeze to come in contact with your skin or painted surfaces of the vehicle. Flush contaminated areas immediately with plenty of water. Don't store new coolant or leave old coolant lying around where it's accessible to children or pets - they're attracted by its sweet smell. Ingestion of even a small amount of coolant can be fatal! Wipe up garage floor and drip pan spills immediately. Keep antifreeze containers covered and repair cooling system leaks as soon as they're noticed.*

8   All vehicles covered by this manual are equipped with a pressurized coolant recovery system, which makes coolant level checks very easy. A coolant reservoir attached to the inner fender panel or the radiator itself is connected by a hose to the radiator filler neck **(see illustration)**. As the engine warms up, some coolant escapes through a valve in the radiator cap and travels through the hose into the reservoir. As the engine cools, the coolant is automatically drawn back into the cooling system to maintain the correct level.

9   The coolant level should be checked when the engine is at normal operating temperature. Simply note the fluid level in the reservoir - it should be above the Cold Fill mark when the engine is at normal operating temperature.

10   If only a small amount of coolant is required to bring the system up to the proper level, regular water can be used. However, to maintain the proper antifreeze/water mixture in the system, both should be mixed together to replenish a low level. High-quality antifreeze/coolant should be mixed with water in the proportion specified on the antifreeze container.

11   Coolant should be added to the reservoir after removing the cap **(see illustration)**. **Warning:** *Don't remove the cap when the engine is warm!* Wait until the engine has cooled, then wrap a thick cloth around the cap and turn it to the first stop. If any steam escapes from the cap, allow the engine to cool further, then remove the cap.

12   As the coolant level is checked, note the condition of the coolant as well. It should be relatively clear. If it's brown or rust colored, the system should be drained, flushed and refilled (see Section 25).

13   If the coolant level drops consistently, there may be a leak in the system. Check the radiator, hoses, filler cap, drain plugs and water pump (see Section 25). If no leaks are noted, have the filler cap pressure tested by a service station.

Windshield washer fluid

Refer to illustration 4.14

14   The fluid for the windshield washer system is stored in a plastic reservoir. The level inside each reservoir should be maintained about one inch below the filler cap. The reservoir is accessible after opening the hood **(see illustration)**.

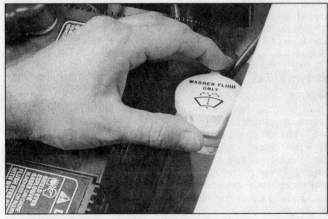

4.14 Flip up the cap to add more fluid to the windshield washer reservoir

4.18 Remove the cell caps to check the water level in the battery - if the level is low add distilled water only

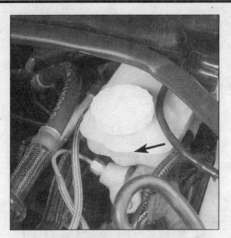

4.21 The brake fluid level on the translucent white plastic brake fluid reservoir should be kept at the Max mark (arrow)

5.2 Use a tire tread depth indicator to monitor tire wear - they are available at auto parts stores and service stations and cost very little

15   In milder climates, plain water can be used in the reservoir, but it should be kept no more than two-thirds full to allow for expansion if the water freezes. In colder climates, use windshield washer system antifreeze, available at any auto parts store, to lower the freezing point of the fluid. Mix the antifreeze with water in accordance with the manufacturer's directions on the container. **Caution:** *Don't use cooling system antifreeze - it'll damage the vehicle's paint. To help prevent icing in cold weather, warm the windshield with the defroster before using the washer.*

Battery electrolyte

Refer to illustration 4.18

Warning: *Certain precautions must be followed when checking or servicing a battery. Hydrogen gas, which is highly flammable, is produced in the cells, so keep lighted tobacco, open flames, bare light bulbs and sparks away from the battery. The electrolyte inside the battery is dilute sulfuric acid, which can burn skin and cause serious injury if splashed in your eyes (wear safety glasses). It'll also ruin clothes and painted surfaces. Remove all metal jewelry which could contact the positive battery terminal and a grounded metal source, causing a direct short.*

16   Vehicles equipped with a maintenance-free battery require no maintenance - the battery case is sealed and has no removable caps for adding water.

17   If a maintenance-type battery is installed, the caps on top of the battery should be removed periodically to check for a low electrolyte level. This check is more critical during warm summer months.

18   Remove each of the caps and add distilled water to bring the level in each cell to the split ring in the filler opening **(see illustration)**.

19   At the same time the battery water level is checked, the overall condition of the battery and related components should be noted. See Section 9 for complete battery check and maintenance procedures.

Brake fluid

Refer to illustration 4.21

20   The brake master cylinder is located on the driver's side of the engine compartment firewall.

21   The level should be maintained at the Max mark on the reservoir **(see illustration)**.

22   If additional fluid is necessary to bring the level up, use a rag to clean all dirt off the top of the reservoir. If any foreign matter enters the master cylinder when the cap is removed, blockage in the brake system lines can occur. Also, make sure all painted surfaces around the master cylinder are covered, since brake fluid will ruin paint. Carefully pour new, clean brake fluid into the master cylinder. Be careful not to spill the fluid on painted surfaces. Be sure the specified

fluid is used; mixing different types of brake fluid can cause damage to the system. See *Recommended lubricants and fluids* at the beginning of this Chapter or your owner's manual.

23   At this time the fluid and the master cylinder can be inspected for contamination. Normally the brake hydraulic system won't need periodic draining and refilling, but if rust deposits, dirt particles or water droplets are seen in the fluid, the system should be dismantled, cleaned and refilled with fresh fluid.

24   Reinstall the master cylinder cap.

25   The brake fluid in the master cylinder will drop slightly as the brake shoes or pads at each wheel wear down during normal operation. If the master cylinder requires repeated replenishing to keep the level up, it's an indication of leaks in the brake system which should be corrected immediately. Check all brake lines and connections, along with the wheel cylinders and booster (see Chapter 9 for more information).

26   If you discover that the reservoir is empty or nearly empty, the brake system should be bled (see Chapter 9).

5   Tire and tire pressure checks (every 250 miles or weekly)

Refer to illustrations 5.2, 5.3, 5.4a, 5.4b and 5.8

1   Periodic inspection of the tires may spare you the inconvenience of being stranded with a flat tire. It can also provide you with vital information regarding possible problems in the steering and suspension systems before major damage occurs.

2   The original tires on this vehicle are equipped with 1/2-inch wide bands that will appear when tread depth reaches 1/16-inch, but they don't appear until the tires are worn out. Tread wear can be monitored with a simple, inexpensive device known as a tread depth indicator **(see illustration)**.

3   Note any abnormal tread wear **(see illustration)**. Tread pattern irregularities such as cupping, flat spots and more wear on one side than the other are indications of front end alignment and/or balance problems. If any of these conditions are noted, take the vehicle to a tire shop or service station to correct the problem.

4   Look closely for cuts, punctures and embedded nails or tacks. Sometimes a tire will hold air pressure for a short time or leak down very slowly after a nail has embedded itself in the tread. If a slow leak persists, check the valve stem core to make sure it's tight **(see illustration)**. Examine the tread for an object that may have embedded itself in the tire or for a "plug" that may have begun to leak (radial tire punctures are repaired with a plug that's installed in a puncture). If a puncture is suspected, it can be easily verified by spraying a solution

Condition	Probable cause	Corrective action	Condition	Probable cause	Corrective action
Shoulder wear	• Underinflation (both sides wear) • Incorrect wheel camber (one side wear) • Hard cornering • Lack of rotation	• Measure and adjust pressure. • Repair or replace axle and suspension parts. • Reduce speed. • Rotate tires.	Feathered edge Toe wear	• Incorrect toe	• Adjust toe-in.
Center wear	• Overinflation • Lack of rotation	• Measure and adjust pressure. • Rotate tires.	Uneven wear	• Incorrect camber or caster • Malfunctioning suspension • Unbalanced wheel • Out-of-round brake drum • Lack of rotation	• Repair or replace axle and suspension parts. • Repair or replace suspension parts. • Balance or replace. • Turn or replace. • Rotate tires.

5.3 This chart will help you determine the condition of the tires, the probable cause(s) of abnormal wear and the corrective action necessary

of soapy water onto the puncture area **(see illustration)**. The soapy solution will bubble if there's a leak. Unless the puncture is unusually large, a tire shop or service station can usually repair the tire.

5   Carefully inspect the inner sidewall of each tire for evidence of brake fluid leakage. If you see any, inspect the brakes immediately.

6   Correct air pressure adds miles to the lifespan of the tires, improves mileage and enhances overall ride quality. Tire pressure cannot be accurately estimated by looking at a tire, especially if it's a radial. A tire pressure gauge is essential. Keep an accurate gauge in the vehicle. The pressure gauges attached to the nozzles of air hoses at gas stations are often inaccurate.

7   Always check tire pressure when the tires are cold. Cold, in this case, means the vehicle has not been driven over a mile in the three

hours preceding a tire pressure check. A pressure rise of four to eight pounds is not uncommon once the tires are warm.

8   Unscrew the valve cap protruding from the wheel or hubcap and push the gauge firmly onto the valve stem **(see illustration)**. Note the reading on the gauge and compare the figure to the recommended tire pressure shown on the placard on the driver's side door pillar. Be sure to reinstall the valve cap to keep dirt and moisture out of the valve stem mechanism. Check all four tires and, if necessary, add enough air to bring them up to the recommended pressure.

9   Don't forget to keep the spare tire inflated to the specified pressure (refer to your owner's manual or the tire sidewall). Note that the pressure recommended for the compact spare is higher than for the tires on the vehicle.

5.4a If a tire loses air on a steady basis, check the valve core first to make sure it's snug (special inexpensive wrenches are commonly available at auto parts stores)

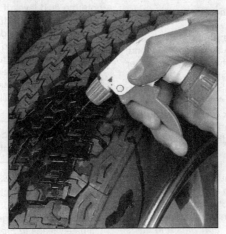

5.4b If the valve core is tight, raise the corner of the vehicle with the low tire and spray a soapy water solution onto the tread as the tire is turned slowly - leaks will cause small bubbles to appear

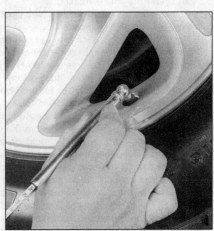

5.8 To extend the life of the tires, check the air pressure at least once a week with an accurate gauge (don't forget the spare!)

6.3 The automatic transaxle fluid is located on the left side of the engine compartment - don't confuse it with the engine oil dipstick

7.5 The power steering fluid dipstick on most models is marked on both sides for checking the fluid cold (as shown) or hot

6   Automatic transaxle fluid level check (every 250 miles or weekly)

Refer to illustrations 6.3 and 6.4

1   The fluid inside the transaxle should be at normal operating temperature to get an accurate reading on the dipstick. This is done by driving the vehicle for several miles, making frequent starts and stops to allow the transaxle to shift through all gears.

2   Park the vehicle on a level surface, place the gear selector lever in Park and leave the engine running.

3   Remove the transaxle dipstick **(see illustration)** and wipe all the fluid from the end with a clean rag.

4   Push the dipstick back into the transaxle until the cap seats completely. Remove the dipstick again and note the fluid on the end. The level should be in the area marked Hot (between the two upper holes in the dipstick) **(see illustration)**. If the fluid isn't hot (temperature about 100-degrees F), the level should be in the area marked Warm (between the two lower holes).

5   If the fluid level is at or below the Add mark on the dipstick, add enough fluid to raise the level to within the marks indicated for the appropriate temperature. Fluid should be added directly into the dipstick hole, using a funnel to prevent spills.

6   Do not overfill the transaxle. Never allow the fluid level to go above the upper hole on the dipstick - it could cause internal transaxle damage. The best way to prevent overfilling is to add fluid a little at a time, driving the vehicle and checking the level between additions.

7   Use only the transaxle fluid specified by the manufacturer. This information can be found in the *Recommended lubricants and fluids* section at the beginning of this Chapter.

8   The condition of the fluid should also be checked along with the level. If it's a dark reddish-brown color, or if it smells burned, it should be changed. If you're in doubt about the condition of the fluid, purchase some new fluid and compare the two for color and smell.

6.4 Check the fluid with the transaxle at normal operating temperature - the level should be kept in the HOT range (between the two upper holes or marks)

7.2 The power steering reservoir dipstick is located at the front of the engine near the radiator

7   Power steering fluid level check (every 250 miles or weekly)

Refer to illustrations 7.2 and 7.5

1   Unlike manual steering, the power steering system relies on fluid which may, over a period of time, require replenishing.

2   The reservoir for the power steering pump is located at the front of the engine on the left (driver's) side of the engine compartment **(see illustration)**.

3   The power steering fluid level can be checked with the engine either hot or cold.

4   With the engine off, use a rag to clean the reservoir cap and the area around the cap. This will help prevent foreign material from falling into the reservoir when the cap is removed.

5   Turn and pull out the reservoir cap, which has a dipstick attached to it. Remove the fluid at the bottom of the dipstick with a clean rag. Reinstall the cap to get a fluid level reading. Remove the cap again and note the fluid level. It should be at the Full Cold mark on the dipstick **(see illustration)**. If the engine is warm, the level can be checked on the other side of the dipstick.

6   If additional fluid is required, pour the specified type directly into the reservoir using a funnel to prevent spills.

7   If the reservoir requires frequent fluid additions, all power steering hoses, hose connections, the power steering pump and the steering box should be carefully checked for leaks.

8   Engine oil and filter change (every 3000 miles or 3 months)

Refer to illustrations 8.3, 8.9, 8.14 and 8.19

1   Frequent oil changes are the most important preventive maintenance procedures that can be done by the home mechanic. When engine oil ages, it gets diluted and contaminated, which ultimately leads to premature engine wear.

2   Although some sources recommend oil filter changes every other oil change, a new filter should be installed every time the oil is changed.

3   Gather together all necessary tools and materials before beginning this procedure **(see illustration)**. **Note:** *To avoid rounding*

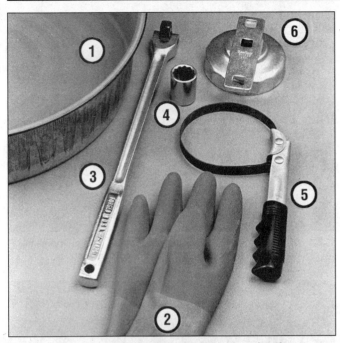

8.3 These tools are required when changing the engine oil and filter

1 **Drain pan** - It should be fairly shallow in depth, but wide to prevent spills
2 **Rubber gloves** - When removing the drain plug and filter, you will get oil on your hands (the gloves will prevent burns)
3 **Breaker bar** - Sometimes the oil drain plug is tight, and a long breaker bar is needed to loosen it
4 **Socket** - To be used with the breaker bar or a ratchet (must be the correct size to fit the drain plug - six-point preferred)
5 **Filter wrench** - This is a metal band-type wrench, which requires clearance around the filter to be effective
6 **Filter wrench** - This type fits on the bottom of the filter and can be turned with a ratchet or breaker bar (different-size wrenches are available for different types of filters)

off the corners of the drain plug, use a six-point wrench or socket.
4   In addition, you should have plenty of clean rags and newspapers handy to mop up any spills. Access to the underside of the vehicle is greatly improved if it can be lifted on a hoist, driven onto ramps or supported by jackstands. **Warning:** *Don't work under a vehicle that is supported only by a jack!*

5   If this is your first oil change on the vehicle, crawl underneath it and familiarize yourself with the locations of the oil drain plug and the oil filter. Since the engine and exhaust components will be warm during the actual work, it's a good idea to figure out any potential problems beforehand.
6   Allow the engine to warm up to normal operating temperature. If oil or tools are needed, use the warm-up time to gather everything necessary for the job. The correct type of oil to buy for your application can be found in the *Recommended lubricants and fluids* section at the beginning of this Chapter.
7   With the engine oil warm (warm oil will drain better and more built-up sludge will be removed with it), raise the vehicle and support it securely on jackstands. They should be placed under the portions of the body designated as hoisting and jacking points (see *Jacking and towing* at the front of this manual).
8   Move all necessary tools, rags and newspapers under the vehicle. Place the drain pan under the drain plug. Keep in mind that the oil will initially flow from the engine with some force, so position the pan accordingly.
9   Being careful not to touch any of the hot exhaust components, use the breaker bar and socket to remove the drain plug near the bottom of the oil pan **(see illustration)**. Depending on how hot the oil is, you may want to wear gloves while unscrewing the plug the final few turns.
10   Allow the oil to drain into the pan. It may be necessary to move the pan further under the engine as the oil flow reduces to a trickle.
11   After all the oil has drained, clean the plug thoroughly with a rag. Small metal particles may cling to it and would immediately contaminate the new oil.
12   Clean the area around the oil pan opening and reinstall the plug. Tighten it securely.
13   Move the drain pan into position under the oil filter.
14   Now use the filter wrench to loosen the oil filter **(see illustration)**.
15   Sometimes the oil filter is on so tight it cannot be loosened, or it's positioned in an area inaccessible with a conventional filter wrench. Other type of tools, which fit over the end of the filter and turned with a ratchet/breaker bar, are available and may be better suited for removing the filter. If the filter is extremely tight, position the filter wrench near the threaded end of the filter, close to the engine.
16   Completely unscrew the old filter. Be careful, it's full of oil. Empty the old oil inside the filter into the drain pan.
17   Compare the old filter with the new one to make sure they're identical.
18   Use a clean rag to remove all oil, dirt and sludge from the area where the oil filter mounts on the engine. Check the old filter to make sure the rubber gasket isn't stuck to the engine mounting surface.
19   Apply a light coat of oil to the rubber gasket on the new oil filter **(see illustration)**.

1

8.9 To avoid rounding off the corners, use the correct size box-end wrench or a socket to remove the engine oil drain plug

8.14 The oil filter is usually on very tight and normally will require a special wrench for removal - DO NOT use the wrench to tighten the filter!

8.19 Lubricate the oil filter gasket with clean engine oil before installing the filter on the engine

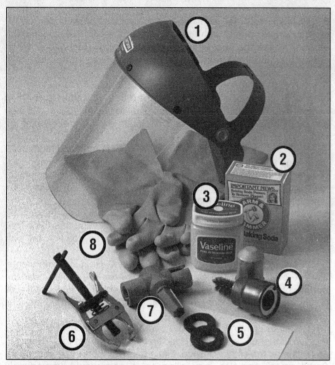

9.1 Tools and materials required for battery maintenance

1 *Face shield/safety goggles - When removing corrosion with a brush, the acidic particles can easily fly up into your eyes*
2 *Baking soda - A solution of baking soda and water can be used to neutralize corrosion*
3 *Petroleum jelly - A layer of this on the battery posts will help prevent corrosion*
4 *Battery post/cable cleaner - This wire brush cleaning tool will remove all traces of corrosion from the battery posts and cable clamps*
5 *Treated felt washers - Placing one of these on each post, directly under the cable clamps, will help prevent corrosion*
6 *Puller - Sometimes the cable clamps are very difficult to pull off the posts, even after the nut/bolt has been completely loosened. This tool pulls the clamp straight up and off the post without damage*
7 *Battery post/cable cleaner - Here is another cleaning tool which is a slightly different version of Number 4 above, but it does the same thing*
8 *Rubber gloves - Another safety item to consider when servicing the battery; remember that's acid inside the battery!*

9.5 On these models the battery is secured by a clamp at the base - make sure the nut is tight (arrow)

9.6a Battery terminal corrosion usually appears as light, fluffy powder

20 Attach the new filter to the engine following the tightening directions printed on the filter canister or packing box. Most filter manufacturers recommend against using a filter wrench due to the possibility of overtightening and damaging the canister.
21 Remove all tools and materials from under the vehicle, being careful not to spill the oil in the drain pan. Lower the vehicle off the jackstands.
22 Move to the engine compartment and locate the oil filler cap on the engine.
23 If the filler opening is obstructed, use a funnel when adding oil.
24 Pour the specified amount of new oil into the engine. Wait a few minutes to allow the oil to drain to the pan, then check the level on the dipstick (see Section 4 if necessary). If the oil level is at or above the Add mark, start the engine and allow the new oil to circulate.
25 Run the engine for only about a minute, then shut it off. Immediately look under the vehicle and check for leaks at the oil pan drain plug and around the oil filter. If either one is leaking, tighten with a bit more force.
26 With the new oil circulated and the filter now completely full,

recheck the level on the dipstick. If necessary, add enough oil to bring the level to the Full mark on the dipstick.
27 During the first few trips after an oil change, make it a point to check for leaks and keep a close watch on the oil level.
28 The old oil drained from the engine cannot be reused in its present state and should be disposed of. Oil reclamation centers, auto repair shops and gas stations will normally accept the oil. After the oil has cooled, it should be drained into containers (plastic bottles with screw-on tops are preferred) for transport to a disposal site.

9   Battery check, maintenance and charging (every 7,500 miles or 6 months)

Refer to illustrations 9.1, 9.5, 9.6a, 9.6b, 9.7a and 9.7b

1   A routine preventive maintenance program for the battery in your vehicle is the only way to ensure quick and reliable starts. But before performing any battery maintenance, make sure that you have the proper equipment necessary to work safely around the battery **(see illustration)**.
2   There are also several precautions that should be taken whenever battery maintenance is performed. Before servicing the battery, always turn the engine and all accessories off and disconnect the cable from the negative terminal of the battery.
3   The battery produces hydrogen gas, which is both flammable and explosive. Never create a spark, smoke or light a match around the battery. Always charge the battery in a ventilated area.

9.6b Removing the cable from a battery post with a wrench - sometimes special battery pliers are required for this procedure if corrosion has caused deterioration of the nut hex (always remove the ground cable first and hook it up last!)

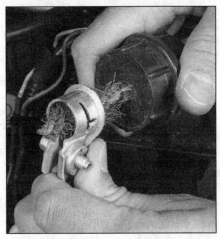

9.7a When cleaning the cable clamps, all corrosion must be removed (the inside of the clamp is tapered to match the taper on the post, so don't remove too much material)

9.7b Regardless of the type of tool used on the battery posts, a clean, shiny surface should be the result

4   Electrolyte contains poisonous and corrosive sulfuric acid. Do not allow it to get in your eyes, on your skin on your clothes. Never ingest it. Wear protective safety glasses when working near the battery. Keep children away from the battery.

5   Note the external condition of the battery. If the positive terminal and cable clamp on your vehicle's battery is equipped with a rubber protector, make sure that it's not torn or damaged. It should completely cover the terminal. Look for any corroded or loose connections, cracks in the case or cover or loose hold-down clamps **(see illustration)**. Also check the entire length of each cable for cracks and frayed conductors.

6   If corrosion, which looks like white, fluffy deposits **(see illustration)** is evident, particularly around the terminals, the battery should be removed for cleaning. Loosen the cable clamp nuts with a wrench, being careful to remove the negative cable first, and slide them off the terminals **(see illustration)**. Then disconnect the hold-down clamp nuts, remove the clamp and lift the battery from the engine compartment.

7   Clean the cable clamps thoroughly with a battery brush or a terminal cleaner and a solution of warm water and baking soda **(see illustration)**. Wash the terminals and the top of the battery case with the same solution but make sure that the solution doesn't get into the battery. When cleaning the cables, terminals and battery top, wear safety goggles and rubber gloves to prevent any solution from coming in contact with your eyes or hands. Wear old clothes too - even diluted, sulfuric acid splashed onto clothes will burn holes in them. If the terminals have been extensively corroded, clean them up with a terminal cleaner **(see illustration)**. Thoroughly wash all cleaned areas with plain water.

8   Before reinstalling the battery in the engine compartment, inspect the plastic battery carrier. If it's dirty or covered with corrosion, remove it and clean it in the same solution of warm water and baking soda. Inspect the metal brackets which support the carrier to make sure that they are not covered with corrosion. If they are, wash them off. If corrosion is extensive, sand the brackets down to bare metal and spray them with a zinc-based primer (available in spray cans at auto paint and body supply stores).

9   Reinstall the battery carrier and the battery back into the engine compartment. Make sure that no parts or wires are laying on the carrier during installation of the battery.

10   Install a pair of specially treated felt washers around the terminals (available at auto parts stores), then coat the terminals and the cable clamps with petroleum jelly or grease to prevent further corrosion. Install the cable clamps and tighten the nuts, being careful to install the negative cable last.

11   Install the hold-down clamp and nuts. Tighten the nut only

enough to hold the battery firmly in place. Overtightening this nut can crack the battery case.

Charging

12   Remove all of the cell caps (if equipped) and cover the holes with a clean cloth to prevent spattering electrolyte. Disconnect the negative battery cable and hook the battery charger leads to the battery posts (positive to positive, negative to negative), then plug in the charger. Make sure it is set at 12 volts if it has a selector switch.

13   If you're using a charger with a rate higher than two amps, check the battery regularly during charging to make sure it doesn't overheat. If you're using a trickle charger, you can safely let the battery charge overnight after you've checked it regularly for the first couple of hours.

14   If the battery has removable cell caps, measure the specific gravity with a hydrometer every hour during the last few hours of the charging cycle. Hydrometers are available inexpensively from auto parts stores - follow the instructions that come with the hydrometer. Consider the battery charged when there's no change in the specific gravity reading for two hours and the electrolyte in the cells is gassing (bubbling) freely. The specific gravity reading from each cell should be very close to the others. If not, the battery probably has a bad cell(s).

15   Some batteries with sealed tops have built-in hydrometers on the top that indicate the state of charge by the color displayed in the hydrometer window. Normally, a bright-colored hydrometer indicates a full charge and a dark hydrometer indicates the battery still needs charging. Check the battery manufacturer's instructions to be sure you know what the colors mean.

16   If the battery has a sealed top and no built-in hydrometer, you can hook up a digital voltmeter across the battery terminals to check the charge. A fully charged battery should read 12.6 volts or higher.

17   Further information on the battery and jump starting can be found in Chapter 5 and at the front of this manual.

10 Cooling system check (every 7,500 miles or 6 months)

Refer to illustration 10.4

Warning: *The electric cooling fan on these models can activate at any time the ignition switch is in the On position. Make sure the ignition is Off when working in the vicinity of the fan.*

1   Many major engine failures can be attributed to a faulty cooling system. If the vehicle is equipped with an automatic transaxle, the cooling system is also used to cool the transaxle fluid.

2   The cooling system should be checked with the engine cold. Do this before the vehicle is driven for the day or after it has been shut off

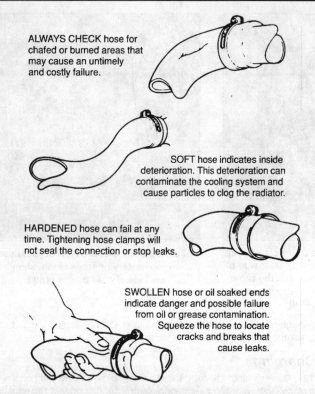

ALWAYS CHECK hose for chafed or burned areas that may cause an untimely and costly failure.

SOFT hose indicates inside deterioration. This deterioration can contaminate the cooling system and cause particles to clog the radiator.

HARDENED hose can fail at any time. Tightening hose clamps will not seal the connection or stop leaks.

SWOLLEN hose or oil soaked ends indicate danger and possible failure from oil or grease contamination. Squeeze the hose to locate cracks and breaks that cause leaks.

10.4 Hoses, like drivebelts, have a habit of failing at the worst possible time - to prevent the inconvenience of a blown radiator or heater hose, inspect them carefully as shown here

for three or four hours.

3   Remove the radiator cap and thoroughly clean the cap (inside and out) with water. Also clean the filler neck on the radiator. All traces of corrosion should be removed.

4   Carefully check the upper and lower radiator hoses along with the smaller diameter heater hoses. Inspect the entire length of each hose, replacing any that are cracked, swollen or deteriorated. Cracks may become more apparent when a hose is squeezed **(see illustration)**.

5   Also check that all hose connections are tight. A leak in the cooling system will usually show up as white or rust-colored deposits on the areas adjoining the leak.

6   Use compressed air or a soft brush to remove bugs, leaves, and other debris from the front of the radiator or air conditioning condenser. Be careful not to damage the delicate cooling fins, or cut yourself on them.

7   Finally, have the cap and system pressure tested. If you do not have a pressure tester, most gas stations and repair shops will do this for a minimal charge.

---

11   Underhood hose check and replacement (every 7,500 miles or 6 months)

Warning: *Replacement of air conditioning hoses must be left to a dealer service department or air conditioning shop equipped to depressurize the system safely. Never remove air conditioning components or hoses until the system has been depressurized.*

General

1   High temperatures under the hood can cause the deterioration of the rubber and plastic hoses used for engine, accessory and emission systems operation. Periodic inspection should be made for cracks, loose clamps, material hardening and leaks.

2   Information specific to the cooling system hoses can be found in Section 25.

3   Some hoses use clamps to secure the hoses to fittings. Where clamps are used, check to be sure they haven't lost their tension, allowing the hose to leak. Where clamps are not used, make sure the hose hasn't expanded and/or hardened where it slips over the fitting, allowing it to leak.

Vacuum hoses

4   It's quite common for vacuum hoses, especially those in the emissions system, to be color coded or identified by colored stripes molded into the hose. Various systems require hoses with different wall thickness, collapse resistance and temperature resistance. When replacing hoses, make sure the new ones are made of the same material.

5   Often the only effective way to check a hose is to remove it completely from the vehicle. Where more than one hose is removed, be sure to label the hoses and their attaching points to insure proper reattachment.

6   When checking vacuum hoses, be sure to include any plastic T-fittings in the check. Check the fittings for cracks and the hose where it fits over the fitting for enlargement, which could cause leakage.

7   A small piece of vacuum hose (1/4-inch inside diameter) can be used as a stethoscope to detect vacuum leaks. Hold one end of the hose to your ear and probe around vacuum hoses and fittings, listening for the "hissing" sound characteristic of a vacuum leak. **Warning:** *When probing with the vacuum hose stethoscope, be careful not to allow your body or the hose to come into contact with moving engine components such as the drivebelt, cooling fan, etc.*

Fuel hose

Warning: *Gasoline is extremely flammable, so take extra precautions when you work on any part of the fuel system. Don't smoke or allow open flames or bare light bulbs near the work area, and don't work in a garage where a natural gas-type appliance (such as a water heater or clothes dryer) with a pilot light is present. If you spill any fuel on your skin, rinse it off immediately with soap and water. When you perform any kind of work on the fuel system, wear safety glasses and have a Class B type fire extinguisher on hand. Before working on any part of the fuel system, relieve the fuel system pressure (see Chapter 4).*

8   Check all rubber fuel hoses for damage and deterioration. Check especially for cracks in areas where the hose bends and just before clamping points, such as where a hose attaches to the fuel injection unit.

9   High quality fuel line, specifically designed for fuel injection systems, should be used for fuel line replacement. **Warning:** *Never use vacuum line, clear plastic tubing or water hose for fuel lines.*

Metal lines

10   Sections of metal line are often used for fuel line between the fuel tank and fuel injection unit. Check carefully to be sure the line has not been bent and crimped and that cracks have not started in the line.

11   If a section of metal fuel line must be replaced, only seamless steel tubing should be used, since copper and aluminum tubing do not have the strength necessary to withstand normal engine operating vibration.

12   Check the metal brake lines where they enter the master cylinder and brake proportioning or ABS unit (if used) for cracks in the lines or loose fittings. Any sign of brake fluid leakage calls for an immediate thorough inspection of the brake system.

---

12   Wiper blade inspection and replacement (every 7,500 miles or 6 months)

Refer to illustrations 12.3 and 12.4

1   The windshield wiper blade elements should be checked periodically for cracks and deterioration.

2   Lift the wiper blade assembly away from the glass.

3   Press the release lever and slide the blade assembly out of the hook in the end of the wiper arm **(see illustration)**.

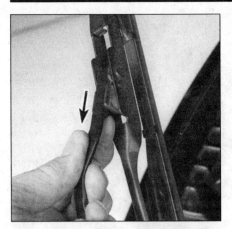

12.3 Depress the release lever and slide the wiper element down out of the hook in the end of the arm

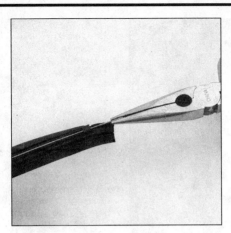

12.4 Use needle-nose pliers to remove the metal rods from the element

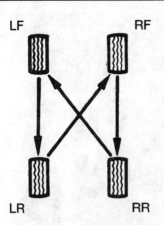

13.2 The recommended tire rotation pattern for these models

4   Use needle-nose pliers to extract the two metal rods, then slide the element out of the frame **(see illustration)**.
5   Slide the new element into the frame and insert the two metal rods to lock it in place.
6   Installation is the reverse of removal.

13   Tire rotation (every 7,500 miles or 6 months)

Refer to illustration 13.2
1   The tires should be rotated at the specified intervals and whenever uneven wear is noticed. Since the vehicle will be raised and the tires removed anyway, this is a good time to check the brakes (see Section 18).
2   Radial tires must be rotated in a specific pattern **(see illustration).**1-14
3   See the information in *Jacking and towing* at the front of this manual for the proper procedures to follow when raising the vehicle and changing a tire; however, if the brakes are to be checked, don't apply the parking brake as stated. Make sure the tires are blocked to prevent the vehicle from rolling.
4   Preferably, the entire vehicle should be raised at the same time. This can be done on a hoist or by jacking up each corner of the vehicle and lowering it onto jackstands. Always use four jackstands and make sure the vehicle is safely supported.
5   After the tire rotation, check and adjust the tire pressures as necessary and be sure to check wheel lug nut tightness.

14   Steering and suspension check (every 7,500 miles or 6 months)

1   Whenever the front of the vehicle is raised for service it is a good idea to visually check the suspension and steering components for wear and damage.
2   Indications of wear and damage include excessive play in the steering wheel before the front wheels react, excessive lean around corners, body movement over rough roads or binding at some point as the steering wheel is turned.
3   Before the vehicle is raised for inspection, test the shock absorbers by pushing down to rock the vehicle at each corner. If it does not come back to a level position within one or two bounces, the shocks are worn and should be replaced. As this is done, check for squeaks and unusual noises from the suspension components. Check the shock absorbers for fluid leakage. Information on shock absorbers and suspension components can be found in Chapter 10.
4   Now raise the front end of the vehicle and support it securely with jackstands placed under the jacking and hoisting points (see *Jacking*

and towing at the front of this manual). Because of the work to be done, the vehicle must be stable and safely supported.
5   Crawl under the vehicle and check for loose bolts, broken or disconnected parts and deteriorated rubber bushings on all suspension and steering components. Look for grease or fluid leaking from around the steering gear boots. Check the power steering hoses and connections for leaks. Check the steering joints for wear.
6   Have an assistant turn the steering wheel from side-to-side and check the steering components for free movement, chafing and binding. If the wheels don't respond the movement of the steering wheel, try to determine where the slack is located.

15   Exhaust system check (every 7,500 or 6 months)

Refer to illustration 15.2
1   With the engine cold (at least three hours after the vehicle has been driven), check the complete exhaust system from its starting point at the engine to the end of the tailpipe. This should be done on a hoist where unrestricted access is available.
2   Check the pipes and connections for signs of leakage and/or corrosion indicating a potential failure. Make sure that all brackets and hangers are in good condition and tight **(see illustration)**.
3   At the same time, inspect the underside of the body for holes, corrosion and open seams which may allow exhaust gases to enter the passenger compartment. Seal all body openings with silicone sealant or body putty.

15.2 Check the exhaust system mounting bolts, brackets and hangers for damage (arrows)

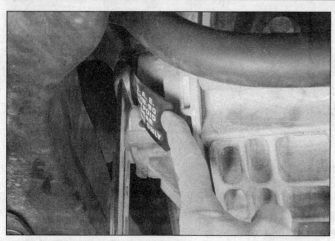

16.1 Use a wrench to unscrew the fill plug from the side of the differential housing - note the plastic tag that contains information on lubricant type

4   Rattles and other noises can often be traced to the exhaust system, especially the mounts and hangers. Try to move the pipes, muffler and catalytic converter. If the components can come into contact with the body, secure the exhaust system with new mounts.
5   This is also an ideal time to check the running condition of the engine by inspecting the very end of the tailpipe. The exhaust deposits here are an indication of engine state-of-tune. If the pipe is black and sooty or coated with white deposits, the engine may be in need of a tune-up (including a thorough fuel injection system inspection).

16 Differential lubricant level check (every 15,000 miles or 12 months)

Refer to illustration 16.1
1   On these models the differential lubricant supply is separate from the transaxle. The differential has a fill plug which must be removed to check the lubricant level **(see illustration)**. If the vehicle is raised to gain access to the plug, be sure to support it safely on jackstands - DO NOT crawl under a vehicle which is supported only by a jack!
2   Remove the plug from the differential and use your little finger to reach inside the housing to feel the lubricant level. The level should be at or near the bottom of the plug hole.
3   If it isn't, add the recommended lubricant through the plug hole with a syringe or squeeze bottle.
4   Install and tighten the plug and check for leaks after the first few miles of driving.

17 Chassis lubrication (every 15,000 miles or 12 months)

Refer to illustration 17.1
1   A grease gun and a cartridge filled with the proper grease (see *Recommended lubricants and fluids*), graphite spray and an oil can filled with engine oil will be required to lubricate the chassis components **(see illustration)**.
2   For easier access under the vehicle, raise it with a jack and place jackstands under the portions of the body designated as hoisting and jacking points front and rear (see *Jacking and towing* at the front of this manual). Make sure it's securely supported by the stands.
3   Before beginning, force a little grease out of the nozzle to remove any dirt from the end of the gun. Wipe the nozzle clean with a rag.
4   With the grease gun and plenty of clean rags, crawl under the vehicle and begin lubricating the components.
5   Wipe the grease fitting clean and push the nozzle firmly over it. Operate the lever on the grease gun to force grease into the fitting until

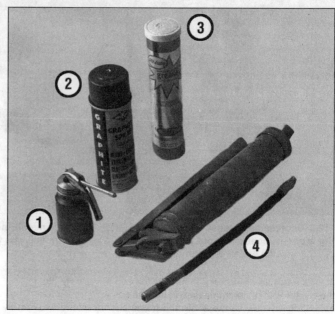

17.1 Materials required for chassis and body lubrication

1   **Engine oil** - *Light engine oil in a can like this can be used for door and hood hinges*
2   *Graphite spray - Used to lubricate lock cylinders*
3   **Grease** - *Grease, in a variety of types and weights, is available for use in a grease gun. Check the Specifications for your requirements*
4   **Grease gun** - *A common grease gun, shown here with a detachable hose and nozzle, is needed for chassis lubrication. After use, clean it thoroughly*

it oozes out of the joint between the two components. If grease escapes around the grease gun nozzle, the fitting is clogged or the nozzle is not completely seated on the fitting. Resecure the gun nozzle to the fitting and try again. If necessary, replace the fitting with a new one.
6   Lubricate the sliding contact and pivot points of the parking brake cable along with the cable guides and levers. This can be done by smearing some of the chassis grease onto the cable and related parts with your fingers.
7   Lower the vehicle to the ground.
8   Open the hood and smear a little chassis grease on the hood latch mechanism. Have an assistant pull the hood release lever from inside the vehicle as you lubricate the cable at the latch.
9   Lubricate all the hinges (door, hood, etc.) with the recommended lubricant to keep them in proper working order.
9   The key lock cylinders can be lubricated with spray-on graphite or silicone lubricant which is available at auto parts stores.
10   Lubricate the door weatherstripping with silicone spray. This will reduce chafing and retard wear.

18 Brake system check (every 15,000 miles or 12 months)

Refer to illustrations 18.5, 18.14 and 18.16
Warning: *Dust created by the brake system may contain asbestos, which is harmful to your health. Never blow it out with compressed air and don't inhale any of it. An approved filtering mask should be worn when working on brakes. Do not, under any circumstances, use petroleum-based solvents to clean brake parts. Use brake system cleaner only!*
1   The brakes should be inspected every time the wheels are removed or whenever a defect is suspected. Indications of a potential brake system problem include the vehicle pulling to one side when the

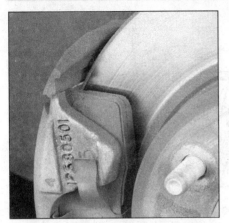

18.5 By looking at the end of the caliper, you can determine the thickness of the remaining friction material on both the inner and outer pads

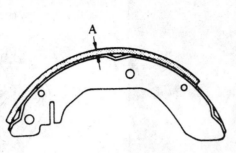

18.14 If the lining is bonded to the brake shoe, measure the lining thickness from the outer surface to the metal shoe, as shown here; if the lining is riveted to the shoe, measure from the lining outer surface to the rivet head

18.16 Use a small screwdriver to carefully pry the boot away from the cylinder and check for fluid leakage

brake pedal is depressed, noises coming from the brakes when they are applied, excessive brake pedal travel, pulsating pedal and leakage of fluid, usually seen on the inside of the tire or wheel.

Disc brakes

2   Disc brakes can be visually checked without removing any parts except the wheels.

3   Raise the vehicle and place it securely on jackstands. Remove the wheels (see *Jacking and towing* at the front of this manual if necessary).

4   Now visible is the disc brake caliper which contains the pads. There is an outer brake pad and an inner pad. Both should be checked for wear.

5   Note the pad thickness by looking at each end of the caliper and through the inspection hole in the caliper body **(see illustration)**. If the combined thickness of the pad lining and metal shoe is 5/16-inch or less, the pads should be replaced.

6   Since it'll be difficult, if not impossible, to measure the exact thickness of the pad, if you're in doubt as to the pad quality, remove them for further inspection or replacement. See Chapter 9 for disc brake pad replacement.

7   Before installing the wheels, check for leakage around the brake hose connections leading to the caliper and for damaged brake hoses (cracks, leaks, chafed areas, etc.). Replace the hoses or fittings as necessary (see Chapter 9).

8   Also check the disc for score marks, wear and burned spots. If these conditions exist, the hub/disc assembly should be removed for servicing (see Chapter 9).

Drum brakes

9   Raise the vehicle and support it securely on jackstands. Block the front tires to prevent the vehicle from rolling; however, don't apply the parking brake or it will lock the drums in place.

10   Remove the rear wheels, referring to *Jacking and towing* at the front of this manual if necessary.

11   Mark the hub so it can be reinstalled in the same position. Use a scribe, chalk, etc. on the drum, hub and backing plate.

12   Remove the brake drum as described in Chapter 9.

13   With the drum removed, carefully clean off any accumulations of dirt and dust using brake system cleaner. **Warning:** *Don't blow the dust out with compressed air and don't inhale any of it (it may contain asbestos, which is harmful to your health).*

14   Note the thickness of the lining material on both front and rear brake shoes. If the material has worn away to within 1/16-inch of the recessed rivets or metal backing, the shoes should be replaced **(see illustration)**. The shoes should also be replaced if they're cracked, glazed (shiny areas), or covered with brake fluid.

15   Make sure all the brake assembly springs are connected and in good condition.

16   Check the brake components for signs of fluid leakage. Carefully pry back the rubber cups on the wheel cylinder located at the top of the brake shoes **(see illustration)**. Any leakage here is an indication that the wheel cylinders should be overhauled immediately (see Chapter 9). Also, check all hoses and connections for signs of leakage.

17   Wipe the inside of the drum with a clean rag and denatured alcohol or brake cleaner. Again, be careful not to breathe the dangerous asbestos dust.

18   Check the inside of the drum for cracks, score marks, deep scratches and "hard spots" which will appear as small discolored areas. If imperfections cannot be removed with fine emery cloth, the drum must be taken to an automotive machine shop for resurfacing.

19   Repeat the procedure for the remaining wheel. If the inspection reveals that all parts are in good condition, reinstall the brake drums. Install the wheels and lower the vehicle to the ground.

Parking brake

20   The parking brake is operated by a foot pedal and locks the rear brake system. The easiest, and perhaps most obvious, method of periodically checking the operation of the parking brake assembly is to park the vehicle on a steep hill with the parking brake set and the transmission in Neutral. If the parking brake cannot prevent the vehicle from rolling, it needs service (see Chapter 9).

---

19   Fuel system check (every 15,000 miles or 12 months)

Refer to illustration 19.6

Warning: *Gasoline is extremely flammable, so take extra precautions when you work on any part of the fuel system. Don't smoke or allow open flames or bare light bulbs near the work area, and don't work in a garage where a natural gas-type appliance (such as a water heater or clothes dryer) with a pilot light is present. If you spill any fuel on your skin, rinse it off immediately with soap and water. When you perform any kind of work on the fuel system, wear safety glasses and have a Class B type fire extinguisher on hand.*

1   On fuel injected models the fuel system is under pressure even when the engine is off. Consequently, the fuel system must be depressurized (see Chapter 4) before servicing the system. Even after depressurization, if any fuel lines are disconnected for servicing, be prepared to catch some fuel as it spurts out. Plug all disconnected fuel lines immediately to prevent the tank from emptying itself.

2   The fuel system is most easily checked with the vehicle raised on a hoist where the components on the underside are readily visible and accessible.

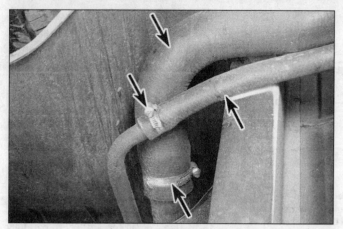

19.6 Check the fuel tank hoses and clamps (arrows) for damage and deterioration

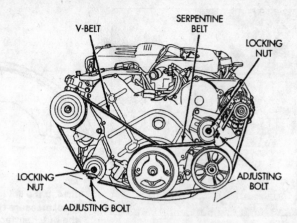

20.2a 3.3L and 3.5L engine drivebelt layout and adjustment details

3   If the smell of gasoline is noticed while driving, or after the vehicle has been parked in the sun, the fuel system should be thoroughly inspected immediately.

4   Remove the gas tank cap and check for damage, corrosion and a proper sealing imprint on the gasket. Replace the cap with a new one if necessary.

5   Inspect the gas tank and filler neck for punctures, cracks and other damage. The connection between the filler neck and the tank is especially critical. Sometimes a rubber filler neck will leak due to loose clamps or deteriorated rubber; problems a home mechanic can usually rectify. **Warning:** *Do not, under any circumstances, try to repair a fuel tank yourself (except to replace rubber components). A welding torch or any open flame can easily cause the fuel vapors to explode if the proper precautions are not taken.*

6   Carefully check all rubber hoses and metal lines leading away from the fuel tank. Check for loose connections, deteriorated hoses, crimped lines and damage of any kind **(see illustration)**. Follow the lines up to the front of the vehicle, carefully inspecting them all the way. Repair or replace damaged sections as necessary (see Chapter 4).

20   Drivebelt check, adjustment and replacement (every 15,000 miles or 12 months)

Refer to illustrations 20.2a, 20.2b, 20.3a, 20.3b, 20.4, 20.5 and 20.8
Warning: *The electric cooling fan on these models can activate at any*

time the ignition switch is in the On position. Make sure the ignition is Off when working in the vicinity of the fan.

1   The drivebelts, or V-belts as they are sometimes called, at the front of the engine, play an important role in the overall operation of the vehicle and its components. Due to their function and material makeup, the belts are prone to failure after a period of time and should be inspected and adjusted periodically to prevent major damage.

2   The number of belts used depends on the engine accessories. On the 3.3L and 3.5L engine, two drivebelts are used; a V-belt to turn the air conditioning compressor and a serpentine belt for the alternator and power steering pump. The 3.3L engine uses a single serpentine belt to drive all components **(see illustrations)**.

3   With the engine off, open the hood and locate the drivebelts at the front of the engine. With a flashlight, check each belt: On V-belts, check for cracks and separation of the belt plies **(see illustration)**. On V-ribbed belts, check for separation of the adhesive rubber on both sides of the core, core separation from the belt side, a severed core, separation of the ribs from the adhesive rubber, cracking or separation of the ribs, and torn or worn ribs or cracks in the inner ridges of the ribs **(see illustration)**. On both belt types, check for fraying and glazing, which gives the belt a shiny appearance. Both sides of the belt should be inspected, which means you will have to twist the belt to check the underside. Use your fingers to feel the belt where you can't see it. If any of the above conditions are evident, replace the belt (go to Step 6).

4   The tightness of each belt is checked by pushing on it at a distance halfway between the pulleys. Apply about 10 pounds of force with your thumb and see how much the belt moves down (deflects).

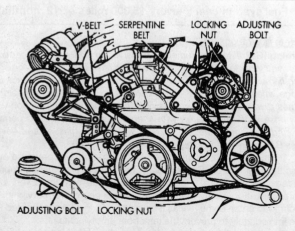

20.2b 3.3L engine serpentine drivebelt layout and adjustment details

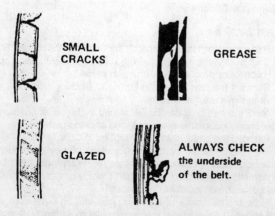

20.3a Here are some of the more common problems associated with V-belts (check the belts very carefully to prevent an untimely breakdown)

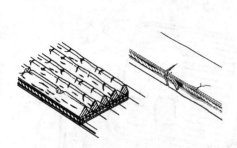

20.3b Check V-ribbed belts for signs of wear like these - if the belt looks worn, replace it

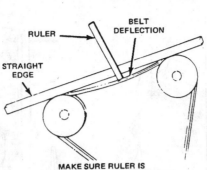

20.4 Measuring drivebelt deflection with a straightedge and ruler

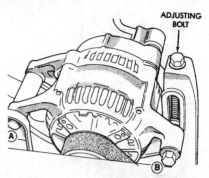

20.5 On 3.3L engines, loosen the alternator pivot bolt (A) and lock bolt (B) and turn the adjusting bolt to achieve the proper belt tension

Measure the deflection with a ruler (see illustration). The belt should deflect about 1/4-inch if the distance between pulleys is between 7 and 11 inches and around 1/2-inch if the distance is between 12 and 16 inches.

Adjustment

5   If adjustment is required on the 3.5L engine belts, loosen the proper tensioner locking nut and turn the adjusting bolt as necessary, then retighten the locking nut (see illustration). On 3.3L engines, loosen the alternator pivot and adjuster lock bolts, then turn the adjusting bolt to achieve the proper belt tension (see illustration).

Replacement

6   To replace a belt, follow the above procedures for drivebelt adjustment but slip the belt off the crankshaft pulley and remove it. If you are replacing the air conditioner compressor belt on 3.5L engines, you have to remove alternator belt first because of the way they are arranged on the crankshaft pulley. Because of this and because belts tend to wear out more or less together, it is a good idea to replace both belts at the same time. Mark each belt and its appropriate pulley groove so the replacement belts can be installed in their proper positions.
7   Take the old belt(s) to the parts store in order to make a direct comparison for length, width and design.
8   After replacing a V-ribbed drivebelt, make sure it fits properly in the ribbed grooves in the pulleys (see illustration). It is essential that the belt be properly centered.
9   Adjust the belt(s) in accordance with the procedure outlined above.

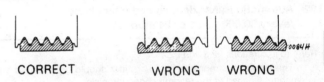

CORRECT   WRONG   WRONG

20.8 When installing the V-ribbed belt, make sure it is centered on the pulley - it must not overlap either edge of the pulley

21 Air filter replacement (every 30,000 miles or 24 months)

Refer to illustrations 21.3 and 21.4
1   At the specified intervals, the air filter element should be replaced.
2   The air filter element is located in a housing in the right front corner of the engine compartment.
3   Remove the screws and lift off the cover (see illustration).
4   Lift the element out (see illustration).
5   Be careful not to drop anything down into the air cleaner assembly. Clean the inside of the housing with a rag.
6   Place the new filter element in position and install the cover. Be sure to tighten any hose clamps which were loosened or removed.

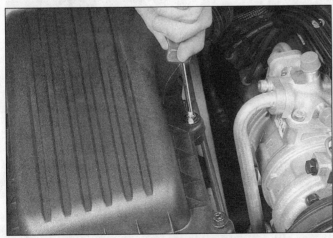

21.3 Use a screwdriver to remove the air cleaner housing cover screws

21.4 Lift the housing cover up for access and removes the element

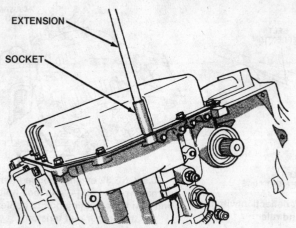

22.3 Use a socket and extension to remove the transaxle pan bolts

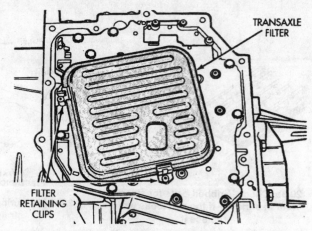

22.4 Detach the clips and lower the filter - be careful, it still contains residual fluid

22 Automatic transaxle fluid and filter change (every 30,000 miles or 24 months)

Refer to illustrations 22.3 and 22.4

1   The automatic transaxle fluid and filter should be changed and the magnet cleaned at the recommended intervals.

2   Raise the front of the vehicle and support it securely on jackstands. Apply the parking brake.

3   Unplug the electrical harness and position a container under the transaxle fluid pan. Loosen the pan bolts **(see illustration)**. Completely remove the bolts along the rear of the pan. Tap the corner of the pan to break the seal and allow the fluid to drain into the container (the remaining bolts will prevent the pan from separating from the transaxle). Remove the remaining bolts and detach the pan.

4   Detach the clips and remove the filter **(see illustration)**.

5   Install the new gasket and filter. Tighten the filter screws securely.

6   Carefully remove all traces of old sealant from the pan and transaxle body (don't nick or gouge the sealing surfaces). Clean the magnet in the pan with a clean, lint-free cloth.

7   Apply a 1/8-inch bead of RTV sealant to the pan sealing surface and position it on the transaxle. Install the bolts and tighten them to the torque listed in this Chapter's Specifications following a criss-cross pattern. Work up to the final torque in three or four steps.

8   Lower the vehicle and add four quarts of the specified fluid (see *Recommended lubricants and fluids* at the beginning of this Chapter) to the transaxle. Start the engine and allow it to idle for at least two

minutes, then move the shift lever through each of the gear positions, ending in Park or Neutral. Check for fluid leakage around the pan.

9   If necessary, add more fluid (a little at a time) until the level is between the Add and Full marks (be careful not to overfill it).

10   Make sure the dipstick is seated completely or dirt could get into the transaxle.

23 Driveaxle boot check (every 30,000 miles or 24 months)

Refer to illustration 23.3

1   If the driveaxle boots are damaged or deteriorated, serious and costly damage can occur to the CV joints the boots are designed to protect. The boots should be inspected very carefully at the recommended intervals.

2   Raise the front of the vehicle and support it securely on jackstands (see *Jacking and towing* at the front of this manual if necessary).

3   Crawl under the vehicle and check the four driveaxle boots (two on each driveaxle) very carefully for cracks, tears, holes, deteriorated rubber and loose or missing clamps **(see illustration)**. If the boots are dirty, wipe them clean before beginning the inspection.

4   If damage or deterioration is evident, replace the boots with new ones and check the CV joints for damage (see Chapter 8).

23.3 Push on the boot to check for damage and signs of leaking grease

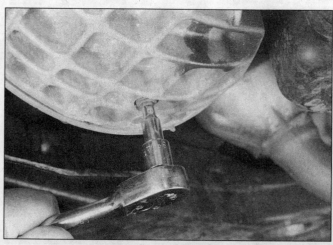

24.3 Use a socket to unscrew the differential drain plug

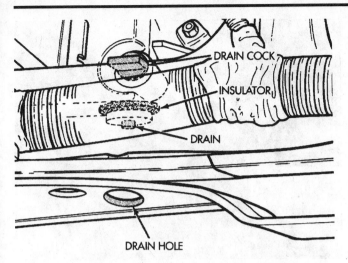

25.5a The drain fitting is located at the bottom of the radiator

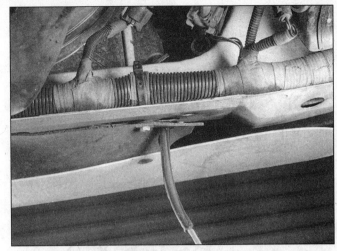

25.5b Connect a piece of 3/8-in hose to the drain fitting to direct the coolant into a container

24 Differential lubricant change (every 30,000 miles or 24 months)

Refer to illustration 24.3

1   Raise the vehicle and support it securely on jackstands.
2   Move a drain pan, rags, newspapers and wrenches under the differential.
3   Remove the differential drain plug at the bottom of the case and allow the lubricant to drain into the pan **(see illustration)**.
4   After the lubricant has drained completely, reinstall the plug and tighten it securely.
5   Remove the fill plug from the side of the differential case (see Section 16). Using a hand pump, syringe or funnel, fill the differential with the specified lubricant until it begins to leak out through the hole. Reinstall the fill plug and tighten it securely.
6   Lower the vehicle.
7   Drive the vehicle for a short distance, then check the drain and fill plugs for leakage.

25 Cooling system servicing (draining, flushing and refilling) (every 30,000 miles or 24 months)

Refer to illustrations 25.5a, 25.5b, 25.6 and 25.12
Warning: *Do not allow engine coolant (antifreeze) to come in contact with your skin or painted surfaces of the vehicle. Rinse off spills immediately with plenty of water. Antifreeze is highly toxic if ingested. Never leave antifreeze lying around in an open container or in puddles on the floor; children and pets are attracted by it's sweet smell and may drink it. Check with local authorities about disposing of used antifreeze. Many communities have collection centers which will see that antifreeze is disposed of safely.*

1   Periodically, the cooling system should be drained, flushed and refilled to replenish the antifreeze mixture and prevent formation of rust and corrosion, which can impair the performance of the cooling system and cause engine damage. When the cooling system is serviced, all hoses and the radiator cap should be checked and replaced, if necessary.

Draining

2   At the same time the cooling system is serviced, all hoses and the coolant reservoir cap should be inspected and replaced if faulty (see Section 10).
3   With the engine cold, remove the coolant reservoir cap and set the heater control to maximum heat.
4   Move a large container under the radiator to catch the coolant

25.6 To allow the system to drain, loosen the bleed valve screw located on the thermostat housing

mixture as it's drained.
5   Open the drain fitting at the bottom of the radiator by hand; don't use pliers **(see illustration)**. Connect a hose to the fitting so the coolant doesn't splash **(see illustration)**.
6   Open the bleed valve screw on the top of the thermostat housing **(see illustration)**.
7   Place a drain pan under the engine and remove the drain plugs located behind the exhaust manifolds on each side of the engine block. Drain the coolant from the block into the drain pan.
8   Disconnect the coolant reservoir hose, remove the reservoir and flush it with clean water.

Flushing

9   In severe cases of contamination or clogging of the radiator, remove it (see Chapter 3) and reverse flush it. This involves inserting the hose in the bottom radiator outlet to allow the clean water to run against the normal flow, draining through the top. A radiator repair shop should be consulted if further cleaning or repair is necessary.
10   Where the coolant is regularly drained and the system refilled with the correct antifreeze mixture there should be no need to employ chemical cleaners or descalers.

Refilling

11   Install the coolant reservoir, reconnect the hoses, close the drain fitting hand tight and install the block drain plugs.

1

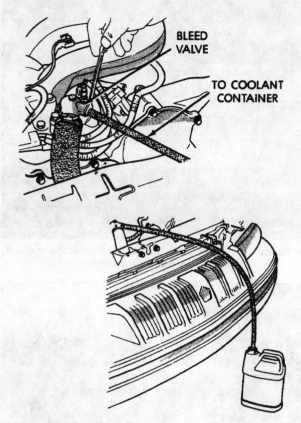

25.12 Connect a hose to the bleed valve screw and run it into an empty coolant container, then open the screw, then fill the coolant reservoir

26.2 Remove the clamp with pliers and pull the PCV valve hose off

26.4 Use a wrench to unscrew the PCV valve from the plenum

12   Connect one end of a four foot long piece of 1/4-inch diameter clear plastic tubing to the bleed screw and run the other end into an empty coolant container (see illustration).

13   Open the bleed valve screw and slowly add coolant to the reservoir until the coolant stream running from the hose is bubble-free. Squeeze the upper radiator hose gently to make sure all remaining air is expelled, then close the bleed valve screw and remove the hose. Fill the coolant reservoir until the level is at the Full Cold mark.

14   Run the engine until normal operating temperature is reached and, with the engine idling, add coolant up the correct level. Install the cap.

15   Always refill the system with a mixture of antifreeze and water in the proportion called for on the antifreeze container or in you owner's manual. Chapter 3 also contains information on antifreeze mixtures.

16   Keep a close watch on the coolant level and the various cooling system hoses during the first few miles of driving. Tighten the hose clamps and add more coolant mixture as necessary.

26   Positive Crankcase Ventilation (PCV) valve check and replacement (every 30,000 miles or 24 months)

Refer to illustrations 26.2 and 26.4

1   The PCV valve is located in the rubber hose connected to the intake manifold plenum.

2   With the engine idling at normal operating temperature, remove the clamp and detach hose from the valve fitting (see illustration).

3   A hissing sound should be heard. Place your finger over the valve opening. If there's no vacuum at the valve, check for a plugged hose, plenum port or valve. Replace any plugged or deteriorated hoses.

4   To replace the valve, use a wrench to unscrew it from the plenum (see illustration).

5   When purchasing a replacement PCV valve, make sure it's for your particular vehicle and engine size. Compare the old valve with the new one to make sure they're the same.

6   Screw the valve into the plenum until it's seated and push the hose securely into position, then install the clamp.

27   Evaporative emissions control system check (every 30,000 miles or 24 months)

1   The function of the evaporative emissions control system is to draw fuel vapors from the gas tank and fuel system, store them in a charcoal canister and route them to the intake manifold during normal engine operation.

2   The most common symptom of a fault in the evaporative emissions system is a strong fuel odor in the engine compartment. If a fuel odor is detected, inspect the charcoal canister, located in the engine compartment on the passenger's side, under the air cleaner assembly. Check the canister and all hoses for damage and deterioration.

3   The evaporative emissions control system is explained in more detail in Chapter 6.

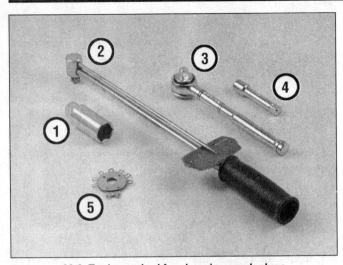

28.2 Tools required for changing spark plugs

1   **Spark plug socket** - *This will have special padding inside to protect the spark plug's porcelain insulator*
2   **Torque wrench** - *Although not mandatory, using this tool is the best way to ensure the plugs are tightened properly*
3   **Ratchet** - *Standard hand tool to fit the spark plug socket*
4   **Extension** - *Depending on model and accessories, you may need special extensions and universal joints to reach one or more of the plugs*
5   **Spark plug gap gauge** - *This gauge for checking the gap comes in a variety of styles. Make sure the gap for your engine is included*

28 Spark plug check and replacement (every 30,000 miles or 24 months)

Refer to illustrations 28.2, 28.5a, 28.5b, 28.7, 28.9a, 28.9b, 28.11 and 28.12

1   On 3.5L engines, the spark plugs are located on the top of the engine. On 3.3L engines, the spark plugs are located on the sides of the engine.

2   In most cases the tools necessary for spark plug replacement include a spark plug socket which fits onto a ratchet (this special socket will be padded inside to protect the porcelain insulators on the new plugs), various extensions and a feeler gauge to check and adjust the spark plug gap **(see illustration)**. A special plug wire removal tool is available for separating the wire boot from the spark plug, but it isn't absolutely necessary. Since these engines are equipped with an aluminum cylinder head, a torque wrench should be used for tightening the spark plugs.
3   The best approach when replacing the spark plugs is to purchase the new spark plugs beforehand, adjust them to the proper gap and then replace each plug one at a time. When buying the new spark plugs, be sure to obtain the correct plug for your specific engine. This information can be found in the Specifications at the front of this Chapter, in the factory owner's manual or on the Vehicle Emissions Control Information label located under the hood. If differences exist between the sources, purchase the spark plug type specified on the VECI label as it was printed for your specific engine.
4   Allow the engine to cool completely before attempting to remove any of the plugs. During this cooling off time, each of the new spark plugs can be inspected for defects and the gaps can be checked.
5   The gap is checked by inserting the proper thickness gauge between the electrodes at the tip of the plug **(see illustration)**. The gap between the electrodes should be as specified on the VECI label in the engine compartment or as listed in this Chapter's Specifications. The wire should touch each of the electrodes. If the gap is incorrect, use the adjuster on the thickness gauge body to bend the curved side electrode slightly until the proper gap is obtained **(see illustration)**. Also, at this time check for cracks in the spark plug body (if any are found, the plug should not be used). If the side electrode is not exactly over the center one, use the adjuster to align the two.

Removal

6   Cover the fender to prevent damage to the paint.
7   With the engine cool, remove the spark plug wire from one spark plug. Pull only on the boot at the end of the wire; don't pull on the wire. Use a twisting motion to free the boot and wire from the plug **(see illustration)**.
8   If compressed air is available, use it to blow any dirt or foreign material away from the spark plug area. A common bicycle pump will also work. The idea here is to eliminate the possibility of material falling into the cylinder through the plug hole as the spark plug is removed.
9   Now place the spark plug socket over the plug and remove it from

28.5a Spark plug manufacturers recommend using a wire-type gauge when checking the gap - if the wire does not slide between the electrodes with a slight drag, adjustment is required

28.5b To change the gap, bend the side electrode only, as indicated by the arrows, and be very careful not to crack or chip the porcelain insulator surrounding the center electrode

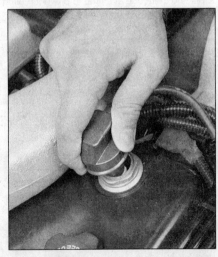

28.7 Pull on the spark plug wire boot and twist it back-and-forth while pulling it

28.9a Use a ratchet and short extension to remove the spark plugs (3.5L engine shown)

28.9b The special socket will hold the spark plug so that it can be withdrawn from the engine

the engine by turning it in a counterclockwise direction **(see illustrations)**.

10   Compare the spark plug with the chart on the inside back cover of this manual to get an indication of the overall running condition of the engine.

Installation

11   It's a good idea to lightly coat the threads of the spark plugs with anti-seize compound **(see illustration)** to insure that the spark plugs do not seize in the aluminum cylinder head.

12   It's often difficult to insert spark plugs into their holes without cross-threading them. To avoid this possibility, fit a piece of 3/8-inch ID rubber hose over the end of the spark plug **(see illustration)**. The flexible hose acts as a universal joint to help align the plug with the plug hole. Should the plug begin to cross-thread, the hose will slip on the spark plug, preventing thread damage. Tighten the spark plug to the torque listed in this Chapter's Specifications.

13   Attach the plug wire to the new spark plug, again using a twisting motion on the boot until it is firmly seated on the end of the spark plug.

14   Follow the above procedure for the remaining spark plugs, replacing them one at a time to prevent mixing up the spark plug wires.

29   Spark plug wire check and replacement (every 30,000 miles or 24 months)

1   The spark plug wires should be checked at the recommended intervals or whenever new spark plugs are installed.

2   The wires should be inspected one at a time to prevent mixing up the order which is essential for proper engine operation.

3   Disconnect the plug wire from the spark plug. A removal tool can be used for this, or you can grab the rubber boot, twist slightly and then pull the wire free. Don't pull on the wire itself, only on the rubber boot.

4   Check inside the boot for corrosion, which will look like a white, crusty powder (don't mistake the white dielectric grease used on some plug wire boots for corrosion).

5   Now push the wire and boot back onto the end of the spark plug. It should be a tight fit on the plug end. If not, remove the wire and use a pair of pliers to carefully crimp the metal connector inside the wire boot until the fit is snug.

6   Now, using a cloth, clean each wire along its entire length. Remove all built-up dirt and grease. As this is done, inspect for burned

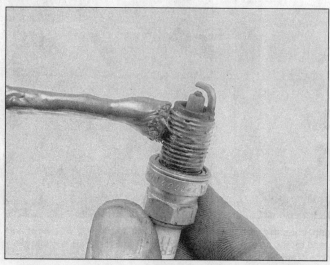

28.11 Apply a thin coat of anti-seize compound to the spark plug threads

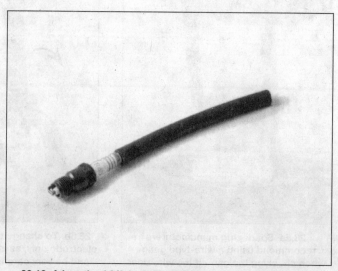

28.12 A length of 3/8-inch ID rubber hose will save time and prevent damaged threads when installing the spark plugs

31.4a Use a small wrench to push on the black plastic ring and release the quick-disconnect fitting at the outlet end of the filter

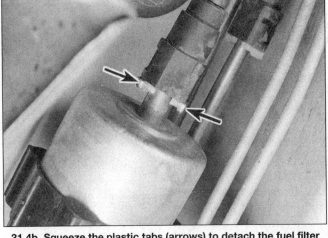

31.4b Squeeze the plastic tabs (arrows) to detach the fuel filter inlet connector

areas, cracks and any other form of damage. Bend the wires in several places to ensure that the conductive material inside hasn't hardened. Repeat the procedure for the remaining wires.
7   If new spark plug wires are needed, purchase a complete pre-cut set for your particular engine. The terminals and rubber boots should already be installed on the wires. Replace the wires one at a time to avoid mixing up the firing order and make sure the terminals are securely seated in the coil pack and on the spark plugs.

30   Seat belt check (every 30,000 miles or 24 months)

1   Check the seat belts, buckles, latch plates and guide loops for obvious damage and signs of wear.
2   See if the seat belt reminder light comes on when the key is turned to the Run or Start positions. A chime should also sound.
3   The seat belts are designed to lock up during a sudden stop or impact, yet allow free movement during normal driving. Make sure the retractors return the belt against your chest while driving and rewind the belt fully when the buckle is unlatched.
4   If any of the above checks reveal problems with the seat belt system, replace parts as necessary.

31   Fuel filter replacement (every 60,000 miles or 48 months)

Refer to illustrations 31.4a, 31.4b and 31.5
Warning: *Gasoline is extremely flammable, so take extra precautions when you work on any part of the fuel system. Don't smoke or allow open flames or bare light bulbs near the work area, and don't work in a garage where a natural gas-type appliance (such as a water heater or clothes dryer) with a pilot light is present. If you spill any fuel on your skin, rinse it off immediately with soap and water. When you perform any kind of work on the fuel system, wear safety glasses and have a Class B type fire extinguisher on hand.*
1   Depressurize the fuel system (see Chapter 4).
2   The fuel filter is a disposable canister type and is located in the

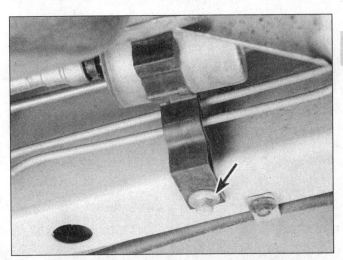

31.5 Remove this bolt (arrow) to detach the filter

fuel line under the right rear of the vehicle, adjacent to the fuel tank.
3   Raise the rear of the vehicle and support it securely on jackstands.
4   Wrap a cloth around the fuel filter to catch the residual fuel (which may still be under slight pressure) and disconnect the hoses. Disconnect the hose on the outlet side by using a small wrench to push the black plastic ring on the quick-disconnect fitting **(see illustration)**. On the inlet side, disconnect the black plastic fuel line connector fitting by squeezing the two white plastic tabs **(see illustration)**.
5   Remove the mounting bolt and detach the bracket and filter from the vehicle **(see illustration)**.
6   Place the new filter in position, install the mounting bolt and tighten it securely.
7   Lubricate the fittings with clean engine oil and insert the quick disconnect fittings into place until they lock in place.
8   Start the engine and check carefully for leaks at the hose connections.

Notes

Chapter 2 Part A
3.3L V6 engine

Contents

2A

Specifications

General

Cylinder numbers (front to rear)	
Left bank	2-4-6
Right bank	1-3-5
Firing order	1-2-3-4-5-6

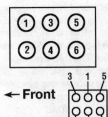

← **Front**

Engine cylinder and coil terminal locations

Camshaft

Endplay	0.005 to 0.012 inch
Lobe lift	0.2667 inch
Camshaft bearing clearance	
Standard	0.001 to 0.004 inch
Service limit	0.005 inch
Camshaft journal diameter	
No. 1	1.9970 to 1.9990 inches
No. 2	1.9809 to 1.9829 inches
No. 3	1.9659 to 1.9679 inches
No. 4	1.9499 to 1.9520 inches
Camshaft bearing diameter (inside)	
No. 1	2.0009 to 1.9999 inches
No. 2	1.9849 to 1.9839 inches
No. 3	1.9699 to 1.9690 inches
No. 4	1.9540 to 1.9529 inches

Oil pump

Cover warpage limit	0.003 inch
Outer rotor thickness (minimum)	0.301 inch
Inner rotor thickness (minimum)	0.301 inch
Rotor-to-pump cover clearance	0.004 inch
Outer rotor-to-housing clearance	0.015 inch
Inner rotor-to-outer rotor lobe clearance	0.008 inch

Torque specification

	Ft-lbs (unless otherwise indicated)
Camshaft sprocket bolt	40
Crankshaft pulley/vibration damper bolt	40
Cylinder head bolts **(see illustration 12.19 for the tightening sequence)**	
Bolts 1 through 8	
First step	45
Second step	65
Third step	65
Fourth step	1/4 turn clockwise (do not use a torque wrench for this step)
Bolt 9 (fifth step)	25
Engine mount bolts	
Insulator to bracket nuts	45
Insulator to frame nuts	45
Exhaust manifold-to-cylinder head bolts...............................	200 in-lbs
Exhaust crossover bolts	25
Driveplate-to-crankshaft bolts	50
Hydraulic lifter retaining plate bolts	105 in-lbs
Intake manifold-to-cylinder head bolts/nuts..........................	200 in-lbs
Intake manifold gasket retaining bolts	105 in-lbs
Oil pan drain plug	25
Oil pan bolts/nuts	105 in-lbs
Oil pump pick-up tube mounting bolts....................................	250 in-lbs
Oil pump cover (plate) bolts (Torx no. 30)	105 in-lbs
Valve cover-to-cylinder head bolts	105 in-lbs
Rocker arm shaft bolts	250 in-lbs
Timing chain cover bolts	
M8	20
M10	40
Rear main oil seal retainer bolts	105 in-lbs

1   General information

This Part of Chapter 2 is devoted to in-vehicle repair procedures for the 3.3L V6 engine. This engine utilizes a cast-iron block with six cylinders arranged in a "V" shape at a 60-degree angle between the two banks. The overhead valve aluminum cylinder heads are equipped with replaceable valve guides and seats. Hydraulic roller lifters actuate the valves through tubular pushrods.

All information concerning engine removal and installation and engine block and cylinder head overhaul can be found in Part C of this Chapter. The following repair procedures are based on the assumption the engine is installed in the vehicle. If the engine has been removed from the vehicle and mounted on a stand, many of the steps outlined in this Part of Chapter 2 will not apply.

The Specifications included in this Part of Chapter 2 apply only to the procedures contained in this Part. Part C of Chapter 2 contains the Specifications necessary for cylinder head and engine block rebuilding.

2   Repair operations possible with the engine in the vehicle

Many major repair operations can be accomplished without removing the engine from the vehicle.

Clean the engine compartment and the exterior of the engine with some type of degreaser before any work is done. It'll make the job easier and help keep dirt out of the internal areas of the engine.

Depending on the components involved, it may be helpful to remove the hood to improve access to the engine as repairs are performed (see Chapter 11 if necessary). Cover the fenders to prevent damage to the paint. Special pads are available, but an old bedspread or blanket will also work.

If vacuum, exhaust, oil or coolant leaks develop, indicating a need for gasket or seal replacement, the repairs can generally be done with the engine in the vehicle. The intake and exhaust manifold gaskets, timing chain cover gasket, oil pan gasket, crankshaft oil seals and cylinder head gaskets are all accessible with the engine in place.

Exterior engine components, such as the intake and exhaust manifolds, the oil pan, timing chain cover (and the oil pump), the water pump, the starter motor, the alternator and the fuel system components can be removed for repair with the engine in place.

Since the cylinder heads can be removed without pulling the engine, valve component servicing can also be accomplished with the engine in the vehicle. Replacement of the timing chain and sprockets is also possible with the engine in the vehicle.

In extreme cases caused by a lack of necessary equipment, repair or replacement of piston rings, pistons, connecting rods and rod bearings is possible with the engine in the vehicle. However, this practice is not recommended because of the cleaning and preparation work that must be done to the components involved.

3   Top Dead Center (TDC) for number 1 piston - locating

1   Disconnect the cable from the negative terminal of the battery.
2   Remove the valve cover closest to the radiator (see Section 4).
3   Remove the spark plugs (see Chapter 1).
4   Using a socket and ratchet on the crankshaft pulley bolt, turn the crankshaft clockwise until there is play in both of the rocker arms for the number 2 cylinder (front cylinder on left side). With the engine set at this position, approximate TDC for cylinder number 2 has been found. To bring the engine to TDC (approximate) for cylinder number 1, make a mark on the crankshaft pulley and a corresponding mark on the engine, then turn the crankshaft 120 degrees counterclockwise.
5   This position will be adequate for most operations requiring the engine to be set at TDC, but if exact TDC must be found, a degree wheel and a dial indicator (with the proper spark plug hole adapter) must be obtained.
6   Install the degree wheel on the crankshaft pulley. These can be found at most auto parts stores.

4.4 Remove the DIS coil pack for access to the left valve cover - two bracket bolts are at the back of the cylinder head

4.5 Remove the valve cover bolts - do not distort the cover by prying it off

6   Detach the valve cover. **Note:** *If the cover sticks to the cylinder head, use a block of wood and a hammer to dislodge it. If the cover still won't come loose, pry on it carefully, but don't distort the sealing flange.*

Installation

7   The mating surfaces of each cylinder head and valve cover must be perfectly clean when the covers are installed. Use a gasket scraper to remove all traces of sealant or old gasket material, then clean the mating surfaces with lacquer thinner or acetone (if there's sealant or oil on the mating surfaces when the cover is installed, oil leaks may develop). Be extra careful not to nick or gouge the mating surfaces with the scraper.

8   Clean the mounting bolt threads with a die if necessary to remove any corrosion and restore damaged threads. Use a tap to clean the threaded holes in the heads.

9   Place the valve cover and new gasket in position, then install the bolts. Tighten the bolts in several steps to the torque listed in this Chapter's Specifications.

10   Complete the installation by reversing the removal procedure. Start the engine and check carefully for oil leaks.

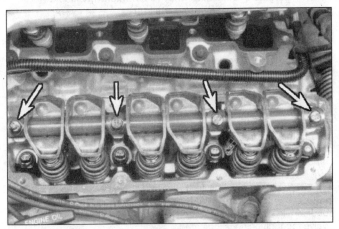

5.2 Remove the rocker arm shaft bolts (arrows) from the cylinder head - be sure to start with the outer ones first

7   Position the engine at TDC (approximate for cylinder number 2 as described in Step 4. Using the proper adapter, install the dial indicator in the number 2 spark plug hole.

8   Slowly turn the crankshaft in a clockwise direction until the dial indicator shows the piston has reached its highest point.

9   Align the zero mark on the degree wheel with the mark made on the engine.

10   Rotate the crankshaft 120 degrees counterclockwise. The engine is now positioned at TDC for cylinder number 1.

11   TDC for any of the remaining cylinders can be located by turning the crankshaft clockwise 120 degrees at a time and following the firing order (see the Specifications at the beginning of this Chapter).

4   Valve cover(s) - removal and installation

Refer to illustrations 4.4 and 4.5

Removal

1   Disconnect the negative battery cable from the battery.

2   Remove the air intake tube, throttle body and intake plenum (see Chapter 4).

3   Remove the ignition wires from the spark plugs (see Chapter 1). Be sure each wire is labeled before removal to ensure correct reinstallation.

4   Referring to Chapter 5, remove the DIS coil pack to access the left valve cover **(see illustration)**.

5   Remove the valve cover bolts **(see illustration)**.

5   Rocker arms, rocker shafts and pushrods - removal, inspection and installation

Refer to illustrations 5.2 and 5.3

Removal

1   Refer to Section 4 and remove the valve cover(s).

2   Loosen each rocker arm shaft bolt a little at a time until they are all loose enough to be removed by hand **(see illustration)**. If the rocker arms are removed from the shaft, be sure to note how they are positioned.

3   Remove the pushrods and store them in order to make sure they don't get mixed up during installation **(see illustration)**.

Inspection

4   Inspect each rocker arm for wear, cracks and other damage, especially where the pushrods and valve stems make contact.

5   Check each rocker arm pivot area and shaft for wear, cracks and galling. If the rocker arms or shafts are worn or damaged, replace them with new ones.

6   Make sure the hole at the pushrod end of each rocker arm is open.

7   Inspect the pushrods for cracks and excessive wear at the ends. Roll each pushrod across a piece of plate glass to see if it's bent (if it wobbles, it's bent).

2A

5.3 Place the pushrods in a box that will hold them in order

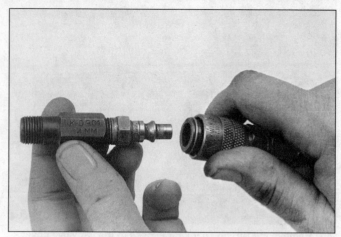

6.5 This is what the air hose adapter that threads into the spark plug hole looks like - they're commonly available in auto parts stores

6.7 Compress the valve spring and use a magnet or needle-nose pliers to remove the keepers

Installation

8   Lubricate the lower end of each pushrod with clean engine oil or moly-base grease and install them in their original locations. Make sure each pushrod seats completely in the lifter socket.

9   Apply moly-base grease to the ends of the valve stems and the upper ends of the pushrods.

10   Apply moly-base grease to the rocker arm shaft. Install the rocker arms on the shaft and lower the assembly onto the cylinder head. Tighten the bolts, a little at a time (working from the center out), to the torque listed in this Chapter's Specifications. As the bolts are tightened, make sure the pushrods engage properly in the rocker arms. **Caution:** *Allow the engine to set for 20 minutes before starting, to allow the lifters to bleed down.*

11   Install the valve cover(s). The rest of the installation is the reverse of the disassembly. Start the engine and check for leaks and tappet noise. **Note:** *There may be some tappet noise during the first five minutes of engine operation.*

6   Valve springs, retainers and seals - replacement

Refer to illustrations 6.5, 6.7 and 6.17
Note: *Broken valve springs and defective valve stem seals can be replaced without removing the cylinder head. Two special tools and a compressed-air source are normally required to perform this operation,*

so read through this Section carefully and rent or buy the tools before beginning the job.

1   Remove the valve covers (see Section 4).

2   Remove the spark plugs (see Chapter 1).

3   Turn the crankshaft until the number one piston is at top dead center on the compression stroke (see Section 3).

4   Remove the rocker arm shafts (see Section 5).

5   Thread an adapter into the spark plug hole and connect an air hose from a compressed air source to it **(see illustration)**. Most auto parts stores can supply the air hose adapter. **Note:** *Many cylinder compression gauges utilize a screw-in fitting that may work with your air hose quick-disconnect fitting.*

6   Apply compressed air to the cylinder. The valves should be held in place by the air pressure. If the valve faces or seats are in poor condition, leaks may prevent the air pressure from retaining the valves - valve reconditioning is indicated.

7   Stuff shop rags into the cylinder head holes around the valves to prevent parts and tools from falling into the engine, then use a valve-spring compressor to compress the spring. Remove the keepers with small needle-nose pliers or a magnet **(see illustration)**.

8   Remove the valve spring and retainer (intake valve) or rotator (exhaust valve).

9   Remove the old valve stem seals.

10   Wrap a rubber band or tape around the top of the valve stem so the valve won't fall into the combustion chamber, then release the air pressure.

11   Inspect the valve stem for damage. Rotate the valve in the guide and check the end for eccentric movement, which would indicate that the valve is bent.

12   Move the valve up-and-down in the guide and make sure it doesn't bind. If the valve stem binds, either the valve is bent or the guide is damaged. In either case, the head will have to be removed for repair.

13   Reapply air pressure to the cylinder to retain the valve in the closed position, then remove the tape or rubber band from the valve stem.

14   Push a new valve stem seal down over the valve guide, using the valve stem as a guide, but don't force the seal against the top of the guide.

15   Install the spring and retainer in position over the valve.

16   Compress the valve spring assembly only enough to install the keepers in the valve stem.

17   Position the keepers in the valve stem groove. Apply a small dab of grease to the inside of each keeper to hold it in place if necessary **(see illustration)**. Remove the pressure from the spring tool and make sure the keepers are seated.

18   Disconnect the air hose and remove the adapter from the spark plug hole.

6.17 Apply a small dab of grease to each keeper before installation to hold it in place on the valve stem until the spring compressor is released

7.4a Disconnect the heater circulation tube from the rear of the intake manifold

7.4b Disconnect the radiator hose and the coolant bypass hose from the front of the intake manifold

2A

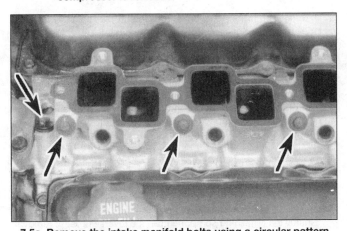

7.5a Remove the intake manifold bolts using a circular pattern and starting with the outer bolts first

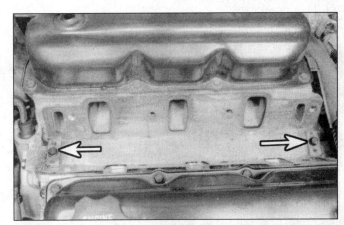

7.5b Remove the intake manifold gasket retaining bolts (arrows)

19 Repeat the above procedure on the remaining cylinders, following the firing order sequence (see the Specifications). Bring each piston to top dead center on the compression stroke before applying air pressure (see Section 3).

20 Reinstall the rocker arm assemblies and the valve covers.

21 Start the engine, then check for oil leaks and unusual sounds coming from the valve cover area. **Caution:** *Allow the engine to set for 20 minutes before starting, to allow the lifters to bleed down.*

7 Intake manifold - removal and installation

Removal

Refer to illustrations 7.4a, 7.4b, 7.5a, 7.5b and 7.9

1 Relieve the fuel system pressure (see Chapter 4), and drain the cooling system (see Chapter 1).

2 Disconnect the negative battery cable from the battery.

3 Remove the air intake plenum, fuel rail and injectors (see Chapter 4). When disconnecting fuel line fittings, be prepared to catch some fuel with a rag, then cap the fittings to prevent contamination.

4 Remove the radiator hose from the thermostat housing, the bypass hose, and the hose at the back of the manifold **(see illustrations)**.

5 Remove the intake manifold mounting bolts and separate the manifold from the engine **(see illustrations)**. If the manifold is stuck, carefully pry on a casting protrusion - don't pry between the manifold

and heads, as damage to the gasket sealing surfaces may result. If you're installing a new manifold, transfer all fittings and sensors to the new manifold.

6 Remove the intake manifold gasket retaining bolts and clamps and lift the gasket from the engine. **Warning:** *The intake gasket is very thin sheetmetal, and the edges are sharp, be careful not to cut your hands while handling the gasket removal or installation.*

Installation

Refer to illustration 7.9

Note: *The mating surfaces of the cylinder heads, block and manifold must be perfectly clean when the manifold is installed. Gasket removal solvents in aerosol cans are available at most auto parts stores and may be helpful when removing old gasket material that's stuck to the heads and manifold (since the manifold is made of aluminum, aggressive scraping can cause damage). Be sure to follow the directions printed on the container.*

7 Lift the old gasket off. Use a gasket scraper to remove all traces of sealant and old gasket material, then clean the mating surfaces with lacquer thinner or acetone. If there's old sealant or oil on the mating surfaces when the manifold is installed, oil or vacuum leaks may develop. Use a vacuum cleaner to remove any gasket material that falls into the intake ports or the lifter valley.

8 Use a tap of the correct size to chase the threads in the bolt holes, if necessary, then use compressed air (if available) to remove the debris from the holes. **Warning:** *Wear safety glasses or a face shield to protect your eyes when using compressed air!*

9 Apply a 3/16-inch (5 mm) bead of RTV sealant or equivalent to the

7.9 Apply RTV sealant to the corners of the cylinder head/block and let it "set-up" (slightly harden) before installing the manifold

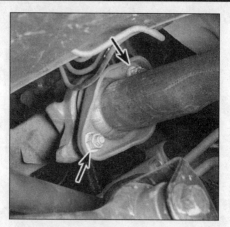

8.4 Remove the nuts (arrows) from the crossover pipe - left manifold shown

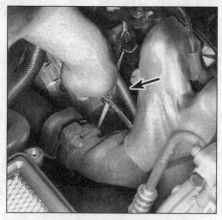

8.5 Disconnect the EGR tube bolts from the engine side of the right exhaust manifold - arrow indicates the tube itself

front and rear ridges of the engine block between the heads **(see illustration)**.

10   Install the intake manifold gasket, end seal retainer plates and bolts.

11   Carefully lower the manifold into place and install the mounting bolts/nuts finger tight.

12   Tighten the mounting bolts/nuts in three steps, working from the center out, in a criss-cross pattern, until they're all at the torque listed in this Chapter's Specifications.

13   Install the remaining components in the reverse order of removal.

14   Change the oil and filter and refill the cooling system (see Chapter 1). Start the engine and check for leaks.

8   Exhaust manifolds - removal and installation

Refer to illustrations 8.4, 8.5 and 8.7

1   Disconnect the negative battery cable from the battery.

2   Remove the air cleaner assembly (see Chapter 4).

3   Allow the engine to cool completely.

4   Unbolt the exhaust crossover pipe where it joins the manifolds. The left manifold is easier to disconnect from underneath, the right manifold is easier to reach from above **(see illustration)**.

5   Disconnect the EGR tube from the right exhaust manifold to the intake manifold **(see illustration)**.

6   Disconnect the electrical connectors at the oxygen sensors.

7   Remove the exhaust manifold heat shield mounting bolts **(see illustration)** and lift the heat shield from the engine.

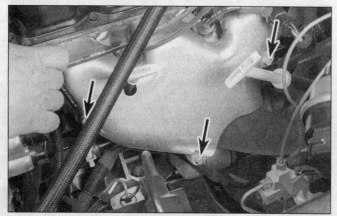

8.7 Remove the mounting bolts (arrows) from the heat shield attached to the manifold

8   Remove the mounting bolts and detach the manifold from the cylinder head. Be sure to spray penetrating lubricant onto the bolts and threads before attempting to remove them.

9   Clean the mating surfaces to remove all traces of old gasket material, then inspect the manifold for distortion and cracks. Warpage can be checked with a precision straightedge held against the mating flange. If a feeler gauge thicker than 0.030-inch can be inserted between the straightedge and flange surface, take the manifold to an automotive machine shop for resurfacing.

10   Place the exhaust manifold in position with a new gasket and install the mounting bolts finger tight. **Note:** *Be sure to identify the exhaust manifold gaskets by the correct cylinder designation and the position of the exhaust ports on the gasket.*

11   Starting in the middle and working out toward the ends, tighten the mounting bolts a little at a time until all of them are at the torque listed in this Chapter's Specifications.

12   Install the remaining components in the reverse order of removal.

13   Start the engine and check for exhaust leaks between the manifold and cylinder head and between the manifold and exhaust pipe.

9   Crankshaft front oil seal - replacement

Refer to illustrations 9.6, 9.7 and 9.8

1   Disconnect the negative battery cable from the battery.

2   Refer to Chapter 1 and remove the drivebelts.

3   Refer to Chapter 3 and remove the cooling fan assembly.

4   Raise the vehicle and support it securely on jackstands.

5   Hold the damper from turning by inserting a bar, and use a wrench to remove the damper bolt.

6   Pull the damper off the crankshaft with a two-jaw puller **(see illustration)**. **Caution:** *The jaws of the puller must only contact the hub of the pulley - not the outer ring.*

7   Note how the old seal is installed - the new one must be installed to the same depth and facing the same way. Carefully pry the old seal out of the cover with a seal puller or a screwdriver. Be very careful not to scratch the crankshaft **(see illustration)**. Wrap tape around the tip of the screwdriver to avoid damage to the crankshaft seal surface.

8   Apply clean engine oil or multi-purpose grease to the outer edge of the new seal, then install it in the cover with the lip (spring side) facing IN. Drive the seal into place **(see illustration)** with a large socket and a hammer, or use a length of large-diameter pipe. make sure the seal enters the bore squarely and stop when the front face is at the proper depth.

9   Installation is the reverse of removal. Be sure to apply clean engine oil or multi-purpose grease to the seal contact surface of the damper hub (if it isn't lubricated, the seal lip could be damaged and oil

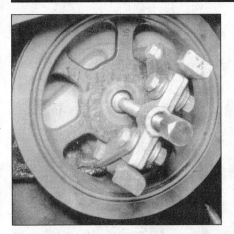

9.6 Remove the vibration damper with a two-jaw puller

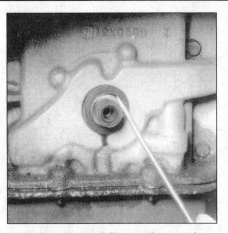

9.7 Be very careful not to damage the crankshaft surface when removing the front seal

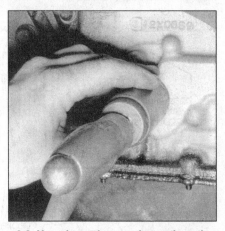

9.8 Use a large deep socket and gently tap the seal into place

2A

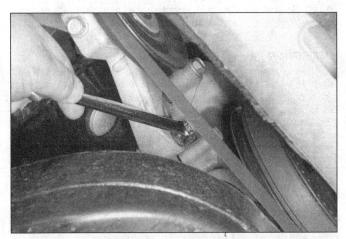

10.8 Unbolt the belt tensioner pulley bracket from underneath on the passenger's side

10.10 Remove the camshaft position sensor (arrow) from the top of the chain housing

leakage would result).
10   Tighten the vibration damper-to-crankshaft bolt to the torque listed in this Chapter's Specifications. the remainder of the installation is the reverse of the removal.

10   Timing chain, cover and sprockets - removal, inspection and installation

Refer to illustrations 10.8, 10.10 and 10.11

Cover removal

1   Disconnect the negative battery cable from the battery.
2   Remove the drivebelts (see Chapter 1).
3   Drain the coolant and remove the water pump pulley and the cooling fan assembly (see Chapter 3).
4   Raise the vehicle and support it on jackstands. Drain the engine oil (see Chapter 1).
5   Disconnect the front anti-sway bar and push it toward the rear of the vehicle. **Note:** *The anti-sway bar clamp mounting bolts are best accessed from underneath the vehicle, but the bolts are on top of the chassis.*
6   Refer to Section 13 and remove the oil pan and oil pump pick-up tube.
7   Unbolt the power steering pump and tie it aside (see Chapter 10).
8   Remove the belt tensioner pulley bracket **(see illustration).**

9   Refer to Section 9 and remove the crankshaft damper.
10   Remove the cam position sensor from the timing cover **(see illustration).**
11   Remove the timing chain cover-to-engine block bolts **(see illustration). Note:** *Draw a diagram showing the locations and sizes of*

10.11 Remove the timing chain cover bolts from the engine (be sure to mark the location of each bolt to aid in proper installation)

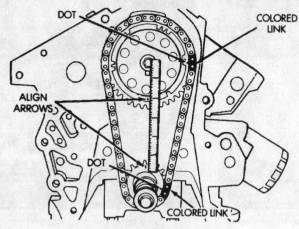

10.13 Timing chain details

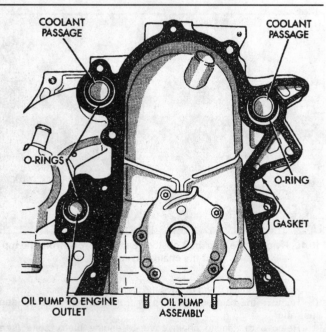

10.23 Use a new gasket and new O-rings when reinstalling the chain cover

10.20 Be sure the timing chain reference links align with marks on the sprockets (arrows)

Inspection

16   Timing chains and sprockets should be replaced in sets. If you intend to install a new timing chain, remove the crankshaft sprocket with a puller and install a new one. Be sure to align the key in the crankshaft with the keyway in the sprocket during installation.

17   Clean the timing chain and sprockets with solvent and dry them with compressed air (if available). **Warning:** *Wear eye protection when using compressed air.*

18   Inspect the components for wear and damage. Look for teeth that are deformed, chipped, pitted and cracked.

19   The timing chain should be replaced with a new one if the engine has high mileage, the chain has visible damage, or total freeplay midway between the sprockets exceeds one-inch. Failure to replace a worn timing chain may result in erratic engine performance, loss of power and decreased fuel mileage. Loose chains can "jump" timing. In the worst case, chain "jumping" or breakage will result in severe engine damage.

Installation

Refer to illustrations 10.20 and 10.23

20   Turn the camshaft to position the dowel pin at 6 o'clock, if necessary Mesh the timing chain with the camshaft sprocket, then engage it with the crankshaft sprocket. The timing marks should be aligned as shown in illustration 10.13. **Note:** *If the crankshaft has been disturbed, turn it until the arrow stamped on the crankshaft sprocket is exactly at the top. If the camshaft was turned, install the sprocket temporarily and turn the camshaft until the sprocket timing mark is at the bottom, opposite the mark on the crankshaft sprocket. The arrows should point to each other. The timing chain reference links should align with the camshaft and crankshaft timing marks that are in the 3 o'clock position* **(see illustration)**. *If you are using factory parts, check this alignment.*

21   Install the camshaft sprocket bolt and tighten it to the torque listed in this Chapter's Specifications.

22   Lubricate the chain and sprocket with clean engine oil. Rotate the engine through two complete revolutions and check the alignment of the timing marks again.

23   Align the flats inside the oil pump with the flats on the crankshaft and install the timing chain cover, using a new cover gasket (apply a thin film of RTV sealant to both sides of the new gasket) and O-rings around the three coolant passages **(see illustration)**. Torque the cover bolts to Specifications.

24   The remaining installation steps are the reverse of removal.

25   Add oil and coolant (see Chapter 1), start the engine and check for leaks.

---

the timing chain cover bolts to aid in installation.

12   Use a gasket scraper to remove all traces of old gasket material and sealant from the cover and engine block. The cover is made of aluminum, so be careful not to nick or gouge it. Clean the gasket sealing surfaces with lacquer thinner or acetone.

Timing chain removal

Refer to illustration 10.13

13   Temporarily install the vibration damper bolt and turn the crankshaft with the bolt to align the timing marks on the crankshaft and camshaft sprockets. The crankshaft sprocket arrow should be at the top (12 o'clock position) and the camshaft sprocket arrow should be in the 6 o'clock position **(see illustration)**.

14   Remove the camshaft sprocket bolt. Do not turn the camshaft in the process (if you do, realign the timing marks before the sprocket is removed).

15   Use two large screwdrivers to carefully pry the camshaft sprocket off the camshaft dowel pin, and remove the sprocket and chain.

11.3 Use a dial indicator on the rocker arm to check for camshaft lobe wear

11.12a Arrange to store the lifters in a partitioned box

11.12b Remove the bolts (arrows) that attach the lifter retaining plate

11.12c Lift off the alignment yokes

2A

11 Camshaft and lifters - removal, inspection and installation

Camshaft lobe lift check

Refer to illustration 11.3

1   In order to determine the extent of cam lobe wear, the lobe lift should be checked prior to camshaft removal.

2   Remove the valve covers (see Section 4).

3   Beginning with the number one cylinder, mount a dial indicator on the engine and position the plunger against the top surface of the first rocker arm. Set the number one cylinder at TDC on the compression stroke (see Section 3). The plunger should be directly above and in line with the pushrod **(see illustration)**.

4   Zero the dial indicator, then very slowly turn the crankshaft in the normal direction of rotation (clockwise) until the indicator needle stops and begins to move in the opposite direction. The point at which it stops indicates maximum cam lobe lift.

5   Record this figure for future reference, then reposition the piston at TDC on the compression stroke.

6   Move the dial indicator to the other number one cylinder rocker arm and repeat the check. Be sure to record the results for each valve.

7   Repeat the check for the remaining valves. Since each piston must be at TDC on the compression stroke for this procedure, work from cylinder-to-cylinder following the firing order sequence. For instance, after checking the number one cylinder rocker arms, turn the engine slowly 120 degrees and you are at TDC for number 2.

8   After the check is complete, compare the results to the specifications in this Chapter. If the valve lift is 0.003 inch less than specified, cam lobe wear has occurred and a new camshaft should be installed.

Removal

Refer to illustrations 11.12a, 11.12b, 11.12c and 11.13

9   Refer to the appropriate Sections and remove the intake manifold, rocker arms, pushrods and the timing chain and camshaft sprockets.

10   Refer to Section 12 to remove the cylinder heads to allow clearance for roller lifter removal. Refer to Chapter 3 and remove the radiator and air conditioning condenser.

11   There are several ways to extract the lifters from the bores. A special tool designed to grip and remove lifters is manufactured by many tool companies and is widely available, but it may not be required in every case. On newer engines without a lot of varnish buildup, the lifters can often be removed with a small magnet or even with your fingers. A machinist's scribe with a bent end can be used to pull the lifters out by positioning the point under the retainer ring inside the top of each lifter. **Caution:** *Do not use pliers to remove the lifters unless you intend to replace them with new ones (along with the camshaft). The pliers will damage the precision machined and hardened lifters, rendering them useless.*

12   Before removing the lifters, arrange to store them in a clearly labeled box to ensure that they are reinstalled in their original locations **(see illustration)**. **Note 1:** *The lifter-aligning yokes and yoke retainer must be removed before the lifters are withdrawn* **(see illustrations)**. Remove the lifters and store them where they will not get dirty. **Note 2:** *The roller-type lifters should have paint dabs showing which side of the*

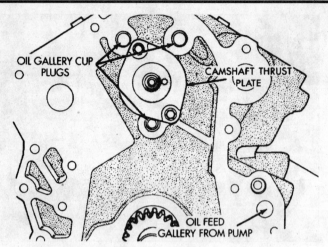

11.13 Remove the camshaft thrust plate

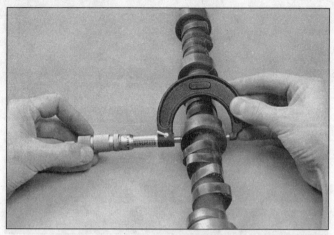

11.16 Use a micrometer to measure the camshaft journals (shown) and the lobes

lifter faces the lifter "valley". If they aren't marked, apply some paint dabs before removing the lifters. *The lifters must be installed the same way to aim the oil feed holes properly.*
Caution: *Do not attempt to withdraw the camshaft with the lifters in place.*
13   Unbolt and remove the camshaft thrust plate **(see illustration)**.
14   Thread a long bolt into the camshaft sprocket bolt hole to use as a handle when removing the camshaft from the block. Support the cam near the block so the lobes do not nick or gouge the bearings as it is withdrawn.

Inspection

Refer to illustrations 11.16 and 11.18

15   After the camshaft has been removed from the engine, cleaned with solvent and dried, inspect the bearing journals for uneven wear, pitting and evidence of seizure. If the journals are damaged, the bearing inserts in the block are probably damaged as well. Both the camshaft and bearings will have to be replaced. **Note:** *Camshaft bearing replacement requires special tools beyond the typical home mechanic. If the bearings are bad, that the engine should be removed and the block taken to an automotive machine shop to ensure that the job is done correctly.*
16   Measure the bearing journals with a micrometer to determine if they are excessively worn or out-of-round **(see illustration)**.
17   Check the camshaft lobes for heat discoloration, score marks, chipped areas, pitting and uneven wear. If the lobes are in good condition and if the lobe lift measurements are as specified in this

Chapter, the camshaft can be reused.
18   Check the rollers carefully for wear and damage and make sure they turn freely without excessive play **(see illustration)**.

Installation

Refer to illustration 11.19

19   Lubricate the camshaft bearing journals and cam lobes with moly-base grease or engine assembly lubricant **(see illustration)**.
20   Slide the camshaft slowly and gently into the engine. Support the cam near the block and be careful not to scrape or nick the bearings. Install the camshaft thrust plate.
21   Install the timing chain and sprockets (see Section 10). Align the timing marks on the crankshaft and camshaft sprockets.
22   Lubricate the lifters with clean engine oil and install them in the block. If the original lifters are being reinstalled, be sure to return them to their original locations. If a new camshaft was installed, be sure to install new lifters as well. Lubricate the lifters with clean engine oil and install them in the block. If the original lifters are being reinstalled, be sure to return them to their original locations, and with the paint marks facing the valley.
23   The remaining installation steps are the reverse of removal.
24   Change the oil, add Mopar Crankcase Conditioner part no. 3419130, or equivalent, and install a new oil filter (see Chapter 1).
25   Start the engine and check for oil pressure and leaks. **Caution:** *Do not run the engine above a fast idle until all the hydraulic lifters have filled with oil and become quiet again.*
26   If a new camshaft and lifters have been installed, the engine

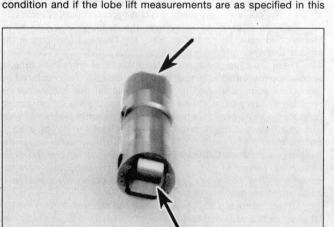

11.18 Check the roller for pitting or excessive looseness and the lifter surfaces for gouges, scoring, wear or damage (arrows)

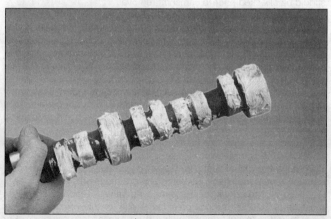

11.19 Lubricate the camshaft lobes and journals with assembly lube before installation

12.10 Do not pry on the cylinder head near the gasket mating surface - use the corners under the casting protrusions

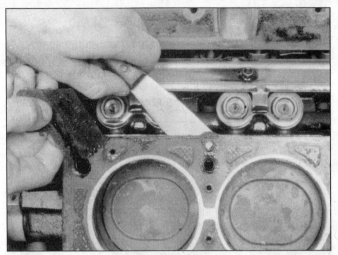

12.13 Use a putty knife or gasket scraper to remove the gasket from the cylinder head

should be brought to operating temperature and run at a fast idle for 15-20 minutes to "break in" the components. Then change the oil and filter once more.

12 Cylinder head(s) - removal and installation

Refer to illustration 12.10
Caution: *Allow the engine to cool completely before loosening the cylinder head bolts.*

Removal

1   Disconnect the negative battery cable from the battery, and drain the cooling system (see Chapter 1).
2   Remove the intake manifold as described in Section 7.
3   Disconnect all wires and vacuum hoses from the cylinder head(s). Be sure to label them to simplify reinstallation.
4   Disconnect the ignition wires and remove the spark plugs (see Chapter 1). Be sure the plug wires are labeled to simplify reinstallation.
5   Detach the exhaust manifold from the cylinder head being removed (see Section 8).
6   Remove the valve cover(s) (see Section 4).
7   Remove the rocker arms and pushrods (see Section 5).
8   Remove the coil wires (see Chapter 1), sending unit wire and heater hoses.
9   Using the new head gasket, outline the cylinders and bolt pattern on a piece of cardboard. Be sure to indicate the front (timing chain end) of the engine for reference. Punch holes at the bolt locations. Loosen each of the cylinder head mounting bolts 1/4-turn at a time until they can be removed by hand - work from bolt-to-bolt in a pattern that's the reverse of the tightening sequence. Store the bolts in the cardboard holder as they're removed - this will ensure they are reinstalled in their original locations, which is absolutely essential.
10   Lift the head(s) off the engine. If resistance is felt, don't pry between the head and block as damage to the mating surfaces will result. Recheck for head bolts that may have been overlooked, then use a hammer and block of wood to tap up on the head and break the gasket seal. Be careful because there are locating dowels in the block which position each head. As a last resort, pry each head up at the corner only and be careful not to damage anything **(see illustration)**. After removal, place the head on blocks of wood to prevent damage to the gasket surfaces.
11   Refer to Chapter 2, Part C, for cylinder head disassembly, inspection and valve service procedures.

Installation

Refer to illustrations 12.13, 12.16, 12.18 and 12.19
12   The mating surfaces of each cylinder head and block must be perfectly clean when the head is installed.
13   Use a gasket scraper to remove all traces of carbon and old gasket material **(see illustration)**, then clean the mating surfaces with lacquer thinner or acetone. If there's oil on the mating surfaces when the head is installed, the gasket may not seal correctly and leaks may develop. When working on the block, it's a good idea to cover the lifter valley with shop rags to keep debris out of the engine. Use a shop rag or vacuum cleaner to remove any debris that falls into the cylinders.
14   Check the block and head mating surfaces for nicks, deep scratches and other damage. If damage is slight, it can be removed with a file; if it's excessive, machining may be the only alternative.
15   Use a tap of the correct size to chase the threads in the head bolt holes. Dirt, corrosion, sealant and damaged threads will affect torque readings.
16   Position the new gasket over the dowel pins in the block. Some gaskets are marked TOP or FRONT to ensure correct installation **(see illustration)**.
17   Carefully position the head on the block without disturbing the gasket.

12.16 Be sure the stamped designations are facing up and forward

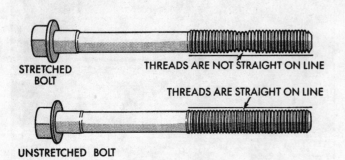

12.18 To check a cylinder head bolt for stretching, lay it against a straightedge - if any threads don't contact the straightedge, replace the bolt

12.19 Cylinder head bolt tightening sequence

13.5 Disconnect the front anti-sway bar clamp bolts and push it to the rear of the vehicle for working room around the oil pan - there are two bolts on each clamp; the arrow indicates one

18   Check the threads of the cylinder head bolts for stretching **(see illustration)**. Replace any bolts that have stretched.
19   Tighten the bolts (numbers 1 through 8) to 45 ft-lbs in the recommended sequence **(see illustration)**. Next, tighten the bolts to 65 ft-lbs following the same recommended sequence. Tighten the same bolts to the same torque again as a double check. Tighten each bolt (except for number 9) an additional 90 degrees (1/4-turn) following

the same sequence. Do not use a torque wrench for this step. **Note:** *After all the head bolts (numbers 1 through 8) have been torqued, tighten head bolt number 9 to 25 ft-lbs.*
20   The remaining installation steps are the reverse of removal.
21   Change the oil and filter (see Chapter 1).

13   Oil pan - removal and installation

Refer to illustrations 13.5, 13.6, 13.7a, 13.7b and 13.10
1   Disconnect the cable from the negative battery terminal.
2   Raise the front of the vehicle and place it securely on jackstands. Apply the parking brake and block the rear wheels to keep it from rolling off the stands. Drain the engine oil (refer to Chapter 1 if necessary).
3   Remove the lower driveplate cover (see Chapter 7).
4   Remove the starter (see Chapter 5).
5   Disconnect and move back the front anti-sway bar **(see illustration)**.
6   Remove the transmission support brackets **(see illustration)**. There is one on either side of the oil pan at the rear of the engine.
7   Remove the bolts and nuts, then carefully separate the oil pan from the block **(see illustration)**. Don't pry between the block and the pan or damage to the sealing surfaces could occur and oil leaks may develop. Instead, tap the pan with a soft-face hammer to break the gasket seal **(see illustration)**.
8   Clean the pan with solvent and remove all old sealant and gasket

13.6 Unbolt and remove the transmission support bracket bolts (arrows) - left bracket shown, right bracket similar

13.7a Remove the bolts from the oil pan

13.7b Use a soft face hammer to loosen the oil pan - be careful not to dent the pan

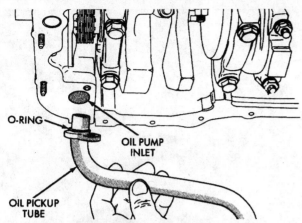

13.10 Remove the oil pump pick-up tube while the pan is off and install a new O-ring

14.2 Remove the oil pump cover bolts with a Torx drive socket

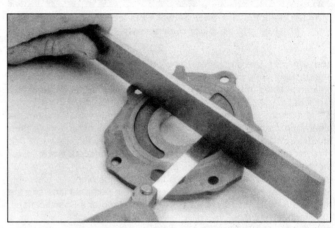

14.4 Place a straightedge across the oil pump cover and check it for warpage with a feeler gauge

2A

material from the block and pan mating surfaces. Clean the mating surfaces with lacquer thinner or acetone and make sure the bolt holes in the block are clear. Check the oil pan flange for distortion, particularly around the bolt holes. If necessary, place the pan on a block of wood and use a hammer to flatten and restore the gasket surface.

9   Apply a bead of RTV sealant to the bottom of the timing chain cover and to the bottom of the rear main oil seal retainer.
10   Remove the oil pump pick-up tube and install a new O-ring while the pan is still off **(see illustration)**.
11   Place the oil pan in position on the block and install the nuts/bolts.
12   After the fasteners are installed, tighten them to the torque listed in this Chapter's Specifications. Starting at the center, follow a crisscross pattern and work up to the final torque in three steps.
13   The remaining steps are the reverse of the removal procedure.
14   Refill the engine with oil (see Chapter 1), run it until normal operating temperature is reached and check for leaks.

14 Oil pump - removal, check and installation

Removal
Refer to illustration 14.2
1   Remove the oil pan (see Section 13).
2   Remove the timing chain cover (see Section 10). Remove the oil pump cover (plate) from the timing chain cover **(see illustration)**.

Check
Refer to illustrations 14.4, 14.6, 14.7, 14.8 and 14.9
3   Clean all parts thoroughly in solvent and carefully inspect the

rotors, pump cover and timing chain cover for nicks, scratches or burrs. Replace the assembly if it is damaged.
4   Use a straightedge and measure the oil pump cover for warpage with a feeler gauge **(see illustration)**. If it's warped more than the limit listed in this Chapter's Specifications, the pump should be replaced.
5   Measure the thickness of the outer rotor. If the thickness is less than the value listed in this Chapter's Specifications, the pump should be replaced.
6   Measure the thickness of the inner rotor **(see illustration)**. If the diameter is less than the value listed in this Chapter's Specifications, the pump should be replaced.
7   Insert the outer rotor into the timing chain cover/oil pump housing

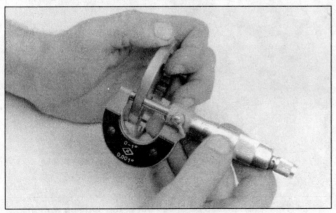

14.6 Use a micrometer to check the thickness of the inner rotor

14.7 Check the outer rotor-to-housing clearance

14.8 Check the clearance between the lobes of the inner and outer rotor (arrow)

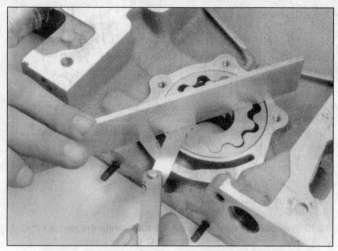

14.9 Using a straightedge and feeler gauges, check the clearance between the surface of the oil pump and the rotors

and measure the clearance between the rotor and housing **(see illustration)**. If the measurement is more than the maximum allowable clearance listed in this Chapter's Specifications, the pump should be replaced.

8   Install the inner rotor in the oil pump assembly and measure the clearance between the lobes on the inner and outer rotors **(see illustration)**. If the clearance is more than the value listed in this Chapter's Specifications, the pump should be replaced. **Note:** *Install the inner rotor with the mark facing up.*

9   Position a straightedge across the face of the oil pump assembly **(see illustration)**. If the clearance between the pump surface and the rotors is greater than the limit listed in this Chapter's Specifications, the pump should be replaced.

Installation

10   Install the pump cover and tighten the bolts to the torque listed in this Chapter's Specifications.

11   To install the pump, turn the flats in the rotor so they align with the flats on the crankshaft.

12   Install the timing chain cover (see Section 10) and tighten the bolts to the torque listed in this Chapter's Specifications.

13   The remainder of installation is the reverse of removal.

15   Driveplate - removal and installation

1   Refer to Chapter 7 and remove the transmission.

2   Paint matching marks on the end of the crankshaft and the flywheel to ensure that it goes back on in the same relationship as before.

3   Jam a large screwdriver through the driveplate to keep the crankshaft from turning, then remove the mounting bolts. **Caution:** *The teeth may be sharp, wear gloves or use rags to protect your hands.*

4   Pull straight back on the driveplate to detach it from the crankshaft.

5   Installation is the reverse of removal. The driveplate must be mounted with the torque converter pads facing the transmission. Be sure to align the matching paint marks. Use thread locking compound on the bolt threads and tighten them to the specified torque in a criss-cross pattern.

16   Rear main oil seal - replacement

Refer to illustrations 16.2, 16.4 and 16.5

1   All engines use a one-piece rear main oil seal which is installed in a bolt-on housing. Replacing this seal requires removal of the

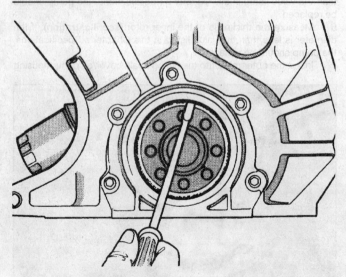

16.2 Pry the old seal from the rear seal housing

16.4 The seal can also be driven out of the housing with the housing removed

16.5 Use a block of wood to drive the new seal into the housing

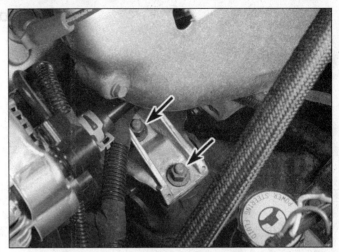

17.7 Remove the nuts (arrows) holding the insulator to the engine bracket . . .

2A

transmission, torque converter and driveplate. Refer to Chapter 7 for the transmission removal procedures.

2   The seal can be removed by prying it out of the housing by inserting a screwdriver, being careful not to nick the crankshaft surface **(see illustration)**. Wrap the screwdriver tip with tape to avoid damage. Be sure to note how far it's recessed into the housing bore before removal so the new seal can be installed to the same depth.

3   The rear main seal housing can also be removed to change the seal, but whenever the housing is removed from the block a new seal and gasket must be installed.

4   If the housing is removed, place it on two blocks of wood and use a small punch to drive out the old seal **(see illustration)**.

5   Clean the housing thoroughly, then apply a thin coat of engine oil to the new seal. Set the seal squarely into the recess of the housing, then, using two pieces of wood, one on each side of the housing, use a hammer to press the seal into place **(see illustration)**.

6   Carefully slide the seal over the crankshaft and bolt the seal housing to the block. Be sure to use a new gasket, but don't use any gasket sealant.

7   The remainder of installation is the reverse of the removal procedure.

17 Engine mounts - check and replacement

Refer to illustrations 17.7 and 17.8
1   Engine mounts seldom require attention, but broken or deteriorated mounts should be replaced immediately or the added strain placed on the driveline components may cause damage.

Check

2   During the check, the engine must be raised slightly to remove the weight from the mounts.

3   Raise the vehicle and support it securely on jackstands, then position the jack under the engine oil pan. Place a large block of wood between the jack head and the oil pan, then carefully raise the engine just enough to take the weight off the mounts.

4   Check the mounts to see if the rubber is cracked, hardened or separated from the metal plates. Sometimes the rubber will split right down the center. Rubber preservative may be applied to the mounts to slow deterioration.

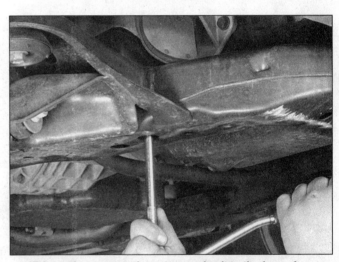

17.8 . . . then remove the nuts securing it to the frame from underneath - access to these nuts is through holes in the frame

5   Check for relative movement between the mount plates and the engine or frame (use a large screwdriver or pry bar to attempt to move the mounts). If movement is noted, lower the engine and tighten the mount fasteners.

Replacement

6   Disconnect the negative cable from the battery, then raise the vehicle and support it securely on jackstands.

7   Remove the nuts holding the insulator to the engine bracket **(see illustration)**.

8   From underneath, remove the nuts holding the insulator to the frame **(see illustration)**.

9   Raise the engine with a jack and block of wood under the oil pan until the studs clear the engine bracket and the frame. remove the insulator and replace it with the new one.

10   Lower the engine and install the top and bottom nuts and torque to this Chapter's Specifications.

Notes

Chapter 2 Part B
3.5L V6 engine

Contents

Specifications

General

Cylinder numbers (front to rear)	
Left bank	2-4-6
Right bank	1-3-5
Firing order	1-2-3-4-5-6
Cylinder head warpage limit	0.002 inch

Camshaft

Endplay	0.004 to 0.014 inch
Lobe lift	
Intake	0.3209 inch
Exhaust	0.2571 inch
Camshaft journal diameter	1.6905 to 1.6913 inches
Camshaft bore diameter (inside)	1.6944 to 1.6952 inches
Camshaft bearing oil clearance	
Standard	0.003 to 0.0047 inch
Service limit	0.0059 inch

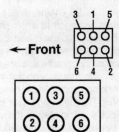

Engine cylinder and coil terminal locations

(diagram showing: 3 1 5 on top, ← Front, 6 4 2 on bottom; cylinders ① ③ ⑤ and ② ④ ⑥)

Oil pump

Cover warpage limit	0.001 inch
Inner and outer rotor thickness (minimum)	0.370 inch
Rotor-to-pump cover clearance	0.003 inch
Outer rotor-to-housing clearance	0.007 inch
Inner rotor-to-outer rotor lobe clearance	0.007 inch

Torque specifications

	Ft-lbs (unless otherwise indicated)
Camshaft sprocket bolts	
Right side	75 plus 1/4-turn
Left side	85 plus 1/4-turn
Camshaft thrust plate bolts	250 in-lbs
Crankshaft damper bolt	85
Cylinder head bolts (in sequence - see illustration 10.22)	
First step	45
Second step	65
Third step	65
Fourth step	Additional 1/4-turn
Engine mount bracket-to-block bolts	65
Engine mount through-bolt nuts	45
Exhaust manifold-to-cylinder head bolts	200 in-lbs
Exhaust crossover bolts	25
Driveplate-to-crankshaft bolts	75
Intake manifold-to-cylinder head bolts	250 in-lbs
Oil pan drain plug	25
Oil pan bolts	105 in-lbs
Oil pump pick-up tube mounting bolt	250 in-lbs
Oil pump cover (plate) bolts (Torx no. 30)	105 in-lbs
Valve cover-to-cylinder head bolts	105 in-lbs
Rocker arm shaft bolts	275 in-lbs
Timing belt cover bolts	
M6	105 in-lbs
M8	250 in-lbs
M10	40
Timing belt tensioner	250 in-lbs
Rear main oil seal retainer bolts	105 in-lbs

1   General information

This Part of Chapter 2 is devoted to in-vehicle repair procedures for the 3.5L V6 engine. This engine utilizes a cast-iron block with six cylinders arranged in a "V" shape at a 60-degree angle between the two banks. The overhead camshaft aluminum cylinder heads are equipped with replaceable valve guides and seats. Aluminum roller rockers on two shafts actuate the valves.

All information concerning engine removal and installation and engine block and cylinder head overhaul can be found in Part C of this Chapter. The following repair procedures are based on the assumption the engine is installed in the vehicle. If the engine has been removed from the vehicle and mounted on a stand, many of the steps outlined in this Part of Chapter 2 will not apply.

The Specifications included in this Part of Chapter 2 apply only to the procedures contained in this Part. Part C of Chapter 2 contains the Specifications necessary for cylinder head and engine block rebuilding.

2   Repair operations possible with the engine in the vehicle

Many major repair operations can be accomplished without removing the engine from the vehicle.

Clean the engine compartment and the exterior of the engine with some type of degreaser before any work is done. It'll make the job easier and help keep dirt out of the internal areas of the engine.

Depending on the components involved, it may be helpful to remove the hood to improve access to the engine as repairs are performed (see Chapter 11 if necessary). Cover the fenders to prevent damage to the paint. Special pads are available, but an old bedspread or blanket will also work.

If vacuum, exhaust, oil or coolant leaks develop, indicating a need for gasket or seal replacement, the repairs can generally be done with the engine in the vehicle. The intake and exhaust manifold gaskets, timing chain cover gasket, oil pan gasket, crankshaft oil seals and cylinder head gaskets are all accessible with the engine in place.

3.4 With the plenum off, remove these two bolts (arrows) from the compressor bracket, loosen the lower bolt and swing it away from the cylinder head

3.5b Remove the valve cover bolts

3.5a Pull the ignition wire harnesses up from the studs on the valve covers

3.6 Remove the nuts and O-rings from each spark plug tube, using either a socket or large pliers

Exterior engine components, such as the intake and exhaust manifolds, the oil pan, timing belt covers (and the oil pump), the water pump, the starter motor, the alternator and the fuel system components can be removed for repair with the engine in place.

Since the cylinder heads can be removed without pulling the engine, valve component servicing can also be accomplished with the engine in the vehicle. Replacement of the timing belt and sprockets is also possible with the engine in the vehicle.

In extreme cases caused by a lack of necessary equipment, repair or replacement of piston rings, pistons, connecting rods and rod bearings is possible with the engine in the vehicle. However, this practice is not recommended because of the cleaning and preparation work that must be done to the components involved.

3 Valve cover(s) - removal and installation

Refer to illustrations 3.4, 3.5a, 3.5b, 3.6 and 3.7

Removal

1 Disconnect the cable from the negative battery terminal.
2 Remove the intake air plenum (see Chapter 4) and cover the lower intake manifold with rags to keep out dirt.
3 Remove the ignition wires from the spark plugs (see Chapter 1). Be sure each wire is labeled before removal to ensure correct reinstallation.
4 Unbolt the air conditioning compressor mount and pull it away from the right cylinder head **(see illustration)**.

3.7 Remove the valve covers

5 Pull the ignition wire harness up from the valve cover studs and remove the valve cover studs/bolts **(see illustrations)**.
6 Remove the retaining nut and O-ring from each spark plug tube **(see illustration)**.
7 Detach the valve cover. **Note:** *If the cover sticks to the cylinder head, use a block of wood and a hammer to dislodge it. If the cover still won't come loose, pry on it carefully, but don't distort the sealing flange* **(see illustration)**.

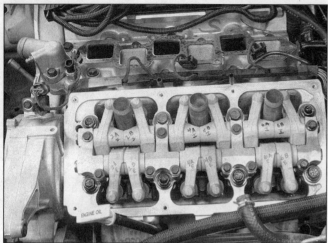

4.2 Use a permanent marker to identify each of the rocker arms and pedestals before removing them from the shaft

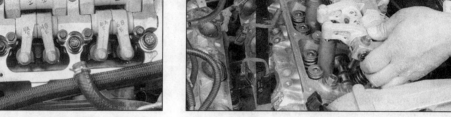

4.3 Remove the rocker arm shaft bolts from the cylinder head - be sure to start with the outer ones first, then remove the rocker arm assembly

Installation

8   The mating surfaces of each cylinder head and valve cover must be perfectly clean when the covers are installed. Use a gasket scraper to remove all traces of sealant or old gasket material, then clean the mating surfaces with lacquer thinner or acetone (if there's sealant or oil on the mating surfaces when the cover is installed, oil leaks may develop). Be extra careful not to nick or gouge the mating surfaces with the scraper.

9   Clean the mounting bolt threads with a die if necessary to remove any corrosion and restore damaged threads. Use a tap to clean the threaded holes in the heads.

10   Place the valve cover and new gasket in position, then install the bolts. Tighten the bolts in several steps to the torque listed in this Chapter's Specifications.

11   Complete the installation by reversing the removal procedure. Start the engine and check carefully for oil leaks.

---

4   Rocker arms and shafts - removal, inspection and installation

Removal

Refer to illustrations 4.2 and 4.3

1   Refer to Section 3 and remove the valve cover(s).

2   Mark the rocker arms and pedestals for identification before removing them **(see illustration)**. There are four per cylinder, two intake and two exhaust.

3   Loosen each rocker arm shaft bolt a little at a time until they are all loose enough to be removed by hand. Remove the shaft and rockers as an assembly **(see illustration)**.

Inspection

Refer to illustrations 4.4 and 4.7

4   Inspect each rocker arm for wear, cracks and other damage. This engine uses aluminum rocker arms with steel roller tips. Make sure the rollers turn freely and show no signs of wear **(see illustration)**.

5   Check each rocker arm pivot area and shaft for wear, cracks and galling. If the rocker arms or shafts are worn or damaged, replace them with new ones.

6   Make sure the axle for the roller tip is not sticking out one side more than the other, and make sure the swivel pads on the hydraulic lash adjusters are in place.

7   To remove the rocker arms and pedestals from the shafts for inspection, the dowel pins at each end must be pulled out. Use a 4mm screw and nut, and a washer and spacer as a puller to extract the dowel pins at each end of the shafts **(see illustration)**.

4.4 Examine the roller tips for signs of wear and make sure they turn freely

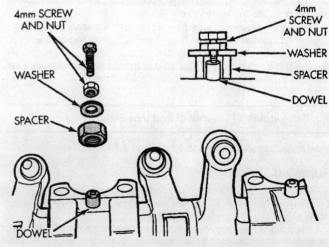

4.7 Use this arrangement of a bolt, nut, washer and spacer to extract the dowel pins from the pedestals

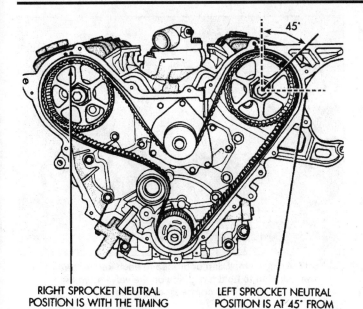

RIGHT SPROCKET NEUTRAL
POSITION IS WITH THE TIMING
MARKS ALIGNED WITH COVER

LEFT SPROCKET NEUTRAL
POSITION IS AT 45° FROM
TIMING MARKS ON COVER

4.10 Position the camshafts in the "neutral" position before installing the rocker arm/shaft assemblies - complete the installation on the right side cylinder head first, then rotate the engine to the neutral position for the left cylinder head

Installation

Refer to illustration 4.10

8   If the rockers arms or pedestals have been removed from the shafts for inspection, lubricate the shafts and install the rocker arms and pedestals in their marked order. Keep the intake rockers on the intake shaft, and exhaust rockers on the exhaust shaft. **Caution:** *Make sure the oil holes in the shafts line up with the oil holes in the pedestal, and with the oil holes in the cylinder head. These are different for left and right rocker shafts.*

9   Reinstall the dowels pins at each end (they press in until they bottom out in the pedestals).

10   The rocker arm assemblies should be installed, and the bolts tightened, with the valvetrain in a "no load" situation. To accomplish this, place the cams in a "neutral" position. Refer to Section 9 and remove the timing belt cover. Rotate the engine until the right side camshaft timing marks align and install the right side rocker arm/shaft assembly **(see illustration)**.

11   For the left cylinder head, rotate the engine until the timing mark on the left camshaft is 45-degrees from the mark on the cover **(see illustration 4.10)**. Install the rocker arm/shaft assembly. Tighten both rocker arm/shaft assembly bolts to the torque listed in this Chapter's Specifications.

12   The remainder of the installation is the reverse of the removal procedures. Start the engine and watch for leaks.

5   Valve springs, retainers and seals - replacement

Refer to illustrations 5.5, 5.7, 5.14 and 5.17

Note: *Broken valve springs and defective valve stem seals can be replaced without removing the cylinder head. Two special tools and a compressed-air source are normally required to perform this operation, so read through this Section carefully and rent or buy the tools before beginning the job.*

1   Remove the valve covers (See Section 3).

2   Remove the spark plugs (see Chapter 1).

3   Rotate the crankshaft until the number one piston is at top dead center on the compression stroke (see Section 9).

4   Remove the rocker arm and shaft assembly (see Section 4).

5   Thread an adapter into the number 1 spark plug hole and connect an air hose from a compressed air source to it **(see illustration)**. Most auto parts stores can supply the air hose adapter. **Note:** *Many cylinder compression gauges utilize a screw-in fitting that may work with your air hose quick-disconnect fitting, and they are usually long enough to reach through the spark plug tubes on the 3.5L engine.*

6   Apply compressed air to the cylinder. The valves should be held in place by the air pressure. If the valve faces or seats are in poor condition, leaks may prevent the air pressure from retaining the valves - valve reconditioning is indicated.

7   Stuff shop rags into the cylinder head holes around the valves to prevent parts and tools from falling into the engine, then use a valve-spring compressor to compress the spring. Remove the keepers with small needle-nose pliers or a magnet **(see illustration)**.

8   Remove the valve spring and retainer.

9   Remove the old valve stem seal.

10   Wrap a rubber band or tape around the top of the valve stem so the valve won't fall into the combustion chamber, then release the air pressure.

11   Inspect the valve stem for damage. Rotate the valve in the guide and check the end for eccentric movement, which would indicate that the valve is bent.

12   Move the valve up-and-down in the guide and make sure it doesn't bind. If the valve stem binds, either the valve is bent or the guide is damaged. In either case, the head will have to be removed for repair.

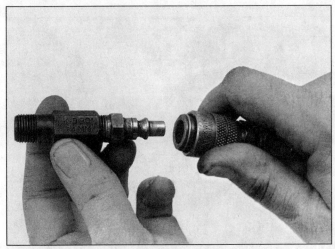

5.5 This is what the air hose adapter that threads into the spark plug hole looks like - they-re commonly available in auto parts stores

5.7 Using a clamp-type spring compressor, compress the spring enough to remove the keepers with small pliers or a magnet

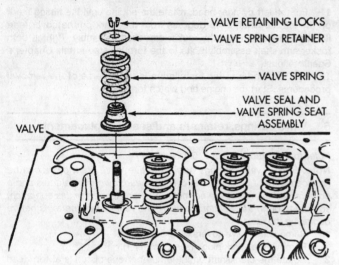

- VALVE RETAINING LOCKS
- VALVE SPRING RETAINER
- VALVE SPRING
- VALVE SEAL AND VALVE SPRING SEAT ASSEMBLY
- VALVE

5.14 Install the new seal on the valve guide - do not displace the garter spring at the top of the seal

5.17 Apply a small dab of grease to each keeper before installation to hold it in place on the valve stem until the spring compressor is released

13   Reapply air pressure to the cylinder to retain the valve in the closed position, then remove the tape or rubber band from the valve stem.
14   Install the new seal on the valve stem and push it down to the top of the valve guide (see illustration), but do not force it, and make sure the garter spring is still in place around the top of the seal.
15   Install the spring and retainer in position over the valve. Caution: *Different length springs are used on the intake and exhaust valves - accidentally installing an intake spring on an exhaust valve can cause major engine damage. The intake springs are identified with a white mark at the top, while the exhaust springs have a pink mark.*
16   Compress the valve spring assembly only enough to install the keepers in the valve stem.
17   Position the keepers in the valve stem groove. Apply a small dab of grease to the inside of each keeper to hold it in place if necessary (see illustration). Remove the pressure from the spring tool and make sure the keepers are seated.
18   Disconnect the air hose and remove the adapter from the spark plug hole.
19   Repeat the above procedure on the remaining cylinders, following the firing order sequence (see the Specifications). Bring each piston to top dead center on the compression stroke before applying air pressure.
20   Reinstall the rocker arm assemblies, valve covers and intake

plenum.
21   Start the engine, then check for oil leaks and unusual sounds coming from the valve cover area.

6   Intake manifold - removal and installation

Removal

Refer to illustrations 6.4 and 6.5
1   Relieve the fuel system pressure (see Chapter 4) and drain the cooling system (see Chapter 1).
2   Disconnect the cable from the negative battery terminal.
3   Remove the air intake plenum, fuel rail and injectors (see Chapter 4). When disconnecting fuel line fittings, be prepared to catch some fuel with a rag, then cap the fittings to prevent contamination.
4   Remove the radiator hose from the thermostat housing and the heater hose from the rear of the intake manifold (see illustration).
5   Remove the intake manifold mounting bolts and separate the manifold from the engine (see illustration). If the manifold is stuck, carefully pry on a casting protrusion - don't pry between the manifold and heads, as damage to the gasket sealing surfaces may result. If you're installing a new manifold, transfer all fittings and sensors to the new manifold.

6.4 After the plenum is removed, disconnect the heater hose fitting at the rear of the manifold (arrows)

6.5 Remove the bolts (arrows) and lift the intake manifold straight up

6.8 Apply a small bead of RTV sealant, on either side of the gaskets, around each water passage at the ends of the heads (arrows)

Installation

Refer to illustration 6.8

Note: *The mating surfaces of the cylinder heads, block and manifold must be perfectly clean when the manifold is installed. Gasket removal solvents are available at most auto parts stores and may be helpful when removing old gasket material that's stuck to the heads and manifold (since the manifold is made of aluminum, aggressive scraping can cause damage). Be sure to follow the directions printed on the container.*

6   Lift the old gasket off. Use a gasket scraper to remove all traces of sealant and old gasket material, then clean the mating surfaces with lacquer thinner or acetone. If there's old sealant or oil on the mating surfaces when the manifold is installed, oil or vacuum leaks may develop. Use a vacuum cleaner to remove any gasket material that falls into the valley.

7   Use a tap of the correct size to chase the threads in the bolt holes, if necessary, then use compressed air (if available) to remove the debris from the holes. **Warning:** *Wear safety glasses or a face shield to protect your eyes when using compressed air!*

8   Apply a bead of RTV sealant or equivalent around the front and rear cylinder head water passages before laying the new gaskets in place **(see illustration)**.

9   Install the intake manifold gaskets and apply RTV sealant to the manifold side of the gaskets, around the water passages.

10   Carefully lower the manifold into place and install the mounting

bolts finger tight.

11   Tighten the mounting bolts/nuts in three steps, working from the center out, in a criss-cross pattern, to the torque listed in this Chapter's Specifications.

12   Install the remaining components in the reverse order of removal.

13   Refill the cooling system (see Chapter 1). Start the engine and check for leaks.

7   Exhaust manifold(s) - removal and installation

Refer to illustrations 7.2, 7.4 and 7.6
Note: *The engine must be completely cool before beginning this procedure.*

Removal

1   Disconnect the cable from the negative battery terminal.

2   Unbolt the exhaust pipes where they join the manifolds **(see illustration)**.

3   Disconnect the oxygen sensor's electrical connector.

4   Remove the exhaust manifold upper heat shield mounting bolts/nuts **(see illustration)** and lift the heat shields from the engine.

5   Remove the nut holding the intake manifold brace and dipstick tube in place (left manifold) and pull the dipstick tube from the engine.

6   Remove the mounting bolts and detach the manifold from the cylinder head **(see illustration)**. Be sure to spray penetrating lubricant onto the bolts and threads before attempting to remove them. **Note:** *The lower heat shield is held in place by the front and rear manifold mounting bolts.*

Installation

7   Clean the mating surfaces to remove all traces of old gasket material, then inspect the manifold for distortion and cracks. Warpage can be checked with a precision straightedge held against the mating flange. If a feeler gauge thicker than 0.030-inch can be inserted between the straightedge and flange surface, take the manifold to an automotive machine shop for resurfacing.

8   Place the exhaust manifold in position with a new gasket (and the lower heat shields) and install the mounting bolts finger tight. **Note:** *Be sure to identify the exhaust manifold gaskets by the correct cylinder designation and the position of the exhaust ports on the gasket.*

9   Starting in the middle and working out toward the ends, tighten the mounting bolts in several increments, to the torque listed in this Chapter's Specifications.

10   Install the remaining components in the reverse order of removal.

11   Start the engine and check for exhaust leaks between the manifold and cylinder head and between the manifold and exhaust pipe.

2B

7.2 Remove the two exhaust pipe-to-manifold flange nuts and slide the flange off the studs

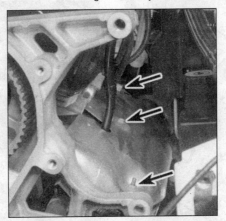

7.4 Two bolts and a nut (arrows) retain the top heat shields on each manifold

7.6 Remove the mounting bolts and separate the exhaust manifold from the cylinder head - the lower heat shields are retained by the front (arrow) and rear manifold bolts

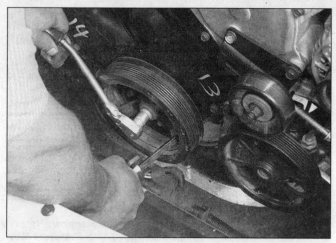

8.3 Insert a prybar or large screwdriver through the balancer to hold it while you loosen the crankshaft damper bolt

8.4 Use a three jaw puller to remove the crankshaft damper. A long Allen bolt must be inserted into the crankshaft for the tool to push against

8   Crankshaft front oil seal - replacement

Refer to illustrations 8.3, 8.4, 8.6, 8.7, 8.8 and 8.9

1   Disconnect the cable from the negative battery terminal. Remove the accessory drivebelts (see Chapter 1).

2   Refer to Chapter 3 and remove the upper radiator crossmember and cooling fan assembly.

3   Position a large screwdriver through the balancer to keep the crankshaft from turning and remove the vibration damper-to-crankshaft bolt **(see illustration)**.

4   Pull the damper off the crankshaft with a puller **(see illustration)**. **Caution:** *The jaws of the puller must only contact the hub of the pulley - not the outer ring.* **Note:** *A long Allen-head bolt must be inserted into the crankshaft nose for the puller's tapered tip to push against.*

5   Refer to Section 9 for removal of the timing belt cover and timing belt.

6   Use a two-bolt puller to remove the crankshaft sprocket, with two bolts threaded into the sprocket **(see illustration)**.

7   With a hammer and punch, tap the dowel pin out of the crankshaft **(see illustration)**. Drive the pin into the hollow, threaded area of the crankshaft snout, where it can be extracted with a small magnet.

8   Pry the old seal out with a hook-type seal tool, being very careful not to scratch the seal surface of the crankshaft **(see illustration)**.

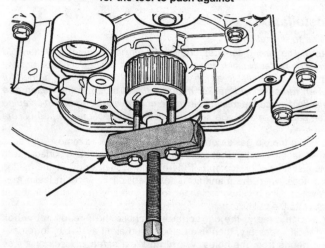

8.6 A two-bolt puller is used to remove the crankshaft sprocket

Note how the seal is installed - the new one must be installed to the same depth and facing the same way.

9   Lubricate the inner lip of the new seal with engine oil and drive it

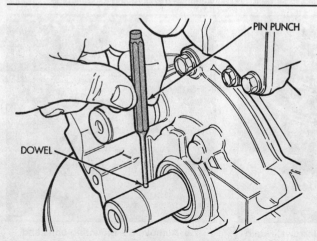

8.7 Tap the dowel pin down into the crankshaft with a punch - it can be extracted from inside the crankshaft snout with a small magnet

8.8 Using a hook-type seal remover, pry out the old seal

8.9 Drive the new seal in to the same depth as the old one, using a large-diameter socket or section of pipe

9.4 Remove the three bolts and the drivebelt tensioner assembly

9.5 Remove the stamped steel timing belt cover

in with a large socket or section of pipe and a hammer **(see illustration)**.

10   Installation is the reverse of removal. Tap the dowel pin back into the crankshaft, with 3/64-inch extending out.

11   Tighten the vibration damper-to-crankshaft bolt to the torque listed in this Chapter's Specifications.

9   Timing belt - replacement

Refer to illustrations 9.4, 9.5, 9.7a, 9.7b, 9.7c, 9.8 and 9.9

Note 1: *The following procedure for timing belt replacement is based on the camshaft sprockets NOT being loosened or removed. If the camshaft sprockets are being removed, follow the cam timing procedure in Section 10.*

Note 2: *Because of work necessary to get at the timing belt and replace it, and because the water pump is in this area, it is recommended that the water pump be replaced at the same time as the belt (see Chapter 3). The factory recommends replacing the timing belt at 105,000 miles or 84 months.*

1   Disconnect the cable from the negative battery terminal. Remove the accessory drivebelts (see Chapter 1).

2   Refer to Section 8 for removal of the crankshaft damper.

3   Refer to Chapter 3 and remove the upper radiator crossmember and the cooling fan assembly.

4   Remove the drivebelt tensioner pulley **(see illustration)**.

5   Unbolt and remove the stamped steel timing belt cover **(see illustration)**.

6   Remove the cast timing belt cover in front of the left cylinder head.

7   Temporarily install the vibration damper bolt and turn the crankshaft with the bolt to align the timing marks on the crankshaft and camshaft sprockets. The crankshaft sprocket arrow should line up with the TDC indicator on the oil pump cover and the camshaft sprocket arrows should line up between the marks on the top of the rear covers **(see illustrations)**.

9.7a Align the notch in the crankshaft sprocket with the TDC mark on the oil pump cover (arrow)

9.7b Align each camshaft sprocket timing mark between the two marks on the rear cover (arrows)

9.7c Mark the timing belt at each camshaft's timing marks for later installation if you plan on reusing the same belt

2B

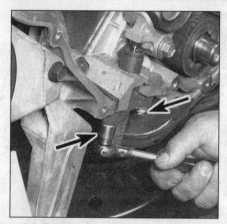

9.8 Remove the timing belt tensioner bolts (arrows), then remove the tensioner and the timing belt

9.9 Compress the plunger on the tensioner in a vise until a drill bit or Allen wrench can be inserted through the hole to retain the plunger - orient the pin in a way that won't interfere with installing the tensioner with the pin in place

10.9a With the engine raised (or the radiator and condenser removed), hold the camshaft sprocket with a wrench while loosening the bolt with a socket and breaker bar - these bolts are very tight

8   Unbolt the timing belt tensioner and remove the belt (see illustration).

9   Compress the timing belt tensioner in a vise until a drill bit or Allen wrench can be inserted through the hole to lock it in (see illustration).

10   Making sure that all timing marks are still aligned, start by installing the new belt at the crankshaft pulley, proceeding counterclockwise up to the left camshaft sprocket. After the belt is on the left camshaft sprocket, keep tension on the belt as it is fed under the water pump pulley, over the right camshaft sprocket, and past the tensioner.

11   Hold the tensioner pulley against the belt and install the tensioner. Tighten the tensioner bolts to the torque listed in this Chapter's Specifications.

12   Remove the Allen key or drill bit from the tensioner, allowing it to tension the pulley on the belt.

13   Rotate the crankshaft pulley through two complete revolutions to check that the timing marks still remain aligned. If not, repeat the belt installation process.

14   The remainder of installation is the reverse of removal. **Note:** *When reinstalling the cast timing cover (which installs before the stamped steel cover), use a thin bead of RTV sealant around the perimeter. The stamped-steel cover has it's own sealant attached, which should be reusable. If there are tears or gaps in the original sealing material, fill the voids with RTV sealant.*

15   Add coolant (see Chapter 1), start the engine and check for leaks.

---

10   Cylinder heads - removal and installation

Caution: *Allow the engine to cool completely before loosening the cylinder head bolts.*

Note: *Special tools are necessary to complete this procedure. Read through the entire procedure and obtain the special tools before beginning work.*

Removal

Refer to illustrations 10.9a, 10.9b, 10.9c, 10.10a, 10.10b, 10.12 and 10.15

1   Disconnect the cable from the negative battery terminal. Drain the cooling system (see Chapter 1).

2   Remove the intake manifold as described in Section 6. If removing the left cylinder head, remove the alternator (see Chapter 5). If removing the right cylinder head, remove the air conditioning compressor (see Chapter 3).

3   Disconnect all wires and vacuum hoses from the cylinder head(s). Be sure to label them to simplify reinstallation.

10.9b The two long camshaft sprocket bolts are not interchangeable - mark them "left" or "right"

4   Disconnect the ignition wires and remove the spark plugs (see Chapter 1). Be sure the plug wires are labeled to simplify reinstallation.

5   Detach the exhaust manifold from the cylinder head being removed (see Section 7).

6   Remove the valve cover(s) (see Section 3).

7   Remove the rocker arms and shafts (see Section 4).

8   Refer to Section 9, remove the timing belt covers, align the TDC marks and remove the timing belt. If the belt is to be reused, mark it's direction of rotation before removing it.

9   Hold the camshaft sprocket hex with a wrench while using a socket and breaker bar to loosen the camshaft bolt, which is under considerable torque (see illustration). It may be necessary to loosen the engine mounts (see Section 16) and raise the engine for sufficient clearance to withdraw the long camshaft bolt (see illustration). As an alternative, remove the radiator and air conditioning condenser (see Chapter 3), it makes the job much easier and the engine does not have to be raised. **Caution:** *The two camshaft sprockets are not interchangeable, nor are the camshaft sprocket bolts. The left camshaft sprocket has the ignition pick-up slots (see illustration), and the left sprocket bolt is longer (10 inches, vs. 8-3/8 inches long for the right bolt).*

10   The power steering pump bracket must be detached to remove the left cylinder head. Also remove the bolt at the bottom, from the power steering bracket to the block (see illustrations).

11   Unbolt and remove the rear timing belt cover(s). On the left

10.9c The two camshaft sprockets are not interchangeable -
the left sprocket has the camshaft position sensor
ring (arrow) on the back

10.10a Remove the five bolts on the rear timing belt cover . . .

10.10b . . . then remove the two power steering pump bracket
bolts (arrows) plus a hidden bolt behind the bracket

10.12 Remove the ground wire terminals from the bottom bolt
of the camshaft retainer plate at the back of the
left cylinder head (arrow)

cylinder head, a steel alternator support bracket behind the rear belt
cover must be removed. **Note:** *The rear cover on the right cylinder
head has water-passage O-rings on the back.*

12   Make sure there are no brackets or connectors attached to the
back of either cylinder head. On the left cylinder head, remove the
ground wire terminals attached with the bottom bolt of the camshaft
retainer plate **(see illustration)**. **Note:** *You may have to bend the water
pipe near it slightly to fully remove the bolt.*

13   Using the new head gasket, outline the cylinders and bolt pattern
on a piece of cardboard. Be sure to indicate the front of the engine for
reference. Punch holes at the bolt locations.

14   Loosen each of the cylinder head mounting bolts 1/4-turn at a
time until they can be removed by hand - work from bolt-to-bolt in a
pattern that's the reverse of the tightening sequence **(see illustration 10.21)**. Store the bolts in the cardboard holder as they're
removed. This will ensure they are reinstalled in their original locations,
which is absolutely essential.

15   Lift the head(s) off the engine **(see illustration)**. If resistance is
felt, don't pry between the head and block as damage to the mating
surfaces will result. Recheck for head bolts that may have been
overlooked, then use a hammer and block of wood to tap up on the
head to break the gasket seal. Be careful because there are locating
dowels in the block which position each head. As a last resort, pry
each head up at the rear corner only and be careful not to damage
anything. After removal, place the head on blocks of wood to prevent
damage to the gasket surfaces.

10.15 Remove the head from the engine, being careful not to
damage the dowel pins in the block

16   Refer to Chapter 2, Part C, for cylinder head disassembly,
inspection and valve service procedures. **Note:** *If the camshaft is to be
removed for examination or replacement, it must be done with the
cylinder head **off** the engine, as it comes out the back of the cylinder
head.*

2B

10.17 Use a putty knife or gasket scraper to remove gasket material from the cylinder head and block

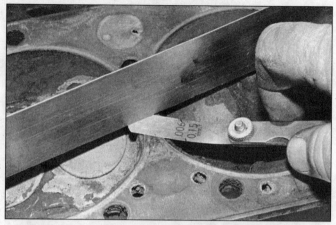

10.18 Check the head for warpage with a straightedge and a feeler gauge - check the Specifications for maximum allowable warpage

Installation

Refer to illustrations 10.17, 10.18, 10.19, 10.20 and 10.22

17   The mating surfaces of each cylinder head and block must be perfectly clean when the head is installed. Use a gasket scraper to remove all traces of carbon and old gasket material **(see illustration)**, then clean the mating surfaces with lacquer thinner or acetone. If there's oil on the mating surfaces when the head is installed, the gasket may not seal correctly and leaks may develop. When working on the block, it's a good idea to cover the valley with shop rags to keep debris out of the engine. Use a shop rag or vacuum cleaner to remove any debris that falls into the cylinders.

18   Check the block and head mating surfaces for nicks, deep scratches and other damage. If damage is slight, it can be removed with a file; if it's excessive, machining may be the only alternative. Use a steel straightedge across the head, trying a feeler gauge underneath to check for warpage **(see illustration)**.

19   Use a tap of the correct size to chase the threads in the head bolt holes. Dirt, corrosion, sealant and damaged threads will affect torque readings. Check the cleaned head bolts for stretch by holding them next to a steel ruler **(see illustration)**. If all the threads don't touch the ruler, the bolt should be replaced.

20   Position the new gasket over the dowel pins in the block. Some gaskets are marked TOP or FRONT to ensure correct installation **(see illustration)**.

21   Carefully position the head on the block without disturbing the gasket.

22   Tighten the bolts to 45 ft-lbs in the recommended sequence **(see illustration)**. Next, tighten the bolts to 65 ft-lbs following the same recommended sequence. Tighten the bolts to 65 ft-lbs again as a

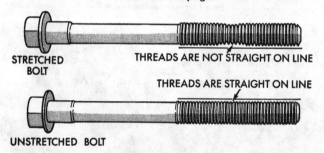

STRETCHED BOLT

THREADS ARE NOT STRAIGHT ON LINE

THREADS ARE STRAIGHT ON LINE

UNSTRETCHED BOLT

10.19 To check a cylinder head bolt for stretching, lay it against a straightedge - if any threads don't contact the straightedge, replace the bolt

double check. Finally, tighten each bolt an additional 90-degrees (1/4-turn) following the same sequence. Do not use a torque wrench for this last step.

Camshaft sprocket timing

Refer to illustrations 10.24 and 10.25

23   Reattach the rear timing belt covers to the cylinder heads and block, making sure new O-rings are in place where used.

24   At this point a special tool is required to lock the camshaft(s) into the TDC position before installing the camshaft sprockets **(see illustration)**. If you cannot obtain the tool from your local dealer, contact Miller Special Tools (1-800-801-5420). Bolt one of these tools at the back of each head, making sure the locating pin fits into the hole in the camshaft.

25   Set up a dial indicator through the number 1 spark plug hole so that it touches the top of the piston **(see illustration)**. If you don't have a long adapter for the indicator, remove the spark plug tube with locking pliers (do not use the pliers on the threaded portion). Using the crankshaft damper bolt in the crankshaft, rotate the engine slightly

10.20 Be sure the stamped designations are facing up and forward when installing the head gasket on the block

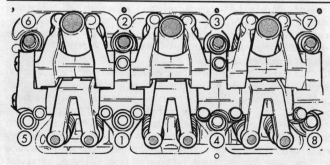

10.22 Cylinder head bolt TIGHTENING sequence

10.24 Bolt these special camshaft alignment tools (Chrysler tool no. 6642, or equivalent) to the back of each cylinder head to hold the camshafts in the TDC position

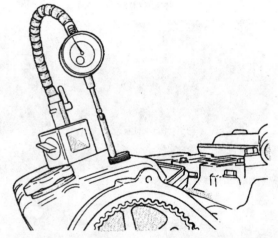

10.25 To properly index the camshaft sprockets, use a dial indicator to determine true TDC for number 1 cylinder

back and forth until there is no piston movement indicated by the dial indicator. This will be the true TDC.

26   Each camshaft sprocket has a D-shaped hole where it fits over the camshaft, and requires precision alignment to properly time the engine. With the camshafts held at the rear by the special tools, and the crankshaft positioned at TDC for number 1 cylinder, place the camshaft sprockets in place with their respective bolts, but **do not tighten the bolts.** Use Loctite 271 sealer on the bolt threads.

27   With the engine in this position, install the timing belt (refer to Section 9). The timing marks on the sprockets should be within the two marks on the rear covers **(see illustration 9.7b).**

28   Install the timing belt tensioner (refer to Section 9) and release the retaining pin.

29   Hold the hex on the camshaft sprockets with a wrench and tighten the camshaft bolts to the torque listed in this Chapter's Specifications **(see illustration 10.9a).**

30   Remove the special camshaft aligning tools on the rear of the cylinder heads. The remaining installation steps are the reverse of removal.

31   Change the oil and filter, refill the cooling system (see Chapter 1), run the engine and check for leaks.

---

11   Camshafts - removal, inspection and installation

Note: *The camshaft lobe lift on the 3.5L engine can be checked with a dial indicator with the cam still in the head. With the rocker arms/shafts removed, place the tip of the dial indicator on one of the camshaft lobes and record the maximum lift as the camshaft is turned through a compete revolution.*

Removal

1   The cylinder head(s) must be removed to withdraw the camshafts from the rear of the heads. Refer to Section 10 for cylinder head removal.

2   Remove the camshaft rear cover and O-ring seal and withdraw the camshaft from the cylinder head, being careful not to nick the cam bearings or journals.

Inspection

Refer to illustrations 11.4, 11.5a, 11.5b, 11.7 and 11.8

3   After the camshaft has been removed from the engine, cleaned with solvent and dried, inspect the bearing journals for uneven wear, pitting and evidence of seizure. If the journals are damaged, the bearing surface in the cylinder head is probably damaged as well. Both the camshaft and the cylinder head will have to be replaced.

4   Measure the bearing journals with a micrometer to determine if they are excessively worn or out-of-round **(see illustration).** Compare your measurements with the journal diameters found in this Chapter's Specifications to determine if the camshaft can be reused.

5   Check the camshaft lobes for heat discoloration, score marks, chipped areas, pitting and uneven wear. Measure a lobe's largest measurement against it's smallest (base circle) to find the lobe lift **(see illustrations).** If the lobes are in good condition and if the lobe lift measurements are as specified in this Chapter's Specifications, the camshaft can be reused.

6   Using a telescoping gauge and outside micrometer, measure the inside diameter of each camshaft journal bearing surface in the cylinder head. Subtract the camshaft bearing journal diameters from the corresponding bearing inside diameters to obtain the bearing oil

2B

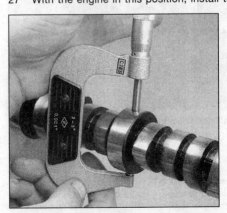

11.4 Use a micrometer to measure the camshaft journal diameters

11.5a Measure the camshaft lobe at its greatest dimension . . .

11.5b . . . and subtract the camshaft lobe diameter at its smallest dimension to obtain the lobe lift specification

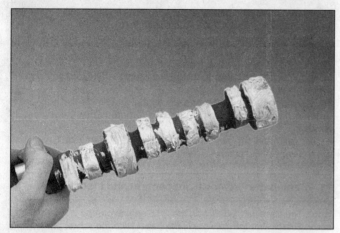

11.7 Coat both the cam lobes and the journals with camshaft installation lube before installing the camshaft

11.8 The camshaft seal can be removed with a hook-type seal remover - use a deep socket or section of pipe to install the new seal

12.3 Disconnect the stabilizer bar bushing brackets above the frame and push the bar toward the rear of the vehicle

12.4 Remove the transmission support brackets (arrows to bolts on left bracket; right bracket similar)

clearance. Compare your findings with the camshaft bearing oil clearance found in this Chapter's Specifications, if it's excessive, a new camshaft and/or cylinder head will be required.

Installation

7   Lubricate the camshaft bearing journals and cam lobes with camshaft installation lube **(see illustration)**.
8   Insert the camshaft carefully into the cylinder head, then install a new seal at the front of the head **(see illustration)**. Using a deep socket or section of pipe, tap the new seal in. Install the camshaft cover at the back of the head with a new O-ring.
9   The remainder of the installation is covered in Sections 9 and 10.

12 Oil pan - removal and installation

Removal

Refer to illustrations 12.3, 12.4, 12.5 and 12.6
1   Disconnect the cable from the negative battery terminal.
2   Raise the front of the vehicle and place it securely on jackstands. Apply the parking brake and block the rear wheels to keep the vehicle from rolling off the stands. Drain the engine oil and remove the oil filter (see Chapter 1).
3   Disconnect the stabilizer bar from the front suspension and move it toward the rear of the vehicle **(see illustration)**.
4   Remove the transmission support brackets, one on each side of the pan at the rear **(see illustration)**, and the lower driveplate cover

12.5 Remove the bolts from the perimeter of the oil pan

(see Chapter 7, Part A).
5   Remove the bolts and nuts, then carefully separate the oil pan from the block **(see illustration)**. Don't pry between the block and the pan or damage to the sealing surfaces could occur and oil leaks may develop. Instead, tap the pan with a soft-face hammer to break the gasket seal.
6   Remove the oil pump pick-up tube, then carefully pull off the oil pan gasket. The 3.5L V6 engine uses a special oil pan gasket which

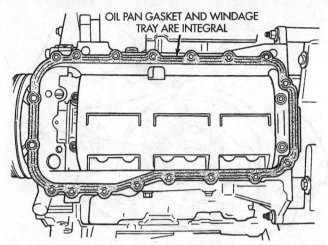

12.6 Details of the combination oil baffle and pan gasket

13.3 Unbolt the oil pump housing from the block

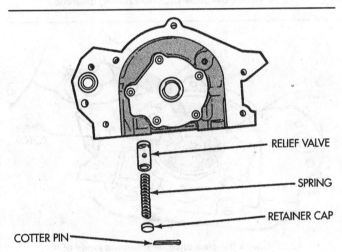

13.4 Remove the oil pressure relief valve for cleaning and inspection

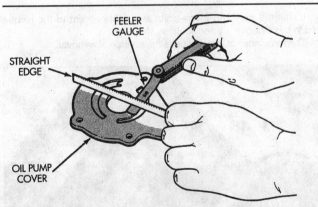

13.8 Place a straightedge across the oil pump cover and check it for warpage with a feeler gauge

combines a sheetmetal oil baffle tray with silicone gasket bonded to the perimeter on both sides. It is meant to be reusable if the sealing material hasn't been damaged **(see illustration)**.

Installation

7   Clean the pan with solvent and remove all old sealant and gasket material from the block and pan mating surfaces. Clean the mating surfaces with lacquer thinner or acetone and make sure the bolt holes

in the block are clear. Check the oil pan flange for distortion, particularly around the bolt holes. If necessary, place the pan on a block of wood and use a hammer to flatten and restore the gasket surface.
8   Apply a bead of RTV sealant to the bottom surface of the oil pump housing and to the bottom of the rear main oil seal retainer. Install the gasket on the block, then the oil pump pick-up tube.
9   Place the oil pan in position on the block and install the nuts/bolts.
10   After the fasteners are installed, tighten them to the torque listed in this Chapter's Specifications. Starting at the center, follow a crisscross pattern and work up to the final torque in three steps.
11   The remaining steps are the reverse of the removal procedure.
12   Refill the engine with oil (see Chapter 1), replace the filter, run it until normal operating temperature is reached and check for leaks.

13 Oil pump - removal, check and installation

Removal

Refer to illustrations 13.3 and 13.4
1   Refer to Sections 9 and 10 for removal of the timing belt and crankshaft sprocket.
2   Refer to Section 12 to remove the oil pan and oil pump pick-up tube.
3   Remove the oil-pump-to-block bolts and pull the oil pump from the block **(see illustration)**.
4   Remove the pressure relief valve and spring by removing the cotter pin **(see illustration)**. Drill a 1/8-inch hole in the cap and screw in a self-tapping screw. Use a vise or locking pliers to pull the cap out, allowing inspection and cleaning.
5   Unbolt the cover from the back of the oil pump housing. Remove the inner and outer rotors from the oil pump body, noting their installed direction for reassembly.

Check

Refer to illustrations 13.8, 13.9, 13.11, 13.12 and 13.13
6   Clean all parts thoroughly in solvent and carefully inspect the rotors, pump cover and oil pump housing for nicks, scratches or burrs. Replace the assembly if it is damaged.
7   Clean the relief valve plunger and inspect it for wear. Small burrs can be removed with 400-grit wet sandpaper and oil. The spring should measure 1.95 inches long.
8   Use a straightedge and measure the oil pump cover for warpage with a feeler gauge **(see illustration)**. If it's warped more than the limit listed in this Chapter's Specifications, the pump should be replaced.
9   Measure the thickness of the outer rotor. If the thickness is less than the value listed in this Chapter's Specifications, the pump should

2B

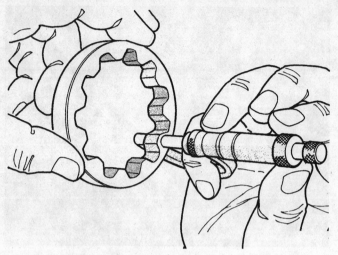

13.9 Use a micrometer to check the thickness of the outer rotor

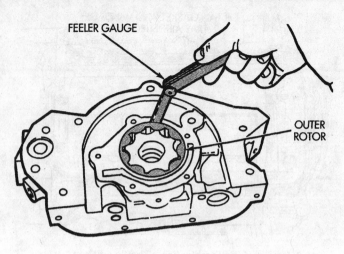

13.11 Check the outer rotor-to-housing clearance

be replaced **(see illustration)**.
10   Measure the thickness of the inner rotor. If the diameter is less than the value listed in this Chapter's Specifications, the pump should be replaced.
11   Insert the outer rotor into the oil pump housing and, while holding the rotor against one side of the housing with your finger, measure the clearance at the opposite side between the rotor and housing **(see illustration)**. If the measurement is more than the maximum allowable clearance listed in this Chapter's Specifications, the pump should be replaced.
12   Install the inner rotor in the oil pump assembly and measure the clearance between the lobes on the inner and outer rotors **(see illustration)**. If the clearance is more than the value listed in this Chapter's Specifications, the pump should be replaced. **Note:** *Install the inner rotor with the mark facing up.*
13   Position a straightedge across the face of the oil pump assembly **(see illustration)**. If the clearance between the pump surface and the rotors is greater than the limit listed in this Chapter's Specifications, the pump should be replaced.

Installation

14   Prime the oil pump by filling the housing with engine oil. Install the pump cover and tighten the bolts to the torque listed in this Chapter's Specifications.
15   To install the pump, turn the flats in the rotor so they align with the flats on the crankshaft.

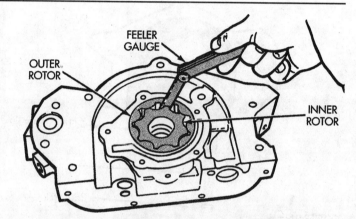

13.12 Check the clearance between the lobes of the inner and outer rotors

16   Install the pump-to-block bolts and tighten them to the torque listed in this Chapter's Specifications.
17   The remainder of installation is the reverse of removal.

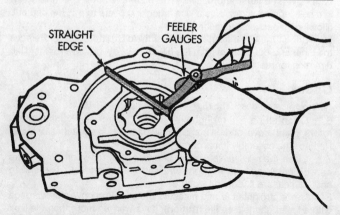

13.13 Using a straightedge and feeler gauge, check the clearance between the surface of the oil pump and the rotors

16.1a Remove the bolt on top that is holding the heat shield over the insulator - remove the heat shield

16.1b With the engine supported by a jack and the weight off the insulator, remove the two upper nuts holding the insulator to the engine bracket

16.1c Through holes in the frame, remove the two lower nuts that retain the insulator to the frame

14 Driveplate - removal and installation

This procedure is essentially the same for both V6 engines. Refer to Part A and follow the procedure outlined there, but use the bolt torque listed in this Chapter's Specifications.

15 Rear main oil seal - replacement

This procedure is essentially the same for both V6 engines. Refer to Part A and follow the procedure outlined there, but use the bolt torque value listed in this Chapter's Specifications.

16 Engine mounts - check and replacement

Refer to illustrations 16.1a, 16.1b and 16.1c

This procedure is essentially the same for both V6 engines **(see illustrations)**. Refer to Part A and follow the procedure outlined there, but use the torque values listed in this Chapter's Specifications. **Note:** *Some models have liquid-filled insulators. These should not be replaced unless there are signs the fluid has leaked out.*

2B

Notes

Chapter 2 Part C
General engine overhaul procedures

Contents

2C

Specifications

3.3L V6 engine

General

Displacement	201 cubic inches
Cylinder compression pressure	100 psi minimum at 250 rpm
Maximum variation between cylinders	25-percent
Oil pressure, warm	30 to 80 psi at 3,000 rpm
	(5 psi minimum at idle)
Firing order	1-2-3-4-5-6

Engine block

Cylinder bore diameter	3.661 inches
Cylinder taper limit	
Standard	0.001 inch
Service limit	0.002 inch
Cylinder out-of-round limit	
Standard	0.001 inch
Service limit	0.003 inch

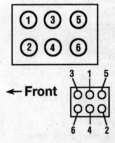

Cylinder and coil terminal locations - 3.3L V6 engine

← **Front**

Pistons and rings

Piston diameter	3.6594 to 3.6602 inches
Piston to bore clearance	0.001 to 0.0022 inch
Piston ring side clearance	
Top compression ring	
Standard	0.0015 to 0.0033 inch
Service limit	0.004 inch
Second compression ring	
Standard	0.0012 to 0.0037 inch
Service limit	0.004 inch
Oil ring	0.0005 to 0.0089 inch
Piston ring end gap	
Compression rings	0.0118 to 0.0217 inch
Oil ring	0.0098 to 0.0394 inch

Crankshaft and connecting rods

Endplay (standard)	
1993 through 1995	0.004 to 0.012 inch
1996 and later	0.004 to 0.009 inch
Main bearing journal	
Diameter	2.519 inches
Taper limit	0.001 inch
Out-of-round limit	0.001 inch
Connecting rod journal	
Diameter	2.283 inches
Out-of-round/taper limits	0.001 inch
Main bearing oil clearance	
1993 through 1995	
Main journals 1, 3 and 4	0.0007 to 0.0022 inch
Main journal 2	0.0007 to 0.0023 inch
1996 and later	
Main journals 1, 3 and 4	0.0004 to 0.0022 inch
Main journal 2	0.0004 to 0.0023 inch
Connecting rod bearing oil clearance	0.00075 to 0.003 inch
Connecting rod endplay (side clearance)	0.005 to 0.015 inch

Cylinder head and valves

Head warpage limit	0.002 inch
Valve seat angle	45 to 45-1/2 degrees
Valve face angle	44-1/2 degrees
Valve margin width	
Intake	1/32 inch
Exhaust	3/64 inch
Valve stem-to-guide clearance	
Intake	
Standard	0.001 to 0.003 inch
Service limit	0.010 inch
Exhaust	
Standard	0.002 to 0.006 inch
Service limit	0.016 inch
Valve spring free length	1.909 inch
Valve spring installed height (spring seat to retainer)	1-17/32 to 1-19/32 inch
Valve stem diameter	
Intake	0.312 to 0.313 inch
Exhaust	0.3112 to 0.3119 inch

Camshaft

Endplay	0.005 to 0.012 inch
Lobe lift	0.2667 inch
Camshaft bearing clearance	
Standard	0.001 to 0.004 inch
Service limit	0.005 inch
Camshaft journal diameter	
No. 1	1.9970 to 1.9990 inches
No. 2	1.9809 to 1.9829 inches
No. 3	1.9659 to 1.9679 inches
No. 4	1.9499 to 1.9520 inches

Camshaft bearing diameter (inside)
    No. 1 .... 2.0009 to 1.9999 inches
    No. 2 .... 1.9849 to 1.9839 inches
    No. 3 .... 1.9699 to 1.9690 inches
    No. 4 .... 1.9540 to 1.9529 inches

Torque specifications*   **Ft-lbs** (unless otherwise indicated)
Main bearing cap bolts
    Step 1 30
    Step 2 .... Rotate an additional 1/4-turn
Connecting rod bearing cap nuts
    Step 1 40
    Step 2 .... Rotate an additional 1/4-turn

*Note: *Refer to Part A for additional torque specifications.*

3.5L V6 engine

General
Displacement .... 215 cubic inches
Cylinder compression pressure .... 155 to 170 psi
Maximum variation between cylinders 25-percent
Oil pressure .... 25 to 80 psi at 3,000 rpm
(5 psi minimum at idle)

Engine block
Cylinder bore diameter .... 3.780 inches
Cylinder taper limit .... 0.002 inch
Cylinder out-of-round limit .... 0.003 inch

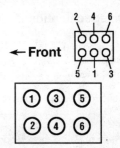

Cylinder and coil terminal
locations - 3.5L V6 engine

Pistons and rings
Piston to bore clearance .... 0.0007 to 0.0020 inch
Piston ring side clearance
    Compression rings
        Standard .... 0.0012 to 0.0031 inch
        Service limit .... 0.004 inch
    Oil rings, steel rails .... 0.0019 to 0.0077 inch
Piston ring end gap
    Top compression ring
        Standard .... 0.008 to 0.014 inch
    Second compression ring
        Standard .... 0.012 to 0.022 inch
    Oil ring
        Standard .... 0.010 to 0.030 inch

Crankshaft and connecting rods
Endplay (standard) .... 0.004 to 0.012 inch
Main bearing journal
    Diameter .... 2.519 to 2.520 inches
    Taper limit .... 0.00025 inch
    Out-of-round limit .... 0.00012 inch
Connecting rod journal
    Diameter .... 2.283 to 2.284 inches
    Out-of-round/taper limits .... 0.0001 inch
Main bearing oil clearance .... 0.0007 to 0.0030 inch
Connecting rod bearing oil clearance .... 0.00075 to 0.0034 inch
Connecting rod endplay (side clearance) .... 0.005 to 0.015 inch

Cylinder head and valves
Head warpage limit .... 0.002 inch
Valve seat angle .... 45 to 45-1/2 degrees
Valve face angle .... 44-1/2 to 45 degrees
Valve margin width
    Intake .... 1/32 inch
    Exhaust .... 3/64 inch
Valve stem-to-guide clearance
    Intake .... 0.0009 to 0.00256 inch
    Exhaust .... 0.002 to 0.037 inch
Valve spring free length
    Intake .... 1.7811 inch
    Exhaust .... 1.7992 inch

Cylinder head and valves (continued)

Valve spring installed height (spring seat to retainer)............................	1-17/32 to 1-19/32 inches
Valve stem diameter	
Intake..	0.2730 to 0.2737 inch
Exhaust..	0.2719 to 0.2726 inch

Camshaft

Endplay..	0.004 to 0.014 inch
Lobe lift	
Intake..	0.3209 inch
Exhaust..	0.2571 inch
Camshaft bearing oil clearance	
Standard..	0.003 to 0.0047 inch
Service limit	0.0059 inch
Camshaft journal diameter, 1 through 4	1.6905 to 1.6913 inches
Camshaft bore diameter (inside), 1 through 4	1.6944 to 1.6952 inches

Torque specifications*

	Ft-lbs (unless otherwise indicated)
Main bearing bolts	
M11 cap bolts	
Step 1..	30
Step 2..	Rotate an additional 1/4-turn
M10 tie bolts...	40
Connecting rod bearing cap nuts	
Step 1..	40
Step 2	Rotate an additional 1/4-turn

***Note:** Refer to Part B for additional torque specifications.*

1   General information

Included in this portion of Chapter 2 are the general overhaul procedures for the cylinder head(s) and internal engine components.

The information ranges from advice concerning preparation for an overhaul and the purchase of replacement parts to detailed, step-by-step procedures covering removal and installation of internal engine components and the inspection of parts.

The following Sections have been written based on the assumption the engine has been removed from the vehicle. For information concerning in-vehicle engine repair, as well as removal and installation of the external components necessary for the overhaul, see Part A (3.3L V6 engine) or B (3.5L V6 engine) of this Chapter.

The Specifications included in this Part are only those necessary for the inspection and overhaul procedures which follow. Refer to Parts A and B for additional Specifications.

2   Engine overhaul - general information

Refer to illustration 2.4

It's not always easy to determine when, or if, an engine should be completely overhauled, as a number of factors must be considered.

High mileage isn't necessarily an indication an overhaul is needed, while low mileage doesn't preclude the need for an overhaul. Frequency of servicing is probably the most important consideration. An engine that's had regular and frequent oil and filter changes, as well as other required maintenance, will most likely give many thousands of miles of reliable service. Conversely, a neglected engine may require an overhaul very early in its life.

Excessive oil consumption is an indication that piston rings, valve seals and/or valve guides are in need of attention. Make sure oil leaks aren't responsible before deciding the rings and/or guides are bad. Perform a cylinder compression check to determine the extent of the work required (see Section 3).

Remove the oil pressure sending unit and check the oil pressure with a gauge installed in its place **(see illustration)**. Compare the results to this Chapter's Specifications. As a general rule, engines

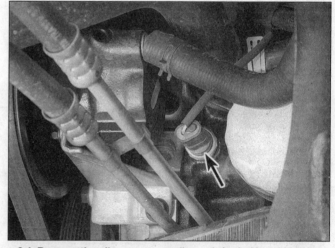

2.4 Remove the oil pressure sending unit (switch) and install a pressure gauge in its place - the oil pressure sending unit (arrow) on 3.3L/3.5L V6 engines is next to the oil filter (here viewed from underneath on the driver's side)

should have ten psi oil pressure for every 1,000 rpm, with 5 psi being the absolute minimum at idle. If the pressure is extremely low, the bearings and/or oil pump are probably worn out.

Loss of power, rough running, knocking or metallic engine noises, excessive valve train noise and high fuel consumption rates may also point to the need for an overhaul, especially if they're all present at the same time. If a complete tune-up doesn't remedy the situation, major mechanical work is the only solution.

An engine overhaul involves restoring the internal parts to the specifications of a new engine. During an overhaul, the piston rings are replaced and the cylinder walls are reconditioned (rebored and/or honed). If a rebore is done by an automotive machine shop, new oversize pistons will also be installed. The main bearings, connecting rod bearings and camshaft bearings are generally replaced with new ones and, if necessary, the crankshaft may be reground to restore the

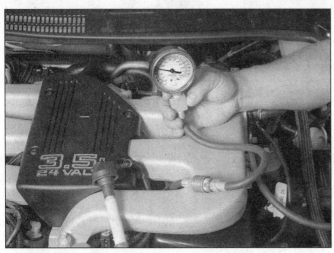

3.6 A compression gauge with a threaded fitting for the spark plug hole and a long hose will be needed for checking the compression on the 3.5L engine

journals. Generally, the valves are serviced as well, since they're usually in less-than-perfect condition at this point. While the engine is being overhauled, other components, such as the starter and alternator, can be rebuilt as well. The end result should be a like new engine that will give many trouble free miles. **Note:** *Critical cooling system components such as the hoses, drivebelts, thermostat and water pump MUST be replaced with new parts when an engine is overhauled. The radiator should be checked carefully to ensure it isn't clogged or leaking (see Chapter 3). Some engine rebuilders will not guarantee their short-blocks or long-blocks unless you have your radiator professionally cleaned and tested.*

Before beginning the engine overhaul, read through the entire procedure to familiarize yourself with the scope and requirements of the job. Overhauling an engine isn't particularly difficult, if you follow all of the instructions carefully, have the necessary tools and equipment and pay close attention to all specifications; however, it can be time consuming. Plan on the vehicle being tied up for a minimum of two weeks, especially if parts must be taken to an automotive machine shop for repair or reconditioning. Check on availability of parts and make sure any necessary special tools and equipment are obtained in advance. Most work can be done with typical hand tools, although a number of precision measuring tools are required for inspecting parts to determine if they must be replaced. Often an automotive machine shop will handle the inspection of parts and offer advice concerning reconditioning and replacement. **Note:** *Always wait until the engine has been completely disassembled and all components, especially the engine block, have been inspected before deciding what service and repair operations must be performed by an automotive machine shop. Since the block's condition will be the major factor to consider when determining whether to overhaul the original engine or buy a rebuilt one, never purchase parts or have machine work done on other components until the block has been thoroughly inspected. As a general rule, time is the primary cost of an overhaul, so it doesn't pay to install worn or substandard parts.*

As a final note, to ensure maximum life and minimum trouble from a rebuilt engine, everything must be assembled with care in a spotlessly clean environment.

3   Cylinder compression check

Refer to illustration 3.6

1   A compression check will tell you what mechanical condition the upper end (pistons, rings, valves, head gaskets) of the engine is in. Specifically, it can tell you if the compression is down due to leakage caused by worn piston rings, defective valves and seats or a blown head gasket. **Note:** *The engine must be at normal operating temperature and the battery must be fully charged for this check.*

2   Begin by cleaning the area around the spark plugs before you remove them. Compressed air should be used, if available, otherwise a small brush or even a bicycle tire pump will work. The idea is to prevent dirt from getting into the cylinders as the compression check is being done. **Warning:** *Wear eye protection when using compressed air.*

3   Remove all of the spark plugs from the engine (see Chapter 1).

4   Block the throttle wide open.

5   Disable the ignition system by disconnecting the primary wires from the coil (see Chapter 5). Also, disable the fuel injection system by unplugging the electrical connector to the injector wiring harness.

6   Install the compression gauge in the number one spark plug hole **(see illustration)**. You will need a gauge with a long hose in order to reach the spark plug threads on the 3.5L V6.

7   Crank the engine over at least seven compression strokes and watch the gauge. The compression should build up quickly in a healthy engine. Low compression on the first stroke, followed by gradually increasing pressure on successive strokes, indicates worn piston rings. A low compression reading on the first stroke, which doesn't build up during successive strokes, indicates leaking valves or a blown head gasket (a cracked head could also be the cause). Deposits on the undersides of the valve heads can also cause low compression. Record the highest gauge reading obtained.

8   Repeat the procedure for the remaining cylinders and compare the results to this Chapter's Specifications.

9   If the readings are below normal, add some engine oil (about three squirts from a plunger-type oil can) to each cylinder, through the spark plug hole, and repeat the test.

10   If the compression increases after the oil is added, the piston rings are definitely worn. If the compression doesn't increase significantly, the leakage is occurring at the valves or head gasket. Leakage past the valves may be caused by burned valve seats and/or faces or warped, cracked or bent valves.

11   If two adjacent cylinders have equally low compression, there's a strong possibility the head gasket between them is blown. The appearance of coolant in the combustion chambers or the crankcase would verify this condition.

12   If one cylinder is about 20-percent lower than the others, and the engine has a slightly rough idle, a worn exhaust lobe on the camshaft could be the cause.

13   If the compression is unusually high, the combustion chambers are probably coated with carbon deposits. If that's the case, the cylinder head(s) should be removed and decarbonized.

14   If compression is way down or varies greatly between cylinders, it would be a good idea to have a leak-down test performed by an automotive repair shop. This test will pinpoint exactly where the leakage is occurring and how severe it is.

4   Vacuum gauge diagnostic checks

A vacuum gauge provides valuable information about what is going on in the engine at a low cost. You can check for worn rings or cylinder walls, leaking head or intake manifold gaskets, incorrect carburetor adjustments, restricted exhaust, stuck or burned valves, weak valve springs, improper ignition or valve timing and ignition problems.

Unfortunately, vacuum gauge readings are easy to misinterpret, so they should be used in conjunction with other tests to confirm the diagnosis.

Both the gauge readings and the rate of needle movement are important for accurate interpretation. Most gauges measure vacuum in inches of mercury (in-Hg). As vacuum increases (or atmospheric pressure decreases), the reading will increase. Also, for every 1,000-foot increase in elevation above sea level, the gauge readings will decrease about one inch of mercury.

2C

Connect the vacuum gauge directly to intake manifold vacuum, not to ported (carburetor) vacuum. Be sure no hoses are left disconnected during the test or false readings will result.

Before you begin the test, allow the engine to warm up completely. Block the wheels and set the parking brake. With the transmission in Park, start the engine and allow it to run at normal idle speed. **Warning:** *Carefully inspect the fan blades for cracks or damage before starting the engine. Keep your hands and the vacuum tester clear of the fan and do not stand in front of the vehicle or in line with the fan when the engine is running.*

Read the vacuum gauge; an average, healthy engine should normally produce about 17 to 22 inches of vacuum with a fairly steady needle. Refer to the following vacuum gauge readings and what they indicate about the engines condition:

1   A low, steady reading usually indicates a leaking gasket between the intake manifold and carburetor or throttle body, a leaky vacuum hose, late ignition timing or incorrect camshaft timing. Check ignition timing with a timing light and eliminate all other possible causes, utilizing the tests provided in this Chapter before you remove the timing chain cover to check the timing marks.

2   If the reading is three to eight inches below normal and it fluctuates at that low reading, suspect an intake manifold gasket leak at an intake port.

3   If the needle has regular drops of about two to four inches at a steady rate, the valves are probably leaking. Perform a compression or leak-down test to confirm this.

4   An irregular drop or down-flick of the needle can be caused by a sticking valve or an ignition misfire. Perform a compression or leak-down test and read the spark plugs.

5   A rapid vibration of about four inches-Hg vibration at idle combined with exhaust smoke indicates worn valve guides. Perform a leak-down test to confirm this. If the rapid vibration occurs with an increase in engine speed, check for a leaking intake manifold gasket or head gasket, weak valve springs, burned valves or ignition misfire.

6   A slight fluctuation, say one inch up and down, may mean ignition problems. Check all the usual tune-up items and, if necessary, run the engine on an ignition analyzer.

7   If there is a large fluctuation, perform a compression or leak-down test to look for a weak or dead cylinder or a blown head gasket.

8   If the needle moves slowly through a wide range, check for a clogged PCV system, incorrect idle fuel mixture, carburetor/throttle body or intake manifold gasket leaks.

9   Check for a slow return after revving the engine by quickly snapping the throttle open until the engine reaches about 2,500 rpm and let it shut. Normally the reading should drop to near zero, rise above normal idle reading (about 5 in-Hg over) and then return to the previous idle reading. If the vacuum returns slowly and doesn't peak when the throttle is snapped shut, the rings may be worn. If there is a long delay, look for a restricted exhaust system (often the muffler or catalytic converter). An easy way to check this is to temporarily disconnect the exhaust ahead of the suspected part and re-test.

Vacuum leak diagnosis procedure

Refer to illustration 4.15

10   If you suspect a vacuum leak, or have just replaced the intake manifold gaskets and want to check for proper sealing, a simple check can be made with a small household propane torch.

11   Place the transmission in Park and apply the emergency brake.

12   Remove the air cleaner assembly for better access to the carburetor or throttle body and intake manifold.

13   Hook up a vacuum gauge and if available, a tachometer.

14   With the engine warmed up and idling, slightly open the valve on the propane bottle. **Warning:** *Do NOT light the torch.*

15   Bring the tip of the torch nozzle around the throttle shaft and the base of the throttle body **(see illustration)**. Allow the torch tip to move slowly around these areas. If the idle speed or vacuum increases, it means that there is a vacuum leak wherever the torch is pointing. The extra combustible gas from the torch makes a temporarily richer mixture if a vacuum leak sucks it into the engine.

16   Move the torch tip slowly around the edges of the intake manifold,

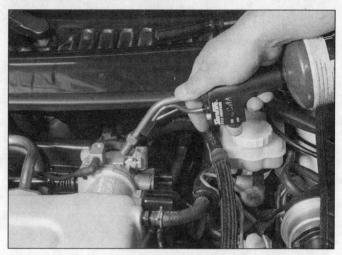

4.15 A turned-on but unlit propane torch can be used to locate vacuum leaks around the throttle body, intake manifold and vacuum lines

especially around the ports at the cylinder head. If there is no increase in vacuum or idle speed, there are no vacuum leaks at the intake. However, vacuum leaks can also occur at a variety of vacuum hoses, which can also be checked with an unlit propane torch.

---

5   Engine removal - methods and precautions

If you've decided the engine must be removed for overhaul or major repair work, several preliminary steps should be taken.

Locating a suitable place to work is extremely important. Adequate work space, along with storage space for the vehicle, will be needed. If a shop or garage isn't available, at the very least a flat, level, clean work surface made of concrete or asphalt is required.
Cleaning the engine compartment and engine before beginning the removal procedure will help keep tools clean and organized.

An engine hoist or A-frame will also be necessary. Make sure the equipment is rated in excess of the combined weight of the engine and transaxle. Safety is of primary importance, considering the potential hazards involved in lifting the engine out of the vehicle.

If the engine is being removed by a novice, a helper should be available. Advice and aid from someone more experienced would also be helpful. There are many instances when one person cannot simultaneously perform all of the operations required when lifting the engine out of the vehicle.

Plan the operation ahead of time. Arrange for or obtain all of the tools and equipment you'll need prior to beginning the job. Some of the equipment necessary to perform engine removal and installation safely and with relative ease are (in addition to an engine hoist) a heavy duty floor jack, complete sets of wrenches and sockets as described in the front of this manual, wooden blocks and plenty of rags and cleaning solvent for mopping up spilled oil, coolant and gasoline. If the hoist must be rented, be sure to arrange for it in advance and perform all of the operations possible without it beforehand. This will save you money and time.

Plan for the vehicle to be out of use for quite a while. A machine shop will be required to perform some of the work which the do-it-yourselfer can't accomplish without special equipment. These shops often have a busy schedule, so it would be a good idea to consult them before removing the engine in order to accurately estimate the amount of time required to rebuild or repair components that may need work.

Always be extremely careful when removing and installing the engine. Serious injury can result from careless actions. Plan ahead, take your time and a job of this nature, although major, can be accomplished successfully.

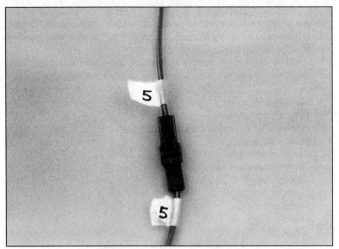

6.4 Label each wire before unplugging the connector

6.23 Lift the engine off the mounts and guide it carefully around any obstacles as an assistant raises the hoist until it clears the front of the vehicle

6   Engine - removal and installation

Refer to illustrations 6.4 and 6.23

Warning 1: *Gasoline is extremely flammable, so take extra precautions when you work on any part of the fuel system. Don't smoke or allow open flames or bare light bulbs near the work area, and don't work in a garage where a natural gas-type appliance (such as a water heater or a clothes dryer) with a pilot light is present. Since gasoline is carcinogenic, wear latex gloves when there's a possibility of being exposed to fuel, and, if you spill any fuel on your skin, rinse it off immediately with soap and water. Mop up any spills immediately and do not store fuel-soaked rags where they could ignite. The fuel system is under constant pressure, so, if any fuel lines are to be disconnected, the fuel pressure in the system must be relieved first (see Chapter 4). When you perform any kind of work on the fuel system, wear safety glasses and have a Class B type fire extinguisher on hand.*

Warning 2: *The air conditioning system is under high pressure - have a dealer service department or service station discharge the system before disconnecting any of the hoses or fittings.*

Warning 3: *These models have airbags. Always disconnect the negative battery cable and wait two minutes before working in the vicinity of the impact sensors, steering column or instrument panel to avoid the possibility of accidental deployment of the airbag, which could cause personal injury (see Chapter 12).*

Note: *Read through the following steps carefully and familiarize yourself with the procedure before beginning work.*

Removal

1   Refer to Chapter 4 and relieve the fuel system pressure, then disconnect the negative cable from the battery.

2   Cover the fenders and cowl and remove the hood (see Chapter 11). Special pads are available to protect the fenders, but an old bedspread or blanket will also work.

3   Remove the air intake tube, intake plenum, and fuel injector rails (see Chapter 4).

4   Label the vacuum lines, emissions system hoses, wiring connectors, ground straps and fuel lines to ensure correct reinstallation, then detach them. Pieces of masking tape with numbers or letters written on them work well **(see illustration)**. If there's any possibility of confusion, make a sketch of the engine compartment and clearly label the lines, hoses and wires.

5   Raise the vehicle and support it securely on jackstands. Drain the cooling system and engine oil (see Chapter 1).

6   Disconnect the exhaust system from the engine (see Chapter 4).

7   Mark the relationship of the torque converter to the driveplate, then remove the torque converter bolts (see Chapter 7).

8   Remove the starter (see Chapter 6) and the two lower

transaxle-to-engine bolts.

9   Remove the upper and lower nuts from the engine mount insulators. Refer to Chapter 2A for illustrations of the engine mounts.

10   Lower the vehicle.

11   Label and detach all coolant hoses from the engine.

12   Remove the coolant reservoir, cooling fan assembly, condenser and radiator (see Chapter 3).

13   Remove the drivebelts (see Chapter 1).

14   Disconnect the fuel lines running from the engine to the chassis (see Chapter 4). Plug or cap all open fittings/lines.

15   Unbolt the power steering pump and set it aside (see Chapter 10). Leave the lines/hoses attached and make sure the pump is kept in an upright position in the engine compartment.

16   Unbolt the air conditioning compressor (see Chapter 3) and set it aside. Do not disconnect the hoses.

17   On vehicles equipped with 3.5L engines, remove the windshield wiper motor and linkage **(see Chapter 12).**

18   Support the transaxle with a jack. Position a block of wood on the jack head to prevent damage to the transaxle.

19   Attach an engine sling or a length of chain to the lifting brackets on the engine.

20   Roll the hoist into position and connect the sling to it. Take up the slack in the sling or chain, but don't lift the engine. **Warning:** *DO NOT place any part of your body under the engine when it's supported only by a hoist or other lifting device.*

21   Remove the left and right engine mount insulators.

22   Remove the upper engine-to-transaxle mounting bolts and recheck to be sure nothing else is still connecting the engine to the chassis or transaxle.

23   Raise the engine slightly to disengage the mounts. Slowly raise the engine out of the vehicle **(see illustration)**. Check carefully to make sure nothing is hanging up as the hoist is raised.

24   Once the engine assembly is out of the vehicle, lower it to the ground and support it on wood blocks.

25   Remove the driveplate and mount the engine on an engine stand.

Installation

26   Check the engine and transaxle mounts. If they're worn or damaged, replace them.

27   **Caution:** *Take great care when installing the torque converter, following the procedure outlined in Chapter 7.*

28   Carefully lower the engine into the engine compartment. Make sure the mounts line up. Reinstall the remaining components in the reverse order of removal. Double-check to make sure everything is hooked up right. **Caution:** *DO NOT use the transaxle-to-engine bolts to force the transaxle and engine together.*

2C

29   Add coolant, oil, power steering and transmission fluid as needed.
30   Run the engine and check for leaks and proper operation of all accessories, then install the hood and test drive the vehicle.
31   If the air conditioning system was discharged, have it evacuated, recharged and leak tested by the shop that discharged it.

7   Engine rebuilding alternatives

The home mechanic is faced with a number of options when performing an engine overhaul. The decision to replace the engine block, piston/connecting rod assemblies and crankshaft depends on a number of factors, with the number one consideration being the condition of the block. Other considerations are cost, access to machine shop facilities, parts availability, time required to complete the project and the extent of prior mechanical experience.

Some of the rebuilding alternatives include:

Individual parts - If the inspection procedures reveal the engine block and most engine components are in reusable condition, purchasing individual parts may be the most economical alternative. The block, crankshaft and piston/connecting rod assemblies should all be inspected carefully. Even if the block shows little wear, the cylinder bores should be surface honed.

Short block - A short block consists of an engine block with a crankshaft and piston/connecting rod assemblies already installed. All new bearings are incorporated and all clearances will be correct. The existing camshaft, valve train components, cylinder head(s) and external parts can be bolted to the short block with little or no machine shop work necessary.

Long block - A long block consists of a short block plus an oil pump, oil pan, cylinder head(s), valve cover(s), camshaft and valve train components, timing sprockets and chain and timing chain cover. All components are installed with new bearings, seals and gaskets incorporated throughout. The installation of manifolds and external parts is all that's necessary.

Give careful thought to which alternative is best for you and discuss the situation with local automotive machine shops, auto parts dealers and experienced rebuilders before ordering or purchasing replacement parts.

8   Engine overhaul - disassembly sequence

1   It's much easier to disassemble and work on the engine if it's mounted on a portable engine stand. A stand can often be rented quite cheaply from an equipment rental yard. Before it's mounted on a stand, the driveplate should be removed from the engine.
2   If a stand isn't available, it's possible to disassemble the engine with it blocked up on the floor. Be extra careful not to tip or drop the engine when working without a stand.
3   If you're going to obtain a rebuilt engine, all external components must come off first, to be transferred to the replacement engine, just as they will if you're doing a complete engine overhaul yourself. These include:

> Alternator and brackets
> Emissions control components
> Ignition coil/module assembly, spark plug wires and spark plugs
> Thermostat and housing cover
> Water pump
> EFI components
> Intake/exhaust manifolds
> Oil filter
> Engine mounts
> Driveplate

Note: *When removing the external components from the engine, pay close attention to details that may be helpful or important during installation. Note the installed position of gaskets, seals, spacers, pins, brackets, washers, bolts and other small items.*

4   If you're obtaining a short block, which consists of the engine block, crankshaft, pistons and connecting rods all assembled, then the cylinder head(s), oil pan and oil pump will have to be removed as well. See Engine rebuilding alternatives for additional information regarding the different possibilities to be considered.
5   If you're planning a complete overhaul, the engine must be disassembled and the internal components removed in the following general order:

> Valve covers
> Exhaust manifolds
> Rocker arm assemblies and shafts (3.5L)
> Rocker arms and pushrods (3.3L)
> Intake manifold
> Timing chain/belt cover
> Timing chain/belt and sprockets
> Cylinder heads
> Camshaft(s)
> Oil pan
> Oil pump
> Piston/connecting rod assemblies
> Rear main oil seal housing
> Crankshaft and main bearings

6   Before beginning the disassembly and overhaul procedures, make sure the following items are available. Also, refer to *Engine overhaul - reassembly sequence* for a list of tools and materials needed for engine reassembly.

> Common hand tools
> Small cardboard boxes or plastic bags for storing parts
> Gasket scraper
> Ridge reamer
> Vibration damper puller
> Micrometers
> Telescoping gauges
> Dial indicator set
> Valve spring compressor
> Cylinder surfacing hone
> Piston ring groove cleaning tool
> Electric drill motor
> Tap and die set
> Wire brushes
> Oil gallery brushes
> Cleaning solvent

9   Cylinder head - disassembly

Refer to illustrations 9.2, 9.3 and 9.4
Note: *New and rebuilt cylinder heads are commonly available for most engines at dealerships and auto parts stores. Due to the fact that some specialized tools are necessary for the disassembly and inspection procedures, and replacement parts aren't always readily available, it may be more practical and economical for the home mechanic to purchase replacement head(s) rather than taking the time to disassemble, inspect and recondition the original(s).*

1   Cylinder head disassembly involves removal of the intake and exhaust valves and related components. The rocker arms and shafts must be removed first (see Part A of this Chapter for 3.3L engines, Part B for 3.5L engines). Label the parts or store them separately so they can be reinstalled in their original locations.
2   Before the valves are removed, arrange to label and store them, along with their related components, so they can be kept separate and reinstalled in their original locations **(see illustration)**.
3   Compress the springs on the first valve with a spring compressor and remove the keepers **(see illustration)**. Carefully release the valve spring compressor and remove the retainer, the spring and the spring seat (if used).
4   Pull the valve out of the head, then remove the oil seal from the guide. If the valve binds in the guide (won't pull through), push it back into the head and deburr the area around the keeper groove with a fine file or whetstone **(see illustration)**.

9.2 A small plastic bag with an appropriate label can be used to store the valve train components so they can be kept together and reinstalled in their original positions

9.3 Use a valve spring compressor to compress the spring, then remove the keepers from the valve stems

9.4 If the valve won't pull through the guide, deburr the edge of the stem end and the area around the top of the keeper groove with a file or whetstone

2C

10.12 Check the cylinder head gasket surface for warpage by trying to slip a feeler gauge under the straightedge (see this Chapter's Specifications for the maximum warpage allowed and use a feeler gauge of that thickness)

5   Repeat the procedure for the remaining valves. Remember to keep all the parts for each valve together so they can be reinstalled in the same locations.

6   Once the valves and related components have been removed and stored in an organized manner, the head should be thoroughly cleaned and inspected. If a complete engine overhaul is being done, finish the engine disassembly procedures before beginning the cylinder head cleaning and inspection process. **Note:** *The 3.5L engine has a camshaft mounted in each head; see Section 13 for camshaft removal and inspection procedures.*

10   Cylinder head - cleaning and inspection

Note: *Be sure to perform all of the following inspection procedures before concluding machine shop work is required. Make a list of the items that need attention.*

Cleaning

1   Thorough cleaning of the cylinder head(s) and related valve train components, followed by a detailed inspection, will enable you to decide how much valve service work must be done during the engine overhaul. **Note:** *If the engine was severely overheated, the cylinder head is probably warped.*

2   Scrape all traces of old gasket material and sealant off the head gasket, intake manifold and exhaust manifold mating surfaces. Be very careful not to gouge the cylinder head. Special gasket removal solvents that soften gaskets and make removal much easier are available at auto parts stores.

3   Remove all built up scale from the coolant passages.

4   Run a stiff wire brush through the various holes to remove deposits that may have formed in them.

5   Run an appropriate size tap into each of the threaded holes to remove corrosion and thread sealant that may be present. If compressed air is available, use it to clear the holes of debris produced by this operation. **Warning:** *Wear eye protection when using compressed air!*

6   Clean the rocker shaft bolt threads with a wire brush.

7   Clean the cylinder head with solvent and dry it thoroughly. Compressed air will speed the drying process and ensure that all holes and recessed areas are clean. **Note:** *Decarbonizing chemicals are available and may prove very useful when cleaning cylinder heads and valve train components. They're very caustic and should be used with caution. Be sure to follow the instructions on the container.*

8   Clean the rocker arm parts with solvent and dry them thoroughly (don't mix them up during the cleaning process). Compressed air will speed the drying process and can be used to clean out the oil passages.

9   Clean all the valve springs, spring seats, keepers and retainers with solvent and dry them thoroughly. Do the components from one valve at a time to avoid mixing up the parts.

10   Scrape off any heavy deposits that may have formed on the valves, then use a motorized wire brush to remove deposits from the valve heads and stems. Again, make sure the valves don't get mixed up.

Inspection

Cylinder head

Refer to illustrations 10.12, 10.14, 10.15, 10.16, 10.17 and 10.18

11   Inspect the head very carefully for cracks, evidence of coolant leakage and other damage. If cracks are found, check with an automotive machine shop concerning repair. If repair isn't possible, a new cylinder head should be obtained.

12   Using a straightedge and feeler gauge, check the head gasket mating surface for warpage **(see illustration)**. If the warpage exceeds the limit in this Chapter's Specifications, it can be resurfaced at an automotive machine shop. **Note 1:** *If the heads are resurfaced, the intake manifold flanges may also require machining.* **Note 2:** *If a head from a 3.5L engine has been warped, it must be straightened by a cylinder head repair shop (the work is done in a special oven) before any machine work is done. If the warpage is removed strictly by machining, the camshaft bores may remain out of alignment.*

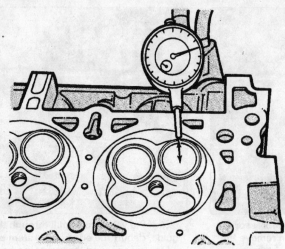

10.14 A dial indicator can be used to determine the valve stem-to-guide clearance - with the valve 1/2-inch off its seat, move the valve head as indicated by the arrows

13   Examine the valve seats in each of the combustion chambers. If they're pitted, cracked or burned, the head will require valve service that's beyond the scope of the home mechanic.
14   Check the valve stem-to-guide clearance by measuring the lateral movement of the valve with a dial indicator attached securely to the head **(see illustration)**. The valve must be in the guide and approximately 1/2-inch off the seat. The total valve head movement indicated by the gauge needle must be divided by two to obtain the actual clearance. After this is done, if there's still some doubt regarding the condition of the valve guides, they should be checked by an automotive machine shop (the cost should be minimal).

Valves

15   Carefully inspect each valve face for uneven wear, deformation, cracks, pits and burned areas. Check the valve stem for scuffing and galling and the neck for cracks. Rotate the valve and check for any obvious indication that it's bent. Look for pits and excessive wear on the end of the stem. The presence of any of these conditions **(see**

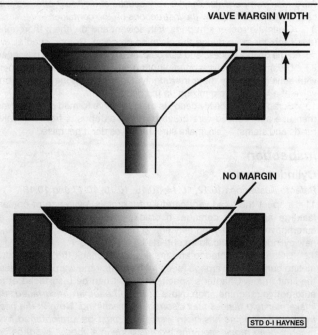

10.16 The margin width on each valve must be as specified - if no margin exists, the valve cannot be reused

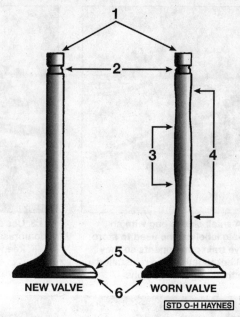

NEW VALVE   WORN VALVE

10.15 Check for valve wear at the points shown here

1	Valve tip	4	Stem (most worn area)
2	Keeper groove	5	Valve face
3	Stem (least worn area)	6	Margin

illustration) indicates the need for valve service by an automotive machine shop.
16   Measure the margin width on each valve **(see illustration)**. Any valve with a margin narrower than specified in this Chapter will have to be replaced with a new one.

Valve components

17   Check each valve spring for wear (on the ends) and pits. Measure the free length and compare it to this Chapter's Specifications **(see illustration)**. Any springs that are shorter than specified have sagged and shouldn't be reused. The tension of all springs should be checked with a special fixture before deciding they're suitable for use in a rebuilt engine (take the springs to an automotive machine shop for this check).
18   Stand each spring on a flat surface and check it for squareness **(see illustration)**. If any of the springs are distorted or sagged, replace all of them with new parts.
19   Check the spring retainers and keepers for obvious wear and cracks. Any questionable parts should be replaced with new ones, as extensive damage will occur if they fail during engine operation.
20   If the inspection process indicates the valve components are in generally poor condition and worn beyond the limits specified, which is

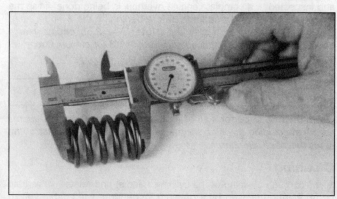

10.17 Measure the free length of each valve spring with a dial or vernier caliper

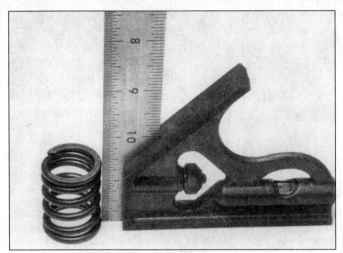

10.18 Check each valve spring for squareness

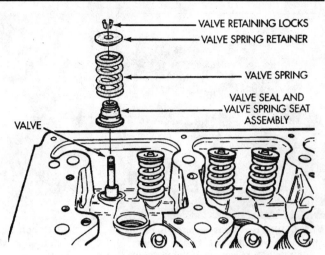

12.4 Make sure the valve stem seals are installed evenly and carefully to avoid damage

usually the case in an engine that's being overhauled, reassemble the valves in the cylinder head and refer to Section 11 for valve servicing recommendations.

11 Valves - servicing

1   Because of the complex nature of the job and the special tools and equipment needed, servicing of the valves, the valve seats and the valve guides, commonly known as a valve job, should be done by a professional.

2   The home mechanic can remove and disassemble the head, do the initial cleaning and inspection, then reassemble and deliver it to a dealer service department or an automotive machine shop for the actual service work. Doing the inspection will enable you to see what condition the head and valvetrain components are in and will ensure that you know what work and new parts are required when dealing with an automotive machine shop.

3   The dealer service department, or automotive machine shop, will remove the valves and springs, recondition or replace the valves and valve seats, recondition the valve guides, check and replace the valve springs, rotators, spring retainers and keepers (as necessary), replace the valve seals with new ones, reassemble the valve components and make sure the installed spring height is correct. The cylinder head gasket surface will also be resurfaced if it's warped.

4   After the valve job has been performed by a professional, the head will be in like-new condition. When the head is returned, be sure to clean it again before installation on the engine to remove any metal particles and abrasive grit that may still be present from the valve service or head resurfacing operations. Use compressed air, if available, to blow out all the oil holes and passages.

12 Cylinder head - reassembly

Refer to illustrations 12.4 and 12.6

1   Regardless of whether or not the head was sent to an automotive repair shop for valve servicing, make sure it's clean before beginning reassembly.

2   If the head was sent out for valve servicing, the valves and related components will already be in place. Begin the reassembly procedure with Step 8.

3   Install the spring seats or valve rotators (if equipped) before the valve seals.

4   Install new seals on each of the valve guides. Using a hammer and a deep socket or seal installation tool, gently tap each seal into place until it's completely seated on the guide **(see illustration)**. Don't

twist or cock the seals during installation or they won't seal properly on the valve stems.

5   Beginning at one end of the head, lubricate and install the first valve. Apply moly-base grease or clean engine oil to the valve stem.

6   Position the valve springs (and shims, if used) over the valves. Compress the springs with a valve spring compressor and carefully install the keepers in the groove, then slowly release the compressor and make sure the keepers seat properly. Apply a small dab of grease to each keeper to hold it in place if necessary **(see illustration)**.

7   Repeat the procedure for the remaining valves. Be sure to return the components to their original locations - don't mix them up!

8   Check the installed valve spring height with a ruler graduated in 1/32-inch increments or a dial caliper. If the head was sent out for service work, the installed height should be correct (but don't automatically assume it is). The measurement is taken from the top of each spring seat to the bottom of the retainer. If the height is greater than specified in this Chapter, shims can be added under the springs to correct it. **Caution:** *Do not, under any circumstances, shim the springs to the point where the installed height is less than specified.*

9   Apply moly-base grease to the rocker arm faces and the shaft, then Refer to Part A or B and install the rocker arm assembly on the cylinder head. **Note:** *On 3.5L engines, install the camshafts before installing the rocker arms/shafts (see Chapter 2B).*

13 Camshaft(s) and bearings - removal and inspection

Refer to Chapter 2, Part A (3.3L engine) or Chapter 2, Part B (3.5L engine) for the camshaft removal and inspection procedures.

12.6 Apply a small dab of grease to each keeper as shown here before installation - it'll hold them in place on the valve stem as the spring is released

14.1 A ridge reamer is required to remove the ridge from the top of each cylinder - do this before removing the pistons!

14.3 Check the connecting rod side clearance with a feeler gauge

14.6 To prevent damage to the crankshaft journals and cylinder walls, slip sections of rubber or plastic hose over the rod bolts before removing the pistons

14 Pistons and connecting rods - removal

Refer to illustrations 14.1, 14.3 and 14.6

Note: *Prior to removing the piston/connecting rod assemblies, remove the cylinder head(s), the oil pan and the oil pump by referring to the appropriate Sections in Parts A or B of Chapter 2.*

1   Use your fingernail to feel if a ridge has formed at the upper limit of ring travel (about 1/4-inch down from the top of each cylinder). If carbon deposits or cylinder wear have produced ridges, they must be completely removed with a special tool **(see illustration)**. Follow the manufacturer's instructions provided with the tool. Failure to remove the ridges before attempting to remove the piston/connecting rod assemblies may result in piston breakage.

2   After the cylinder ridges have been removed, turn the engine upside-down so the crankshaft is facing up.

3   Before the connecting rods are removed, check the endplay with feeler gauges. Slide them between the first connecting rod and the crankshaft throw until the play is removed **(see illustration)**. The endplay is equal to the thickness of the feeler gauge(s). If the endplay exceeds the service limit, new connecting rods will be required. If new rods (or a new crankshaft) are installed, the endplay may fall under the minimum specified in this Chapter (if it does, the rods will have to be machined to restore it - consult an automotive machine shop for advice if necessary). Repeat the procedure for the remaining connecting rods.

4   Check the connecting rods and caps for identification marks. If they aren't plainly marked, use a small center-punch to make the appropriate number of indentations on each rod and cap (1, 2, 3, etc., depending on the engine type and cylinder they're associated with).

5   Loosen each of the connecting rod cap nuts 1/2-turn at a time until they can be removed by hand. Remove the number one connecting rod cap and bearing insert. Don't drop the bearing insert out of the cap.

6   Slip a short length of plastic or rubber hose over each connecting rod cap bolt to protect the crankshaft journal and cylinder wall as the piston is removed **(see illustration)**.

7   Remove the bearing insert and push the connecting rod/piston assembly out through the top of the engine. Use a wooden or plastic hammer handle to push on the upper bearing surface in the connecting rod. If resistance is felt, double-check to make sure all of the ridge was removed from the cylinder.

8   Repeat the procedure for the remaining cylinders.

9   After removal, reassemble the connecting rod caps and bearing inserts in their respective connecting rods and install the cap nuts finger tight. Leaving the old bearing inserts in place until reassembly will help prevent the connecting rod bearing surfaces from being accidentally nicked or gouged.

10   Don't separate the pistons from the connecting rods (see Section 19 for additional information).

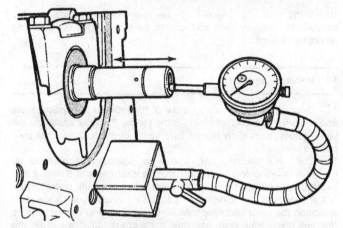

15.1 Checking crankshaft endplay with a dial indicator

15 Crankshaft - removal

Refer to illustrations 15.1, 15.3, 15.4 and 15.5

Note: *The crankshaft can be removed only after the engine has been removed from the vehicle. It's assumed the driveplate, crankshaft balancer/vibration damper, timing chain or belt, oil pan, oil pump and piston/connecting rod assemblies have already been removed. The rear main oil seal housing must be unbolted and separated from the block before proceeding with crankshaft removal.*

1   Before the crankshaft is removed, check the endplay. Mount a dial indicator with the stem in line with the crankshaft, touching the nose of the crank **(see illustration)**.

2   Push the crankshaft all the way to the rear and zero the dial indicator. Next, pry the crankshaft to the front as far as possible and check the reading on the dial indicator. The distance it moves is the endplay. If it's greater than the value listed in this Chapter's Specifications, check the crankshaft thrust surfaces for wear. If no wear is evident, new main bearings should correct the endplay.

3   If a dial indicator isn't available, feeler gauges can be used. Gently pry or push the crankshaft all the way to the front of the engine. Slip feeler gauges between the crankshaft and the front face of the thrust main bearing to determine the clearance **(see illustration)**.

4   Check the main bearing caps to see if they're marked to indicate their locations. They should be numbered consecutively from the front of the engine to the rear. If they aren't, mark them with number stamping dies or a center-punch **(see illustration)**. Main bearing caps generally have a cast-in arrow, which points to the front of the engine.

15.3 To check crankshaft endplay with a feeler gauge, place the gauge between the thrust main bearing and the crank

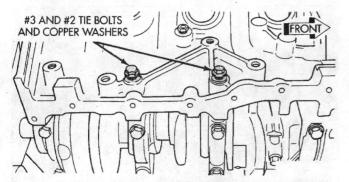

15.5 Remove the tie bolts from the no. 2 and no. 3 main bearing caps

Loosen the main bearing cap bolts 1/4-turn at a time each, until they can be removed by hand. Note if any stud bolts are used and make sure they're returned to their original locations when the crankshaft is reinstalled.
5   On 3.5L engines, also remove the main cap tie bolts that enter the #2 and #3 caps through the side of the block just above the oil pan mounting surface **(see illustration)**.
6   Gently tap the caps with a soft-face hammer, then separate them from the engine block. If necessary, use the bolts as levers to remove the caps. Try not to drop the bearing inserts if they come out with the caps.

16.4a A hammer and large punch can be used to knock the core plugs sideways in their bores

15.4 Use a center punch or number stamping dies to mark the main bearing caps to ensure installation in their original locations of the block (make the punch marks near one of the bolt heads)

7   Carefully lift the crankshaft out of the engine. It may be a good idea to have an assistant available, since the crankshaft is quite heavy. With the bearing inserts in place in the engine block and main bearing caps, return the caps to their respective locations on the engine block and tighten the bolts finger tight.

16 Engine block - cleaning

Refer to illustrations 16.4a, 16.4b, 16.8 and 16.10
1   Remove the main bearing caps and separate the bearing inserts from the caps and the engine block. Tag the bearings, indicating which cylinder they were removed from and whether they were in the cap or the block, then set them aside.
2   Using a gasket scraper, remove all traces of gasket material from the engine block. Be very careful not to nick or gouge the gasket sealing surfaces.
3   Remove all of the covers and threaded oil gallery plugs from the block. The plugs are usually very tight - they may have to be drilled out and the holes retapped. Use new plugs when the engine is reassembled.
4   Remove the core plugs from the engine block. To do this, knock one side of each plug into the block with a hammer and punch, then grasp them with large pliers and pull them out **(see illustrations)**.
5   If the engine is extremely dirty, it should be taken to an automotive machine shop for cleaning.

2C

16.4b Pull the core plugs from the block with pliers

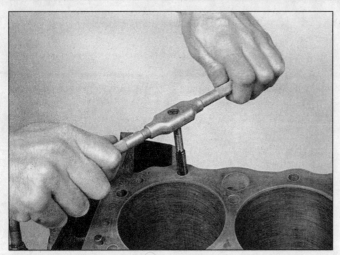

16.8 All bolt holes in the block - particularly the main bearing cap and head bolt holes - should be cleaned and restored with a tap (be sure to remove debris from the holes after this is done)

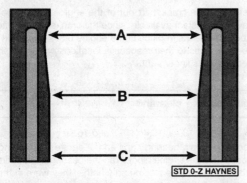

17.4a Measure the diameter of each cylinder just under the wear ridge (A), at the center (B) and at the bottom (C)

16.10 A large socket on an extension can be used to drive the new core plugs into the bores

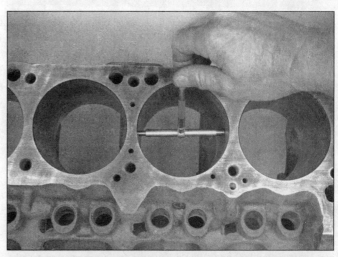

17.4b The ability to "feel" when the telescoping gauge is at the correct point will be developed over time, so work slowly and repeat the check until you're satisfied the bore measurement is accurate

6   After the block is returned, clean all oil holes and oil galleries one more time. Brushes specifically designed for this purpose are available at most auto parts stores. Flush the passages with warm water until the water runs clear, dry the block thoroughly and wipe all machined surfaces with a light, rust preventive oil. If you have access to compressed air, use it to speed the drying process and blow out all the oil holes and galleries. **Warning:** *Wear eye protection when using compressed air!*

7   If the block isn't extremely dirty or sludged up, you can do an adequate cleaning job with hot soapy water and a stiff brush. Take plenty of time and do a thorough job. Regardless of the cleaning method used, be sure to clean all oil holes and galleries very thoroughly, dry the block completely and coat all machined surfaces with light oil.

8   The threaded holes in the block must be clean to ensure accurate torque readings during reassembly. Run the proper size tap into each of the holes to remove rust, corrosion, thread sealant or sludge and restore damaged threads **(see illustration)**. If possible, use compressed air to clear the holes of debris produced by this operation. Now is a good time to clean the threads on the head bolts and the main bearing cap bolts as well.

9   Reinstall the main bearing caps and tighten the bolts finger tight.

10   After coating the sealing surfaces of the new core plugs with Permatex no. 2 sealant, install them in the engine block. Make sure they're driven in straight and seated properly or leakage could result. Special tools are available for this purpose, but a large socket, with an outside diameter that will just slip into the core plug, a 1/2-inch drive extension and a hammer will work just as well **(see illustration)**.

11   Apply non-hardening sealant (such as Permatex no. 2 or Teflon pipe sealant) to the new oil gallery plugs and thread them into the holes in the block. Make sure they're tightened securely.

12   If the engine isn't going to be reassembled right away, cover it with a large plastic trash bag to keep it clean.

17 Engine block - inspection

Refer to illustrations 17.4a, 17.4b and 17.4c

1   Before the block is inspected, it should be cleaned as described in Section 16.

2   Visually check the block for cracks, rust and corrosion. Look for stripped threads in the threaded holes. It's also a good idea to have the block checked for hidden cracks by an automotive machine shop that has the special equipment to do this type of work. If defects are found, have the block repaired, if possible, or replaced.

3   Check the cylinder bores for scuffing and scoring.

4   Check the cylinders for taper and out-of-round by performing the following steps **(see illustrations)**:

5   Measure the diameter of each cylinder at the top (just under the ridge area), center and bottom of the cylinder bore, parallel to the crankshaft axis.

6   Next, measure each cylinder's diameter at the same three

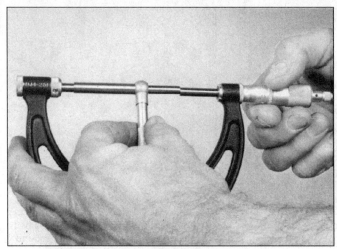

17.4c The gauge is then measured with a micrometer to determine the bore size

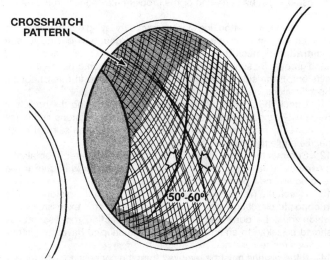

CROSSHATCH PATTERN

50°-60°

18.3b The cylinder hone should leave a smooth, crosshatch pattern with the lines intersecting at approximately a 60-degree angle

18.3a A "bottle brush" hone will produce better results if you've never honed cylinders before

2C

locations perpendicular to the crankshaft axis.

7   The taper of each cylinder is the difference between the bore diameter at the top of the cylinder and the diameter at the bottom. The out-of-round specification of the cylinder bore is the difference between the parallel and perpendicular readings. Compare your results to this Chapter's Specifications.

8   If the cylinder walls are badly scuffed or scored, or if they're out-of-round or tapered beyond the limits given in this Chapter's Specifications, have the engine block rebored and honed at an automotive machine shop. If a rebore is done, oversize pistons and rings will be required.

9   If the cylinders are in reasonably good condition and not worn to the outside of the limits, and if the piston-to-cylinder clearances can be maintained properly, they don't have to be rebored. Honing is all that's necessary (see Section 18).

18   Cylinder honing

Refer to illustrations 18.3a and 18.3b

1   Prior to engine reassembly, the cylinder bores must be honed so the new piston rings will seat correctly and provide the best possible combustion chamber seal. **Note:** *If you don't have the tools or don't*

want to tackle the honing operation, most automotive machine shops will do it for a reasonable fee.

2   Before honing the cylinders, install the main bearing caps and tighten the bolts to the torque listed in this Chapter's Specifications.

3   Two types of cylinder hones are commonly available - the flex hone or "bottle brush" type and the more traditional surfacing hone with spring-loaded stones. Both will do the job, but for the less experienced mechanic the "bottle brush" hone will probably be easier to use. You'll also need some honing oil (kerosene will work if honing oil isn't available), rags and an electric drill motor. Proceed as follows:

a) *Mount the hone in the drill motor, compress the stones and slip it into the first cylinder* **(see illustration)**. *Be sure to wear safety goggles or a face shield!*

b) *Lubricate the cylinder with plenty of honing oil, turn on the drill and move the hone up-and-down in the cylinder at a pace that will produce a fine crosshatch pattern on the cylinder walls. Ideally, the crosshatch lines should intersect at approximately a 60-degree angle* **(see illustration)**. *Be sure to use plenty of lubricant and don't take off any more material than is absolutely necessary to produce the desired finish.* **Note:** *Piston ring manufacturers may specify a smaller crosshatch angle than the traditional 60-degrees - read and follow any instructions included with the new rings.*

c) *Don't withdraw the hone from the cylinder while it's running. Instead, shut off the drill and continue moving the hone up-and-down in the cylinder until it comes to a complete stop, then compress the stones and withdraw the hone. If you're using a "bottle brush" type hone, stop the drill motor, then turn the chuck in the normal direction of rotation while withdrawing the hone from the cylinder.*

d) *Wipe the oil out of the cylinder and repeat the procedure for the remaining cylinders.*

4   After the honing job is complete, chamfer the top edges of the cylinder bores with a small file so the rings won't catch when the pistons are installed. Be very careful not to nick the cylinder walls with the end of the file.

5   The entire engine block must be washed again very thoroughly with warm, soapy water to remove all traces of the abrasive grit produced during the honing operation. **Note:** *The bores can be considered clean when a lint-free white cloth - dampened with clean engine oil - used to wipe them out doesn't pick-up any more honing residue, which will show up as gray areas on the cloth. Be sure to run a brush through all oil holes and galleries and flush them with running water.*

6   After rinsing, dry the block and apply a coat of light rust preventive oil to all machined surfaces. Wrap the block in a plastic trash bag to keep it clean and set it aside until reassembly.

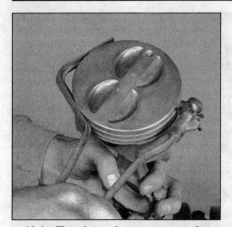

19.4a The piston ring grooves can be cleaned with a special tool, as shown here . . .

19.4b . . . or a section of a broken ring

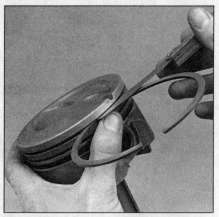

19.10 Check the ring side clearance with a feeler gauge at several points around the groove, using a new piston ring

19 Pistons and connecting rods - inspection

Refer to illustrations 19.4a, 19.4b, 19.10 and 19.11

1   Before the inspection process can be carried out, the piston/connecting rod assemblies must be cleaned and the original piston rings removed from the pistons. **Note:** *Always use new piston rings when the engine is reassembled.*

2   Using a piston ring installation tool, carefully remove the rings from the pistons. Be careful not to nick or gouge the pistons in the process.

3   Scrape all traces of carbon from the top of the piston. A hand-held wire brush or a piece of fine emery cloth can be used once the majority of the deposits have been scraped away. Do not, under any circumstances, use a wire brush mounted in a drill motor to remove deposits from the pistons. The piston material is soft and may be eroded away by the wire brush.

4   Use a piston ring groove cleaning tool to remove carbon deposits from the ring grooves. If a tool isn't available, a piece broken off the old ring will do the job. Be very careful to remove only the carbon deposits. Don't remove any metal and do not nick or scratch the sides of the ring grooves **(see illustrations)**.

5   Once the deposits have been removed, clean the piston/rod assemblies with solvent and dry them with compressed air (if available). **Warning:** *Wear eye protection. Make sure the oil return holes in the back sides of the ring grooves are clear.*

6   If the pistons and cylinder walls aren't damaged or worn excessively, and if the engine block isn't rebored, new pistons won't be necessary. Normal piston wear appears as even, vertical wear on the piston thrust surfaces and slight looseness of the top ring in its groove. New piston rings, however, should always be used when an engine is rebuilt.

7   Carefully inspect each piston for cracks around the skirt, at the pin bosses and at the ring lands.

8   Look for scoring and scuffing on the thrust faces of the skirt, holes in the piston crown and burned areas at the edge of the crown. If the skirt is scored or scuffed, the engine may have been suffering from overheating and/or abnormal combustion, which caused excessively high operating temperatures. The cooling and lubrication systems should be checked thoroughly. A hole in the piston crown is an indication that abnormal combustion (preignition) was occurring. Burned areas at the edge of the piston crown are usually evidence of spark knock (detonation). If any of the above problems exist, the causes must be corrected or the damage will occur again. The causes may include intake air leaks, incorrect fuel/air mixture, low octane fuel, ignition timing and EGR system malfunctions.

9   Corrosion of the piston, in the form of small pits, indicates coolant is leaking into the combustion chamber and/or the crankcase. Again,

the cause must be corrected or the problem may persist in the rebuilt engine.

10   Measure the piston ring side clearance by laying a new piston ring in each ring groove and slipping a feeler gauge in beside it **(see illustration)**. Check the clearance at three or four locations around each groove. Be sure to use the correct ring for each groove - they are different. If the side clearance is greater than listed in this Chapter's Specifications, new pistons will have to be used.

11   Check the piston-to-bore clearance by measuring the bore (see Section 17) and the piston diameter. Make sure the pistons and bores are correctly matched. Measure the piston across the skirt, at a 90-degree angle to the piston pin **(see illustration)**.

12   Subtract the piston diameter from the bore diameter to obtain the clearance. If it's greater than specified, the block will have to be rebored and new pistons and rings installed.

13   Check the piston-to-rod clearance by twisting the piston and rod in opposite directions. Any noticeable play indicates excessive wear, which must be corrected. The piston/connecting rod assemblies should be taken to an automotive machine shop to have the pistons and rods resized and new pins installed.

14   If the pistons must be removed from the connecting rods for any reason, they should be taken to an automotive machine shop. While they are there have the connecting rods checked for bend and twist, since automotive machine shops have special equipment for this purpose. **Note:** *Unless new pistons and/or connecting rods must be installed, do not disassemble the pistons and connecting rods.*

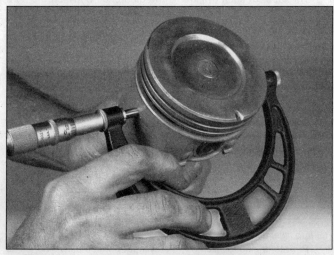

19.11 Measure the piston diameter at a 90-degree angle to the piston pin and in line with it

20.1 The oil holes should be chamfered so sharp edges don't gouge or scratch the new bearings

20.2 Use a wire or stiff plastic bristle brush to clean the oil passages in the crankshaft

15   Check the connecting rods for cracks and other damage. Temporarily remove the rod caps, lift out the old bearing inserts, wipe the rod and cap bearing surfaces clean and inspect them for nicks, gouges and scratches. After checking the rods, replace the old bearings, slip the caps into place and tighten the nuts finger tight. **Note:** *If the engine is being rebuilt because of a connecting rod knock, be sure to install new rods.*

20 Crankshaft - inspection

Refer to illustrations 20.1, 20.2, 20.5 and 20.7

1   Remove all burrs from the crankshaft oil holes with a stone, file or scraper **(see illustration)**.
2   Clean the crankshaft with solvent and dry it with compressed air (if available). **Warning:** *Wear eye protection when using compressed air. Be sure to clean the oil holes with a stiff brush* **(see illustration)** *and flush them with solvent.*
3   Check the main and connecting rod bearing journals for uneven wear, scoring, pits and cracks.
4   Check the rest of the crankshaft for cracks and other damage. It should be magnafluxed to reveal hidden cracks - an automotive machine shop will handle the procedure.
5   Using a micrometer, measure the diameter of the main and connecting rod journals and compare the results to this Chapter's Specifications **(see illustration)**. By measuring the diameter at a number of points around each journal's circumference, you'll be able to determine whether or not the journal is out-of-round. Take the measurement at each end of the journal, near the crank throws, to determine if the journal is tapered.
6   If the crankshaft journals are damaged, tapered, out-of-round or worn beyond the limits given in the Specifications, have the crankshaft reground by an automotive machine shop. Be sure to use the correct size bearing inserts if the crankshaft is reconditioned.
7   Check the oil seal journals at each end of the crankshaft for wear and damage. If the seal has worn a groove in the journal, or if it's nicked or scratched **(see illustration)**, the new seal may leak when the engine is reassembled. In some cases, an automotive machine shop may be able to repair the journal by pressing on a thin sleeve. If repair isn't feasible, a new or different crankshaft should be installed.
8   Refer to Section 21 and examine the main and rod bearing inserts.

21 Main and connecting rod bearings - inspection

Refer to illustration 21.1

1   Even though the main and connecting rod bearings should be replaced with new ones during the engine overhaul, the old bearings should be retained for close examination, as they may reveal valuable information about the condition of the engine **(see illustration)**.

2C

20.5 Measure the diameter of each crankshaft journal at several points to detect taper and out-of-round conditions

20.7 If the seals have worn grooves in the crankshaft journals, or if the seal contact surfaces are nicked or scratched, the new seals will leak

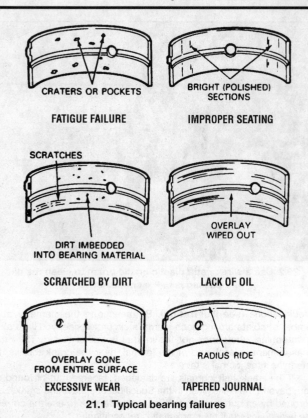

CRATERS OR POCKETS

FATIGUE FAILURE

BRIGHT (POLISHED) SECTIONS

IMPROPER SEATING

SCRATCHES

DIRT IMBEDDED INTO BEARING MATERIAL

SCRATCHED BY DIRT

OVERLAY WIPED OUT

LACK OF OIL

OVERLAY GONE FROM ENTIRE SURFACE

EXCESSIVE WEAR

RADIUS RIDE

TAPERED JOURNAL

21.1 Typical bearing failures

2   Bearing failure occurs because of lack of lubrication, the presence of dirt or other foreign particles, overloading the engine and corrosion. Regardless of the cause of bearing failure, it must be corrected before the engine is reassembled to prevent it from happening again.

3   When examining the bearings, remove them from the engine block, the main bearing caps, the connecting rods and the rod caps and lay them out on a clean surface in the same general position as their location in the engine. This will enable you to match any bearing problems with the corresponding crankshaft journal.

4   Dirt and other foreign particles get into the engine in a variety of ways. It may be left in the engine during assembly, or it may pass through filters or the PCV system. It may get into the oil, and from there into the bearings. Metal chips from machining operations and normal engine wear are often present. Abrasives are sometimes left in engine components after reconditioning, especially when parts aren't thoroughly cleaned using the proper cleaning methods. Whatever the source, these foreign objects often end up embedded in the soft bearing material and are easily recognized. Large particles won't embed in the bearing and will score or gouge the bearing and journal. The best prevention for this cause of bearing failure is to clean all parts thoroughly and keep everything spotlessly clean during engine assembly. Frequent and regular engine oil and filter changes are also recommended.

5   Lack of lubrication (or lubrication breakdown) has a number of interrelated causes. Excessive heat (which thins the oil), overloading (which squeezes the oil from the bearing face) and oil leakage or throw off (from excessive bearing clearances, worn oil pump or high engine speeds) all contribute to lubrication breakdown. Blocked oil passages, which usually are the result of misaligned oil holes in a bearing shell, will also oil starve a bearing and destroy it. When lack of lubrication is the cause of bearing failure, the bearing material is wiped or extruded from the steel backing of the bearing. Temperatures may increase to the point where the steel backing turns blue from overheating.

6   Driving habits can have a definite effect on bearing life. Low speed operation in too high a gear (lugging the engine) puts very high loads on bearings, which tend to squeeze out the oil film. These loads cause the bearings to flex, which produces fine cracks in the bearing face (fatigue failure). Eventually the bearing material will loosen in pieces and tear

away from the steel backing. Short trip driving leads to corrosion of bearings because insufficient engine heat is produced to drive off the condensed water and corrosive gases. These products collect in the engine oil, forming acid and sludge. As the oil is carried to the engine bearings, the acid attacks and corrodes the bearing material.

7   Incorrect bearing installation during engine assembly will lead to bearing failure as well. Tight fitting bearings leave insufficient oil clearance and will result in oil starvation. Dirt or foreign particles trapped behind a bearing insert result in high spots on the bearing which lead to failure.

22 Engine overhaul - reassembly sequence

1   Before beginning engine reassembly, make sure you have all the necessary new parts, gaskets and seals as well as the following items on hand:

Common hand tools
Torque wrench (1/2-inch drive)
Piston ring installation tool
Piston ring compressor
Vibration damper installation tool
Short lengths of rubber or plastic hose to fit over
    connecting rod bolts
Plastigage
Feeler gauges
Fine-tooth file
New engine oil
Engine assembly lube or moly-base grease
Gasket sealant
Thread locking compound

2   In order to save time and avoid problems, engine reassembly must be done in the following general order:

3.3L V6 engine

Crankshaft and main bearings
Rear main oil seal housing
Piston/connecting rod assemblies
Oil pump
Camshaft
Timing chain and sprockets
Timing chain cover
Oil pan
Cylinder heads
Valve lifters
Rocker arms and pushrods
Intake and exhaust manifolds
Valve covers

3.5L V6 engine

Crankshaft and main bearings
Rear main oil seal housing
Piston/connecting rod assemblies
Oil pump
Oil pan
Timing belt cover
Timing belt and sprockets
Cylinder heads and camshafts
Intake and exhaust manifolds
Valve covers
Driveplate

23 Piston rings - installation

Refer to illustrations 23.3, 23.4, 23.5, 23.9a, 23.9b, 23.12 and 23.13

1   Before installing the new piston rings, the ring end gaps must be checked. It's assumed the piston ring side clearance has been checked and verified correct (see Section 19).

2   Lay out the piston/connecting rod assemblies and the new ring

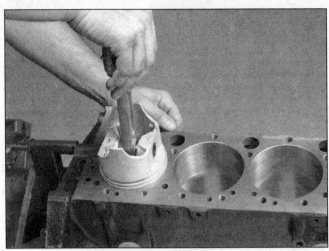

23.3 When checking piston ring end gap, the ring must be square in the cylinder bore (this is done by pushing the ring down with the top of a piston)

23.4 With the ring square in the cylinder, measure the end gap with a feeler gauge

sets so the ring sets will be matched with the same piston and cylinder during the end gap measurement and engine assembly.

3   Insert the top (number one) ring into the first cylinder and square it up with the cylinder walls by pushing it in with the top of the piston **(see illustration)**. The ring should be near the bottom of the cylinder, at the lower limit of ring travel.

4   To measure the end gap, slip feeler gauges between the ends of the ring until a gauge equal to the gap width is found **(see illustration)**. The feeler gauge should slide between the ring ends with a slight amount of drag. Compare the measurement to this Chapter's Specifications. If the gap is larger or smaller than specified, double-check to make sure you have the correct rings before proceeding.

5   If the gap is too small, it must be enlarged or the ring ends may come in contact with each other during engine operation, which can cause serious engine damage. The end gap can be increased by filing the ring ends very carefully with a fine file. Mount the file in a vise equipped with soft jaws, slip the ring over the file with the ends contacting the file teeth and slowly move the ring to remove material from the ends. When performing this operation, file only from the outside in **(see illustration)**.

6   Excess end gap isn't critical unless it's greater than 0.040-inch. Again, double-check to make sure you have the correct rings for the engine.

7   Repeat the procedure for each ring that will be installed in the first cylinder and for each ring in the remaining cylinders. Remember to keep rings, pistons and cylinders matched up.

8   Once the ring end gaps have been checked/corrected, the rings can be installed on the pistons.

23.5 If the end gap is too small, clamp a file in a vise and file the ring ends (from the outside in only) to enlarge the gap slightly

9   The oil control ring (lowest one on the piston) is usually installed first. It's composed of three separate components. Slip the spacer/expander into the groove **(see illustration)**. If an anti-rotation tang is used, make sure it's inserted into the drilled hole in the ring groove. Next, install the lower side rail. Don't use a piston ring installation tool on the oil ring side rails, as they may be damaged. Instead, place one end of the side rail into the groove between the spacer/expander and the ring land, hold it firmly in place and slide a finger around the piston while pushing the rail into the groove **(see illustration)**. Next, install the upper side rail in the same manner.

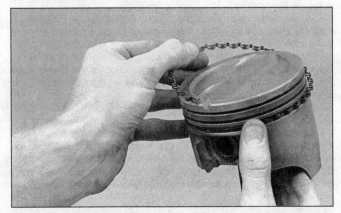

23.9a Installing the spacer/expander in the oil control ring groove

23.9b DO NOT use a piston ring installation tool when installing the oil ring side rails

2C

23.12 Install the compression rings with a ring expander - the mark must face up

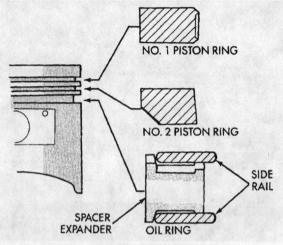

23.13 Piston ring details

10   After the three oil ring components have been installed, check to make sure both the upper and lower side rails can be turned smoothly in the ring groove.

11   The number two (middle) ring is installed next. It's usually stamped with a mark, which must face up, toward the top of the piston. **Note:** *Always follow the instructions printed on the ring package or box - different manufacturers may require different approaches. Don't mix up the top and middle rings, as they have different cross sections.*

12   Use a piston ring installation tool and make sure the identification mark is facing the top of the piston, then slip the ring into the middle groove on the piston **(see illustration)**. Don't expand the ring any more than necessary to slide it over the piston.

13   Install the number one (top) ring in the same manner. Make sure the mark is facing up. Be careful not to confuse the number one and number two rings **(see illustration)**.

14   Repeat the procedure for the remaining pistons and rings.

24   Crankshaft - installation and main bearing oil clearance check

Refer to illustrations 24.11 and 24.15

1   Crankshaft installation is the first step in engine reassembly. It's assumed at this point that the engine block and crankshaft have been cleaned, inspected and repaired or reconditioned.

2   Position the engine with the bottom facing up.

3   Remove the main bearing cap bolts and lift out the caps. Lay them out in the proper order to ensure correct installation.

4   If they're still in place, remove the original bearing inserts from the block and the main bearing caps. Wipe the bearing surfaces of the block and caps with a clean, lint-free cloth. They must be kept spotlessly clean.

Main bearing oil clearance check

Note: *Don't touch the faces of the new bearing inserts with your fingers. Oil and acids from your skin can etch the bearings.*

5   Clean the back sides of the new main bearing inserts and lay one in each main bearing saddle in the block. If one of the bearing inserts from each set has a large groove in it, make sure the grooved insert is installed in the block. Lay the other bearing from each set in the corresponding main bearing cap. Make sure the tab on the bearing insert fits into the recess in the block or cap. **Caution:** *The oil holes in the block must line up with the oil holes in the bearing inserts. Do not hammer the bearing into place and don't nick or gouge the bearing faces. No lubrication should be used at this time.*

6   Install the thrust bearing in the number two cap and saddle.

7   Clean the faces of the bearings in the block and the crankshaft main bearing journals with a clean, lint-free cloth.

24.11 Lay the Plastigage strips (arrow) on the main bearing journals, parallel to the crankshaft centerline

8   Check or clean the oil holes in the crankshaft, as any dirt here can go only one way - straight through the new bearings.

9   Once you're certain the crankshaft is clean, carefully lay it in position in the main bearings.

10   Before the crankshaft can be permanently installed, the main bearing oil clearance must be checked.

11   Cut several pieces of the appropriate size Plastigage (they should be slightly shorter than the width of the main bearings) and place one piece on each crankshaft main bearing journal, parallel with the journal axis **(see illustration)**.

12   Clean the faces of the bearings in the caps and install the caps in their original locations (don't mix them up) with the arrows pointing toward the front of the engine. Don't disturb the Plastigage.

13   Starting with the center main and working out toward the ends, tighten the main bearing cap bolts, in three steps, to the torque figure listed in this Chapter's Specifications. Don't rotate the crankshaft at any time during this operation.

14   Remove the bolts and carefully lift off the main bearing caps. Keep them in order. Don't disturb the Plastigage or rotate the crankshaft. If any of the main bearing caps are difficult to remove, tap them gently from side-to-side with a soft-face hammer to loosen them.

15   Compare the width of the crushed Plastigage on each journal to the scale printed on the Plastigage envelope to obtain the main bearing oil clearance **(see illustration)**. Check the Specifications to make sure it's correct.

16   If the clearance is not as specified, the bearing inserts may be the wrong size (which means different ones will be required). Before deciding different inserts are needed, make sure no dirt or oil was

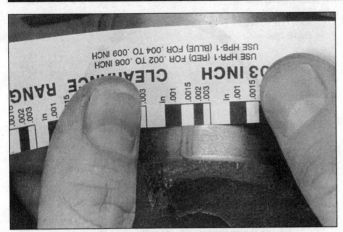

24.15 Compare the width of the crushed Plastigage to the scale on the envelope to determine the main bearing oil clearance (always take the measurement at the widest point of the Plastigage); be sure to use the correct scale - standard and metric ones are included

26.2 To install the new seal in the housing, simply lay the housing on a clean, flat workbench, lay a block of wood on the seal and carefully tap it into place with a hammer

between the bearing inserts and the caps or block when the clearance was measured. If the Plastigage was wider at one end than the other, the journal may be tapered (see Section 20).

17   Carefully scrape all traces of the Plastigage material off the main bearing journals and/or the bearing faces. Use your fingernail or the edge of a credit card - don't nick or scratch the bearing faces.

Final crankshaft installation

18   Carefully lift the crankshaft out of the engine.

19   Clean the bearing faces in the block, then apply a thin, uniform layer of moly-base grease or engine assembly lube to each of the bearing surfaces. Be sure to coat the thrust faces as well as the journal face of the thrust bearing.

20   Make sure the crankshaft journals are clean, then lay the crankshaft back in place in the block.

21   Clean the faces of the bearings in the caps, then apply lubricant to them.

22   Install the caps in their original locations with the arrows pointing toward the front of the engine.

23   Install the bolts.

24   Tighten the number 1, 3, and 4 main caps to the torque listed in this Chapter's Specifications (work from the center out). **Note:** *Don't forget to install the tie bolts to the number 3 cap with new copper washers.*

25   Tighten the thrust bearing cap bolts to 10-to-12 ft-lbs.

26   Tap the ends of the crankshaft forward and backward with a lead

26.1 To remove the old rear main oil seal from the housing, support the housing on a pair of wood blocks and drive out the seal with a punch or screwdriver and hammer - make sure you don't damage the seal bore

or brass hammer to line up the main bearing and crankshaft thrust surfaces. Drive a wedge of some type between the rear of the block and the rear crankshaft counterweight (engine turned to TDC for cylinder number 6) to apply light pressure forward on the crankshaft.

27   Now tighten the number 2 main cap bolts to Specifications, then the number 2 tie bolts with new copper washers and tighten them to the torque listed in this Chapter's Specifications.

28   Rotate the crankshaft a number of times by hand to check for any obvious binding.

29   The final step is to check the crankshaft endplay with feeler gauges or a dial indicator as described in Section 15. The endplay should be correct if the crankshaft thrust faces aren't worn or damaged and new bearings have been installed.

30   Refer to Section 26 and install the new rear main oil seal.

25   Camshaft - installation

Refer to Chapter 2, Part A (3.3L engine) or Chapter 2, Part B (3.5L engine) for the camshaft installation procedure.

26   Rear main oil seal - installation

Refer to illustrations 26.1 and 26.2
Note: *The crankshaft must be installed and the main bearing caps bolted in place before the new seal and housing assembly can be bolted to the block.*

1   Remove the old seal from the housing with a hammer and punch by driving it out from the back side **(see illustration)**. Be sure to note how far it's recessed into the housing bore before removing it; the new seal will have to be recessed an equal amount. Be very careful not to scratch or otherwise damage the bore in the housing or oil leaks could develop.

2   Make sure the housing is clean, then apply a thin coat of engine oil to the outer edge of the new seal. The seal must be pressed squarely into the housing bore, so hammering it into place isn't recommended. If you don't have access to a press, sandwich the housing and seal between two smooth pieces of wood and press the seal into place with the jaws of a large vise. If you don't have a vise big enough, lay the housing on a workbench and drive the seal into place with a block of wood and hammer **(see illustration)**. The pieces of wood must be thick enough to distribute the force evenly around the entire circumference of the seal. Work slowly and make sure the seal enters the bore squarely.

3   Lubricate the seal lips with clean engine oil or multi-purpose grease before you slip the seal/housing over the crankshaft and bolt it to the block, using a new gasket between the block and the retainer.

4   Tighten the housing bolts a little at a time until they're all snug.

2C

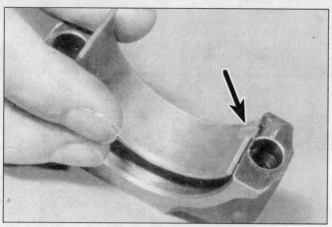

27.4 The tab on the bearing (arrow) must fit into the cap recess so the bearing will seat properly

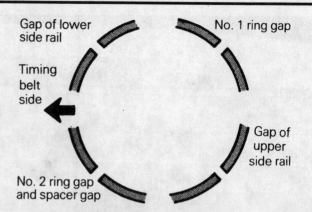

27.5 Position the ring gaps as shown here before installing the piston/connecting rod assemblies in the engine

27   Pistons and connecting rods - installation and rod bearing oil clearance check

Refer to illustrations 27.4, 27.5, 27.9, 27.11, 27.13 and 27.17

1   Before installing the piston/connecting rod assemblies, the cylinder walls must be perfectly clean, the top edge of each cylinder must be chamfered, and the crankshaft must be in place.
2   Remove the cap from the end of the number one connecting rod (check the marks made during removal). Remove the original bearing inserts and wipe the bearing surfaces of the connecting rod and cap with a clean, lint-free cloth. They must be kept spotlessly clean.

Connecting rod bearing oil clearance check

Note: *Don't touch the faces of the new bearing inserts with your fingers. Oil and acids from your skin can etch the bearings.*
3   Clean the back side of the new upper bearing insert, then lay it in place in the connecting rod. Make sure the tab on the bearing fits into the recess in the rod. Don't hammer the bearing insert into place and be very careful not to nick or gouge the bearing face. Don't lubricate the bearing at this time.
4   Clean the back side of the other bearing insert and install it in the rod cap. Again, make sure the tab on the bearing fits into the recess in the cap **(see illustration)**, and don't apply any lubricant. It's critically important that the mating surfaces of the bearing and connecting rod are perfectly clean and oil free when they're assembled.

5   Position the piston ring gaps as shown **(see illustration)**.
6   Slip a section of plastic or rubber hose over each connecting rod cap bolt.
7   Lubricate the piston and rings with clean engine oil and attach a piston ring compressor to the piston. Leave the skirt protruding about 1/4-inch to guide the piston into the cylinder. The rings must be compressed until they're flush with the piston.
8   Rotate the crankshaft until the number one connecting rod journal is at BDC (bottom dead center) and apply a coat of engine oil to the cylinder walls.
9   With the mark or notch on top of the piston **(see illustration)** facing the front of the engine, gently insert the piston/connecting rod assembly into the number one cylinder bore and rest the bottom edge of the ring compressor on the engine block. **Note:** *On 3.5L engines, the pistons are marked "L" or "R", for left or right bank. They should not be interchanged from one bank to the other.*
10   Tap the top edge of the ring compressor to make sure it's contacting the block around its entire circumference.
11   Gently tap on the top of the piston with the end of a wooden or plastic hammer handle **(see illustration)** while guiding the end of the connecting rod into place on the crankshaft journal. The piston rings may try to pop out of the ring compressor just before entering the cylinder bore, so keep some pressure on the ring compressor. Work slowly, and if any resistance is felt as the piston enters the cylinder, stop immediately. Find out what's hanging up and fix it before proceeding. Do not, for any reason, force the piston into the cylinder - you might break a ring and/or the piston.
12   Once the piston/connecting rod assembly is installed, the connecting rod bearing oil clearance must be checked before the rod cap is permanently bolted into place.

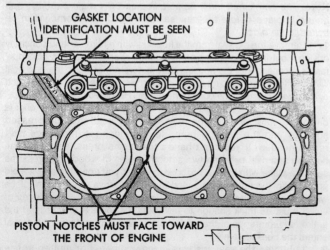

27.9 The pistons must be installed with the notch or arrow pointing to the front of the engine - on 3.5L engines, the pistons are also marked "L" or "R" to indicate which bank they must go in

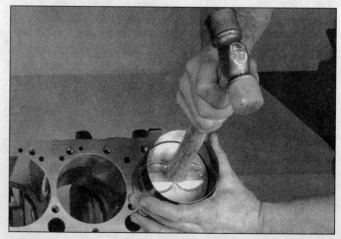

27.11 Gently drive the piston into the cylinder bore with the end of a wooden or plastic hammer handle

27.13 Lay the Plastigage strips on each rod bearing journal, parallel to the crankshaft centerline

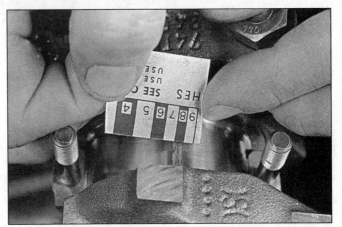

27.17 Measuring the width of the crushed Plastigage to determine the rod bearing oil clearance (be sure to use the correct scale - standard and metric ones are included)

13 Cut a piece of the appropriate size Plastigage slightly shorter than the width of the connecting rod bearing and lay it in place on the number one connecting rod journal, parallel with the journal axis (see illustration).

14 Clean the connecting rod cap bearing face, remove the protective hoses from the connecting rod bolts and install the rod cap. Make sure the mating mark on the cap is on the same side as the mark on the connecting rod.

15 Install the nuts and tighten them to the torque listed in this Chapter's Specifications. **Note:** *Use a thin-wall socket to avoid erroneous torque readings that can result if the socket is wedged between the rod cap and nut. If the socket tends to wedge itself between the nut and the cap, lift up on it slightly until it no longer contacts the cap. Do not rotate the crankshaft at any time during this operation.*

16 Remove the nuts and detach the rod cap, being very careful not to disturb the Plastigage.

17 Compare the width of the crushed Plastigage to the scale printed on the Plastigage envelope to obtain the oil clearance (see illustration). Compare it to this Chapter's Specifications to make sure the clearance is correct.

18 If the clearance is not as specified, the bearing inserts may be the wrong size (which means different ones will be required). Before deciding different inserts are needed, make sure no dirt or oil was between the bearing inserts and the connecting rod or cap when the clearance was measured. Also, recheck the journal diameter. If the Plastigage was wider at one end than the other, the journal may be tapered (refer to Section 21).

Final connecting rod installation

19 Carefully scrape all traces of the Plastigage material off the rod journal and/or bearing face. Be very careful not to scratch the bearing - use your fingernail or the edge of a credit card.

20 Make sure the bearing faces are perfectly clean, then apply a uniform layer of clean moly-base grease or engine assembly lube to both of them. You'll have to push the piston into the cylinder to expose the face of the bearing insert in the connecting rod - be sure to slip the protective hoses over the rod bolts first.

21 Slide the connecting rod back into place on the journal, remove the protective hoses from the rod cap bolts, install the rod cap and tighten the nuts to the torque listed in this Chapter's Specifications.

22 Repeat the entire procedure for the remaining pistons/connecting rods.

23 The important points to remember are:

a) *Keep the back sides of the bearing inserts and the insides of the connecting rods and caps perfectly clean when assembling them.*
b) *Make sure you have the correct piston/rod assembly for each cylinder.*
c) *The arrow or mark on the piston must face the front of the engine.*
d) *Lubricate the cylinder walls with clean oil.*

e) *Lubricate the bearing faces when installing the rod caps after the oil clearance has been checked.*

24 After all the piston/connecting rod assemblies have been properly installed, rotate the crankshaft a number of times by hand to check for any obvious binding.

25 As a final step, the connecting rod endplay (side clearance) must be checked. Refer to Section 14 for this procedure.

26 Compare the measured endplay to this Chapter's Specifications to make sure it's correct. If it was correct before disassembly and the original crankshaft and rods were reinstalled, it should still be right. If new rods or a new crankshaft were installed, the endplay may be inadequate. If so, the rods will have to be removed and taken to an automotive machine shop for resizing.

28 Initial start-up and break-in after overhaul

Warning: *Have a fire extinguisher handy when starting the engine for the first time.*

1 Once the engine has been installed in the vehicle, double-check the engine oil and coolant levels.

2 With the spark plugs out of the engine and the ignition and fuel systems disabled (see Section 3), crank the engine until oil pressure registers on the gauge or the light goes out.

3 Install the spark plugs, hook up the plug wires and restore the ignition/fuel system functions (see Section 3).

4 Start the engine. It may take a few moments for the fuel system to build up pressure, but the engine should start without a great deal of effort. **Note:** *If backfiring occurs through the throttle body, recheck the valve timing.*

5 After the engine starts, it should be allowed to warm up to normal operating temperature. While the engine is warming up, make a thorough check for fuel, oil and coolant leaks.

6 Shut the engine off and recheck the engine oil and coolant levels.

7 Drive the vehicle to an area with no traffic, accelerate from 30 to 50 mph, then allow the vehicle to slow to 30 mph with the throttle closed. Repeat the procedure 10 or 12 times. This will load the piston rings and cause them to seat properly against the cylinder walls. Check again for oil and coolant leaks.

8 Drive the vehicle gently for the first 500 miles (no sustained high speeds) and keep a constant check on the oil level. It isn't unusual for an engine to use oil during the break-in period.

9 At approximately 500 to 600 miles, change the oil and filter.

10 For the next few hundred miles, drive the vehicle normally. Don't pamper it or abuse it.

11 After 2000 miles, change the oil and filter again and consider the engine broken in.

2C

Notes

Chapter 3
Cooling, heating and air conditioning systems

Contents

Specifications

General

Radiator cap pressure rating	14 to 18 psi
Thermostat rating (opening temperature)	195-degrees F
Cooling system capacity	See Chapter 1
Refrigerant capacity	28 ounces

Torque specifications

	In-lbs
Thermostat housing bolts/nuts	250 in-lbs
Water pump pulley screws (3.3L)	250 in-lbs
Water pump mounting bolts (all models)	105 in-lbs

1   General information

Engine cooling system

All vehicles covered by this manual employ a pressurized engine cooling system with thermostatically controlled coolant circulation. An impeller-type water pump mounted on the front of the engine pumps coolant through the engine. The pump mounts on the timing chain case on the 3.3L engine, and directly on the engine block on the 3.5L. The coolant flows around the combustion chambers and toward the rear of the engine. Cast-in coolant passages direct coolant near the intake ports, exhaust ports, and spark plug areas.

A wax pellet-type thermostat is located in a housing near the front of the engine. During warm-up, the closed thermostat prevents coolant from circulating through the radiator. As the engine nears normal operating temperature, the thermostat opens and allows hot coolant to travel through the radiator, where it's cooled before returning to the engine.

The cooling system is sealed by a pressure-type cap, which raises the boiling point of the coolant and increases the cooling efficiency of the system. If the system pressure exceeds the cap pressure relief value, the excess pressure in the system forces the spring-loaded valve inside the cap off its seat and allows the coolant to escape through the overflow tube into a coolant reservoir. When the system cools the excess coolant is automatically drawn from the reservoir back into the radiator.

The coolant reservoir does double duty as both the point at which fresh coolant is added to the cooling system to maintain the proper fluid level and as a holding tank for overheated coolant. This type of cooling system is known as a closed design because coolant that escapes past the pressure cap is saved and reused. Unlike most conventional coolant recovery tanks, these models have a *pressurized* tank which is connected directly to the engine and water pump. The location of the tank compared to the radiator makes it the highest point in the system, and the best place to keep air out of the system.

Heating system

The heating system consists of a blower fan and heater core located in the heater box, with hoses connecting the heater core to the engine cooling system. Hot engine coolant is circulated through the heater core. When the heater mode on the heater/air conditioning control head on the dashboard is activated, a flap door opens to expose the heater box to the passenger compartment. A fan switch on the control head activates the blower motor, which forces air through the core, heating the air.

Air conditioning system

The air conditioning system consists of a condenser mounted in front of the radiator, an evaporator mounted adjacent to the heater core, a compressor mounted on the engine, receiver/drier which contains a high pressure relief valve and the plumbing connecting all of the above components.

A blower fan forces the warmer air of the passenger compartment through the evaporator core, transferring the heat from the air to the refrigerant (sort of a "radiator in reverse"). The liquid refrigerant boils off into low pressure vapor, taking the heat with it when it leaves the evaporator.

2   Antifreeze - general information

Refer to illustration 2.4

Warning: *Do not allow antifreeze to come in contact with your skin or painted surfaces of the vehicle. Rinse off spills immediately with plenty of water. Antifreeze is highly toxic if ingested. Never leave antifreeze lying around in an open container or in puddles on the floor; children and pets are attracted by it's sweet smell and may drink it. Antifreeze is also flammable, so don't store or use it near open flames. Check with*

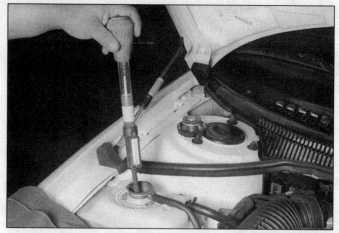

2.4 An inexpensive hydrometer can be used to test the level of anti-freeze protection in your coolant

local authorities about disposing of used antifreeze. Many communities have collection centers which will see that antifreeze is disposed of safely. Never dump used anti-freeze on the ground or into drains.
Note: *Non-Toxic coolant is available at local auto parts stores. Although the coolant is non-toxic when fresh, proper disposal is still required.*

The cooling system should be filled with a water/ethylene glycol based antifreeze solution, which will prevent freezing down to at least 20-degrees F, or lower if local climate requires it. It also provides protection against corrosion and increases the coolant boiling point.

The cooling system should be drained, flushed and refilled at the specified intervals (see Chapter 1). Old or contaminated antifreeze solutions are likely to cause damage and encourage the formation of rust and scale in the system. Use distilled water with the antifreeze.

Before adding antifreeze, check all hose connections, because antifreeze tends to leak through very minute openings. Engines don't normally consume coolant, so if the level goes down, find the cause and correct it.

The exact mixture of antifreeze-to-water which you should use depends on the relative weather conditions. The mixture should contain at least 50-percent antifreeze, but should never contain more than 70 percent antifreeze. Consult the mixture ratio chart on the antifreeze container before adding coolant. Hydrometers are available at most auto parts stores to test the coolant **(see illustration)**. Use antifreeze that meets the vehicle manufacturer's specifications.

3   Thermostat - check and replacement

Warning: *Do not remove the coolant tank cap, drain the coolant or replace the thermostat until the engine has cooled completely.*

Check

1   Before assuming the thermostat is to blame for a cooling system problem, check the coolant level, drivebelt tension (see Chapter 1) and temperature gauge operation.
2   If the engine seems to be taking a long time to warm up (based on heater output or temperature gauge operation), the thermostat is probably stuck open. Replace the thermostat with a new one.
3   If the engine runs hot, use your hand to check the temperature of the upper radiator hose. If the hose isn't hot, but the engine is, the thermostat is probably stuck closed, preventing the coolant inside the engine from escaping to the radiator. Replace the thermostat.
Caution: *Don't drive the vehicle without a thermostat. The computer may stay in open loop and emissions and fuel economy will suffer.*
4   If the upper radiator hose is hot, it means that the coolant is flowing and the thermostat is open. Consult the Troubleshooting Section at the front of this manual for cooling system diagnosis.

3.10 Thermostat mounting bolts, 3.5L engine (3.3L similar)

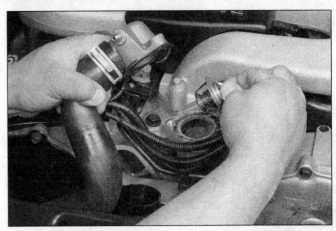

3.11 Remove the thermostat, noting which end is up

4.1a The high-speed and low-speed fans are mounted in one housing, with a harness connecting them to the RFI module (arrow)

4.1b Disconnect the fan connector (arrow) and try operating the fan with a fused battery-voltage jumper wire and a ground wire

3

Replacement

Refer to illustrations 3.10 and 3.11

5   Disconnect the negative battery cable from the battery.

6   Drain the cooling system (see Chapter 1). If the coolant is relatively new or in good condition, save it and reuse it.

7   Follow the upper radiator hose to the engine to locate the thermostat housing.

8   Loosen the hose clamp, then detach the hose from the fitting. If it's stuck, grasp it near the end with a pair of adjustable pliers and twist it to break the seal, then pull it off. If the hose is old or deteriorated, cut it off and install a new one.

9   If the outer surface of the large fitting that mates with the hose is deteriorated (corroded, pitted, etc.) it may be damaged further by hose removal. If it is, the thermostat housing cover will have to be replaced.

10   Remove the fasteners and detach the housing cover **(see illustration)**. If the cover is stuck, tap it with a soft-face hammer to jar it loose. Be prepared for some coolant to spill as the gasket seal is broken.

11   Note how it's installed (which end is facing up), then remove the thermostat **(see illustration)**.

12   Remove all traces of old gasket material and sealant from the housing and cover with a gasket scraper.

13   Install the thermostat on the housing, spring-end first **(see illustration 3.11)**. Dip a new gasket in water and place it over the thermostat, lining up the bolt holes.

14   Install the cover and fasteners. Tighten the fasteners to the torque listed in this Chapter's Specifications.

15   Reattach the hose to the fitting and tighten the hose clamp securely.

16   Refill the cooling system (see Chapter 1).

17   Start the engine and allow it to reach normal operating temperature, then check for leaks and proper thermostat operation (as described in Steps 2 through 4). See Chapter 1 for cooling system air-bleeding procedure.

4   Engine cooling fans and circuit - check and replacement

Warning: *To avoid possible injury or damage, DO NOT operate the engine with a damaged fan. Do not attempt to repair fan blades - replace a damaged fan with a new one.*

Note: *Always be sure to check for blown fuses before attempting to diagnose an electrical circuit problem.*

Check

Refer to illustrations 4.1a, 4.1b, 4.3, 4.4a and 4.4b

1   If the engine is overheating and the cooling fan is not coming on, unplug the electrical connector at the motor and use jumper wires to connect the fan directly to the battery. If the fan still doesn't work, replace the motor. test each motor separately. They are connected to an RFI module (Radio Frequency Interference), with the low-speed motor having a two-pin connector and a three-pin connector on the high-speed fan **(see illustrations)**.

4.3 The coolant temperature sensor (arrow) is located at the front of the engine, next to the thermostat

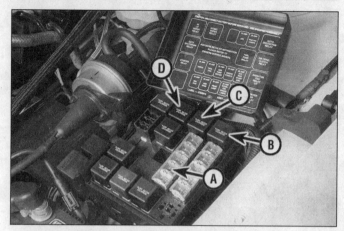

4.4a Location of cooling/air conditioning circuit components in the power distribution center:

A   40-amp radiator fan fuse
B   High speed fan relay
C   Low-speed fan relay
D   Air conditioning clutch relay

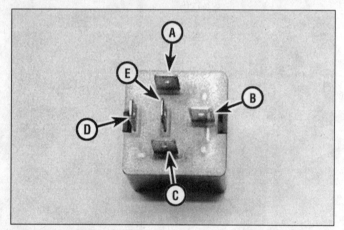

4.4b Pins on the fan relays - there should be continuity between A and C, and no continuity between D and B unless power is applied to A and ground applied to C

thermostat housing and varies resistance with temperature to signal the PCM **(see illustration)**. A test for checking the resistance values of the sensor is found in Chapter 6, Section 5.

4   Pull the fan relays (one low-speed and one high-speed relay) from the Power Distribution Center and test the relays for resistance between terminals A and C, which should read around 75 ohms. Check the pins for continuity **(see illustrations)**.

5   Carefully check all wiring and connections (wiring diagrams are included at the end of Chapter 12). If no obvious problems are found, further diagnosis should be done by a dealer service department or repair shop with a scan tool.

Fan replacement

Refer to illustrations 4.7a, 4.7b, 4.8a, 4.8b, 4.8c, 4.9a and 4.9b

6   Disconnect the negative battery cable, then unplug the electrical connector if you haven't already done so **(see illustration 4.1)**

7   Remove the upper radiator crossmember, either detaching the four bolts and laying it aside, or also removing the two bolts to the latch and removing the crossmember entirely **(see illustrations)**.

8   Remove the fan shroud mounting bolts, detach the clips at the top and bottom of the shroud with a small screwdriver, detach the wire harness clips from the shroud, then carefully lift the fan assembly out of the engine compartment **(see illustrations)**. **Note:** *It is easier to*

2   If the motor is OK, but the cooling fan doesn't come on when the engine gets hot, the fault may be in the coolant temperature sensor in the thermostat housing, the fan relays, the engine control computer or the wiring which connects the components.

3   The engine coolant temperature sensor is located in the

4.7a Remove the four bolts (arrows) on the upper radiator crossmember and lay it aside with the cable attached or . . .

4.7b . . . remove the two bolts at the latch (arrows) and remove the crossmember completely out of the way

4.8a Remove the four screws holding the fan assembly to the radiator - two are accessible from the top, two from the bottom

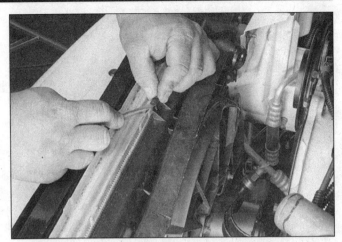

4.8b There are also two clips at the top of the radiator

4.8c Pull the fan assembly straight up and out

4.9a One fan blade is held on with a clip, the other with a nut (arrow)

remove the fan assembly if the upper radiator hose is disconnected first from the radiator.

9   To detach the fan blade from the motor, remove the clip from the motor shaft with a small screwdriver **(see illustration)**. If the fan blade is stuck on the shaft, apply a little penetrating oil to the end of the shaft and fan bushing, let it sit for awhile and try again. If the fan is still stuck, gently tap the tip of the shaft with a small hammer or rubber mallet. To detach the motor from the shroud, remove the retaining nuts or Torx screws **(see illustration)** and slide the motor out of the shroud.

10   Installation is the reverse of removal. **Note:** *When reinstalling the fan assembly, make sure the rubber air shields around the assembly are still in place - without them, the cooling system may not work efficiently.*

---

5   Radiator and de-aeration coolant tank - removal and installation

---

Warning: *Wait until the engine is completely cool before beginning this procedure.*

Radiator

Removal

Refer to illustrations 5.6, 5.7, 5.8 and 5.9

1   Disconnect the negative battery cable.

2   Drain the cooling system (see Chapter 1). If the coolant is

4.9b To remove the low-speed fan motor from the shroud, remove these three Torx socket screws (arrows) - the other motor has male Torx head screws

relatively new and in good condition, save it and reuse it.

3   Remove the upper radiator crossmember and cooling fan assembly (see Section 4). **Note:** *On some New Yorker models, a shield in front of the radiator will have to be removed, and the headlight assemblies removed for access (see Chapter 12).*

3

5.6 Detach the transmission cooler lines (arrows)

5.7 Remove the upper left (driver's side) mounting bolt (arrow) - right side similar

5.8 Location of the four condenser-to-radiator mounting screws (arrows)

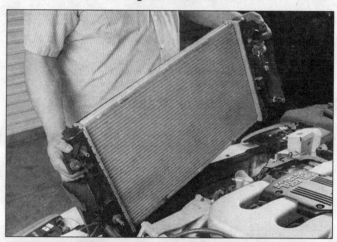

5.9 Carefully lift the radiator out of the engine compartment - it can be removed with the condenser either attached or left in the vehicle

5.17 Detach the hoses from the reservoir tank, and remove the three mounting bolts

4   Disconnect the overflow hose from the radiator filler neck.

5   Loosen the hose clamps, then detach the upper and lower coolant hoses from the radiator. If they're stuck, grasp each hose near the end with a pair of adjustable pliers and twist it to break the seal, then pull it off - be careful not to distort the radiator fittings! If the hoses are old or deteriorated, cut them off and install new ones.

6   Disconnect and plug the transmission fluid cooler lines **(see illustration)**.

7   Remove the two upper radiator-to-body mounting bolts **(see illustration)**. At this point, if the vehicle is equipped with air conditioning, there are two ways to remove the radiator. If the condenser is staying in the vehicle, remove the four condenser-to-radiator mounting screws (accessible through the lower openings in the front of the body) and the one screw in the air conditioning line clip on the passenger side, and the radiator can be pulled up. **Note:** *Make sure the rubber radiator insulators (they fit on the bottom of the radiator and into sockets in the body) remain in place in the body for proper reinstallation of the radiator.*

8   The alternative to Step 7 if the condenser is being removed (and the air conditioning system has already been evacuated of refrigerant) is to disconnect the condenser lines (see Section 15) and remove the radiator and condenser as a unit, separating the two components outside of the car where the fasteners are easier to get at **(see illustration)**. **Warning:** *The air conditioning system is under high pressure. Do not loosen any hose fittings or remove any components until after the system has been discharged by a dealer service department or service station. Always wear eye protection when disconnecting air conditioning system fittings.*

9   Carefully lift out the radiator. Don't spill coolant on the vehicle or

scratch the paint **(see illustration)**.

10   Check the radiator for leaks and damage. If it needs repair, have a radiator shop or dealer service department perform the work, as special techniques are required.

11   Remove bugs and dirt from the radiator with compressed air and a soft brush (don't bend the cooling fins).

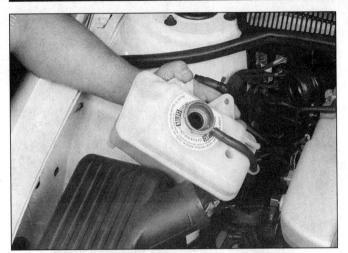

5.18 Remove the tank from the vehicle for cleaning or replacement

7.4 Remove the water pump pulley bolts - 3.3L engine

Installation

12 Inspect the radiator mounts for deterioration and make sure there's no dirt or gravel in them when the radiator is installed.
13 Installation is the reverse of the removal procedure. Make sure the radiator is properly seated on the lower mounting insulators before fastening the top brackets.
14 After installation, fill the cooling system with the proper mixture of antifreeze and water (see Chapter 1).
15 Start the engine and check for leaks. Allow the engine to reach normal operating temperature, indicated by the upper radiator hose becoming hot. Recheck the coolant level and add more if required.
16 If you're working on an automatic transmission equipped vehicle, check and add fluid as needed.

Coolant de-aeration/recovery tank

Refer to illustrations 5.17 and 5.18
17 Detach the hoses at the reservoir **(see illustration)**. Plug the hose to prevent leakage.
18 Remove the reservoir retaining bolts and lift the reservoir out of the engine compartment **(see illustration)**.
19 Installation is the reverse of removal. While the tank is off the vehicle, it should be cleaned with soapy water and a brush to remove any deposits inside.

6 Water pump - check

1 A failure in the water pump can cause serious engine damage due to overheating.
2 There are three ways to check the operation of the water pump while it's installed on the engine. If the pump is defective, it should be replaced with a new or rebuilt unit.
3 Water pumps are equipped with weep or vent holes. If a failure occurs in the pump seal, coolant will leak from the hole. In most cases you'll need a flashlight to find the hole on the water pump from underneath to check for leaks. **Note:** *Some small black staining around the weep hole is normal. If the stain is heavy brown or actual coolant is evident, replace the pump.*
4 If the water pump shaft bearings fail there may be a howling sound at the front of the engine while it's running. With the engine off, shaft wear can be felt if the water pump pulley is rocked up-and-down. Don't mistake drivebelt slippage, which causes a squealing sound, for water pump bearing failure.
5 A quick water pump performance check is to put the heater on. If the pump is failing, it won't be able to efficiently circulate hot water all the way to the heater core like it used to.

7 Water pump - replacement

Warning: *Wait until the engine is completely cool before beginning this procedure.*
1 Disconnect the negative battery cable from the battery.
2 Drain the cooling system (see Chapter 1). If the coolant is relatively new or in good condition, save and reuse it.

3.3L engines

Refer to illustrations 7.4 and 7.5
3 Remove the drivebelt (see Chapter 1).
4 Remove the water pump pulley bolts **(see illustration)**.
5 Remove the bolts and detach the water pump from the front cover **(see illustration)**.
6 Clean the bolt threads and the threaded holes in the front cover to remove any corrosion and sealant.
7 Remove the old O-ring and clean the mating surfaces. Be careful not to gouge or scratch the mating surfaces.
8 Apply a thin bead of RTV sealant to the mating surface of the water pump and install a new O-ring in the groove.
9 Install the new pump to the front cover and tighten the bolts to the torque listed in this Chapter's Specifications.
10 Reinstall the pulley and drivebelt and check the tension (see Chapter 1).
11 Refill the cooling system (see Chapter 1). Run the engine and check for leaks.

7.5 The water pump on 3.3L engines is retained by five bolts

7.13 Remove the timing belt tensioner (arrows to mounting bolts) and pull the belt from the water pump - 3.5L engine

7.14 Remove the water pump bolts - 3.5L engine

3.5L engines

Refer to illustrations 7.13, 7.14 and 7.15

12   The water pump on this engine is driven by the timing belt. Refer to Chapter 2, Part B for procedures to access the timing belt.

13   Remove the timing belt tensioner and pull the belt away from the water pump, leaving it in place on the other components **(see illustration)**. **Caution:** *Do not turn the crankshaft or camshafts while the belt is disconnected, or camshaft timing will be disturbed.*

14   Remove the water pump bolts and remove the pump from the engine **(see illustration)**.

15   Install the new pump with a new O-ring, wetting it with water for easier installation in the groove. Apply a thin coat of RTV sealant on the flange outside the O-ring and install the pump, tightening the bolts to this Chapter's Specifications **(see illustration)**.

16   Refer to Chapter 2, Part B for the procedures to reinstall the timing belt and timing belt tensioner.

17   Refill the cooling system and operate the engine to check for leaks.

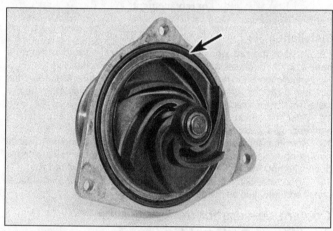

7.15 Ready the new 3.5L water pump for installation with a new O-ring (arrow) and a thin coat of sealant around the flange

8   Coolant temperature sending unit - check and replacement

Warning: *Wait until the engine is completely cool before beginning this procedure.*

Check

1   The coolant temperature indicator system is composed of a light or temperature gauge mounted in the dash and a coolant temperature sending unit mounted on the engine **(see illustration 4.3)**. In the models covered by this manual, there is only one coolant temperature sensor, which functions as indicator to both the PCM and the instrument panel.

2   If an overheating indication occurs, check the coolant level in the system and then make sure the wiring between the light or gauge and the sending unit is secure and all fuses are intact.

3   When the ignition switch is turned on and the starter motor is turning, the indicator light (if equipped) should be on (overheated engine indication).

4   If the light is not on, the bulb may be burned out, the ignition switch may be faulty or the circuit may be open.

5   As soon as the engine starts, the light should go out and remain out unless the engine overheats. Failure of the light to go out may be due to a grounded wire between the light and the sending unit, a defective sending unit or a faulty ignition switch. See Chapter 6, Section 5 for a diagnostic check of the coolant temperature switch. Check the coolant to make sure it's the proper type. **Note:** *Plain water may have too low a boiling point to activate the sending unit.*

Replacement

Warning: *Wait until the engine is completely cool before beginning this procedure.*

6   Disconnect the electrical connector from the sensor.

7   Wrap the threads of the new sensor with Teflon tape to prevent leaks.

8   Unscrew the sensor. Be prepared for some coolant spillage (read the Warning in Section 2).

9   Install the sensor and tighten it securely.

10   Connect the electrical connector.

11   Check the coolant level after the replacement unit has been installed and top up the system, if necessary (see Chapter 1). Check now for proper operation of the gauge and sending unit. Observe the system for leaks after operation.

9   Blower motor and circuit - check and replacement

Check

Refer to illustrations 9.2, 9.7a, 9.7b and 9.7c

1   Check the fuse and all connections in the circuit for looseness and corrosion. Make sure the battery is fully charged.

2   Remove the lower right dash insulator panel (below the glove box) for access to the blower motor **(see illustration)**. **Note:** *When reinstalling this panel, be sure the left end fits properly into its recess in the ducting.*

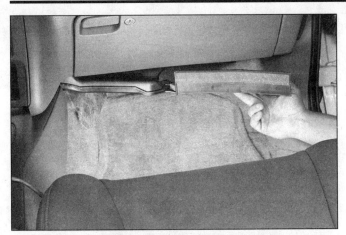

9.2 To access the blower motor or resistor, carefully pull down the lower right under-dash panel

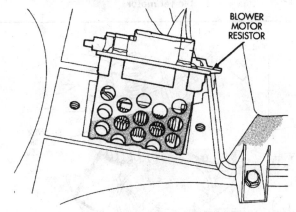

9.7b Blower motor resistor - manual air-conditioned models

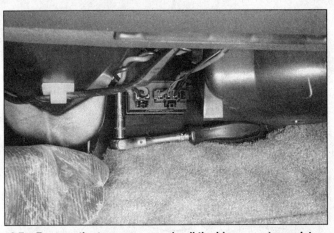

9.7a Remove the two screws and pull the blower motor resistor from the heater housing - shown with a socket on one of the screws - the twisted pair of wires are the ones going to the blower motor

9.7c Models with Automatic Temperature Control (ATC) have a 14-speed Blower Power Module instead of a conventional resistor

3   Backprobe the blower motor electrical connector with two small paper clips (straightened out) and connect a voltmeter to the blower motor connector and ground at the resistor **(see illustrations 9.7a through 9.7c).**

4   With the transmission in Park, the parking brake securely set, turn the ignition switch to the Run position. It isn't necessary to start the vehicle.

5   Move the blower switch through each of its positions and note the voltage readings. Changes in voltage indicate that the motor speeds will also vary as the switch is moved to the different positions.

6   If there is voltage present, but the blower motor does not operate, the blower motor is probably faulty. Disconnect the blower motor connector and hook one side to a chassis ground and the other to a fused source of battery voltage. If the blower doesn't operate, it is faulty.

7   If voltage wasn't present at the blower motor at all speeds, and the motor itself tested OK, the problem is in the switch, wiring or blower motor resistor. To replace the resistor, remove the two screws and pull the resistor from the heater housing **(see illustrations)**. **Note:** *Models with Automatic Temperature Control do not have a resistor. They are equipped with a Blower Power Module* **(see illustration)**, *which receives signals from the Body Control Module (computer) and regulates the blower at fourteen different speeds. The ATC system requires a factory scan tool to diagnose completely, however see Section 12 for the self-diagnosis procedures that do not require a factory scanning tool.*

Blower motor replacement

Refer to illustrations 9.10, 9.11a, 9.11b and 9.12

8   Disconnect the battery negative cable.

9   Detach the panel underneath the right end of the dash. It has four fasteners, all of them facing up - two screws in front (side toward the passenger seat) and two sheet metal nuts on the backside (toward the firewall).

10   Disconnect the wiring plug at the blower motor resistor and push the harness grommet through the blower motor cover **(see illustration)**.

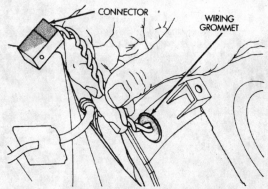

9.10 Disconnect the blower harness plug (twisted pair of wires) from the blower motor resistor and push the harness and grommet through the blower cover

3

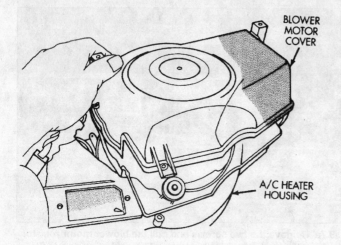

9.11a Remove the screws and remove the blower motor cover

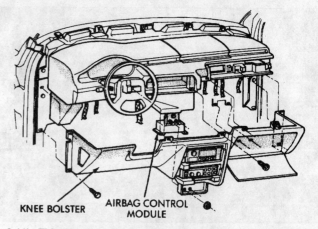

9.11b This drawing oversimplifies the procedure, but the full-width knee bolster must be removed for access to the blower motor

11   Remove the screws holding the blower motor cover **(see illustration)**. These screws are difficult to access without taking off the dashboard knee bolster (see Chapter 11), which is a long procedure **(see illustration)**. There are a lot of hidden fasteners to remove.
12   Remove the three screws and pull out the blower motor and fan assembly **(see illustration)**.
13   The fan is balanced with the blower motor, and is available only as an assembly. If the fan is damaged, both fan and blower motor must be replaced.
14   Installation is the reverse of removal.

10   Heater core - replacement

Refer to illustrations 10.2a, 10.2b, 10.12 and 10.13
Warning: *The air conditioning system is under high pressure. Do not loosen any hose fittings or remove any components until after the system has been discharged by a dealer service department or service station. Always wear eye protection when disconnecting air conditioning system fittings.*
Note: *Heater core removal on these models is a difficult undertaking for the home mechanic. It can be done, but requires discharging the air conditioning system, removing most of the dash, and disconnecting the passenger airbag system and a great many wiring connectors under the dash. The heater core and air conditioning evaporator are contained in a two-piece "box" which must be removed from under the*

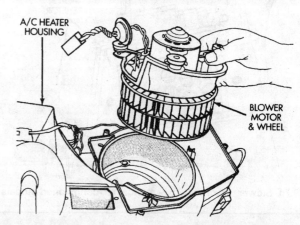

9.12 Remove three screws and pull down the blower motor and fan assembly

dash and separated into halves.
1   Have the air conditioning system discharged, drain the cooling system (see Chapter 1) and disconnect the battery.
2   Disconnect the heater hoses at the firewall and unbolt the air conditioning lines from the expansion valve **(see illustrations)**.
Caution: *Plug the air conditioning lines to prevent the entry of air into*

10.2a Disconnect the heater hoses at the firewall (arrow)

10.2b Unbolt the air conditioning lines (arrows) from the expansion valve

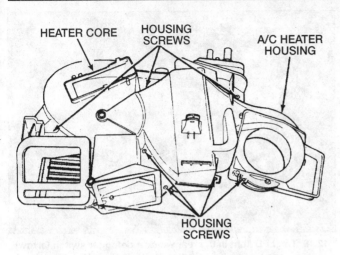

10.12 Heater/air conditioning housing and heater core location

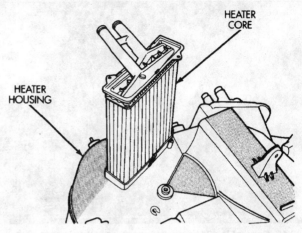

10.13 Remove the heater core retaining screws and pull the heater core from the housing

the system, since the lubricant absorbs air.

3   Remove the three nuts from the studs protruding through the firewall into the engine compartment.

4   Open the doors and pry the plastic end cap bezels from each side of the dashboard (see Chapter 11).

5   Remove the heater/air-conditioner control from the dash (see Section 11), the glove box, instrument panel and dash panels and the radio (see Chapter 11).

6   Remove the center console, if equipped (see Chapter 7), the steering column covers (see Chapter 11), and then drop the steering column down (see Chapter 10), but don't remove the column.

7   Disconnect the airbags (see Chapter 12).

8   Remove the left and right windshield pillar trim pieces and carefully pry up the dashboard top cover (along the base of the windshield).

9   Disconnect the DRB scan-tool connector (see Chapter 6) and the dashboard ground strap, then remove the five bolts holding the dashboard panel to the cowl and pull out the panel. There are also two screws in the door jambs that must be removed. **Note:** *The factory recommends that this is a two-person job.*

10   Disconnect the 60-way connector to the PCM, the ten-way connector to the body controller, and the electrical connector to the blower motor.

11   Remove the airbag module and brace, and the floor air ducts and

air ducts for the rear heat.

12   Remove the three bolts which hold the heater/air conditioning housing to the cowl, and roll the housing out and down to remove it **(see illustration).**

13   Remove the retaining screws and pull the heater core from the housing **(see illustration).**

14   Installation is the reverse of removal. Be sure to refill the cooling system (see Chapter 1) and recharge the air conditioning system (see Section 13). **Note:** *Since the heater core replacement is so difficult, it is recommended that once the housing is removed from the vehicle, the heater core should be replaced with a new unit, not repaired.*

11 Heater/air conditioner control assembly - removal and installation

Refer to illustrations 11.3 and 11.4

1   Disconnect the negative battery cable.

2   Remove the center bezel (see Chapter 11).

3   Remove the three control mounting screws **(see illustration).**

4   Pull the control assembly back, disconnect the two electrical connectors **(see illustration)**, then remove the control unit.

5   Installation is the reverse of removal.

11.3 To detach the heater/air conditioner control assembly from the dash, remove these three screws (arrows) . . .

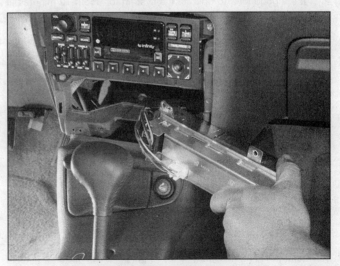

11.4 . . .then pull the unit out and disconnect the two electrical connectors

3

12.12 Cans of R-134A refrigerant are available in auto parts stores that can be added to your system with a simple recharging kit

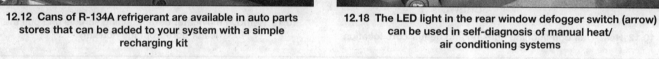

12.18 The LED light in the rear window defogger switch (arrow) can be used in self-diagnosis of manual heat/ air conditioning systems

12 Air conditioning and heating system - check and maintenance

Warning: *The air conditioning system is under high pressure. Do not loosen any hose fittings or remove any components until after the system has been discharged by a dealer service department or service station. Always wear eye protection when disconnecting air conditioning system fittings.*

1   The following maintenance checks should be performed on a regular basis to ensure the air conditioner continues to operate at peak efficiency.

a) *Check the compressor drivebelt. If it's worn or deteriorated, replace it* (see Chapter 1).

b) *Check the drivebelt tension and, if necessary, adjust it* (see Chapter 1).

c) *Check the system hoses. Look for cracks, bubbles, hard spots and deterioration. Inspect the hoses and all fittings for oil bubbles and seepage. If there's any evidence of wear, damage or leaks, replace the hose(s).*

d) *Inspect the condenser fins for leaves, bugs and other debris. Use a "fin comb" or compressed air to clean the condenser.*

e) *Make sure the system has the correct refrigerant charge.*

f) *Check the evaporator housing drain tube for blockage.*

2   It's a good idea to operate the system for about 10 minutes at least once a month, particularly during the winter. Long term non-use can cause hardening, and subsequent failure, of the seals.

3   Because of the complexity of the air conditioning system and the special equipment necessary to service it, in-depth troubleshooting and repairs are not included in this manual (refer to the *Haynes Automotive Heating and Air Conditioning Repair Manual*). However, simple checks and component replacement procedures are provided in this Chapter.

4   The most common cause of poor cooling is simply a low system refrigerant charge. If a noticeable drop in cool air output occurs, the following quick check will help you determine if the refrigerant level is low.

Checking the refrigerant charge

5   Warm the engine up to normal operating temperature.

6   Place the air conditioning temperature selector at the coldest setting and the blower at the highest setting. Open the doors (to make sure the air conditioning system doesn't cycle off as soon as it cools the passenger compartment).

7   With the compressor engaged - the clutch will make an audible click and the center of the clutch will rotate. If the compressor discharge line feels warm and the compressor inlet pipe feels cool, the

system is properly charged.

8   Place a thermometer in the dashboard vent nearest the evaporator and add refrigerant to the system until the indicated temperature is around 40 to 45 degrees F. If the ambient (outside) air temperature is very high, say 110 degrees F, the duct air temperature may be as high as 60 degrees F, but generally the air conditioning is 30-50 degrees F cooler than the ambient air. **Note:** *Humidity of the ambient air also affects the cooling capacity of the system. Higher ambient humidity lowers the effectiveness of the air conditioning system.*

Adding refrigerant

Refer to illustration 12.12

9   Buy an automotive charging kit at an auto parts store. A charging kit includes a 14-ounce can of refrigerant, a tap valve and a short section of hose that can be attached between the tap valve and the system low side service valve. Because one can of refrigerant may not be sufficient to bring the system charge up to the proper level, it's a good idea to buy a couple of additional cans. Make sure that one of the cans contains red refrigerant dye. If the system is leaking, the red dye will leak out with the refrigerant and help you pinpoint the location of the leak. **Caution:** *There are two types of refrigerant, R-12, used on vehicles up to 1992, and the more environmentally-friendly R-134a used in all the models covered by this book. These two refrigerants (and their appropriate refrigerant oils) are not compatible and must never be mixed or components will be damaged. Use only R-134a refrigerant in the models covered by this book.* **Warning:** *Never add more than two cans of refrigerant to the system.*

10   Hook up the charging kit by following the manufacturer's instructions. **Warning:** *DO NOT hook the charging kit hose to the system high side! The fittings on the charging kit are designed to fit* **only** *on the low side of the system.*

11   Back off the valve handle on the charging kit and screw the kit onto the refrigerant can, making sure first that the O-ring or rubber seal inside the threaded portion of the kit is in place. **Warning:** *Wear protective eyewear when dealing with pressurized refrigerant cans.*

12   Remove the dust cap from the low-side charging connection and attach the quick-connect fitting on the kit hose **(see illustration)**.

13   Warm up the engine and turn on the air conditioner. Keep the charging kit hose away from the fan and other moving parts. **Note:** *The charging process requires the compressor to be running. Your compressor may cycle off if the pressure is low due to a low charge. If the clutch cycles off, you can pull the low-pressure cycling switch plug and attach a jumper wire. This will keep the compressor ON.*

14   Turn the valve handle on the kit until the stem pierces the can, then back the handle out to release the refrigerant. You should be able to hear the rush of gas. Add refrigerant to the low side of the system

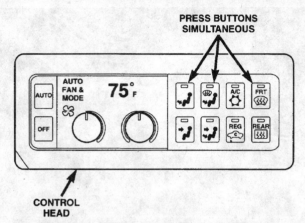

PRESS BUTTONS SIMULTANEOUS

CONTROL HEAD

12.31 With ATC systems, set the display for 75 degrees and depress these three buttons until the display blinks

23 . . . . .   ATC blend door feedback control
24 . . . . .   ATC mode door feedback failure
25 . . . . .   Ambient temperature sensor
26 . . . . .   ATC in-car sensor
27 . . . . .   Sun sensor failure
31 . . . . .   ATC recirculation door stall failure
32 . . . . .   ATC blend door stall failure
33 . . . . .   ATC mode door stall failure
34 . . . . .   Engine temperature message not received
35 . . . . .   Evaporator temperature sensor failure
36 . . . . .   ATC head communication failure

12.32 ATC system trouble codes

until both the receiver-drier surface and the evaporator inlet pipe feel about the same temperature . Allow stabilization time between each addition.

15   If you have an accurate thermometer, you can place it in the center air conditioning duct inside the vehicle and keep track of the "conditioned" air temperature. A charged system that is working properly should put out air that is 40 degrees F. If the ambient (outside) air temperature is very high, say 110 degrees F, the duct air temperature may be as high as 60 degrees F, but generally the air conditioning is 30-50 degrees F cooler than the ambient air.

16   When the can is empty, turn the valve handle to the closed position and release the connection from the low-side port. Replace the dust cap.

17   Remove the charging kit from the can and store the kit for future use with the piercing valve in the UP position, to prevent inadvertently piercing the can on the next use.

Self-diagnostic checks
Manual heat/air conditioning
Refer to illustration 12.18

18   On manual (non-ATC) systems, the LED light on the rear-window defogger will display some diagnostic codes by blinking **(see illustration)**.

19   To begin the diagnostic mode, run the vehicle at idle with the controls set as follows: the blower speed knob should be on any position other than OFF, the temperature knob should be in full COOL, and the right knob should be in the DEFROST mode.

20   To enter the diagnostic mode, press the defogger switch in for five seconds, until it begins to blink, then release it. It will continue to blink for about 30 seconds while it calibrates. If the light goes out, calibration is OK, and you can skip to Step 14.

21   If the light stayed on, switch the mode knob to the MIX position. If the light still remains on there a problem with the control head.

22   Switch the mode knob to the FLOOR position; if the light stays on, it indicates a problem in the blend door or the blend door actuator wiring.

23   Move the knob to the Bi-Level position, where a continuing light indicates a problem with the mode actuator or circuit.

24   Position the knob in the MIX mode. The LED should now flash twice then pause, and continue a two-flash sequence, indicating that the MIX mode is OK.

25   In the FLOOR mode, the light should flash in threes, meaning that the FLOOR mode is OK.

26   In the Bi-Level mode, a four-flash sequence indicates that mode is OK.

27   In the PANEL mode, the light should flash five times to indicate no problems there, and in the Recirculate-Panel mode six times, and seven times in the Recirculate Bi-Level mode.

28   The temperature control can be checked by switching the mode

knob to Defrost and rotating the temperature knob. If the temperature control is OK, the light will flash faster the more you turn the temperature knob up, until the light goes out at the hottest setting.

29   Switch the knob between Panel and Recirculate-Panel and watch the recirculation door. Proper operation means that circuit and components are OK.

30   To get out of the self-diagnostic mode, turn off the blower or push the air conditioning button once.

Automatic Temperature Control (ATC)
Refer to illustrations 12.31, 12.32 and 12.35

31   To use the diagnostic mode on Automatic Temperature Control models, have the engine idling and set the temperature on the panel to 75 degrees and push in and hold the Floor, Mix and Defrost buttons all at the same time until the display section blinks, then release the buttons **(see illustration)**.

32   The control display will continue to blink, and then show two-digit trouble codes, if any are present. The codes range from 23 to 36 **(see illustration)**.

33   Only one code can be displayed at a time, but pressing and releasing the Panel button will display the next code, if present.

34   If there is a code indicating the problem is with the in-car ambient temperature sensor, test the sensor's fan by turning on the system and placing a small section of a tissue over the marquee nameplate above the glovebox. behind the nameplate is the sensor, which incorporates a small fan that circulates interior air past the sensor. If the tissue stays in place over the name-plate (which acts as a grille over the sensor), the fan is working.

35   If the tissue won't stay in place, the fan is not running, and the sensor/fan assembly needs to be replaced. Remove the dash end cap (see Chapter 11) for access to one screw holding the right dash bezel in place, then pry out the bezel **(see illustration)** for access to the sensor.

3

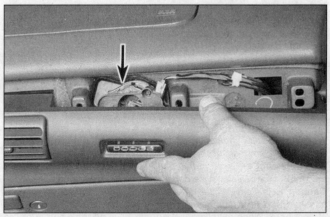

12.35 Remove the right dash bezel for access to the in-car ambient temperature sensor (arrow)

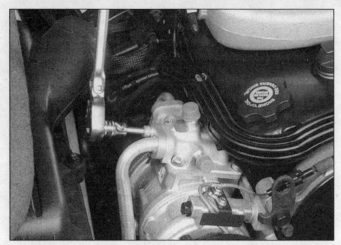

13.5 Remove the socket-head bolts and pull off and plug the refrigerant lines at the compressor

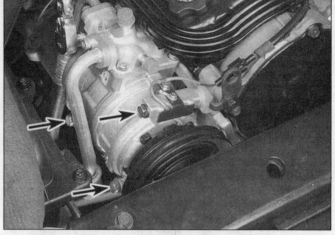

13.6 Remove these bolts (arrows) to take the compressor from its mounting bracket

13 Air conditioning compressor - removal and installation

Refer to illustrations 13.5 and 13.6

Warning: *The air conditioning system is under high pressure. DO NOT disassemble any part of the system (hoses, compressor, line fittings, etc.) until after the system has been evacuated and the refrigerant recovered by a dealer service department or air conditioning service station.*

Note: *The filter-drier/receiver-drier (see Section 14) should be replaced whenever the compressor is replaced.*

1   Have the system discharged (see Warning above).
2   Disconnect the negative cable from the battery.
3   Unplug the electrical connector from the compressor clutch. On some models, the connector is on the compressor clutch; on others, it's at the end of a short lead **(see illustration 13.5)**.
4   Remove the drivebelt (see Chapter 1).
5   Disconnect the refrigerant lines from the compressor **(see illustration)**. Plug the open fittings to prevent entry of dirt and moisture.
6   Unbolt the compressor from the mounting bracket **(see illustration)** and lift it out of the vehicle.
7   If a new compressor is being installed, pour out the oil from the old compressor into a graduated container and add that amount of new refrigerant oil to the new compressor. Also follow any directions included with the new compressor.
8   The clutch may have to be transferred from the original to the new compressor.
9   Installation is the reverse of removal. Replace all O-rings with new ones specifically made for use with R-134a refrigerant and lubricate them with R-134a-compatible refrigerant oil.
10   Have the system evacuated, recharged and leak tested by the shop that discharged it.

14 Air conditioning receiver-drier - removal and installation

Refer to illustration 14.4

Warning: *The air conditioning system is under high pressure. DO NOT disassemble any part of the system (hose, compressor, line fittings, etc.) until after the system has been evacuated and the refrigerant recovered by a dealer service department or service station.*

Caution: *Replacement filter-drier/receiver-drier units are so effective at absorbing moisture that they can quickly saturate upon exposure to the atmosphere. When installing a new unit, have all tools and supplies ready for quick reassembly to avoid having the system open any longer than necessary.*

14.4 Use two wrenches when disconnecting the receiver-drier fitting (arrow) from the condenser

1   The receiver-drier acts as a reservoir for the system refrigerant. It's located on the right side of the engine compartment, next to the radiator and condenser **(see illustration 13.4a)**.
2   Have the system discharged (see the Warning at the beginning of this Section).
3   Disconnect the cable from the negative terminal of the battery.
4   Disconnect the refrigerant lines from the receiver-drier **(see illustration)**. Use a back-up wrench to prevent twisting the tubing where it joins the condenser. The other line requires using a quick-disconnect-fitting tool to uncouple it, see Section 15 for use of the tool.
5   Plug the open fittings to prevent entry of dirt and moisture.
6   Remove the top condenser-mounting bolt and the screw from the aluminum line support above the receiver/drier, spread the aluminum clamp and remove the receiver/drier.
7   Installation is the reverse of removal. If a new receiver-drier is being installed add one ounce of refrigerant oil to it before installation.
8   Take the vehicle back to the shop that discharged it. Have the system evacuated, recharged and leak tested.

15 Air conditioning condenser - removal and installation

Warning: *The air conditioning system is under high pressure. DO NOT disassemble any part of the system (hoses, compressor, line fittings, etc.) until after the system has been evacuated and the refrigerant recovered by a dealer service department or service station.*

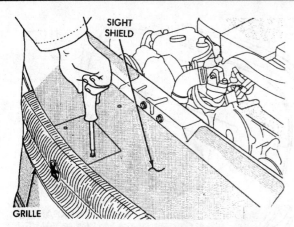

15.3 Remove this sight shield, if equipped (New Yorker/LHS models)

15.11a Disconnect the refrigerant lines (arrows) from the condenser and receiver/drier

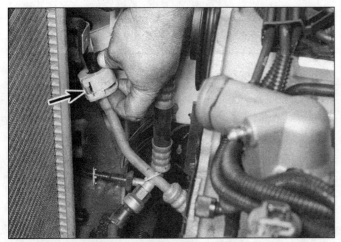

15.11b Slip the proper size quick-disconnect tool (arrow) over the line connections - this pulls the spring back and allows the two slip-fit, O-ringed tubes to be pulled apart

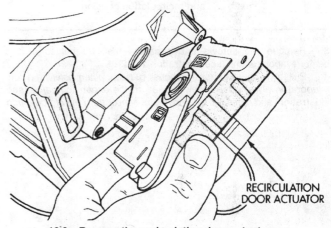

16.2a Remove the recirculation door actuator . . .

Note: *The receiver-drier should be replaced whenever the condenser is replaced* (see Section 14).

1   Have the system discharged (see Warning above).
2   Disconnect the negative battery cable.

New Yorker and LHS models

Refer to illustration 15.3

3   Remove the sight-shield ahead of the radiator **(see illustration)** and the right and left headlight modules (see Chapter 12).
4   Disconnect the refrigerant lines from the condenser **(see illustrations 15.11a and 15.11b)**.
5   Remove the left and right headlight modules (see Chapter 12).
6   Drain the cooling system and remove the fan assembly and radiator (refer to Sections 4 and 5) with the condenser attached, then remove the four screws to separate the condenser from the radiator **(see illustration 4.8)**. Plug the open ends of the condenser and the disconnected refrigerant lines to prevent entry of dirt or moisture.
7   Inspect the rubber insulator pads (on the lower crossmember) on which the radiator sits. Replace them if they're dried or cracked.
8   If the original condenser will be reinstalled, store it with the line fittings on top to prevent oil from draining out. If a new condenser is being installed, pour one ounce of R-134a-compatible refrigerant oil into it prior to installation.
9   Reinstall the components in the reverse order of removal. Be sure the rubber pads are in place under the condenser.
10   Have the system evacuated, recharged and leak tested by the shop that discharged it.

Concorde, Intrepid, Vision models

Refer to illustrations 15.11a and 15.11b

11   Disconnect and plug the air conditioning lines at the condenser. The lower fitting at the right side of the condenser is accessed through one of the air-holes in the front bumper cover **(see illustrations)**.
12   Remove the four screws holding the condenser to the radiator, two are accessed from above, between the radiator and the grille area, and two are accessed through the lower openings in the front bumper cover **(see illustration 4.8)**. Remove the condenser.
13   Reinstall the components in the reverse order of removal.
14   Have the system evacuated, recharged and leak tested by the shop that discharged it.

16   Air conditioning evaporator and expansion valve - removal and installation

Refer to illustrations 16.2a, 16.2b and 16.4
Warning: *The air conditioning system is under high pressure. DO NOT disassemble any part of the system (hoses, compressor, line fittings, etc.) until after the system has been evacuated and the refrigerant recovered by a dealer service department or service station.*
1   Remove the heater and air conditioning unit assembly (see Section 10).
2   Remove the recirculating door actuator and housing **(see illustrations)**.

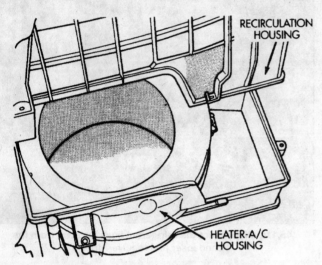

RECIRCULATION
HOUSING

HEATER-A/C
HOUSING

16.2b . . . and recirculation housing

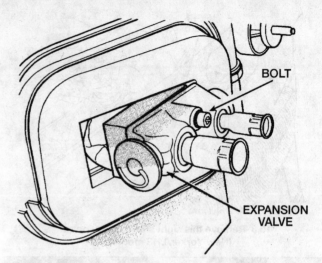

BOLT

EXPANSION
VALVE

**16.4 Remove the two bolts (one shown here) holding the
expansion valve to the evaporator and replace the gasket**

3   Remove the screws and separate the two halves of the
heater/evaporator unit **(see illustration 10.12)**.
4   Pull the evaporator from the housing. **Note:** *When installing a new
evaporator, always use a new gasket on the expansion valve* **(see
illustration)** *and reinstall the temperature sensor from the old core into*

the new core before installation.
5   Installation is the reverse of removal. If a new evaporator is being
installed, pour one ounce of new, R-134a-compatible refrigerant oil
into it prior to installation.

Chapter 4
Fuel and exhaust systems

Contents

Specifications

General

Fuel pressure
  3.3L engine
    With regulator vacuum hose attached .... 46 psi
    With regulator vacuum hose disconnected .... 55 psi
  3.5L engine
    With regulator vacuum hose attached .... 39 psi
    With regulator vacuum hose disconnected .... 48 psi
Fuel injector resistance .... 12.4 ohms

Torque specifications

	Ft-lbs (unless otherwise indicated)
Air intake plenum bolts	250 in-lbs
Throttle body mounting nuts	19
Throttle linkage locknut (3.5L engine)	36 in-lbs
Fuel rail mounting bolts	
3.3L engine	200 in-lbs
3.5L engine	100 in-lbs

1   General information

Refer to illustration 1.6

General

The vehicles covered by this manual are equipped with a Sequential Multi Port Fuel Injection (MPFI) system. This system uses timed impulses to sequentially inject the fuel directly into the intake ports of each cylinder. The injectors are controlled by the Powertrain Control Module (PCM). The PCM monitors various engine parameters and delivers the exact amount of fuel, in the correct sequence, into the intake ports.

All models are equipped with an electric fuel pump, mounted in the fuel tank. It is necessary to remove the fuel tank for access to the fuel pump. The fuel level sending unit is an integral component of the fuel pump and it must be removed from the fuel tank in the same manner.

The exhaust system consists of exhaust manifolds, a catalytic converter, an exhaust pipe and a muffler. Each of these components is replaceable. For further information regarding the catalytic converter, refer to Chapter 6.

Flexible Fuel Vehicles (FFV)

A certain percentage of the Chrysler LH models are equipped with the Flexible Fuel system. These Flexible Fuel Vehicles (FFV) are designed to accept methanol fuel mixture as well as 100 percent unleaded fuel mixture. The methanol fuel mixture can be as high as 85 percent methanol and 15 percent gasoline. Pure methanol (100 percent) should be avoided as it's properties make cold starting below 50 degrees Fahrenheit very difficult.

Servicing FFV vehicles and fuel injection components is identical with gasoline system components, but there are other precautions the home mechanic must realize. Methanol is more toxic than gasoline. Before servicing the fuel system release fuel system pressure and wear METHANOL-RESISTANT gloves and eye protection to avoid contact. Avoid breathing methanol vapors and do not ingest methanol because it will cause sickness and even death. Methanol vapors are extremely flammable and can collect along the ground. Be sure to work in a well ventilated area. Use only factory designed replacement parts or damage to the system will occur. Here is a list of the fuel injection system components that have been specially designed for FFV's.

> Fuel pump module and fuel level sending unit
> Fuel gauge
> Fuel tank
> Fuel pressure regulator
> Fuel rail
> Fuel injectors and O-rings
> Fuel inlet pipes
> Fuel filter
> Fuel filler cap
> Fuel pressure relief rollover valve

The fuel injection system can adapt to the different fuel mixtures because of a specially designed sensor. The Methanol Concentration Sensor detects the type of fuel that has been added to the fuel tank, analyzes it content and signals the PCM to adjust the working parameters of the fuel system **(see illustration)**. This sensor's output voltage will vary with the percent of methanol in the fuel mixture. The sensor output ranges from 0.5 volts for pure methanol to 4.75 volts for the 85/15 percent methanol/gasoline mixture. The methanol sensor is attached to the fuel tank on the driver's side.

2   Fuel pressure relief procedure

Refer to illustrations 2.2a, 2.2b and 2.3

Warning: *Gasoline is extremely flammable, so take extra precautions when you work on any part of the fuel system. Don't smoke or allow open flames or bare light bulbs near the work area, and don't work in a garage where a natural gas-type appliance (such as a water heater or a*

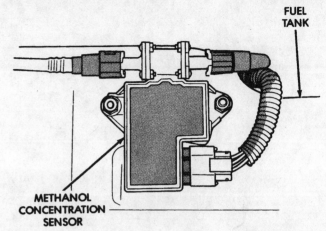

1.6 The Methanol Concentration Sensor is attached to the right side of the fuel tank

clothes dryer) with a pilot light is present. Since gasoline is carcinogenic, wear latex gloves when there's a possibility of being exposed to fuel, and, if you spill any fuel on your skin, rinse it off immediately with soap and water. Mop up any spills immediately and do not store fuel-soaked rags where they could ignite. The fuel system is under constant pressure, so, if any fuel lines are to be disconnected, the fuel pressure in the system must be relieved first. When you perform any kind of work on the fuel system, wear safety glasses and have a Class B type fire extinguisher on hand.

1   Detach the cable from the negative battery terminal. Unscrew the fuel filler cap to relieve pressure built up in the fuel tank.

2   Remove the cap from the fuel pressure test port located on the fuel rail **(see illustrations)**.

3   Use one of the two following methods:

a) *Attach a fuel pressure gauge (special tool no. J 34730-1) or equivalent to the Schrader valve on the fuel rail **(see illustration)**. Place the gauge bleeder hose in an approved fuel container. Open the valve on the gauge to relieve pressure, then disconnect the cable from the negative terminal of the battery.*

b) *Locate the fuel pressure test port and carefully place several shop towels around the test port and the fuel rail. Remove the cap and using the tip of a screwdriver, depress the Schrader valve and let the fuel drain into the shop towels. Be careful to catch any fuel that might spray upward by using another shop towel.*

4   Unless this procedure is followed before servicing fuel lines or connections, fuel spray (and possible injury) may occur.

5   Install the cap onto the fuel pressure test port.

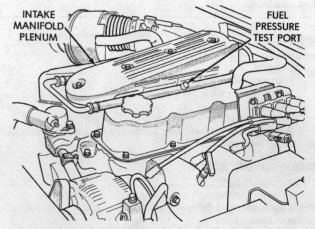

2.2a Location of the fuel pressure test port on the 3.3L engine

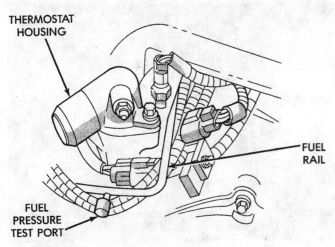

2.2b Location of the fuel pressure test port on the 3.5L engine

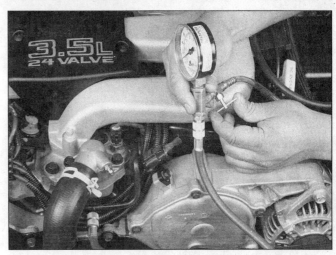

2.3 Install a fuel pressure gauge to the fuel rail at the test port and use the valve to bleed off the excess fuel into a suitable container

3 Fuel pump/fuel pressure - check

Refer to illustration 3.2

Warning: *Gasoline is extremely flammable, so take extra precautions when you work on any part of the fuel system. Don't smoke or allow open flames or bare light bulbs near the work area, and don't work in a garage where a natural gas-type appliance (such as a water heater or a clothes dryer) with a pilot light is present. Since gasoline is carcinogenic, wear latex gloves when there's a possibility of being exposed to fuel, and, if you spill any fuel on your skin, rinse it off immediately with soap and water. Mop up any spills immediately and do not store fuel-soaked rags where they could ignite. The fuel system is under constant pressure, so, if any fuel lines are to be disconnected, the fuel pressure in the system must be relieved first (see Section 2 for more information). When you perform any kind of work on the fuel system, wear safety glasses and have a Class B type fire extinguisher on hand.*

Preliminary check

Note: *On all models, the fuel pump is located inside the fuel tank (see Section 5).*

1   If you suspect insufficient fuel delivery, first inspect all fuel lines to ensure that the problem is not simply a leak in a line.

2   Set the parking brake and have an assistant turn the ignition switch to the ON position while you listen to the fuel pump (inside the fuel tank). You should hear a "whirring" sound, lasting for a couple of seconds. Start the engine. The whirring sound should now be continuous (although harder to hear with the engine running). If there is

no sound, either the fuel pump fuse **(see illustration)**, fuel pump, fuel pump relay, ASD relay or related circuits are defective (proceed to Step 16).

Pressure check

Refer to illustrations 3.4a and 3.4b

3   Relieve the fuel pressure (see Section 2).

4   Remove the cap from the fuel pressure test port located on the fuel rail and attach a fuel pressure gauge **(see illustrations)**.

5   Start the engine and check the pressure on the gauge, comparing your reading with the pressure listed in this Chapter's Specifications. Now, detach the vacuum hose from the fuel pressure regulator. With the engine idling, measure the fuel pressure. It should be as listed in this Chapter's Specifications. Reconnect the vacuum hose.

6   If the fuel pressure is not within specifications, check the following:

a) *If the pressure is within specifications when the vacuum hose is connected to the pressure regulator but does not increase when the vacuum hose is disconnected, check for vacuum at the hose. If there is vacuum present, replace the pressure regulator (see Section 14). If there is no vacuum, check the hose for a break or an obstruction.*

b) *If the pressure is higher than specified, check for a pinched or clogged fuel return hose or pipe. If the return line is not obstructed, replace the fuel pressure regulator (see Section 14).*

4

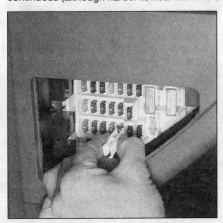

3.2 First check to make sure the fuel pump fuse is not blown (3.5L engine shown)

3.4a Install the fuel pressure gauge to the fuel rail and observe the fuel pressure with the engine idling (3.3L engine shown)

3.4b Fuel pressure test set-up on the 3.5L engine

3.8a Install a vacuum pump to the fuel pressure regulator and check for fuel pressure without vacuum applied . . .

3.8b . . . next, apply vacuum and check the fuel pressure - the fuel pressure should decrease as the vacuum is applied

c) If the pressure is lower than specified:
   1) Inspect the fuel filter - make sure it's not clogged (see Chapter 1).
   2) Look for a pinched or clogged fuel hose between the fuel tank and the fuel rail.
   3) Check the pressure regulator for a malfunction (see below).
   4) Look for leaks in the fuel line.

7   If there are no problems with any of the above-listed components, check the fuel pump (see below).

Component checks

Fuel pressure regulator
Refer to illustrations 3.8a and 3.8b

8   Connect a vacuum pump to the fuel pressure regulator **(see illustrations)**. Read the fuel pressure gauge without vacuum applied to the fuel pressure regulator and also with vacuum applied. The fuel pressure should decrease as vacuum increases. Compare your readings with the values listed in this Chapter's Specifications.

9   Reconnect the vacuum hose to the regulator and check the fuel pressure at idle, comparing your reading with the value listed in this Chapter's Specifications. Disconnect the hose and watch the gauge - the pressure should jump up to the maximum specified pressure as soon as the hose is disconnected. If the pressure at idle was too high (with the hose disconnected), connect a vacuum gauge to the hose and check for vacuum.

10   If the fuel pressure is LOW, pinch the fuel return line shut and watch the gauge. If the pressure doesn't rise, the fuel pump is defective or there is a restriction in the fuel feed line. If the pressure rises sharply, replace the fuel pressure regulator (see Section 14). **Note:** *It will be necessary to fabricate special rubber fuel lines to be installed between the fuel rail and the fuel return line. The braided metal lines cannot be collapsed for testing purposes.*

11   If the indicated fuel pressure is too high, disconnect the fuel return line and blow through it to check for blockage. If there is no blockage, replace the fuel pressure regulator (see Section 14).

Fuel pump
Refer to illustration 3.15

12   If you suspect a problem with the fuel pump, verify the pump actually runs. Have an assistant turn the ignition switch to ON - you should hear a brief "whirring" noise as the pump comes on and pressurizes the system. Have the assistant start the engine. This time you should hear a constant whirring sound from the pump (but it's more difficult to hear with the engine running).

13   If the pump does not come on (makes no sound), proceed to the next step.

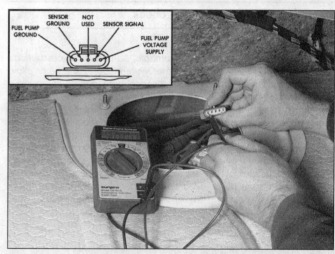

3.15 Check for battery voltage to the fuel pump at the fuel pump connector. Power will be delivered for only two seconds through the fuel pump relay so watch carefully when the assistant turns the ignition key on

14   Remove the trunk liner and fuel pump access cover (see Section 5). Disconnect the electrical connector from the fuel pump.

15   Working on the harness side of the fuel pump electrical connector, check for battery voltage to the fuel pump with the ignition key ON (engine not running) **(see illustration)**. Battery voltage should be present. Also check for continuity to ground on the fuel pump ground circuit. If voltage is available, the ground is good and the fuel pump doesn't run when connected, replace the fuel pump (see Section 5). If no voltage is available, check the main relays (see below).

Main relays
Refer to illustrations 3.17, 3.19 and 3.20
Note: *The Automatic Shutdown (ASD) relay and the fuel pump relay must both be tested to insure proper fuel pump operation. Testing procedures for the ASD relay and the fuel pump relay are identical.*

16   To test a relay, first remove it from its location in the engine compartment Power Distribution Center.

17   Remove the relay from the connector and verify that there is battery voltage (ignition switch ON) at the connector **(see illustration)**.

18   If there is no voltage, check the fuel pump fuse. If voltage is not present at the fuse, check the fuel pump circuit (see Wiring Diagrams at the end of Chapter 12).

3.17 Locate the fuel pump relay in the Power Distribution Center and check for battery voltage to the relay

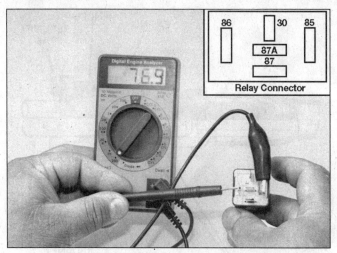

3.19 Check the resistance between terminals number 86 and number 85. It should be approximately 75 ohms

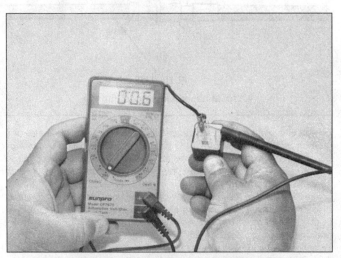

3.20 Also check for continuity between terminals number 87A and 30. Continuity should exist

19   Using an ohmmeter, connect the positive probe (+) onto terminal number 86 and the negative probe (-) onto terminal number 85 and check the resistance. There should be approximately 75 ohms resistance **(see illustration)**.

20   Using an ohmmeter, connect the positive probe (+) onto terminal number 30 and the negative probe (-) onto terminal number 87A and check for continuity. Continuity should be present **(see illustration)**.

21   Using an ohmmeter, connect the positive probe (+) onto terminal number 30 and the negative probe (-) onto terminal number 87 and check for continuity. There should be no continuity.

22   Connect battery voltage to the no. 86 terminal, ground the number 85 terminal and verify there's continuity between the number 87 and number 30 terminals. If there isn't, replace the relay.

---

4   Fuel lines and fittings - repair and replacement

Warning: *Gasoline is extremely flammable, so take extra precautions when you work on any part of the fuel system. Don't smoke or allow open flames or bare light bulbs near the work area, and don't work in a garage where a natural gas-type appliance (such as a water heater or a clothes dryer) with a pilot light is present. Since gasoline is carcinogenic, wear latex gloves when there's a possibility of being exposed to*

fuel, and, if you spill any fuel on your skin, rinse it off immediately with soap and water. Mop up any spills immediately and do not store fuel-soaked rags where they could ignite. The fuel system is under constant pressure, so, if any fuel lines are to be disconnected, the fuel pressure in the system must be relieved first (see Section 2 for more information). When you perform any kind of work on the fuel system, wear safety glasses and have a Class B type fire extinguisher on hand.

1   Always relieve the fuel pressure before servicing fuel lines or fittings (see Section 2).

2   The fuel feed, return and vapor lines extend from the fuel tank to the engine compartment. The lines are secured to the underbody with clip and screw assemblies. These lines must be occasionally inspected for leaks, kinks and dents.

3   If evidence of dirt is found in the system or fuel filter during disassembly, the line should be disconnected and blown out. Check the fuel strainer on the fuel gauge sending unit (see Section 6) for damage and deterioration.

Steel tubing

4   If replacement of a fuel line or emission line is called for, use tubes/hoses meeting Chrysler specification or its equivalent.

5   Don't use copper or aluminum tubing to replace steel tubing. These materials cannot withstand normal vehicle vibration.

6   Because fuel lines used on fuel-injected vehicles are under high pressure, they require special consideration.

7   Some fuel lines have threaded fittings with O-rings. Any time the fittings are loosened to service or replace components:

 a) *Use a backup wrench while loosening and tightening the fittings.*
 b) *Check all O-rings for cuts, cracks and deterioration. Replace any that appear hardened, worn or damaged.*
 c) *If the lines are replaced, always use original equipment parts, or parts that meet the original equipment standards specified in this Section.*

Flexible hose

Warning: *Use only original equipment replacement hoses or their equivalent. Others may fail from the high pressures of this system.*

8   Don't route fuel hose within four inches of any part of the exhaust system or within ten inches of the catalytic converter. Metal lines and rubber hoses must never be allowed to chafe against the frame. A minimum of 1/4-inch clearance must be maintained around a line or hose to prevent contact with the frame.

Removal and installation

Refer to illustrations 4.11a, 4.11b and 4.11c

9   Relieve the fuel pressure.

10   Remove all fasteners attaching the lines to the vehicle body.

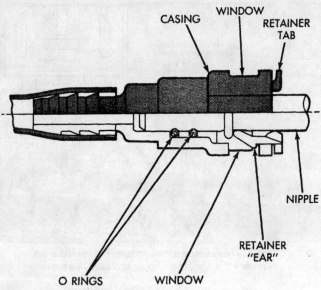

**4.11a Cross-sectional view of a two-tab quick
connect fuel line fitting**

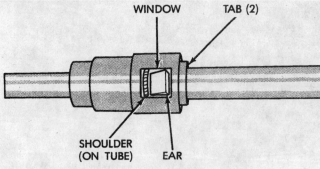

**4.11b Plastic tab type quick connect fitting with
a window style body**

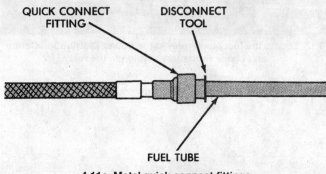

4.11c Metal quick connect fittings

11   There are various methods depending upon the type of quick-disconnect fitting on the fuel line **(see illustrations)**. Carefully remove the fuel lines from the chassis. **Caution:** *The plastic ring type fittings are not serviced separately. Do not attempt to service these types of fuel lines in the event the clip or line becomes damaged. Replace the entire fuel line as an assembly.*

12   Installation is the reverse of removal. Be sure to use new O-rings at the threaded fittings (if equipped).

Repair

13   In the event of any fuel line damage (metal or flexible lines) it is necessary to replace the damaged lines with factory replacement parts. Others may fail from the high pressures of this system.

5   Fuel pump - removal and installation

Refer to illustrations 5.3a, 5.3b, 5.4, 5.5, 5.6, 5.7, 5.8, 5.9, 5.10 and 5.11

Warning: *Gasoline is extremely flammable, so take extra precautions when you work on any part of the fuel system. Don't smoke or allow open flames or bare light bulbs near the work area, and don't work in a*

garage where a natural gas-type appliance (such as a water heater or a clothes dryer) with a pilot light is present. Since gasoline is carcinogenic, wear latex gloves when there's a possibility of being exposed to fuel, and, if you spill any fuel on your skin, rinse it off immediately with soap and water. Mop up any spills immediately and do not store fuel-soaked rags where they could ignite. The fuel system is under constant pressure, so, if any fuel lines are to be disconnected, the fuel pressure in the system must be relieved first (see Section 2) for more information). When you perform any kind of work on the fuel system, wear safety glasses and have a Class B type fire extinguisher on hand.*

1   Detach the cable from the negative battery terminal.

2   Relieve the fuel system pressure (see Section 2).

3   Remove the trunk liner (carpet) **(see illustrations)**.

4   Remove the nuts from the fuel pump access cover **(see illustration)** and lift the cover from the trunk.

5   Remove the fuel lines from the inlet and return pipe connectors

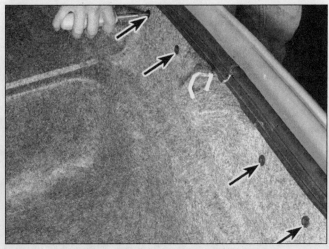

**5.3a Remove the screws (arrows) that retain the
trunk carpet to the body**

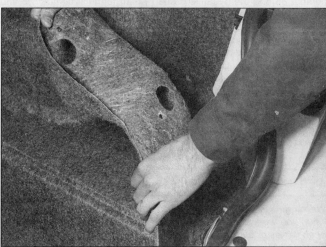

5.3b Lift the trunk liner (carpet) from the trunk

5.4 Remove the access cover mounting nuts (arrows)

5.5 Pinch the tabs on the fuel lines and remove them from the fuel pump module

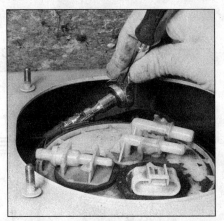

5.6 Remove the clamp from the perimeter of the fuel pump module

5.7 Lift the fuel pump module from the trunk

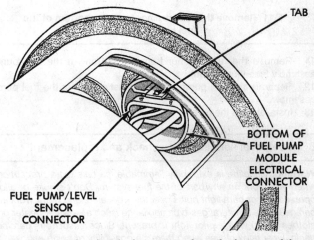

5.8 Remove the electrical connector from the bottom of the sending unit connector

(see illustration). Remove the fuel vent line.
6   Remove the clamp from the perimeter of the fuel pump module **(see illustration)**.
7   Remove the fuel pump/fuel level sending unit from the tank **(see illustration)**.
8   Press the retaining tab and remove the electrical connector from the bottom of the connector assembly **(see illustration)**.
9   Remove the wire retaining clip from the electrical connector **(see**

illustration).
10   Note the wire colors and terminal designations for the fuel level sending unit **(see illustration)**. Carefully remove each wire from the electrical connector. This will separate the fuel level sending unit from the fuel pump electrical harness. **Note:** *This step will require a very small screwdriver or special electrical tool to depress the terminal release clip in the connector body.*

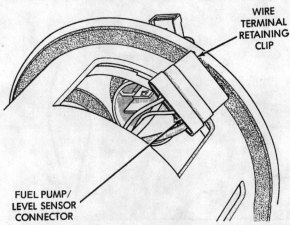

5.9 Pull the connector through the module window and remove the wire terminal retaining clip

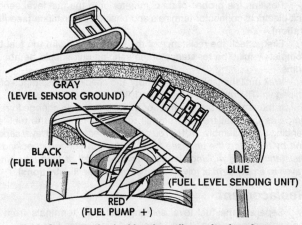

5.10 Separate the fuel level sending unit wires from the fuel pump connector

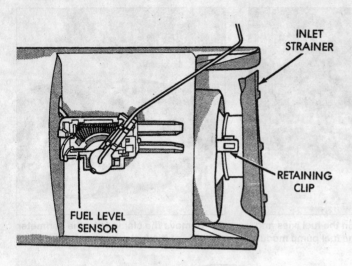

5.11 Remove the fuel strainer from the bottom of the fuel pump module

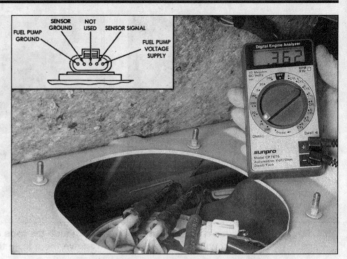

6.2 Working in the trunk area, disconnect the fuel pump/fuel level sending unit assembly connector and check the resistance of the fuel level sending unit by probing the correct wire terminals

11   Remove the fuel strainer from the bottom of the fuel pump assembly **(see illustration)**.
12   Separate the fuel pump from the plastic body of the fuel pump assembly.
13   Installation is the reverse of removal.

6   Fuel level sending unit - check and replacement

Warning: *Gasoline is extremely flammable, so take extra precautions when you work on any part of the fuel system. Don't smoke or allow open flames or bare light bulbs near the work area, and don't work in a garage where a natural gas-type appliance (such as a water heater or a clothes dryer) with a pilot light is present. Since gasoline is carcinogenic, wear latex gloves when there's a possibility of being exposed to fuel, and, if you spill any fuel on your skin, rinse it off immediately with soap and water. Mop up any spills immediately and do not store fuel-soaked rags where they could ignite. The fuel system is under constant pressure, so, if any fuel lines are to be disconnected, the fuel pressure in the system must be relieved first (see Section 2 for more information). When you perform any kind of work on the fuel system, wear safety glasses and have a Class B type fire extinguisher on hand.*

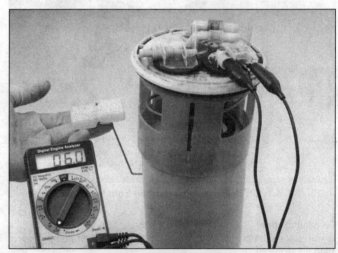

6.5a Measure the resistance of the fuel level sending unit with the float raised (full tank) . . .

Check

Refer to illustrations 6.2, 6.5a, 6.5b, 6.7, 6.8 and 6.10
1   Remove the trunk liner (carpet) (see Section 5).
2   Position the probes of an ohmmeter onto the fuel level sending unit electrical connector terminals and check for resistance **(see illustration)**.
3   First, check the resistance of the sending unit with the fuel tank completely full. The resistance of the sending unit should be about 6 ohms.
4   Wait until the tank is nearly empty and check the resistance of the unit again. The resistance should be 1,035 ohms.
5   If the readings are incorrect or there is very little change in resistance as the float travels from full to empty, replace the fuel level sending unit assembly. **Note:** *You can also check the fuel level sending unit by removing the unit (see Steps 6 through 10) and checking the resistance while moving the float from full (arm at highest point of travel) to empty (arm at lowest point of travel* **(see illustrations)***.*

Replacement

6   Separate the fuel level sending unit wire terminals from the module connector (see Steps 1 through 10 in Section 5).
7   Insert a screwdriver between the fuel pump module and the top of

6.5b . . . and then with the float lowered (empty tank)

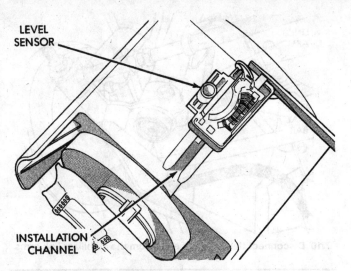

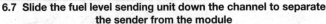

6.7 Slide the fuel level sending unit down the channel to separate the sender from the module

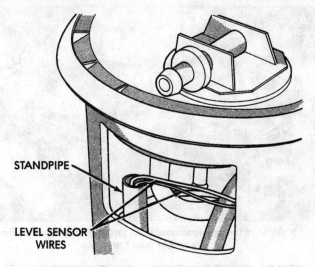

6.8 Insert the wires through the standpipe

the fuel level sending unit **(see illustration)**. Push the sending unit down slightly to separate it from the module.

8   Slide the fuel level sensor wires through the standpipe inside the fuel pump module assembly **(see illustration)**.

9   Lift the fuel level sending unit from the assembly.

10   Installation is the reverse of removal. Feed the wires into the standpipe and slide the fuel level sensor up into the channel until it snaps into place. Ensure that the tab at the bottom of the sensor locks into place **(see illustration)**.

7   Fuel tank - removal and installation

Refer to illustrations 7.6, 7.8, 7.10, 7.11a and 7.11b

Warning: *Gasoline is extremely flammable, so take extra precautions when you work on any part of the fuel system. Don't smoke or allow open flames or bare light bulbs near the work area, and don't work in a garage where a natural gas-type appliance (such as a water heater or a clothes dryer) with a pilot light is present. Since gasoline is carcinogenic, wear latex gloves when there's a possibility of being exposed to fuel, and, if you spill any fuel on your skin, rinse it off immediately with*

soap and water. Mop up any spills immediately and do not store fuel-soaked rags where they could ignite. The fuel system is under constant pressure, so, if any fuel lines are to be disconnected, the fuel pressure in the system must be relieved first (see Section 2 for more information). When you perform any kind of work on the fuel system, wear safety glasses and have a Class B type fire extinguisher on hand.

Note: *The following procedure is much easier to perform if the fuel tank is empty. Some tanks have a drain plug for this purpose. If the tank does not have a drain plug, the fuel can be siphoned from the tank using a siphoning kit, available at most auto parts stores. NEVER start the siphoning action with your mouth!*

1   Remove the fuel tank filler cap to relieve fuel tank pressure.

2   Relieve the fuel system pressure (see Section 2).

3   Detach the cable from the negative terminal of the battery.

4   Siphon the fuel into an approved gasoline container, using a siphoning kit (available at most auto parts stores).

5   Remove the exhaust pipe from the rubber hangers on the frame rail at the rear of the vehicle and in front of the fuel tank.

6   Remove the fuel inlet and vent hose clamps and remove the hoses from the vehicle **(see illustration)**.

7   Disconnect the fuel lines from the fuel filter (see Chapter 1).

4

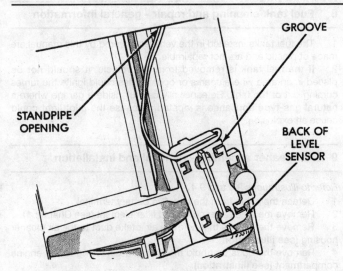

6.10 Slide the sending unit up into the channel until it snaps into place

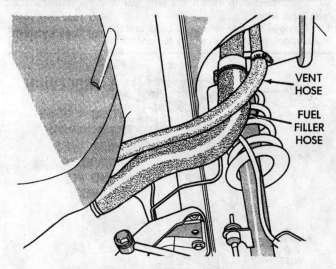

7.6 Remove the fuel filler hose and vent hose

7.8 Remove the crossmember bolts (arrows) and separate the crossmember from the frame

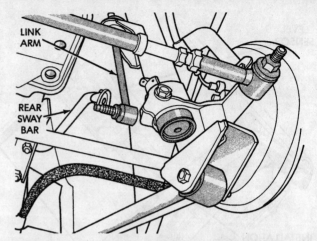

7.10 Disconnect the sway bar ends from the stabilizer link arms

7.11a Remove the fuel tank strap bolts (arrows) and separate the tank strap from the frame

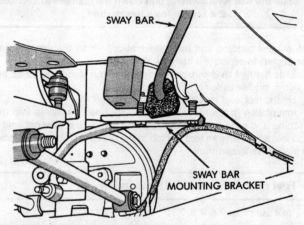

7.11b Hold the sway bar in place with the mounting brackets

8   Carefully mark the position of the crossmember in relation to the frame using a grease pencil or white paint. Remove the crossmember mounting bolts and lower the crossmember **(see illustration)**.

9   Support the fuel tank with a floor jack. Position a piece of wood between the jack head and the fuel tank to protect the tank.

10   Disconnect both ends of the sway bar from the stabilizer links **(see illustration)**. .

11   Remove the fuel tank strap bolts and the fuel tank strap **(see illustration)**. It will be necessary to reinstall the sway bar mounting

brackets to prevent the sway bar from falling down **(see illustration)**.

12   Remove the tank from the vehicle.

13   Installation is the reverse of removal.

8   Fuel tank cleaning and repair - general information

1   The fuel tanks installed in the vehicles covered by this manual are made of plastic and are not repairable.

2   If the fuel tank is removed from the vehicle, it should not be placed in an area where sparks or open flames could ignite the fumes coming out of the tank. Be especially careful inside a garage where a natural gas-type appliance is located, because the pilot light could cause an explosion.

9   Air cleaner assembly - removal and installation

Refer to illustrations 9.3 and 9.4

1   Detach the cable from the negative battery terminal.

2   Remove the air cleaner cover and filter element (see Chapter 1).

3   Remove the clamps that hold the air intake duct to the air cleaner housing **(see illustration)**.

4   Remove the bolts that hold the air cleaner housing to the engine compartment **(see illustration)**.

5   Lift the assembly up and detach it from the fresh air intake duct, then remove it from the engine compartment.

6   Installation is the reverse of removal.

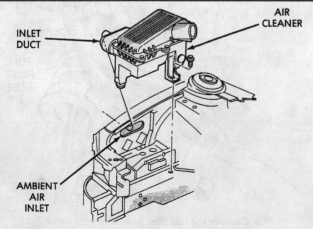

9.3 Air cleaner housing installation details

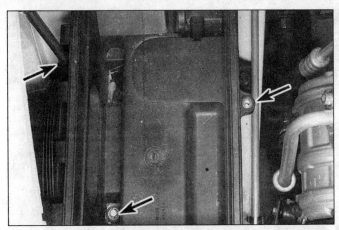

9.4 Remove the bolts (arrows) and lift the air cleaner housing from the vehicle

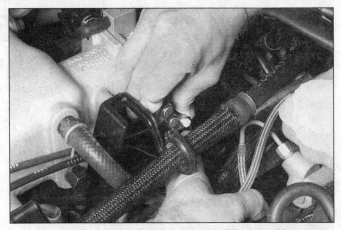

10.2 Rotate the throttle lever and slide the cable end out of the recess

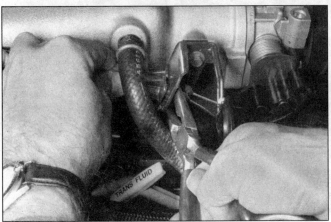

10.3 Use needlenose pliers to depress the tabs, disconnecting the cable from the bracket

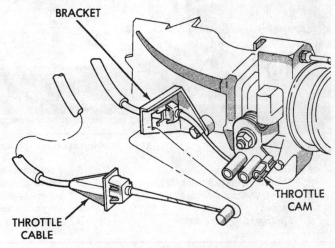

10.4a Accelerator cable details on the 3.3L engine

10 Accelerator cable - replacement

Refer to illustrations 10.2, 10.3, 10.4a, 10.4b and 10.5

1   Detach the cable from the negative battery terminal.
2   Rotate the throttle lever and separate the cable end from the slotted portion of the throttle lever (see illustration).
3   Using needlenose pliers, squeeze the tabs on the housing

and release the accelerator cable retainer from the bracket (see illustration).
4   Separate the accelerator cable from the throttle body assembly (see illustrations).
5   Working underneath the dash, detach the cable from the accelerator pedal (see illustration).
6   Pull the grommet from the firewall and pull the cable through the firewall from the engine compartment side.
7   Installation is the reverse of removal.

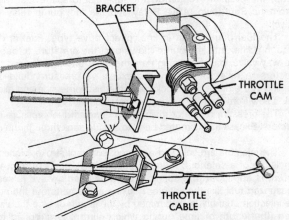

10.4b Accelerator cable details on the 3.5L engine

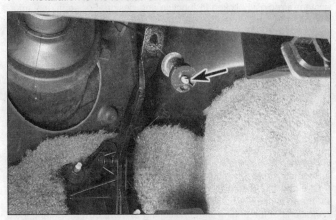

10.5 Pull the accelerator cable out of the grommet and slide the cable through the slot (arrow) in the grommet

4

11.1a Fuel injection component locations on the 3.3L V6 engine

1	Throttle body	
2	Throttle Position Sensor (TPS)	
3	Manifold Absolute Pressure (MAP) sensor	
4	Fuel pressure regulator	
5	Fuel pressure test port	
6	Power distribution center	
7	Air intake plenum	
8	Engine coolant temperature sensor	
9	Fuel injector	
10	Idle Air Control (IAC) valve	
11	Powertrain Control Module (PCM) (under air cleaner housing)	
12	Air cleaner housing	

11 Fuel injection system - general information

Refer to illustrations 11.1a and 11.1b

The Sequential Electronic Fuel Injection (SEFI) system consists of three sub-systems: air intake, electronic control and fuel delivery. The system uses a Powertrain Control Module (PCM) along with the sensors (coolant temperature sensor, Throttle Position Sensor (TPS), Manifold Absolute Pressure (MAP) sensor, oxygen sensor, etc.) to determine the proper air/fuel ratio under all operating conditions **(see illustrations)**.

The fuel injection system and the emissions and engine control system are closely linked in function and design. For additional information, refer to Chapter 6.

Air intake system

The air intake system consists of the air cleaner, the air intake ducts, the throttle body, the idle control system, the air intake plenum and the intake manifold.

A throttle position sensor is attached to the throttle shaft to monitor changes in the throttle opening. On models equipped with the 3.3L engine, the MAP sensor is attached to the rear of the air intake plenum while on the 3.5L, the MAP sensor is attached to the side of the air intake plenum

When the engine is idling, the air/fuel ratio is controlled by the idle air control system, which consists of the Powertrain Control Module (PCM) and the Idle Air Control (IAC) valve. The IAC valve is controlled by the PCM and is opened and closed depending upon the running conditions of the engine (air conditioning system, power steering, cold and warm running etc.). This valve regulates the amount of airflow past the throttle plate and into the intake manifold, thus increasing or

decreasing the engine idle speed. The PCM receives information from the sensors (vehicle speed, coolant temperature, air conditioning, power steering mode etc.) and adjusts the idle according to the demands of the engine and driver.

Electronic emissions and engine control system

The electronic emissions and engine control system is explained in detail in Chapter 6.

Fuel delivery system

The fuel delivery system consists of these components: The fuel pump, the pressure regulator, the fuel injectors, the fuel rail, the Automatic Shutdown (ASD) Relay and the fuel pump relay (main relays).

The fuel pump is an in-line, direct drive type. Fuel is drawn through a filter into the pump, flows past the armature through the one-way valve, passes through another filter and is delivered to the injectors. A relief valve prevents excessive pressure build-up by opening in the event of a blockage in the discharge side and allowing fuel to flow from the high to the low pressure side.

The pressure regulator maintains a constant fuel pressure to the injectors. Excess fuel is routed back to the fuel tank through the return line.

The injectors are solenoid-actuated, constant stroke, pintle types consisting of a solenoid, plunger, needle valve and housing. When current is applied to the solenoid coil, the needle valve raises and pressurized fuel fills the injector housing and squirts out the nozzle. The injection quantity is determined by the length of time the valve is open (the length of time during which current is supplied to the solenoid coils).

Because it determines opening and closing intervals, which in

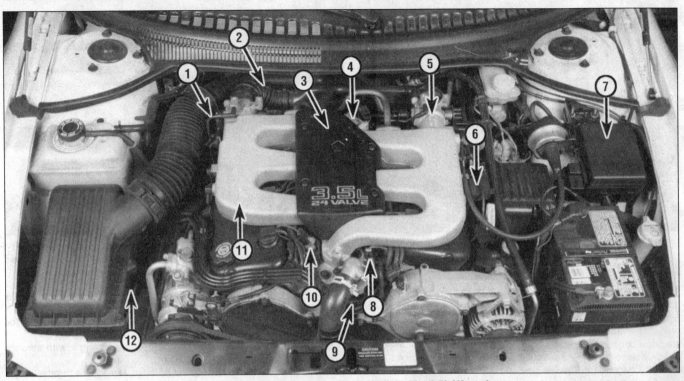

11.1b Fuel injection component locations on the 3.5L V6 engine

1   Throttle Position Sensor (TPS) (attached to throttle body)
2   Air intake duct
3   Air temperature sensor (under plenum)
4   Idle Air Control (IAC) valve
5   Throttle body (left side)
6   Manifold Absolute Pressure (MAP) sensor

7   Power distribution center
8   Coolant temperature sensor
9   Fuel pressure test port
10 Fuel injector
11 Air intake plenum
12 Powertrain Control Module (PCM) (under air cleaner housing)

turn, determines the air-fuel mixture ratio - injector timing must be quite accurate. To attain the best possible injector response, the current rise time, when voltage is being applied to each injector coil, must be as short as possible.

The Automatic Shutdown (ASD) relay and the fuel pump relay are contained within Power Distribution Center, which is located in the left side of the engine compartment. The ASD relay connects battery voltage to the fuel injectors and the ignition coil while the fuel pump relay connects battery voltage only to the fuel pump. If the PCM senses there is NO signal from the camshaft or crankshaft sensors

while the ignition key is RUN or cranking, the PCM will de-energize both relays.

12   Fuel injection system - check

Refer to illustrations 12.7, 12.8 and 12.9

Note: *The following procedure is based on the assumption that the fuel pressure is adequate (see Section 3).*

1   Check all wiring harness connectors that are related to the system. Check the ground wire connections on the intake manifold for tightness. Loose connectors and poor grounds can cause many problems that resemble more serious malfunctions.
2   Check to see that the battery is fully charged, as the control unit and sensors depend on an accurate supply voltage in order to properly meter the fuel.
3   Check the air filter element - a dirty or partially blocked filter will severely impede performance and economy (see Chapter 1).
4   If a blown fuse is found, replace it and see if it blows again. If it does, search for a grounded wire in the harness to the fuel pump.
5   Check the air intake duct to the intake manifold for leaks, which will result in an excessively lean mixture. Also check the condition of all vacuum hoses connected to the intake manifold.
6   Remove the air intake duct from the throttle body and check for dirt, carbon or other residue build-up. If it's dirty, clean it with aerosol carburetor cleaner and a toothbrush.
7   With the engine running, place an automotive stethoscope against each injector, one at a time, and listen for a clicking sound, indicating operation **(see illustration)**. If you don't have a stethoscope, place the tip of a screwdriver against the injector and listen through the handle.

12.7 Use a stethoscope to determine if the injectors are working properly - they should make a steady clicking sound that rises and falls with engine speed changes

4

12.8 Measure the resistance of each injector. It should be approximately 12 ohms

12.9 Install the "noid" light (available at most auto parts stores) into each injector electrical connector and confirm that it blinks when the engine is cranking or running

8   Unplug the injector electrical connectors and test the resistance of each injector **(see illustration)**. Compare the values to the Specifications listed in this Chapter.

9   Install an injector test light ("noid" light) into each injector electrical connector, one at a time **(see illustration)**. Crank the engine over. Observe that the light flashes evenly on each connector. This will test for voltage to the injector.

10   The remainder of the system checks can be found in the following Sections.

13   Throttle body - check, removal and installation

Check

Refer to illustration 13.1

1   On top of the throttle body, locate the vacuum hose that goes to the purge control solenoid. Detach it from the throttle body and attach a vacuum gauge in its place **(see illustration)**.

2   Start the engine and warm it to its normal operating temperature (wait until the cooling fan comes on twice). Verify the gauge indicates no vacuum.

3   Open the throttle slightly from idle and verify that the gauge indicates vacuum. If the gauge indicates no vacuum, check the port to make sure it is not clogged. Clean it with aerosol carburetor cleaner if necessary.

4   Stop the engine and verify the accelerator cable and throttle valve operate smoothly without binding or sticking.

5   If the accelerator cable or throttle valve binds or sticks, check for a build-up of sludge on the cable or throttle shaft.

6   If a build-up of sludge is evident, try removing it with aerosol carburetor cleaner or a similar solvent.

7   If cleaning fails to remedy the problem, replace the throttle body.

Removal and installation

Refer to illustration 13.13

Warning: *Wait until the engine is completely cool before beginning this procedure.*

3.3L engine

8   Detach the cable from the negative battery terminal.

9   Remove the air duct that connects the air cleaner assembly to the throttle body.

10   Unplug the throttle position sensor connector from the throttle body. Also label and detach all vacuum hoses from the throttle body.

11   Detach the accelerator cable (see Section 10) and, if equipped, the transmission throttle valve cable (see Chapter 7B).

12   Detach the coolant hoses from the throttle body. Plug the lines to prevent coolant loss.

13   Unscrew the two mounting bolts/nuts and remove the throttle body and gasket **(see illustration)**. Remove all traces of old gasket material from the throttle body and intake manifold.

13.1 Remove the hose that connects the throttle body to the purge control solenoid and attach a vacuum gauge (3.5L engine shown)

13.13 Remove the two bolts (arrows) and separate the throttle body from the intake manifold (3.3L engine shown)

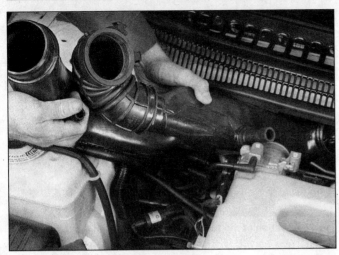

13.17 Remove the dual throttle body air intake duct

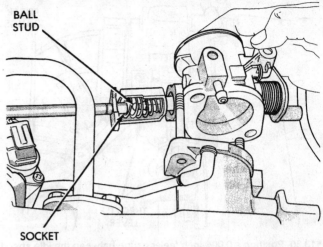

BALL STUD

SOCKET

13.19 Remove the left throttle body from the air intake plenum and separate it from the synchonization shaft

14   Installation is the reverse of removal. Be sure to use a new gasket. Adjust the accelerator cable (see Section 10) and, if equipped, the throttle valve cable (see Chapter 7). Check the coolant level and add some, if necessary (see Chapter 1).

3.5L engine
Refer to illustrations 13.17, 13.19 and 13.26

Left throttle body
15   Detach the cable from the negative battery terminal.
16   Hold the throttle lever in wide open position and remove the throttle cable and cruise control cables from the throttle lever (see Section 10).
17   Remove the air intake duct that is attached to both throttle bodies **(see illustration)**.
18   Disconnect the purge hose and PCV hose from the throttle body.
19   Unscrew the mounting nuts and remove the throttle body and gasket. Carefully separate the throttle body from the synchronization shaft **(see illustration)**.
20   Remove all traces of old gasket material from the throttle body and air intake plenum.
21   Installation is the reverse of removal. Be sure to use a new gasket. Adjust the accelerator cable (see Section 10) and, if equipped, the throttle valve cable (see Chapter 7). **Note:** *Be sure to check the throttle body synchronization after the throttle body has been installed (see Steps 29 through 32).*

Right throttle body
22   Detach the cable from the negative battery terminal.
23   Remove the air intake duct that is attached to both throttle bodies **(see illustration 13.17)**.
24   Disconnect the purge hose from the throttle body.
25   Disconnect the electrical connector from the TPS (see Chapter 6).
26   Unscrew the mounting nuts and remove the throttle body and gasket. Carefully separate the throttle body from the synchronization shaft. Be careful to separate the tang on the end of the throttle shaft from the throttle linkage without bending or damaging the alignment **(see illustration)**.
27   Remove all traces of old gasket material from the throttle body and air intake plenum.
28   Installation is the reverse of removal. Be sure to use a new gasket. Adjust the accelerator cable (see Section 10) and, if equipped, the throttle valve cable (see Chapter 7B). **Note:** *Be sure to check the throttle body synchronization after the throttle body has been installed (see Steps 29 through 32).*

Throttle body synchronization (3.5L engine)
Refer to illustrations 13.29 and 13.30
29   The throttle bodies must be synchronized in the event there is a gap between the adjustment screw and the linkage lever **(see illustration)**. This adjustment must be checked after the throttle bodies have been removed or repaired.

4

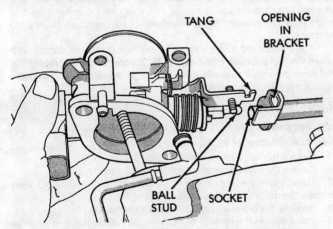

TANG   OPENING IN BRACKET

BALL STUD   SOCKET

13.26 Remove the right throttle body from the air intake plenum and separate it from the synchonization shaft

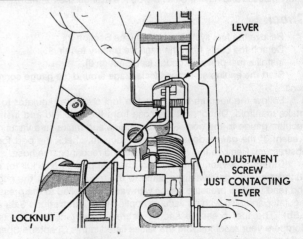

LEVER

ADJUSTMENT SCREW JUST CONTACTING LEVER

LOCKNUT

13.29 Check the gap between the linkage lever and the adjusting screw

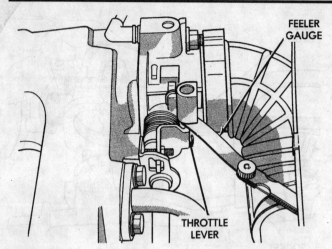

13.30 Position a 0.004-inch feeler gauge between the idle speed screw and the throttle body

14.12 Location of the fuel pressure regulator on the 3.3L engine

30   Position a 0.004-inch feeler gauge between the idle speed screw and the right throttle body **(see illustration)**.
31   Loosen the adjustment screw locknut on the synchronization shaft **(see illustration 13.29)**. Turn the adjustment screw until it just touches the lever on the synchronization shaft. Tighten the locknut to the torque listed in this Chapter's Specifications.
32   Check the clearance between the throttle lever and the idle speed screw. The 0.004-inch feeler gauge should now "drag" slightly when it is being removed. A 0.006-inch feeler gauge should not fit between the throttle lever and the idle speed screw.

14   Fuel pressure regulator - check and replacement

Warning: *Gasoline is extremely flammable, so take extra precautions when you work on any part of the fuel system. Don't smoke or allow open flames or bare light bulbs near the work area, and don't work in a garage where a natural gas-type appliance (such as a water heater or a clothes dryer) with a pilot light is present. Since gasoline is carcinogenic, wear latex gloves when there's a possibility of being exposed to fuel, and, if you spill any fuel on your skin, rinse it off immediately with soap and water. Mop up any spills immediately and do not store fuel-soaked rags where they could ignite. The fuel system is under constant pressure, so, if any fuel lines are to be disconnected, the fuel pressure in the system must be relieved first (see Section 2 for more information). When you perform any kind of work on the fuel system, wear safety glasses and have a Class B type fire extinguisher on hand.*

Check

1   Relieve the fuel system pressure (see Section 2).
2   Detach the cable from the negative battery terminal.
3   Install a fuel pressure gauge (see Section 3).
4   Start the engine and check for leakage around the gauge connections.
5   Follow the vacuum hose from the fuel pressure regulator to the intake manifold. Disconnect the hose from the manifold and install a vacuum gauge to the port. Start the engine and make sure vacuum is present. If the gauge doesn't indicate vacuum, check the port for an obstruction. Remove the vacuum gauge and reconnect the hose.
6   Detach the vacuum hose from the fuel pressure regulator and connect a hand-held vacuum pump to the regulator. Start the engine and read the fuel pressure gauge with vacuum applied to the pressure regulator and also with no vacuum applied **(see illustrations 3.8a and 3.8b)**. The fuel pressure should decrease as vacuum increases. Compare your readings with the values listed in this Chapter's Specifications.
7   Reconnect the vacuum hose to the regulator and check the fuel pressure at idle, comparing your reading with the value listed in this

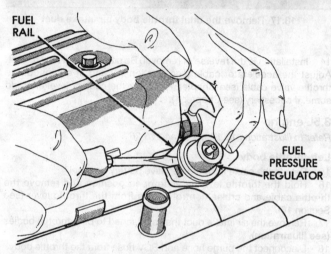

14.13 Carefully pry the fuel pressure regulator from the fuel rail using a flat bladed screwdriver

Chapter's Specifications. Disconnect the vacuum hose and watch the gauge - the pressure should jump up to the maximum specified pressure as soon as the hose is disconnected. If the pressure doesn't fluctuate, replace the fuel pressure regulator.
8   If the fuel pressure is low, pinch the fuel return line shut and watch the gauge. If the pressure doesn't rise, the fuel pump is defective or there is a restriction in the fuel feed line. If the pressure rises sharply, replace the pressure regulator. **Note:** *It will be necessary to fabricate special rubber fuel lines to be installed between the fuel rail and the fuel return line. The braided metal lines cannot be collapsed for testing purposes.*
9   If the indicated fuel pressure is too high, stop the engine and relieve the fuel pressure (see Section 2). Disconnect the fuel return line and blow through it to check for a blockage. If there is no blockage, replace the fuel pressure regulator.

Replacement

3.3L engine

Refer to illustrations 14.12, 14.13 and 14.14

10   Relieve the fuel system pressure (see Section 2).
11   Detach the cable from the negative battery terminal.
12   Detach the vacuum hose from the pressure regulator, then unscrew the mounting bolt **(see illustration)**.
13   Remove the pressure regulator **(see illustration)**.
14   Installation is the reverse of removal. Be sure to use new O-rings **(see illustration)**. Lubricate the O-rings with a light coat of clean engine oil before installation.
15   Check for fuel leaks after installing the pressure regulator.

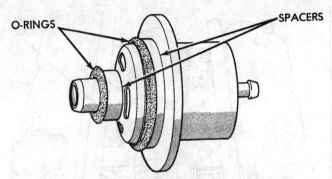

14.14 Be sure to change both O-rings with new ones before installation

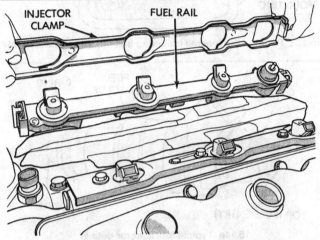

14.21 Lift the injector clamp from the fuel rail

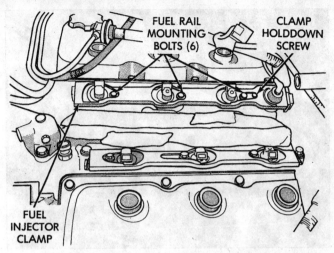

14.20 Remove the hold down screw from the fuel rail

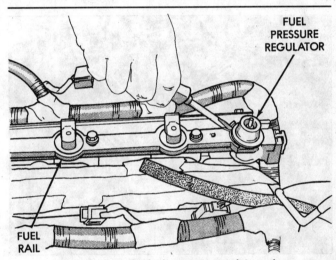

14.23 Remove the fuel pressure regulator using a flat bladed screwdriver

3.5L engine

Refer to illustrations 14.20, 14.21 and 14.23

16   Relieve the fuel system pressure (see Section 2).
17   Detach the cable from the negative battery terminal.
18   Remove the air intake plenum (see Section 18).
19   Remove the electrical connectors from the injectors and vacuum hose from the fuel pressure regulator.
20   Remove the fuel rail mounting bolts **(see illustration)**
21   Remove the hold down clamp screw and slide the fuel injector clamp toward the rear of the engine. Lift the hold down clamp off the fuel rail assembly **(see illustration)**.
22   Install the fuel rail mounting bolts finger tight.
23   Carefully pry the fuel pressure regulator out of the fuel rail **(see illustration)**.
24   Installation is the reverse of removal. Be sure to use new O-rings **(see illustration 14.14)**. Lubricate the O-rings with a light coat of clean engine oil before installation.
25   Check for fuel leaks after installing the pressure regulator.

15   Fuel injectors - check, removal and installation

Warning: *Gasoline is extremely flammable, so take extra precautions when you work on any part of the fuel system. Don't smoke or allow open flames or bare light bulbs near the work area, and don't work in a garage where a natural gas-type appliance (such as a water heater or a clothes dryer) with a pilot light is present. Since gasoline is carcinogenic, wear latex gloves when there's a possibility of being exposed to fuel, and, if you spill any fuel on your skin, rinse it off immediately with soap and water. Mop up any spills immediately and do not store fuel-soaked rags where they could ignite. The fuel system is under constant pressure, so, if any fuel lines are to be disconnected, the fuel pressure*

in the system must be relieved first (see Section 2 for more information). When you perform any kind of work on the fuel system, wear safety glasses and have a Class B type fire extinguisher on hand.

Check

1   Start the engine and warm it to its normal operating temperature.
2   With the engine idling, unplug each injector one-at-a-time, note the change in idle speed then reconnect the injector. If the idle speed drop is almost the same for each cylinder, the injectors are operating correctly. If unplugging a particular injector fails to change the idle speed, proceed to the next step.
3   Turn the engine off. Remove the connector from the injector, and measure the resistance between the two terminals of the injector **(see illustration 12.8)**.
4   The resistance should be approximately 12.4 ohms. If not, replace it with a new one.
5   If the resistance is as specified, connect a 12-volt test light or a special injector harness test light (noid light), (available at most auto parts stores) to the electrical connector **(see illustration 12.9)**.

   a) *If the light flashes as the engine is cranked or started, the injector is receiving proper voltage.*
   b) *If the light doesn't flash, check the wiring harness (see Chapter 12).*
   c) *If the wiring harness is not damaged or shorted, check the wiring between the PCM and the injector(s) for a short circuit, or a break in the wire or bad connection.*

4

15.12 Pinch the fuel line and remove it from the fuel rail

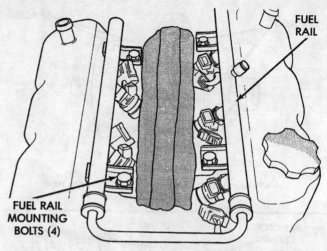

15.13a Remove the fuel rail mounting bolts (3.3L engine shown)

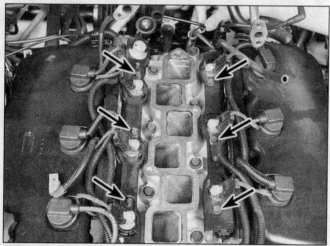

**15.13b Fuel rail mounting bolt locations (arrows)
on the 3.5L engine**

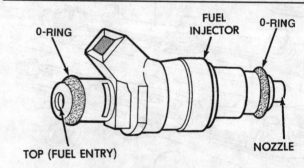

15.14a Typical fuel injector details

Removal

Refer to illustrations 15.12, 15.13a, 15.13b, 15.14a and 15.14b

6   Detach the cable from the negative battery terminal.
7   Relieve the fuel pressure (see Section 2).
8   Remove the air intake plenum (see Section 18).
9   Unplug the injector connectors.
10   Detach the vacuum hose from the fuel pressure regulator (see Section 14).
11   Detach any ground cables from the fuel rail.
12   Detach the fuel feed line and return line from the fuel rail **(see illustration)**.
13   Remove the mounting nuts **(see illustrations)** and detach the fuel rail from the injectors.
14   Remove the injector(s) from the intake manifold and remove and discard the O-rings **(see illustrations)**. **Note:** *Whether you're replacing an injector or a leaking O-ring, it's a good idea to remove all the injectors from the fuel rail and replace all the O-rings.*

Installation

15   Coat the new seal rings with clean engine oil and slide them onto the injectors.
16   Coat the new O-rings with clean engine oil and install them on the injector(s), then insert each injector into its corresponding bore in the fuel rail.
17   Install the injector and fuel rail assembly on the intake manifold.

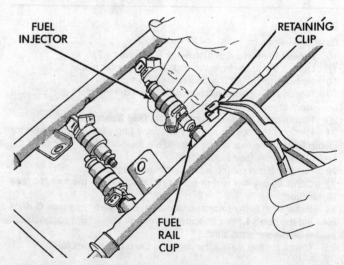

15.14b On 3.3L engines, remove the clip and separate the fuel injector from the fuel rail

Tighten the fuel rail mounting nuts to the torque listed in this Chapter's Specifications.
18   The remainder of installation is the reverse of removal.
19   After the injector/fuel rail assembly installation is complete, turn the ignition switch to ON, but don't operate the starter (this activates the fuel pump for about two seconds, which builds up fuel pressure in the fuel lines and the fuel rail). Repeat this about two or three times, then check the fuel lines, rail and injectors for fuel leakage.

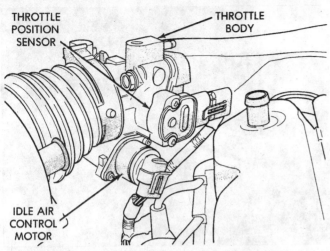

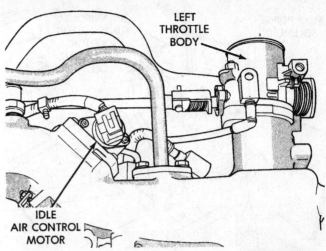

16.1a Idle Air Control (IAC) valve location on the 3.3L engine

16.1b Idle Air Control (IAC) valve location on the 3.5L engine

16.4 Check for battery voltage on the IAC connector Terminal A (purple wire) and then again on Terminal C (yellow wire)

16.7 Plug the SCAN tool into the diagnostic test connector (arrow) under the driver's dash

16   Idle Air Control (IAC) system - check and component replacement

Refer to illustrations 16.1a, 16.1b, 16.4 and 16.7

1   The idle speed is controlled by the IAC valve **(see illustrations)**. This valve changes the amount of air that will bypass into the intake manifold. The IAC valve is controlled by the PCM and is opened and closed depending upon the running conditions of the engine (air conditioning system, power steering, cold and warm running etc.).

Check

2   Chrysler recommends the use of a special IAC "exerciser" tool installed in series between the IAC valve and the harness electrical connector for testing purposes. There are several tests the home mechanic can perform on the IAC system to verify operation but they are limited and are useful only in the case of definite problems rather than intermittent failure.

3   Disconnect the electrical connector from the IAC valve and listen carefully for a change in the idle. Connect the IAC valve electrical connector and turn the air conditioning on and listen for a change in idle rpm. When the engine is cold, the IAC valve should vary the idle as the engine begins to warm-up and also when the air conditioning compressor is turned ON. If there are no obvious signs that the IAC valve is working, continue testing.

4   Use a voltmeter and test for voltage to the IAC valve with the ignition key ON (engine not running). Backprobe the IAC valve electrical connector and check for battery voltage on the purple/white wire (+) (3.3L engine) or the purple wire (+) (3.5L engine) **(see illustration)**. Next, check for battery voltage on the yellow wire (+). **Note:** *Voltage should also be present when the engine is running but monitoring the voltage changes as the engine rpm fluctuates is difficult without a factory designed SCAN tool.*

5   If there is no voltage present, have the electrical circuit for the IAC valve diagnosed by a dealer service department or other qualified repair shop.

6   If the computer is delivering voltage to the IAC valve, check that the IAC valve is not frozen or defective. Remove the IAC valve and leaving the IAC valve connected, turn the ignition key ON (engine not running). The pintle should retract (pull in).

7   There is an alternate method for testing the IAC valve. A SCAN tool is available from some automotive parts stores and specialty tool companies that can be plugged into the ALDL for the purpose of monitoring the computer and the sensors. Install the SCAN tool and switch to the IAC position mode and monitor the steps (valve winding position) **(see illustration)**. The SCAN tool should indicate between 10 to 200 steps depending upon the rpm range. Allow the engine to idle for several minutes and while observing the count reading, snap the throttle to achieve high rpm (under 3,500). Repeat the procedure several times and observe the SCAN tool steps when the engine returns to idle. The readings should be within 5 to 10 steps each time. If the readings fluctuate greatly, replace the IAC valve. **Note:** *When the*

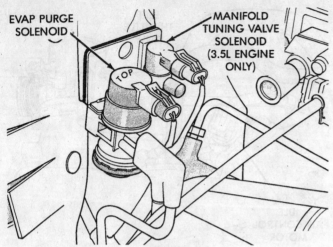

17.1 Location of the MTV solenoid on the 3.5L engine

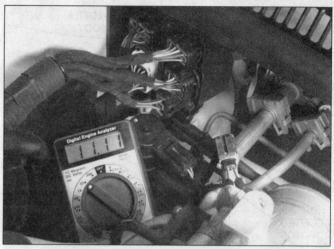

17.3 Check for battery voltage on the MTV solenoid
electrical connector

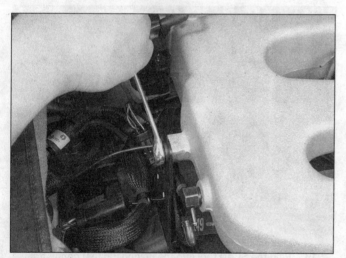

18.10 Remove the brackets from the sides of the air intake
plenum (3.5L engine shown)

18.11a Remove the plenum bolts (3.3L engine)

IAC valve electrical connector is disconnected for testing, the PCM will have to "relearn" its idle mode. In other words, it will take a certain amount of time before the idle valve resets for the correct idle speed. Make sure the idle is smooth before plugging in the SCAN tool.

Replacement

8   Disconnect the electrical connector from the IAC valve.
9   Remove the two mounting screws from the valve and lift it from the intake plenum or throttle body.
10   Installation is the reverse of removal. Be sure to install a new O-ring.

17 Manifold tuning system (3.5L engine) - check and component replacement

Refer to illustrations 17.1 and 17.3
1   The Manifold tuning system is designed to improve low end torque by controlling the length of the intake passage. During wide open throttle, the valve opens a crossover passage that connects both sides of the air intake plenum. The system components are the PCM, Manual Tuning Valve (MTV), MTV solenoid **(see illustration)** and air intake plenum.
2   Check the general condition of all the Manifold Tuning system

components visually. Check for broken hoses, damaged air ducts, a cracked or leaking plenum or a stuck valve. The MTV actuator is located on top of the air intake plenum and it opens and closes the valve inside the plenum using vacuum from the MTV solenoid. The MTV solenoid is controlled by the PCM.
3   Check for battery voltage to the MTV solenoid with the ignition key ON (engine not running) **(see illustration)**.
4   If battery voltage is available and the MT system is suspect, have the system checked at a dealer service department.

18 Air intake plenum - removal and installation

Refer to illustrations 18.10, 18.11a, 18.11b, 18.12a and 18.12b
1   Detach the cable from the negative battery terminal.
2   Relieve the fuel pressure (see Section 2).
3   Disconnect the air intake duct(s) from the throttle body (see Section 9).
4   Disconnect the accelerator cable (see Section 10) and the cruise control cable.
5   Detach the electrical connectors from the TPS, MAP sensor, IAC valve and the EGR transducer solenoid.
6   Disconnect the PCV hose and the brake booster hose from the rear of the air intake plenum.

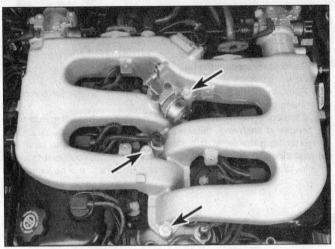

18.11b Remove the plenum bolts (arrows) (3.5L engine)

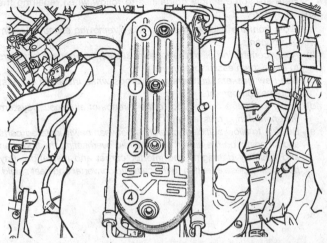

18.12a Air intake plenum tightening sequence on the 3.3L engine

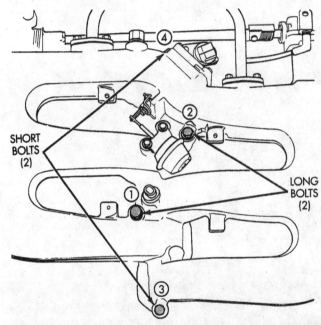

18.12b Air intake plenum tightening sequence on the 3.5L engine

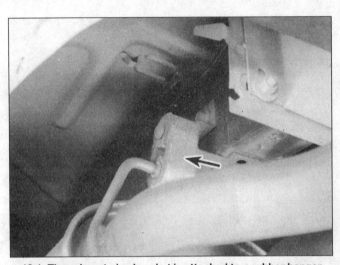

19.1 The exhaust pipe bracket is attached to a rubber hanger

7   Disconnect the vacuum line from the fuel pressure regulator (see Section 14).
8   Disconnect the purge control solenoid hose from the throttle body.
9   Remove the EGR tube from the air intake plenum (see Chapter 6).
10   On 3.5L engines, remove the mounting bracket bolt from each side of the plenum (see illustration).
11   Remove the air intake plenum mounting bolts (see illustrations). Lift the plenum from the engine compartment.
12   Installation is the reverse of removal. Follow the correct tightening sequence and tighten the plenum bolts to the torque listed in this Chapter's Specifications (see illustrations).

19   Exhaust system servicing - general information

Refer to illustration 19.1

Warning: *Inspection and repair of exhaust system components should be done only after enough time has elapsed after driving the vehicle to allow the system components to cool completely. Also, when working under the vehicle, make sure it is securely supported on jackstands.*

1   The exhaust system consists of the exhaust manifold(s), the catalytic converter, the muffler, the tailpipe and all connecting pipes, brackets, hangers and clamps. The exhaust system is attached to the body with mounting brackets and rubber hangers (see illustration). If any of the parts are improperly installed, excessive noise and vibration will be transmitted to the body.

Muffler and pipes

2   Conduct regular inspections of the exhaust system to keep it safe and quiet. Look for any damaged or bent parts, open seams, holes, loose connections, excessive corrosion or other defects which could allow exhaust fumes to enter the vehicle. Also check the catalytic converter when you inspect the exhaust system (see below). Deteriorated exhaust system components should not be repaired; they should be replaced with new parts.
3   If the exhaust system components are extremely corroded or rusted together, welding equipment will probably be required to remove them. The convenient way to accomplish this is to have a muffler repair shop remove the corroded sections with a cutting torch. If, however, you want to save money by doing it yourself (and you don't have a welding outfit with a cutting torch), simply cut off the old components with a hacksaw. If you have compressed air, special pneumatic cutting chisels can also be used. If you do decide to tackle the job at home, be sure to wear safety goggles to protect your eyes from metal chips and work gloves to protect your hands.

4

4   Here are some simple guidelines to follow when repairing the exhaust system:

a) *Work from the back to the front when removing exhaust system components.*

b) *Apply penetrating oil to the exhaust system component fasteners to make them easier to remove.*

c) *Use new gaskets, hangers and clamps when installing exhaust systems components.*

d) *Apply anti-seize compound to the threads of all exhaust system fasteners during reassembly.*

e) *Be sure to allow sufficient clearance between newly installed parts and all points on the underbody to avoid overheating the floor pan and possibly damaging the interior carpet and insulation. Pay particularly close attention to the catalytic converter and heat shield.*

Catalytic converter

Warning: *The converter gets very hot during operation. Make sure it has cooled down before you touch it.*

Note: *See Chapter 6 for more information on the catalytic converter.*

5   Periodically inspect the heat shield for cracks, dents and loose or missing fasteners.

6   Remove the heat shield and inspect the converter for cracks or other damage.

7   If the converter must be replaced, remove the mounting nuts from the flanges at each end, detach the rubber mounts and separate the converter from the exhaust system (you should be able to push the exhaust pipes at each end out of the way to clear the converter studs.

8   Installation is the reverse of removal. Be sure to use new gaskets.

Chapter 5
Engine electrical systems

Contents

Specifications

Ignition system

Ignition coil
Primary resistance	0.45 to 0.65 ohms
Secondary resistance	7,000 to 15,800 ohms

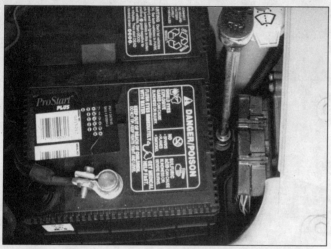

4.2 Remove the bolt and detach the hold-down clamp from the battery tray

1   General information

The engine electrical systems include all ignition, charging and starting components. Because of their engine-related functions, these components are discussed separately from chassis electrical devices such as the lights, the instruments, etc. (which are included in Chapter 12).

Always observe the following precautions when working on the electrical systems:

a) *Be extremely careful, when servicing engine electrical components. They are easily damaged if checked, connected or handled improperly.*

b) *Never leave the ignition switch on for long periods of time with the engine off.*

c) *Don't disconnect the battery cables while the engine is running.*

d) *Maintain correct polarity when connecting a battery cable from another vehicle during jump starting.*

e) *Always disconnect the negative cable first and hook it up last or the battery may be shorted by the tool being used to loosen the cable clamps.*

It's also a good idea to review the safety-related information regarding the engine electrical systems located in the *Safety First* section near the front of this manual before beginning any operation included in this Chapter.

2   Battery - emergency jump starting

Refer to the *Booster battery (jump) starting* procedure at the front of this manual.

3   Battery cables - check and replacement

1   Periodically inspect the entire length of each battery cable for damage, cracked or burned insulation and corrosion. Poor battery cable connections can cause starting problems and decreased engine performance.

2   Check the cable-to-terminal connections at the ends of the cables for cracks, loose wire strands and corrosion. The presence of white, fluffy deposits under the insulation at the cable terminal connection is a sign that the cable is corroded and should be replaced. Check the terminals for distortion, missing mounting bolts and corrosion.

3   When removing the cables, always disconnect the negative cable first and hook it up last or the battery may be shorted by the tool used to loosen the cable clamps. Even if only the positive cable is being

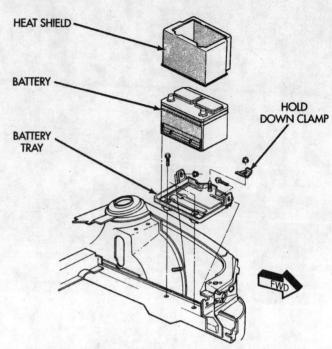

4.4 Battery tray and hold-down assembly installation details

replaced, be sure to disconnect the negative cable from the battery first (see Chapter 1 for further information regarding battery cable removal).

4   Disconnect the old cables from the battery, then trace each of them to their opposite ends and detach them from the starter solenoid and ground terminals. Note the routing of each cable to ensure correct installation.

5   If you are replacing either or both of the old cables, take them with you when buying new cables. It is vitally important that you replace the cables with identical parts. Cables have characteristics that make them easy to identify: positive cables are usually red and larger in cross-section; ground cables are usually black and smaller in cross section.

6   Clean the threads of the solenoid or ground connection with a wire brush to remove rust and corrosion. Apply a light coat of battery terminal corrosion inhibitor, or petroleum jelly, to the threads to prevent future corrosion.

7   Attach the cable to the solenoid or ground connection and tighten the mounting nut/bolt securely.

8   Before connecting a new cable to the battery, make sure that it reaches the battery post without having to be stretched.

9   Connect the positive cable first, followed by the negative cable.

4   Battery - removal and installation

Refer to illustrations 4.2 and 4.4

1   Disconnect both cables from the battery terminals. **Caution:** *Always disconnect the negative cable first and hook it up last or the battery may be shorted by the tool being used to loosen the cable clamps.*

2   Remove the battery hold-down clamp **(see illustration).**

3   Lift out the battery. Be careful - it's heavy. **Note:** *Battery straps and handlers are available at most auto parts stores for a reasonable price. They make it easier to remove and carry the battery.*

4   While the battery is out, remove and inspect the carrier (tray) for corrosion **(see illustration).**

5   If corrosion has leaked down to the battery support, remove the bolts and lift the support out. Use baking soda to clean the deposits from the metal to prevent the support from further oxidation.

6.3 To use a calibrated ignition tester, simply disconnect a spark plug wire, connect it to the tester, clip the tester to a convenient ground and crank the engine over - if there's enough power to fire the plug, sparks will be visible between the electrode tip and the tester body

6   If you are replacing the battery, make sure you get one that's identical, with the same dimensions, amperage rating, cold cranking rating, etc.

7   Installation is the reverse of removal.

5   Ignition system - general information

All models are equipped with a distributorless ignition system (DIS). The entire ignition system consists of the ignition switch, the battery, the coil packs, the primary (low voltage) and secondary (high voltage) wiring circuits, the ignition wires and spark plugs, the camshaft position sensor, the crankshaft position sensor and the Powertrain Control Module (PCM). The PCM controls the ignition timing, spark and advance characteristics for the engine. The ignition timing is not adjustable. The crankshaft and camshaft sensors are both Hall Effect timing devices. Refer to Chapter 6 for testing and replacement procedures for the crankshaft sensor and camshaft sensor.

The crankshaft sensor and camshaft sensor generate pulses that are input to the Powertrain Control Module. The PCM determines crankshaft position from these two sensors. The PCM calculates injector sequence and ignition timing from the crankshaft position.

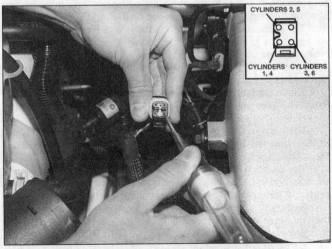

6.9 Touch the probe of an LED test light to each coil driver circuit and observe that the test light flashes while the engine is cranked over

The PCM regulates the ignition system. The PCM supplies battery voltage to the ignition coil packs through the Automatic Shutdown Relay (ASD). The PCM also controls the ground circuit for the ignition coil.

The computerized ignition system provides complete control of the ignition timing by determining the optimum timing using a micro computer in response to engine speed, coolant temperature, throttle position and vacuum pressure in the intake manifold. These parameters are relayed to the PCM by the camshaft position sensor, crankshaft position sensor, the Throttle Position Sensor (TPS), coolant temperature sensor and Manifold Absolute Pressure (MAP) sensor. Ignition timing is altered during warm-up, idling and warm running conditions by the PCM.

Refer to a dealer parts department or auto parts store for any questions concerning the availability of the ignition parts and assemblies. Testing the camshaft position sensor and the crankshaft position sensor is covered in Chapter 6.

6   Ignition system - check

Refer to illustrations 6.3 and 6.9

Warning: *Because of the very high voltage generated by the ignition system, extreme care should be taken whenever an operation is performed involving ignition components. This not only includes the coil, camshaft position sensor and spark plug wires, but related items connected to the system as well, such as the plug connections, tachometer and any test equipment.*

1   With the ignition switch turned to the "ON" position, a glowing instrument panel "Battery" light or "Oil Pressure" light is a basic check for battery supply to the ignition system and PCM.

2   Check all ignition wiring connections for tightness, cuts, corrosion or any other signs of a bad connection.

3   Use a calibrated ignition tester (available at most auto parts stores or specialty tool companies) to verify adequate secondary voltage (25,000 volts) at each spark plug **(see illustration).** Make sure you use an ignition tester calibrated for electronic ignition systems. A faulty or poor connection at that plug could also result in a misfire. Also, check for carbon deposits inside the spark plug boot.

4   If NO spark or INTERMITTENT sparks occur, disconnect the coil pack electrical connector and check for battery voltage to the ignition coil pack on the dark green/orange wire with the ignition On. You may have to cycle the ignition key on and off several times to make this check because the computer shuts off the ignition feed if it senses the engine is not cranking. Refer to the ignition wiring schematic at the end of Chapter 12 for additional wiring harness information.

5   Using an ohmmeter, check the resistance between the coil terminals (see Section 7). If an open is found (verified by an infinite reading), replace the coil.

6   Using an ohmmeter, check the resistance of the spark plug wires. Each wire should measure less than 25,000 ohms.

7   Check the operation of the Automatic Shutdown (ASD) relay (see Chapter 4).

8   Check the operation of the camshaft position sensor (see Chapter 6) and the crankshaft position sensor (see Chapter 6).

9   If all the checks are correct, check the coil driver circuits from the computer. Using a test light (an LED-type test light works best for this check) connected to the positive battery terminal, disconnect the coil pack electrical connector and probe the white, red and black connector terminals while an assistant cranks the engine **(see illustration). Caution:** *Do not touch the dark green/red wire terminal with the test light connected to the positive battery terminal or damage to the PCM may result.* If the circuits are functioning properly, the light will rapidly blink on and off as the PCM grounds the circuit. If there is no flashing from the test light, most likely the computer is defective. Have the PCM diagnosed by a dealer service department.

10   Additional checks should be performed by a dealer service department or an automotive repair shop.

5

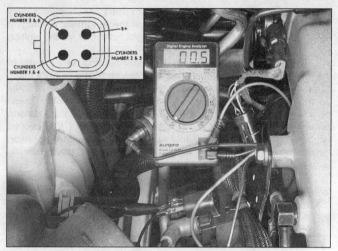

7.3 Connect the positive probe of the ohmmeter to the B+ terminal and with the negative probe, test each cylinder terminal for the primary circuit resistance value. They all should be within specifications

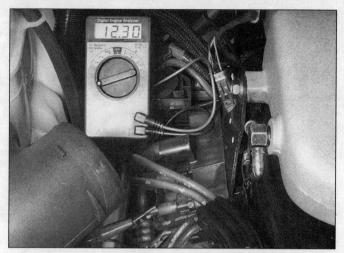

7.4 Connect the ohmmeter probes to the secondary tower for each coil pack pair. Each coil pair should fall within the secondary resistance specification value

7   Ignition coil - check and replacement

Check

Refer to illustrations 7.3 and 7.4

1   Clearly label the six spark plug wires, then detach them from the coil pack. Measure the resistance of each cable. It should be 3 to 12 k-ohms per foot of cable. Replace any cable not within this range.
2   Unplug the electrical connector on the coil pack.
3   Working on the coil connector, measure the resistance on the primary side of each coil with a digital ohmmeter **(see illustration)**. At the coil, connect an ohmmeter between the B+ pin and the pin corresponding to the particular cylinder. Compare your readings with the resistance values listed in this Chapter's Specifications.
4   Measure the secondary resistance of the coil between the paired high tension towers of each group of cylinders **(see illustration)**. Compare your readings with the resistance values listed in this Chapter's Specifications.
5   If any coil in the coil pack fails either of the above tests, replace the coil pack.
6   Installation is the reverse of removal.

Replacement

Refer to illustration 7.9

7   Clearly label the six spark plug wires, then detach them from the coil pack.
8   Unplug the electrical connector from the coil pack.
9   Remove the coil pack mounting bolts **(see illustration)** and lift the coil pack from the engine compartment.

8   Charging system - general information and precautions

Refer to illustration 8.1

The charging system includes the alternator, a charge indicator light, the battery, the Powertrain Control Module (PCM), the ASD relay, a fusible link and the wiring between all the components **(see illustration)**. The charging system supplies electrical power to maintain the battery at its full charge capacity. The alternator is driven by a serpentine drivebelt.

The alternator control system within the PCM varies the voltage generated at the alternator in accordance with driving conditions. Depending on electric load, vehicle speed, engine coolant

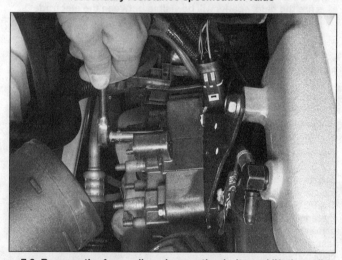

7.9 Remove the four coil pack mounting bolts and lift the coil from the engine compartment (3.5L engine shown)

temperature, accessories (air conditioning system, radio, cruise control etc.) and the intake air temperature, the system will adjust the amount of voltage generated, creating less load on the engine.

The purpose of the voltage regulator is to limit the alternator's voltage to a preset value. This prevents power surges, circuit overloads, etc., during peak voltage output. The voltage regulator is contained within the PCM and in the event of failure, the PCM must be replaced as a single unit.

These models are equipped with a Nippondenso 90 amp alternator. The alternator must be replaced as a single unit in the event of failure.

The charging system doesn't ordinarily require periodic maintenance. However, the drivebelt, battery, harness wires and connections should be inspected at the intervals outlined in Chapter 1.

The dashboard warning light should come ON when the ignition key is turned to ON, but it should go off immediately after the engine is started. If it remains on, there is a malfunction in the charging system (see Section 11). Some vehicles are also equipped with a voltmeter. If the voltmeter indicates abnormally high or low voltage, check the charging system.

Be very careful when making electrical circuit connections to a vehicle equipped with an alternator and note the following:

a) *When reconnecting wires to the alternator from the battery, be sure to note the polarity.*

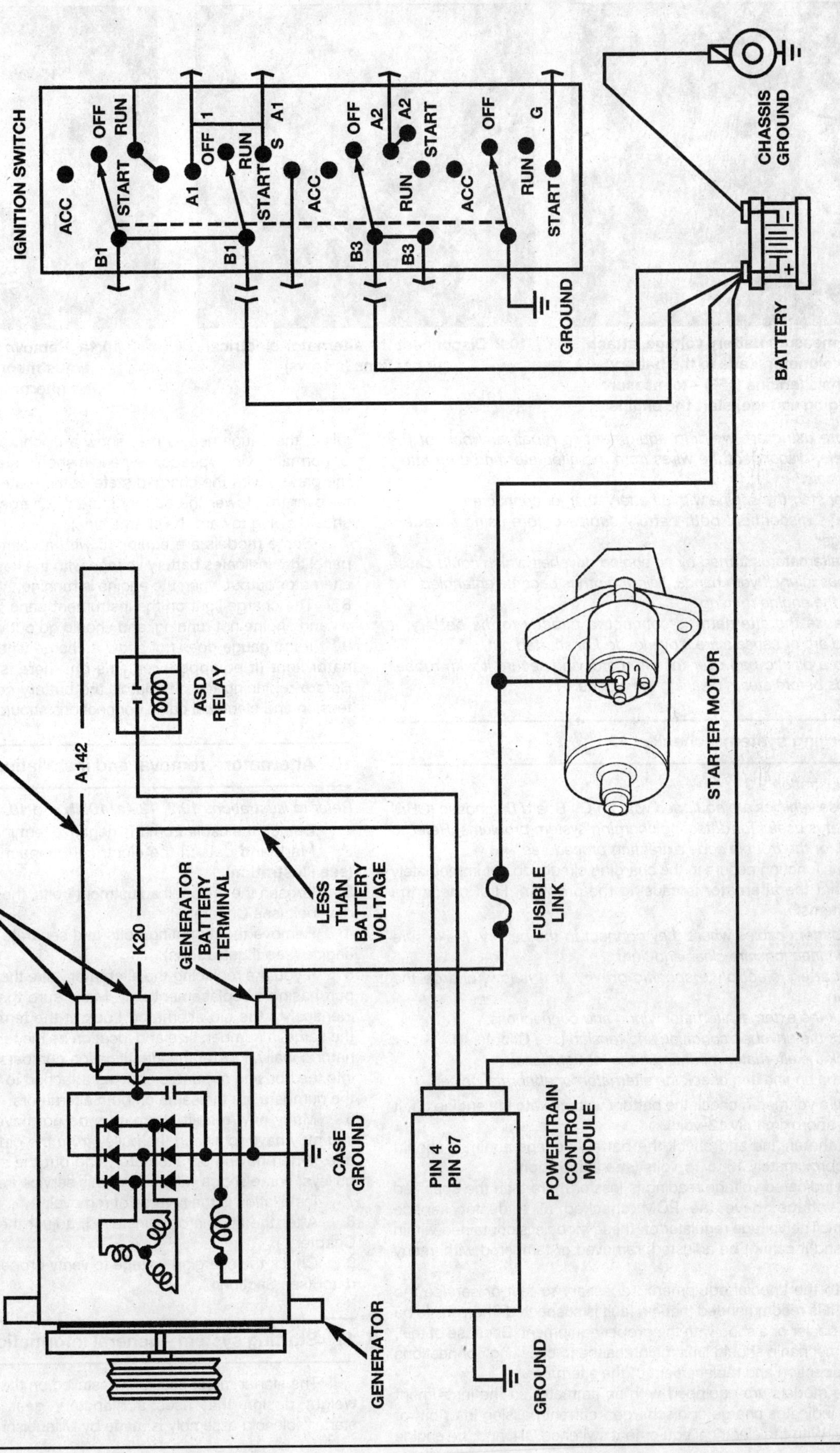

IGNITION SWITCH

ACC OFF RUN START A1 OFF RUN START S A1 ACC OFF RUN START A2 A2 ACC OFF RUN G START

B1 B1 B3 B3

GROUND

CHASSIS GROUND

BATTERY

BATTERY VOLTAGE

FIELD TERMINALS

A142

ASD RELAY

K20

GENERATOR BATTERY TERMINAL

LESS THAN BATTERY VOLTAGE

CASE GROUND

STARTER MOTOR

FUSIBLE LINK

PIN 4
PIN 67

POWERTRAIN CONTROL MODULE

GROUND

GENERATOR

8.1 Typical charging system schematic

5

9.3 To measure battery voltage, attach the voltmeter leads to the battery terminals (engine OFF) - to measure charging voltage, start the engine

10.2 Disconnect the alternator electrical connections (arrows)

10.4a Remove the pivot bolt and adjustment bolt from the alternator (arrows)

b) *Before using arc welding equipment to repair any part of the vehicle, disconnect the wires from the alternator and the battery terminals.*
c) *Never start the engine with a battery charger connected.*
d) *Always disconnect both battery cables before using a battery charger.*
e) *The alternator is turned by an engine drivebelt which could cause serious injury if your hands, hair or clothes become entangled in it with the engine running.*
f) *Because the alternator is connected directly to the battery, it could arc or cause a fire if overloaded or shorted out.*
g) *Wrap a plastic bag over the alternator and secure it with rubber bands before steam cleaning the engine.*

9 Charging system - check

Refer to illustration 9.3
Note: *These vehicles are equipped with an On Board Diagnostic (OBD) system that is useful for detecting charging system problems. Refer to Chapter 6 for the trouble code extracting procedures.*
1   If a malfunction occurs in the charging circuit, do not immediately assume that the alternator is causing the problem. First check the following items:

a) *The battery cables where they connect to the battery. Make sure the connections are clean and tight.*
b) *The battery electrolyte specific gravity. If it is low, charge the battery.*
c) *Check the external alternator wiring and connections.*
d) *Check the drivebelt condition and tension (see Chapter 1).*
e) *Check the alternator mounting bolts for tightness.*
f) *Run the engine and check the alternator for abnormal noise.*

2   Using a voltmeter, check the battery voltage with the engine off. It should be approximately 12-volts.
3   Start the engine and check the battery voltage again. It should now be approximately 13 to 15-volts **(see illustration)**.
4   If the indicated voltage reading is less or more than the specified charging voltage, have the PCM checked at a dealer service department. The voltage regulator on these models is contained within the PCM and it cannot be adjusted, removed or tampered with in any way.
5   Due to the special equipment necessary to test or service the alternator, it is recommended that if a fault is suspected, the vehicle be taken to a dealer or a shop with the proper equipment. Because of this, the home mechanic should limit maintenance to checking cohnections and the inspection and replacement of the alternator.
6   Some models are equipped with an ammeter on the instrument panel that indicates charge or discharge - current passing in or out of the battery. With the electrical equipment switched ON, and the engine

idling, the gauge needle may show a discharge condition. At fast idle or normal driving speeds the needle should stay on the charge side of the gauge, with the charged state of the battery determining just how far over (the lower the battery state of charge, the farther the needle should swing toward the charge side).
7   Some models are equipped with a voltmeter on the instrument panel that indicates battery voltage with the key on and engine off, and alternator output when the engine is running.
8   The charge light on the instrument panel illuminates with the key on and engine not running, and should go out when the engine runs.
9   If the gauge does not show a charge when it should or the alternator light (if equipped) remains on, there is a fault in the system. Before replacing the alternator, the battery condition, alternator belt tension and electrical cable connections should be checked.

10 Alternator - removal and installation

Refer to illustrations 10.2, 12.4a, 10.4b and 10.4c
1   Detach the cable from the negative terminal of the battery.
2   Mark and detach the electrical connectors from the alternator **(see illustration).**
3   Loosen the drivebelt adjustment bolts, then detach the serpentine drivebelt (see Chapter 1).
4   Remove the mounting bolts and separate the alternator from the engine **(see illustrations)**.
5   If you are replacing the alternator, take the old one with you when purchasing a replacement unit. Make sure the new/rebuilt unit looks identical to the old alternator. Look at the terminals - they should be the same in number, size and location as the terminals on the old alternator. Finally, look at the identification numbers - they will be stamped into the housing or printed on a tag attached to the housing. Make sure the numbers are the same on both alternators.
6   Many new/rebuilt alternators do not have a pulley installed, so you may have to switch the pulley from the old unit to the new/rebuilt one. When buying an alternator, find out the shop's policy regarding pulleys; some shops will perform this service free of charge.
7   Installation is the reverse of removal.
8   After the alternator is installed, adjust the drivebelt tension (see Chapter 1).
9   Check the charging voltage to verify proper operation of the alternator (see Section 9).

11 Starting system - general information and precautions

The starter motor assembly installed on the 3.5L engines is a light-weight design that uses a planetary gear reduction drive. This starter/solenoid assembly is made by Mitsubishi (MELCO) and provides

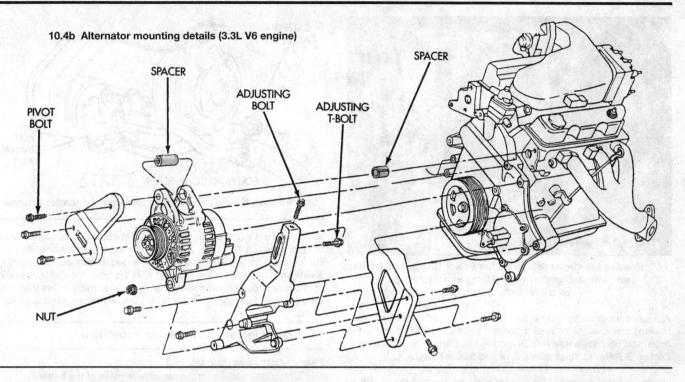

10.4b Alternator mounting details (3.3L V6 engine)

higher rotational speeds for starting. This unit has a removable solenoid that can be purchased at most automotive parts stores. The starter motor assembly on the 3.3L engines is a Nippondenso offset gear reduction design that uses different size output gears to achieve the same effect. This unit is sold strictly as a complete assembly. Check with your local dealer parts department before disassembly.

The starting system consists of the battery, the starter motor, the starter solenoid and the wires connecting them. The solenoid is mounted directly on the starter motor.

The solenoid/starter motor assembly is installed on the upper part of the engine, next to the transmission bellhousing.

When the ignition key is turned to the Start position, the starter solenoid is actuated through the starter control circuit which includes a starter relay located in the Power Distribution Center. The starter solenoid then connects the battery to the starter. The battery supplies the electrical energy to the starter motor, which does the actual work of cranking the engine.

Always observe the following precautions when working on the starting system:

a) *Excessive cranking of the starter motor can overheat it and cause serious damage. Never operate the starter motor for more than 15 seconds at a time without pausing to allow it to cool for at least two minutes.*
b) *The starter is connected directly to the battery and could arc or cause a fire if mishandled, overloaded or shorted out.*
c) *Always detach the cable from the negative terminal of the battery before working on the starting system.*

12 Starter motor - in-vehicle check

Refer to illustration 12.7
Note: *Before diagnosing starter problems, make sure the battery is fully charged.*

1   If the starter motor does not turn at all when the switch is operated, make sure the shift lever is in Neutral or Park.
2   Make sure the battery is charged and all cables, both at the battery and starter solenoid terminals, are clean and secure.
3   If the starter motor spins but the engine is not cranking, the overrunning clutch in the starter motor is slipping and the starter motor

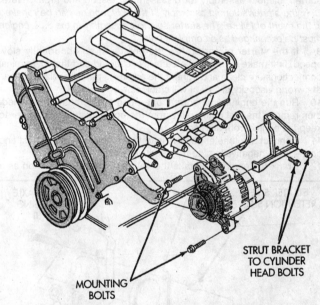

10.4c Alternator mounting details (3.5L V6 engine)

STRUT BRACKET TO CYLINDER HEAD BOLTS

MOUNTING BOLTS

must be replaced. Also, the ring gear on the flywheel or driveplate may be worn.
4   If, when the switch is actuated, the starter motor does not operate at all but the solenoid clicks, the problem lies with either the battery, the main solenoid contacts or the starter motor itself (or the engine is seized).
5   If the solenoid plunger cannot be heard when the switch is actuated, the battery is bad, the fusible link is burned (the circuit is open) or the solenoid itself is defective.
6   To check the solenoid, connect a remote starter switch between the battery and the ignition switch wire terminal (the small terminal) on the solenoid. If the starter motor operates when the remote switch is activated, the solenoid is OK and the problem is in the ignition switch, neutral start switch, starter relay or the wiring.

5

12.7 Remove the starter relay from the Power Distribution Center and with the ignition key ON (engine not running), check for battery voltage

7   Locate the starter relay in the power distribution center **(see illustration)**. Remove the relay and perform the identical tests as for the Automatic Shutdown Relay (ASD) and the fuel pump relay in Chapter 4, Section 3. **Refer to illustrations 3.19 and 3.20** in Chapter 4.
8   If the starter motor still does not operate, remove the starter/solenoid assembly for disassembly, testing and repair. **Note:** *Only the starter/solenoid assembly in the 3.5L engine can be repaired in the event of failure. The starter/solenoid assembly in the 3.3L engine must be exchanged as a complete unit.*
9   If the starter motor cranks the engine at an abnormally slow speed, first make sure that the battery is charged and that all terminal connections are clean and tight. If the engine is partially seized, or has the wrong viscosity oil in it, it will crank slowly.
10   Run the engine until normal operating temperature is reached, then remove the fuel pump relay from the power distribution center to keep the engine from starting.
11   Connect a voltmeter positive lead to the positive battery post and connect the negative lead to the negative post.
12   Crank the engine and take the voltmeter readings as soon as a

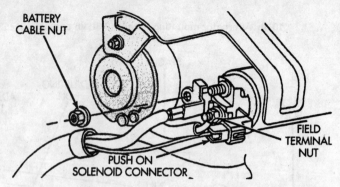

13.2 Remove the electrical connectors from the starter solenoid

steady figure is indicated. Do not allow the starter motor to turn for more than 15 seconds at a time. A reading of nine volts or more, with the starter motor turning at normal cranking speed, is normal. If the reading is nine volts or more but the cranking speed is slow, the motor, solenoid contacts or circuit connections are faulty. If the reading is less than nine volts and the cranking speed is slow, the starter motor is probably bad.

13   Starter motor - removal and installation

Refer to illustrations 13.2 and 13.3
1   Detach the cable from the negative terminal of the battery.
2   Clearly label, then disconnect the wires from the terminals on the starter motor solenoid. Disconnect any clips securing the wiring harness to the starter **(see illustration)**.
3   Remove the mounting bolts and detach the starter **(see illustration)**.
4   Installation is the reverse of removal.

14   Starter solenoid (3.5L engine) - removal and installation

Refer to illustrations 14.4
1   Disconnect the cable from the negative terminal of the battery.
2   Remove the starter motor (see Section 12).
3   Disconnect the strap from the solenoid to the starter motor terminal.
4   Remove the screws which secure the solenoid to the starter motor gear housing and detach the solenoid from the gear housing **(see illustration)**.
5   While the solenoid is removed, check the starter gear teeth. If the starter gear teeth are damaged, you should also inspect the flywheel or driveplate ring gear for damage.
6   Installation is the reverse of removal.

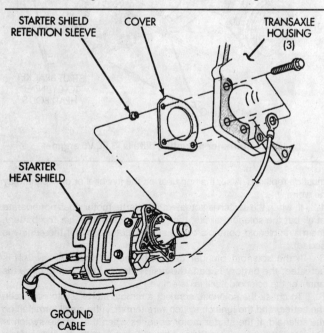

13.3 Starter motor installation details (3.5L V6 engine)

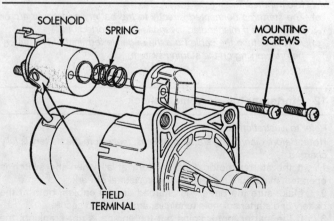

14.4 Starter solenoid mounting details (MELCO starter)

Chapter 6
Emissions and engine control systems

Contents

Specifications

Torque specifications

Crankshaft sensor retaining bolt	105 inch-lbs
Camshaft sensor retaining bolt	105 inch-lbs
EGR tube mounting nuts	95 inch-lbs
EGR valve bolts	200 inch-lbs

1 General information

Refer to illustrations 1.3a, 1.3b, 1.6a and 1.6b

To prevent pollution of the atmosphere from incompletely burned and evaporating gases, and to maintain good driveability and fuel economy, a number of emission control systems are incorporated. The principal systems are:

   Positive Crankcase Ventilation (PCV) system
   Evaporative Emission Control (EVAP) system
   Exhaust Gas Recirculation (EGR) system
   Oxygen sensor (O$_2$) system
   Catalytic converter (TWC)
   Manifold Tuning system (see Chapter 4)
   Powertrain Control Module (PCM) (computer) and
     information sensors

The Sections in this Chapter include general descriptions, checking procedures within the scope of the home mechanic and component replacement procedures (when possible) for each of the systems listed above.

Before assuming an emissions control system is malfunctioning, check the fuel and ignition systems carefully. The diagnosis of some emission control devices requires specialized tools, equipment and

training. If checking and servicing become too difficult or if a procedure is beyond your ability, consult a dealer service department. Remember, the most frequent cause of emissions problems is simply a loose or broken vacuum hose or wire, so always check the hose and electrical connections first **(see illustrations)**.

This doesn't mean, however, that emission control systems are particularly difficult to maintain and repair. You can quickly and easily perform many checks and do most of the regular maintenance at home with common tune-up and hand tools. **Note:** *Because of a Federally mandated extended warranty which covers the emission control system components, check with your dealer about warranty coverage before working on any emissions-related systems. Once the warranty has expired, you may wish to perform some of the component checks and/or replacement procedures in this Chapter to save money.*

Pay close attention to any special precautions outlined in this Chapter. It should be noted that the illustration of the various systems may not exactly match the system installed on your vehicle because of changes made by the manufacturer during production or from year-to-year.

A Vehicle Emissions Control Information (VECI) label is located in the engine compartment **(see illustrations)**. This label contains important emissions specifications and adjustment information. When servicing the engine or emissions systems, the VECI label in your particular vehicle should always be checked for up-to-date information.

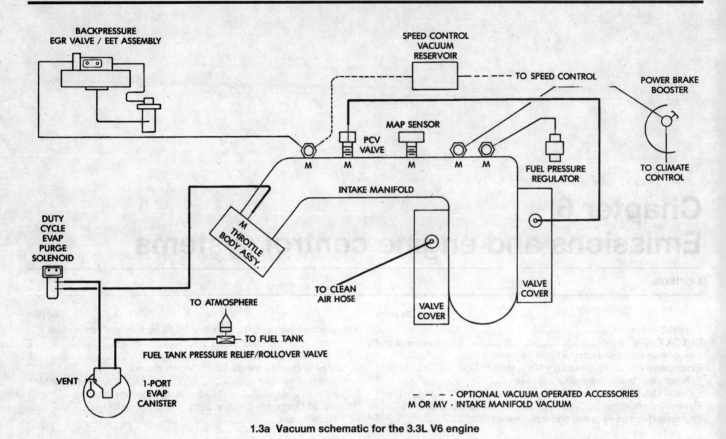

1.3a Vacuum schematic for the 3.3L V6 engine

1.3b Vacuum schematic for the 3.5L V6 engine

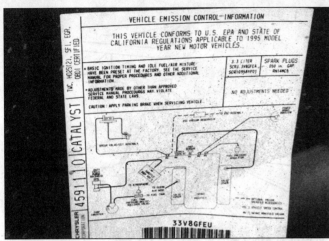

1.6a The Vehicle Emission Control Information (VECI) label is located on the underside of the hood and contains information on idle speed adjustment, ignition timing, location of the emissions control devices on your vehicle, vacuum line routing, etc (3.3L engine shown)

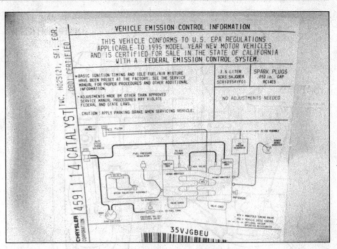

1.6b VECI label on the 3.5L engine

2 Sequential Electronic Fuel Injection (SEFI) system and information sensors - description

Refer to illustration 2.3

1   The engines are equipped with "sequentially" operated fuel injectors. A fuel injector is located in each intake port. The system fires each injector in sequence, timed with the opening of each intake valve. The Sequential Electronic Fuel Injection (SEFI) system provides the correct air-fuel ratio under all driving conditions.

2   The "brain" of all SEFI systems is a computer known as a Power-train Control Module (PCM). The PCM is located at the front corner of the engine compartment.

3   The PCM receives variable voltage inputs from a variety of sensors, switches and relays **(see illustration)**. All inputs are converted into digital signals which are "read" by the PCM, which constantly fine-tunes such variables as ignition timing, spark advance, ignition coil dwell, fuel injector pulse width and idle speed to minimize exhaust emissions and

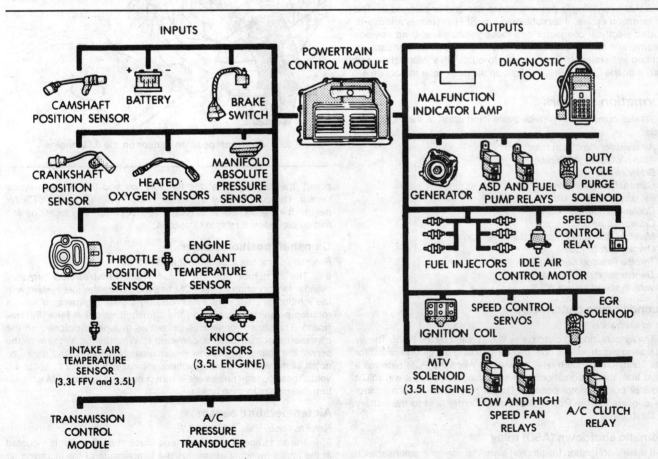

2.3 Emission and engine control components on the 3.3L and 3.5L engines

6

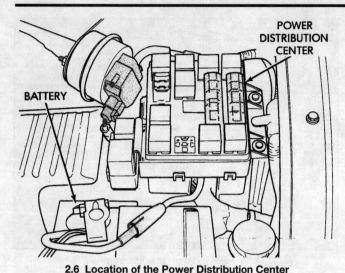

2.6 Location of the Power Distribution Center

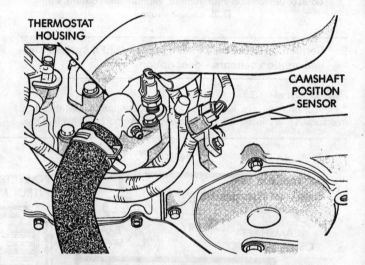

2.8a Camshaft position sensor on the 3.3L engine

enhance driveability. It also controls the operation of the radiator cooling fan, the alternator charging rate and such emissions-related components as the EGR solenoids and the purge solenoid for the EVAP canister. The PCM even updates and revises its own programming in response to changing operating conditions.

4   The PCM also constantly monitors many of its own input and output circuits. If a fault is found in the SEFI system, the information is stored in the PCM memory. The diagnosis process begins with reading any stored fault codes to identify the general location of a problem, followed by a thorough visual inspection of the system components to ensure that everything is properly connected and/or plugged in. The most common cause of a problem in any SEFI system is a loose or corroded electrical connector or a loose vacuum line. If no obvious problems are found, proceed to check the relevant sensors as described in Section 4. To learn how to output this information and display it on the CHECK ENGINE light on the dash, refer to Section 4.

Information sensors

5   Various components provide basic information to the PCM; they include:

    Air conditioning clutch relay
    Auto shutdown (ASD) relay
    Brake switch
    Camshaft position sensor
    Air temperature sensor
    Coolant temperature sensor
    Crankshaft position sensor
    Manifold Absolute Pressure (MAP) sensor
    Oxygen sensor (O2)
    Throttle Position Sensor (TPS)
    Transmission neutral-safety switch
    Vehicle speed sensor (VSS)

Air conditioning clutch relay

Refer to illustration 2.6

6   The air conditioning clutch relay is controlled by the PCM. The air conditioning clutch relay is operated by switching the ground circuit for the air conditioning clutch relay on and off. When the PCM receives a request from the air conditioning (climate control system) it will adjust the idle air control motor position. The air conditioning clutch control relay is located in the Power Distribution Center next to the battery **(see illustration)**.

Automatic shutdown (ASD) relay

7   If there's no ignition (distributor) signal, or cam or crank reference sensor signal, present when the ignition key is turned to the RUN position, the auto shutdown relay interrupts power to the electric fuel

2.8b Camshaft position sensor on the 3.5L engine

pump, the fuel injectors, the ignition coil and the heated oxygen sensor. The cut-out relay is located in the Power Distribution Center next to the battery. For ASD relay and fuel pump relay locations and testing procedures, refer to Chapter 4.

Camshaft position sensor

Refer to illustrations 2.8a, 2.8b, 2.8c and 2.8d

8   The camshaft position sensor **(see illustrations)** provides cylinder identification to the PCM to synchronize the fuel system with the ignition system. The synchronizing signal is generated from a rotating pulse ring located on the camshaft sprocket **(see illustrations)**. The sensor generates pulses as groups of notches on the camshaft sprocket pass underneath it. When metal aligns with the sensor the voltage pulses low (approximately 0.3 volts) and when the notch aligns with the sensor, voltage increases suddenly to about 5.0 volts. These voltage pulses are in turn processed by the PCM which in turn determines ignition timing.

Air temperature sensor

Refer to illustrations 2.9a and 2.9b

9   The air temperature sensor **(see illustrations)**, which is mounted in the intake manifold, measures the temperature of the incoming air and sends this information to the PCM. This data is used by the PCM to modify the air/fuel mixture.

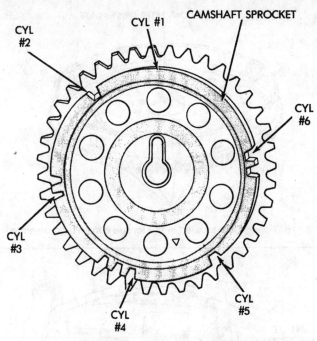

2.8c Camshaft sprocket on the 3.3L engine

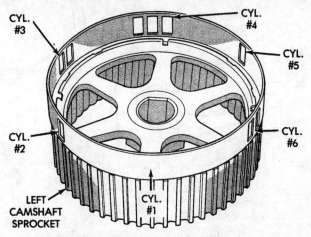

2.8d Camshaft sprocket on the 3.5L engine

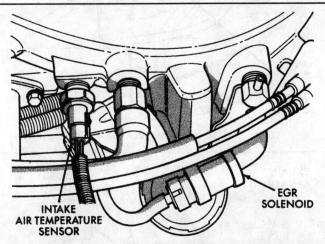

2.9a Location of the air temperature sensor on the 3.3L engine

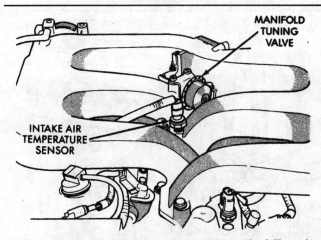

2.9b Location of the air temperature sensor on the 3.5L engine

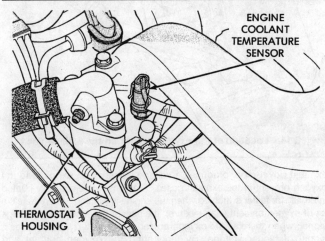

2.10a Location of the coolant temperature sensor
on the 3.3L engine

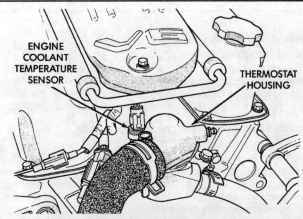

2.10b Location of the coolant temperature sensor
on the 3.5L engine

Coolant temperature sensor

Refer to illustrations 2.10a and 2.10b

10   The coolant temperature sensor **(see illustrations)**, which is threaded into the intake manifold near the thermostat housing, monitors coolant temperature and sends this information to the PCM. This data, along with the information from the air temperature sensor, is used by the PCM to determine the correct air/fuel mixture and idle speed while the engine is warming up. The sensor is also used to turn on the radiator fan.

6

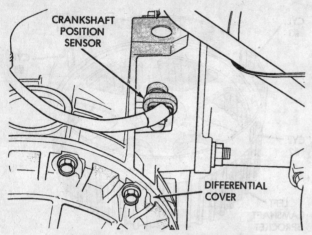

2.11a Location of the crankshaft position sensor on the 3.3L engine

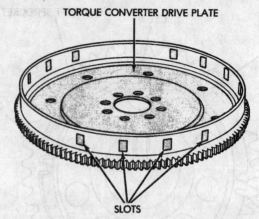

2.11b Timing slots located in the torque converter driveplate

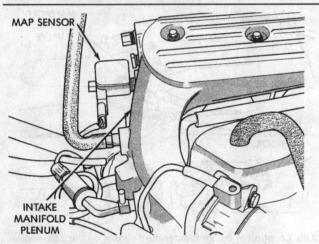

2.12a MAP sensor location on the 3.3L engine

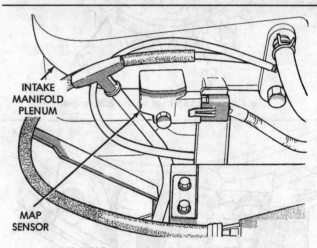

2.12b MAP sensor location on the 3.5L engine

Crankshaft position sensor

Refer to illustrations 2.11a and 2.11b

11   The crankshaft position sensor **(see illustration)** is mounted on the passenger side of the transmission bellhousing. This sensor sends information to the PCM regarding engine crankshaft position. The sensor "reads" the slots on the torque converter driveplate **(see illustration)**.

Manifold Absolute Pressure (MAP) sensor

Refer to illustrations 2.12a and 2.12b

12   The MAP sensor **(see illustrations)** is located on the intake manifold plenum. It monitors intake manifold vacuum. The MAP sensor transmits this data, along with data on barometric pressure, in the form of a variable voltage output to the PCM. When combined with data from other sensors, this information helps the PCM determine the correct air-fuel mixture ratio.

Miscellaneous switches

13   Various switches (such as the transmission neutral safety switch, the air conditioning switch, the speed control switch and the brake light switch) provide information to the PCM, which adjusts engine operation in accordance with what switch states are present at these inputs. The state of these switch inputs (high/low) is difficult to determine without the DRB II diagnostic meter.

Oxygen sensor

Refer to illustrations 2.14a and 2.14b

14   The oxygen sensor **(see illustrations)**, which is mounted in the

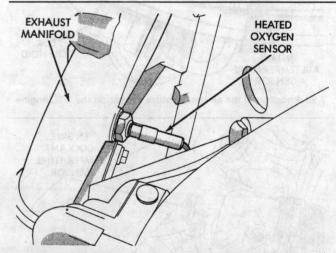

2.14a Location of the oxygen sensor on the 3.3L engine

exhaust down-pipe, produces a voltage signal when exposed to the oxygen present in the exhaust gases. The sensor is electrically heated internally for faster switching when the engine is running. When there's a lot of oxygen present (lean mixture), the sensor produces a low voltage signal; when there's little oxygen present (rich mixture), it produces a signal of higher voltage. By monitoring the oxygen content and converting it to electrical voltage, the sensor acts as a lean-rich switch. The voltage signal to the PCM alters the pulse width of the injectors.

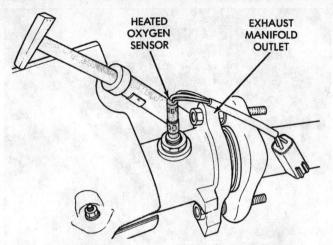

2.14b Location of the oxygen sensor on the 3.5L engine

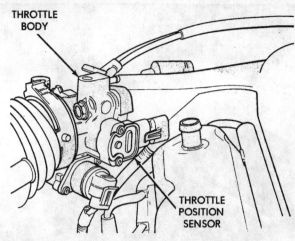

2.15a Location of the TPS (3.3L engine)

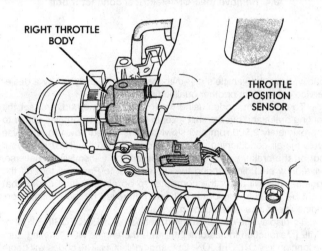

2.15b Location of the TPS (3.5L engine)

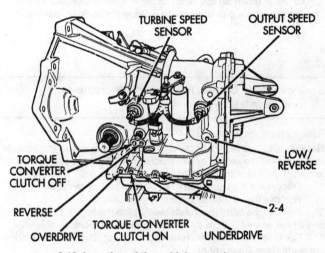

2.16 Location of the vehicle speed sensors

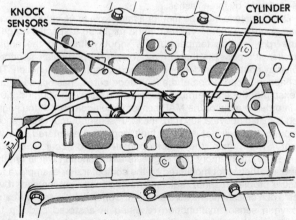

2.17 Location of the knock sensors on the 3.5L engine

Throttle Position Sensor (TPS)

Refer to illustrations 2.15a and 2.15b

15   The TPS **(see illustrations)**, which is located on the throttle body, monitors the angle of the throttle plate. The voltage produced increases or decreases in accordance with the opening angle of the throttle plate. This data, when relayed to the PCM, along with data from several other sensors, enables the computer to adjust the air/fuel ratio in accordance with the operating conditions, such as acceleration, deceleration, idle and wide open throttle.

Vehicle distance (speed) sensor

Refer to illustration 2.16

16   The vehicle distance (speed) sensors, which are located in the transmission extension housing **(see illustration),** senses vehicle motion. The sensor generates pulses for every revolution of the driveaxle and transmits them as voltage signals to the PCM. These signals are compared by the PCM with the throttle signal from the throttle position sensor so it can distinguish between a closed throttle deceleration and normal idle (vehicle stopped) condition. Under deceleration conditions, the PCM controls the IAC valve to maintain the desired MAP value; under idle conditions, the PCM adjusts the IAC valve to maintain the desired engine speed.

Knock sensor (3.5L engine only)

Refer to illustration 2.17

17   The 3.5L engine is equipped with two knock sensors **(see illustration)**. The knock sensor detects a knock in the cylinder during the combustion process and it sends an electrical signal to the PCM. The PCM, in turn, retards the ignition timing by a certain amount to reduce the uncontrolled detonation. The knock sensor consists of a small crystal that vibrates with engine vibration. If the engine detonation exceeds the normal limit, the vibration causes an increase of the voltage signal from the knock sensor.

6

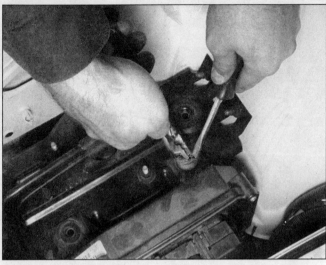

3.3 Push down on the collar using a screwdriver and lift the center pin with a pair of pliers to release the locking mechanism

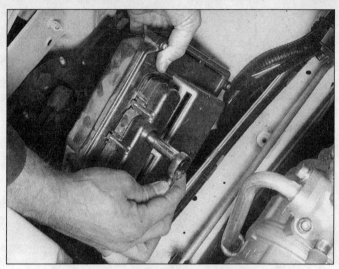

3.4 Remove the PCM electrical connector bolt

3   Powertrain Control Module (PCM) - removal and installation

Refer to illustrations 3.3 and 3.4
Note: *Avoid static electricity damage to the PCM by grounding yourself to the body of the vehicle before touching the PCM and using a special anti-static pad to store the PCM on once it is removed.*
1   Disconnect the cable from the negative battery terminal.
2   Remove the air cleaner assembly (see Chapter 4).
3   Remove the bolts that retain the PCM to the engine compartment and lift the assembly from the vehicle **(see illustration)**.
4   Remove the harness retaining bolt for the PCM electrical connector **(see illustration)**.
5   Installation is the reverse of removal.

4   On Board Diagnosis (OBD) system - description and trouble code access

Note 1: *On the models covered by this manual, the CHECK ENGINE light or MIL light, located in the instrument panel, flashes on for three seconds as a bulb test when the engine is started. The light comes on and stays on when there's a problem in the SEFI system.*
Note 2: *1996 and later models are equipped with the OBD-II system. The engine codes can be accessed using the ignition key but it will be necessary to use a special factory SCAN tool (DRB-II) to read and interpret the various levels of diagnostic information.*
Note 3: *Before outputting the trouble codes, thoroughly inspect ALL electrical connectors and hoses. Make sure all electrical connections are tight, clean and free of corrosion; make sure all hoses are properly connected, fit tightly and are in good condition (no cracks or tears).*
1   The self-diagnosis information contained in the PCM (computer) can be accessed either by the ignition key or by using a special tool called the Diagnostic Readout Box (DRB II). This tool is attached to the diagnostic connector in the engine compartment and reads the codes and parameters on the digital display screen. The tool is expensive and most home mechanics prefer to use the alternate method. The drawback with the ignition key method is that it does not access all the available codes for display. Most problems can be solved or diagnosed quite easily and if the information cannot be obtained

readily, have the vehicle's self-diagnosis system analyzed by a dealer service department or other qualified repair shop.
2   To obtain the codes using the ignition key method, first set the parking brake and put the shift lever in Park. Raise the engine speed to approximately 2,500 rpm and slowly let the speed down to idle. Also cycle the air conditioning system (on briefly, then off). Next, with your foot on the brake, select each position on the transmission (Reverse, Drive, Low etc.), finally bring the shifter back to Park and turn off the engine. This will allow the computer to obtain any fault codes that might be linked to any of the sensors controlled by the transmission, engine speed or air conditioning system.
3   To display the codes on the dashboard (CHECK ENGINE light or a MIL [Malfunction Indicator light]), with the engine NOT running, turn the ignition key ON, OFF, ON, OFF and finally ON. The codes will begin to flash. The light will blink the number of the first digit then pause and blink the number of the second digit. For example: Code 23, air temperature sensor circuit, would be indicated by two flashes, then a pause followed by three flashes.
4   Certain criteria must be met for a fault code to be entered into the engine controller memory. The criteria might be a specific range of engine rpm, engine temperature or input voltage to the engine controller. It's possible that a fault code for a particular monitored circuit may not be entered into the memory despite a malfunction. This may happen because one of the fault code criteria has not been met. For example, the engine must be operating between 750 and 2,000 rpm in order to monitor the MAP sensor circuit correctly. If the engine speed is raised above 2,400 rpm, the MAP sensor output circuit shorts to ground and will not allow a fault code to be entered into the memory. Then again, the exact opposite could occur: A code is entered into the memory that suggests a malfunction within another component that is not monitored by the computer. For example, a fuel pressure problem cannot register a fault directly but instead, it will cause a rich or lean fuel mixture problem. Consequently, this will cause an oxygen sensor malfunction resulting in a stored code in the computer for the oxygen sensor. Be aware of the interrelationship of the sensors and circuits and the overall relationship of the emissions control and fuel injection systems.
5   The accompanying table is a list of the typical trouble codes which may be encountered while diagnosing the system. Also included are simplified troubleshooting procedures. If the problem persists after these checks have been made, more detailed service procedures will have to be performed by a dealer service department or other qualified repair shop.

Trouble codes

Note: *Not all trouble codes apply to all models.*

Code 11   No distributor reference signal detected during engine cranking. Check the circuit between the distributor and the PCM.

Code 12   Problem with the battery connection. Direct battery input to controller disconnected within the last 50 ignition key-on cycles.

Code 13**   Indicates a problem with the MAP sensor pneumatic (vacuum) system.

Code 14**   MAP sensor voltage too low or too high.

Code 15**   A problem with the vehicle distance/speed signal. No distance/speed sensor signal detected during road load conditions.

Code 16   Loss of battery voltage.

Code 17   Engine is cold too long. Engine coolant temperature remains below normal operating temperatures during operation (check the thermostat).

Code 21**   Problem with oxygen sensor signal circuit. Sensor voltage to computer not fluctuating.

Code 22**   Coolant sensor voltage too high or too low. Test coolant temperature sensor.

Code 23**   Indicates that the air temperature sensor input is below the minimum acceptable voltage or sensor input is above the maximum acceptable voltage.

Code 24**   Throttle position sensor voltage high or low. Test the throttle position sensor.

Code 25**   Idle Air Control (IAC) valve circuits. A shorted condition is detected in one or more of the IAC valve circuits.

Code 27   One of the injector control circuit output drivers does not respond properly to the control signal. Check the circuits.

Code 31**   Problem with the canister purge solenoid circuit.

Code 32**   An open or shorted condition detected in the EGR solenoid circuit. Possible air/fuel ratio imbalance not detected during diagnosis.

Code 33   Air conditioning clutch relay circuit. An open or shorted condition detected in the compressor clutch relay circuit.

Code 34   Open or shorted condition detected in the speed control vacuum or vent solenoid circuits.

Code 35   Open or shorted condition detected in the radiator fan low speed relay circuit.

Code 41**   Problem with the charging system. Occurs when battery voltage from the ASD relay is below 11.75-volts.

Code 42   Auto shutdown relay (ASD) control circuit indicates an open or shorted circuit condition.

Code 43**   Peak primary circuit current not achieved with the maximum dwell time.

Code 44   Battery temperature sensor volts malfunction. Problem with the battery temperature voltage circuit in the PCM.

Code 46**   Charging system voltage too high. Computer indicates that the battery voltage is not properly regulated.

Code 47**   Charging system voltage too low. Battery voltage sense input below target charging voltage during engine operation and no significant change in voltage detected during active test of alternator output.

Code 51*   Oxygen sensor signal input indicates lean fuel/air ratio condition during engine operation.

Code 52**   Oxygen sensor signal input indicates rich fuel/air ratio condition during engine operation.

Code 53   Internal PCM failure detected.

Code 54   No camshaft position sensor signal from distributor. Problem with the distributor synchronization circuit.

Code 55   Completion of fault code display on CHECK ENGINE lamp. This is an end of message code.

Code 62   Unsuccessful attempt to update EMR mileage in the controller EEPROM.

Code 63   Controller failure. EEPROM write denied. Check the PCM.

Code 64**   The Flexible Fuel sensor voltage is low. Methanol concentration sensor input below the maximum acceptable voltage requirements.

Code 65   An open or shorted condition detected in the Manifold Tuning Valve (MTV) solenoid circuit.

Code 66   PCM is not receiving CCD Bus signals.

Code 77   Speed Control Power relay circuit is open or shorted.

** *These codes light up the CHECK ENGINE light on the instrument panel during engine operation once the trouble code has been recorded.*

6

5   Information sensors - check and replacement

Note 1: *After performing checking procedures to any of the information sensors, be sure to clear the PCM of all trouble codes by disconnecting the cable from the negative terminal of the battery for at least ten seconds*

Note 2: *1996 models are equipped with the OBD-II system. The engine codes can be accessed using the ignition key but it will be necessary to use a special factory SCAN tool (DRB-II) to read and interpret the various levels of diagnostic information. Have the vehicle diagnosed by a dealer service department if following the sensor checking procedures fails to turn up a problem.*

Oxygen sensor

General description

1   The oxygen sensor, which is located in the exhaust manifold **(see illustrations 2.14a and 2.14b)**, monitors the oxygen content of the exhaust gas stream. The oxygen content in the exhaust reacts with the oxygen sensor to produce a voltage output which varies from 0.1-volt (high oxygen, lean mixture) to 0.9-volts (low oxygen, rich mixture). The PCM constantly monitors this variable voltage output to determine the ratio of oxygen to fuel in the mixture. The PCM alters the air/fuel mixture ratio by controlling the pulse width (open time) of the fuel injectors. A mixture ratio of 14.7 parts air to 1 part fuel is the ideal mixture ratio for minimizing exhaust emissions, thus allowing the catalytic converter to operate at maximum efficiency. It is this ratio of 14.7 to 1 which the PCM and the oxygen sensor attempt to maintain at all times. **Note:** *1996 models are equipped with four oxygen sensors; right bank and left bank upstream oxygen sensors and left and right downstream (after the catalytic converter) oxygen sensors.*

2   The oxygen sensor produces no voltage when it is below its normal operating temperature of about 600-degrees F. During this initial period before warm-up, the PCM operates in OPEN LOOP mode.

3   If the engine reaches normal operating temperature and/or has been running for two or more minutes, and if the oxygen sensor is producing a steady signal voltage below 0.45-volts at 1,500 rpm or greater, the PCM will set a Code 51 or 52. The PCM will also set a code 21 if it detects any problem with the oxygen sensor circuit.

4   When there is a problem with the oxygen sensor or its circuit, the PCM operates in the open loop mode - that is, it controls fuel delivery in accordance with a programmed default value instead of feedback information from the oxygen sensor.

5   The proper operation of the oxygen sensor depends on four conditions:

a) *Electrical - The low voltages generated by the sensor depend upon good, clean connections which should be checked whenever a malfunction of the sensor is suspected or indicated.*

b) *Outside air supply - The sensor is designed to allow air circulation to the internal portion of the sensor. Whenever the sensor is removed and installed or replaced, make sure the air passages are not restricted.*

c) *Proper operating temperature - The PCM will not react to the sensor signal until the sensor reaches approximately 600-degrees F. This factor must be taken into consideration when evaluating the performance of the sensor.*

d) *Unleaded fuel - The use of unleaded fuel is essential for proper operation of the sensor. Make sure the fuel you are using is of this type.*

6   In addition to observing the above conditions, special care must be taken whenever the sensor is serviced.

a) *The oxygen sensor has a permanently attached pigtail and electrical connector which should not be removed from the sensor. Damage or removal of the pigtail or electrical connector can adversely affect operation of the sensor.*

b) *Grease, dirt and other contaminants should be kept away from the electrical connector and the louvered end of the sensor.*

c) *Do not use cleaning solvents of any kind on the oxygen sensor.*

d) *Do not drop or roughly handle the sensor.*

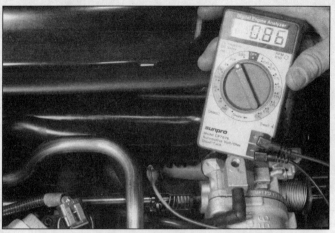

5.7a Install a pin into the electrical connector and backprobe the oxygen sensor electrical connector dark green/black wire terminal to monitor the sensor output signal voltage. The oxygen sensor electrical connector is located behind the throttle body on the 3.5L engine

e) *The silicone boot must be installed in the correct position to prevent the boot from being melted and to allow the sensor to operate properly.*

Check

Refer to illustrations 5.7a, 5.7b, 5.7c, 5.7d, 5.12 and 5.14

7   Locate the oxygen sensor electrical connector and insert a long pin into the oxygen sensor connector black/dark green (left O2 sensor) or tan/white (right O2 sensor) signal voltage wire **(see illustrations).**

8   Install the positive probe of a voltmeter onto the correct pin and the negative probe to ground. **Note:** *Consult the wiring diagrams at the end of Chapter 12 for additional information on the oxygen sensor electrical connector wire color designations.*

9   Start the engine and monitor the voltage signal (millivolts) as the engine goes from cold to warm.

10   The oxygen sensor will produce a steady voltage signal at first (open loop) of approximately 0.1 to 0.2 volts with the engine cold. After a period of approximately two minutes, the engine will reach operating temperature and the oxygen sensor will start to fluctuate between 0.1 to 0.9 volts (closed loop). If the oxygen sensor fails to reach the closed loop mode or there is a very long period of time until it does switch into closed loop mode, replace the oxygen sensor with a new part.

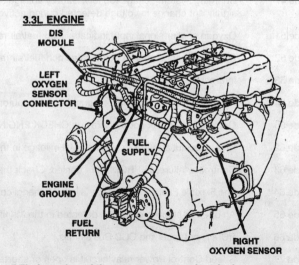

5.7b Location of the oxygen sensor electrical connectors on the 3.3L engine

11   Also inspect the oxygen sensor heater. Disconnect the oxygen sensor electrical connector and connect an ohmmeter between the two white wires. It should measure approximately 5 to 7 ohms.
12   Check for proper supply voltage to the heater **(see illustration)**. Measure the voltage on the oxygen sensor electrical connector between the:

Light green/black wire terminal (+) and the black wire terminal (-) on 1993 through 1995 models, or the

Dark green/orange wire terminal (+) and the black wire terminal (-) on 1996 models.

There should be battery voltage with the ignition key ON (engine not running). If there is no voltage, check the circuit between the main relay, the PCM and the sensor. **Note:** *It is important to remember that supply voltage will only last approximately 2 seconds because the system uses a relay to turn off the voltage if the engine is not started.*
13   Using an ohmmeter, check the resistance of the oxygen sensor heater elements. Unplug the oxygen sensor electrical connectors and attach the leads of an ohmmeter to the wire terminals. The resistance should be approximately 5 to 7 ohms. If not, replace the sensor.
14   Access to the oxygen sensors electrical connectors can make monitoring the SIGNAL voltage changes difficult without removing several components to allow room for connecting the volt/ohmmeter electrical leads. A SCAN tool is available from some automotive parts stores and specialty tool companies that can be plugged into the test connector for the purpose of monitoring the computer and the sensors **(see illustration)**. Install the SCAN tool and switch to the Oxygen Sensor

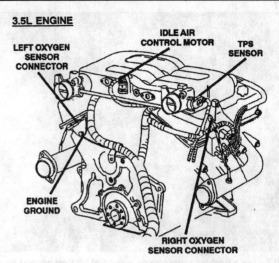

5.7c Location of the O2 electrical connectors on the 3.5L engine

mode and monitor the O2 sensor crosscounts (varying millivolt signals). The SCAN tool should indicate approximately 100 to 200 millivolts when cold (LEAN condition) and then fluctuate from 300 to 800 millivolts warm (CLOSED LOOP).

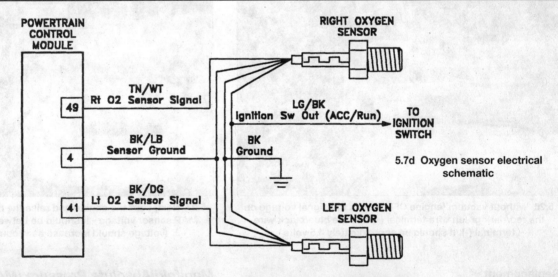

5.7d Oxygen sensor electrical schematic

5.12 Measure the voltage to the oxygen sensor heater on the light green/black wire terminal (+).

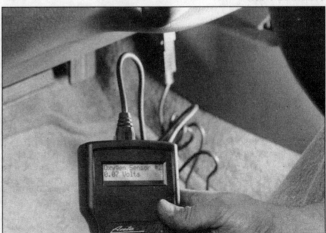

5.14 Install the SCAN tool into the test connector under the dash and monitor the O2 sensor crosscounts (millivolt signal)

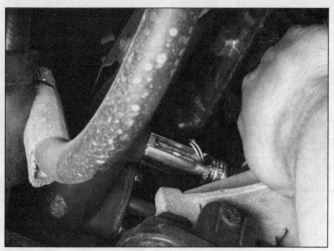

5.17 Use a box-end wrench or a special slotted socket to remove
the O₂ sensor from the exhaust manifold

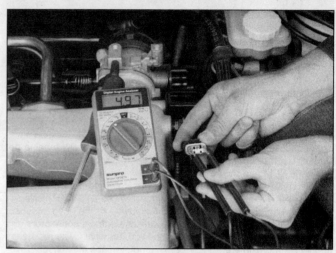

5.25 Using a voltmeter, check for reference voltage to the MAP
sensor on the purple/white (+) wire terminal and blue/black (-)
wire terminal. It should be approximately 5.0 volts

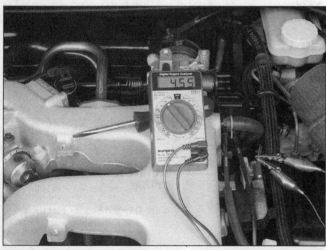

5.26 Without vacuum (engine OFF), check the signal voltage on
the red/dark green wire terminal (+) and the blue/black wire
terminal (-). It should be approximately 4.5 volts

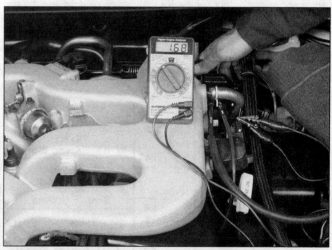

5.27 Next, start the engine and raise the rpm and check for the
MAP sensor voltage - it should be between 0.5 and 2.0 volts
(voltage should increase as vacuum decreases)

Replacement

Refer to illustration 5.17

Note: *Because it is installed in the exhaust manifold or pipe, which contracts when cool, the oxygen sensor may be very difficult to loosen when the engine is cold. Rather than risk damage to the sensor (assuming you are planning to re-use it in another manifold or pipe), start and run the engine for a minute or two, then shut it off. Be careful not to burn yourself during the following procedure.*

15   Disconnect the cable from the negative battery terminal.

16   Raise the vehicle and place it securely on jackstands.

17   Carefully disconnect the electrical connector from the sensor and unscrew the sensor from the exhaust manifold **(see illustration)**.

18   Anti-seize compound must be used on the threads of the sensor to facilitate future removal. The threads of new sensors will already be coated with this compound, but if an old sensor is removed and reinstalled, recoat the threads.

19   Install the sensor and tighten it securely.

20   Reconnect the electrical connector of the pigtail lead to the main engine wiring harness.

21   Lower the vehicle, take it on a test drive and check to see that no trouble codes set.

Manifold Absolute Pressure (MAP) sensor

General description

22   The Manifold Absolute Pressure (MAP) sensor **(see illustrations 2.12a and 2.12b)** monitors the intake manifold pressure changes resulting from changes in engine load and speed and converts the information into a voltage output. The PCM uses the MAP sensor to control fuel delivery and ignition timing. The PCM will receive information as a voltage signal that will vary from 1.0 to 1.5 volts at closed throttle (high vacuum) and 4.0 to 4.5 volts at wide open throttle (low vacuum). The MAP sensor is located on the side of the intake manifold plenum.

23   A failure in the MAP sensor circuit should set a Code 13 or a Code 14.

Check

Refer to illustrations 5.25, 5.26 and 5.27

24   Check the electrical connector at the sensor for a snug fit. Check the terminals in the connector and the wires leading to it for looseness and breaks. Repair as required.

25   Disconnect the MAP sensor connector, turn the ignition key ON

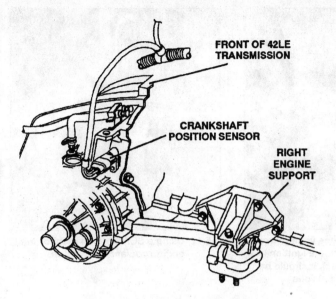

5.33a Location of the crankshaft sensor

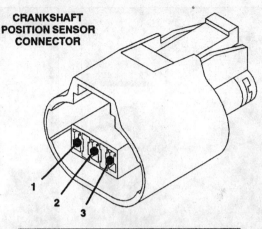

CAV	COLOR	FUNCTION
1	OR	8-VOLT SUPPLY
2	BK/LB	SENSOR GROUND
3	LB/DB	CKP SENSOR SIGNAL

5.33b Check the reference voltage on the orange wire terminal. It should be approximately 8.0 volts

(engine not running) and check for voltage on the reference wire (purple/white wire) (+) and ground wire (blue/black) (-) **(see illustration)**. There should be approximately 5 volts.

26　Connect the electrical connector to the MAP sensor and check for voltage on the signal wire (red/dark green wire) (+) with the ignition key on (engine not running). There should be approximately 4.5 volts. This checks signal voltage to the PCM **(see illustration)**.

27　Start the engine and slowly raise the rpm while probing the signal wire (red/dark green wire terminal) with the positive probe of the voltmeter **(see illustration)**. Voltage should increase as vacuum decreases. If the readings are incorrect, replace the MAP sensor with a new part.

28　An alternate method of diagnosing the MAP sensor is by the use of an electronic SCAN tool. SCAN tools can be plugged into the test connector for the purpose of monitoring the computer and the sensors and are available from some automotive parts stores and specialty tool companies. Install the SCAN tool and switch to the MAP mode and monitor the voltage signal with the engine at idle and high rpm **(see illustration 5.14)**. The SCAN tool should indicate between 1.2 to 1.6 volts. Raise the engine rpm and observe that as engine rpm increases (decreasing vacuum) the MAP SIGNAL voltage increases. The SCAN tool must be able to access the data stream to read real-time values. If the MAP sensor voltage readings are incorrect, replace the MAP sensor.

Replacement

29　Disconnect the electrical connector from the MAP sensor.
30　Unscrew the MAP sensor from the intake plenum.
31　Installation is the reverse of removal.

Crankshaft position sensor

General description

32　On these models, the crankshaft position sensor determines the timing for the fuel injection and ignition on each cylinder. It also detects engine RPM. The crankshaft position sensor is a Hall-Effect device that is mounted on the bellhousing and detects notches in the driveplate **(see illustrations 2.11a and 2.11b)**. The engine will not operate if the PCM does not receive a crankshaft position sensor input.

Check

Refer to illustrations 5.33a and 5.33b

33　Check the reference voltage to the crankshaft sensor from the PCM. Locate the crankshaft sensor electrical connector **(see**

illustration) near the bellhousing, remove the connector and with the ignition key ON (engine not running) install the positive probe of the voltmeter to the orange wire terminal (+) **(see illustration)**. There should be 8.0 volts.

34　If reference voltage is present, check for the crank sensor signal. Install the electrical connector onto the crank sensor, backprobe the light blue/dark blue wire terminal (+) using a pin or paper clip and monitor the voltage changes as you turn the engine over slowly using a socket and wrench on the crankshaft pulley or by tapping the ignition key without starting the engine. The voltage will fluctuate from 0.3 (metal under sensor) to 5.0 volts (slots under sensor). Refer to Chapter 2B for additional information.

35　Because the crankshaft sensor is very difficult to reach, it may be easier to use a SCAN tool or have the system checked at a dealer service department. The SCAN tool can be plugged into the test connector for the purpose of monitoring the computer and the sensors. This special tool is available from some automotive parts stores and specialty tool companies.

Replacement

36　Disconnect the crankshaft sensor wiring harness connector.
37　Remove the crankshaft sensor mounting bolts. Use only the original bolts to mount the sensor, they are machined to correctly space the sensor to the flywheel.
38　Installation is the reverse of removal. Tighten the bolt(s) to the torque listed in this Chapter's Specifications.

Engine Coolant Temperature (ECT) sensor

General description

39　The coolant temperature sensor is a thermistor (a resistor which varies the value of its resistance in accordance with temperature changes) **(see illustrations 2.10a and 2.10b)**. The change in the resistance values will directly affect the voltage signal from the coolant thermosensor. As the sensor temperature DECREASES, the resistance values will INCREASE. As the sensor temperature INCREASES, the resistance values will DECREASE. A failure in the coolant sensor circuit should set either a Code 14 or a Code 15. These codes indicate a failure in the coolant temperature circuit, so the appropriate solution to the problem will be either repair of a wire or replacement of the sensor. The sensor can also be checked with an ohmmeter, by measuring its resistance when cold, then warming up the engine and taking another measurement.

6

5.40 Position the probes of the ohmmeter on the coolant temperature sensor and check the resistance

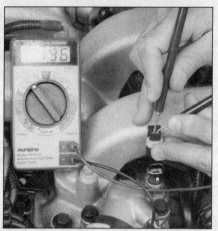

5.41 Check the reference voltage from the PCM to the ECT with the ignition key ON (engine not running). It should be approximately 5.0 volts

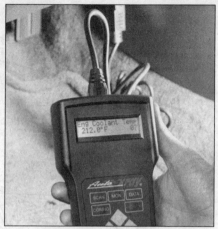

5.42 Using a SCAN tool to monitor the engine coolant temperature

Check

Refer to illustrations 5.40, 5.41 and 5.42

40   To check the sensor, check the resistance values of the coolant temperature sensor while it is completely cold (50 to 80-degrees F = 15,700 to 9,200 ohms) **(see illustration)**. Next, start the engine and warm it up until it reaches operating temperature. The resistance should be lower (170 to 200-degrees F = 900 to 600 ohms).

41   Check the reference voltage with the ignition key ON (engine not running) **(see illustration)**. Place the positive probe of the voltmeter on the tan/black (+) wire terminal and the negative probe on the black/blue (-) wire terminal. It should be approximately 5.0 volts.

42   A SCAN tool is available from some automotive parts stores and specialty tool companies that can be plugged into the diagnostic connector for the purpose of monitoring the computer and the sensors. Install the SCAN tool and switch to the ECT mode and monitor the temperature of the engine COLD **(see illustration)**. The SCAN tool should indicate between 75 to 90-degrees F. Allow the engine to idle for several minutes and observe the coolant temperature increase as the engine progressively warms-up. The temperature should indicate between 180 to 210-degrees F when fully warmed-up. **Note:** *If there is not a definite change in temperature, remove the coolant temperature sensor and check the resistance in a pan of heated water to simulate warm-up conditions. If the sensor tests are good, check the wiring harness from the sensor to the computer.*

Replacement

Warning: *Wait until the engine is completely cool before beginning this procedure.*

43   To remove the sensor, release the locking tab, unplug the electrical connector, then carefully unscrew the sensor. **Caution:** *Handle the coolant sensor with care. Damage to this sensor will affect the operation of the entire fuel injection system.*

44   Before installing the new sensor, wrap the threads with Teflon sealing tape to prevent leakage and thread corrosion.

45   Installation is the reverse of removal.

Throttle Position Sensor (TPS)

General description

46   The Throttle Position Sensor (TPS) is located on the end of the throttle shaft on the throttle body **(see illustrations 2.15a and 2.15b)**. By monitoring the output voltage from the TPS, the PCM can determine fuel delivery based on throttle valve angle (driver demand). A broken or loose TPS can cause intermittent bursts of fuel from the injector and an unstable idle because the PCM thinks the throttle is moving.

Check

Refer to illustrations 5.48, 5.49a, 5.49b, 5.50a and 5.50b

47   Locate the Throttle Position Sensor (TPS) on the throttle body.

48   Disconnect the TPS electrical connector and using a voltmeter, check the reference voltage from the PCM. Install the positive probe (+) onto the purple/white wire terminal and the negative probe (-) onto the black/blue wire terminal **(see illustration)**. The voltage should read approximately 5.0 volts.

49   Next, install the electrical connector onto the TPS and check the TPS signal voltage. With the throttle fully closed, connect the positive probe (+) of the voltmeter onto the orange/blue wire terminal and the negative probe to ground **(see illustrations)**. Gradually open the throttle valve and observe the TPS sensor voltage. With the throttle valve fully closed, the voltage should read approximately 0.5 to 1.0 volt. Slowly move the throttle valve and observe a distinct change in the voltage values as the sensor travels from idle to full throttle. The voltage should increase to approximately 3.5 to 5.0 volts. If the readings are incorrect, replace the TPS sensor.

50   An alternate method of diagnosing the TPS sensor is by the use of an electronic SCAN tool. SCAN tools can be plugged into the test connector for the purpose of monitoring the computer and the sensors and are available from some automotive parts stores and specialty tool companies **(see illustrations)**. Install the SCAN tool and switch to the TPS mode and monitor the voltage signal with the engine at idle and

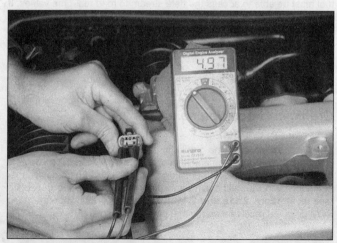

5.48 Check for reference voltage to the TPS sensor on the purple/white wire terminal (+) and the black/blue wire terminal (-) (ground). It should be approximately 5.0 volts

5.49a Check the voltage signal from the signal wire terminal (orange/blue) (+) and ground wire terminal (black/blue) (-). First, check the voltage with the throttle completely closed. It should be approximately 0.5 volts

high rpm. The SCAN tool should indicate between 0.5 to 1.0 volt at idle. Raise the engine rpm and observe that as engine rpm increases the TPS voltage increases to approximately 3.5 to 5.0 volts. The SCAN

tool must be able to access the data stream to read real-time values. If the TPS sensor voltage readings are incorrect, replace the TPS sensor.

51   A problem in any of the TPS circuits will set a Code 24. Once a trouble code is set, the PCM will use an artificial default value for throttle position and some vehicle performance will return.

Replacement

Refer to illustrations 5.54a and 5.54b

52   Disconnect the electrical connector from the TPS.

53   Remove the mounting screws from the TPS and remove the TPS from the throttle body.

54   When installing the TPS, be sure to align the socket locating tangs on the TPS with the throttle shaft in the throttle body **(see illustrations).**

55   Installation is the reverse of removal. Be sure the throttle valve is fully closed once the TPS is mounted. If it isn't, rotate the TPS to allow complete closure (idle) before tightening the mounting screws.

Air Temperature sensor

General information

56   The air temperature sensor is located in the intake manifold. This sensor is also referred to as the Intake Air Temperature (IAT) sensor. This sensor operates as a negative temperature coefficient (NTC) device. As the sensor temperature DECREASES, the resistance values will INCREASE. As the sensor temperature INCREASES, the resistance values will DECREASE. Most cases, the appropriate solution to the problem will be either repair of a wire or replacement of the sensor.

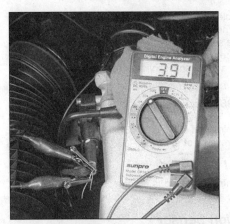

5.49b Next, using your hand, rotate the throttle valve until wide open throttle is attained and check the voltage signal. It should be 3.5 to 5.0 volts

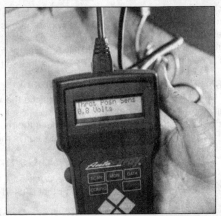

5.50a Monitor the TPS voltage using a SCAN tool with the engine idling

5.50b Depress the accelerator pedal and see if the voltage value increases

6

5.54a Align the tangs on the TPS with the throttle shaft on the throttle body before installing the sensor (3.3L engine shown)

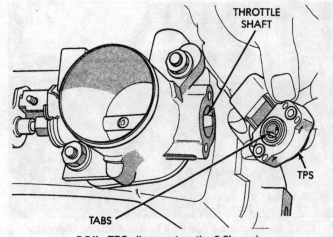

5.54b TPS alignment on the 3.5L engine

5.57 Checking the resistance of the air temperature sensor on the 3.5L engine

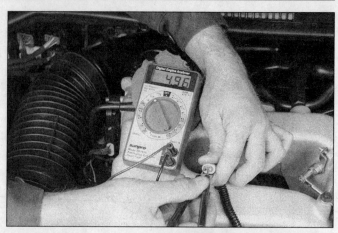

5.58 Checking the reference voltage to the air temperature sensor on the 3.5L engine

Check

Refer to illustrations 5.57 and 5.58

57   To check the sensor, check the resistance values **(see illustration)** of the air temperature sensor while it is completely cold (50 to 80-degrees F = 7,900 to 1,800 ohms). Next, start the engine and warm it up until it reaches operating temperature. The resistance should be lower (180 to 200-degrees F = 170 to 20 ohms). With the ignition switch OFF, disconnect the electrical connector from the air temperature sensor, which is located on the intake manifold. Using an ohmmeter, measure the resistance between the two terminals on the sensor.

58   With the ignition key ON (engine not running), check for reference voltage on the harness connector to the sensor **(see illustration)**. It should be approximately 5.0 volts.

59   If the sensor resistance test results are incorrect, replace the air temperature sensor.

60   If the sensor checks out okay but there is still a problem, have the vehicle checked at a dealer service department or other qualified repair shop, as the PCM may be malfunctioning.

Replacement

61   Unplug the electrical connector from the air temperature sensor.

62   Unscrew the sensor from the intake manifold and remove the air temperature sensor.

63   Installation is the reverse of removal.

Vehicle Speed Sensor

General description

64   The Vehicle Speed Sensor (VSS) is located on the transmission

depending upon the model and equipment package **(see illustration 2.16)**. This sensor is a permanent magnetic variable reluctance sensor that produces a pulsing voltage whenever vehicle speed is over 3 mph. These pulses are translated by the PCM and provided to other systems for fuel and transmission shift control.

Check

65   To check the vehicle speed sensor, remove the electrical connector in the wiring harness near the sensor. Using a voltmeter, check for reference voltage to the sensor. The reference wire should have approximately 5.0 volts or more available. If there is no voltage available, have the PCM diagnosed by a dealership service department.

Replacement

66   To replace the VSS, disconnect the electrical connector from the VSS.

67   Remove the retaining bolt and lift the VSS from the transmission.

68   Installation is the reverse of removal.

Lock-up Control Solenoid

69   The Lock-up Control Solenoid is a computer controlled output actuator that is used to activate the lock-up torque converter.

Camshaft Position Sensor

General description

70   The camshaft position sensor **(see illustration 2.8a, 2.8b, 2.8c and 2.8d)** provides cylinder identification to the PCM to synchronize

5.73a Backprobe the camshaft sensor electrical connector tan/yellow (+) and black/light blue (-) wire terminals (3.3L engine shown)

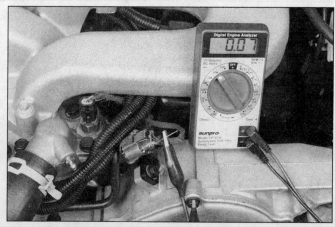

5.73b Turn the engine over slowly using a breaker bar and socket on the front pulley and observe the voltage fluctuate between 0.3 volts and 5.0 volts (3.5L engine shown)

5.80 Location of the knock sensors on the 3.5L engine (the cylinder head is removed for clarity)

the fuel system with the spark system. The synchronizing signal is generated from a rotating pulse ring located on the camshaft sprocket. The sensor generates pulses as groups of notches on the camshaft sprocket pass underneath it. When metal aligns with the sensor the voltage pulses low (approximately 0.3 volts) and when the notch aligns with the sensor, voltage increases suddenly to about 5.0 volts. These voltage pulses are in turn processed by the PCM which in turn determines ignition timing.

Check

Refer to illustrations 5.73a and 5.73b

71 To check the cam sensor circuit, disconnect the cam sensor electrical connector. Turn the ignition key to ON but do not start the engine.
72 Check the reference voltage. Measure the voltage between orange wire terminal (+) and the black/light blue wire terminal (-). It should be 8 volts.
73 If reference voltage is present, check for the cranking signal. Install the electrical connector onto the camshaft sensor, backprobe the tan/yellow wire terminal (+) and the black/light blue wire terminal (-) using a pin or paper clip and monitor the voltage changes as you turn the engine over slowly using a socket and wrench on the crankshaft pulley or by tapping the ignition key without starting the engine. **(see illustrations)**. The voltage will fluctuate from 0.3 (metal under sensor) to 5.0 volts (slots under sensor). Refer to Chapter 2B for additional information.
74 If the voltage readings are both correct, have the cam sensor diagnosed by a dealer service department or other qualified repair shop.
75 It may be necessary to observe the actual camshaft sensor signal

while the engine is running. A SCAN tool is available from some automotive parts stores and specialty tool companies that can be plugged into the test connector for the purpose of monitoring the computer and the sensors. Install the SCAN tool and switch to the Camshaft sensor mode and monitor the voltage signal from the cam sensor.

Replacement

76 Disconnect the negative terminal from the battery.
77 Disconnect the electrical connector from the cam sensor.
78 Remove the bolt from the camshaft sensor and lift the sensor from the timing cover.
79 Installation is the reverse of removal. Be sure to install the paper spacer onto the camshaft sensor and tighten the camshaft sensor bolt to the torque listed in this Chapter's Specifications.

Knock sensors (3.5L engine only)
General information

Refer to illustration 5.80

80 The 3.5L engine is equipped with two knock sensors **(see illustration)**. If the knock sensor detects a knock in the cylinder during the combustion process it sends an electrical signal to the PCM. The PCM, in turn, retards the ignition timing by a certain amount to reduce the uncontrolled detonation. The knock sensor consists of a small crystal that oscillates with engine vibration. If the engine detonation supersedes the normal limit, the vibration causes an increase in the voltage signal from the knock sensor

Check

81 In the event of knock sensor failure, have the system checked at a dealer service department.

Replacement

82 Remove the intake manifold (see Chapter 2B).
83 Disconnect the electrical connector(s) and unscrew the knock sensor(s) from the engine block.
84 Installation is the reverse of removal.

Park Neutral position switch

85 Refer to Chapter 7 for all the checks and replacement procedures for the Park/Neutral position switch.

---

6 Positive Crankcase Ventilation (PCV) system

Refer to illustrations 6.1a, 6.1b and 6.1c

1 The Positive Crankcase Ventilation (PCV) system **(see illustrations)** reduces hydrocarbon emissions by scavenging crankcase vapors. It does this by circulating fresh air from the air cleaner through

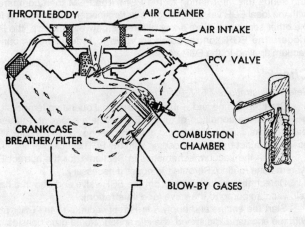

6.1a Schematic of a typical PCV system

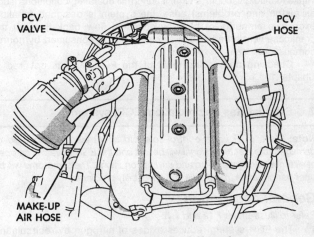

6.1b PCV system on the 3.3L engine

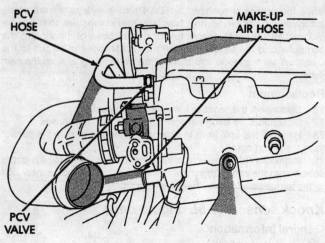

6.1c PCV system on the 3.5L engine

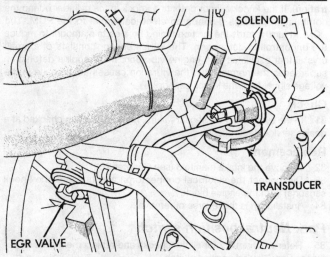

7.1b EGR components on the 3.5L engine

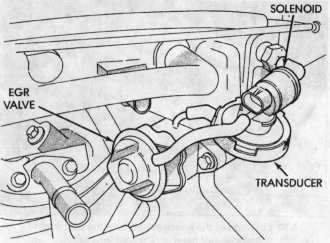

7.1a EGR components on a 3.3L engine

7.6 Install a hand-held vacuum pump onto the EGR valve and observe that the valve diaphragm moves up and down freely without any binding - the engine should stall with vacuum applied

the crankcase, where it mixes with blow-by gases and is then rerouted through a PCV valve to the intake manifold.

2   The main components of the PCV system are the PCV valve, a blow-by filter and the vacuum hoses connecting these two components with the engine.

3   To maintain idle quality, the PCV valve restricts the flow when the intake manifold vacuum is high. If abnormal operating conditions (such as piston ring problems) arise, the system is designed to allow excessive amounts of blow-by gases to flow back through the crankcase vent tube into the air cleaner to be consumed by normal combustion.

4   Checking and replacement of the PCV valve is covered in Chapter 1.

7   Exhaust Gas Recirculation (EGR) system

Note: *If the EGR valve control solenoid becomes disconnected or damaged, the electrical signal will be lost and the EGR valve will be open at all times during warm-up and driving conditions. The symptoms will be poor performance, rough idle and driveability problems.*

General description

Refer to illustrations 7.1a and 7.1b

1   The EGR system reduces oxides of nitrogen by recirculating exhaust gas through the EGR valve and intake manifold into the combustion chambers **(see illustrations)**.

2   The EGR system consists of the EGR valve, EGR backpressure transducer and the EGR control solenoid valve (EET), the Powertrain Control Module (PCM) and various sensors. The PCM memory is programmed to produce the ideal EGR valve lift for each operating condition. An EGR valve lift sensor detects the amount of EGR valve lift and sends this information to the PCM. The PCM then compares it with the ideal EGR valve lift, which is determined by data received from the other sensors. If there's any difference between the two, the PCM triggers the EGR control solenoid valve to reduce the amount of vacuum applied to the EGR valve.

Check

Refer to illustrations 7.6, 7.10 and 7.11

3   Start the engine and warm it to its normal operating temperature.

4   Check the condition of all the EGR system hoses and tubes for leaks, cracks, kinks or hardening of the rubber hoses. Make sure all the hoses are intact before proceeding with the EGR check.

5   Check the vacuum schematics in Section 1 for the correct EGR system hose routing. Reroute the hoses if necessary.

6   Detach the vacuum hose from the EGR valve and attach a hand-held vacuum pump to the valve **(see illustration)**.

7   Start the engine and apply 5 in-Hg. of vacuum to the EGR valve. With the engine at idle speed, the idle speed should drop considerably or even stall as vacuum is applied. This indicates that the EGR system is operating properly.

7.10 Check for vacuum to the EET solenoid with the engine running

7.11 With the ignition key ON (engine not running) there should be battery voltage present at the EET solenoid electrical connector

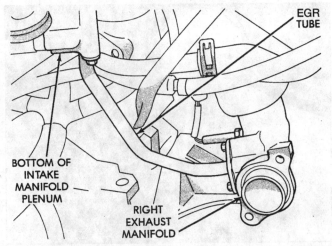

7.14a Remove the EGR tube and check for blockage or damage (3.3L engine shown)

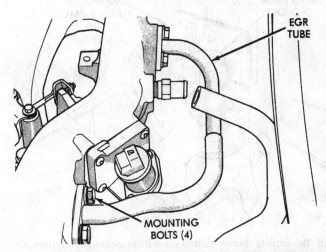

7.14b EGR tube mounting details on the 3.5L engine

8   If the engine speed does not change, this indicates a possible faulty EGR valve, blocked or plugged EGR tube or passages in the intake and exhaust manifolds that may be plugged with carbon.

9   Apply vacuum to the EGR valve and observe the stem on the EGR valve for movement. If the valve opens and closes correctly and the engine does not stall, check the passages.

10   Install a vacuum gauge into the Electronic EGR Transducer (EET) vacuum line, start the engine and verify that the EET is receiving the proper amount of vacuum **(see illustration)**.

11   Also, disconnect the EET solenoid electrical connector and check for battery voltage with the ignition key ON (engine not running) **(see illustration)**.

12   Remove the EGR tube and check for plugged ports in the manifolds, bent tubes or other problems. If necessary replace the EGR tube with a new part. **Note:** *If the EGR valve is severely plugged with carbon deposits, do not attempt to scrape them out. Replace the unit.*

Component replacement

EGR valve

Refer to illustrations 7.14a and 7.14b

13   Unplug the electrical connector for the EGR valve control solenoid (EET).

14   Remove the EGR tube mounting bolts **(see illustrations)** and separate the tube from the engine. **Note:** *It is not necessary to completely remove the EGR tube on the 3.3L to gain access to the*

EGR valve.

15   Remove the nuts that secure the EGR valve and detach the EGR valve. Lift the EGR valve and the EET out as a single unit.

16   Clean the mating surfaces of the EGR valve and adapter.

17   Install the EGR valve, using a new gasket. Tighten the nuts securely.

18   Plug in the electrical connector to the EGR valve control solenoid (EET).

EET control solenoid

19   Disconnect the electrical connector to the EET solenoid.

20   Disconnect the vacuum hoses from the EET to the EGR valve.

21   Lift the EET solenoid from the engine compartment.

22   Installation is the reverse of removal.

8   Evaporative emissions control (EVAP) system

General description

Refer to illustrations 8.5a, 8.5b and 8.6

1   The fuel evaporative emissions control system absorbs fuel vapors and, during engine operation, releases them into the engine intake where they mix with the incoming air-fuel mixture.

2   Every evaporative system employs a canister filled with activated charcoal to absorb fuel vapors.

6

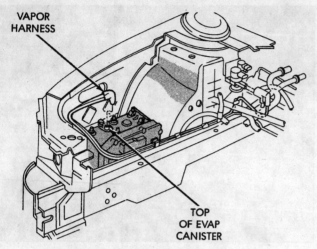

8.5a Location of the EVAP canister

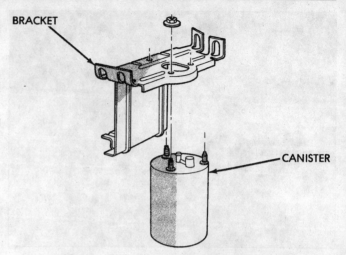

8.5b The EVAP canister can be lowered below the fenderwell after the mounting bolts have been removed

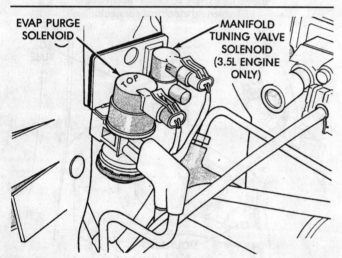

8.6 The canister purge control solenoid is located in the right side corner of the engine compartment

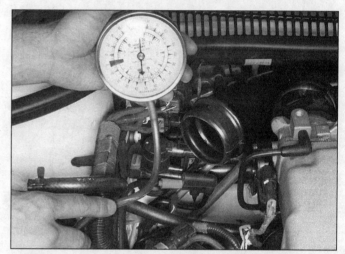

8.8 Disconnect the dual vacuum line from the purge control solenoid, install the vacuum gauge into the bottom port and confirm that there is vacuum to the purge control solenoid

3   The fuel filler cap is fitted with a two-way valve as a safety device. The valve vents fuel vapors to the atmosphere if the evaporative control system fails.

4   Another fuel cut-off valve (fuel tank rollover valve), mounted on the fuel tank, regulates fuel vapor flow from the fuel tank to the charcoal canister, based on the pressure or vacuum caused by temperature changes.

5   After passing through the two-way valve, fuel vapor is carried by vent hoses to the charcoal canister in the engine compartment **(see illustrations)**. The activated charcoal in the canister absorbs and stores these vapors.

6   When the engine is running and warmed to a pre-set temperature, a purge control solenoid **(see illustration)**, allows a purge control diaphragm valve in the charcoal canister to be opened by intake manifold vacuum. Fuel vapors from the canister are then drawn through the purge control diaphragm valve by intake manifold vacuum. The duty cycle of the EVAP purge control solenoid regulates the rate of flow of the fuel vapors from the canister to the throttle body. The PCM controls the purge control solenoid. During cold running conditions and hot start time delay, the PCM does not energize the solenoid (NO PURGING VAPORS). After the engine has warmed up to the correct operating temperatures the PCM purges the vapors into the throttle body according to the running conditions of the engine. The PCM will cycle (ON then OFF) the purge control solenoid about 5 to 10 times per second. The flow rate will be controlled by the pulse width or length of time the solenoid is allowed to be energized.

Check

Refer to illustrations 8.8, 8.10 and 8.17

Note: *The evaporative control system, like all emission control systems, is protected by a Federally-mandated extended warranty (5 years or 50,000 miles at the time this manual was written). The EVAP system probably won't fail during the service life of the vehicle; however, if it does, the hoses or charcoal canister are usually to blame.*

7   Always check the hoses first. A disconnected, damaged or missing hose is the most likely cause of a malfunctioning EVAP system. Refer to the Vacuum Hose Routing Diagram (attached to the radiator support) to determine whether the hoses are correctly routed and attached. Repair any damaged hoses or replace any missing hoses as necessary.

8   Disconnect the vacuum hose from the purge control diaphragm valve (located on the intake manifold) and connect a vacuum gauge to the hose **(see illustration)**. Start the engine and allow it to idle. There should be NO vacuum present with the engine temperature below 167-degrees F.

9   If there is no vacuum present, proceed to Step 13.

10   If there is vacuum present, disconnect the electrical connector on the purge control solenoid and check for battery voltage **(see illustration)**.

11   If battery voltage is present, replace the purge cut-off solenoid valve.

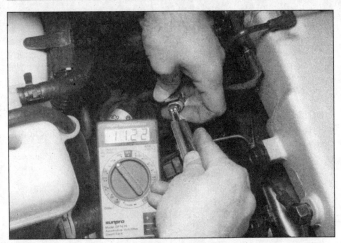

8.10 Check for battery voltage at the purge control solenoid electrical connector

8.17 Monitor the purge control solenoid duty cycle (ON TIME) as the engine goes from cold to warm running conditions

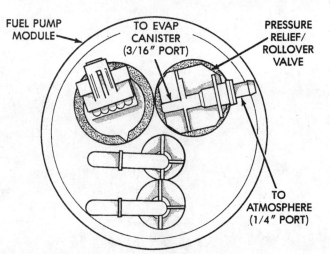

8.19 The fuel tank pressure relief/rollover valve is located on top of the fuel pump/fuel level sending unit module

9.1 Location of the catalytic converter in the exhaust system

12   If there is no battery voltage, repair the wiring harness to the PCM.
13   Warm the engine up to normal operating temperature. If there originally was no vacuum on the purge control diaphragm valve, check the vacuum source.
14   If there is vacuum present, proceed to Step 16.
15   If there is no vacuum present, trace the vacuum line to the manifold and look for damaged hoses or blocked ports.
16   If vacuum was originally present, have the fuel tank rollover valve tested by a dealer service department.
17   An alternate method of diagnosing the purge control solenoid sensor is by the use of an electronic SCAN tool. SCAN tools can be plugged into the test connector for the purpose of monitoring the computer, sensors and output actuators and are available from some automotive parts stores and specialty tool companies. Install the SCAN tool and switch to the Purge Control Solenoid mode and monitor the voltage signal (duty cycle) **(see illustration)**. The SCAN tool should indicate a percentage of dwell time (ON time). Allow the engine to warm up and observe the purge control solenoid open to circulate the crankcase vapors. The SCAN tool must be able to access the data stream to read real-time values.

Fuel tank rollover valve

Refer to illustration 8.19
18   Remove fuel pump access cover to expose the fuel pressure and vent lines (see Chapter 4).
19   The valve is seated in a rubber grommet **(see illustration)**.

Remove the valve by prying one side up and rolling the grommet out of the tank along with the valve.
20   Installation is the reverse of removal.

9   Catalytic converter

Note: *Because of a Federally mandated extended warranty which covers emissions-related components such as the catalytic converter, check with a dealer service department before replacing the converter at your own expense.*

General description

Refer to illustration 9.1
1   The catalytic converter **(see illustration)** is an emission control device added to the exhaust system to reduce pollutants from the exhaust gas stream. There are two types of converters. The conventional oxidation catalyst reduces the levels of hydrocarbon (HC) and carbon monoxide (CO). The three-way catalyst lowers the levels of oxides of nitrogen (NOx) as well as hydrocarbons (HC) and carbon monoxide (CO).

Check

2   The test equipment for a catalytic converter is expensive and highly sophisticated. If you suspect that the converter on your vehicle is malfunctioning, take it to a dealer or authorized emissions inspection facility for diagnosis and repair.

6

3   Whenever the vehicle is raised for servicing of underbody components, check the converter for leaks, corrosion, dents and other damage. Check the welds/flange bolts that attach the front and rear ends of the converter to the exhaust system. If damage is discovered, the converter should be replaced.

4   Although catalytic converters don't break too often, they can become plugged. The easiest way to check for a restricted converter is to use a vacuum gauge to diagnose the effect of a blocked exhaust on intake vacuum.

  a) *Open the throttle until the engine speed is about 2000 rpm.*
  b) *Release the throttle quickly.*

  c) *If there is no restriction, the gauge will quickly drop to not more than 2 in-Hg or more above its normal reading.*
  d) *If the gauge does not show 5 in-Hg or more above its normal reading, or seems to momentarily hover around its highest reading for a moment before it returns, the exhaust system, or the converter, is plugged (or an exhaust pipe is bent or dented, or the core inside the muffler has shifted).*

Replacement

5   Refer to the exhaust system removal and installation section in Chapter 4.

Chapter 7
Automatic transaxle

Contents

Specifications

Torque specifications

	Ft-lbs (unless otherwise indicated)
Transaxle-to-engine bolts	75
Torque converter-to-driveplate bolts	60

1   General information

All vehicles covered in this manual are equipped with a 42LE electronic 4-speed automatic transaxle. All information on the automatic transaxle is included in this Chapter.

Due to the complexity of the automatic transaxles covered in this manual and to the specialized equipment necessary to perform most service operations, this Chapter contains only those procedures related to general diagnosis, routine maintenance, adjustment and removal and installation.

If the transaxle requires major repair work, it should be left to a dealer service department or a transmission repair shop. You can, however, remove and install the transaxle yourself and save the expense, even if the repair work is done by a transmission shop.

Some 1996 and later models are equipped with a driver-interactive system known as "Autostick." This system allows the transaxle to be shifted manually. When the shift lever is moved into the Autostick position, the transaxle remains in whatever gear it was using before Autostick was activated. Moving the shift lever to the left (towards the driver) downshifts the transaxle and moving it to the right (towards the passenger seat) upshifts it. The instrument cluster illuminates the gear you have selected. In the Autostick mode, the vehicle can be driven away in first, second or third gear. The cruise control system can be used while in the Autostick mode as long as the shift lever is in third or fourth gear. If the shift lever is moved to second, however, it shuts off the cruise control. Shifting into Overdrive cancels the Autostick mode and the transaxle control module resumes its overdrive shift program.

2   Diagnosis - general

Automatic transaxle malfunctions may be caused by five general conditions:

a) *Poor engine performance*
b) *Improper adjustments*
c) *Hydraulic malfunctions*
d) *Mechanical malfunctions*
e) *Malfunctions in the computer or its signal network*

Diagnosis of these problems should always begin with a check of the easily repaired items: fluid level and condition (see Chapter 1) and shift linkage adjustment. Next, perform a road test to determine if the problem has been corrected or if more diagnosis is necessary. If the problem persists after the preliminary tests and corrections are completed, additional diagnosis should be done by a dealer service department or transmission repair shop. Refer to the *Troubleshooting* Section at the front of this manual for information on symptoms of transaxle problems.

Preliminary checks

1 Drive the vehicle to warm the transaxle to normal operating temperature.
2 Check the fluid level as described in Chapter 1.
  a) *If the fluid level is unusually low, add enough fluid to bring the level within the designated area of the dipstick, then check for external leaks (see below).*
  b) *If the fluid level is abnormally high, drain off the excess, then check the drained fluid for contamination by coolant. The presence of engine coolant in the automatic transmission fluid indicates that a failure has occurred in the internal radiator walls that separate the coolant from the transmission fluid (see Chapter 3).*
  c) *If the fluid is foaming, drain it and refill the transaxle, then check for coolant in the fluid, or a high fluid level.*
3 Check the engine idle speed. **Note:** *If the engine is malfunctioning, do not proceed with the preliminary checks until it has been repaired and runs normally.*
4 Inspect the shift control linkage (see Section 3). Make sure that it's properly adjusted and that the linkage operates smoothly.

Fluid leak diagnosis

5 Most fluid leaks are easy to locate visually. Repair usually consists of replacing a seal or gasket. If a leak is difficult to find, the following procedure may help.
6 Identify the fluid. Make sure it's transmission fluid and not engine oil or brake fluid (automatic transmission fluid is a deep red color).
7 Try to pinpoint the source of the leak. Drive the vehicle several miles, then park it over a large sheet of cardboard. After a minute or two, you should be able to locate the leak by determining the source of the fluid dripping onto the cardboard.
8 Make a careful visual inspection of the suspected component and the area immediately around it. Pay particular attention to gasket mating surfaces. A mirror is often helpful for finding leaks in areas that are hard to see.
9 If the leak still cannot be found, clean the suspected area thoroughly with a degreaser or solvent, then dry it.
10 Drive the vehicle for several miles at normal operating temperature and varying speeds. After driving the vehicle, visually inspect the suspected component again.
11 Once the leak has been located, the cause must be determined before it can be properly repaired. If a gasket is replaced but the sealing flange is bent, the new gasket will not stop the leak. The bent flange must be straightened.
12 Before attempting to repair a leak, check to make sure that the following conditions are corrected or they may cause another leak. **Note:** *Some of the following conditions cannot be fixed without highly specialized tools and expertise. Such problems must be referred to a transmission shop or a dealer service department.*

Gasket leaks

13 Check the pan periodically. Make sure the bolts are tight, no bolts are missing, the gasket is in good condition and the pan is flat (dents in the pan may indicate damage to the valve body inside).
14 If the pan gasket is leaking, the fluid level or the fluid pressure may be too high, the vent may be plugged, the pan bolts may be too tight, the pan sealing flange may be warped, the sealing surface of the transaxle housing may be damaged, the gasket may be damaged or the transaxle casting may be cracked or porous. If sealant instead of

gasket material has been used to form a seal between the pan and the transaxle housing, it may be the wrong sealant.

Seal leaks

15 If a transaxle seal is leaking, the fluid level or pressure may be too high, the vent may be plugged, the seal bore may be damaged, the seal itself may be damaged or improperly installed, the surface of the shaft protruding through the seal may be damaged or a loose bearing may be causing excessive shaft movement.
16 Make sure the dipstick tube seal is in good condition and the tube is properly seated. Periodically check the area around the speedometer gear or sensor for leakage. If transmission fluid is evident, check the O-ring for damage.

Case leaks

17 If the case itself appears to be leaking, the casting is porous and will have to be repaired or replaced.
18 Make sure the oil cooler hose fittings are tight and in good condition.

Fluid comes out vent pipe or fill tube

19 If this condition occurs, the transaxle is overfilled, there is coolant in the fluid, the case is porous, the dipstick is incorrect, the vent is plugged or the drain-back holes are plugged.

---

3 Shift cable - replacement and adjustment

1 The shift cable must be adjusted when:
  a) *The shift cable is replaced*
  b) *The column shifter is replaced*
  c) *The shift/ignition interlock cable is replaced*
  d) *The transaxle is replaced*
  e) *The valve body is repaired or replaced*
  f) *The engine won't crank over in Park or Neutral.*
2 The cable must also be adjusted if:
  a) *The transaxle can be shifted without the key in the ignition*
  b) *The key can be removed with the shifter in Reverse*
  c) *The key cannot be removed with the shift lever in the Park position*

Column-shift cable

Replacement

Refer to illustrations 3.3, 3.5, 3.6, 3.9, 3.10, 3.11, 3.15 and 3.18
3 Remove the duct assembly from underneath the dash **(see illustration)**.

3.3 Remove the duct assembly from underneath the dash

SILENCER/DUCT ASSEMBLY

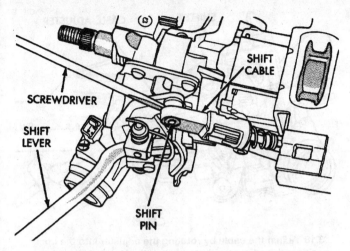

3.5 Disconnect the shift cable from the shift lever pin

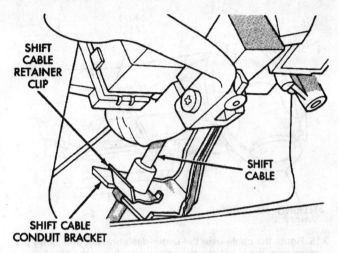

3.6 Remove the cable retainer clip from the shift cable bracket

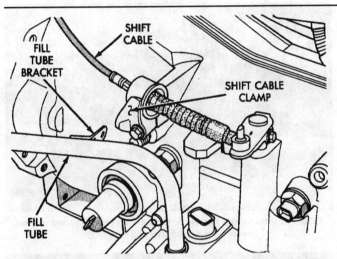

3.9 Unbolt the fill tube bracket and rotate the fill tube out of the way to gain access to the shift cable clamp

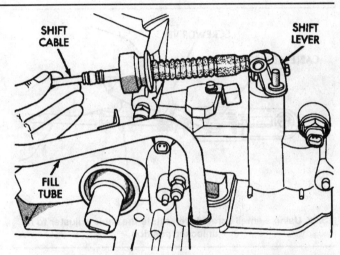

3.10 Loosen the shift cable clamp, disconnect the shift cable from the shift lever on the transaxle and remove the cable

4   Remove the column-cover screws, tilt the column down, remove the upper half of the column cover, raise the column back up, remove the tilt lever and, with the key removed, remove the lower column cover (see Chapter 11).

5   Disconnect the shift cable from the shift lever pin (see illustration).

6   Remove the cable retainer clip from the shift cable bracket (see illustration).

7   From the engine compartment side of the firewall, pry the grommet out of the firewall and pull out the rear end of the cable from the interior of the vehicle.

8   Raise the front of the vehicle and place it securely on jackstands.

9   Unbolt the fill tube bracket (see illustration) and rotate the fill tube out of the way to gain access to the shift cable clamp.

10   Loosen the shift cable clamp and disconnect the shift cable from the shift lever on the transaxle (see illustration). Remove the cable.

11   Route the new cable from underneath the vehicle, between the engine block and the heater return tube (see illustration).

12   Connect the new cable to the transaxle shift lever, then set the shift lever to the Park position (the position farthest to the rear).

13   Place the cable in the clamp and tighten the clamp mounting bolt securely. Rotate the fill tube to its proper location and install and tighten the fill tube bracket bolt.

14   Route the cable through the hole in the firewall and install the grommet in the hole.

7

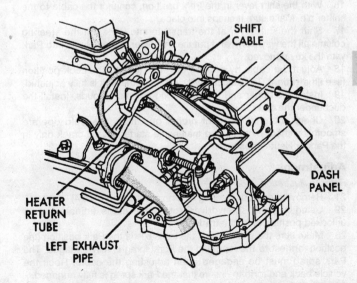

3.11 Route the new cable from underneath the vehicle, between the engine block and the heater return tube

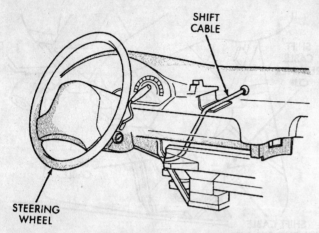

3.15 Route the cable over the under-dash bracket and along the steering column; secure the cable to the bracket with a new retainer clip.

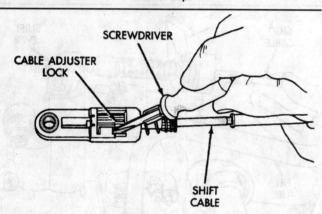

3.22 Using a small screwdriver, rotate the cable adjuster to its unlocked position

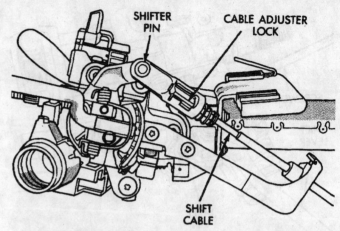

3.18 Adjust the cable by rotating the adjuster into the Lock position; the adjuster will click when the lock is fully adjusted

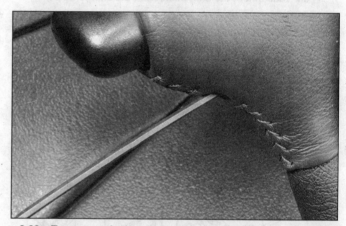

3.28a To remove the handle from the shift lever, loosen the set screw with a 3/32-inch Allen key . . .

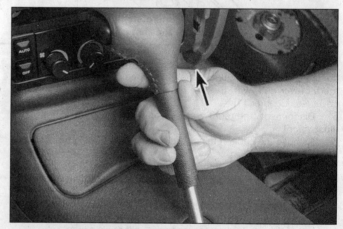

3.28b . . . then slide the handle straight up

15   Route the cable over the under-dash bracket and along the steering column **(see illustration)**. Secure the cable to the bracket with a new retainer clip.

16   With the shift lever in the Park position, connect the cable to the shifter pin. Make sure it snaps into place.

17   Shift the shift lever at the transaxle into Park. Tilt the steering column all the way down and put the shift lever at the column into Park with the key removed.

18   Adjust the cable by rotating the adjuster into the Lock position **(see illustration)**. The adjuster will click when the lock is fully adjusted.

19   Install the upper and lower steering column shrouds. Install the duct under the dash.

20   Check the shift lever for proper operation. It should operate smoothly without binding, and the engine starter should crank only in the Park or Neutral positions.

Adjustment

Refer to illustration 3.22

21   Remove the upper steering column shroud (see Step 4).

22   Using a small screwdriver, rotate the cable adjuster to its unlocked position **(see illustration)**.

23   Make sure the shift lever at the transaxle is the Park position (the position farthest to the rear) and the Park sprag is fully engaged. The Park sprag must be engaged when adjusting the cable. Rock the vehicle back and forth to ensure that the Park sprag is fully engaged.

24   Tilt the steering column to its full down position and place the shift lever in the Park position with the key removed.

25   Using a small screwdriver, rotate the cable adjuster to its locked position.

26   Install the upper steering column shroud.

27   Check the shift lever for proper operation. It should operate smoothly, without binding. The vehicle should crank only in Park or Neutral.

Floor-shift cable

Replacement

Refer to illustrations 3.28a, 3.28b, 3.30, 3.31, 3.32 and 3.34

28   Remove the shift lever handle **(see illustrations)**.

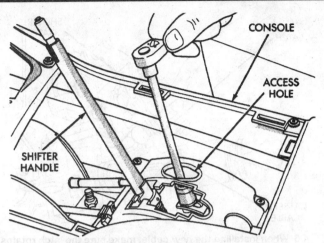

3.30 Loosen the shift cable adjustment nut

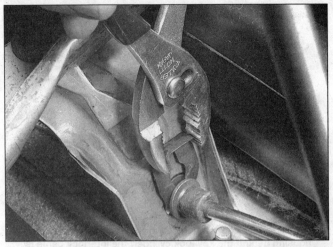

3.31 Remove the retaining clip from the shift cable bracket with a pair of pliers

3.32 To disconnect the cable from the pin on the shift lever, pop it off with a screwdriver

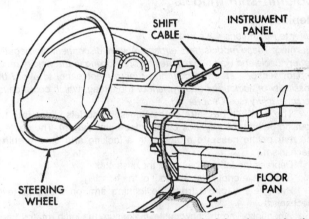

3.34 Route the new cable over the under-dash bracket, under the air conditioning duct, over the central distribution duct, through the support strut and air bag mounting bracket, over the carpeting and down to the shift lever bracket

29   Remove the console bezel (see Chapter 11).
30   Loosen the nut on the shift cable adjust lever **(see illustration)**.
31   Remove the retaining clip from the shift cable bracket **(see illustration)**.
32   Disconnect the cable from the pin on the shift lever **(see illustration)**.
33   Follows Steps 7 through 14.
34   Route the new cable under the air conditioning duct, over the central distribution duct, through the support strut and air bag mounting bracket. Then route it over the carpeting and down to the shift lever bracket **(see illustration)**.
35   Place the shift lever in the Park position.
36   Route the cable through the hole in the shift lever bracket and attach the end of the cable to the pin on the shift lever.
37   Install a new retainer clip on the cable at the shift lever bracket.
38   Tighten the adjuster nut securely.
39   Install the console bezel and the shift lever handle.
40   Check the shift lever for proper operation. It should operate smoothly, without binding. The vehicle should crank only in Park or Neutral.

Adjustment

41   Remove the shift lever handle and the console bezel (see Chapter 11).
42   Loosen the nut on the shift cable adjuster **(see illustration 3.30)**.
43   Make sure the shift lever at the transaxle is the Park position (the position farthest to the rear). The Park sprag must be engaged when

adjusting the cable. Rock the vehicle back and forth to ensure that the Park sprag is fully engaged.
44   Place the shift lever inside the vehicle in the Park position.
45   Place the ignition in Lock with the key removed.
46   Tighten the adjuster nut at the bezel.
47   Install the console bezel and shift lever handle.
48   Check the shift lever for proper operation. It should operate smoothly without binding. The engine should crank only in Park or Neutral.

4   Shift/ignition interlock system - description, replacement and adjustment

Description

1   The ignition interlock system connects the automatic transmission shift lever and the lock system. With the ignition key in the Off or Accessory position, the interlock system holds the transmission shift lever in Park. When the key is the in the Unlock or Run position, the shift lever is unlocked and can be moved to any position. And if the shift lever is not in Park, the system prevents the operator from turning the ignition switch to the Off or Accessory positions.

7

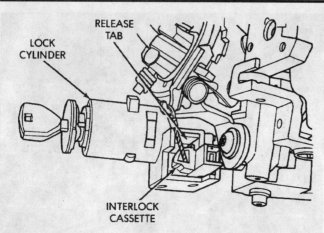

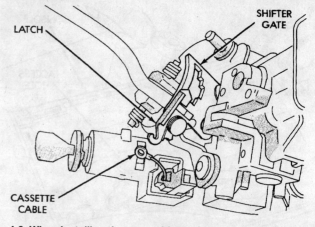

4.2 The interlock cassette on column-shift models slides into its housing behind the key lock cylinder; the interlock cable is attached to a locking arm on the shifter mechanism

4.6 When installing the new cable, make sure the latch rotates freely on the shifter gate

Column-shift models

Replacement

Refer to illustrations 4.2 and 4.6

Warning: *These models have airbags. Always disconnect the negative battery cable and wait two minutes before working in the vicinity of the impact sensors, steering column or instrument panel to avoid the possibility of accidental deployment of the airbag, which could cause personal injury (see Chapter 12).*

2   The interlock cassette on column-shift models slides into the housing behind the key lock cylinder **(see illustration)**. The cable at the rear of the cassette attaches to a locking arm on the shifter mechanism.
3   Depress the tab on the top of the cassette.
4   Slide the interlock cassette out of the housing.
5   Remove the cable from the locking arm on the shift lever mechanism.
6   When installing the new cable, make sure the latch rotates freely on the shifter gate **(see illustration)**.
7   With the shifter in Park and the key removed, install the cable over the hook on the locking arm of the shifter mechanism.
8   Slide the cassette into the housing until it locks in place.

Adjustment

9   The column shift interlock system is adjusted only after installing a new cassette. It cannot be adjusted more than once. If the system operates improperly, install and adjust a new interlock cassette.

10   Push the release tab in until it stops **(see illustration 4.2)**. The adjustment tab will click as it moves into position. Ensure the tab is fully depressed.

Floor-shift models

Replacement

Refer to illustrations 4.16, 4.18, 4.19, 4.20a and 4.20b

Warning: *These models have airbags. Always disconnect the negative battery cable and wait two minutes before working in the vicinity of the impact sensors, steering column or instrument panel to avoid the possibility of accidental deployment of the airbag, which could cause personal injury (see Chapter 12).*

11   The interlock cable slides into the housing behind the lock cylinder and attaches to the shift lever base. The floor-shift interlock system is adjusted by a nut at the shift lever assembly. If the system must be adjusted (but not replaced), adjust it as described below.
12   Remove the shift lever handle **(see illustrations 3.28a and 3.28b)**.
13   Remove the console bezel (see Chapter 11).
14   Remove the under-panel silencer from the driver's side.
15   Remove the tilt lever and the steering column covers from the steering column (see Chapter 11).
16   Loosen the nut on the interlock adjustment lever **(see illustration)**.
17   Turn the ignition key to the Run position.
18   Detach the interlock cable from the shift lever base **(see illustration)**.

4.16 The first step in removing a floor-mounted interlock cable is to loosen the nut on the interlock lever with a deep socket

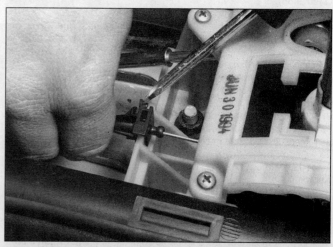

4.18 To disengage the interlock cable housing from the shift lever base, pry up on this small locking tab

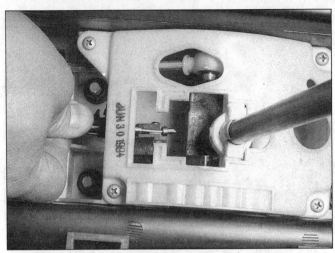

4.19 Disengage the cable end plug from its groove in the interlock lever

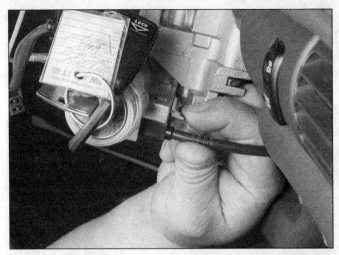

4.20a To disengage the forward end of the interlock cable from the key lock cylinder, squeeze this tab . . .

19   Slide the cable end plug out of its groove in the interlock lever **(see illustration)**.
20   At the ignition key lock cylinder, squeeze the lock tab on the interlock cable and pull the cable out of the lock cylinder housing **(see illustrations)**.
21   Make sure the ignition switch is in the On position.
22   Route the interlock cable down the steering column and above the air distribution center duct. Route the cable between the support strut and the air bag module mounting bracket and down to the shift lever assembly.
23   Insert the forward end of the interlock cable into the lock cylinder housing and push it in until it snaps into place.
24   Turn the ignition key to the Off/Lock position and put the shift lever in the Park position.
25   Insert the cable end plug into its groove in the interlock lever. Make sure the plug is properly seated in the groove.
26   Reattach the cable to the shift lever base. The cable housing is fully seated when it snaps into place.
27   Adjust the interlock cable (see Steps 29 through 32).
28   The remainder of installation is the reverse of removal.

Adjustment

29   Remove the ignition key from the lock cylinder with the switch in the Lock position. Make sure the shift lever is still in Park.
30   When the adjustment nut on the interlock lever is loosened, the

cable automatically indexes itself to the correct position. Loosen the adjustment nut and allow the cable to do so. Tighten the adjustment nut.
31   With the ignition key in the Off (locked) position, the shift lever should be locked in the Park position. If it isn't, inspect the system for binding and repeat the adjustment procedure.
32   Without starting the engine, place the ignition switch in the Run position. Move the shift lever to the Reverse position. You should be unable to remove the ignition key from the lock cylinder. If you can remove the key at this point, inspect the system for binding and repeat the adjustment procedure.

5   Shift lever - removal and installation

Standard shifter

Refer to illustration 5.5
1   Remove the shift lever handle **(see illustrations 3.28a and 3.28b)**.
2   Remove the console bezel (see Chapter 11).
3   Disconnect the shift cable (see Section 3).
4   Disconnect the shift/ignition interlock cable (see Section 4).
5   Remove the shift lever assembly retaining nuts **(see illustration)**.
6   Installation is the reverse of removal.

7

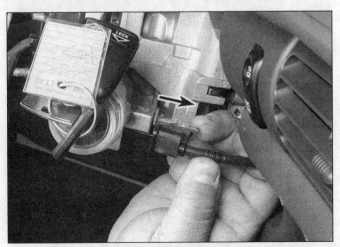

4.20b . . . then pull the cable housing straight out of the lock cylinder

5.5 To remove the shift lever assembly, remove these mounting nuts (arrows)

6.1a To check the transaxle mount, insert a prybar or large screwdriver between the mount and the bracket (shown inserted on the left side of mount in this photo, and on the right side in next photo), then move it back and forth and up and down; if the mount rubber is cracked or torn, replace the mount, which is bolted to the crossmember by this bolt (arrow) . . .

Autostick shifter (some 1996 and later models)

7   The Autostick shifter (see Section 1 for description of operation) is replaced in the same manner as the standard floor shifter. Aside from unplugging the switch in the shift lever base, the replacement procedure is identical to the procedure described above for a conventional shift lever assembly.

6   Transaxle mount - check and replacement

Refer to illustrations 6.1a, 6.1b and 6.3

Check

1   Insert a large screwdriver or prybar between the mount bracket and the rubber portion of the mount and pry up **(see illustrations)**.
2   The transaxle should not move excessively away from the mount. If it does, or if the rubber is torn or badly cracked, replace the mount.

6.3 To detach the mount from the transaxle, remove this nut and through-bolt (arrows)

6.1b . . . and this bolt (arrow) (the arrows point to the lower ends of the bolts protruding through the crossmember - the bolt heads are on top of the mount flange)

Replacement

3   To replace a mount, remove the long through-bolt that attaches the transaxle to the mount **(see illustration)**, support the transaxle with a jack, remove the two bolts that attach the mount to the crossmember **(see illustrations 6.1a and 6.1b)**, raise the jack slightly and remove the mount. **Warning:** *Never place your hands between the transaxle and crossmember when the transaxle is supported by a jack, since the jack could slip and serious injury could result. Use a long screwdriver or other tool to remove the mount.*
4   Installation is the reverse of removal.

7   Transaxle - removal and installation

Removal

Refer to illustrations 7.6, 7.10, 7.11, 7.12a, 7.12b, 7.14 and 7.19
1   Place protective covers on the fenders and cowl and remove the hood (see Chapter 11).
2   Relieve the fuel system pressure (see Chapter 4).
3   Disconnect the negative cable from the battery.
4   Remove the engine air intake duct (see Chapter 4).

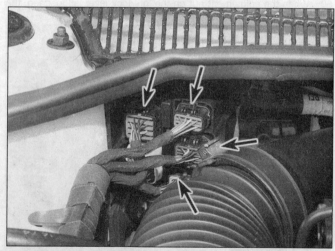

7.6 The four electrical connectors (arrows) for the transaxle are located next to the right shock tower (you'll have to cut some cable ties to free the connector from the harness)

7.10 Remove the four engine-to-transaxle bracket bolts (arrows)

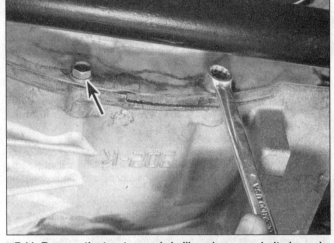

7.11 Remove the two transaxle bellhousing cover bolts (arrow)

5   Unplug the electrical connector for the crankshaft position sensor, which is located on the upper right side of the transaxle bellhousing (see Chapter 6).

6   Unplug the electrical connector **(see illustration)** for the transaxle, which is located on the right shock tower. You'll have to cut some cable ties to free the connector from the harness - use new ties (available at auto parts stores) upon installation.

7   Loosen the wheel lug nuts, raise the vehicle and support it securely on jackstands. Remove the wheels. Drain the transaxle fluid and the differential lubricant (see Chapter 1). Disconnect the shift cable from the transaxle (see Section 3).

8   Remove the ABS wheel speed sensors, if equipped, from the steering knuckles (see Chapter 9), then detach the struts from the steering knuckles (see Chapter 10).

9   Using a prybar, detach the inner CV joints from the transaxle (see Chapter 8) and suspend the driveaxles with wire. **Caution:** *Allowing the driveaxles to hang freely could damage the CV joints.*

10   Remove the engine-to-transaxle brackets **(see illustration)**.

11   Remove the transaxle bellhousing cover **(see illustration)**.

12   Mark the relationship of the torque converter to the driveplate **(see illustration)**. Rotate the crankshaft by turning the damper pulley and remove the torque converter bolts **(see illustration)**.

13   Unbolt the starter assembly (see Chapter 5) and set it aside. It's not necessary to actually remove the starter or disconnect the electrical wiring; simply secure the starter aside, between the engine and the frame.

14   Disconnect the transaxle cooler lines at the transaxle **(see**

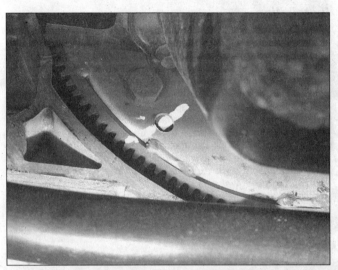

7.12a Mark the relationship of the torque converter to the driveplate . . .

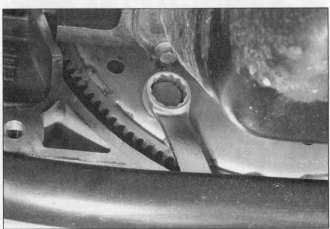

7.12b . . . then rotate the crankshaft by turning the damper pulley to remove each torque converter bolt

7.14 Unscrew the transaxle cooler line fittings (arrows) from the transaxle (use a flare-nut wrench on the nut and a back-up wrench on the transaxle fitting)

7

illustration).

15   Remove the dipstick.

16   Remove the exhaust pipes (see Chapter 4).

17   Support the transmission with a jack - preferably a jack made for this purpose. Safety chains will help steady the transmission on the jack.

18   Raise the jack slightly to remove the weight of the transaxle on the rear transaxle mount, then remove the rear mount through bolt.

19   Remove the rear crossmember mounting bolts **(see illustration)**.

20   Pry the transaxle mount to the rear to separate it from the transaxle.

21   Remove the rear crossmember.

22   Recheck to be sure nothing is still connecting the transaxle to the engine or to the vehicle. Label and disconnect anything still attached.

23   Lower the rear of the transaxle to gain access to the bellhousing bolts. Remove the bellhousing bolts.

24   Remove the dipstick tube from the transaxle. Be prepared to plug the dipstick hole with a shop rag to prevent fluid from leaking out.

25   Remove the engine-to-transaxle bolts.

26   Carefully lower the transaxle from the vehicle. Keep the transaxle level and make sure the torque converter at the front does not fall out.

Installation

27   If removed, install the torque converter on the transaxle input shaft. Make sure the converter hub splines are properly engaged with the splines on the transaxle input shaft.

28   With the transaxle secured to the jack as on removal, and with an assistant holding the torque converter in place, raise the transaxle into position and turn the converter to align the bolt holes in the converter with the bolt holes in the driveplate. Do not use excessive force to install the transaxle - if something binds and the transaxle won't mate with the engine, alter the angle of the transaxle slightly until it does mate. **Caution**: *Do NOT use transaxle-to-engine bolts to force the engine and transaxle into alignment. Doing so could crack or damage major components. If you experience difficulties, have an assistant help you line up the dowel pins on the block with the transaxle. Some wiggling of the engine and/or the transaxle will probably be necessary to secure proper alignment of the two.*

7.19 Remove the rear crossmember mounting bolts (arrows)

29   Install the engine-to-transaxle and bellhousing-to-engine bolts. Tighten all bolts to the torque listed in this Chapter's Specifications.

30   Install the rear transaxle mount and through bolt and tighten the bolt and nut securely.

31   Reinstall the remaining components in the reverse order of removal.

32   Remove all jacks and lower the vehicle. Tighten the wheel lug nuts to the torque listed in the Chapter 1 Specifications.

33   Add the specified amounts of automatic transmission fluid and differential lubricant (see Chapter 1).

34   Connect the negative battery cable.

35   Adjust the shift cable (see Section 3).

36   Road test the vehicle to check for proper transaxle operation and check for leakage.

37   Run the engine and check for proper operation and leaks. Shut off the engine and recheck the fluid levels.

Chapter 8   Driveaxles

Contents

Specifications

Torque specifications

Ft-lbs (unless otherwise indicated)

Driveaxle/hub nut...

Wheel lug nuts ....

120

See Chapter 1

1   Driveaxles - general information and inspection

Refer to illustration 1.1

1   Power is transmitted from the transaxle to the wheels through a pair of driveaxles **(see illustration)**. The inner end of each driveaxle is splined to a stub shaft protruding from the differential side gears; the outer end of each driveaxle has a stub shaft that is splined to the front hub and bearing assembly and locked in place with a large nut.

2   The inner ends of the driveaxles are equipped with sliding constant velocity (CV) joints, which are capable of both angular and axial motion. Each inner CV joint assembly consists of a tripot-type bearing and a housing in which the joint is free to slide in-and-out as the driveaxle moves up-and-down with the wheel.

3   The outer ends of the driveaxles are equipped with "ball-and-cage" type CV joints, which are capable of angular but not axial movement. Each outer CV joint consists of six ball bearings running between an inner race and an outer cage.

8

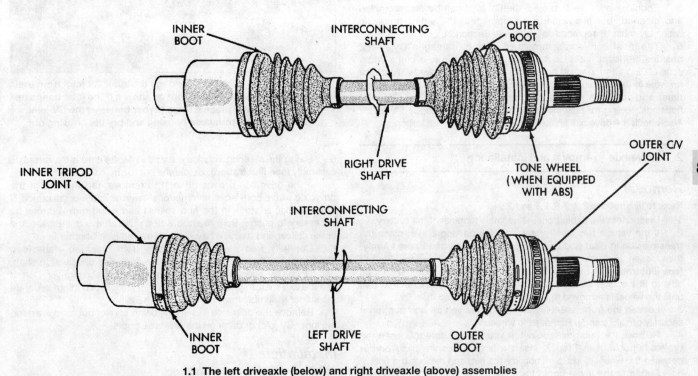

1.1 The left driveaxle (below) and right driveaxle (above) assemblies

2.2 To loosen the hub/driveaxle nut on a vehicle with steel wheels, apply the parking brake, place the transaxle in gear and have an assistant apply the brakes firmly, then loosen the nut with a socket and breaker bar

2.6 To separate the outer end of the driveaxle from the steering knuckle, swing the knuckle out until it clears the splined stub shaft of the outer CV joint (be extremely careful - if the splines of the stub shaft nick the lip of the seal on the backside of the knuckle, water could get into the hub bearing assembly

4   The boots should be inspected periodically for damage and leaking lubricant. Torn CV joint boots must be replaced immediately or the joints will be damaged. If either boot of a driveaxle is damaged, that driveaxle must be removed in order to replace the boot (see Section 2). **Note 1:** *Some auto parts stores carry "split" type replacement boots, which can be installed without removing the driveaxle from the vehicle. This is convenient, but we recommend that the driveaxle be removed and the CV joint disassembled and cleaned to ensure that the joint is free from contaminants, such as moisture and dirt, which will accelerate CV joint wear.* **Note 2:** *The inner tripot joint boots on the vehicles covered in this manual are constructed from different materials: The left inner boot is made from a high-temperature application silicone material; the right inner boot is made from hytrel plastic. Make sure you obtain a boot made of the correct material for the CV joint boot you're replacing.*

5   Should a boot be damaged, the CV joint can be disassembled and cleaned, but if any parts are damaged, the entire driveaxle assembly must be replaced as a unit (see Section 3).

6   The most common symptom of worn or damaged CV joints, besides lubricant leaks, is a clicking noise in turns, a clunk when accelerating after coasting and vibration at highway speeds. To check for wear in the CV joints and driveaxle shafts, grasp each axle (one at a time) and rotate it in both directions while holding the CV joint housings, feeling for play indicating worn splines or sloppy CV joints. Also check the driveaxle shafts for cracks, dents and distortion.

2.8 You might be able to disengage the inner CV joint from the stub shaft by simply pulling it out as shown; if the joint hangs up on the snap-ring, place a large prybar between the CV joint housing and the transaxle housing and pry the housing out

---

2   Driveaxle - removal and installation

Removal

Refer to illustrations 2.2, 2.6, 2.8 and 2.9

1   Disconnect the cable from the negative terminal of the battery.

2   If the vehicle has steel wheels, set the parking brake, place the transmission in gear and have an assistant apply the brakes firmly, then loosen the hub/driveaxle nut with a large socket and breaker bar **(see illustration)**. If the vehicle has aluminum wheels, you may not be able to fit a socket through the opening for the nut; you'll have to wait until the wheel is removed to loosen the nut (see Step 4).

3   Loosen the front wheel lug nuts, raise the vehicle and support it securely on jackstands. Remove the wheel.

4   Remove the hub/driveaxle nut. If you weren't able to loosen the driveaxle/hub nut in Step 2, insert a large screwdriver or prybar between the wheel studs to immobilize the hub and remove the nut.

5   Separate the lower control arm from the steering knuckle (see Chapter 10).

6   Swing the steering knuckle out and separate it from the driveaxle assembly **(see illustration)**. Be careful not to strain the brake hose.

7   If the driveaxle proves difficult to remove, tap the end of the driveaxle with a soft-faced hammer or a hammer and a brass punch. If the driveaxle is stuck in the hub splines and won't move, it may be necessary to push it from the hub with a puller. If this is the case, the brake caliper and disc will have to be removed (see Chapter 9).

8   Carefully free the inner CV joint from the stub shaft **(see illustration)**. If the joint hangs up on the snap-ring on the stub shaft, pop it loose by levering it out with a large prybar or screwdriver. Do not use the axleshaft to pull on the inner CV joint. Doing so might separate the spider assembly from the tripot joint housing.

9   Remove the driveaxle assembly, being careful not to overextend the inner CV joint or damage the driveaxle boots.

Installation

Refer to illustrations 2.10a and 2.10b

10   Installation is the reverse of the removal procedure, but note the

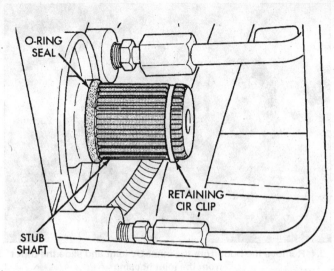

2.10a Be sure to replace the O-ring seal and the retaining circlip on the stub shaft

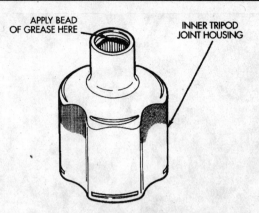

2.10b Apply an even coat of multi-purpose grease to the indicated area, where the inner CV joint seats against the O-ring on the stub shaft

following additional points:

a) *Be sure to install a new O-ring seal and retainer circlip on the stub shaft* **(see illustration)***.*

b) *Apply an even bead of multi-purpose grease around the spline of the inner CV joint, where the joints seats against the O-ring on the stub shaft* **(see illustration)***.*

c) *When installing the driveaxle, push it sharply in to seat the snapring on the stub shaft into its groove inside the splined female end of the inner CV joint housing.*

d) *Tighten the driveaxle/hub nut to the torque listed in this Chapter's Specifications.*

e) *Install the wheel and lug nuts, lower the vehicle and tighten the lug nuts to the torque listed in the Chapter 1 Specifications.*

3   Driveaxle boot replacement and CV joint inspection

Caution: *The inner CV joint boots on the vehicles covered in this manual are constructed from different materials: The left boot is a high-temperature application silicone; the right boot is hytrel plastic. Make sure you obtain a boot of the correct material for the CV joint boot you're replacing.*
Note: *If the CV joints must be overhauled (usually due to torn boots), explore all options before beginning the job. Complete, rebuilt driveaxles may be available on an exchange basis, eliminating much time and work. Whichever route you choose to take, check on the cost and availability of parts before disassembling the vehicle.*
1   Remove the driveaxle (see Section 2).
2   Mount the driveaxle in a vise with wood lined jaws (to prevent damage to the axleshaft). Check the CV joint for excessive play in the radial direction, which indicates worn parts. Check for smooth operation throughout the full range of motion for each CV joint. If a boot is torn, the recommended procedure is to disassemble the joint, clean the components and inspect for damage due to loss of lubrication and possible contamination by foreign matter. If the CV joint is in good condition, lubricate it with CV joint grease and install a new boot.

Inner CV joint

Disassembly
Refer to illustrations 3.3a, 3.3b, 3.4, 3.5, 3.6 and 3.7
3   Using diagonal cutters, cut the boot clamps **(see illustrations)**, remove the clamps and discard them.

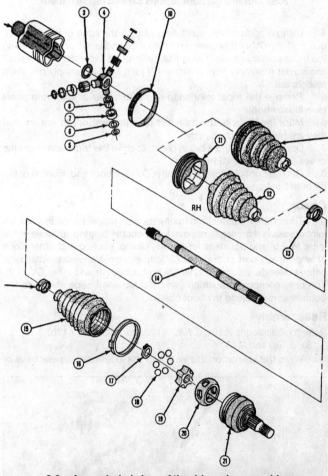

3.3a An exploded view of the driveaxle assembly:

1	Not used	12	Driveaxle inner boot
2	Inner CV joint housing	13	Boot retaining clamp
3	Spacer ring	14	Axleshaft
4	Tripot joint spider	15	Driveaxle outer boot
5	Retaining ring	16	Boot retaining clamp
6	Ball and roller retainer	17	Race retaining ring
7	Tripot joint ball	18	Ball bearings
8	Needle roller bearing	19	CV joint inner race
9	Not used	20	CV joint cage
10	Boot retaining clamp	21	CV joint outer race
11	Tripot bushing		

8

3.3b Cut the old boot clamps off and discard them

3.4 Remove the boot from the inner CV joint and slide the tripot from the joint housing

4 Using a screwdriver, carefully pry up on the edge of the CV boot, pull it off the CV joint housing and slide it down the axleshaft, exposing the tripot spider assembly **(see illustration)**. To separate the axleshaft and spider assembly from the inner CV joint housing, simply pull them straight out.

5 Remove the tripot joint snap-ring with a pair of snap-ring pliers **(see illustration)**.

6 Mark the tripot to the axleshaft **(see illustration)** to ensure that they are reassembled properly.

7 Use a hammer and a brass punch to drive the tripot joint from the driveaxle **(see illustration)**.

8 Cut the boot clamps for the outer CV joint boot and slide off or cut off both boots.

Check

9 Thoroughly clean all components with solvent until the old CV joint grease is completely removed. Inspect the bearing surfaces of the inner tripots and housings for cracks, pitting, scoring and other signs of wear. If any part of the inner CV joint is worn, you must replace the entire driveaxle assembly (inner CV joint, axleshaft and outer CV joint). The only components which can be purchased separately are the boots themselves and the boot clamps.

Reassembly

Refer to illustrations 3.10a, 3.10b, 3.10c, 3.10d, 3.11a, 3.11b, 3.12, 3.13a, 3.13b and 3.13c

10 Wrap the splines on the inner end the axleshaft with electrical or

3.5 Remove the snap-ring with a pair of snap-ring pliers

duct tape to protect the boots from the sharp edges of the splines **(see illustration)**. Slide the clamps and boot onto the axleshaft, then remove the tape and place the tripot on the shaft. Apply grease to the tripot assembly and inside the housing. Insert the tripot into the housing and pack the remainder of the grease around the tripot **(see**

3.6 Mark the relationship of the tripot bearing assembly to the axleshaft

3.7 Drive the tripot joint off the axleshaft with a brass punch and hammer; be careful not to damage the bearing surfaces or the splines on the shaft

3.10a Wrap the axleshaft splines with electrical tape to prevent damaging the boot as it's slid onto the shaft

3.10b Install the tripot spider on the axleshaft (make sure your match mark is facing out)

3.10c Place grease at the bottom of the CV joint housing

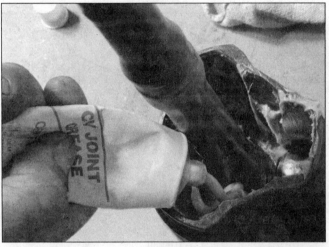

3.10d Install the boot and clamps onto the axleshaft, then insert the tripot into the housing, followed by the rest of the grease

illustrations). If you're repacking the outer joint, be sure to work the entire tube of CV joint grease (included with the boot kit) into the bearing assembly.

11   Slide the boot into place, making sure the small end seats in the

flat spot on the axleshaft between the locating shoulders (see illustration). Also make sure that the thinnest groove on the axleshaft is the only one showing (see illustration).

12   Slide the axleshaft in or out of the inner CV joint so that the

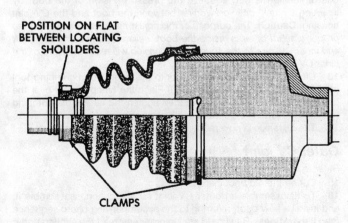

3.11a Slide the boot into place, making sure the small end seats in the flat spot on the axleshaft between the locating shoulders

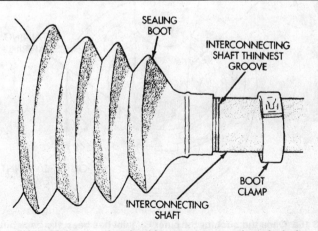

3.11b Make sure that the thinnest groove on the axleshaft is the only one showing

8

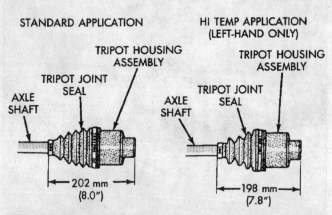

3.12 Slide the axleshaft in or out of the inner CV joint so that the dimensions of the boot and joint are as shown (the purpose of this adjustment is to ensure that the proper amount of air is inside the boot; if you neglect this adjustment, the inner CV joint boot could fail)

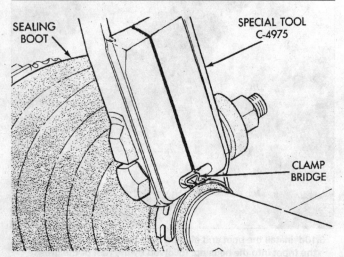

3.13b ... then tighten the nut on the crimping tool until the jaws are closed

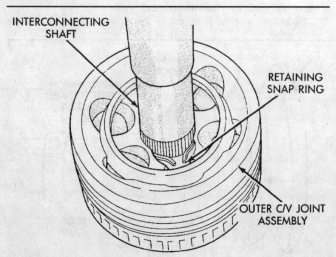

3.16a Once the boot for the outer CV joint has been slid back out of the way and some of the old grease is wiped off, you'll see a snap-ring buried in there

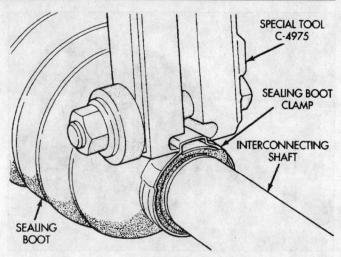

3.13a Clamp the new boot clamps onto the boot with a crimping tool (tool number C-4975, or the equivalent): Place the crimping tool over the bridge of each new boot clamp ...

3.13c A typical aftermarket alternative to the factory tool: Instead of using a nut to crimp the clamp, it relies on hand pressure

dimensions of the boot and joint are as shown (see illustration). Once this dimension is set, equalize the pressure inside of the boot by inserting a small, dull screwdriver between the boot and the CV joint housing. Caution: The purpose of this adjustment is to ensure that the proper amount of air is inside the boot. Failure to adjust the axleshaft and inner CV joint to the specified dimension will result in failure of the inner CV joint boot.

13 Clamp the new boot clamps onto the boot with a crimping tool (tool number C-4975, or equivalent). Place the crimping tool over the bridge of each new boot clamp, then tighten the nut on the crimping tool until the jaws are closed (see illustrations).

14 The driveaxle is now ready for installation (see Section 2).

Outer CV joint

Refer to illustrations 3.16a through 3.16s

15 Cut off the old boot clamps.

16 To disassemble an outer CV joint for inspection, reassemble it, and install a new boot, referring to the accompanying photo sequence (see illustrations). Be sure to stay in order and read the caption under each illustration.

17 The driveaxle is now ready for installation (see Section 2).

3.16b Use a pair of snap-ring pliers to release the snap-ring, then slide the outer CV joint assembly off the axleshaft and discard the old boot

3.16c Place the outer CV joint assembly in a vise, then press down on the inner race far enough to allow a ball bearing to be removed; if it's difficult to tilt, gently tap the cage and inner race with a brass punch and hammer

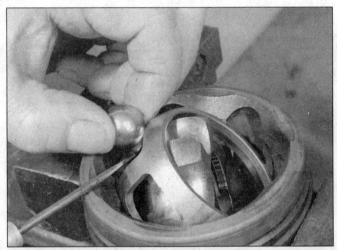

3.16d Pry the balls out of the cage, one at a time, with a dull screwdriver or wooden tool

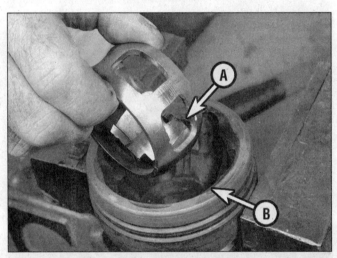

3.16e Tilt the inner race and cage 90-degrees, then align the windows (A) in the cage with the lands (B) of the housing and rotate the inner race up and out of the outer race

3.16f Align the inner race lands with the cage window and rotate the inner race out of the cage

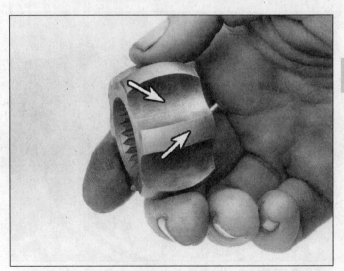

3.16g After cleaning the components with solvent, check the inner race lands and grooves for pitting and score marks

8

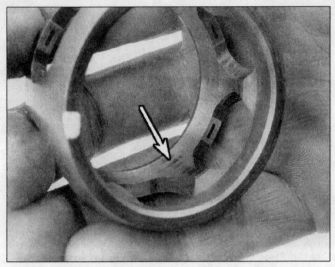

3.16h Check the cage for cracks, pitting and score marks -
shiny spots are normal and don't affect operation

3.16i With the race and cage tilted at 90-degrees, lower the
assembly into the housing

3.16j Rotate the assembly by gently tapping with a hammer and
brass punch . . .

3.16k . . . then press the balls into the cage windows, repeating
until all of the balls are installed

3.16l Use needle-nose pliers to lower the snap-ring
into the groove . . .

3.16m . . . then seat it into the groove with snap-ring pliers

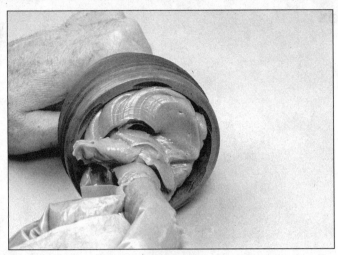

3.16n Pack the outer CV joint assembly with lubricant through the inner splined hole . . .

3.16o . . . then insert a wooden dowel (with a diameter slightly less than that of the axle) through the splined hole and push down - the dowel will force the grease into the joint - repeat until the bearing is completely packed

3.16p Install the boot on the driveaxle (see illustration 3.10a), then apply grease to the inside of the boot until . . .

3.16q . . . the level is up to the end of the axle

3.16r Position the CV joint assembly on the driveaxle, aligning the splines, then use a soft-face hammer to drive the joint onto the driveaxle until the snap-ring is seated in the groove

3.16s Seat the small end of the boot in the flat area on the axleshaft between the locating shoulders, with only one groove (the thinnest) showing (see illustrations 3.11a and 3.11b) and install the new retaining clamp. Then install the other clamp on the larger end of the boot, again making sure the boot is properly seated. Crimp the clamps with the special factory tool or a suitable equivalent (see illustrations 3.13a, 3.13b and 3.13c)

8

Notes

Chapter 9 Brakes

Contents

Specifications

General

Brake fluid type	See Chapter 1

Disc brakes

Brake pad minimum thickness	See Chapter 1
Disc lateral runout limit	0.005 inch
Disc minimum thickness	Cast into disc
Thickness variation	0.0005 inch

Drum brakes

Minimum brake lining thickness	See Chapter 1
Maximum drum diameter	Cast into drum

Torque specifications

Brake booster mounting nuts	250 in-lbs
Brake hose banjo bolt-to-caliper	24 ft-lbs
Caliper guide pin bolts	192 in-lbs
Master cylinder-to-brake booster mounting nuts	250 in-lbs
Parking brake pedal assembly mounting bolts	250 in-lbs
Wheel cylinder-to-brake backing plate mounting nuts	75 in-lbs

9

1   General information

General

All models covered by this manual are equipped with a hydraulically-operated brake system. All front brakes are discs; rear brakes are either drums or discs. All brakes are self-adjusting. Disc brakes automatically compensate for pad wear, while drum brakes incorporate an adjustment mechanism which is activated as the brakes are applied.

The hydraulic system is split diagonally - the left front and right rear brakes are on one circuit, the right front and left rear on the other. If one circuit fails, the other circuit will remain functional and a warning indicator will light up on the dashboard when a substantial amount of brake fluid is lost, showing that a failure has occurred.

Calipers

All disc brakes used by the vehicles covered in this manual are equipped with a double-pin floating caliper, a single-piston design that "floats" on two steel guide pins. When the brake pedal is depressed, hydraulic pressure pushing on the piston is transmitted to the inner brake pad and against the inner surface of the brake disc. As the force against the disc from the inner pad is increased, the caliper assembly moves in, sliding on the guide pins and pulling the outer pad against the disc, providing a pinching force on the disc.

Master cylinder

The master cylinder is located under the hood on the driver's side, and can be identified by the large fluid reservoir on top. The master cylinder has two separate circuits to accommodate the diagonally split system.

Power brake booster

The power brake booster uses engine manifold vacuum to provide assistance to the brakes. It is mounted on the firewall in the engine compartment, directly behind the master cylinder.

Parking brake system

The parking brake pedal actuates the rear brakes via two cables. The parking brake cables pull on a lever attached to the brake shoe assembly, causing the shoes to expand against the drum (or, on rear disc brake models, a pair of small brake shoes inside the disc/hub assembly).

Precautions

There are some general precautions and warnings related to the brake system:

a) *Use only brake fluid conforming to DOT 3 specifications.*
b) *The brake pads and linings may contain asbestos fibers which are hazardous to your health if inhaled. Whenever you work on brake system components, clean all parts with brake system cleaner. Do not allow the fine dust to become airborne.*
c) *Safety should be paramount whenever any servicing of the brake components is performed. Do not use parts or fasteners which are not in perfect condition, and be sure all clearances and torque specifications are adhered to. If you are at all unsure about a certain procedure, seek professional advice. Upon completion of any brake system work, test the brakes carefully in a controlled area before driving the vehicle in traffic.*
d) *If a problem is suspected in the brake system, don't drive the vehicle until it's fixed.*

2   Anti-lock Brake System (ABS) - general information

Description

The Teves Mark IV (1993 and 1994 models) and Mark IV-G (1995 and 1996 models) Anti-lock Brake System (ABS) prevents wheel lock-up under heavy braking conditions on virtually any road surface.

Preventing the wheels from locking up maintains vehicle maneuverability, preserves directional stability, and allows optimal deceleration. How does ABS work? Basically, by monitoring the rotational speed of the wheels and controlling the brake line pressure to the calipers/wheel cylinders at each wheel during braking.

Principle components

Controller Anti-lock Brake (CAB)

The CAB consists of a pair of microprocessors which monitor wheel speeds and control the anti-lock and traction control functions. The CAB receives two identical signals and process the information independently of one another. The results are compared to make sure that they agree. If they don't, the CAB turns off the ABS and traction control functions, and turns on the warning lights.

Hydraulic control unit

The Hydraulic Control Unit (HCU) is located in the engine compartment on the left frame rail, just below and ahead of the master cylinder. The HCU contains the valve block assembly, the pump/motor assembly and the fluid accumulator.

Valve block assembly

The valve block assembly contains eight valve/solenoids: four inlet valves and four outlet valves. The inlet valves are spring-loaded in the open position and the outlet valves are spring-loaded in the closed position. During ABS operation, these valves are cycled to maintain the proper slip ratio for each channel. If a wheel locks, the inlet valve is closed to prevent a further increase in pressure. Simultaneously, the outlet valve is opened to release the pressure back to the accumulators until the wheel is no longer slipping. Once the wheel no longer slips, the outlet valve closes and the inlet valve opens to allow pressure to the wheel caliper or wheel cylinder.

Pump/motor assembly

The pump/motor assembly consists of an electric motor and a dual-piston pump. The pump provides high-pressure brake fluid to the hydraulic control unit when the ABS system is activated.

Fluid accumulators

The two fluid accumulators in the HCU are for the primary and secondary hydraulic circuits, respectively. The accumulators temporarily store brake fluid that is blocked during ABS operation. This fluid is re-routed to the pump.

Proportioning valves

See Section 9.

Wheel speed sensors

A speed sensor is mounted at each wheel. The speed sensors send variable voltage signals to the HCU. These analog voltage outputs are proportional to the speed of rotation of each wheel.

Diagnosis and repair

The ABS system has self-diagnostic capabilities. Each time the ignition key is turned to On, the system runs a self-test. If it finds a problem, the ABS and traction control warning lights come on and remain on. If there's no problem with the system, the lights go out after a second or two.

If the ABS and traction control warning lights come on and stay on during vehicle operation, there is a problem in the ABS system. Two things now happen: The controller stores a diagnostic trouble code (which can be displayed with a DRB II scanner at the dealer) and the ABS system is shut down. Once the ABS system is disabled, it will remain disabled until the problem is fixed and the trouble code is erased. However, the regular brake system will continue to function normally.

Although a DRB II (a special electronic tester) is necessary to properly diagnose the system, you can make a few preliminary checks before taking the vehicle to a dealer:

a) *Make sure the brake calipers are in good condition.*
b) *Check the electrical connector at the controller.*

3.3 Use a C-clamp to depress the piston into its bore; this aids removal of the caliper and installation of the new pads (rear caliper shown)

3.4a Wash down the disc and brake pads with brake cleaner to remove brake dust; DO NOT blow brake dust off with compressed air

c) *Check the fuses.*
d) *Follow the wiring harness to the speed sensors and brake light switch and make sure all connections are secure and the wiring isn't damaged.*

If the above preliminary checks don't rectify the problem, the vehicle should be diagnosed by a dealer service department.

3 Disc brake pads - replacement

Refer to illustrations 3.3, 3.4a through 3.4l
Warning: *Disc brake pads must be replaced on both front or rear wheels at the same time - never replace the pads on only one wheel. Also, the dust created by the brake system may contain asbestos, which is harmful to your health. Never blow it out with compressed air and don't inhale any of it. An approved filtering mask should be worn when working on the brakes. Do not, under any circumstances, use petroleum-based solvents to clean brake parts. Use brake system cleaner only!*
Note: *This procedure applies to both the front and the rear disc brakes.*
1   Loosen the front wheel lug nuts, raise the front of the vehicle and support it securely on jackstands. Apply the parking brake. Remove the front wheels (or the rear wheels, if you're working on a vehicle with rear discs).
2   Remove about two-thirds of the fluid from the master cylinder reservoir and discard it. Position a drain pan under the brake assembly

and clean the caliper and surrounding area with brake system cleaner.
3   Push the piston back into its bore to provide room for the new brake pads with a C-clamp **(see illustration)**. As the piston is depressed to the bottom of the caliper bore, the fluid in the master cylinder will rise. Make sure it doesn't overflow. If necessary, siphon off some of the fluid.
4   To replace the brake pads, follow the accompanying photos, beginning with **illustration 3.4a**. Be sure to stay in order and read the caption under each illustration.
5   While the pads are removed, inspect the caliper for brake fluid leaks and ruptures of the piston boot. Overhaul or replace the caliper as necessary (see Section 4). Also inspect the brake disc carefully (see Section 5). If machining is necessary, follow the information in that Section to remove the disc.
6   Before installing the caliper guide pin bolts, clean them and check them for corrosion and damage. If they're significantly corroded or damaged, replace them. Be sure to tighten the caliper guide pin bolts to the torque listed in this Chapter's Specifications.
7   Install the brake pads on the opposite wheel, then install the wheels and lower the vehicle. Tighten the lug nuts to the torque listed in the Chapter 1 Specifications. Add brake fluid to the reservoir until it's full (see Chapter 1).
8   Pump the brakes several times to seat the pads against the disc, then check the fluid level again.
9   Check the operation of the brakes before driving the vehicle in traffic. Try to avoid heavy brake applications until the brakes have been applied lightly several times to seat the pads.

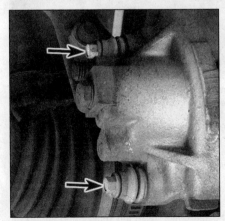

3.4b To remove the front caliper, remove these guide pin bolts (arrows)

3.4c To remove the rear caliper, remove these guide pin bolts (arrows)

3.4d Hang the caliper from the strut coil spring with a piece of wire - don't let it hang by the brake hose

9

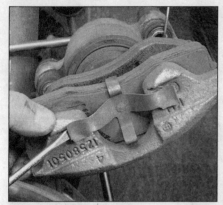

3.4e Pry the outer brake pad retaining spring from the caliper . . .

3.4f . . . and remove the outer brake pad

3.4g Pull the inner brake pad retaining spring loose from the piston and remove the pad

3.4h Remove the guide pin bushings

3.4i Remove the bushing boots, inspect them for tears and replace as necessary

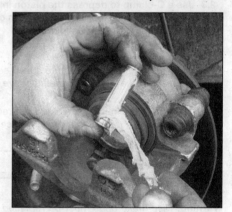

3.4j Lubricate the guide pin bushings with multi-purpose grease before installing them

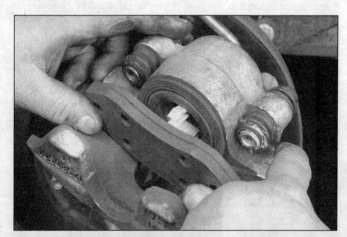

3.4k Install the inner brake pad - make sure the retaining spring is fully seated into its bore in the piston

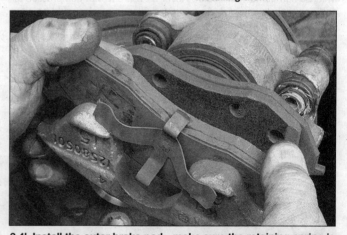

3.4l Install the outer brake pad - make sure the retaining spring is properly engaged with the caliper body

4   Disc brake caliper - removal, overhaul and installation

Warning: *Dust created by the brake system may contain asbestos, which is harmful to your health. Never blow it out with compressed air and don't inhale any of it. An approved filtering mask should be worn when working on the brakes. Do not, under any circumstances, use petroleum-based solvents to clean brake parts. Use brake system cleaner only.*

Note: *If an overhaul is indicated (usually because of fluid leaks, a stuck piston or broken bleeder screw) explore all options before beginning*

this procedure. New and factory rebuilt calipers are available on an exchange basis, which makes this job quite easy. If you decide to rebuild the calipers, make sure rebuild kits are available before proceeding. Always rebuild or replace the calipers in pairs - never rebuild just one of them.

Removal

1   Loosen the front wheel lug nuts, raise the vehicle and support it securely on jackstands. Remove the front wheels.

2   Unscrew the banjo bolt from the caliper and detach the hose. **Note:** *If you're just removing the caliper for acess to other components, don't*

4.4 With a block of wood placed between the piston and the caliper frame, use compressed air to ease the piston out of the bore

disconnect the hose. Discard the sealing washers on each side of the fitting and use new ones during installation. Wrap a plastic bag around the end of the hose to prevent fluid loss and contamination.

3   Refer to the first few steps in Section 3 (caliper removal is the first part of the brake pad replacement procedure). Clean the caliper assembly with brake system cleaner. DO NOT use kerosene, gasoline or petroleum-based solvents. Be sure to check the pads as well and replace them if necessary (see Section 3).

Overhaul

Refer to illustrations 4.4, 4.5a, 4.5b, 4.6, 4.10, 4.11a, 4.11b and 4.12

4   Place several shop towels or a block of wood in the center of the caliper to act as a cushion, then use compressed air, directed into the fluid inlet, to remove the piston **(see illustration)**. Use only enough air pressure to ease the piston out of the bore. If the piston is blown out, even with the cushion in place, it may be damaged. **Warning:** *Never place your fingers in front of the piston in an attempt to catch or protect it when applying compressed air, as serious injury could occur.*

5   Pry the dust boot from the caliper bore **(see illustrations)**.

6   Using a wood or plastic tool, remove the piston seal from the groove in the caliper bore **(see illustration)**. Metal tools may cause bore damage.

7   Remove the bleeder screw, then remove and discard the guide

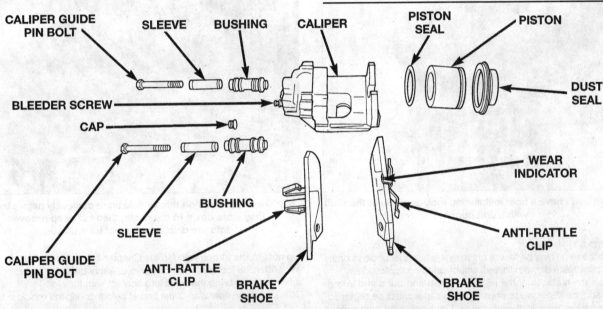

4.5a An exploded view of the caliper assembly

CALIPER GUIDE PIN BOLT — SLEEVE — BUSHING — CALIPER — PISTON SEAL — PISTON — DUST SEAL — BLEEDER SCREW — CAP — WEAR INDICATOR — BUSHING — SLEEVE — ANTI-RATTLE CLIP — CALIPER GUIDE PIN BOLT — ANTI-RATTLE CLIP — BRAKE SHOE — BRAKE SHOE

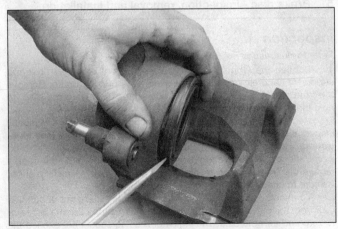

4.5b Carefully pry the dust boot out of the caliper

4.6 The piston seal should be removed with a plastic or wooden tool to avoid damage to the bore and the seal groove (a pencil will do the job)

9

4.10 Position the new seal in the cylinder groove - make sure it isn't twisted

4.11a Slip the boot over the piston

4.11b Push the piston straight into the cylinder - make sure it doesn't become cocked in the bore

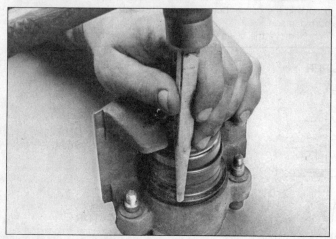

4.12 If you don't have a boot installation tool, gently seat the boot with a drift punch

pin bushings and sleeves.

8   Clean the remaining parts with brake system cleaner or clean brake fluid, then blow them dry with filtered, unlubricated compressed air.

9   Inspect the surfaces of the piston for nicks and burrs and loss of plating. If surface defects are present, the caliper must be replaced. Check the caliper bore in a similar way. Light polishing with crocus cloth is permissible to remove slight corrosion and stains. Discard the caliper pins if they're severely corroded or damaged.

10   Lubricate the new piston seal with clean brake fluid and position the seal in the cylinder groove using your fingers only **(see illustration)**.

11   Install the new dust boot in the groove in the end of the piston **(see illustration)**. Dip the piston in clean brake fluid and insert it squarely into the cylinder. Depress the piston to the bottom of the cylinder bore **(see illustration)**.

12   Seat the boot in the caliper counterbore using a boot installation tool or a blunt punch **(see illustration)**.

13   Install the new guide pin boots and bushings.

14   Install the bleeder screw and tighten it securely.

Installation

15   Install the caliper assembly, tightening the caliper guide pin bolts to the torque listed in this Chapter's Specifications.

16   Connect the brake hose to the caliper using new sealing washers. Tighten the banjo bolt to the torque listed in this Chapter's Specifications.

17   Bleed the brakes (see Section 11).

18   Install the wheels and lug nuts. Lower the vehicle and tighten the

lug nuts to the torque listed in the Chapter 1 Specifications.

19   After the job has been completed, firmly depress the brake pedal a few times to bring the pads into contact with the disc.

20   Check the operation of the brakes before driving the vehicle in traffic.

---

5   Brake disc - inspection, removal and installation

Inspection

Refer to illustrations 5.2, 5.3, 5.4a and 5.4b

1   Loosen the wheel lug nuts, raise the front of the vehicle and support it securely on jackstands. Apply the parking brake. Remove the front wheels. Reinstall the lug nuts, flat side toward the disc, to hold the disc firmly against the hub.

2   Remove the brake caliper as described in Section 4. Visually inspect the disc surface for score marks and other damage **(see illustration)**. Light scratches and shallow grooves are normal after use and won't affect brake operation. Deep grooves - over 0.015-inch deep - require disc removal and refinishing by an automotive machine shop. Be sure to check both sides of the disc.

3   To check disc runout, place a dial indicator at a point about 1/2-inch from the outer edge of the disc **(see illustration)**. Set the indicator to zero and turn the disc. The indicator reading should not exceed the runout limit listed in this Chapter's Specifications. If it does, the disc should be refinished by an automotive machine shop. **Note:** *Professionals recommend resurfacing the brake discs regardless of the dial*

5.2 The brake pads on this vehicle were obviously neglected, as they wore down to the rivets, then cut deep grooves into the disc, which must be replaced

5.3 Use a dial indicator to check disc runout - if the reading exceeds the specified runout limit, the disc will have to be machined or replaced

5.4a On some models, the minimum thickness is cast into the inside of the disc - on others, it's located on the outside of the disc

5.4b Use a micrometer to measure the thickness of the disc at several points

5.8 Cut off and discard the disc retaining washers, if present (it isn't necessary to reinstall them)

6.2 Before disassembling the brake shoe assembly, wash it thoroughly with brake system cleaner

indicator reading (to produce a smooth, flat surface that will eliminate brake pedal pulsations and other undesirable symptoms related to questionable discs). At the very least, if you elect not to have the discs resurfaced, deglaze them with sandpaper or emery cloth.

4   The disc must not be machined to a thickness less than the specified minimum thickness. The minimum (or discard) thickness is cast into the disc **(see illustration)**. The disc thickness can be checked with a micrometer **(see illustration)**.

Removal and installation

Refer to illustration 5.8

5   Loosen the wheel lug nuts, raise the vehicle and place it securely on jackstands.

6   Remove the wheel. If you're removing a rear disc, block the front wheels and release the parking brake.

7   Remove the caliper (see Section 4).

8   Remove the retaining clips, if present, from the wheel studs **(see illustration)**.

9   Pull the disc off the hub.

10   If you're removing a rear disc and the disc won't come off, remove the plug from the parking brake adjusting access hole. Turn the adjusting star wheel with a suitable tool (such as a screwdriver or brake adjusting tool) and retract the parking brake shoes (see Section 13 for details on the parking brake shoes on models with rear disc brakes).

11   Installation is the reverse of removal. Make sure you tighten the caliper guide pin bolts to the torque listed in this Chapter's Specifications.

6   Drum brake shoes - replacement

Refer to illustrations 6.2, 6.4a through 6.4v and 6.5

Warning: *Drum brake shoes must be replaced on both wheels at the same time - never replace the shoes on only one wheel. Also, the dust created by the brake system may contain asbestos, which is harmful to your health. Never blow it out with compressed air and don't inhale any of it. An approved filtering mask should be worn when working on the brakes. Do not, under any circumstances, use petroleum-based solvents to clean brake parts. Use brake system cleaner only!*

Caution: *Whenever the brake shoes are replaced, the hold-down springs should also be replaced. Due to the continuous heating/cooling cycle that the springs are subjected to, they lose their tension over a period of time and may allow the shoes to drag on the drum and wear at a much faster rate than normal.*

1   Loosen the wheel lug nuts, raise the rear of the vehicle and support it securely on jackstands. Block the front wheels to keep the vehicle from rolling. Release the parking brake. Remove the wheel. **Note:** *All four front or rear brake shoes must be replaced at the same time, but to avoid mixing up parts, work on only one brake assembly at a time.*

2   Remove the brake drum. **Note:** *If the drum won't come off, retract the brake shoes by inserting a screwdriver or brake adjusting tool through the hole in the backing plate and turning the adjuster screw star wheel. The drum should now come off.* Wash down the brake assembly with brake cleaner **(see illustration)**.

3   Remove the hub and bearing assembly (see Chapter 10).

9

6.4a Remove the rear brake shoe hold-down spring

6.4b Remove the front brake shoe hold-down spring

6.4c Spread the upper ends of the brake shoes apart and pull them out just enough to clear the wheel cylinder (this takes some tension off the upper return spring

6.4d Lift the automatic adjuster lever off the adjuster star wheel and back off the wheel to retract the shoes (this takes even more tension of the upper return spring)

6.4e Unhook the upper end of the automatic adjuster lever spring from the lever

6.4f Unhook the rear end of the upper return spring from the rear shoe (diagonal cutting pliers are being used here because they grip the spring well, but care must be taken not to damage the spring)

6.4g Unhook the front end of the upper return spring from the front shoe

6.4h Disengage the automatic adjuster from the rear shoe

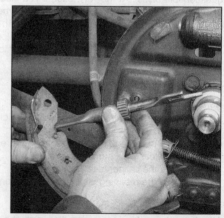

6.4i Disengage the automatic adjuster from the front shoe

4   Follow **illustrations 6.4a through 6.4v** for the inspection and replacement of the brake shoes. Be sure to stay in order and read the caption under each illustration.

5   Before reinstalling the drum it should be checked for cracks, score marks, deep scratches and hard spots, which will appear as small discolored areas. If the hard spots cannot be removed with fine emery cloth or if any of the other conditions listed above exist, the drum must be taken to an automotive machine shop to have it turned. **Note:** *Professionals recommend resurfacing the drums whenever a brake job is done. Resurfacing will eliminate the possibility of out-of-*

6.4j Unhook the lower return spring from the front brake shoe

6.4k Unhook the rear lower return spring from the anchor plate, then remove the rear shoe and detach the parking brake cable from the lever (see illustration 15.31a). Transfer the parking brake lever to the new rear shoe

6.4l Connect the lower return springs to the shoes and the anchor plate

6.4m Engage the automatic adjuster with the front shoe

6.4n Engage the adjuster with the rear shoe

6.4o Hook the front end of the upper return spring into the front brake shoe

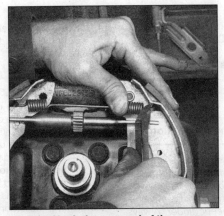

6.4p Hook the rear end of the upper return spring into the rear brake shoe

6.4q Spread the upper ends of the brake shoes apart and push the brake shoe assembly against the brake backing plate; make sure the shoes are both properly seated against the wheel cylinder pistons

round drums. If the drums are worn so much that they can't be resurfaced without exceeding the maximum allowable diameter (stamped into the drum) **(see illustration)**, then new ones will be required. At the very least, if you elect not to have the drums resurfaced, remove the glazing from the surface with emery cloth or sandpaper using a swirling motion.

6   Install the hub and bearing assembly (see Chapter 10).

7   Install the brake drum. Pump the brake pedal several times, then turn the adjuster star wheel using a screwdriver inserted through the hole in the backing plate until the brake shoes slightly drag on the drum as the drum is turned. Now, back-off the adjuster until the shoes don't drag on the drum.

9

6.4r Install the front brake shoe
hold-down spring

6.4s Install the rear brake shoe
hold-down spring

6.4t Hook the lower end of the automatic
adjuster lever spring into its hole (arrow)
in the front brake shoe

6.4u Install the automatic adjuster lever
onto its pivot pin; make sure the small
lever at the upper left is installed
between the adjuster and the
front brake shoe as shown

6.4v Hook the upper end of the automatic
adjuster lever spring into its hole (arrow)
in the lever

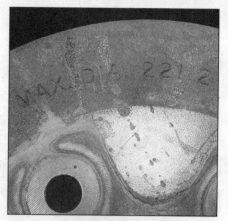

6.5 The maximum allowable diameter is
stamped into the drum

8   Mount the wheel, install the lug nuts, then lower the vehicle. Tighten the lug nuts to the torque listed in the Chapter 1 Specifications.

9   Make a number of forward and reverse stops to adjust the brakes until satisfactory pedal action is obtained.

10   Check brake operation before driving the vehicle in traffic.

---

7   Wheel cylinder - removal, overhaul and installation

Note: *If an overhaul is indicated (usually because of fluid leakage or sticky operation) explore all options before beginning the job. New wheel cylinders are available, which makes this job quite easy. If you decide to rebuild the wheel cylinder, make sure a rebuild kit is available before proceeding. Never overhaul only one wheel cylinder. Always rebuild both of them at the same time.*

Removal

Refer to illustration 7.2

1   Remove the brake shoes (see Section 6).

2   Unscrew the brake line fitting from the rear of the wheel cylinder **(see illustration)**. If available, use a flare-nut wrench to avoid rounding off the corners on the fitting. Don't pull the metal line out of the wheel cylinder - it could bend, making installation difficult.

3   Remove the two bolts securing the wheel cylinder to the brake backing plate.

4   Remove the wheel cylinder.

5   Plug the end of the brake line to prevent the loss of brake fluid and the entry of dirt.

Overhaul

Refer to illustration 7.6

6   To disassemble the wheel cylinder, remove the rubber dust boot from each end of the cylinder, then push out the two pistons, the cups and the cup expanders and spring assembly **(see illustration)**. Discard the rubber parts and use new ones from the rebuild kit when reassembling the wheel cylinder.

7   Inspect the pistons for scoring and scuff marks. If present, the wheel cylinder should be replaced.

8   Examine the inside of the cylinder bore for score marks and corrosion. If these conditions exist, the cylinder can be honed slightly to restore it, but replacement is recommended.

9   If the cylinder is in good condition, clean it with brake system cleaner. **Warning:** *DO NOT, under any circumstances, use gasoline or petroleum-based solvents to clean brake parts!*

10   Remove the bleeder screw and make sure the hole is clean.

11   Lubricate the cylinder bore with clean brake fluid, then insert one of the new rubber cups into the bore. Make sure the lip on the rubber cup faces in.

12   Install the cup expander and spring assembly from the other side of the cylinder, then install the remaining cup in the cylinder bore.

13   Install the pistons.

14   Install the boots.

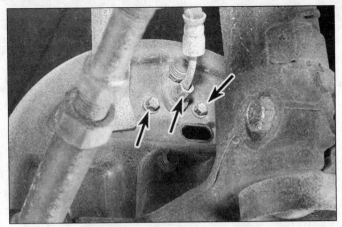

7.2 To detach the wheel cylinder from the brake backing plate, disconnect the brake line fitting and remove the wheel cylinder bolts (arrows)

Installation

15 Installation is the reverse of removal. Attach the brake line to the wheel cylinder before installing the mounting bolts and tighten the line fitting after the wheel cylinder mountings bolts have been tightened. If

available, use a flare-nut wrench to tighten the line fitting. Make sure you tighten the line fitting securely and the wheel cylinder mounting bolts to the torque listed in this Chapter's Specifications.

16 Install the brake shoes and brake drum (see Section 6).

17 Bleed the brakes (see Section 11). Don't drive the vehicle in traffic until brake operation has been thoroughly tested.

8 Master cylinder - removal, reservoir replacement and installation

Removal

Refer to illustrations 8.2, 8.3 and 8.4

1 Place rags under the brake line fittings and prepare caps or plastic bags to cover the ends of the lines once they're disconnected. **Caution:** *Brake fluid will damage paint. Cover all painted surfaces and avoid spilling fluid during this procedure.*

2 Unplug the electrical connector from the brake fluid level sensor **(see illustration)**.

3 Loosen the tube nuts at the ends of the brake lines where they enter the master cylinder. To prevent rounding off the flats on these nuts, a flare-nut wrench, which wraps around the nut, should be used **(see illustration)**. Pull the brake lines away from the master cylinder slightly and plug the ends to prevent contamination. Also plug the openings in the master cylinder to prevent fluid spillage.

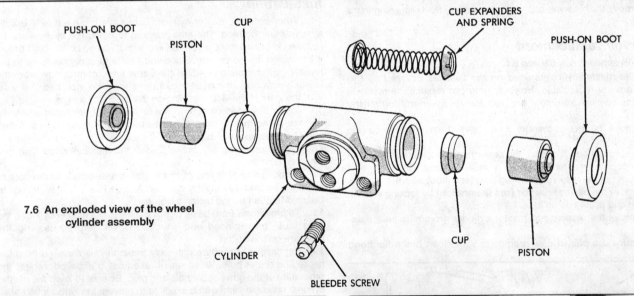

7.6 An exploded view of the wheel cylinder assembly

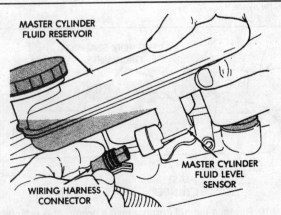

8.2 Unplug the electrical connector from the brake fluid level sensor, which is located on the left side of the reservoir

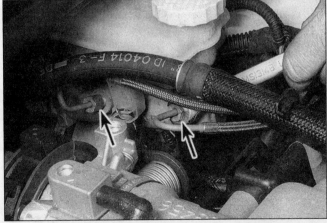

8.3 Disconnect the brake line fittings (arrows) with a flare-nut wrench

9

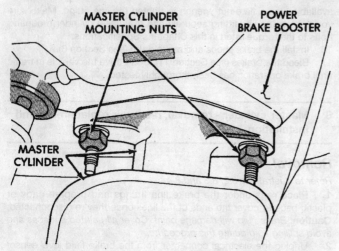

8.4 To detach the master cylinder from the power brake booster, remove these nuts (arrows), then pull the master cylinder assembly straight off the mounting studs

4   Remove the two master cylinder mounting nuts **(see illustration)** and unbolt the bracket. Move the bracket aside slightly, taking care not to kink the hydraulic lines. Remove the master cylinder from the vehicle.
5   Remove the reservoir cap, then discard any fluid remaining in the reservoir.

Reservoir replacement

Refer to illustrations 8.8, 8.9 and 8.10
Note: *The master cylinders used on the vehicles covered by this manual are not rebuildable. However, you can replace the reservoir and/or the sealing grommets between the reservoir and the master cylinder.*
6   Remove the master cylinder, if you haven't already done so (see Steps 1 through 5).
7   Remove the cap and drain the brake fluid into a container. Clean the exterior of the master cylinder with brake system cleaner.
8   Knock out the reservoir retaining pins **(see illustration)**.
9   Remove the plastic reservoir **(see illustration)** by rocking it back-and-forth and pulling up on it.
10 Remove the reservoir-to-master cylinder grommets **(see illustration)**.
11 Lubricate a pair of new grommets with clean brake fluid and

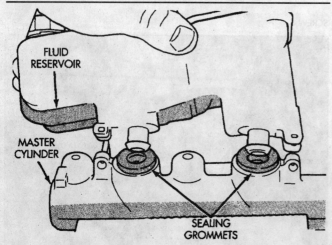

8.9 To separate the reservoir from the master cylinder, rock the reservoir back and forth and pull up at the same time

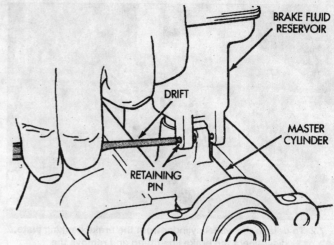

8.8 Remove the reservoir retaining pins with a small punch

install them into their bores in the master cylinder.
12 Install the reservoir into the grommets; make sure the reservoir is completely seated and the reservoir cap is at the front.
13 Install the reservoir retaining pins.

Installation

14 Whenever the master cylinder is removed, the entire hydraulic system must be bled. The time required to bleed the system can be reduced is the master cylinder is filled with fluid and bench bled before it's installed on the vehicle. Since you'll have to apply pressure to the master cylinder piston and, at the same time, control flow from the brake line outlets, the master cylinder should be mounted in a vise, with the jaws of the vise clamping on the mounting flange.
15 Insert threaded plugs into the brake line outlet holes and snug them down so that air won't leak past them - but not so tight that they can't be easily loosened.
16 Fill the reservoir with brake fluid of the recommended type (see Chapter 1).
17 Remove one plug and push the piston assembly into the bore to expel the air from the master cylinder. A large Phillips screwdriver can be used to push on the piston assembly.
18 To prevent air from being drawn back into the master cylinder, the plug must be replaced and snugged down before releasing the pressure on the piston.
19 Repeat the procedure until only brake fluid is expelled from the brake line outlet hole. When only brake fluid is expelled, repeat the procedure at the other outlet hole and plug. Be sure to keep the master cylinder reservoir filled with brake fluid to prevent the introduction of air into the system.

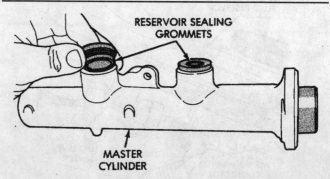

8.10 Remove the old grommets; if a grommet is difficult to remove, pry it out carefully with a small screwdriver but make sure you don't gouge the aluminum master cylinder housing

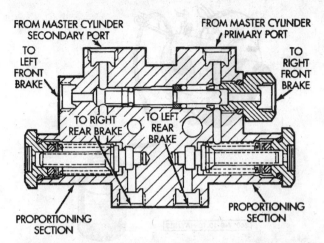

9.1 Non-ABS models use a conventional proportioning valve; it's located in the engine compartment, below the master cylinder

20   Since high pressure isn't involved in the bench bleeding procedure, an alternative to the removal and replacement of the plugs with each stroke of the piston assembly is available. Before pushing in on the piston assembly, remove the plug as described in Step 18. Before releasing the piston, however, instead of replacing the plug, simply put your finger tightly over the hole to keep air from being drawn back into the master cylinder. Wait several seconds for brake fluid to be drawn from the reservoir into the bore, then depress the piston again, removing your finger as brake fluid is expelled. Be sure to put your finger back over the hole each time before releasing the piston, and when the bleeding procedure is complete for that outlet, replace the plug and tighten it before going on to the other port.
21   Carefully install the master cylinder by reversing the removal steps. Make sure you tighten the master cylinder mounting nuts to the torque listed in this Chapter's Specifications.
22   Bleed the brake system (see Section 11).

9   Proportioning valve - description, check and replacement

Description

Refer to illustrations 9.1, 9.2a and 9.2b
1   All non-ABS models have a proportioning valve **(see illustration)** that balances front to rear braking by controlling the increase in rear system hydraulic pressure above a preset level. Under light pedal pressure, the valve allows full hydraulic pressure to the front and rear

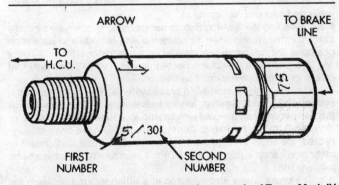

9.2b ABS models with traction control use a pair of Teves Mark IV traction control/ABS proportioning valves, one of which is located in each rear brake line, near the rear suspension crossmember

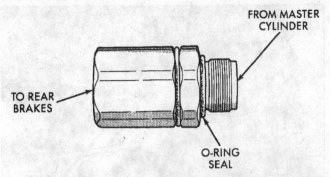

9.2a ABS models without traction control use a pair of Teves Mark IV-G ABS proportioning valves, one of which is located in each rear brake line, near the rear suspension crossmember

brakes. But above a certain pressure - known as the "split point" - the proportioning valve reduces the amount of pressure increase to the rear brakes in accordance with a predetermined ratio. This lessens the chance of rear wheel lock-up and skidding.
2   Models with ABS use a screw-in proportioning valve **(see illustrations)** in each rear brake hydraulic circuit. Below a preset level of pressure, the valves do nothing. Above a certain pressure, the valves limit brake pressure to the rear brakes.

Check

3   If either rear wheel skids prematurely under hard braking, it could indicate a defective proportioning valve. If this occurs, drive the vehicle to a dealer immediately and have the system checked out by a competent professional in the dealer service department. A pair of special pressure gauges are required for diagnosing the proportioning valve.

Replacement

Non-ABS models

Refer to illustration 9.4
Caution: *Brake fluid will damage paint. Cover all painted surfaces and avoid spilling fluid during this procedure.*
4   Loosen the brake hydraulic fluid lines from the proportioning valve with a flare-nut wrench **(see illustration)** to prevent rounding off the corners of the fittings. Back off the fittings and detach the lines. Plug the ends of the lines to prevent loss of brake fluid and the entry of dirt.
5   Unbolt the valve and remove it.
6   Installation is the reverse of removal.
7   Bleed the system after the replacement valve has been installed.

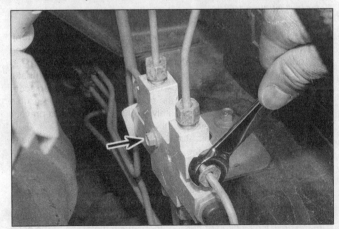

9.4 On non-ABS models, unscrew the brake fluid hydraulic line fittings with a flare-nut wrench to prevent rounding off the corners of the nuts, then remove this bolt (arrow) to detach the valve from its mounting bracket

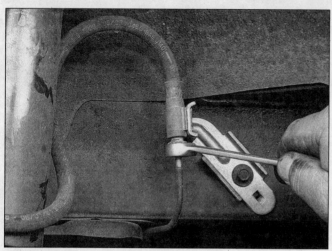

10.3 To disconnect a flexible brake hose from a metal brake line, simply unscrew the threaded fitting nut as shown, but make sure you don't kink the metal line; if the fitting nut is frozen, soak it with penetrant and try again

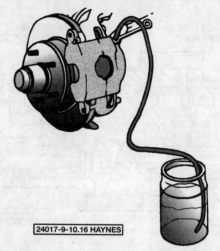

24017-9-10.16 HAYNES

11.8 When bleeding the brakes, a hose is connected to the bleed screw at the caliper or wheel cylinder and then submerged in brake fluid - air will be seen as bubbles in the tube and container (all air must be expelled before moving to the next wheel)

Models with ABS

8   Raise the rear of the vehicle and place it securely on jackstands.
9   Unscrew the proportioning valve from the brake lines **(see illustrations 9.2a and 9.2b)**. Use a flare-nut wrench to prevent rounding off the corners of the fittings. Back off the fittings and detach the lines. Plug the ends of the lines to prevent loss of brake fluid and the entry of dirt.
10   Installation is the reverse of removal.
11   Bleed the system after the replacement valve has been installed.

10 Brake hoses and lines - check and replacement

1   About every six months, with the vehicle raised and placed securely on jackstands, the flexible hoses which connect the steel brake lines with the front and rear brake assemblies should be inspected for cracks, chafing of the outer cover, leaks, blisters and other damage. These are important and vulnerable parts of the brake system and inspection should be complete. A light and mirror will be needed for a thorough check. If a hose exhibits any of the above defects, replace it with a new one.

Flexible hose replacement

Refer to illustration 10.3
2   Clean all dirt away from the ends of the hose.
3   Disconnect the brake line from the hose fitting **(see illustration)**. Be careful not to bend the frame bracket or line. If the threaded fitting is corroded, soak it with penetrating oil and allow the penetrant time to loosen it up, then try again. If you try to break loose a brake nut that's frozen, you will kink the metal line, which will then have to be replaced.
4   Separate the metal line from the connection and pull the flexible hose through the bracket. Immediately plug the metal line to prevent excessive fluid loss or contamination.
5   Unscrew the banjo bolt at the caliper and disconnect the hose from the caliper, discarding the sealing washers on either side of the fitting.
6   Using new sealing washers, attach the new brake hose to the caliper. Tighten the banjo bolt to the torque listed this Chapter's Specifications.
7   Insert the other end of the new hose through the bracket. Make sure the hose isn't kinked or twisted, then attach metal line to the hose and tighten the brake line fitting nut securely.
8   Carefully check to make sure the suspension or steering components don't make contact with the hose. Have an assistant push down on the vehicle while you watch to see whether the hose interferes with

suspension operation. If you're replacing a front hose, have your assistant turn the steering wheel lock-to-lock while you make sure the hose doesn't interfere with the steering linkage or the steering knuckle.
9   Bleed the brake system (see Section 11).

Metal brake lines

10   When replacing brake lines, be sure to use the correct parts. Don't use copper tubing for any brake system components. Purchase steel brake lines from a dealer parts department or auto parts store.
11   Prefabricated brake line, with the tube ends already flared and fittings installed, is available at auto parts stores and dealer parts departments. These lines are also sometimes bent to the proper shapes.
12   When installing the new line make sure it's well supported in the brackets and has plenty of clearance between moving or hot components. Make sure you tighten the fittings securely.
13   After installation, check the master cylinder fluid level and add fluid as necessary. Bleed the brake system as outlined in Section 11 and test the brakes carefully before placing the vehicle into normal operation.

11 Brake system bleeding

Refer to illustration 11.8
Warning: *Wear eye protection when bleeding the brake system. If the fluid comes in contact with your eyes, immediately rinse them with water and seek medical attention.*
Note: *Bleeding the brake system is necessary to remove any air that's trapped in the system when it's opened during removal and installation of a hose, line, caliper, wheel cylinder or master cylinder.*
1   If a brake line was disconnected only at a wheel, then only that caliper or wheel cylinder must be bled.
2   On conventional (non-ABS) brake systems, if air has entered the system due to low fluid level, all four brakes must be bled. **Warning:** *If this has occurred on a model with an Anti-lock Brake System (ABS), or if the lines to the Hydraulic Control Unit (HCU) have been disconnected, the vehicle must be towed to a dealer service department or other repair shop equipped with a DRB II scan tool to have the system properly bled.*
3   If a brake line is disconnected at a fitting located between the master cylinder and any of the brakes, that part of the system served by the disconnected line must be bled.
4   Remove any residual vacuum from the brake power booster (if equipped) by applying the brake several times with the engine off.

5   Remove the master cylinder reservoir cover and fill the reservoir with brake fluid. Reinstall the cover. **Note:** *Check the fluid level often during the bleeding operation and add fluid as necessary to prevent the fluid level from falling low enough to allow air bubbles into the master cylinder.*

6   Have an assistant on hand, as well as a supply of new brake fluid, an empty clear container, a length of 3/16-inch clear plastic or vinyl tubing to fit over the bleeder valve and a wrench to open and close the bleeder valve.

7   Beginning at the right rear wheel, loosen the bleeder screw slightly, then tighten it to a point where it's snug but can still be loosened quickly and easily.

8   Place one end of the tubing over the bleeder screw fitting and submerge the other end in brake fluid in the container **(see illustration).**

9   Have the assistant pump the brakes a few times to get pressure in the system, then hold the pedal firmly depressed.

10   While the pedal is held depressed, open the bleeder screw just enough to allow a flow of fluid to leave the valve. Watch for air bubbles to exit the submerged end of the tube. When the fluid flow slows after a couple of seconds, tighten the screw and have your assistant release the pedal.

11   Repeat Steps 9 and 10 until no more air is seen leaving the tube, then tighten the bleeder screw and proceed to the left rear wheel, the right front wheel and the left front wheel, in that order, and perform the same procedure. Be sure to check the fluid in the master cylinder reservoir frequently.

12   Never use old brake fluid. It contains moisture which will deteriorate the brake system components and can even boil if the temperature of the brake fluid rises high enough, which will render the brakes useless.

13   Refill the master cylinder with fluid at the end of the operation.

14   Check the operation of the brakes. The pedal should feel solid when depressed, with no sponginess. If necessary, repeat the entire process. **Warning:** *Do not operate the vehicle if the pedal feels low or spongy, if the ABS light on the dash won't go off or if you are in doubt about the effectiveness of the brake system.*

12   Power brake booster - check, removal and installation

Operating check

1   Depress the brake pedal several times with the engine off and make sure that there is no change in the pedal reserve distance.

2   Depress the pedal and start the engine. If the pedal goes down slightly, operation is normal.

Airtightness check

3   Start the engine and turn it off after one or two minutes. Depress the brake pedal several times slowly. If the pedal goes down farther the first time but gradually rises after the second or third depression, the booster is airtight.

4   Depress the brake pedal while the engine is running, then stop the engine with the pedal depressed. If there is no change in the pedal reserve travel after holding the pedal for 30 seconds, the booster is airtight.

Removal

Refer to illustration 12.9

5   The power brake booster unit requires no special maintenance apart from periodic inspection of the vacuum hose and the case. Disassembly of the power unit requires special tools and is not ordinarily performed by the home mechanic. If a problem develops, it's recommended that a new or factory rebuilt unit be installed.

6   Remove the cowl cover (see Chapter 11) and the windshield wiper module (see Chapter 12).

7   Remove the master cylinder (see Section 8). It isn't necessary to actually disconnect the brake lines from the master cylinder; simply slide the master cylinder off the mounting studs and push it aside (just

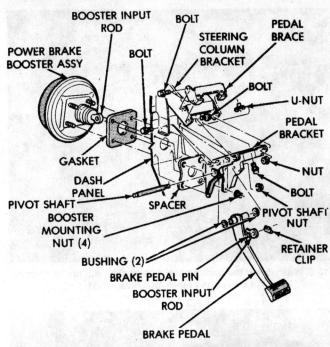

12.9 Power brake booster and brake pedal mounting details

make sure you don't kink the metal brake lines).

8   Disconnect the vacuum hose from the power brake booster.

9   Working under the dash, disconnect the power brake pushrod from the top of the brake pedal by prying off the retainer clip **(see illustration).** Discard the old retainer clip and buy a new clip for reassembly.

10   Remove the nuts attaching the booster to the firewall.

11   Carefully lift the booster unit away from the firewall and out of the engine compartment.

Installation

12   To install the booster, place it into position and tighten the retaining nuts to the torque listed in this Chapter's Specifications. Connect the brake pedal. **Warning:** *Use a new retainer clip. Do not re-use the old clip.*

13   Install the master cylinder and vacuum hose.

14   Carefully test the operation of the brakes before placing the vehicle in normal operation.

13   Parking brake shoes (models with rear disc brakes) - removal, inspection and installation

Warning: *Dust created by the brake system may contain asbestos, which is harmful to your health. Never blow it out with compressed air and don't inhale any of it. An approved filtering mask should be worn when working on the brakes. Do not, under any circumstances, use petroleum-based solvents to clean brake parts. Use brake system cleaner only.*

Note: *Parking brake shoes should be replaced on both wheels at the same time - never replace the shoes on only one wheel.*

Removal

Refer to illustrations 13.5 and 13.6a through 13.6h

1   The parking brake system should be checked as a normal part of driving. With the vehicle parked on a hill, apply the brake, place the transmission in Neutral and verify that the parking brake alone with hold the vehicle (be sure to stay in the vehicle during this check). Additionally, every 24 months - and any time a fault is suspected - the assembly itself should be visually inspected.

9

13.5 Wash down the parking brake assembly with brake cleaner
so you don't inhale any brake dust

13.6a Remove the front brake shoe hold-down clip by pushing in
on the clip and turning the retaining pin 90-degrees

13.6b Remove the rear brake shoe hold-down clip

13.6c Pull the upper end of the rear brake shoe away from the
parking brake actuator lever . . .

13.6d . . . then unhook the upper spring from the rear shoe

2   Loosen the rear wheel lug nuts, raise the rear of the vehicle and
support it securely on jackstands. Block the front wheels and remove
the rear wheels. Release the parking brake.
3   Remove the rear calipers (see Section 4). Support the caliper
assemblies with a coat hanger or heavy wire and don't disconnect the
brake line from the caliper.
4   Remove the rear discs (see Section 5). Remove the rear hub and
bearing assemblies (see Chapter 10).
5   Clean the parking brake assembly with brake system cleaner **(see
illustration)**.
6   Follow the accompanying sequence of photos to remove the
parking brake shoes **(see illustrations)**. Be sure to stay in order and
read the caption under each illustration.

Inspection

7   Inspect the lining contact pattern o determine whether the shoes
are bent or have been improperly adjusted. The lining should show
contact across the entire width, extending from head to toe. Shoes
showing contact only on one side should be replaced.
8   Clean the backing plate with a suitable solvent.
9   Inspect the drum (see Section 6).

13.6e Disengage the lower end of the rear shoe from the adjuster . . .

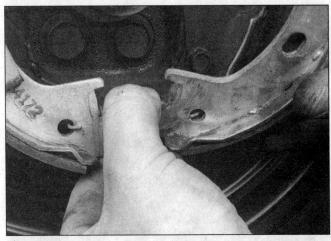

13.6f . . . then unhook the lower spring from the rear shoe and remove the rear shoe

13.6g Unhook the lower spring from the front brake shoe

13.6h Unhook the upper spring from the front brake shoe

Installation

Refer to illustrations 13.10a through 13.10l

10 Follow the accompanying sequence of photos to install the new shoes (see illustrations), then install the hub and bearing assemblies (see Chapter 10).

11 Before installing the disc, rotate the star wheel on the adjuster until the distance across the friction surfaces of the parking brake shoes is 6-3/4 inches.

12 Install the disc (see Section 5). Using a screwdriver or brake adjusting tool, turn the star wheel on the parking brake shoe adjuster

13.10a Lubricate the friction points on the brake backing plate with high-temperature grease

13.10b Insert the end of the parking brake cable into the parking brake actuator lever, if removed

9

13.10c Insert the pin for the hold-down clip through the brake backing plate

13.10d Install the front parking brake shoe

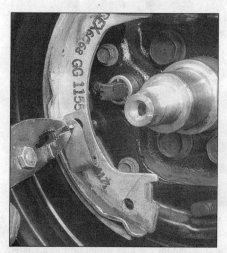

13.10e Install the front brake shoe hold-down clip

13.10f Hook the upper return spring to the front parking brake shoe

13.10g Hook the lower return spring to the front parking brake shoe

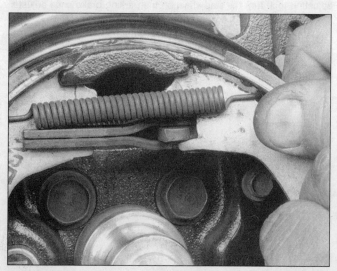

13.10h Hook the upper return spring to the rear parking brake shoe

13.10i Hook the lower return spring to the rear parking brake shoe

  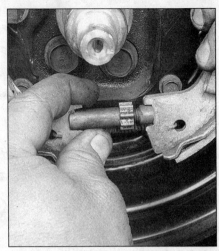

13.10j Pull the rear parking brake shoe back and engage it with the actuator lever

13.10k Insert the pin for the rear hold-down clip through the backing plate and install the rear hold-down clip

13.10l Install the adjuster between the parking brake shoes, then turn the adjuster star wheel until the distance across the friction surfaces of the shoes is 6-3/4 inches

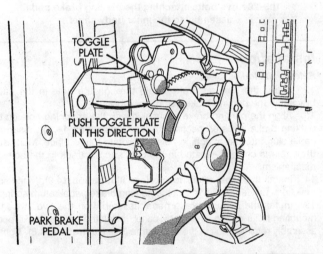 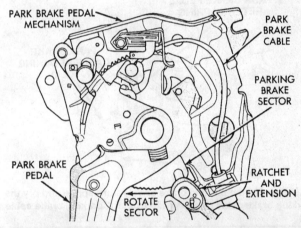

14.3 To release the toggle plate, reach up under the dash while keeping pressure on the parking brake pedal and push the toggle plate in the indicated direction

14.5 Insert a 1/4-inch drive ratchet extension into the 1/4-inch square hole located in the sector of the parking brake mechanism and rotate the sector toward the rear of the vehicle until the ratchet extension contacts the back of the parking brake pedal. This winds up the sector spring

until the shoes slightly drag as the disc is turned, then back-off the adjuster until the shoes don't drag.

13   Install the caliper (see Section 4).

14   Repeat this sequence for the other parking brake shoes at the other rear wheel.

14 Parking brake pedal assembly - removal and installation

Removal

Refer to illustrations 14.3, 14.5, 14.7, 14.8, 14.9 and 14.11

1   On floor-shift models, remove the shift lever handle (see Chapter 7).

2   Remove the center console and the lower knee bolster panel (see Chapter 11).

3   Release the parking brake pedal. If the parking brake pedal is jammed and won't release, the toggle plate may be stuck. To release the toggle plate, reach up under the dash while keeping pressure on the parking brake pedal, and push the toggle plate in the indicated direction **(see illustration)**. You should now be able to release the parking brake. **Warning:** *When releasing the toggle plate, be sure to keep pressure on the parking brake pedal. If there's no pressure applied to the pedal when the toggle is released, the pedal can snap back, causing injury.*

4   Reload the parking brake self-adjuster (see Steps 5 through 7). **Note:** *The self-adjuster mechanism in the parking brake pedal assembly automatically adjusts the parking brake cables. No routine cable adjustment is necessary. However, anytime the parking brake pedal or a parking brake cable is removed or replaced, the automatic adjustment mechanism must be reloaded and locked out.*

5   Insert a 1/4-inch-drive ratchet extension into the 1/4-inch square hole located in the sector of the parking brake mechanism **(see illustration)**.

6   Rotate the sector toward the rear of the vehicle until the ratchet extension contacts the back of the parking brake pedal. This winds up

9

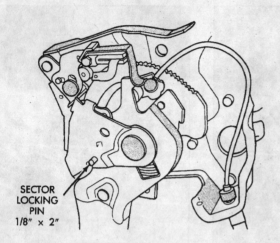

14.7 To lock the sector into place, insert a 1/8 X 2-inch pin, drill bit or Allen wrench into the parking brake lever mechanism; the pin must go all the way through both sidesof the parking brake mechanism

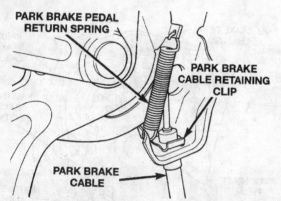

14.9 Remove the parking brake pedal return spring and pry the parking brake cable retaining clip from the parking brake cable

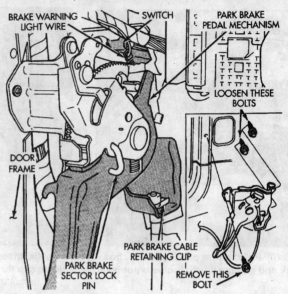

14.8 Unplug the electrical connector from the brake warning light switch, remove the bolt attaching the parking brake pedal assembly to the door frame and loosen - but don't remove - th9-20e two bolts attaching the parking brake pedal assembly to the inner body panel

Installation

Refer to illustration 14.16

12   Insert the parking brake cable through the hole in the cable bracket in the parking brake pedal assembly.

13   Align the parking brake cable slug with the attaching hole on the parking brake adjuster mechanism **(see illustration 14.11)**. Insert the cable slug into the attaching hole and rotate it into place. Make sure the cable is correctly seated in the cam surface track in the adjuster mechanism.

14   Install the cable retaining clip **(see illustration 14.9)**. Make sure the clip is fully engaged. Install the parking brake pedal return spring.

15   Install the parking brake pedal assembly on the two loosened mounting bolts on the inner body panel; install the parking brake pedal assembly retaining bolt in the door frame **(see illustration 14.8)**. Tighten

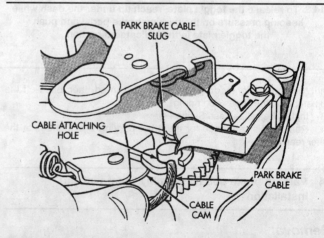

14.11 Rotate the parking brake cable to align it with the notch in the cable attaching hole on the parking brake adjuster mechanism, lift the cable slug out of the attaching hole, pull the cable through the hole in the cable bracket and separate the cable from the parking brake pedal assembly.

the sector spring.

7   Insert a 1/8 X 2-inch pin, drill bit or Allen wrench into the parking brake lever mechanism **(see illustration)**. The pin must go all the way through both sides of the parking brake mechanism. This locks the sector into place. **Warning:** *The self-adjusting mechanism of the parking brake pedal assembly contains a clock spring loaded to about eight pounds. Use care in handling the parking brake pedal assembly. Do not release the self-adjuster lockout device before installing the cables into the equalizer. Keep your hands away from the self-adjuster sector and pawl. Careless handling of the parking brake pedal adjuster mechanism could cause serious injury.*

8   Unplug the electrical connector from the brake warning light switch **(see illustration)**.

9   Remove the parking brake pedal return spring **(see illustration)**. Using a screwdriver, pry the parking brake cable retaining clip from the parking brake cable.

10   Remove the bolt attaching the parking brake pedal assembly to the door frame; loosen - but don't remove - the two bolts attaching the parking brake pedal assembly to the inner body panel **(see illustration 14.8)**.

11   Rotate the parking brake cable to align it with the notch in the cable attaching hole on the parking brake adjuster mechanism **(see illustration)**. Lift the cable slug out of the attaching hole, then pull the cable through the hole in the cable bracket and separate the cable from the parking brake pedal assembly.

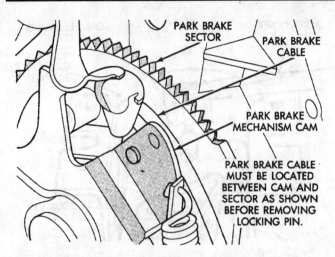

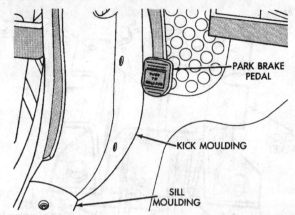

15.5 Remove the left (driver's side) sill molding and kick molding

14.16 Before releasing the self-adjuster mechanism, make sure that the front parking brake cable is correctly engaged with the parking brake mechanism

all three bolts to the torque listed in this Chapter's Specifications.

16   Before releasing the self-adjuster mechanism, make sure that all three parking brake cables are properly attached to the equalizer bracket (see Section 15) and that the front cable is correctly engaged with the parking brake mechanism **(see illustration)**.

17   Using a pair of pliers, pull out the lock pin installed in the parking brake mechanism with a firm and quick motion. When the locking pin is removed from the parking brake pedal adjuster mechanism, the adjuster automatically adjusts the parking brake cables.

18   Apply and release the parking brake pedal several times. The rear wheels should rotate freely without the brakes dragging.

19   Install the lower knee bolster panel and the center console (see Chapter 11).

20   On floor-shift models, install the shift lever handle (see Chapter 7).

15   Parking brake cables - replacement

Front cable

Removal

Refer to illustrations 15.5, 15.6, 15.7, 15.9, 15.10 and 15.11

1   Remove the driver's seat from the vehicle (see Chapter 11).

2   On bucket seat models, remove the handle from the shift lever **(see illustrations 3.28a and 3.28b in Chapter 7)**.

3   On bucket seat models, remove the center console (see Chapter 11).

4   On bench seat models, remove the rear seat lower cushion (see Chapter 11).

5   Remove the left (driver's side) sill molding and kick molding **(see illustration)**.

6   On bucket seat models, remove the rear console mounting bracket from the parking brake cable reaction bracket, and remove the rear passenger compartment heat duct **(see illustration)**.

7   On bench seat models, remove the accelerator pedal and bracket, and peel back the carpet to expose the front parking brake cable, the reaction bracket cover and the equalizer **(see illustration)**.
Note: *As an alternative to removing the accelerator pedal and bracket, cut the carpet around the accelerator pedal bracket and peel it back. When you're done, glue it back in place. Remove the equalizer cover from the reaction bracket.*

8   Reload the parking brake adjuster mechanism (see Steps 4 through 7 in Section 14).

9   Disconnect the front parking brake cable from the parking brake

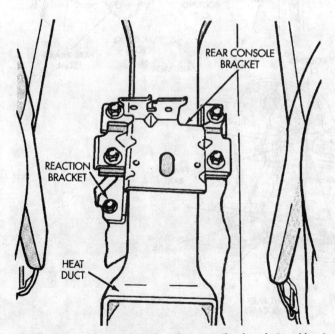

15.6 Rear console mounting bracket, reaction bracket and heat duct (bucket seat models)

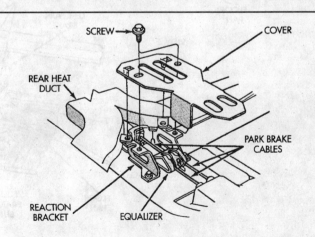

15.7 Reaction bracket cover and equalizer (bench seat models)

9

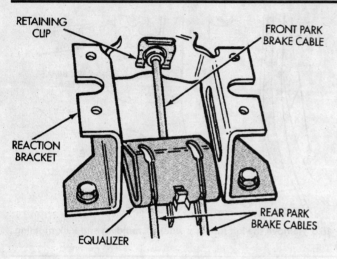

15.9 Front parking brake cable connection at the equalizer

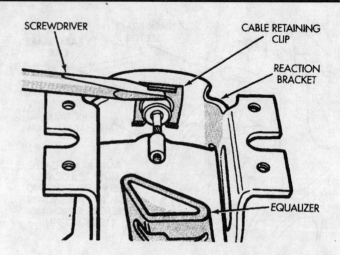

15.10 Using a screwdriver, pry off the cable retaining clip and pull the cable out of the reaction bracket

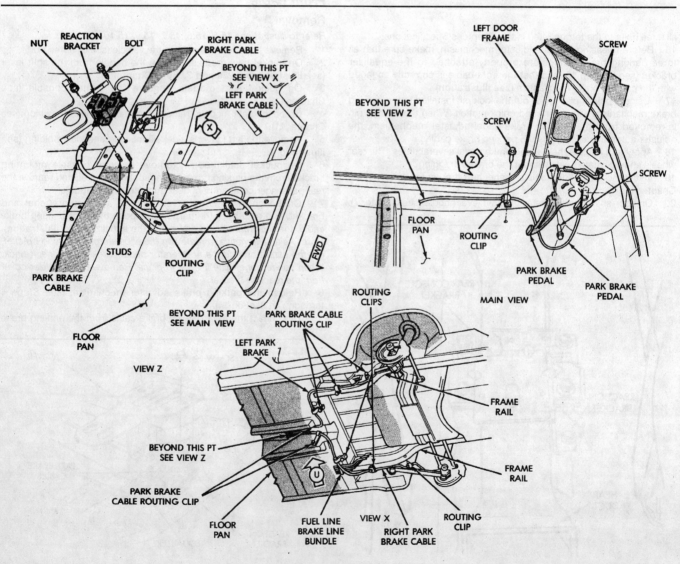

15.11 Forward cable retaining clip and floorpan crossmember routing clips

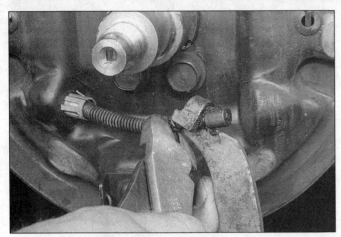

15.31a On models with rear drum brakes, pull back the spring and disengage the cable from the parking brake lever . . .

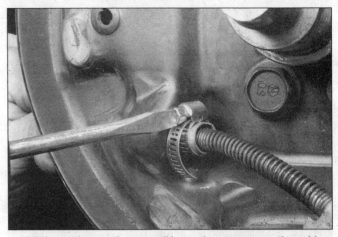

15.31b . . . then, using a small hose clamp, squeeze the cable housing retainer tabs and pull the cable through the brake backing plate; if you don't have a clamp handy, use a 1/2-inch box-end wrench or a pair of pliers (using pliers isn't as easy)

cable equalizer **(see illustration)**.
10 Using a screwdriver, pry off the cable retaining clip **(see illustration)**. Pull the cable out of the reaction bracket.
11 Remove the screw from the forward cable retaining clip, and remove the cable from the two routing clips attached to the floorpan crossmember **(see illustration)**.
12 Remove the parking brake pedal assembly (see Section 14).
13 Using a screwdriver, pry the parking brake cable retaining clip from the parking brake cable **(see illustration 14.9)**.
14 Rotate the parking brake cable to align it with the notch in the cable attaching hole on the parking brake adjuster mechanism **(see illustration 14.11)**. Lift the cable slug out of the attaching hole, then pull the cable through the hole in the cable bracket and separate the cable from the parking brake pedal assembly.

Installation

15 Install the parking brake cable through the cable bracket in the parking brake pedal assembly.
16 Align the parking brake cable with the notch in the cable attaching hole, insert the cable slug into the hole and rotate the cable into place. Make sure the cable is properly seated in the cam surface track of the parking brake pedal assembly **(see illustration 14.11)**.
17 Install the cable retaining clip **(see illustration 14.9)**. Make sure the hooked ends of the parking brake pedal return spring are properly engaged.
18 Install the parking brake pedal assembly (see Section 14). Don't forget to plug in the electrical connector for the brake warning light switch.
19 Route the front parking brake cable along the floor of the vehicle, insert the end of the cable through the mounting hole in the reaction bracket and install the retaining clip **(see illustration 15.10)**. Carefully tap the retaining clip with a small hammer until it's fully seated. Attach the cable to the equalizer **(see illustration 15.9)**.
20 Install the parking brake cable routing clip screw and tighten it securely. Install the crossmember routing clips **(see illustration 15.11)**.
21 Make sure that the parking brake cable is properly seated in the cam surface track of the parking brake mechanism **(see illustration 14.16)**.
22 Using a pair of pliers, pull out the lock pin installed in the parking brake mechanism with a firm and quick motion. When the locking pin is removed from the parking brake pedal adjuster mechanism, the adjuster automatically adjusts the parking brake cables.
23 On bench seat models, fold the carpeting back into position and install the accelerator pedal and bracket assembly (or, if you cut the carpet, glue the carpet down to the pan).
24 On bucket seat models, install the rear passenger compartment heat duct and the rear console mounting bracket **(see illustration 15.6)**.
25 Install the left (driver's side) sill molding and kick molding **(see illustration 15.5)**.
26 On bench seat models, install the rear seat lower cushion (see Chapter 11).
27 On bucket seat models, install the center console (see Chapter 11).
28 On bucket seat models, install the shift lever handle (see Chapter 7).
29 Install the driver's seat (see Chapter 11).

Rear cables

Removal

Refer to illustrations 15.31a, 15.31b, 15.32a, 15.32b, 15.33 and 15.36
Note: *Disconnect only one rear parking brake cable from the rear brakes at a time. If you disconnect both cables simultaneously, it will be extremely difficult to connect both of them to the equalizer.*
30 Loosen the rear wheel lug nuts, raise the rear of the vehicle and place it securely on jackstands. Remove the rear wheels.
31 On models with rear drum brakes, remove the rear drum (see Section 6) and the rear hub and bearing assembly (see Chapter 10). Disassemble the brake shoe assembly (see Section 6). Disconnect the cable from the parking brake lever **(see illustration)**. Using a small hose clamp, squeeze the cable housing retainer tabs **(see illustration)** and pull the cable through the brake backing plate. If you don't have a clamp handy, use a 1/2-inch box wrench or a pair of pliers (using pliers isn't as easy).
32 On models with rear disc brakes, remove the rear caliper (see

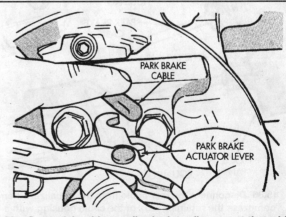

15.32a On models with rear disc brakes, disconnect the cable from the parking brake actuator lever . . .

15.32b . . . then, squeeze the retainer tabs on the cable housing and pull the cable through the brake backing plate

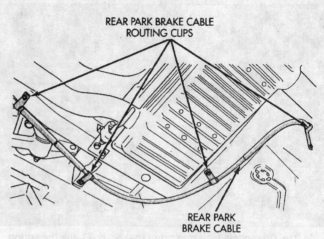

15.33 Remove the four cable retaining clips attaching the rear cable to the floorpan and frame

Section 4) and disc (see Section 5). Disassemble the parking brake shoe assembly (see Section 13). Disconnect the cable from the parking brake actuator lever **(see illustration)**, then squeeze the retainer tabs on the cable housing **(see illustration)** and pull the cable through the backing plate.

33   Remove the four cable retaining clips attaching the rear cable to the floorpan and frame **(see illustration)**.

34   On bucket seat models, remove the handle from the shift lever (see Chapter 7), remove the center console (see Chapter 11) and remove the rear console mounting bracket from the parking brake cable reaction bracket, and remove the rear passenger compartment heat duct **(see illustration 15.6)**.

35   On bench seat models, move the front passenger seat to its full-forward position. Remove the driver's seat and the rear seat lower cushion (see Chapter 11). Remove both lower rear door opening sill moldings and fold the rear carpet forward, exposing the parking brake equalizer cover **(see illustration 15.7)**. Remove the cover from the reaction bracket.

36   Disconnect the rear cable from the equalizer **(see illustration)**, then compress the retaining tabs of the cable housing with a 1/2-inch box wrench, a pair of pliers or a small hose clamp and pull the cable through the floorpan.

Installation

Refer to illustration 15.44

37   Insert the rear end of the new rear cable through the hole in the brake backing plate. Make sure the cable is pulled through the hole far enough to allow the retaining tabs to expand all the way around the cable, locking the cable to the backing plate.

38   Insert the front end of the rear cable through the hole in the floorpan. Again, make sure the cable is pulled through the hole far enough to allow the retaining tabs to expand all the way around the cable, locking the cable to the floorpan.

39   Install the four retaining clips that attach the rear cable to the floorpan and tighten the screws securely **(see illustration 15.33)**.

40   Grasp the equalizer firmly, pull it to the rear and connect the front end of the rear cable to the equalizer **(see illustration 15.9)**.

41   On bucket seat models, install the rear passenger compartment heat duct **(see illustration 15.6)**, install the rear console mounting bracket on the parking brake cable reaction bracket, install the center console (see Chapter 11) and install the handle on the shift lever **(see illustrations 3.28a and 3.28b in Chapter 7)**.

42   On bench seat models, install the cover from the reaction bracket. Fold back the rear carpet and install both lower rear door opening sill

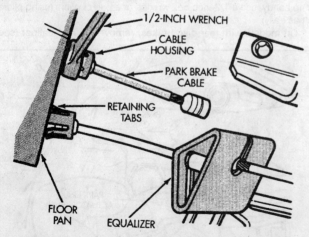

15.36 Disconnect the rear cable from the equalizer, then compress the retaining tabs of the cable housing with a 1/2-inch box wrench (shown), a pair of pliers or a small hose clamp and pull the cable through the floorpan

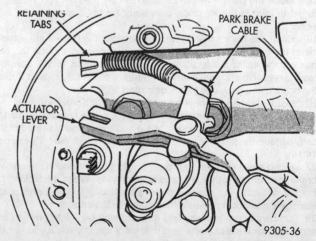

15.44 On models with rear disc brakes, engage the actuator lever with the rear end of the parking brake cable as shown, then install the actuator lever

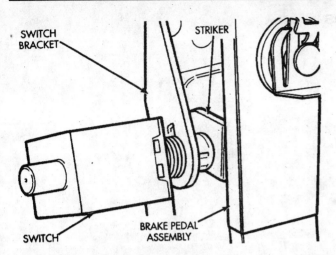

16.1a A typical earlier brake light switch (without cruise control)

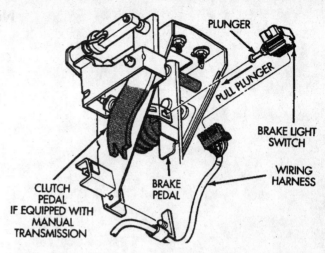

16.1b A typical later brake light switch (with cruise control)

moldings. Move the front passenger seat back to its normal position. Install the driver's seat and the rear seat lower cushion (see Chapter 11).
43   On models with rear drum brakes, connect the cable to the parking brake lever, reassemble the rear brake assembly (see Section 6), install the rear hub and bearing assembly (see Chapter 10) and install the rear drum.
44   On models with rear disc brakes, connect the cable to the parking brake actuator lever **(see illustration)**, reassemble the parking brake shoe assembly (see Section 13), install the disc (see Section 5) and install the rear caliper (see Section 3).
45   Repeat this procedure for the other rear cable, if you're replacing both cables.
46   Install the rear wheels, hand tighten the wheel lug nuts, remove the jackstands and lower the vehicle. Tighten the rear wheel lug nuts to the torque listed in the Chapter 1 Specifications.

16 Brake light switch - check, replacement and adjustment

Refer to illustrations 16.1a and 16.1b
1   The brake light switch **(see illustrations)** is a normally-open switch that controls the operation of the vehicle brake lights. The switch is located near the top of the brake pedal, either on the left side of the brake pedal bracket or on the steering column support. When the brake pedal is applied, a spring-loaded plunger closes the circuit to the left and right brake lights.
2   On models with cruise control, the brake light switch also deactivates the cruise control system when the brake pedal is depressed. When the brake pedal is applied on these models, the switch opens the ground circuit for the switch sensor inside the and the powertrain control module deactivates the cruise control system.

Check

3   If the brake lights don't come on when the brake pedal is applied, check the brake light fuse (see Chapter 12). If the fuse is bad, look for a short in the brake light circuit.
4   If the fuse is okay, use a test light or voltmeter to verify that there's voltage to the switch. If there's no voltage to the switch, look for an open or short in the power wire to the switch. Repair the power wire.

5   If the brake lights still don't come on when the brake pedal is applied, unplug the electrical connector from the brake light switch and, using an ohmmeter, verify that there's continuity between the switch terminals when the brake pedal is applied, i.e. the switch is closed. If there isn't, replace the switch.
6   If there is continuity between the switch terminals when the brake is applied, but the brake lights don't come on when the brake pedal is applied, check the wiring between the switch and the brake lights for an open circuit.

Replacement

7   Depress and hold the brake pedal, then rotate the brake light switch about 30-degrees in a counterclockwise direction.
8   Pull the switch to the rear and remove it from its mounting bracket.
9   Unplug the electrical connector from the switch.
10   Install and adjust the new switch (see below).

Adjustment

1993 through 1995 models

11   Install the switch in the retaining bracket and push it forward as far as it will go. The brake pedal will move forward slightly.
12   Gently pull back on the brake pedal, bringing the striker back toward the switch until the brake pedal will go back no further. The switch will ratchet backward to the correct position. Very little movement is required, and no further adjustment is necessary.

1996 and later models

13   Hold the brake light switch firmly and pull out on the plunger until it ratchets out to its fully extended position.
14   Plug the electrical connector into the switch.
15   Depress the brake pedal as far as it will go, then install the switch in the bracket by aligning the index key on the switch with the slot at the top of the square hole in the mounting bracket. **Caution:** *Don't use excessive force when pulling back on the brake pedal to adjust the switch. If you use too much force, you will damage the switch or the striker.* When the switch is fully installed in the bracket, rotate the switch clockwise about 30-degrees to lock the switch into the bracket.
16   Gently pull back on the brake pedal until the pedal stops moving. The switch plunger will ratchet backward to the correct position.

9

Notes

Chapter 10
Suspension and steering systems

Contents

Specifications

Torque specifications

Ft-lbs (unless otherwise indicated)

Front suspension

Control arm pivot bushing-to-cradle bracket bolt	90
Hub and bearing-to-steering knuckle bolts	80
Stabilizer bar link-to-steering arm nut	17
Stabilizer bar link-to-stabilizer bar nut	70
Stabilizer bushing/retainer bolts	40
Steering knuckle-to-balljoint stud pinch bolt	40
Strut upper mounting nuts	25
Strut shaft nut	70
Strut-to-steering knuckle nuts	125
Tension strut-to-cradle bracket nut	110
Tension strut-to-control arm nut	110

Rear suspension

Hub and bearing assembly-to-spindle nut	125
Lateral link-to-spindle bolt	105
Lateral link-to-rear crossmember bolt	105
Stabilizer-to-link nuts	70
Stabilizer bushing bracket bolts	44
Strut upper mounting nuts	20
Strut shaft nut	70
Spindle-to-strut pinch bolt	40
Trailing arm-to-body bolt	75
Trailing arm-to-spindle bolt	75

10

Steering system

	Ft-lbs (unless otherwise indicated)
Airbag module retaining screws	96 in-lbs
Power steering pump mounting bolts	40
Power steering fluid pressure line fitting	25
Steering gear mounting bolts	50
Power steering fluid line tube fittings	23
Inner tie rod-to-steering gear bolts	55
Steering wheel nut	45
Tie-rod end	
Stud nut	27
Wheel lug nuts	See Chapter 1

1 General information

Refer to illustrations 1.1a, 1.1b, 1.2a and 1.2b

The front suspension **(see illustrations)** is a Macpherson strut design. The upper end of each strut/coil spring assembly is attached to the vehicle body. The lower end of each strut is bolted to the upper end of the steering knuckle. The lower end of the steering knuckle is attached to a balljoint mounted in the outer end of the control arm. The control arm is positioned longitudinally by a tension strut. A stabilizer bar bolted to the frame and connected to the strut/coil assemblies reduces body roll during cornering.

The rear suspension **(see illustrations)** also uses strut/coil spring assemblies. The upper end of each strut is attached to the vehicle body. The lower end of the strut is attached to a spindle. The spindle is located by a pair of lateral links on each side, and a longitudinally mounted trailing arm between the body and each spindle.

The power-assisted rack-and-pinion steering gear is located above the transaxle, behind the engine and in front of the firewall. The steering gear actuates the tie-rods. The tie-rod ends are connected to steering arms on the strut assemblies. The steering column is designed to collapse in the event of an accident.

Frequently, when working on the suspension or steering system components, you may come across fasteners which seem impossible

1.1a Front suspension and steering components

1	Stabilizer bar	3	Strut assembly	5	Driveaxle assembly
2	Tension strut	4	Control arm		

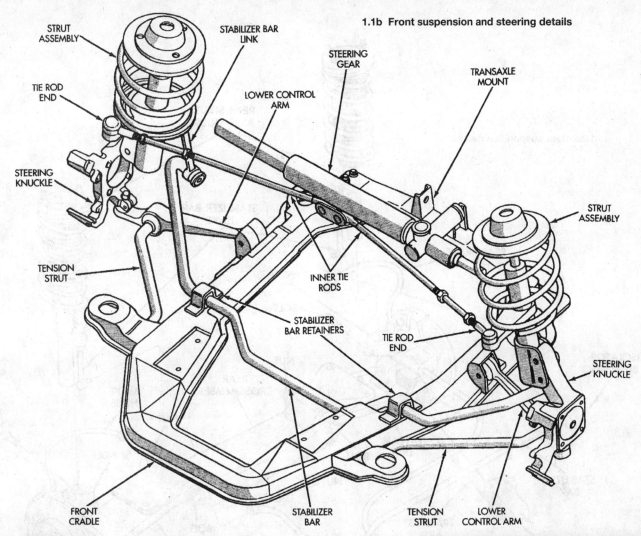

1.1b Front suspension and steering details

STRUT
ASSEMBLY

STABILIZER BAR
LINK

STEERING
GEAR

TRANSAXLE
MOUNT

TIE ROD
END

LOWER CONTROL
ARM

STRUT
ASSEMBLY

STEERING
KNUCKLE

INNER TIE
RODS

TENSION
STRUT

STABILIZER
BAR RETAINERS

TIE ROD
END

STEERING
KNUCKLE

FRONT
CRADLE

STABILIZER
BAR

TENSION
STRUT

LOWER
CONTROL ARM

1.2a Rear suspension components

1	Rear lateral link	3	Front lateral link	5	Spindle
2	Rear wheel toe adjuster	4	Trailing arm	6	Strut assembly

10

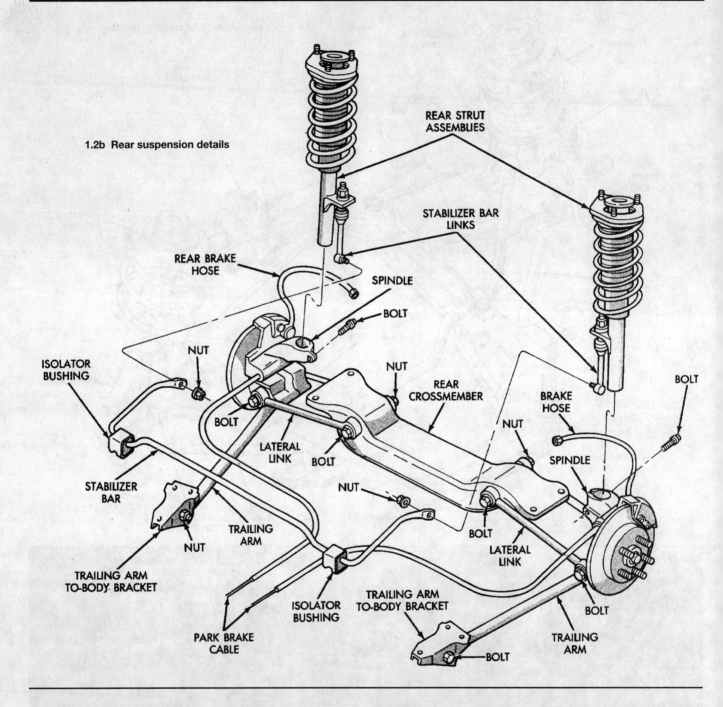

1.2b Rear suspension details

to loosen. These fasteners on the underside of the vehicle are continually subjected to water, road grime, mud, etc., and can become rusted or "frozen," making them extremely difficult to remove. In order to unscrew these stubborn fasteners without damaging them (or other components), be sure to use lots of penetrating oil and allow it to soak in for a while. Using a wire brush to clean exposed threads will also ease removal of the nut or bolt and prevent damage to the threads. Sometimes a sharp blow with a hammer and punch will break the bond between a nut and bolt threads, but care must be taken to prevent the punch from slipping off the fastener and ruining the threads. Heating the stuck fastener and surrounding area with a torch sometimes helps too, but isn't recommended because of the obvious dangers associated with fire. Long breaker bars and extension, or "cheater," pipes will increase leverage, but never use an extension pipe on a ratchet - the ratcheting mechanism could be damaged. Sometimes tightening the nut or bolt first will help to

break it loose. Fasteners that require drastic measures to remove should always be replaced with new ones.

Since most of the procedures dealt with in this Chapter involve jacking up the vehicle and working underneath it, a good pair of jackstands will be needed. A hydraulic floor jack is the preferred type of jack to lift the vehicle, and it can also be used to support certain components during various operations. **Warning:** *Never, under any circumstances, rely on a jack to support the vehicle while working on it. Whenever any of the suspension or steering fasteners are loosened or removed they must be inspected and, if necessary, replaced with new ones of the same part number or of original equipment quality and design. Torque specifications must be followed for proper reassembly and component retention. Never attempt to heat or straighten any suspension or steering components. Instead, replace any bent or damaged part with a new one.*

2.2 After removing the front wheels, you'll find the stabilizer bar retainers by lifting up the flap of the wheelhouse cover; to detach either stabilizer bar retainer from the engine cradle, remove the retainer bolts

2.3a To disconnect the upper end of the stabilizer bar link from the strut/coil spring assembly, remove this nut (arrow)

2   Stabilizer bar and bushings (front) - removal and installation

Bushings

Refer to illustrations 2.2, 2.3a, 2.3b and 2.6

1   Loosen the front wheel lug nuts. Raise the front of the vehicle and support it securely on jackstands. Apply the parking brake and block the rear wheels to keep the vehicle from rolling off the stands. Remove the front wheels.

2   Peel back the wheelhouse cover and remove the bolts from the stabilizer bar bushing retainers **(see illustration)**. Remove the retainer bolts and remove the retainers.

3   Remove the nuts that attach the upper and lower ends of the stabilizer links to the strut/coil spring assembly and to the stabilizer bar **(see illustrations)**. Detach the links.

4   Inspect the retainer bushings for cracks and tears. If either bushing is broken, damaged, distorted or worn, replace both of them. If the ballstuds on the links are loose or othrwise worn, replace the links.

5   Install the links and bushings. Tighten the link nuts to the torque listed in this Chapter's Specifications.

6   Install the retainer bushings. Clean the areas on the stabilizer bar where the bushings are located. Lubricate the inside and outside of the new bushings with vegetable oil (used in cooking) to simplify reassembly. **Caution:** *Don't use petroleum or mineral-based lubricants or brake fluid - they will lead to deterioration of the bushings.* These bushings are split so that you can install them without having to slide them onto the ends of the stabilizer bar. Install the new bushings with the slit in each bushing facing forward **(see illustration)**.

7   Install the retainers, align the bolt holes in the retainers with the mounting holes in the cradle and hand tighten - but do not torque - the retainer bolts. Do not torque these bolts until the vehicle is back on the ground. **Caution:** *Make sure the lower part of the stabilizer bar is centered in the middle of the cradle assembly. If it isn't, the stabilizer bar could contact other suspension components.*

8   Install the wheels and wheel lug nuts and snug the wheel lug nuts. Remove the jackstands and lower the vehicle. Tighten the wheel lug nuts to the torque listed in the Chapter 1 Specifications.

9   With the full weight of the vehicle supported by the suspension, use a long extension to tighten the stabilizer bushing retainer bolts to the torque listed in this Chapter's Specifications.

Stabilizer bar

Stabilizer bar removal requires the removal of the engine cradle assembly. Stabilizer bars rarely wear out, and if one becomes damaged it is most likley the result of an accident that was severe enough to damage other major components (such as the cradle itself). Damage this severe will require the services of an auto body shop. For this reason, front stabilizer bar removal and installation is not covered in this manual.

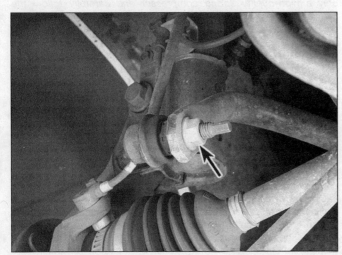

2.3b To disconnect the lower end of the stabilizer bar link from the stabilizer bar itself, remove this nut (arrow)

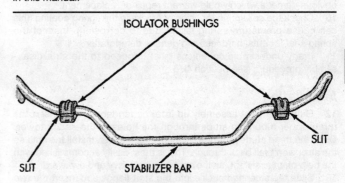

2.6 When installing the stabilizer bar bushings, make sure that the slit on each bushing faces forward

10

3.4 If the vehicle is equipped with ABS, remove the ABS wire harness grommets from the small bracket on the strut, then remove the bracket retaining bolt (arrow) and detach the bracket

3.6 To detach the lower end of the strut from the steering knuckle, remove these two large nuts and knock out the bolts with a punch and hammer

3.8 To detach the upper end of the strut from the body, remove these three nuts; be sure to have a helper hold the strut while you're removing the nuts or it will fall out when you remove the last nut!

3   Struts (front) - removal, inspection and installation

Removal

Refer to illustrations 3.4, 3.6 and 3.8

1   Loosen the wheel lug nuts, raise the vehicle and support it securely on jackstands. Remove the wheel.

2   Disconnect the stabilizer bar link from the strut assembly **(see illustration 2.3a)**.

3   Disconnect the tie-rod end from the steering arm (see Section 18).

4   If the vehicle is equipped with ABS, remove the speed sensor wire harness grommets from the wire harness bracket **(see illustration)** and remove the bracket.

5   Remove the brake caliper assembly from the steering knuckle and remove the brake disc (see Chapter 9). Suspend the caliper with a piece of wire to prevent damage to the brake hose. Support the control arm with a floor jack.

6   Remove the strut-to-knuckle nuts **(see illustration)** and knock the bolts out with a hammer and punch.

7   Separate the strut from the steering knuckle. Be careful not to overextend the inner CV joint. Also, don't let the steering knuckle fall out, as the brake hose could be damaged.

8   Support the strut and spring assembly with one hand and remove the three strut-to-shock tower nuts **(see illustration)**. It would be a good idea to have an assistant help you do this. Remove the assembly out from the fenderwell.

Inspection

9   Check the strut body for leaking fluid, dents, cracks and other obvious damage which would warrant repair or replacement.

10   Check the coil spring for chips or cracks in the spring coating (this can cause premature spring failure due to corrosion). Inspect the spring seat for cuts, hardness and general deterioration.

11   If any undesirable conditions exist, proceed to the strut disassembly procedure (see Section 4).

Installation

12   Guide the strut assembly up into the fenderwell and insert the three upper mounting studs through the holes in the shock tower. Once the three studs protrude from the shock tower, install the nuts so the strut won't fall back through. This is most easily accomplished with the help of an assistant, as the strut is quite heavy and awkward.

13   Slide the steering knuckle into the strut flange and insert the two bolts. Install the nuts and tighten them to the torque listed in this Chapter's Specifications. Do not turn the bolts; hold them while you tighten the nuts.

14   If the vehicle is equipped with ABS, install the speed sensor wiring harness bracket, tighten the bolt securely and push the wire harness grommets back into the bracket.

15   Install the wheel and lug nuts, then lower the vehicle and tighten the lug nuts to the torque listed in the Chapter 1 Specifications.

16   Tighten the three upper mounting nuts to the torque listed in this Chapter's Specifications.

17   Drive the vehicle to an alignment shop to have the front end alignment checked, and if necessary, adjusted.

4   Strut/coil spring - replacement

1   If the struts or coil springs exhibit the telltale signs of wear (leaking fluid, loss of damping capability, chipped, sagging or cracked coil springs) explore all options before beginning any work. The strut/shock absorber assemblies are not serviceable and must be replaced if a problem develops. However, strut assemblies complete with springs may be available on an exchange basis, which eliminates much time and work. Whichever route you choose to take, check on the cost and availability of parts before disassembling your vehicle. **Warning:** *Disassembling a strut is potentially dangerous and utmost attention must be directed to the job, or serious injury may result. Use only a high-quality spring compressor and carefully follow the manufacturer's instructions furnished with the tool. After removing the coil spring from the strut assembly, set it aside in a safe, isolated area.*

Disassembly

Refer to illustrations 4.2, 4.4, 4.5, 4.6, 4.7 and 4.8

2   Remove the strut and spring assembly following the procedure described in the previous Section. Mount the strut assembly in a vise. Line the vise jaws with wood or rags to prevent damage to the unit and don't tighten the vise excessively. To ensure proper reassembly, use paint to mark the relationship of the upper end of the coil spring to the seat/bearing assembly and upper strut mount, and the lower end of the spring to the strut as shown **(see illustration)**.

3   Following the tool manufacturer's instructions, install the spring compressor (which can be obtained at most auto parts stores or equipment yards on a daily rental basis) on the spring and compress it sufficiently to relieve all pressure from the upper spring seat **(see illustration 4.2)**. This can be verified by wiggling the spring.

4   Loosen and remove the strut shaft nut **(see illustration)** while holding the shaft with a 10mm wrench or socket. If you don't have access to the special tool (L-4558A) shown in the accompanying photo, use an offset box-end wrench to break the nut loose.

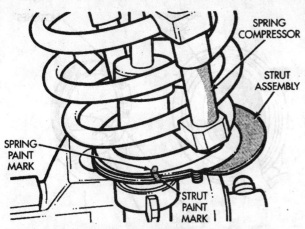

4.2 To ensure proper reassembly, use paint to mark the relationship of the upper end of the coil spring to the seat/bearing assembly and upper strut mount (not shown), and the lower end of the spring to the strut

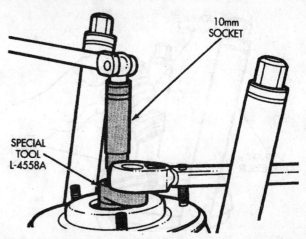

4.4 Loosen and remove the strut shaft nut with a special tool like this one, or use an offset box-end wrench to break the nut loose while holding the shaft with a 10mm wrench or socket

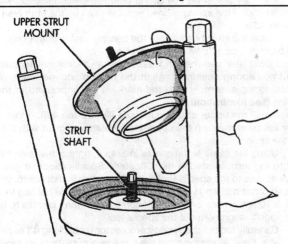

4.5 Remove the upper strut mount

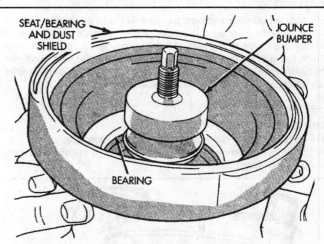

4.6 Remove the seat/bearing and dust shield assembly, then remove the jounce bumper

5   Remove the upper strut mount **(see illustration)**.
6   Remove the seat/bearing, dust shield and jounce bumper **(see illustration)**.
7   Carefully lift the compressed spring from the assembly **(see** illustration) and set it in a safe place. **Warning:** *Never place your head near the end of the spring!*
8   Remove the lower spring isolator from the strut assembly **(see illustration)**.

4.7 Carefully lift the compressed spring from the assembly, keeping the ends of the spring pointed away from your body

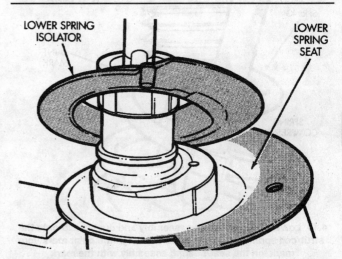

4.8 Remove the lower spring isolator from the strut assembly

10

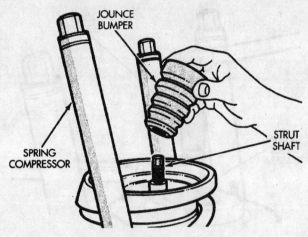

4.11 Install the jounce bumper

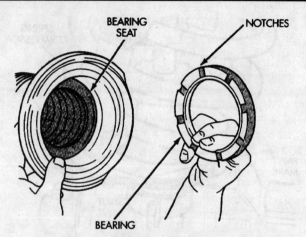

4.13 Install the strut bearing into the bearing seat with the
notches on the bearing facing down

Inspection

9   Inspect all disassembled parts for signs of excessive wear or failure. Replace all broken, damaged or worn parts. Inspect the strut unit for excessive oil leakage. If the strut is leaking, replace it. Also check the strut for loss of gas charge by pushing the strut shaft into the body of the strut and releasing it. The strut shaft should return to its fully extended position. If it doesn't, replace the strut.

Reassembly

Refer to illustrations 4.11, 4.13 and 4.14

10   Install the lower spring isolator **(see illustration 4.8)**.
11   Extend the damper rod to its full length and install the jounce bumper **(see illustration)**.

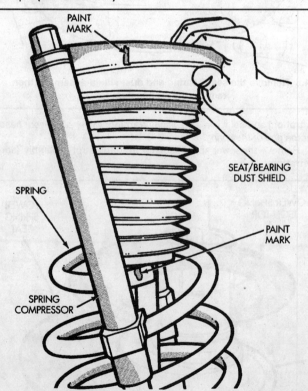

4.14 Lower the seat/bearing assembly and dust shield onto the
strut/coil spring assembly; be sure to align the paint mark you
made on the seat/bearing assembly with the mark
on the upper end of the coil spring

12   Carefully place the coil spring onto the lower insulator, with the marked end of the spring aligned with the mark on the strut **(see illustration 4.2)**.
13   Install the strut bearing into the bearing seat with the notches on the bearing facing down **(see illustration)**.
14   Lower the seat/bearing assembly and dust shield onto the strut/coil spring assembly. Align the paint mark you made on the seat/bearing assembly with the mark on the upper end of the coil spring **(see illustration)**.
15   Install the upper strut mount **(see illustration 4.5)**. Again, make sure the paint mark on the upper strut mount is aligned with the mark on the spring.
16   Using the same technique as in Step 4, tighten the damper shaft nut to the torque listed in this Chapter's Specifications. If you don't have access to the special tool (L-4558A) shown in that photo, you can use an offset box-end wrench to tighten the nut while holding the shaft with a 10mm wrench or socket (of course, you won't be able to tighten it to specifications without the special tool).
17   Carefully loosen the spring compressor by backing off each nut a turn at a time, alternating between the two nuts, until all tension is removed from the coil spring.
18   Install the strut in the vehicle (see Section 3).
19   Repeat this procedure for the other strut.
20   Drive the vehicle to an alignment shop and have the front end aligned.

5.2 Remove the pinch bolt which secures the balljoint stud to the
steering knuckle (do NOT remove the big nut that attaches the rear
end of the tension strut to the control arm unless the control arm
and tension strut have already been removed from the vehicle)

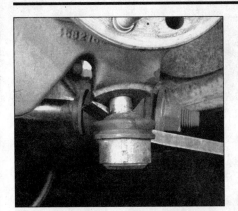

5.3 Using a prybar, separate the control arm from the steering knuckle

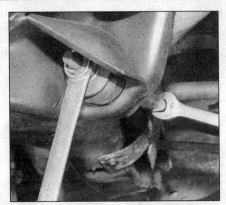

5.4 To loosen the nut that attaches the tension strut to the cradle, hold the tension strut with a wrench on its machined flat

5.5 Remove the pivot bolt and nut (arrows) that attach the control arm to the cradle

5 Control arm - removal, inspection and installation

Removal

Refer to illustrations 5.2, 5.3, 5.4 and 5.5

1   Loosen the wheel lug nuts, raise the front of the vehicle, support it securely on jackstands and remove the wheel.

2   Remove the pinch bolt which secures the balljoint stud to the steering knuckle **(see illustration)**.

3   Using a prybar, separate the control arm from the steering knuckle **(see illustration)**.

4   Remove the nut that attaches the tension strut to the cradle **(see illustration)**.

5   Remove the pivot bolt that attaches the control arm to the engine cradle **(see illustration)**.

6   Remove the control arm and the tension strut as a single assembly. First, remove the pivot bushing from the cradle, then slide the tension strut out of the isolator bushing.

Inspection

Refer to illustration 5.8

7   Make sure the control arm and tension strut are straight. If either component is bent, replace it. Do not attempt to straighten a bent control arm or tension strut.

8   Inspect all bushings **(see illustration)** for cracks and tears. If any bushing is torn or worn out, take the assembly to an automotive machine shop and have it replaced.

Installation

9   Insert the tension strut through the cradle, slip the isolator bushing over the threaded end of the strut, then install the lower control arm pivot bushing into the cradle.

10   Install the control arm-to-cradle bolt and nut, and tighten - but don't torque - the nut yet.

11   Install the washer on the tension strut isolator bushing, then install a NEW nut on the tension strut and tighten it to the torque listed in this Chapter's Specifications. While tightening the new nut, prevent the tension strut from turning by holding it at the machined flat with a wrench **(see illustration 5.4)**.

12   Install the lower balljoint stud into the steering knuckle, install the pinch bolt and tighten it to the torque listed in this Chapter's Specifications.

13   Install the wheel and lug nuts, lower the vehicle and tighten the lug nuts to the torque listed in the Chapter 1 Specifications.

14   With the suspension supporting the vehicle's weight and the control arm at its normal height, tighten the lower control arm pivot bolt to the torque listed in this Chapter's Specifications.

15   It's a good idea to have the front wheel alignment checked and, if necessary, adjusted after this job has been performed.

6 Tension strut - removal and installation

1   Loosen the wheel lug nuts, raise the front of the vehicle, support it securely on jackstands and remove the wheel.

2   Remove the control arm and tension strut (see Steps 1 through 6 in Section 5).

3   Remove the large nut that attaches the tension strut to the control arm.

4   Inspect the tension strut bushings for cracks and tears **(see illustration 5.8)**. If any bushing is damaged or excessively worn, take the strut to an automotive machine shop and have the bushing replaced.

5   Reattach the tension strut to the control arm. Install the strut with the word "FRONT," which is stamped into the strut, positioned *away* from the control arm **(see illustration 5.8)**.

6   Install a NEW strut-to-control arm retaining nut and, using a wrench on the machined flat of the tension strut to hold the strut, tighten the nut securely. (It's easier to torque the nut to specification after the control arm/tension strut assembly is installed in the vehicle.)

7   Install the control arm and tension strut in the vehicle (see Steps 9 through 14 in Section 5). Using a floor jack placed under the control arm, raise the control arm to simulate normal ride height. Tighten the lower control arm pivot bolt and the tension strut-to-control arm nut to the torque values listed in this Chapter's Specifications.

8   It's a good idea to have the front wheel alignment checked and, if necessary, adjusted after this job has been performed.

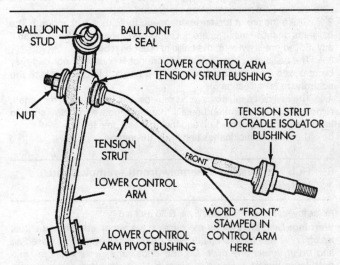

5.8 Inspect all control arm and tension strut bushings for cracks and tears; if any bushing is torn or worn out, take the assembly to an automotive machine shop and have it replaced

10

8.3 Insert a large screwdriver or prybar between the studs to hold the hub and use a large breaker bar to break loose the driveaxle hub nut

8.4 Remove the three steering knuckle-to-hub and bearing retaining bolts (arrows) (upper bolt not visible in this photo)

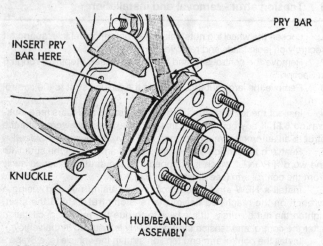

8.5a If the hub and bearing assembly is stuck in the steering knuckle, use a prybar to gently work it out

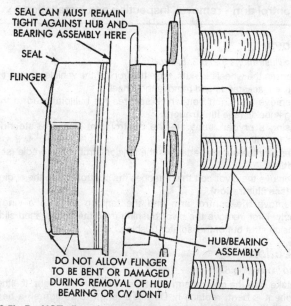

8.5b Do NOT allow the metal seal on the backside of the hub and bearing assembly to be bent or damaged during removal of the hub and bearing assembly; if it's frozen to the steering knuckle and becomes bent, damaged or dislodged removal of the hub and bearing assembly, do NOT reuse the old hub and bearing assembly

7   Balljoints - check and replacement

1   Raise the vehicle and support it securely on jackstands. Make sure the tires are not contacting the ground.
2   Grasp the tire at top and bottom and try to rock it in and out. The balljoints on these vehicles are not supposed to have any freeplay, so if any movement is evident, the balljoint must be replaced.
3   The balljoints on these vehicles are not serviceable, nor can they be removed from the control arms. If a balljoint is bad, replace the control arm (see Section 5).
4   The balljoint seal, however, is replaceable. If the seal is damaged, remove the control arm and take it to an automotive machine shop to have the old seal pressed off and the new seal pressed on.
5   Remove the jackstands and lower the vehicle.

8   Hub and bearing assembly (front) - removal and installation

Refer to illustrations 8.3, 8.4, 8.5a, 8.5b and 8.6
Warning: *Dust created by the brake system may contain asbestos, which is harmful to your health. Never blow it out with compressed air and don't inhale any of it. Do not, under any circumstances, use petroleum-based solvents to clean brake parts. Use brake system cleaner only.*
1   If the vehicle has steel wheels, loosen the driveaxle/hub nut (see Chapter 8); if the vehicle has aluminum wheels, the nut can't be

loosened until the wheel is removed because the hole in the center of the wheel is too small for a regular socket (you need a special thin-walled socket to fit through the hole for the nut). Loosen the wheel lug nuts, raise the front of the vehicle, support it securely on jackstands and remove the wheel.
2   Remove the front caliper assembly, support it with a piece of wire and remove the brake disc from the hub and bearing assembly (see Chapter 9).
3   Remove the driveaxle/hub nut **(see illustration)**.
4   Remove the three steering knuckle-to-hub and bearing retaining bolts **(see illustration)**.
5   Remove the hub and bearing assembly from the steering knuckle by sliding it straight out of the steering knuckle and off the end of the stub shaft. If the hub and bearing assembly is stuck in the steering knuckle, use a prybar **(see illustration)** to gently work it out. If the stub shaft is frozen to the hub and bearing assembly, gently tap the nose of the shaft with a soft-face hammer to free it up. Do NOT allow the metal seal **(see illustration)** on the backside of the hub and bearing assembly to be bent or damaged during removal of the hub and bearing assembly. If the metal seal is frozen to the steering knuckle

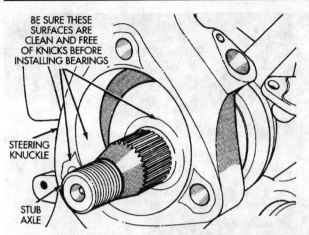

8.6 Make sure that the mounting surface inside the steering knuckle is smooth and free of burrs and nicks

9.3 To remove the speed sensor from the steering knuckle, remove the sensor retaining bolt (arrow), then pull out the sensor; if the sensor is stuck, dislodge it by tapping it gently with a small soft-face hammer (do NOT try to pull it out with a pair of pliers)

10.3 To disconnect the rear stabilizer from each link, remove this big nut; if the link stud turns with the nut, hold the stud with a wrench or socket

and becomes bent, damaged or dislodged removal of the hub and bearing assembly, do NOT reuse the old hub and bearing assembly.

6   Make sure that the mounting surface inside the steering knuckle **(see illustration)** is smooth and free of burrs and nicks.

7   Carefully slide the hub and bearing assembly onto the stub shaft and into the steering knuckle until it's fully seated. Be careful not to damage the flinger disc **(see illustration 8.5b)** on the backside of the hub and bearing assembly. If the flinger is damaged, a NEW hub and bearing assembly must be used.

8   Install the three hub and bearing assembly retaining bolts and tighten them gradually and evenly until the hub and bearing assembly is seated squarely against the front of the steering knuckle. Then tighten the bolts to the torque listed in this Chapter's Specifications.

9   Install a NEW driveaxle/hub nut and tighten it securely. If the vehicle has factory aluminum wheels, you'll have to tighten the nut to the torque listed in this Chapter's Specifications now; if it has steel wheels, you can torque the nut after the vehicle is on the ground. If the vehicle has aluminum wheels, place a large screwdriver or prybar between the studs and tighten the nut to the torque listed in the Chapter 8 Specifications.

10   Install the brake disc and the caliper assembly (see Chapter 9).

11   Install the wheel and hand tighten the wheel lug nuts. Remove the jackstands and lower the vehicle.

12   If the vehicle has steel wheels, place the transmission in gear, apply the parking brake and have an assistant apply firm pressure to the brake pedal, then tighten the driveaxle nut to the torque listed in the Chapter 8 Specifications.

9   Steering knuckle - removal and installation

Refer to illustration 9.3
Warning: *Dust created by the brake system may contain asbestos, which is harmful to your health. Never blow it out with compressed air and don't inhale any of it. Do not, under any circumstances, use petroleum-based solvents to clean brake parts. Use brake system cleaner only.*

1   If the vehicle has steel wheels, loosen the driveaxle/hub nut now (see Chapter 8); if the vehicle has aluminum wheels, the nut can't be loosened until the wheel is removed **(see illustration 8.3)** because the hole in the center of the wheel is too small for a regular socket (you need a special thin-walled socket to fit through the hole for the nut). Loosen the wheel lug nuts, raise the vehicle and support it securely on jackstands. Remove the wheel.

2   Remove the brake caliper, support it with a piece of wire, and remove the brake disc from the hub and bearing assembly (see Chapter 9).

3   If the vehicle is equipped with ABS, remove the speed sensor **(see illustration)** from the steering knuckle. If the sensor has seized in the knuckle, do NOT try to extricate it with a pair of pliers! Instead,

dislodge it by tapping on it gently with a small soft-face hammer.

4   Remove the hub and bearing assembly (see Section 8).

5   Remove the balljoint stud pinch bolt and separate the control arm from the steering knuckle (see Section 5).

6   Unbolt the strut assembly from the steering knuckle (see Section 3).

7   Remove the steering knuckle assembly.

8   Installation is the reverse of removal. Be sure to tighten all suspension fasteners to the torque listed in this Chapter's Specifications. If the vehicle has aluminum wheels, be sure to torque the driveaxle/hub nut before installing the wheel (see Section 8).

9   Install the wheel. Lower the vehicle and tighten the wheel lug nuts to the torque listed in the Chapter 1 Specifications. If the vehicle has steel wheels, tighten the driveaxle/hub nut and tighten it to the torque listed in the Chapter 8 Specifications.

10   Drive the vehicle to an alignment shop and have the front end alignment checked.

10   Stabilizer bar (rear) - removal and installation

Refer to illustrations 10.3 and 10.6

1   Loosen the rear wheel lug nuts. Raise the rear of the vehicle and place it securely on jackstands. Block the front wheels and remove the rear wheels.

2   Remove the fuel tank (see Chapter 4).

3   Remove the stabilizer bar-to-link nuts **(see illustration)**.

10

10.6 Be sure to use NEW bolts (arrows) for the stabilizer bushing brackets

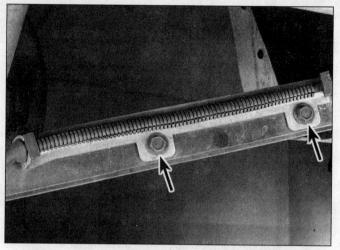

11.3a To protect the ABS sensor wire from damage, remove these bolts and detach the wire from the trailing arm . . .

4   Remove the stabilizer bar from the vehicle.
5   Inspect the stabilizer bushings for cracks and tears. If the bushings are damaged, distorted or excessively worn, replace them.
6   Installation is the reverse of removal. Be sure to use NEW stabilizer bushing bracket bolts and tighen the stabilizer bar-to-link nuts and the stabilizer bushing bracket bolts **(see illustration)** to the torque listed in this Chapter's Specifications.
7   Install the rear wheels, tighten the wheel lug nuts, remove the jackstands and lowe the vehicle. Tighten the wheel lug nuts to the torque listed in this Chapter's Specifications.

11   Struts (rear) - removal, inspection and installation

Removal

Refer to illustrations 11.3a, 11.3b, 11.6, 11.7, 11.8 and 11.9
1   Loosen the rear wheel lug nuts, raise the rear of the vehicle and support it securely on jackstands. Block the front wheels and remove the rear wheels.
2   If the vehicle is equipped with rear drum brakes, disconnect the rear brake hose from the wheel cylinder (see Chapter 9). If the vehicle is equipped with rear disc brakes, remove the rear caliper assembly and hang it out of the way with a piece of wire, then remove the brake disc (see Chapter 9).

3   If the vehicle is equipped with ABS, detach the ABS sensor wire from the strut bracket and from the trailing arm **(see illustrations)**. **Caution:** *If the spindle and trailing arm assembly is lowered from the strut with the ABS sensor wire attached to the strut bracket and the trailing arm, the sensor wire will be damaged.*
4   Remove the through-bolt that attaches the lateral links to the spindle **(see illustration 11.3a)**.
5   Disconnect the stabilizer bar from the link **(see illustration 10.3)**.
6   Loosen and remove the spindle-to-strut pinch bolt **(see illustration)**.
7   Insert a center punch into the hole on the inside of the spindle **(see illustration)** and tap the punch until it's jammed into the hole. This spreads the spindle casting enough to disengage it from the lower end of the strut.
8   Using a hammer, tap on the top of the spindle casting **(see illustration)** until it drops down far enough to fall off the lower end of the strut.
9   Open the trunk. Have an assistant support the strut. Locate the three upper strut-to-body mounting nuts **(see illustration)** in the upper front corner of the trunk and remove them.
10   Remove the strut assembly.

Inspection

11   Follow the inspection procedures described in Section 3. If you

11.3b . . . then remove the bolt (center arrow) from the ABS sensor wire bracket; to disconnect the lateral links from the spindle, remove the nut and long through-bolt (arrows)

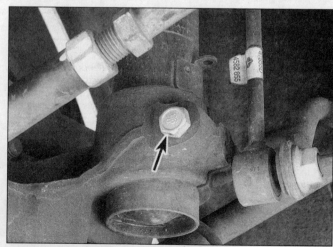

11.6 To separate the spindle from the lower end of the strut, remove this pinch bolt (arrow)

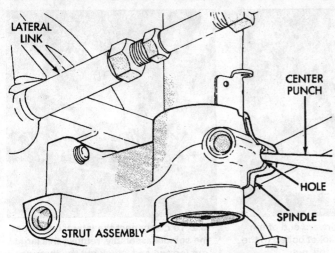

11.7 To spread the spindle so it can be knocked off the end of the strut, jam a center punch into the hole in the split in the spindle and drive it in until it won't go any further

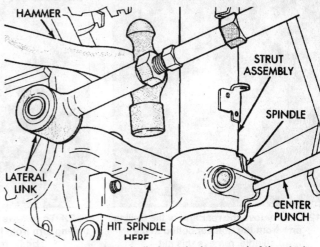

11.8 To separate the spindle from the lower end of the strut, knock it off with a hammer

determine that the strut assembly must be disassembled for replacement of the strut or the coil spring, refer to Section 4.

Installation

Refer to illustration 11.13

12   Maneuver the strut assembly up into the wheel housing and insert the mounting studs through the holes in the body. Install the three nuts, but don't tighten them yet.

13   With the center punch in its hole, push the spindle onto the lower end of the strut assembly. Tap the spindle up the strut until the notch in the spindle is tightly seated against the locating tab on the strut body **(see illustration)**. Remove the center punch from the hole. Install the pinch bolt and tighten it to the torque listed in this Chapter's Specifications.

14   Attach the lateral links to the spindle with the through-bolt and tighten the bolt to the torque listed in this Chapter's Specifications.

15   Connect the stabilizer bar to the link and tighten the nut to the torque listed in this Chapter's Specifications.

16   Attach the ABS sensor wire brackets to the spindle and trailing arm.

17   If the vehicle is equipped with rear drum brakes, connect the rear brake hose to the wheel cylinder (see Chapter 9). If the vehicle is

equipped with rear disc brakes, install the brake disc and brake caliper (see Chapter 9).

18   Repeat this procedure for the other strut.

19   Install the wheel and lug nuts, lower the vehicle and tighten the lug nuts to the torque listed in the Chapter 1 Specifications.

20   If you disconnected the rear brake hoses from the wheel cylinders, bleed the brakes (see Chapter 9).

21   Drive the vehicle to an alignment shop and have the rear wheel toe checked.

12   Trailing arm - removal and installation

Refer to illustrations 12.3 and 12.4

1   Loosen the rear wheel lug nuts, raise the vehicle and support it securely on jackstands. Block the front wheels and remove the rear wheel.

2   If the vehicle is equipped with ABS, detach the ABS sensor wire from the strut bracket and from the trailing arm **(see illustration 11.3a)**. **Caution:** *If the trailing arm assembly is removed with the ABS sensor wire attached, the sensor wire will be damaged.*

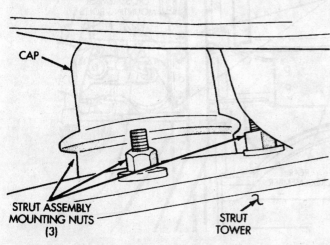

11.9 The three upper strut-to-body nuts are located in the front upper corner of the trunk

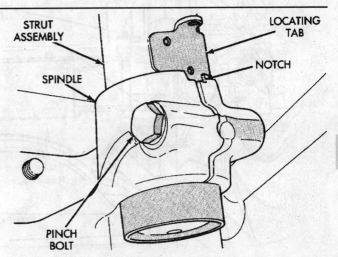

11.13 When installing the spindle onto the lower end of the strut, tap the spindle on until it's fully seated against the locating tab on the strut body

10

12.3 To remove the rear end of the trailing arm from the bracket bolted to the spindle, remove this nut

12.4 To remove the forward end of the trailing arm from the bracket bolted to the body, remove this nut

13.2 To disconnect the lateral links from the spindle assembly, remove this large nut (arrow) and knock out the through-bolt with a long punch

3   Remove the nut from the trailing arm-to-spindle bracket bolt (**see illustration**).

4   Remove the nut from the trailing arm-to-body bracket bolt (**see illustration**) and detach the trailing arm from the vehicle.

5   Installation is the reverse of the removal procedure. Be sure to tighten the nuts to the torque listed in this Chapter's Specifications.

13   Lateral links - removal and installation

Refer to illustrations 13.2, 13.3 and 13.4

1   Loosen the rear wheel lug nuts, raise the rear of the vehicle and support it securely on jackstands. Remove the rear wheel.

2   Remove the nut and bolt that attach the lateral link to the spindle (**see illustration**).

3   If you're removing the right lateral links, place a floor jack under the fuel tank to support the tank while the crossmember is removed. Put a block of wood between the jack head and the fuel tank to protect the tank. Remove the four rear crossmember bolts (**see illustration**) and lower the crossmember far enough so that the right lateral link-to-crossmember bolt clears the fuel tank.

4   Remove the lateral link-to-crossmember nut and bolt (**see illustration**).

5   Installation is the reverse of removal. Make sure the heads of all lateral link bolts are facing *forward*, then tighten all fasteners to the torque listed in this Chapter's Specifications.

6   Install the wheel and lug nuts, then lower the vehicle to the ground. Tighten the rear wheel lug nuts to the torque listed in the Chapter 1 Specifications.

7   Have the rear wheel toe checked by an alignment shop.

14   Hub and bearing assembly (rear) - removal and installation

Refer to illustrations 14.3a through 14.3g

Warning: *Dust created by the brake system may contain asbestos, which is harmful to your health. Never blow it out with compressed air and don't inhale any of it. Do not, under any circumstances, use petroleum-based solvents to clean brake parts. Use brake system cleaner only.*

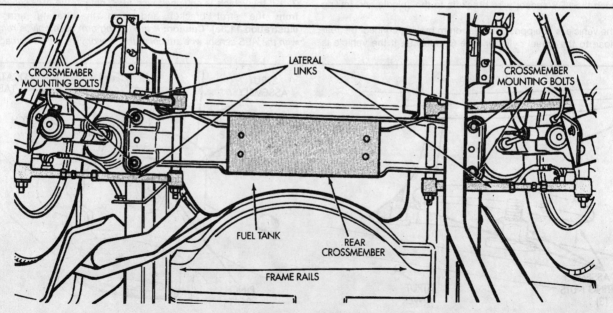

13.3 Before removing the right lateral link-to-crossmember bolt and nut, support the fuel tank with a floor jack, remove the four rear crossmember mounting bolts and lower the crossmember far enough to allow the right lateral link-to-crossmember bolt to clear the fuel tank

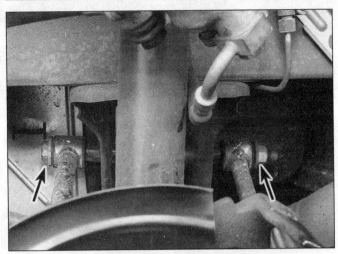

13.4 To remove the left lateral link-to-crossmember nut and bolt (arrows), simply remove the nut and knock out the bolt with a long punch

14.3a Remove the dust cap (doesn't apply to models with rear disc brakes)

1   Loosen the wheel lug nuts, raise the vehicle and support it securely on jackstands. Remove the wheel.
2   On models with rear drum brakes, remove the drum; on models with rear disc brakes, remove the caliper and the brake disc (see Chapter 9).
3   Follow the accompanying photos to remove the hub and bearing assembly **(see illustrations)**. Installation is the reverse of removal. Be sure to tighten the hub-to-spindle nut to the torque listed in this Chapter's Specifications.
4   Install the brake drum, or disc and caliper (see Chapter 9).
5   Install the wheel and hand tighten the wheel lug nuts. Remove the jackstands, lower the vehicle and tighten the lug nuts to the torque listed in the Chapter 1 Specifications.

14.3b Remove the cotter pin (doesn't apply to model with rear disc brakes)

14.3c Remove the nut retainer (doesn't apply to models with rear disc brakes)

14.3d Remove the wave washer (doesn't apply to models with rear disc brakes)

14.3e Remove the hub retaining nut

14.3f Remove the large washer

14.3g Remove the hub and bearing assembly

10

15.4a Remove the wheel speed sensor retaining bolt . . .

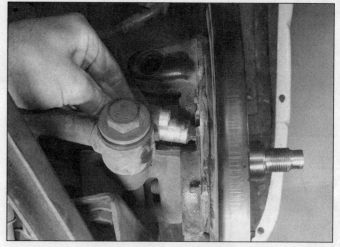

15.4b . . . and pull out the sensor

15 Spindle - removal and installation

Refer to illustration 15.4a, 15.4b and 15.5
Warning: *Dust created by the brake system may contain asbestos, which is harmful to your health. Never blow it out with compressed air and don't inhale any of it. Do not, under any circumstances, use petroleum-based solvents to clean brake parts. Use brake system cleaner only.*

1   Loosen the rear wheel lug nuts, raise the vehicle and support it on jackstands. Block the front wheels and remove the rear wheel.
2   On models with rear drum brakes, remove the rear brake drum and brake shoe assembly, disconnect the parking brake cable from the parking brake lever and disconnect the brake hose from the wheel cylinder (see Chapter 9). On models with rear disc brakes, remove the caliper and brake disc, remove the parking brake shoes and disconnect the parking brake cable from the actuator lever (see Chapter 9).
3   Remove the rear hub and bearing assembly (see Section 14).
4   On models with ABS, remove the wheel speed sensor from the brake backing plate **(see illustrations)**.
5   Unbolt the brake backing plate **(see illustration)** and remove it.
6   If the vehicle is equipped with ABS, detach the ABS sensor wire from the strut bracket and from the trailing arm **(see illustrations 11.3a and 11.3b)**. **Caution:** *If the trailing arm assembly is lowered from the strut with the ABS sensor wire attached to the strut bracket and the trailing arm, the sensor wire will be damaged.*
7   Remove the nut and bolt which attach the trailing arm to the bracket on the spindle **(see illustration 12.3)**.
8   Remove the nut and bolt which attach the lateral links to the spindle **(see illustration 13.2)**.
9   Disconnect the spindle from the strut (see Section 11).
10   Installation is the reverse of removal. Be sure to tighten all suspension fasteners to the torque listed in this Chapter's Specifications.
11   Install the wheel and lug nuts. Lower the vehicle and tighten the lug nuts to the torque listed in the Chapter 1 Specifications.

16 Steering system - general information

All models are equipped with rack-and-pinion steering. The steering gear - which is located behind the engine, above the transaxle, in front of the firewall - operates the steering knuckles via tie rods connected to steering arms on the strut assemblies. The tie-rod ends can be replaced by unscrewing them from the inner tie rods. Adjustment sleeves between the inner tie rods and the tie-rod ends are

15.5 To remove the brake backing plate, remove these four bolts

used to adjust front wheel toe.
The power assist system consists of a belt-driven pump and associated lines and hoses. The fluid level in the power steering pump reservoir should be checked periodically (see Chapter 1).
The steering wheel operates the steering shaft, which actuates the steering gear through a short steering column and a couple of universal joints (referred to by Chrysler as the upper and lower intermediate column shafts). Looseness in the steering can be caused by wear in these universal joints, the steering gear, the tie-rod ends and loose retaining bolts.

17 Steering wheel - removal and installation

Removal

Refer to illustrations 17.3a, 17.3b, 17.4, 17.5, 17.7 and 17.8
Warning: *These models have airbags. Always disconnect the negative battery cable and wait two minutes before working in the vicinity of the impact sensors, steering column or instrument panel to avoid the possibility of accidental deployment of the airbag, which could cause personal injury (see Chapter 12).*

1   Lock the steering column as follows: Turn the steering wheel clockwise 1/2-turn from the straight-ahead position, turn the ignition key to the Lock position and remove the key from the key lock cylinder. This ensures that no damage occurs to the airbag clockspring when

17.3a On models with cruise control, remove the cruise control switch screws (arrows) and pull off each switch . . .

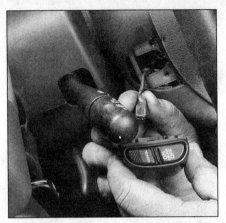

17.3b . . . then unplug the electrical connector (left switch shown, right switch identical)

17.4 To detach the airbag module from the steering wheel, remove the two module retaining bolts (left bolt shown, right bolt identical)

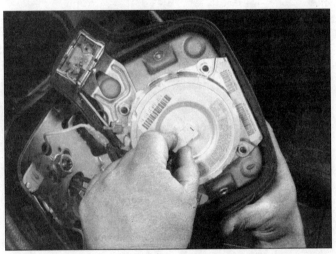

17.5 Lift the airbag module off the steering wheel, unplug the module electrical connector and unplug the horn switch lead

17.7 Mark the relationship of the steering wheel to the steering shaft

the steering wheel is removed.

2   Disconnect the cable from the negative terminal of the battery. Wait at least two minutes before proceeding.

3   Remove the two cruise control switches (see illustrations) from the steering wheel to gain access to the airbag module retaining screws. If the vehicle isn't equipped with cruise control, pry off the covers on the sides of the steering wheel for access.

4   Remove the two airbag module retaining bolts (see illustration).

5   Lift the airbag module off the steering wheel and unplug the airbag electrical connector (see illustration). Also unplug the electrical connector for the horn. Warning: Set the airbag module aside in a safe, isolated location. Carry the airbag module with the trim side facing away from you and set it down with the trim side facing up.

6   Remove the steering wheel retaining nut.

7   Mark the relationship of the steering wheel to the steering shaft (see illustration).

8   Use a puller to disconnect the steering wheel from the shaft (see illustration).

Installation

9   Align the mark on the steering wheel with the mark on the shaft and slip the wheel onto the shaft. Install the nut and tighten it to the torque listed in this Chapter's Specifications.

10   Plug in the horn and airbag module electrical connectors.

11   Install the airbag module and tighten the module retaining bolts to the torque listed in this Chapter's Specifications.

17.8 Use a steering wheel puller to remove the wheel from the shaft

12   Plug in and install the cruise control switches and tighten the screws securely. On vehicles without cruise control, install the covers.

13   Connect the negative battery cable.

10

18.3 Holding the machined flat on the adjustment sleeve with an open-end wrench, loosen the tie-rod end jam nut

18.4 Prevent the tie-rod end stud from turning by holding it with a wrench, then break the stud nut loose with another wrench, but don't remove it yet

18.5 Install a small puller and push the tie-roe end stud out of the steering arm

18 Tie-rod ends - removal and installation

Removal

Refer to illustrations 18.3, 18.4 and 18.5
1   Loosen the wheel lug nuts. Raise the front of the vehicle, support it securely on jackstands, block the rear wheels and set the parking brake. Remove the front wheel.
2   Measure the distance from the center of the tie-rod end to the outer edge of the adjustment sleeve and write down this measurement.
3   Hold the adjustment sleeve with a wrench on the machined flat and loosen the jam nut with another wrench **(see illustration)**.
4   Loosen - but don't remove - the nut on the tie-rod end stud **(see illustration)**.
5   Disconnect the tie-rod from the steering arm with a puller **(see illustration)**. Remove the nut and separate the tie-rod.
6   Unscrew the tie-rod end from the adjustment sleeve.

Installation

7   Thread the jam nut onto the new tie-rod end and screw the tie-rod end into the adjustment sleeve until the distance from the center of the new tie-rod end to the outer edge of the adjustment sleeve matches the measurement you made before removing the old tie-rod end.
8   Install the tie-rod end stud into the steering arm, install the stud nut and tighten it to the torque listed in this Chapter's Specifications.
9   Tighten the jam nut securely.
10   Install the wheel and lug nuts. Lower the vehicle and tighten the lug nuts to the torque listed in the Chapter 1 Specifications.
11   Have the front end alignment checked by an alignment shop.

19 Steering gear - removal and installation

Removal

Refer to illustrations 19.9, 19.10, 19.11, 19.13, 19.14, 19.15 and 19.16
Warning: *These models are equipped with airbags. Make sure the steering shaft is not turned while the steering gear is removed or you could damage the airbag system. To prevent the shaft from turning, turn the ignition key to the lock position before beginning work or run the seat belt through the steering wheel and clip the seat belt into place. Due to the possible damage to the airbag system, we recommend only experienced mechanics attempt this procedure.*
1   Disconnect the negative battery cable.
2   Raise the vehicle and place it securely on jackstands. Disconnect the shift cable from the shift lever on the transaxle (see Chapter 7, Part A). Lower the vehicle.

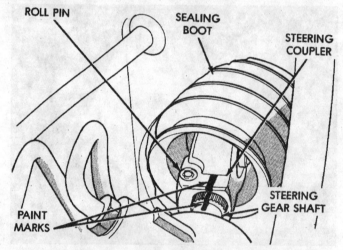

19.9 Slide the sealing boot up the steering intermediate shaft until you can see the lower U-joint steering coupler; using paint, mark the relationship of the steering coupler to the steering gear shaft to ensure proper reassembly

3   If the vehicle is equipped with a 3.5L engine, disconnect the throttle cable from the throttle body and remove it from the throttle cable bracket (see Chapter 4).
4   Remove both wiper arm assemblies from the wiper arm pivots (see Chapter 12).
5   Remove the six screws which attach the cowl panel to the cowl and remove the cowl panel and weatherstripping (see Chapter 11).
6   Remove the air intake plenum assembly (see Chapter 4).
7   Unplug the wiper module electrical connector and remove the five screws attaching the wiper module assembly to the cowl panel (see Chapter 12). Remove the wiper module from the cowl panel.
8   Detach the vacuum hose for the power brake booster at the intake manifold and place the hose out of the way.
9   Slide the sealing boot up the steering intermediate shaft until you can see the lower U-joint steering coupler **(see illustration)**. Turn the front wheels of the vehicle to the full-left position, then turn them back until the roll pin in the coupler is accessible. Turn the ignition key to the Lock position to keep the steering column from rotating after the coupler is disengaged from the steering gear. **Caution:** *Failure to lock the steering shaft could allow it to rotate beyond its normal number of turns in either direction, which will damage the airbag module clock-spring.* Using paint, mark the relationship of the steering coupler to the steering gear shaft to ensure proper reassembly.

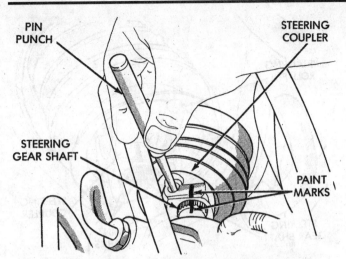

19.10 Using a small pin punch, knock out the roll pin which attaches the coupler to the steering gear shaft

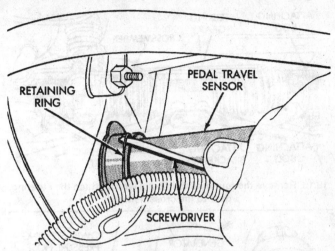

19.11 Lift the pedal travel sensor retaining ring from its notch with a small screwdriver and remove the ring

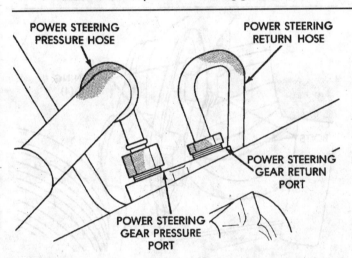

19.13 Detach the power steering pressure and return lines and cap the ends to prevent excessive fluid loss and contamination

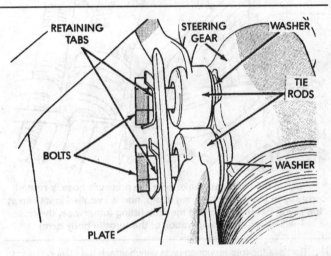

19.14 Bend back the retaining tabs for the bolts which attach the inner tie rods to the steering gear, then remove the bolts (note the location of the washers - between the inner tie rods and the steering gear)

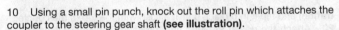

10 Using a small pin punch, knock out the roll pin which attaches the coupler to the steering gear shaft (see illustration).
11 Pump the brake pedal about 20 times to evacuate any vacuum

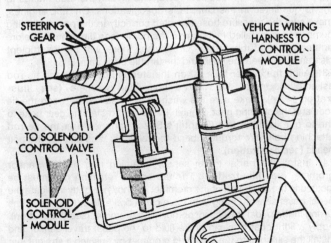

19.15 If the vehicle is equipped with speed-proportional steering, unplug the electrical connector from the solenoid control module

stored in the pedal travel sensor. Locate the travel sensor on the front of the brake booster, just below the master cylinder assembly. Unplug the electrical connector from the sensor. Lift the sensor retaining ring from its notch with a small screwdriver (see illustration) and remove the ring. Remove the pedal travel sensor from the brake booster by pulling it straight out of its mounting grommet. Do NOT twist the sensor.
12 Loosen and remove the two nuts which attach the master cylinder to the power brake booster. Remove the master cylinder (with the brake lines connected) from the booster (see Chapter 9). Carefully position the master cylinder out of the way, against the left shock tower.
13 Place a drain pan under the steering gear. Detach the power steering pressure and return lines (see illustration) and cap the ends to prevent excessive fluid loss and contamination. Detach the bracket from the top of the steering gear assembly.
14 Bend back the retaining tabs for the bolts which attach the inner tie rods to the steering gear (see illustration). Remove these bolts. Carefully lay the tie rods, bolts and plate as an assembly on the transaxle bellhousing.
15 If the vehicle is equipped with speed-proportional steering, unplug the electrical connector from the solenoid control module (see illustration).

10

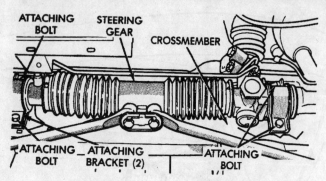

19.16 Remove the four mounting bolts which attach the steering gear to the crossmember

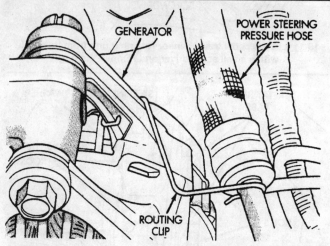

19.22 On 3.5L engines, make sure the pressure hose is routed correctly to the power steering pump, and is installed in its clip at the pump before tightening the tube fitting (otherwise, the hose will interfere with operation of the throttle body cam)

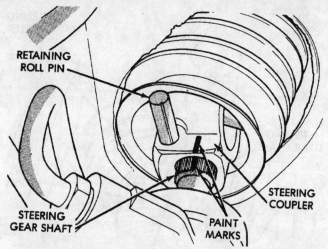

19.21 Install the steering coupler-to-steering shaft roll pin and tap it into place until it's flush with the top of the coupler

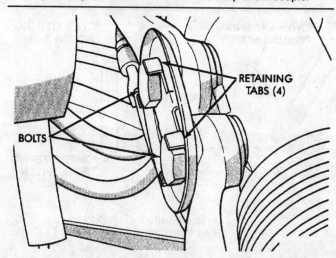

19.23 After the tie-rod attaching bolts are torqued, bend the retaining tabs against the bolt heads

16   Remove the four mounting bolts which attach the steering gear to the crossmember **(see illustration)**, slide the steering gear forward in the vehicle to disengage the coupler from the steering gear shaft. Once the steering gear is disengaged, do NOT turn the steering gear shaft or the steering column shaft (see the Warning at the beginning of this Section). Remove the steering gear assembly from the vehicle through the area in the cowl from which the windshield wiper module was previously removed.

Installation

Refer to illustrations 19.21, 19.22, 19.23, 19.24a and 19.24b

17   If you're installing a new steering gear assembly, carefully grasp the steering gear in your left hand and rotate the shaft counter-clockwise with your right hand until the steering gear center take-off for the tie rods is in the full-left position.

18   Install the steering gear assembly through the area in the cowl from which the windshield wiper module was previously removed.

19   If you're installing the old steering gear, align the paint mark on the steering coupler with the mark on the steering gear shaft and insert the shaft into the coupler. If you're installing a new steering gear assembly, rotate the steering gear shaft back from its full-left position until the master spline on the steering gear shaft is aligned with the master spline on the coupler, then insert the shaft into the coupler.

20   Align the steering gear with the four mounting holes in the crossmember and install the four mounting bolts. Make sure the brake line routing clip is installed under the left steering gear mounting bracket. Tighten the steering gear mounting bolts to the torque listed in this Chapter's Specifications.

21   Install the steering coupler-to-steering shaft roll pin **(see illus-**

tration) and tap it into place until it's flush with the top of the coupler.

22   Attach the power steering fluid pressure and return lines to the steering gear **(see illustration 19.13)** and tighten the tube fittings to the torque listed in this Chapter's Specifications. On 3.5L engines, make sure the pressure hose is routed correctly to the power steering pump, and is installed in its clip at the pump **(see illustration)** before tightening the tube fitting. Otherwise, there will be insufficient clearance between the hose and the throttle body cam.

23   Align the center take off on the steering gear with the tie-rod assemblies. Install the tie-rod bolts and washers **(see illus-tration 19.14)**. Make sure the washers are installed between the tie rods and the steering gear. Tighten the tie rod-to-steering gear bolts to the torque listed in this Chapter's Specifications. After the tie-rod attaching bolts are torqued, bend the retaining tabs against the bolt heads **(see illustration)**.

24   Install the pedal travel sensor retaining ring on the sensor grommet **(see illustration)**. The tab on the retaining ring must be located in the top notch of the grommet as shown. Lightly lubricate the pedal travel sensor O-ring with fresh clean brake fluid, then install the O-ring in the pedal travel sensor mounting grommet **(see illustration)**. Apply a light coat of clean brake fluid to the pedal travel sensor and install the sensor into the mounting grommet by pushing it straight into the grommet. Make sure the sensor is inserted into the grommet until the tab on the sensor is past the retaining ring on the grommet. Plug the electrical connector into the pedal travel sensor.

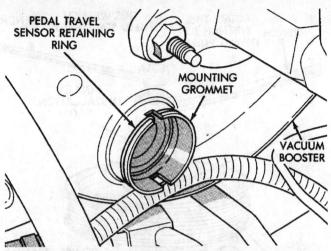

19.24a Install the pedal travel sensor retaining ring on the sensor grommet; make sure the tab on the retaining ring is located in the top notch of the grommet as shown

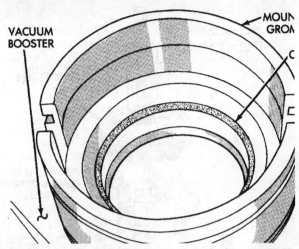

19.24b Lightly lubricate the pedal travel sensor O-ring with clean brake fluid, then install the O-ring in the pedal travel sensor mounting grommet

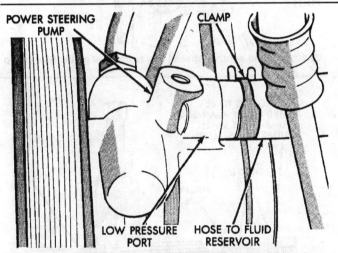

20.5 Remove the hose clamp from the hose coming from the reservoir to the power steering pump and detach the hose from the pump

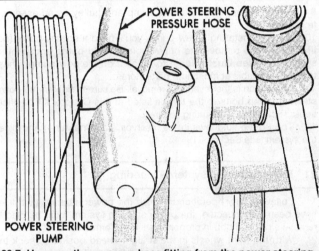

20.7 Unscrew the pressure hose fitting from the power steering pump discharge port

25 The remainder of installation is the reverse of removal. After lowering the vehicle, bleed the power steering system (see Section 21).

20 Power steering pump - removal and installation

Refer to illustrations 20.5, 20.7, 20.8, 20.10a, 20.10b and 20.10c

1 Disconnect the cable from the negative battery terminal.
2 Remove the serpentine drivebelt (see Chapter 1).
3 Raise the vehicle and support it securely on jackstands.
4 Using a large syringe or suction gun, suck as much fluid out of the power steering fluid reservoir as possible.
5 Place a drain pan under the vehicle to catch any fluid that spills out when the hoses are disconnected. Remove the hose clamp **(see illustration)** from the hose coming from the reservoir to the power steering pump and detach the hose from the pump.
6 On 3.5L engines, remove the power steering pressure clip **(see illustration 19.22)** which is attached to the alternator bracket.
7 Unscrew the power steering pressure hose fitting from the power steering pump discharge port **(see illustration)**.
8 Remove the three bolts which attach the power steering pump to the pump bracket. The bolts can be accessed through the holes in the power steering pump pulley **(see illustration)**.

10

20.8 To remove the three bolts which attach the power steering pump to the pump bracket, turn the pulley so that one of its holes is aligned with each bolt

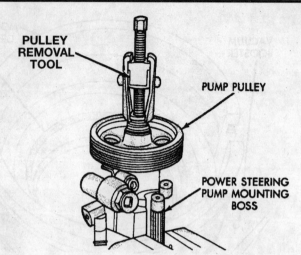

20.10a If you're installing a new pump, you'll need a special puller to remove the pulley from the old pump . . .

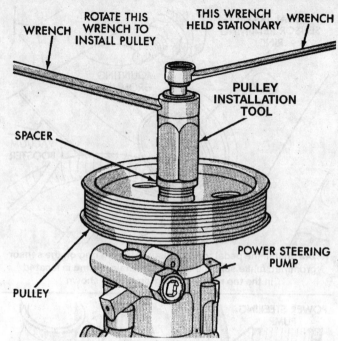

20.10b . . . and another special tool to install it on the new pump

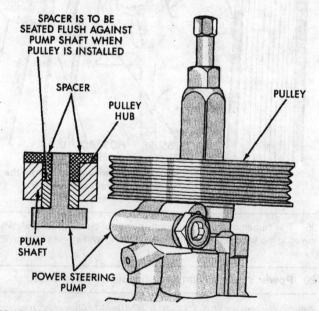

20.10c When you install the pulley on the new pump, make sure the spacer is fully seated as shown

9   Remove the power steering pump and pulley as an assembly from below.
10   If you're installing a new pump, you'll need a special puller (see illustration) to remove the pulley from the old pump and another special tool (see illustrations) to install it on the new pump. These tools are available at most auto parts stores.
11   Installation is the reverse of removal. Be sure to tighten the power steering pump bolts to the torque listed in this Chapter's Specifications. Tighten the hose fitting securely.
12   Top up the fluid level in the reservoir (see Chapter 1) and bleed the system (see Section 21).

21   Power steering system - bleeding

1   Following any operation in which the power steering fluid lines have been disconnected, the power steering system must be bled to remove all air and obtain proper steering performance.
2   With the front wheels in the straight ahead position, check the power steering fluid level and, if low, add fluid until it reaches the Cold mark on the dipstick.
3   Start the engine and allow it to run at fast idle. Recheck the fluid level and add more if necessary to reach the Cold mark on the dipstick.
4   Bleed the system by turning the wheels from side to side, without hitting the stops. This will work the air out of the system. Keep the reservoir full of fluid as this is done.
5   When the air is worked out of the system, return the wheels to the straight ahead position and leave the vehicle running for several more minutes before shutting it off.
6   Road test the vehicle to be sure the steering system is functioning normally and noise free.
7   Recheck the fluid level to be sure it is up to the Hot mark on the dipstick while the engine is at normal operating temperature. Add fluid if necessary (see Chapter 1).

22   Wheels and tires - general information

Refer to illustration 22.1
1   All vehicles covered by this manual are equipped with metric-sized fiberglass or steel belted radial tires (see illustration). Use of other size or type of tires may affect the ride and handling of the vehicle. Don't mix different types of tires, such as radials and bias belted, on the same vehicle as handling may be seriously affected. It's recommended that tires be replaced in pairs on the same axle, but if only one tire is being replaced, be sure it's the same size, structure and tread design as the other.

2   Because tire pressure has a substantial effect on handling and wear, the pressure on all tires should be checked at least once a month or before any extended trips (see Chapter 1).
3   Wheels must be replaced if they are bent, dented, leak air, have elongated bolt holes, are heavily rusted, out of vertical symmetry or if the lug nuts won't stay tight. Wheel repairs that use welding or peening are not recommended.
4   Tire and wheel balance is important in the overall handling, braking and performance of the vehicle. Unbalanced wheels can adversely affect handling and ride characteristics as well as tire life. Whenever a tire is installed on a wheel, the tire and wheel should be balanced by a shop with the proper equipment.

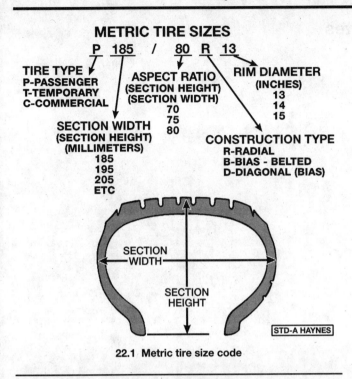

22.1 Metric tire size code

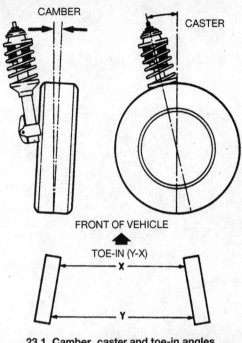

23.1 Camber, caster and toe-in angles

23 Wheel alignment - general information

Refer to illustration 23.1

A wheel alignment refers to the adjustments made to the wheels so they are in proper angular relationship to the suspension and the ground. Wheels that are out of proper alignment not only affect vehicle control, but also increase tire wear. The alignment angles normally measured are camber, caster and toe-in **(see illustration)**. Toe-in is the only adjustable angle on the front or the rear. The other angles should be measured to check for bent or worn suspension parts.

Getting the proper wheel alignment is a very exacting process, one in which complicated and expensive machines are necessary to perform the job properly. Because of this, you should have a technician with the proper equipment perform these tasks. We will, however, use this space to give you a basic idea of what is involved with a wheel alignment so you can better understand the process and deal intelligently with the shop that does the work.

Toe-in is the turning in of the wheels. The purpose of a toe specification is to ensure parallel rolling of the wheels. In a vehicle with

zero toe-in, the distance between the front edges of the wheels will be the same as the distance between the rear edges of the wheels. The actual amount of toe-in is normally only a fraction of an inch. On the front end, toe-in is controlled by the tie-rod end position on the tie-rod. On the rear end, it's controlled by a threaded adjuster on the rear lateral link. Incorrect toe-in will cause the tires to wear improperly by making them scrub against the road surface.

Camber is the tilting of the wheels from vertical when viewed from one end of the vehicle. When the wheels tilt out at the top, the camber is said to be positive (+). When the wheels tilt in at the top the camber is negative (-). The amount of tilt is measured in degrees from vertical and this measurement is called the camber angle. This angle affects the amount of tire tread which contacts the road and compensates for changes in the suspension geometry when the vehicle is cornering or traveling over an undulating surface.

Caster is the tilting of the front steering axis from the vertical. A tilt toward the rear is positive caster and a tilt toward the front is negative caster.

Notes

Chapter 11   Body

Contents

1   General information

The Chrysler LH models feature a "unibody" layout, using a floor pan with front and rear frame side rails which support the body components, front and rear suspension systems and other mechanical components. Certain components are particularly vulnerable to accident damage and can be unbolted and repaired or replaced. Among these parts are the body moldings, bumpers, front fenders, the hood and trunk lids and all glass. Only general body maintenance practices and body panel repair procedures within the scope of the do-it-yourselfer are included in this chapter.

Although all models are very similar, some procedures may differ somewhat from one body to another. The body designations are as follows:

XP and XS	Eagle Vision ESI and TSI
DH and DP	Dodge Intrepid and ES
LP	Chrysler Concorde
CH and CP	Chrysler New Yorker and LHS

2   Body - maintenance

1   The condition of your vehicle's body is very important, because the resale value depends a great deal on it. It's much more difficult to repair a neglected or damaged body than it is to repair mechanical components. The hidden areas of the body, such as the wheel wells, the frame and the engine compartment, are equally important, although they don't require as frequent attention as the rest of the body.
2   Once a year, or every 12,000 miles, it's a good idea to have the underside of the body steam cleaned. All traces of dirt and oil will be removed and the area can then be inspected carefully for rust, damaged brake lines, frayed electrical wires, damaged cables and other problems. The front suspension components should be greased after completion of this job.
3   At the same time, clean the engine and the engine compartment with a steam cleaner or water-soluble degreaser.
4   The wheel wells should be given close attention, since under-coating can peel away and stones and dirt thrown up by the tires can

11

These photos illustrate a method of repairing simple dents. They are intended to supplement *Body repair - minor damage* in this Chapter and should not be used as the sole instructions for body repair on these vehicles.

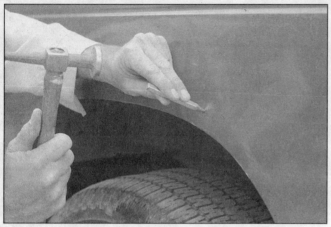

1   If you can't access the backside of the body panel to hammer out the dent, pull it out with a slide-hammer-type dent puller. In the deepest portion of the dent or along the crease line, drill or punch hole(s) at least one inch apart . . .

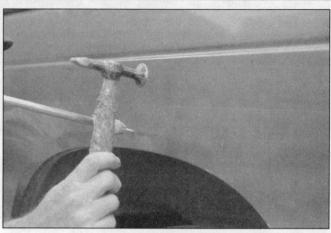

2   . . . then screw the slide-hammer into the hole and operate it. Tap with a hammer near the edge of the dent to help 'pop' the metal back to its original shape. When you're finished, the dent area should be close to its original contour and about 1/8-inch below the surface of the surrounding metal

3   Using coarse-grit sandpaper, remove the paint down to the bare metal. Hand sanding works fine, but the disc sander shown here makes the job faster. Use finer (about 320-grit) sandpaper to feather-edge the paint at least one inch around the dent area

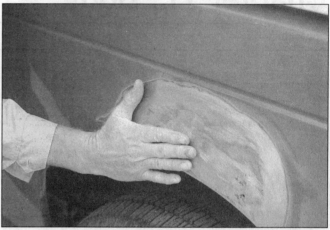

4   When the paint is removed, touch will probably be more helpful than sight for telling if the metal is straight. Hammer down the high spots or raise the low spots as necessary. Clean the repair area with wax/silicone remover

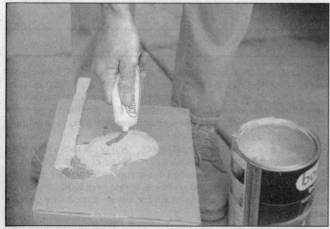

5   Following label instructions, mix up a batch of plastic filler and hardener. The ratio of filler to hardener is critical, and, if you mix it incorrectly, it will either not cure properly or cure too quickly (you won't have time to file and sand it into shape)

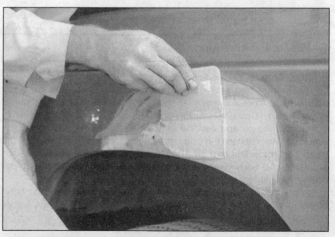

6   Working quickly so the filler doesn't harden, use a plastic applicator to press the body filler firmly into the metal, assuring it bonds completely. Work the filler until it matches the original contour and is slightly above the surrounding metal

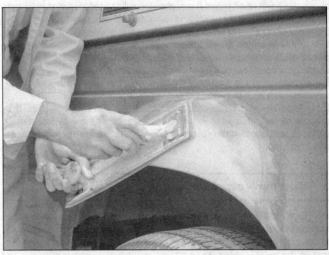

7   Let the filler harden until you can just dent it with your fingernail. Use a body file or Surform tool (shown here) to rough-shape the filler

8   Use coarse-grit sandpaper and a sanding board or block to work the filler down until it's smooth and even. Work down to finer grits of sandpaper - always using a board or block - ending up with 360 or 400 grit

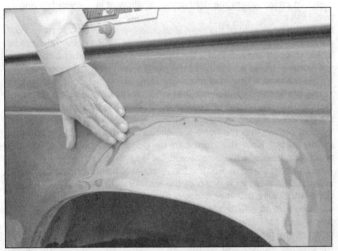

9   You shouldn't be able to feel any ridge at the transition from the filler to the bare metal or from the bare metal to the old paint. As soon as the repair is flat and uniform, remove the dust and mask off the adjacent panels or trim pieces

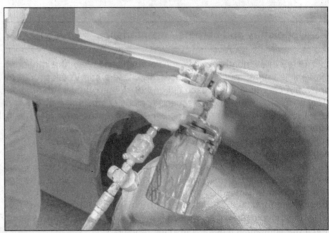

10   Apply several layers of primer to the area. Don't spray the primer on too heavy, so it sags or runs, and make sure each coat is dry before you spray on the next one. A professional-type spray gun is being used here, but aerosol spray primer is available inexpensively from auto parts stores

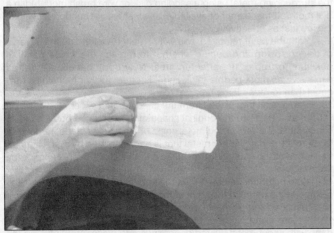

11   The primer will help reveal imperfections or scratches. Fill these with glazing compound. Follow the label instructions and sand it with 360 or 400-grit sandpaper until it's smooth. Repeat the glazing, sanding and respraying until the primer reveals a perfectly smooth surface

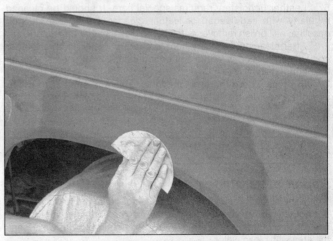

12   Finish sand the primer with very fine sandpaper (400 or 600-grit) to remove the primer overspray. Clean the area with water and allow it to dry. Use a tack rag to remove any dust, then apply the finish coat. Don't attempt to rub out or wax the repair area until the paint has dried completely (at least two weeks)

cause the paint to chip and flake, allowing rust to set in. If rust is found, clean down to the bare metal and apply an anti-rust paint.

5   The body should be washed about once a week. Wet the vehicle thoroughly to soften the dirt, then wash it down with a soft sponge and plenty of clean soapy water. If the surplus dirt is not washed off very carefully, it can wear down the paint.

6   Spots of tar or asphalt thrown up from the road should be removed with a cloth soaked in solvent.

7   Once every six months, wax the body and chrome trim. If a chrome cleaner is used to remove rust from any of the vehicle's plated parts, remember that the cleaner also removes part of the chrome, so use it sparingly.

3   Vinyl trim - maintenance

Don't clean vinyl trim with detergents, caustic soap or petroleum-based cleaners. Plain soap and water works just fine, with a soft brush to clean dirt that may be ingrained. Wash the vinyl as frequently as the rest of the vehicle. After cleaning, application of a high-quality rubber and vinyl protectant will help prevent oxidation and cracks. The protectant can also be applied to weatherstripping, vacuum lines and rubber hoses, which often fail as a result of chemical degradation, and to the tires.

4   Upholstery and carpets - maintenance

1   Every three months remove the floormats and clean the interior of the vehicle (more frequently if necessary). Use a stiff whisk broom to brush the carpeting and loosen dirt and dust, then vacuum the upholstery and carpets thoroughly, especially along seams and crevices.

2   Dirt and stains can be removed from carpeting with basic household or automotive carpet shampoos available in spray cans. Follow the directions and vacuum again, then use a stiff brush to bring back the "nap" of the carpet.

3   Most interiors have cloth or vinyl upholstery, either of which can be cleaned and maintained with a number of material-specific cleaners or shampoos available in auto supply stores. Follow the directions on the product for usage, and always spot-test any upholstery cleaner on an inconspicuous area (bottom edge of a backseat cushion) to ensure that it doesn't cause a color shift in the material.

4   After cleaning, vinyl upholstery should be treated with a protectant. **Note:** *Make sure the protectant container indicates the product can be used on seats - some products make may a seat too slippery.* **Caution:** *Do not use protectant on vinyl-covered steering wheels.*

5   Leather upholstery requires special care. It should be cleaned regularly with saddlesoap or leather cleaner. Never use alcohol, gasoline, nail polish remover or thinner to clean leather upholstery.

6   After cleaning, regularly treat leather upholstery with a leather conditioner, rubbed in with a soft cotton cloth. Never use car wax on leather upholstery.

7   In areas where the interior of the vehicle is subject to bright sunlight, cover leather seating areas of the seats with a sheet if the vehicle is to be left out for any length of time.

5   Body repair - minor damage

Repair of scratches

1   If the scratch is superficial and does not penetrate to the metal of the body, repair is very simple. Lightly rub the scratched area with a fine rubbing compound to remove loose paint and built up wax. Rinse the area with clean water.

2   Apply touch-up paint to the scratch, using a small brush. Continue to apply thin layers of paint until the surface of the paint in the scratch is level with the surrounding paint. Allow the new paint at least

two weeks to harden, then blend it into the surrounding paint by rubbing with a very fine rubbing compound. Finally, apply a coat of wax to the scratch area.

3   If the scratch has penetrated the paint and exposed the metal of the body, causing the metal to rust, a different repair technique is required. Remove all loose rust from the bottom of the scratch with a pocket knife, then apply rust inhibiting paint to prevent the formation of rust in the future. Using a rubber or nylon applicator, coat the scratched area with glaze-type filler. If required, the filler can be mixed with thinner to provide a very thin paste, which is ideal for filling narrow scratches. Before the glaze filler in the scratch hardens, wrap a piece of smooth cotton cloth around the tip of a finger. Dip the cloth in thinner and then quickly wipe it along the surface of the scratch. This will ensure that the surface of the filler is slightly hollow. The scratch can now be painted over as described earlier in this section.

Repair of dents

See photo sequence

4   When repairing dents, the first job is to pull the dent out until the affected area is as close as possible to its original shape. There is no point in trying to restore the original shape completely as the metal in the damaged area will have stretched on impact and cannot be restored to its original contours. It is better to bring the level of the dent up to a point which is about 1/8-inch below the level of the surrounding metal. In cases where the dent is very shallow, it is not worth trying to pull it out at all.

5   If the back side of the dent is accessible, it can be hammered out gently from behind using a soft-face hammer. While doing this, hold a block of wood firmly against the opposite side of the metal to absorb the hammer blows and prevent the metal from being stretched.

6   If the dent is in a section of the body which has double layers, or some other factor makes it inaccessible from behind, a different technique is required. Drill several small holes through the metal inside the damaged area, particularly in the deeper sections. Screw long, self tapping screws into the holes just enough for them to get a good grip in the metal. Now the dent can be pulled out by pulling on the protruding heads of the screws with locking pliers.

7   The next stage of repair is the removal of paint from the damaged area and from an inch or so of the surrounding metal. This is easily done with a wire brush or sanding disk in a drill motor, although it can be done just as effectively by hand with sandpaper. To complete the preparation for filling, score the surface of the bare metal with a screwdriver or the tang of a file or drill small holes in the affected area. This will provide a good grip for the filler material. To complete the repair, see the subsection on *filling and painting*.

Repair of rust holes or gashes

8   Remove all paint from the affected area and from an inch or so of the surrounding metal using a sanding disk or wire brush mounted in a drill motor. If these are not available, a few sheets of sandpaper will do the job just as effectively.

9   With the paint removed, you will be able to determine the severity of the corrosion and decide whether to replace the whole panel, if possible, or repair the affected area. New body panels are not as expensive as most people think and it is often quicker to install a new panel than to repair large areas of rust.

10   Remove all trim pieces from the affected area except those which will act as a guide to the original shape of the damaged body, such as headlight shells, etc. Using metal snips or a hacksaw blade, remove all loose metal and any other metal that is badly affected by rust. Hammer the edges of the hole on the inside to create a slight depression for the filler material.

11   Wire brush the affected area to remove the powdery rust from the surface of the metal. If the back of the rusted area is accessible, treat it with rust inhibiting paint.

12   Before filling is done, block the hole in some way. This can be done with sheet metal riveted or screwed into place, or by stuffing the hole with wire mesh.

13   Once the hole is blocked off, the affected area can be filled and painted. See the following subsection on *filling and painting*.

Filling and painting

14   Many types of body fillers are available, but generally speaking, body repair kits which contain filler paste and a tube of resin hardener are best for this type of repair work. A wide, flexible plastic or nylon applicator will be necessary for imparting a smooth and contoured finish to the surface of the filler material. Mix up a small amount of filler on a clean piece of wood or cardboard (use the hardener sparingly). Follow the manufacturer's instructions on the package, otherwise the filler will set incorrectly.

15   Using the applicator, apply the filler paste to the prepared area. Draw the applicator across the surface of the filler to achieve the desired contour and to level the filler surface. As soon as a contour that approximates the original one is achieved, stop working the paste. If you continue, the paste will begin to stick to the applicator. Continue to add thin layers of paste at 20-minute intervals until the level of the filler is just above the surrounding metal.

16   Once the filler has hardened, the excess can be removed with a body file. From then on, progressively finer grades of sandpaper should be used, starting with a 180-grit paper and finishing with 600-grit wet-or-dry paper. Always wrap the sandpaper around a flat rubber or wooden block, otherwise the surface of the filler will not be completely flat. During the sanding of the filler surface, the wet-or-dry paper should be periodically rinsed in water. This will ensure that a very smooth finish is produced in the final stage.

17   At this point, the repair area should be surrounded by a ring of bare metal, which in turn should be encircled by the finely feathered edge of good paint. Rinse the repair area with clean water until all of the dust produced by the sanding operation is gone.

18   Spray the entire area with a light coat of primer. This will reveal any imperfections in the surface of the filler. Repair the imperfections with fresh filler paste or glaze filler and once more smooth the surface with sandpaper. Repeat this spray-and-repair procedure until you are satisfied that the surface of the filler and the feathered edge of the paint are perfect. Rinse the area with clean water and allow it to dry completely.

19   The repair area is now ready for painting. Spray painting must be carried out in a warm, dry, windless and dust free atmosphere. These conditions can be created if you have access to a large indoor work area, but if you are forced to work in the open, you will have to pick the day very carefully. If you are working indoors, dousing the floor in the work area with water will help settle the dust which would otherwise be in the air. If the repair area is confined to one body panel, mask off the surrounding panels. This will help minimize the effects of a slight mismatch in paint color. Trim pieces such as chrome strips, door handles, etc., will also need to be masked off or removed. Use masking tape and several thicknesses of newspaper for the masking operations.

20   Before spraying, shake the paint can thoroughly, then spray a test area until the spray painting technique is mastered. Cover the repair area with a thick coat of primer. The thickness should be built up using several thin layers of primer rather than one thick one. Using 600-grit wet-or-dry sandpaper, rub down the surface of the primer until it is very smooth. While doing this, the work area should be thoroughly rinsed with water and the wet-or-dry sandpaper periodically rinsed as well. Allow the primer to dry before spraying additional coats.

21   Spray on the top coat, again building up the thickness by using several thin layers of paint. Begin spraying in the center of the repair area and then, using a circular motion, work out until the whole repair area and about two inches of the surrounding original paint is covered. Remove all masking material 10 to 15 minutes after spraying on the final coat of paint. Allow the new paint at least two weeks to harden, then use a very fine rubbing compound to blend the edges of the new paint into the existing paint. Finally, apply a coat of wax.

6   Body repair - major damage

1   Major damage must be repaired by an auto body shop specifically equipped to perform unibody repairs. These shops have the specialized equipment required to do the job properly.

2   If the damage is extensive, the body must be checked for proper alignment or the vehicle's handling characteristics may be adversely affected and other components may wear at an accelerated rate.

3   Due to the fact that all of the major body components (hood, fenders, etc.) are separate and replaceable units, any seriously damaged components should be replaced rather than repaired. Sometimes the components can be found in a wrecking yard that specializes in used vehicle components, often at considerable savings over the cost of new parts.

7   Hinges and locks - maintenance

Once every 3000 miles, or every three months, the hinges and latch assemblies on the doors, hood and trunk should be given a few drops of light oil or lock lubricant. The door latch strikers should also be lubricated with a thin coat of grease to reduce wear and ensure free movement. Lubricate the door and trunk locks with spray-on graphite lubricant.

8   Windshield and fixed glass - replacement

Replacement of the windshield and fixed glass requires the use of special fast-setting adhesive/caulk materials and some specialized tools and techniques. These operations should be left to a dealer service department or a shop specializing in glass work.

9   Hood - removal, installation and adjustment

Refer to illustrations 9.2, 9.10 and 9.11
Note: *The hood is heavy and somewhat awkward to remove and install - at least two people should perform this procedure.*

Removal and installation

1   Use blankets or pads to cover the cowl area of the body and the fenders. This will protect the body and paint as the hood is lifted off.
2   Scribe alignment marks around the bolt heads to insure proper alignment during installation (a permanent-type felt-tip marker also will work for this) **(see illustration)**.
3   Disconnect any cables or wire harnesses which will interfere with removal.
4   Have an assistant support the weight of the hood. Remove the hinge-to-hood bolts.
5   Lift off the hood.
6   Installation is the reverse of removal.

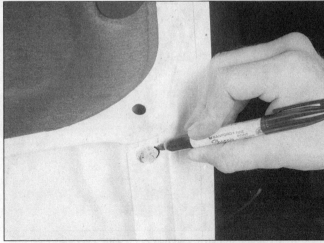

9.2 **Use a marking pen to outline the hinge plate and bolt heads**

11

9.10 Adjust the hood height by screwing the hood bumpers in or out

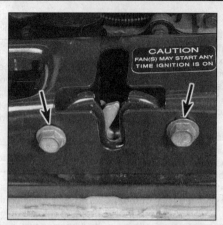

9.11 Loosen the bolts (arrows) and move the latch to adjust the hood in closed position

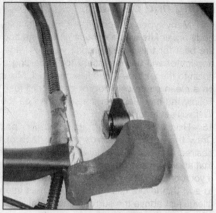

10.2 Use a screwdriver to remove the plastic retainer from the end of the strut

Adjustment

7   Fore-and-aft and side-to-side adjustment of the hood is done by moving the hood in relation to the hinge plate after loosening the bolts.
8   Scribe or trace a line around the entire hinge plate so you can judge the amount of movement.
9   Loosen the bolts or nuts and move the hood into correct alignment. Move it only a little at a time. Tighten the hinge bolts or nuts and carefully lower the hood to check the alignment.
10   Adjust the hood bumpers on the radiator support so the hood is flush with the fenders when closed **(see illustration)**.
11   The safety latch assembly can also be adjusted up-and-down and side-to-side after loosening the bolts **(see illustration)**.
12   The hood latch assembly, as well as the hinges, should be periodically lubricated with white lithium-base grease to prevent sticking and wear.

10 Hood support struts - replacement

Refer to illustrations 10.2 and 10.3
Note: The hood is heavy and somewhat awkward to hold - at least two people should perform this procedure.
1   Open the hood and support it.
2   Use a screwdriver to pry out the plastic retainers from each end of the strut **(see illustration)**.
3   Use large screwdriver or a prybar to pry sharply on the ends of the strut to detach it from the vehicle **(see illustration)**.
4   Installation is the reverse of removal.

10.3 Detach the strut end by prying with a screwdriver

11 Hood latch and cable - removal and installation

Refer to illustrations 11.1, 11.4 and 11.6
Warning: These models have airbags. Always disconnect the negative battery cable and wait two minutes before working in the vicinity of the impact sensors, steering column or instrument panel to avoid the possibility of accidental deployment of the airbag, which could cause personal injury (see Chapter 12).

Latch

1   Remove the bolts and detach the latch assembly **(see illustration)**.
2   Referring to Step 4, detach the cable, the remove the latch.
3   Installation is the reverse of removal.

Cable

4   Use a screwdriver to release the cable end, then detach the cable case from the bracket **(see illustration)**.
5   In the passenger compartment, remove the three screws and detach the door sill trim cover for access to the hood release handle.
6   Remove the bolts and detach the hood release cable and handle assembly **(see illustration)**.
7   Under the dash, remove the cable grommet from the firewall.
8   Connect a string or piece of wire to the engine compartment end

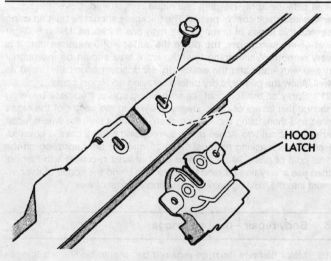

11.1 Hood latch details

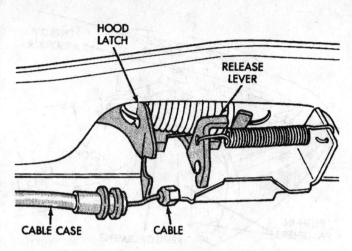

11.4 Detach the cable from the latch and bracket

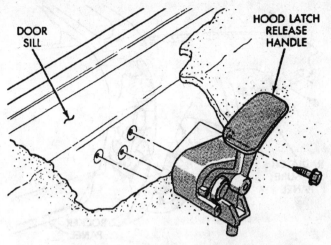

11.6 Hood release cable and handle attachment details

of the cable, then detach the cable and pull it through the firewall into the passenger compartment.
9   Connect the string or wire to the new cable and pull it through the firewall into the engine compartment.
10   The remainder of installation is the reverse of removal.

12 Radiator grille (CH and CP models only) - removal and installation

Refer to illustrations 12.2, 12.3 and 12.5
Warning: *These models have airbags. Always disconnect the negative battery cable and wait two minutes before working in the vicinity of the impact sensors, steering column or instrument panel to avoid the possibility of accidental deployment of the airbag, which could cause personal injury (see Chapter 12).*
1   Open the hood.
2   On some models it will be necessary to remove the screws and detach the radiator closure panel sight shield for access **(see illustration)**.
3   Some models use plastic fasteners to retain the grille. Use a small screwdriver to pry out the plastic push-in fasteners retaining the grille to the fascia, then disengage the tabs at the bottom and detach the grille **(see illustration)**.
4   To install, place the grille in position and seat the tabs into the holes in the fascia, then secure the grille with the push-in fasteners.

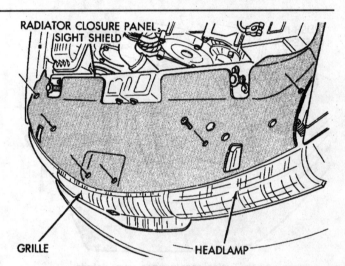

12.2 On some models you'll have to remove the sight shield for access to the grille

5   Other models use bolts to hold the grille in place. Remove the bolts and pull the grille straight out to remove it **(see illustration)**.
6   Installation is the reverse of removal.

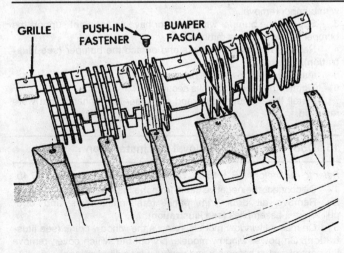

12.3 Remove the push-in fasteners and detach the grille

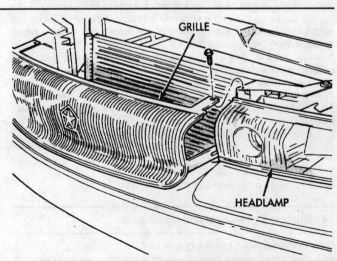

12.5 On some models the grille is retained with bolts

11

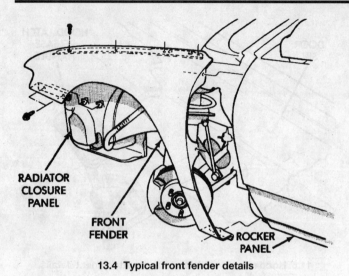

13.4 Typical front fender details

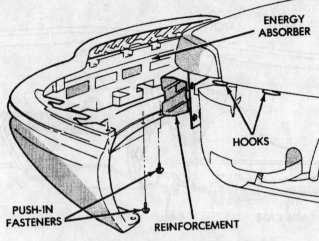

14.1a Typical front bumper cover details

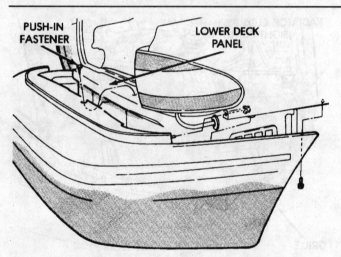

14.1b Typical rear bumper cover details

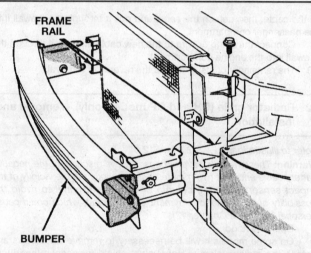

14.4 Typical bumper mounting details

13 Front fender - removal and installation

Refer to illustration 13.4

Warning: *These models have airbags. Always disconnect the negative battery cable and wait two minutes before working in the vicinity of the impact sensors, steering column or instrument panel to avoid the possibility of accidental deployment of the airbag, which could cause personal injury (see Chapter 12).*

1   Loosen the front wheel lug nuts, raise the vehicle, support it securely on jackstands and remove the front wheel.

2   Remove the headlight assembly (see Chapter 12).

3   Detach the front bumper cover from the fender (see Section 14).

4   Remove the fender-to-rocker panel mounting bolts **(see illustration)**.

5   Remove the bolts at the front and rear edges of the fender.

6   Working in the engine compartment, remove the fender-to-inner wheelhouse bolts and detach the fender.

7   Installation is the reverse of removal.

8   Tighten all nuts, bolts and screws securely.

14 Bumpers - removal and installation

Refer to illustrations 14.1a, 14.1b and 14.4

Warning: *These models have airbags. Always disconnect the negative battery cable and wait two minutes before working in the vicinity of the*

impact sensors, steering column or instrument panel to avoid the possibility of accidental deployment of the airbag, which could cause personal injury (see Chapter 12).

1   Detach the bumper cover **(see illustrations)**.

2   Disconnect any wiring or other components that would interfere with bumper removal.

3   Support the bumper with a jack or have an assistant support the bumper as the bolts are removed.

4   Remove the mounting bolts and detach the bumper **(see illustration)**.

5   Installation is the reverse of removal.

6   Tighten the mounting bolts securely.

7   Install the bumper cover and any other components that were removed.

15 Door trim panel - removal and installation

Refer to illustrations 15.2, 15.3a, 15.3b, 15.3c, 15.3d, 15.4a and 15.4b

1   Disconnect the negative cable from the battery.

2   Remove all door trim panel retaining screws and door pull/armrest assemblies **(see illustration)**.

3   On manual window models, remove the window crank **(see illustration)**. On power window models, pry out the switch cover, remove the control switch assembly and unplug it **(see illustrations)**.

4   Grasp the trim panel and pull up sharply to detach it from the door

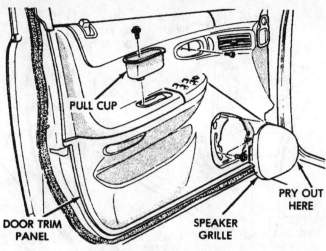

15.2 Door trim panel details

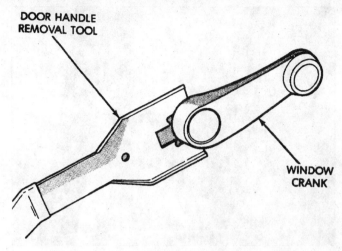

15.3a A tool like this one will make window crank removal much easier

15.3b Pry off the door switch cover, . . .

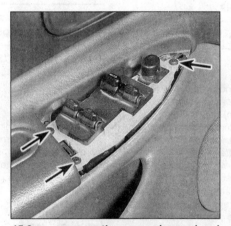

15.3c . . . remove the screws (arrows) and lift the switch out . . .

15.3d . . . and unplug it

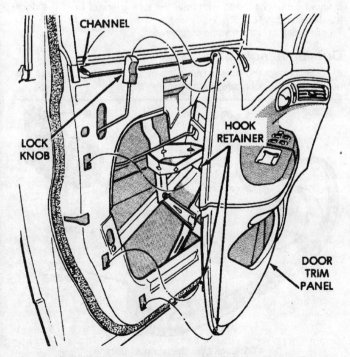

15.4a Pull up sharply to detach the door trim panel

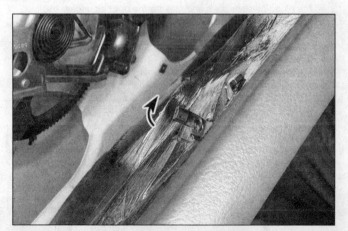

15.4b Rotate the clip in the direction shown to disconnect the door handle rod

11

(see illustration). Disconnect the inner door handle lock rod from the handle (see illustration). Unplug any electrical connectors and remove the door panel.

5   Connect the wire harness connectors and place the panel in position in the door. Press the trim panel down into place until the clips are seated.

6   Install the armrest/door pulls and the window switch or crank. Reconnect the negative battery cable.

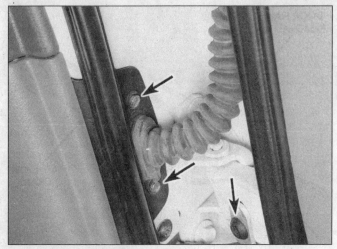

16.2 Remove the bolts and unplug the electrical connector (arrows) - remove the Torx-head bolt (lower right arrow) to detach the door stay from the hinge

16   Door - removal, installation and adjustment

Refer to illustrations 16.2 and 16.4

1   Remove the door trim panel.

2   Disconnect any wire harness connectors and push them through the door opening so they won't interfere with door removal and detach check strap from the door hinge **(see illustration).**

3   Place a jack under the door or have an assistant on hand to support it when the hinge bolts are removed. **Note:** *If a jack is used, place a rag between it and the door to protect the door's painted surfaces.*

4   Scribe around the mounting bolt heads with a marking pen, remove the bolts and carefully lift off the door **(see illustration).**

5   Installation is the reverse of removal, making sure to align the hinge with the marks made during removal before tightening the bolts.

6   Following installation of the door, check the alignment and adjust it if necessary as follows:

   a) *Up-and-down and in-and-out adjustments are made by loosening the hinge-to-door bolts and moving the door as necessary.*

   b) *Forward-and-backward adjustments are made by loosening the hinge-to-body bolts and moving the door as necessary.*

   c) *The door lock striker can also be adjusted both up-and-down and sideways to provide positive engagement with the lock mechanism. This is done by loosening the mounting screws and moving the striker as necessary.*

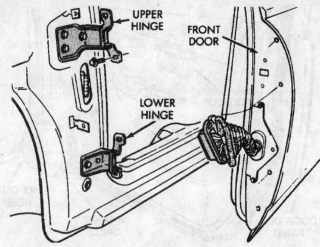

16.4 Remove the hinge bolts and lift the door off

17   Door latch, lock cylinder and outside handle - removal and installation

Refer to illustrations 17.3, 17.6 and 17.8

1   Close the window completely and remove the door trim panel (see Section 15).

Latch

2   Disconnect the link rods from the latch.

3   Remove the three Torx-head mounting screws from the end of the door (it may be necessary to use an impact-type screwdriver to loosen them) and detach the latch from the door **(see illustration).**

4   Place the latch in position, install the screws and tighten them securely.

5   Connect the link rods to the latch.

Lock cylinder

6   Disconnect the link, use a screwdriver to push the key lock cylinder retainer off and withdraw the lock cylinder from the door handle assembly.

7   Installation is the reverse of removal.

Outside handle

8   Disconnect the links, remove the mounting nut and detach the handle from the door **(see illustration).**

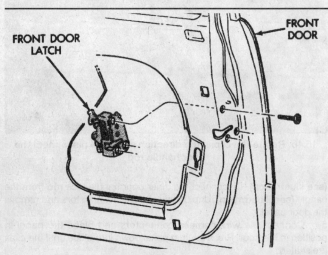

17.3 A Torx-head tool may be required to remove the door latch screws

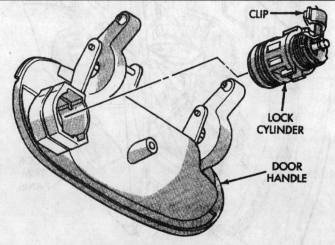

17.6 Lock cylinder removal details

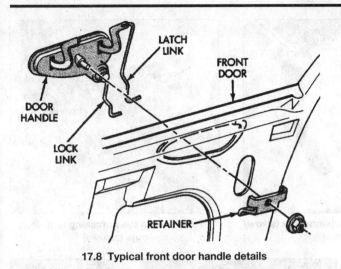

17.8 Typical front door handle details

9   Place the handle in position, attach the links and install the nut. Tighten the nut securely.

18   Door window glass - removal, installation and adjustment

Refer to illustrations 18.1, 18.3, 18.5a and 18.5b

1   Remove the door trim panel (see Section 15). Remove the upper trim retainer channel and, on rear doors, the applique from the door frame **(see illustration)**.

Removal

2   Lower the glass to within two inches of the bottom of its travel.
3   Loosen the screws retaining the regulator roller channel to the glass, slide the channel toward the rear so the screw heads pass through the key hole slots, then detach the glass and lift it up and out of the door **(see illustration)**.

Installation

4   Lower the glass into the door, insert the screw heads through the key hole slots in the channel, then slide the channel forward to lock the glass in place. Tighten the screws.

Adjustment

5   If adjustment is necessary, loosen the adjustment nuts, then adjust the glass position **(see illustration)**. Tighten the adjustment screws **(see illustration)**.

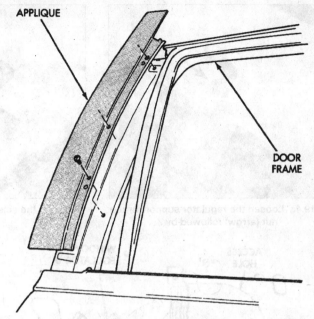

18.1 Rear door applique details

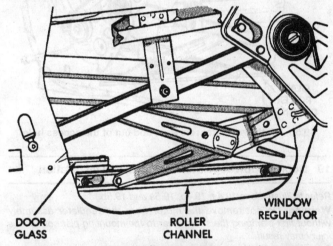

18.3 Loosen the screws and slide the roller channel rearward so the screw heads line up with the key hole slots

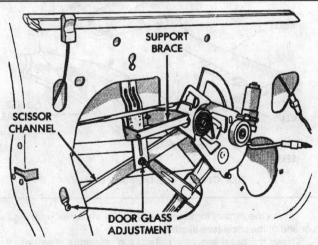

18.5a Front door adjustment details

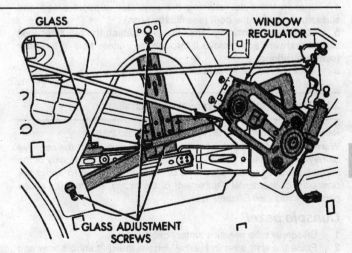

18.5b Rear door adjustment details

11

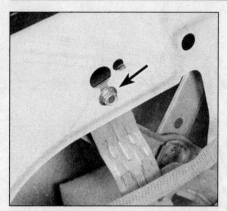

19.4a Loosen the regulator support brace nut (arrow) followed by . . .

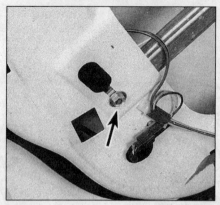

19.4b . . . the scissors channel nut (arrow)

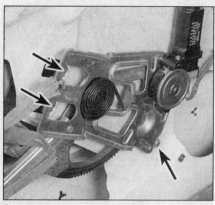

19.5a Loosen the remaining regulator nuts (arrows)

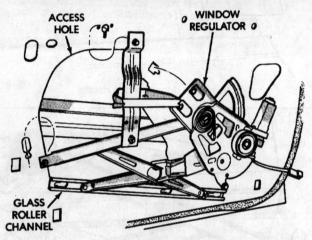

19.5b Lift the regulator rearward and out of the access hole

20.3 The console bezel screw is accessible after removing the ashtray

19 Door window regulator - removal and installation

Refer to illustrations 19.4a, 19.4b, 19.5a and 19.5b

Warning: *Do not remove the motor from the regulator assembly without first clamping the sector gear to the mounting plate or serious injury may result.*

1   Remove the door trim panel (see Section 15).
2   Remove the door window glass (see Section 17).
3   On power window models, unplug the electrical connector.
4   Loosen the nuts retaining the regulator support brace and scissors channel to the door **(see illustrations)**.
5   Loosen the remaining nuts, lift up to detach the regulator then slide it rearward and remove it through the access hole in the door **(see illustrations)**.
6   Installation is the reverse of removal.

20 Center console - removal and installation

Refer to illustrations 20.3, 20.4, 20.6a, 20.6b and 20.6c

Warning: *These models have airbags. Always disconnect the negative battery cable and wait two minutes before working in the vicinity of the impact sensors, steering column or instrument panel to avoid the possibility of accidental deployment of the airbag, which could cause personal injury (see Chapter 12).*

Console bezel

1   Disconnect the negative battery cable.
2   Place the shift lever in Neutral, loosen the shift knob screw and remove the knob.

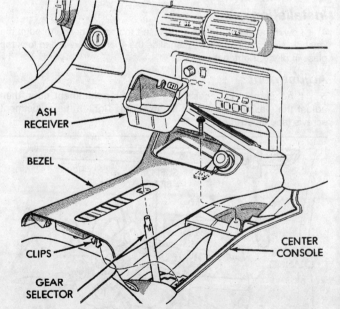

20.4 Console bezel removal details

3   Lift out the ashtray for access and remove the screw retaining the front end of the bezel **(see illustration)**.
4   Grasp the bezel securely, detach the rear edge clips from the console and remove the bezel **(see illustration)**.

20.6a Remove the console front retaining screws (arrows) and . . .

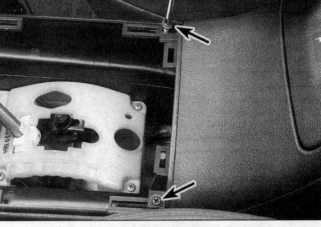

20.6b . . . after removing the bezel, the lower two screws (arrows) . . .

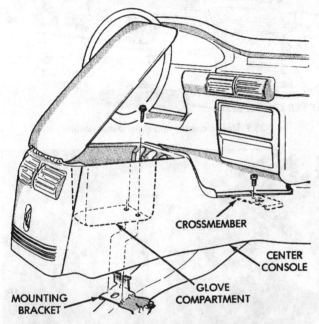

CROSSMEMBER

CENTER
CONSOLE

MOUNTING
BRACKET

GLOVE
COMPARTMENT

20.6c . . . followed by the two screws inside the console

Center console

5   Remove the bezel (see above).
6   Remove the console retaining screws **(see illustrations)**.
7   Detach the console and lift it up, then unplug any electrical connectors and remove the console from the vehicle.
8   Installation is the reverse of removal.

21 Trunk lid - removal, installation and adjustment

Refer to illustration 21.3

1   Open the trunk lid and cover the edges of the trunk compartment with pads or cloths to protect the painted surfaces when the lid is removed.
2   Disconnect any cables or electrical connectors attached to the trunk lid that would interfere with removal.
3   Use a marking pen to make alignment marks around the hinge bolt heads **(see illustration)**.
4   While an assistant supports it's weight, remove the hinge bolts from both sides and lift the trunk lid off.
5   Installation is the reverse of removal. **Note:** *When reinstalling the*

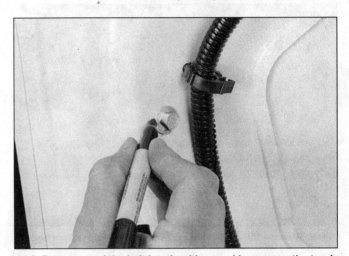

21.3 Draw around the bolt heads with a marking pen so the trunk lid can be installed in the same position

trunk lid, align the hinge bolt heads with the marks made during removal.
6   After installation, close the lid and see if it's in proper alignment with the surrounding panels. Fore-and-aft and side-to-side adjustments of the lid are controlled by the position of the hinge bolts in the holes. To adjust it, loosen the hinge bolts, reposition the lid and retighten the bolts.
7   The height of the lid in relation to the surrounding body panels when closed can be adjusted by loosening the lock striker bolts, repositioning the striker and retightening the bolts.

22 Instrument cluster bezel - removal and installation

Refer to illustration 22.4
Warning: *These models have airbags. Always disconnect the negative battery cable and wait two minutes before working in the vicinity of the impact sensors, steering column or instrument panel to avoid the possibility of accidental deployment of the airbag, which could cause personal injury (see Chapter 12).*

1   Remove the left dashboard end cap and the headlight switch bezel and the upper center bezel (see Section 23).
2   Remove the headlight switch (see Chapter 12).
3   Lower the steering wheel to it's lowest position.
4   Remove the screws and detach the bezel **(see illustration)**.
5   Installation is the reverse of removal.

11

22.4 Remove the screws retaining the cluster bezel

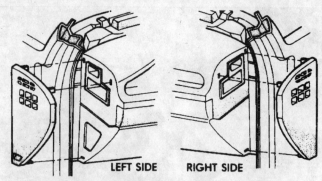

23.2 The end caps are held in place by clips

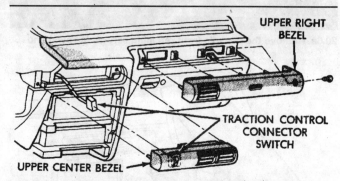

UPPER RIGHT BEZEL

TRACTION CONTROL CONNECTOR SWITCH

UPPER CENTER BEZEL

23.7 Upper center and right bezel details

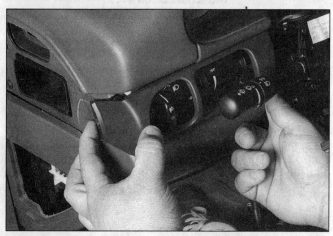

23.5 Remove the screw and detach the headlight switch bezel

23.11 Use a screwdriver to pry off the lower center bezel

23 Dashboard panels - removal and installation

Warning: *These models have airbags. Always disconnect the negative battery cable and wait two minutes before working in the vicinity of the impact sensors, steering column or instrument panel to avoid the possibility of accidental deployment of the airbag, which could cause personal injury (see Chapter 12).*

Dashboard end caps

Refer to illustration 23.2

1   The end caps are held in place by clips.
2   Grasp the cover securely (by the fuse box on the left cap or the heater vane on the right cap) and pull sharply to remove it **(see illustration)**. If necessary, gently pry with a screwdriver.
3   Installation is the reverse of removal.

Headlight switch bezel

Refer to illustration 23.5

4   Remove the left side end cap.
5   Remove the screw at the end of the dashboard and detach the bezel **(see illustration)**.
6   Installation is the reverse of removal.

Upper center bezel

Refer to illustration 23.7

7   Using a hooked tool, detach the bezel and unplug the electrical connector **(see illustration)**.
8   Installation is the reverse of removal.

Upper right bezel

9   Remove the screw and detach the bezel from the dashboard **(see illustration 23.7)**.
10   Installation is the reverse of removal.

Lower center bezel

Refer to illustration 23.11

11   Use a screwdriver to detach the bezel from the dashboard **(see illustration)**.
12   Installation is the reverse of removal.

Glove box

13   Remove the three screws along the bottom edge and open the glove box.
14   Squeeze the sidewalls in and remove the glove box from the dashboard.
15   Installation is the reverse of removal.

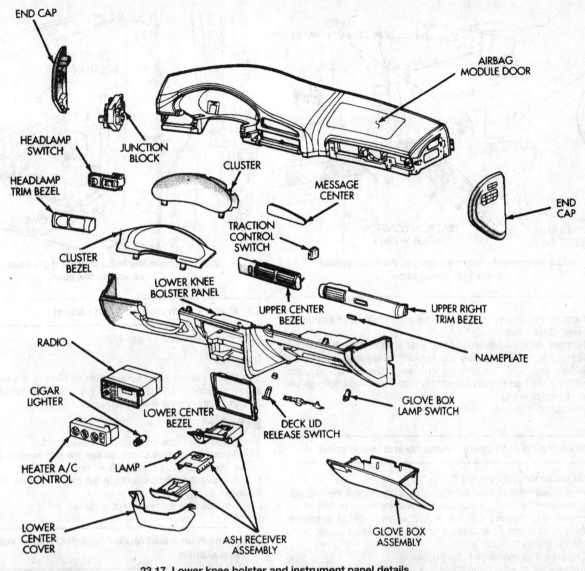

END CAP

AIRBAG
MODULE DOOR

HEADLAMP
SWITCH

JUNCTION
BLOCK

CLUSTER

MESSAGE
CENTER

HEADLAMP
TRIM BEZEL

END
CAP

TRACTION
CONTROL
SWITCH

CLUSTER
BEZEL

LOWER KNEE
BOLSTER PANEL

UPPER CENTER
BEZEL

UPPER RIGHT
TRIM BEZEL

NAMEPLATE

RADIO

GLOVE BOX
LAMP SWITCH

CIGAR
LIGHTER

LOWER CENTER
BEZEL

DECK LID
RELEASE SWITCH

HEATER A/C
CONTROL

LAMP

LOWER
CENTER
COVER

ASH RECEIVER
ASSEMBLY

GLOVE BOX
ASSEMBLY

23.17 Lower knee bolster and instrument panel details

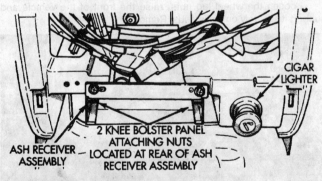

ASH RECEIVER
ASSEMBLY

2 KNEE BOLSTER PANEL
ATTACHING NUTS
LOCATED AT REAR OF ASH
RECEIVER ASSEMBLY

CIGAR
LIGHTER

23.18 Knee bolster center support bracket screw locations

Lower knee bolster panel

Refer to illustration 23.17, 23.18, 23.19, 23.20 and 23.21

16   Open the front doors and remove the dashboard end caps.

17   Remove the console bezel, lower center cover and lower center bezel **(see illustration)**.

18   Remove the radio ground strap bolt and the two retaining screws from the center support bracket **(see illustration)**.

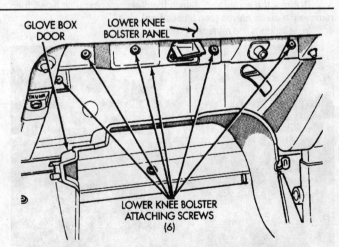

GLOVE BOX
DOOR

LOWER KNEE
BOLSTER PANEL

LOWER KNEE BOLSTER
ATTACHING SCREWS
(6)

**23.19 Lower the glove box door for access to the
knee bolster screws**

19   Open the glove box, squeeze in the sides and swing the glove box down out of the dashboard, then remove the screws along the top **(see illustration)**.

11

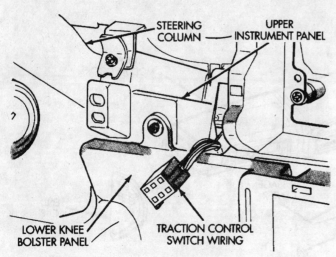

23.20 Remove the screws retaining the knee bolster to the instrument panel

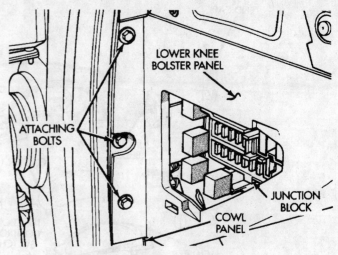

23.21 Remove the bolts attaching the ends of the bolster to the cowl

20   Remove the screws retaining the bolster to the upper instrument panel **(see illustration)**.
21   Remove the knee bolster-to-cowl bolts at either end, then detach and lower the assembly **(see illustration)**. Unplug the electrical connectors and, with the steering column in the full up position, remove the knee bolster panel assembly from the vehicle through the right side door opening.
22   Installation is the reverse of removal.

24   Steering column cover - removal and installation

Refer to illustrations 24.2 and 24.3
Warning: *These models have airbags. Always disconnect the negative battery cable and wait two minutes before working in the vicinity of the impact sensors, steering column or instrument panel to avoid the possibility of accidental deployment of the airbag, which could cause personal injury (see Chapter 12).*
1   Disconnect the negative battery cable.
2   Remove the three column cover screws **(see illustration)**.
3   Remove the screw and detach the steering column tilt lever, then remove the cover halves **(see illustration)**.
4   Installation is the reverse of removal.

25   Mirrors - removal and installation

Refer to illustrations 25.1 and 25.5

Interior
1   Use a Phillips head screwdriver to remove the set screw, then slide the mirror up off the button on the windshield **(see illustration)**.
2   Installation is the reverse of removal.

Exterior
3   Remove the door trim panel (see Section 15).
4   Remove the screws and detach the mirror knob and bezel. On power mirrors, unplug the electrical connector.
5   Remove the nuts and detach the mirror from the door **(see illustration)**.
6   Installation is the reverse of removal.

26   Wheelhouse and fender splash shields - removal and installation

Refer to illustrations 26.2 and 26.3
1   Loosen the wheel lug nuts, raise the front of the vehicle and support it securely on jackstands. Remove the wheel(s).

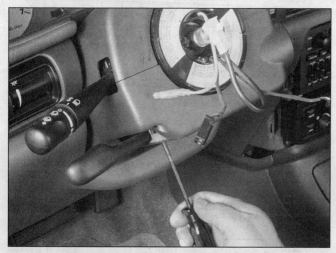

24.2 Remove the three column cover screws

24.3 Remove the screw and detach the tilt lever to allow the column cover half to be lifted off

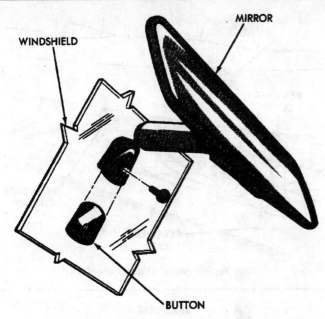

25.1 The interior mirror fits over a button on the glass and is held in position by a screw

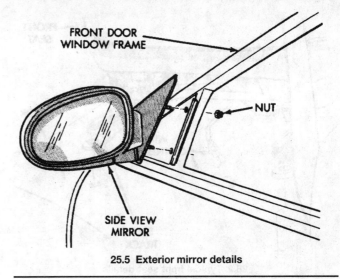

25.5 Exterior mirror details

2   The wheelhouse splash shield is retained by plastic push-in fasteners. Carefully pry out the fasteners out with pliers or wire cutters and detach the splash shield (see illustration).
3   The fender splash shield is held in place by screws. Remove the screws, detach the splash shield and detach the wire harness, then lower the splash shield from the fender well (see illustration).
4   Installation is the reverse of removal.

27 Cowl cover - removal and installation

Refer to illustration 27.2
1   Disconnect the windshield washer hoses and remove the wiper arms.
2   Remove the plastic expanding fasteners. While these look like plastic Phillips head screws, they are actually press-in fasteners. Remove the plastic screws, then gently pry out the push-in fasteners. To install these fasteners, press the expander into place then insert the screw fully by pushing it in with a Phillips head screwdriver (see illustration).
3   After removing the fasteners, detach the weatherstrip.
4   Remove the clips along the front edge and lift the cowl cover toward the windshield.
5   Installation is the reverse of removal.

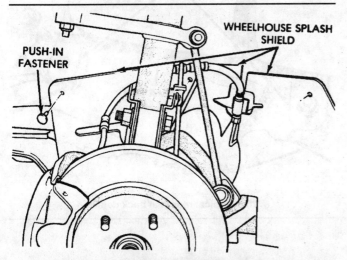

26.2 Wheelhouse splash shield details

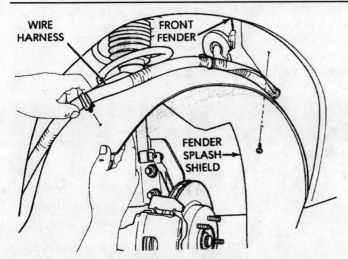

26.3 Fender splash shield details

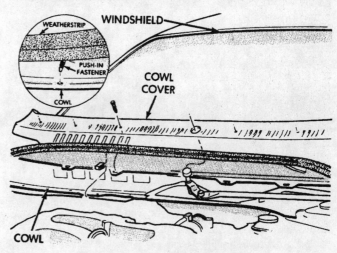

27.2 Cowl cover removal details

11

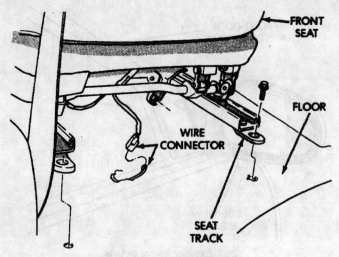

28.2 Typical front seat details

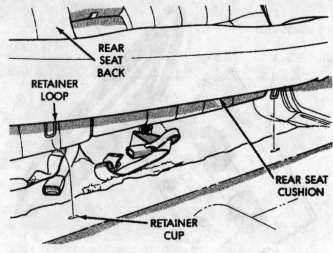

28.5 Typical rear seat cushion details

28   Seats - removal and installation

Refer to illustrations 28.2, 28.5 and 28.6

Front

1   Move the seat forward.
2   Remove the front seat track bolts, followed by the rear seat track bolts and unplug any electrical connectors attached to the seat **(see illustration)**.
3   Lift the seat from the vehicle.
4   Installation is the reverse of removal.

Rear

5   Remove the seat cushion by grasping the front edge securely, then pulling up sharply to detach the cushion **(see illustration)**.
6   Remove the seat back and seat belt retaining nuts and lift the seat back out of the vehicle **(see illustration)**.
7   Installation is the reverse of removal.

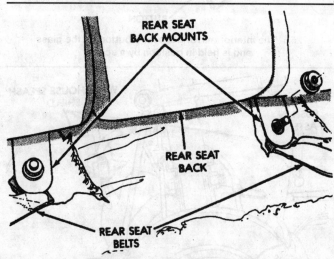

28.6 Typical rear seat back details

Chapter 12
Chassis electrical system

Contents

Specifications

Light bulb types

Front

Headlight bulb	9007
Park/turn signal/side marker light	3157NA
Fog light bulb	H3
Underhood light bulb	105

Interior

Speedometer and instrument cluster light	PC194
Door courtesy light	212-2
Ignition lock light	ASC
Overhead console light	192
Glove compartment light	194
Reading light (front or rear)	192
Visor vanity light	6501966

Rear

License plate light	168
Back-up light	3157
Brake/turn signal (Eagle)	3157
Brake/turn signal/taillight (Dodge/Chrysler)	3057
Taillight (Eagle)	916
Trunk	98
High-mounted brake light	921
Side marker light	
Dodge	168
Chrysler	921

12

1   General information

The electrical system is a 12-volt, negative ground type. Power for the lights and all electrical accessories is supplied by a lead/acid-type battery which is charged by the alternator.

This Chapter covers repair and service procedures for the various electrical components not associated with the engine. Information on the battery, alternator, distributor and starter motor can be found in Chapter 5. **Warning:** *When working on the electrical system, disconnect the negative battery cable from the battery to prevent electrical shorts and/or fires.*

Although all models are very similar, some procedures differ somewhat from one body to another. The body designations are as follows:

XP and XS	*Eagle Vision ESI and TSI*
DH and DP	*Dodge Intrepid and ES*
LP	*Chrysler Concorde*
CH and CP	*Chrysler New Yorker and LHS*

2   Electrical troubleshooting - general information

A typical electrical circuit consists of an electrical component, any switches, relays, motors, fuses, fusible links or circuit breakers related to the component and the wiring and connectors that link the component to both the battery and the chassis. To help pinpoint an electrical circuit problem, wiring diagrams are included at the end of this Chapter.

Before tackling any troublesome electrical circuit, first study the appropriate wiring diagrams to get a complete understanding of what makes up that individual circuit. Trouble spots, for instance, can often be narrowed down by noting if other components related to the circuit are operating properly. If several components or circuits fail at one time, chances are the problem is in a fuse or ground connection, because several circuits are often routed through the same fuse and ground connections.

Electrical problems usually stem from simple causes, such as loose or corroded connections, a blown fuse, a melted fusible link or a bad relay. Visually inspect the condition of all fuses, wires and connections in a problem circuit before troubleshooting it.

If testing instruments are going to be utilized, use the diagrams to plan ahead of time where to make the necessary connections to accurately pinpoint the trouble spot.

The basic tools needed for electrical troubleshooting include a circuit tester or voltmeter (a 12-volt bulb with a set of test leads can also be used), a continuity tester (which includes a bulb, battery and set of test leads) and a jumper wire, preferably with a circuit breaker incorporated, which can be used to bypass electrical components. Before attempting to locate a problem with test instruments, use the wiring diagram(s) to decide where to make the connections.

Voltage checks

Voltage checks should be performed if a circuit isn't functioning properly. Connect one lead of a circuit tester to either the negative battery terminal or a known good ground. Connect the other lead to a connector in the circuit being tested, preferably nearest to the battery or fuse. If the bulb of the tester lights, voltage is present, which means the part of the circuit between the connector and the battery is problem free. Continue checking the rest of the circuit in the same fashion. When you reach a point where no voltage is present, the problem lies between that point and the last test point with voltage. Most of the time the problem can be traced to a loose connection. **Note:** *Keep in mind that some circuits receive voltage only when the ignition key is in the Accessory or Run position.*

Finding a short

One method of finding a short in a circuit is to remove the fuse and connect a test light or voltmeter in its place to the fuse terminals.

There should be no voltage present in the circuit. Move the wiring harness from side-to-side while watching the test light. If the bulb lights, there's a short to ground somewhere in that area, probably where the insulation has rubbed through. The same test can be performed on each component in the circuit, even a switch.

"Short finders" are also commonly available. These reasonably priced tools connect in place of a fuse and pulse voltage through the circuit. An inductive meter (included with the kit) is then run along the wiring for the circuit. When the needle on the meter stops moving, you've found the point of the short.

Ground check

Perform a ground test to check whether a component is properly grounded. Disconnect the battery and connect one lead of a self-powered test light, known as a continuity tester, to a known good ground. Connect the other lead to the wire or ground connection being tested. If the bulb lights, the ground is good. If the bulb doesn't light, the ground is no good.

Continuity check

A continuity check is done to determine if there are breaks in a circuit - if it's capable of passing electricity properly. With the circuit off (no power in the circuit), a self-powered continuity tester can be used to check it. Connect the test leads to both ends of the circuit (or to the "power" end and a good ground) - if the test light comes on the circuit is passing current properly. If the light doesn't come on, there's a break (open) somewhere in the circuit. The same procedure can be used to test a switch by connecting the continuity tester to the switch terminals. With the switch on, the test light should come on.

Finding an open circuit

When diagnosing for possible open circuits, it's often difficult to locate them by sight because oxidation or terminal misalignment are hidden by the connectors. Merely wiggling a connector on a sensor or in the wiring harness may correct the open circuit condition. Remember this when an open is indicated when troubleshooting a circuit. Intermittent problems may also be caused by oxidized or loose connections. Electrical troubleshooting is simple if you keep in mind that all electrical circuits are basically electricity running from the battery, through the wires, switches, relays, fuses and fusible links to each electrical component (light bulb, motor, etc.) and to ground, where it's passed back to the battery. Any electrical problem is an interruption in the flow of electricity to and from the battery.

3   Fuses - general information

Refer to illustrations 3.1a, 3.1b and 3.3

The electrical circuits of the vehicle are protected by a combination of fuses, circuit breakers and fusible links. The fuse block is located in the left side of the dashboard under a cover, easily accessible by opening the driver's door **(see illustration)**. A fuse and relay block, called the Power Distribution Center (PDC) is located on the left side of the engine compartment **(see illustration)**.

Each of the fuses is designed to protect a specific circuit, and the various circuits are identified on the fuse panel itself.

Miniaturized fuses are employed in the fuse block. These compact fuses, with blade terminal design, allow fingertip removal and replacement. If an electrical component fails, always check the fuse first. A blown fuse is easily identified through the clear plastic body. Visually inspect the element for evidence of damage **(see illustration)**. If a continuity check is called for, the blade terminal tips are exposed in the fuse body.

Be sure to replace blown fuses with the correct type. Fuses of different ratings are physically interchangeable, but only fuses of the proper rating should be used. Replacing a fuse with one of a higher or lower value than specified is not recommended. Each electrical circuit needs a specific amount of protection. The amperage value of each fuse is molded into the fuse body.

3.1a The fuse block is located at the left end of the instrument panel on these models - open the driver's door and unclip the cover for easy access

3.1b The power distribution center is located in the engine compartment and contains both fuses and relays

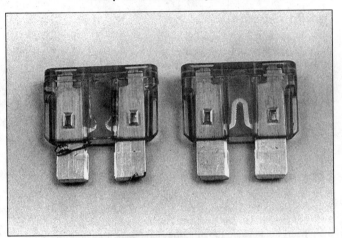

3.3 The fuses used on these models can be easily checked visually to determine if they are blown

If the replacement fuse immediately fails, don't replace it again until the cause of the problem is isolated and corrected. In most cases, the cause will be a short circuit in the wiring caused by a broken or deteriorated wire.

4   Fusible links - general information

Refer to illustration 4.2

Some circuits are protected by fusible links. The links are used in circuits which are not ordinarily fused, such as the ignition circuit.

Although the fusible links appear to be a heavier gauge than the wires they're protecting, the appearance is due to the thick insulation. All fusible links are four wire gauges smaller than the wire they're designed to protect. fusible links can't be repaired, but a new link of the same size wire can be installed. The procedure is as follows:

a) *Disconnect the negative cable from the battery.*
b) *Disconnect the fusible link from the wiring harness.*
c) *Cut the damaged fusible link out of the wire just behind the connector.*
d) *Strip the insulation back approximately 1-inch.*
e) *Spread the strands of the exposed wire apart, push them together and twist them in place* **(see illustration)**.
f) *Use rosin core and solder the wires together to obtain a good connection.*

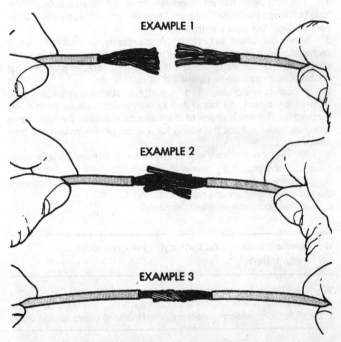

4.2 To repair a fusible link, cut out the damaged section, then join a new section by stripping the wire and twisting it together, as shown here. When securely joined, solder the connections and wrap them with electrical tape

g) *Use plenty of electrical tape around the soldered joint. No wires should be exposed.*
h) *Connect the negative battery cable. Test the circuit for proper operation.*

5   Circuit breakers - general information

Circuit breakers protect components such as power windows, power door locks and headlights. Some circuit breakers are located in the fuse box. On some models the circuit breaker resets itself automatically, so an electrical overload in the circuit will cause it to fail momentarily, then come back on. If the circuit doesn't come back on, check it immediately. Once the condition is corrected, the circuit breaker will resume its normal function. Some circuit breakers must be reset manually.

12

6   Relays - general information

Several electrical accessories in the vehicle utilize relays to transmit current to the component. If the relay is defective, the component won't operate properly. The fuse block and power distribution center, located in the engine compartment contain several relays **(see illustrations 3.1a and 3.1b)**.

If a faulty relay is suspected, it can be removed and tested by a dealer service department or a repair shop. Defective relays must be replaced as a unit.

7   Turn signal/hazard flasher - check and replacement

Refer to illustration 7.1

Warning: *These models have airbags. Always disconnect the negative battery cable and wait two minutes before working in the vicinity of the impact sensors, steering column or instrument panel to avoid the possibility of accidental deployment of the airbag, which could cause personal injury (see Section 27).*

1   The turn signal/hazard flasher is a small unit located between the fuse block and the brake pedal on a bracket under the driver's side air conditioning duct **(see illustration)**.

2   When the flasher unit is functioning properly, an audible click can be heard during its operation. If the turn signals fail on one side or the other and the flasher unit doesn't make its characteristic clicking sound, a faulty turn signal bulb is indicated.

3   If both turn signals fail to blink, the problem may be due to a blown fuse, a faulty flasher unit, a broken switch or a loose or open connection. If a quick check of the fuse box indicates the turn signal fuse has blown, check the wiring for a short before installing a new fuse.

4   To replace the flasher, simply detach it from its electrical connector and plug in the new one.

5   Make sure the replacement is identical to the original. Compare the old one to the new one before installing it.

6   Installation is the reverse of removal.

8   Ignition switch and lock cylinder - removal and installation

Warning: *These models have airbags. Always disconnect the negative battery cable and wait two minutes before working in the vicinity of the impact sensors, steering column or instrument panel to avoid the*

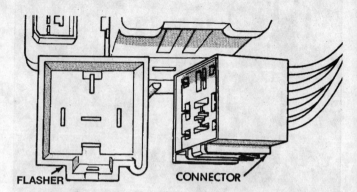

7.1 The turn signal/hazard flasher is mounted under the dash near the brake pedal

possibility of accidental deployment of the airbag, which could cause personal injury (see Section 27).

Ignition switch

Refer to illustrations 8.1 and 8.6

1   The ignition switch is located on the left side of steering column and is actuated by the key lock cylinder **(see illustration)**.

2   Disconnect the negative cable from the battery.

3   Remove the steering column cover (see Chapter 11).

4   Remove the multi-function switch (see Section 9).

5   Unplug the electrical connector, remove the screws, then detach the switch and lower it from the steering column.

6   Insert the switch and index the tab on the switch with the notch in the lock cylinder and install the screws securely **(see illustration)**.

Lock cylinder

Refer to illustration 8.10

7   Disconnect the negative cable from the battery.

8   Remove the steering column cover (see Chapter 11).

9   Insert the key and turn it to the Run position.

10   Depress the retaining pin (on some models a small screwdriver may be required) to unseat the lock cylinder, then remove the lock cylinder from the ignition switch **(see illustration)**.

11   Insert the lock cylinder in the Lock position and, while pushing the lock cylinder in, insert the key and turn it clockwise to the Run position.

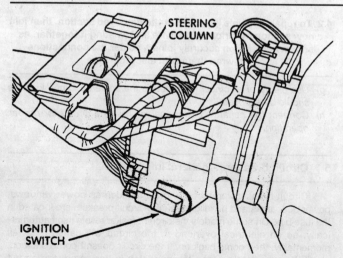

8.1 The ignition switch is located on the left side of the steering column

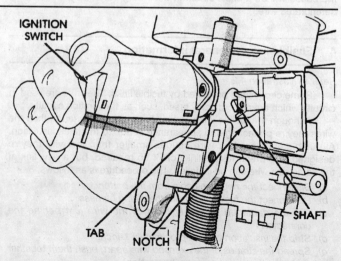

8.6 Align the ignition switch tab with the notch in the housing

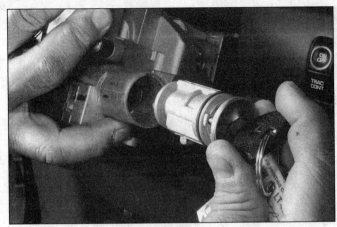

8.10 With the key in the Run position, depress the release button and pull the lock cylinder out

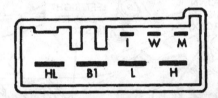

SWITCH POSITION		TERMINALS	RESISTANCE VALUE
OFF		PIN I to M	OPEN ≥ 300 K OHMS
DELAY LEVEL	1	PIN I to M	9.72 K OHMS
	2	PIN I to M	8.22 K OHMS
	3	PIN I to M	6.61 K OHMS
	4	PIN I to M	5.12 K OHMS
	5	PIN I to M	3.67 K OHMS
	6	PIN I to M	2.22 K OHMS
LOW		PIN I to M	1.02 K OHMS
HIGH		PIN I to M	0.51 K OHMS
WASH		PIN I to W	OPEN
RESISTANCE AT MAXIMUM DELAY POSITION SHOULD BE			9,720 OHMS
RESISTANCE AT MINIMUM DELAY POSITION SHOULD BE			2,220 OHMS

9.4a Wiper/washer switch terminal details

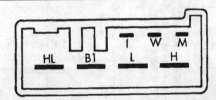

SWITCH POSITION	CONTINUITY BETWEEN
LOW BEAM	HL and L
HIGH BEAM	HL and H
OPTICAL HORN	B1 and H

9.4b Headlight dimmer switch continuity check details - the switch must be in the indicated position for each check

9 Multi-function switch - check and replacement

Warning: *These models have airbags. Always disconnect the negative battery cable and wait two minutes before working in the vicinity of the impact sensors, steering column or instrument panel to avoid the possibility of accidental deployment of the airbag, which could cause personal injury (see Section 27).*

1   The multi-function switch is located on the left side of the steering column. It incorporates the turn signal, headlight dimmer and windshield wiper/washer functions into one switch.
2   Remove the steering column cover (see Chapter 11).
3   Unplug the electrical connector(s).

Check

Refer to illustrations 9.4a, 9.4b and 9.4c

4   Use an ohmmeter or self-powered test light and the accompanying diagrams to check for continuity between the switch terminals with the switch in each position **(see illustrations)**.

Replacement

5   Remove the bolts, then detach the switch from the steering column.
6   Installation is the reverse of removal.

10 Headlight bulb - replacement

Refer to illustrations 10.4a, 10.4b and 10.5
Warning: *Halogen bulbs are gas-filled and under pressure and may shatter if the surface is scratched or the bulb is dropped. Wear eye protection and handle the bulbs carefully, grasping only the base whenever possible. Don't touch the surface of the bulb with your fingers because the oil from your skin could cause it to overheat and fail prematurely. If you do touch the bulb surface, clean it with rubbing alcohol.*

1   Open the hood. On some models it will be necessary to remove the radiator closure panel sight shield for access (see Chapter 11, Section 12).
2   Disconnect the negative cable from the battery.
3   Remove the headlight housing (see Section 12)

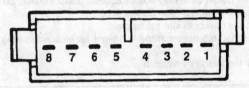

SWITCH POSITION		CONTINUITY BETWEEN
TURN SIGNAL	HAZARD WARNING	
NEUTRAL	OFF	1 and 3
LEFT	OFF	7 and 6
RIGHT	OFF	7 and 8
NEUTRAL	ON	2 and 3 7 and 8 7 and 6 4 and 5

9.4c Turn signal and hazard flasher continuity check details

12

10.4a Unscrew the plastic collar . . .

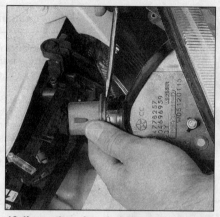
10.4b . . . then detach the bulb holder and pull it out of the housing

10.5 Pull the bulb out of the holder

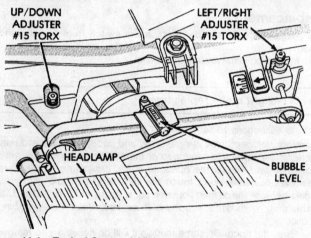
11.1a Typical Concord, Vision and Intrepid model bubble indicator and adjustment details

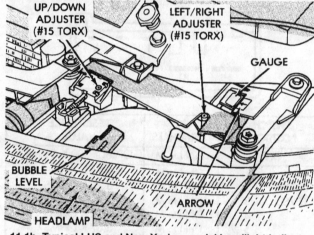
11.1b Typical LHS and New Yorker model headlight indicator and adjuster layout

4   Unscrew the bulb retaining ring and detach the holder **(see illustrations)**.
5   Pull the holder assembly out for access, grasp the bulb base and unplug it from the holder **(see illustration)**.
6   Insert the new bulb into the holder.
7   Install the bulb holder in the headlight assembly and plug in the connector.
8   Install the headlight assembly.

11   Headlights - adjustment

Refer to illustrations 11.1a, 11.1b, 11.3 and 11.5
Warning: *The headlights must be aimed correctly. If adjusted incorrectly, they could temporarily blind the driver of an oncoming vehicle and cause an accident or seriously reduce your ability to see the road. The headlights should be checked for proper aim every 12 months and any time a new headlight housing is installed or front end body work is performed.*
1   The headlights on these models feature integral vertical and horizontal adjustment indicators with Torx-head adjusting screws that allow the owner to check and adjust headlight alignment **(see illustrations)**.
2   Adjustment should be made with the vehicle sitting level, the gas tank full and a normal load in the vehicle.
3   Open the hood and check the vertical bubble indicator to make sure the bubble is centered over the "0" (yellow) area of the indicator **(see illustration)**.
4   If necessary, center the bubble by turning the up-and-down

(vertical) adjusting screw. **Note:** *Do not turn the calibration screw on the indicator itself.*
5   Check the arrow on the horizontal indicator decal to make sure the arrow is pointing at the "0" **(see illustration)**. Turn the right-and-left (horizontal) adjusting screw to adjust if necessary.
6   If you have any problems achieving proper adjustment, take the vehicle to have the headlights checked by a dealer service department or service station as soon as possible.

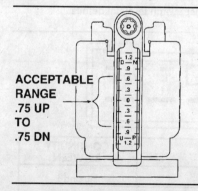
ACCEPTABLE RANGE .75 UP TO .75 DN

11.3 Keep the vertical adjustment bubble in the acceptable range

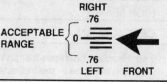
11.5 Horizontal adjustment acceptable range

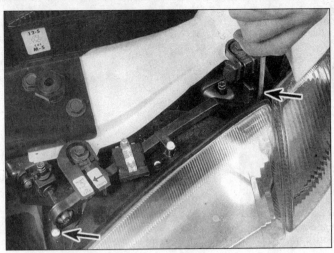

12.3a Remove the two Torx-head screws (arrows) . . .

12.3b . . . then pull the housing out and unplug the bulb connector

12   Headlight housing removal and installation

Refer to illustrations 12.3a and 12.3b
Warning: *These models have airbags. Always disconnect the negative battery cable and wait two minutes before working in the vicinity of the impact sensors, steering column or instrument panel to avoid the possibility of accidental deployment of the airbag, which could cause personal injury (see Section 27).*
1   Open the hood.
2   On some models it will be necessary to remove the radiator closure panel sight shield for access (see Chapter 11, Section 12).
3   Remove the retaining screws, pull the housing out and unplug the electrical connector **(see illustrations)**.
4   Installation is the reverse of removal. After you're done, check the headlight adjustment (see Section 11).

13   Bulb replacement

Front parking/side marker/turn signal light
Refer to illustrations 13.1a, 13.1b, 13.2 and 13.3
1   Open the hood, press the release clip that retains the parking/marker light housing, then pull the housing straight forward **(see illustrations)**.
2   Turn the bulb holder counterclockwise and pull it out of the housing **(see illustration)**.

13.1a Detach the clip (arrow) . . .

3   Squeeze the clips and pull the bulb out of the holder **(see illustration)**.
4   Installation is the reverse of removal.

Fog light
Refer to illustrations 13.5, 13.6, 13.7a and 13.7b
5   Remove the two Phillips head retaining screws and lower the

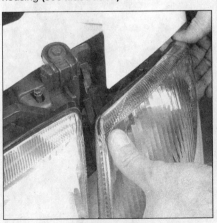

13.1b . . . then remove the housing by pulling it forward

13.2 Turn the bulb holder counterclockwise and pull it straight out of the housing

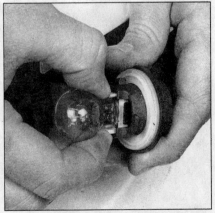

13.3 Squeeze the clips and remove the bulb

12

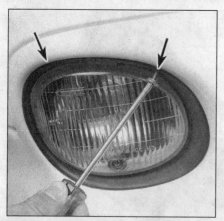

13.5 Remove the two screws (arrows) and pull the fog light housing out

13.6 Detach the clips and remove the back of the housing

13.7a Squeeze the spring clips and remove the bulb holder

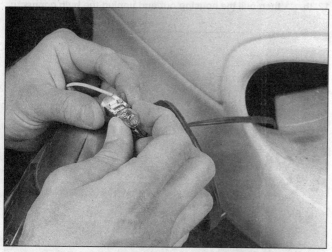

13.7b The bulb pulls straight out of the holder

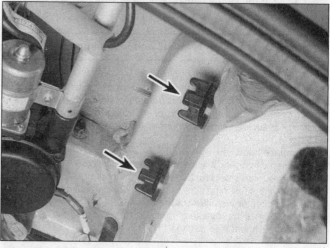

13.9a Unscrew the plastic nuts (arrows) . . .

housing out for access to the bulb holder (see illustration).
6   Release the clips and detach the housing cover (see illustration).
7   Detach the bulb holder clip, pull the bulb from the housing, then pull the bulb straight out (see illustrations).
8   Installation is the reverse of removal.

Tail light bulb

Refer to illustrations 13.9a, 13.9b, 13.10 and 13.11
9   Open the trunk, remove the plastic nuts and rotate the housing out for access to the bulb holders (see illustrations).
10   Rotate the holder counterclockwise and pull it straight out (see illustration).

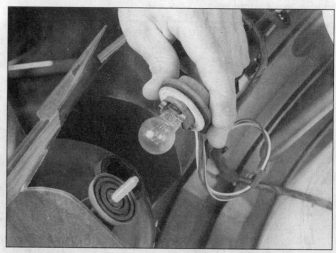

13.9b . . . and remove the taillight housing for access to the bulbs

13.10 Rotate the bulb holder counterclockwise to remove it

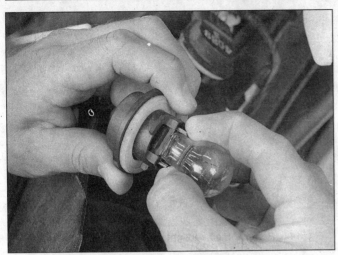

13.11 Squeeze the tabs and pull the bulb out of the holder

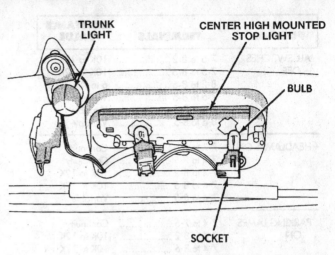

13.13 Typical high-mounted brake light details
(except CP and CH models)

11   Remove the bulb, squeezing the clips and pulling it straight out **(see illustration)**
12   Installation is the reverse of removal.

Center high-mounted brake light

All models except CP and CH

Refer to illustration 13.13
13   Open the trunk, reach under the rear parcel panel and remove the bulb socket assemblies from the center high-mounted brake light housing **(see illustration)**.
14   Pull the bulb straight out of the socket and install the new one.
15   Installation is the reverse of removal.

CP and CH models

Refer to illustration 13.18
16   Open the trunk and unplug the brake light electrical connector.
17   Remove the upper rear deck panel.
18   Remove the brake light housing retaining screws and detach the housing **(see illustration)**.
19   Pull the bulb straight out of the holder.
20   Installation is the reverse of removal.

Rear side marker light (CP and CH models only)

21   Reach up behind the rear bumper fascia and remove the bulb holder by rotating it counterclockwise.
22   Pull the bulb straight out of the holder.
23   Installation is the reverse of removal.

Instrument panel lights

24   To gain access to the instrument panel lights, the instrument cluster will have to be removed first (see Section 20).
25   Rotate the bulb holder counterclockwise and remove it from the instrument cluster.
26   Pull the bulb straight out of the holder.
27   Installation is the reverse of removal.

License plate lights

Refer to illustration 13.28
28   Remove the two screws and pull out the lamp assembly **(see illustration)**.
29   Remove the bulb holder.
30   Pull the bulb straight out of the holder.
31   Installation is the reverse of removal.

14   Headlight switch - check and replacement

Warning: *These models have airbags. Always disconnect the negative battery cable and wait two minutes before working in the vicinity of the impact sensors, steering column or instrument panel to avoid the possibility of accidental deployment of the airbag, which could cause personal injury (see Section 27).*
1   Disconnect the negative battery cable.
2   Remove the headlight switch (see Steps 4 through 6 below).

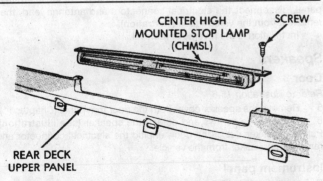

13.18 CP and CH model high-mounted brake light details

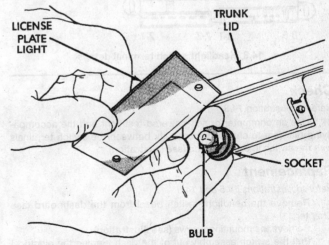

13.28 License plate light bulb replacement details

12

POSITION	TERMINALS	RESISTANCE VALUE
ALL SWITCHES OFF	7-5 to 8-2	10K to 12K
	7-5 to 8-6	10K to 12K
	8-2 to 8-6	6 to 7
	7-5 to 8-5	Variable
	8-2 to 8-5	Variable
	8-6 to 8-5	Variable
HEADLAMPS ON	7-7 to 7-6	Continuity
	7-4 to 7-5	Continuity
	7-4 to 8-2	10K to 12K
	7-4 to 8-6	10K to 12K
	7-4 to 8-5	Variable
PARKING LAMPS ON	7-4 to 7-5	Continuity
	7-4 to 8-2	10K to 12K
	7-4 to 8-6	10K to 12K
	7-4 to 8-5	Variable
THUMBWHEEL- DIM POSITION	7-5 to 8-5	Continuity
	8-2 to 8-5	10K to 12K
	8-6 to 8-5	10K to 12K
THUMBWHEEL- BRIGHT POSITION	7-5 to 8-5	10K to 12K
	8-2 to 8-5	900 to 1.1K
	8-6 to 8-5	900 to 1.1K
THUMBWHEEL- DOME LAMPS POSITION	7-5 to 8-5	10K to 12K
	8-2 to 8-5	900 to 1.1K
	8-6 to 8-5	900 to 1.1K
	8-2 to 8-5	Continuity
	8-2 to 8-3	Continuity
FRONT FOG LAMPS ON	7-7 to 7-6	Continuity
	7-4 to 7-5	Continuity
	7-4 to 8-2	10K to 12K
	7-4 to 8-6	10K to 12K
	7-4 to 8-5	Variable
	7-1 to 7-2	Continuity
	8-2 to 7-1	Continuity
	8-6 to 7-1	6 to 7
	8-5 to 7-1	Variable

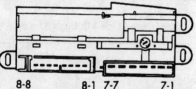

8-8   8-1 7-7   7-1

14.3 Headlight switch terminal details

Check

Refer to illustration 14.3

3   Use an ohmmeter or self-powered test light and the accompanying diagram to check for continuity between the switch terminals with the switch in each position **(see illustration)**.

Replacement

Refer to illustrations 14.5 and 14.6

4   Remove the headlight switch bezel from the dashboard (see Chapter 11).
5   Remove the mounting screws **(see illustration)**.
6   Pull the switch assembly out of the dash, unplug the electrical connector and remove the switch **(see illustration)**.
7   Installation is the reverse of removal.

14.5 Remove the headlight switch mounting screws

14.6 Pull the switch out and unplug it

15   Radio and speakers - removal and installation

Refer to illustration 15.3
Warning: *These models have airbags. Always disconnect the negative battery cable and wait two minutes before working in the vicinity of the impact sensors, steering column or instrument panel to avoid the possibility of accidental deployment of the airbag, which could cause personal injury (see Section 27).*

Radio

1   Disconnect the negative battery cable from the battery.
2   Remove the dashboard lower center bezel (Chapter 11).
3   Remove the mounting screws, pull the radio out of the instrument panel, disconnect the electrical connectors and antenna lead, then remove it from the vehicle **(see illustration)**.
4   Installation is the reverse of removal.

Speakers

Door

Refer to illustration 15.6
5   Remove the speaker cover from the door trim panel (Chapter 11).
6   Remove the screws and detach the speaker **(see illustration)**. Pull the speaker out of the door, unplug the electrical connector and remove the speaker from the vehicle.

Instrument panel

Refer to illustration 15.7
7   Remove the instrument panel top cover by prying and detaching

15.3 A unique type of anti-theft screw (arrow) is used to secure the radio on these models - a special tool, available from Chrysler, is required

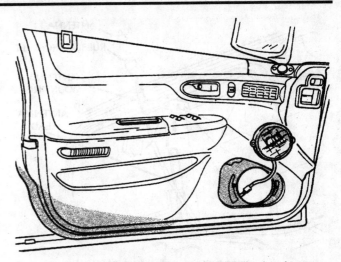

15.6 The speakers are held in place by two Phillips head screws - after removing the screws, pull the speaker out and disconnect the electrical connector

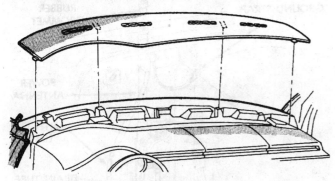

15.7 Detach the instrument panel cover clips at the points shown for access to the speakers

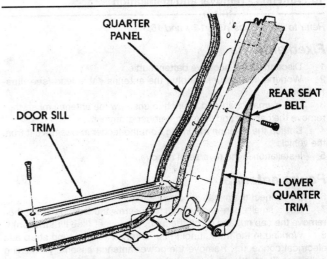

15.10a Remove the door sill quarter trim . . .

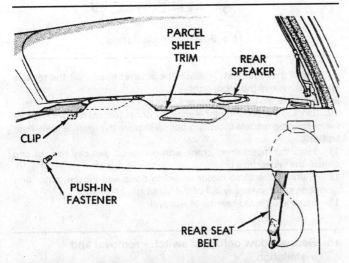

15.10b . . . then detach the parcel shelf trim for access to the rear speakers

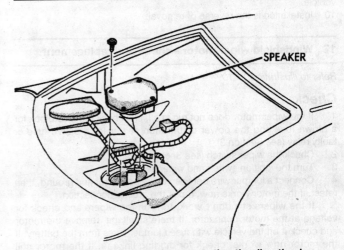

15.11 Lift the rear speaker out, noting the direction in which the connector faces

the clips at each end. Next, lift the rear edge and disengage the clips along the front edge **(see illustration)**.

8   Remove the screws, lift the speaker up, then unplug the electrical connector and remove the speaker from the vehicle.

Rear speakers

Refer to illustrations 15.10a, 15.10b and 15.11

9   Open the trunk and unplug the electrical connectors.
10   Remove the rear parcel shelf trim panel **(see illustrations)**.

11   Remove the screws and detach the speaker **(see illustration)**.
12   Installation is the reverse of removal, making sure that the wire connectors face forward.

12

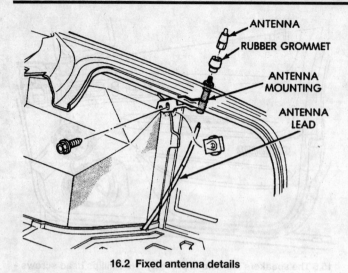

16.2 Fixed antenna details

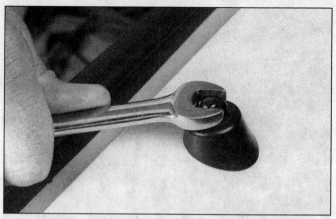

16.7 Unscrew the antenna nut with a small wrench (power antenna shown)

16 Antenna - removal and installation

Refer to illustrations 16.2, 16.7 and 16.8

Fixed antenna

1   Disconnect the negative battery cable.
2   Working in the trunk, unplug the antenna cable lead **(see illustration)**.
3   Use a small open-end wrench to unscrew the antenna mast, then remove the cap nut and lift off the rubber grommet.
4   Detach the antenna mounting from the fender and remove it from the vehicle.
5   Installation is the reverse of removal.

Power antenna

6   Disconnect the negative battery cable.
7   Use a small open-end wrench to unscrew the antenna mast, then remove the cap nut and lift off the rubber grommet **(see illustration)**.
8   Working in the trunk, unplug the antenna lead, ground strap and electrical connector. Remove the power antenna assembly retaining bolts **(see illustration)**.
9   Detach the antenna from the fender and remove it from the vehicle.
10   Installation is the reverse of removal.

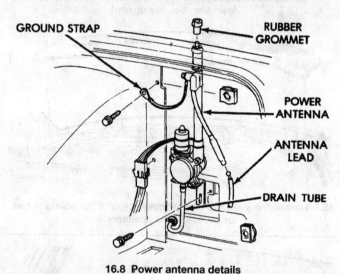

16.8 Power antenna details

17 Windshield wiper motor - check and replacement

Refer to illustration 17.10

Check

1   If the wiper motor does not run at all, first check the fuse block for a blown fuse and the power distribution center for a blown fuse or faulty relay (see Section 3).
2   Check the wiper switch (see Section 9).
3   Turn the ignition switch and wiper switch on.
4   Connect a jumper wire between the wiper motor and ground, then retest. If the motor works now, repair the ground connection.
5   If the wipers still don't work, turn on the wipers and check for voltage at the motor connector. If there's voltage, remove the motor and check it off the vehicle with fused jumper wires from the battery. If the motor now works, check for binding linkage. If the motor still doesn't work, replace it.
6   If there's no voltage at the motor, the problem is in the switch or wiring.

Replacement

7   Disconnect the negative cable from the battery.

8   Mark their locations, detach the washer hoses, lift the release lever and remove the wiper arms.
9   Remove the cowl cover (see Chapter 11).
10   Unplug the wiper motor electrical connector and remove the four wiper housing module mounting bolts. Remove the module **(see illustration)**.
11   Hold the motor drive crank with a wrench, remove the nut and detach the wiper drive link.
12   Remove the three motor retaining bolts and lift the motor and mounting plate assembly out of the housing.
13   Installation is the reverse of removal.

18 Rear window defogger switch - removal and installation

Warning: *These models have airbags. Always disconnect the negative battery cable and wait two minutes before working in the vicinity of the impact sensors, steering column or instrument panel to avoid the possibility of accidental deployment of the airbag, which could cause personal injury (see Section 27).*
1   The defogger switch is part of the heater and air conditioning system control switch.
2   Remove the dashboard lower center bezel (see Chapter 11).
3   Remove the screws, detach the switch assembly, unplug the electrical connector and remove the assembly from the panel.
4   Installation is the reverse of removal.

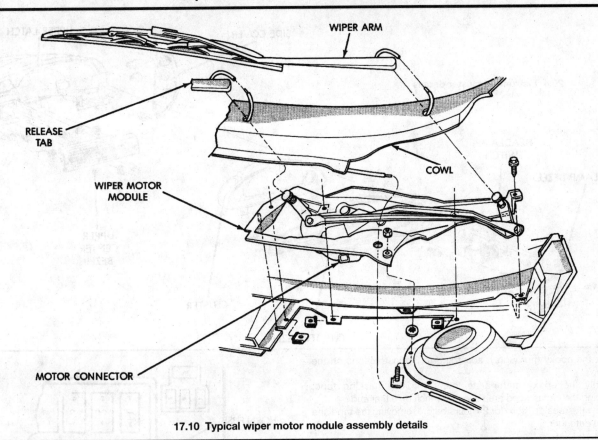

17.10 Typical wiper motor module assembly details

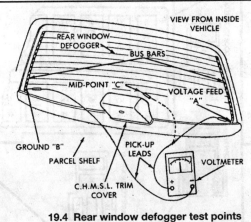

19.4 Rear window defogger test points

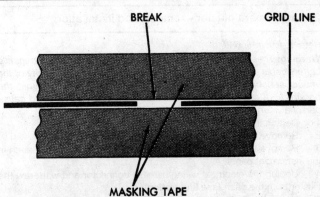

19.13 To repair a broken grid, first apply a strip of tape to either side of the grid to mask off the area

19   Rear window defogger - check and repair

Refer to illustrations 19.4 and 19.13

1   The rear window defogger consists of a number of horizontal elements baked onto the glass surface.

2   Small breaks in the element can be repaired without removing the rear window.

Check

3   Turn the ignition switch and defogger system switches On.

4   Ground the negative lead of a voltmeter to terminal B and the positive lead to terminal A **(see illustration)**.

5   The voltmeter should read between 10 and 15 volts. If the reading is lower, there is a poor ground connection.

6   Contact the negative lead to a good body ground. The reading should stay the same.

7   Connect the negative lead to terminal B, then touch each grid line

at the mid-point with the positive lead.

8   The reading should be approximately six volts. If the reading is 0, there is a break between mid-point "C" and terminal "A".

9   A 10 to 14 volt reading is an indication of a break between mid-point "C". Move the lead toward the break; the voltage will change when the break is crossed.

Repair

10   Repair the break in the line using repair kit recommended specifically for this purpose, such as Mopar Repair Kit No. 4267922 (or equivalent). Included in this kit is plastic conductive epoxy.

11   Prior to repairing a break, turn off the system and allow it to de-energize for a few minutes.

12   Lightly buff the element area with fine steel wool, then clean it thoroughly with rubbing alcohol.

13   Use masking tape to mask off the area of repair **(see illustration)**.

12

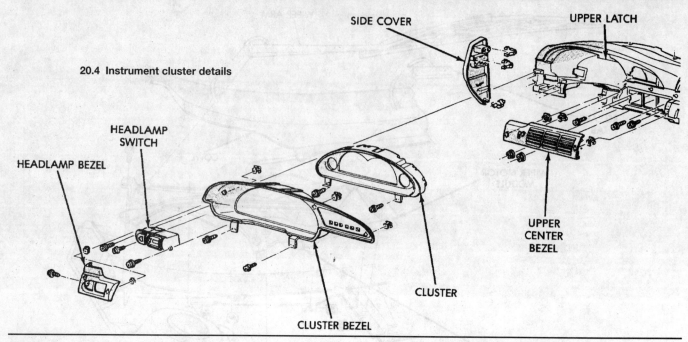

20.4 Instrument cluster details

14   Mix the epoxy thoroughly, according to the instructions on the package.
15   Apply the epoxy material to the slit in the masking tape, overlapping the undamaged area about 3/4-inch on either end.
16   Allow the repair to cure for 24 hours before removing the tape and using the defogger.

20 Instrument cluster - removal and installation

Refer to illustration 20.4

Warning: *These models have airbags. Always disconnect the negative battery cable and wait two minutes before working in the vicinity of the impact sensors, steering column or instrument panel to avoid the possibility of accidental deployment of the airbag, which could cause personal injury (see Section 27).*

1   Detach the cable from the negative battery terminal.
2   Remove instrument cluster bezel (see Chapter 11).
3   Remove the bolts and detach the cluster from the upper latch in the instrument panel.
4   Unplug the electrical wiring harness connector and withdraw the cluster from the dash **(see illustration)**.
5   Installation is the reverse of removal.

21 Horn - check and replacement

Refer to illustrations 21.1, 21.2 and 21.4

Warning: *These models have airbags. Always disconnect the negative battery cable and wait two minutes before working in the vicinity of the impact sensors, steering column or instrument panel to avoid the possibility of accidental deployment of the airbag, which could cause personal injury (see Section 27).*

Check

1   If the horns do not sound, check the horn fuse in the fuse block located in the end of the instrument panel **(see illustration)**. If the fuse is blown, replace it and retest. If it blows again, there is a short circuit in the horn or wiring between the horn and fuse block.
2   If the fuse is good, remove the horn relay and use an ohmmeter to check for continuity between ground and terminal 12 of the fuse block **(see illustration)**. There should be continuity only when the horn is depressed. If this isn't the case there is a problem with the horn switch or wiring.

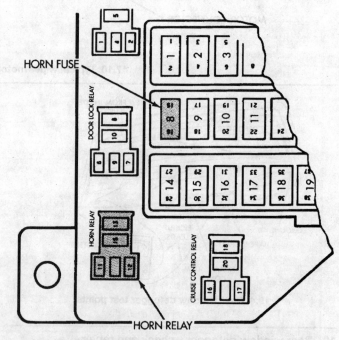

21.1 The horn fuse and relay are located in the fuse block

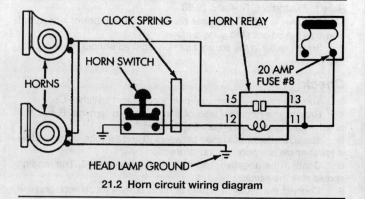

21.2 Horn circuit wiring diagram

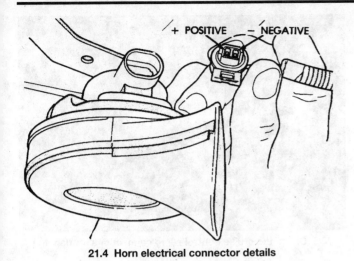

21.4 Horn electrical connector details

3   Connect a jumper wire between terminals 13 and 15 of the fuse block. If the horn sounds, the relay is faulty. Replace it.
4   To test the horn, unplug the electrical connector. Connect one lead of a voltmeter to ground and the other to the positive terminal **(see illustration)**. If no voltage is present, there is a fault in the wiring. If there is voltage, use an ohmmeter to check for continuity to ground. If there is continuity and the horn still doesn't sound, it is faulty.

Replacement

5   Unplug the electrical connector and remove the bracket bolt.
6   Installation is the reverse of removal.

22   Electric rear view mirrors - description and check

Refer to illustration 22.7
1   Electric rear view mirrors use two motors to move the glass; one for up-and-down adjustments and one for left-to-right adjustments.
2   The control switch has a selector portion which sends voltage to the left or right side mirror. With the ignition ON but the engine OFF, roll down the windows and operate the mirror control switch through all functions (left-right and up-down) for both the left and right side mirrors.
3   Listen carefully for the sound of the electric motors running in the mirrors.
4   If the motors can be heard but the mirror glass doesn't move, there's probably a problem with the drive mechanism inside the mirror. Remove and disassemble the mirror to locate the problem.
5   If the mirrors don't operate and no sound comes from the mirrors, check the fuse (see Section 3).
6   If the fuse is OK, remove the mirror control switch from its mounting without disconnecting the wires attached to it. Turn the ignition ON and check for voltage at the switch. There should be voltage at one terminal. If there's no voltage at the switch, check for an open or short in the wiring between the fuse panel and the switch.
7   If there's voltage at the switch, disconnect it. Check the switch for continuity in all its operating positions **(see illustration)**. If the switch does not have continuity, replace it.
8   Reconnect the switch. Locate the wire going from the switch to ground. Leaving the switch connected, connect a jumper wire between this wire and ground. If the mirror works normally with this wire in place, repair the faulty ground connection.
9   If the mirror still doesn't work, remove the cover and check the wires at the mirror for voltage with a test light. Check with ignition ON and the mirror selector switch on the appropriate side. Operate the mirror switch in all its positions. There should be voltage at one of the switch-to-mirror wires in each switch position (except the neutral "off" position).
10   If there's not voltage in each switch position, check the wiring

SWITCH POSITION Move Button	CONTINUITY BETWEEN TERMINALS
Mirror in L Position	
▲	PIN 8 to 10 PIN 7 to 4
▶	PIN 2 to 8 PIN 10 to 4
▼	PIN 8 to 7 PIN 10 to 4
◀	PIN 8 to 10 PIN 3 to 4
Mirror in R Position	
▲	PIN 8 to 1 PIN 2 to 4
▶	PIN 3 to 8 PIN 1 to 4
▼	PIN 8 to 2 PIN 1 to 4
◀	PIN 1 to 8 PIN 9 to 4

22.7 Electric mirror switch continuity check details

between the mirror and control switch for opens and shorts.
11   If there's voltage, remove the mirror and test it off the vehicle with jumper wires. Replace the mirror if it fails this test (see Chapter 11).

23   Cruise control system - description and check

Refer to illustration 23.5
1   The cruise control system maintains vehicle speed with a vacuum-actuated servo motor located in the engine compartment, which is connected to the throttle linkage by a cable. The system consists of the electronic Powertrain Control Module (PCM), brake switch, control switches, a relay, the vehicle speed sensor and associated wiring. Listed below are some general procedures that may be used to locate common cruise control problems.
2   Locate and check the fuse (see Section 3). Also check the vacuum hose to the cruise control servo to make sure it's not plugged, cracked or soft (which will cause it to collapse in operation. With the engine off, check the servo by applying vacuum (with a hand vacuum pump) to the vacuum fitting on the servo - the servo should move the throttle linkage if it's working properly.
3   Have an assistant operate the brake lights while you check their operation (voltage from the brake light switch deactivates the cruise control).
4   If the brake lights don't come on or don't shut off, correct the problem and retest the cruise control.
5   Inspect the cable linkage between the cruise control servo and the throttle linkage. The cruise control servo is located on the left (driver's) side of the vehicle **(see illustration)**.
6   Visually inspect the wires connected to the cruise control servo and check for damage and broken wires.
7   Cruise controls use a variety of speed sensing devices. On these models the speed sensor pickup is located in the transaxle. Refer to Chapter 6 for information on checking this sensor.
8   Test drive the vehicle to determine if the cruise control is now working. If it isn't, take it to a dealer service department or an automotive electrical specialist for further diagnosis and repair.

12

24 Power door lock system - description and check

Refer to illustration 24.5

1   Power door lock systems are operated by bi-directional solenoids located in the doors. The lock switches have two operating positions: Lock and Unlock. These switches activate a relay which in turn connects voltage to the door lock solenoids. Depending on which way the relay is activated, it reverses polarity, allowing the two sides of the circuit to be used alternately as the feed (positive) and ground side.

2   Always check the circuit protection first. These vehicles use a combination of circuit breakers and fuses.

3   Operate the door lock switches in both directions (Lock and Unlock) with the engine off. Listen for the faint click of the relay operating.

4   If there's no click, check for voltage at the switches. If no voltage is present, check the wiring between the fuse panel and the switches for shorts and opens.

5   If voltage is present but no click is heard, test the switch for continuity **(see illustration)**. Replace it if there's not continuity in both switch positions.

6   If the switch has continuity but the relay doesn't click, check the wiring between the switch and relay for continuity. Repair the wiring if there's no continuity.

7   If the relay is receiving voltage from the switch but is not sending voltage to the solenoids, check for a bad ground at the relay case. If the relay case is grounding properly, replace the relay.

8   If all but one lock solenoid operates, remove the trim panel from the affected door (see Chapter 11) and check for voltage at the solenoid while the lock switch is operated. One of the wires should have voltage in the Lock position; the other should have voltage in the unlock position.

9   If the inoperative solenoid is receiving voltage, replace the solenoid.

10   If the inoperative solenoid isn't receiving voltage, check for an open or short in the wire between the lock solenoid and the relay.

Note: *It's common for wires to break in the portion of the harness between the body and door (opening and closing the door fatigues and eventually breaks the wires).*

25 Power window system - description and check

Refer to illustration 25.9

1   The power window system consists of the control switches, the motors, glass mechanisms (regulators), and associated wiring.

2   Power windows are wired so they can be lowered and raised from the master control switch by the driver or by remote switches located at the individual windows. Each window has a separate motor which is reversible. The position of the control switch determines the polarity and therefore the direction of operation. The system is equipped with a relay that controls current flow to the motors.

3   The power window system operates when the ignition switch is ON. In addition, these models have a window lockout switch at the master control switch which, when activated, disables the switches at the rear windows. Always check these items before troubleshooting a window problem.

4   These procedures are general in nature, so if you can't find the problem using them, take the vehicle to a dealer service department or other qualified repair shop.

5   If the power windows don't work at all, check the fuse or circuit breaker.

6   If only the rear windows are inoperative, or if the windows only operate from the master control switch, check the rear window lockout switch for continuity in the unlocked position. Replace it if it doesn't have continuity.

7   Check the wiring between the switches and fuse panel for continuity. Repair the wiring, if necessary.

8   If only one window is inoperative from the master control switch, try the other control switch at the window. **Note:** *This doesn't apply to the drivers door window.*

9   If the same window works from one switch, but not the other,

23.5 Check the cruise control servo connections for damage

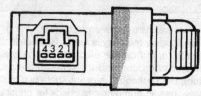

SWITCH POSITION	CONTINUITY BETWEEN	RESISTANCE VALUE
UNLOCK	1 and 4	2700 Ω ± 10%
LOCK	1 and 4	620 Ω ± 10%

24.5 Door lock switch continuity check details - the switch must be in the indicated position for each check

check the switch for continuity **(see illustration)**.

10   If the switch tests OK, check for a short or open in the wiring between the affected switch and the window motor.

11   If one window is inoperative from both switches, remove the trim panel from the affected door (see Chapter 11) and check for voltage at the motor while the switch is operated.

12   If voltage is reaching the motor, disconnect the glass from the regulator (see Chapter 11). Move the window up and down by hand while checking for binding and damage. Also check for binding and damage to the regulator. If the regulator is not damaged and the window moves up and down smoothly, replace the motor (see Chapter 11). If there's binding or damage, lubricate, repair or replace parts, as necessary.

13   If voltage isn't reaching the motor, check the wiring in the circuit for continuity between the switches and motors. Check that the relay is grounded properly and receiving voltage from the switches. Also check that the relay sends voltage to the motor when the switch is turned on. If it doesn't, replace the relay.

14   Test the windows after you are done to confirm proper repairs.

26 Power seats - description and check

Refer to illustration 26.8

1   Power seats allow you to adjust the position of the seat with little effort. The optional power seats on these models adjust forward and backward, up and down, tilt forward and backward and recline up and down.

2   The power seat system consists of a motor, a switch on the seat and a relay and fuse in the engine compartment fuse block.

3   Look under the seat for any objects which may be preventing the seat from moving.

4   If the seat won't work at all, check the fuse.

SWITCH POSITION		CONTINUITY BETWEEN TERMINALS
OFF		PIN 8 to 10
		PIN 8 to 11
		PIN 8 to 7
		PIN 8 to 6
		PIN 8 to 3
		PIN 8 to 4
		PIN 8 to 9
		PIN 8 to 2
UP	DRIVER'S	PIN 8 to 10
		PIN 5 to 11
UP	RIGHT FRONT	PIN 8 to 7
		PIN 5 to 6
UP	LEFT REAR	PIN 8 to 3
		PIN 5 to 4
UP	RIGHT REAR	PIN 8 to 9
		PIN 5 to 2
DOWN	DRIVER'S	PIN 8 to 11
		PIN 5 to 10
DOWN	RIGHT FRONT	PIN 8 to 6
		PIN 5 to 7
DOWN	LEFT REAR	PIN 8 to 4
		PIN 5 to 3
DOWN	RIGHT REAR	PIN 8 to 2
		PIN 5 to 9
WINDOW LOCK		PIN 5 to 1

SWITCH POSITION	CONTINUITY BETWEEN PINS	
	DRIVER	PASSENGER
OFF	PIN 8 to 10	PIN 8 to 0
	PIN 8 to 11	PIN 8 to 11
	PIN 8 to 7	PIN 8 to 11
	PIN 8 to 6	PIN 8 to 6
	PIN 8 to 3	PIN 8 to 3
	PIN 8 to 4	PIN 8 to 4
	PIN 8 to 9	PIN 8 to 9
	PIN 8 to 2	PIN 8 to 2
FRONT RISER UP	PIN 8 to 10	PIN 8 to 10
	PIN 5 to 11	PIN 5 to 11
FRONT RISER DOWN	PIN 8 to 7	PIN 8 to 7
	PIN 5 to 6	PIN 5 to 6
CENTER SWITCH FORWARD	PIN 8 to 3	PIN 8 to 3
	PIN 5 to 4	PIN 5 to 4
CENTER SWITCH REARWARD	PIN 8 to 9	PIN 8 to 9
	PIN 5 to 2	PIN 5 to 2
REAR RISER UP	PIN 8 to 11	PIN 8 to 11
	PIN 5 to 10	PIN 5 to 10
REAR RISER DOWN	PIN 8 to 6	PIN 8 to 6
	PIN 5 to 7	PIN 5 to 7
RECLINER UP	PIN 8 to 4	PIN 8 to 4
	PIN 5 to 3	PIN 5 to 3
RECLINER DOWN	PIN 8 to 2	PIN 8 to 2
	PIN 5 to 9	PIN 5 to 9

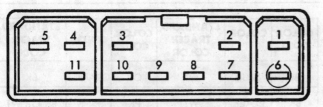

25.9 Continuity check details for the power window master control switch

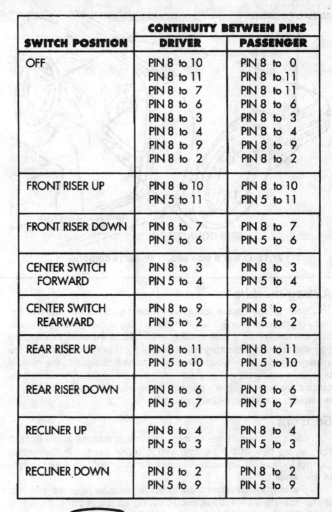

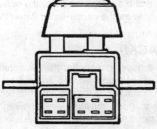

26.8 Power seat switch continuity check details

5   With the engine off to reduce the noise level, operate the seat controls in all directions and listen for sound coming from the seat motor(s).

6   If the motor runs or clicks but the seat doesn't move, the integral seat drive mechanism is damaged and the motor assembly must be replaced.

7   If the motor doesn't work or make noise, check for voltage at the motor while an assistant operates the switch. If it still doesn't work, replace it.

8   If the motor isn't getting voltage, check for voltage at the switch. If there's no voltage at the switch, check the wiring between the fuse panel and the switch. If there's voltage at the switch, check the switch for continuity in all its operating positions **(see illustration)**. Replace the switch if there's no continuity.

9   If the switch is OK, check for a short or open in the wiring between the switch and motor. If there's a relay between the switch and motor, check that it's grounded properly and there's voltage to the relay. Also check that there's voltage going from the relay to the motor when the when the switch is operated. If there's not, and the relay is grounded properly, replace the relay.

10   Test the completed repairs.

27 Airbag system - general information

Refer to illustrations 27.1a and 27.1b

These models are equipped with a Supplemental Restraint System (SRS), more commonly called an airbag system. This system is designed to protect the driver and front seat passenger from serious injury in the event of head-on or frontal collision. It consists of airbag modules in the center of the steering wheel and the right side of the dashboard, two crash sensors mounted at the front of the vehicle and an Airbag Control Module (ACM), mounted in the passenger compartment, which contains a safing sensor **(see illustrations)**.

12

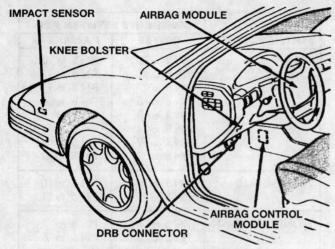

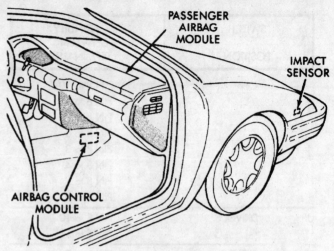

27.1a Driver's side airbag system components

27.1b Passenger's side airbag system components

Airbag module

Each airbag module contains a housing incorporating the cushion (airbag) and inflator unit. The inflator assembly is mounted on the back of the housing over a hole through which gas is expelled, inflating the bag almost instantaneously when an electrical signal is sent from the system. The specially wound wire that carries this signal to the module is called a clockspring. The clockspring is a flat, ribbon-like electrically conductive tape which is wound so it can transmit an electrical signal regardless of steering wheel position.

Sensors

The system has three sensors: two crash sensors at the front of the vehicle behind the bumper and a safing sensor in the Airbag Control Module (ACM) located under the instrument panel, just in front of the center console.

The front crash sensors are basically pressure sensitive switches that complete an electrical circuit during an impact of sufficient G force. The electrical signal from the crash sensors is sent to the safing sensor in the ACM, which then completes the circuit and inflates the airbags.

Airbag Control Module (ACM)

The ACM contains the safing sensor, a capacitor that maintains electrical system power if the battery is damaged and an on-board microprocessor which monitors the operation of the system. It checks this system every time the vehicle is started, causing the AIRBAG light to go on, then off, if the system is operating properly. If there is a fault in the system, the light will go on and stay on and the ACM will store fault codes indicating the nature of the fault. If the AIRBAG light does go on and stay on, the vehicle should be taken to your dealer immediately for service.

28 Wiring diagrams - general information

Refer to illustrations 28.4a, 28.4b and 28.4c

Since it isn't possible to include all wiring diagrams for every year covered by this manual, the following diagrams are those that are typical and most commonly needed.

Prior to troubleshooting any circuits, check the fuse and circuit breakers (if equipped) to make sure they're in good condition. Make sure the battery is properly charged and check the cable connections (see Chapter 1).

When checking a circuit, make sure that all connectors are clean, with no broken or loose terminals. When unplugging a connector, do not pull on the wires. Pull only on the connector housings themselves.

Refer to the accompanying table and legend for the wire color codes applicable to your vehicle **(see illustrations)**.

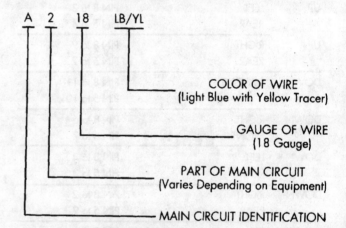

28.4a Wire color code identification key

COLOR CODE	COLOR	STANDARD TRACER COLOR	COLOR CODE	COLOR	STANDARD TRACER CODE
BL	BLUE	WT	OR	ORANGE	BK
BK	BLACK	WT	PK	PINK	BK OR WT
BR	BROWN	WT	RD	RED	WT
DB	DARK BLUE	WT	TN	TAN	WT
DG	DARK GREEN	WT	VT	VIOLET	WT
GY	GRAY	BK	WT	WHITE	BK
LB	LIGHT BLUE	BK	YL	YELLOW	BK
LG	LIGHT GREEN	BK	*	WITH TRACER	

28.4b Wire color code chart

LEGEND OF SYMBOLS USED ON WIRING DIAGRAMS

Symbol	Description	Symbol	Description
+	POSITIVE		BY-DIRECTIONAL ZENER DIODE
−	NEGATIVE		MOTOR
	GROUND		ARMATURE AND BRUSHES
	FUSE	C100	CONNECTOR IDENTIFICATION
	GANG FUSES WITH BUSS BAR		MALE CONNECTOR
	CIRCUIT BREAKER		FEMALE CONNECTOR
	CAPACITOR		DENOTES WIRE CONTINUES ELSEWHERE
Ω	OHMS		DENOTES WIRE GOES TO ONE OF TWO CIRCUITS
	RESISTOR		SPLICE
	VARIABLE RESISTOR	S100	SPLICE IDENTIFICATION
	SERIES RESISTOR		THERMAL ELEMENT
	COIL	TIMER	TIMER
	STEP UP COIL		MULTIPLE CONNECTOR
	OPEN CONTACT		OPTIONAL — WIRING WITH / WIRING WITHOUT
	CLOSED CONTACT		"Y" WINDINGS
	CLOSED SWITCH	88:88	DIGITAL READOUT
	OPEN SWITCH		SINGLE FILAMENT LAMP
	CLOSED GANGED SWITCH		DUAL FILAMENT LAMP
	OPEN GANGED SWITCH		L.E.D. — LIGHT EMITTING DIODE
	TWO POLE SINGLE THROW SWITCH		THERMISTOR
	PRESSURE SWITCH		GAUGE
	SOLENOID SWITCH		SENSOR
	MERCURY SWITCH		FUEL INJECTOR
	DIODE OR RECTIFIER		

28.4c Wiring diagram symbol legend

12

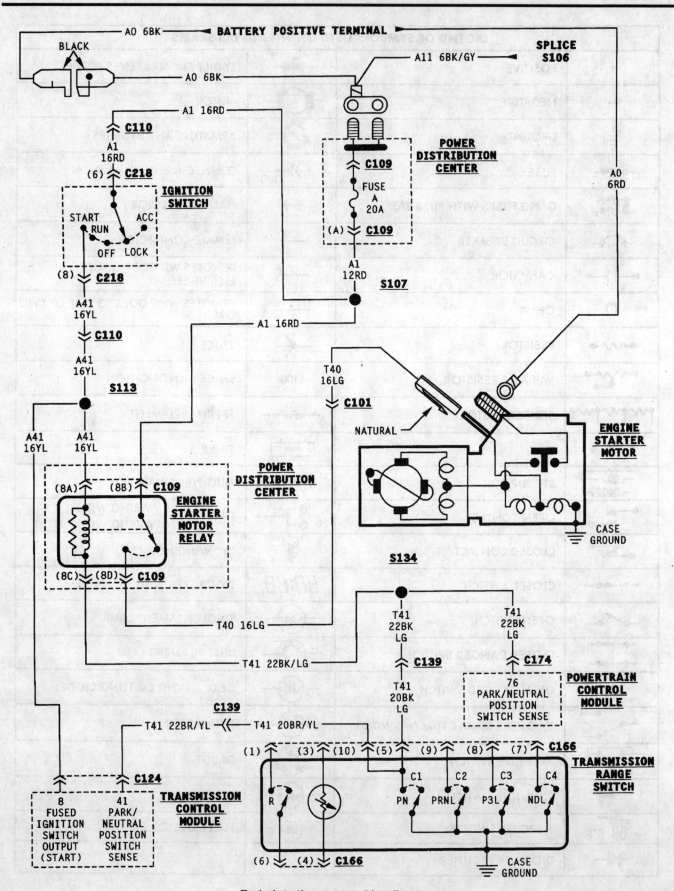

Typical starting system wiring diagram

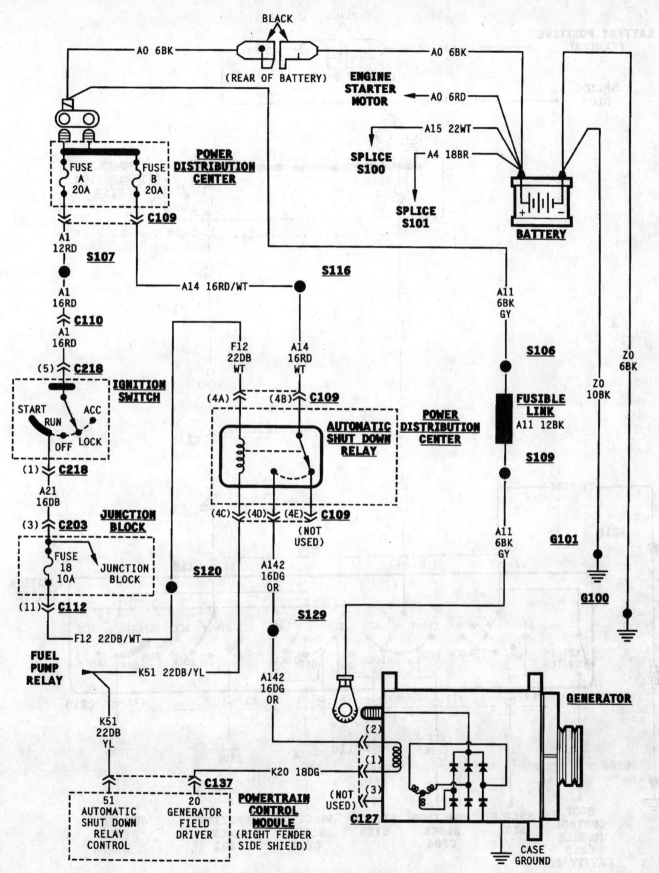

Typical charging system wiring diagram

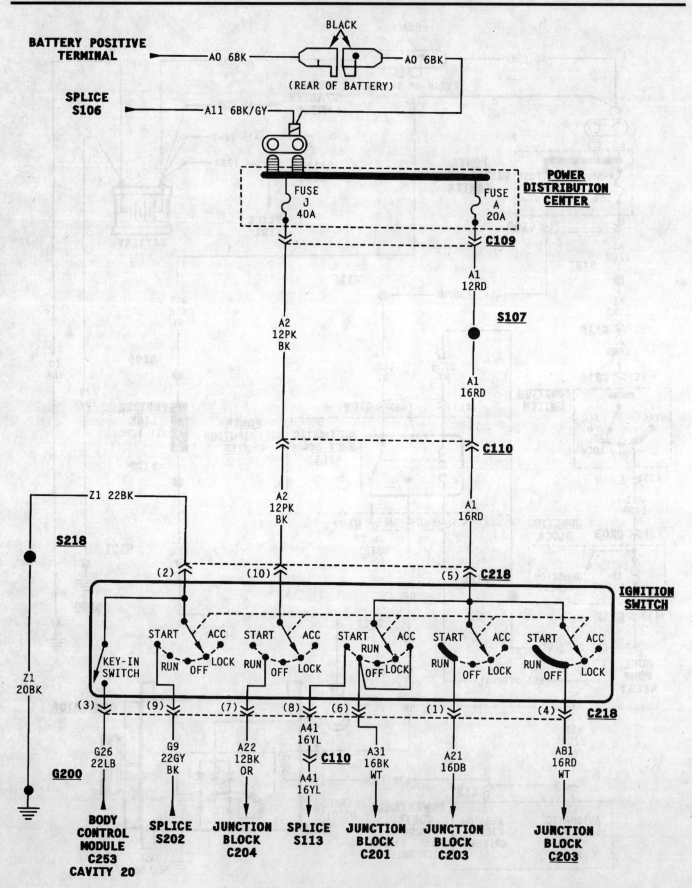

Typical ignition switch wiring diagram

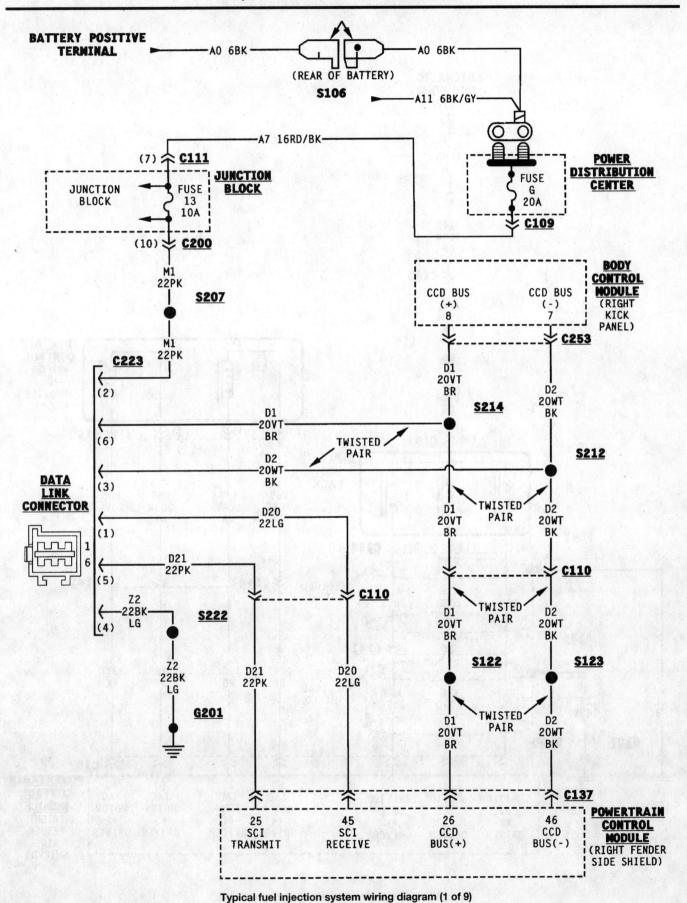

Typical fuel injection system wiring diagram (1 of 9)

12

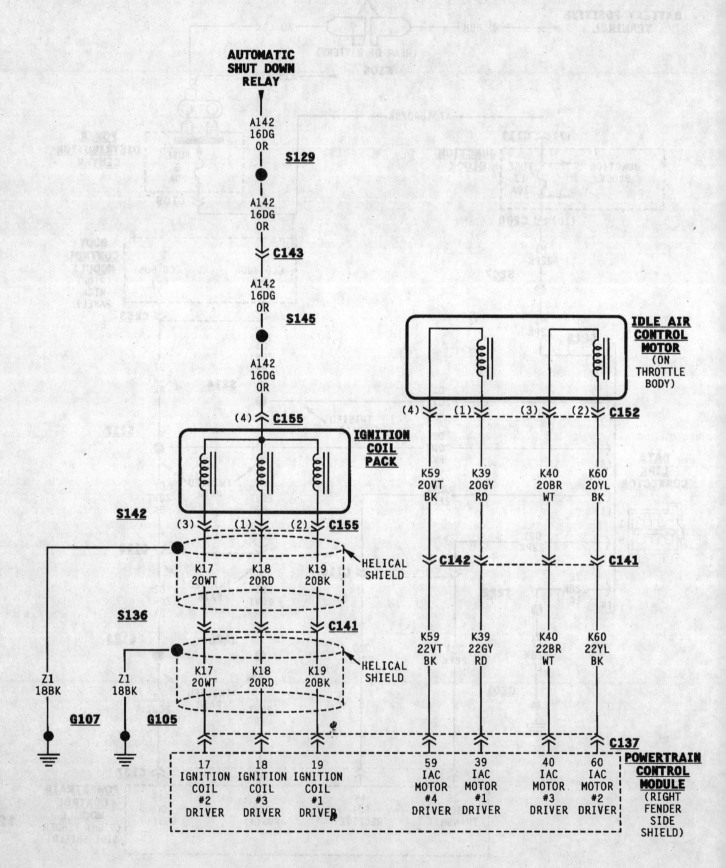

Typical fuel injection system wiring diagram (2 of 9)

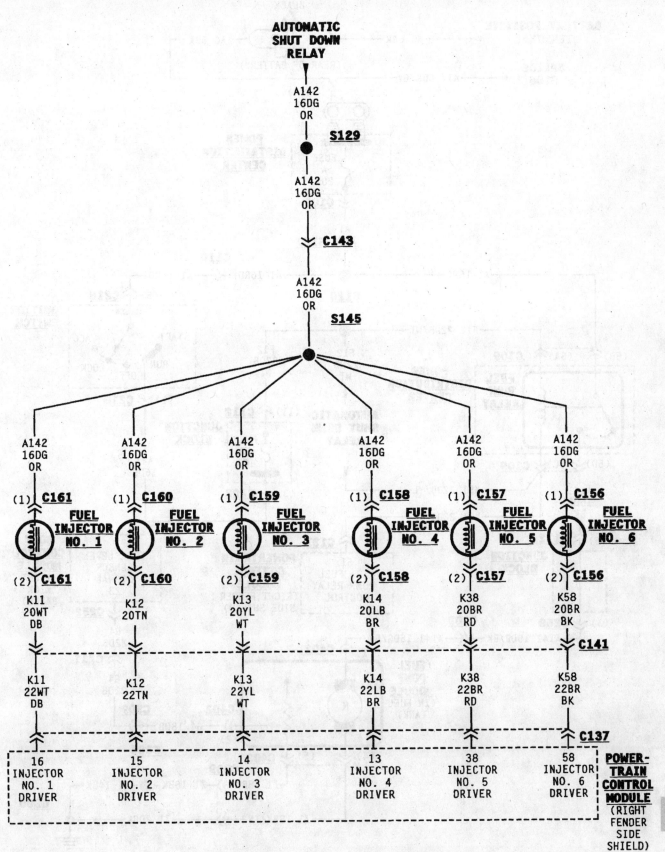

Typical fuel injection system wiring diagram (3 of 9)

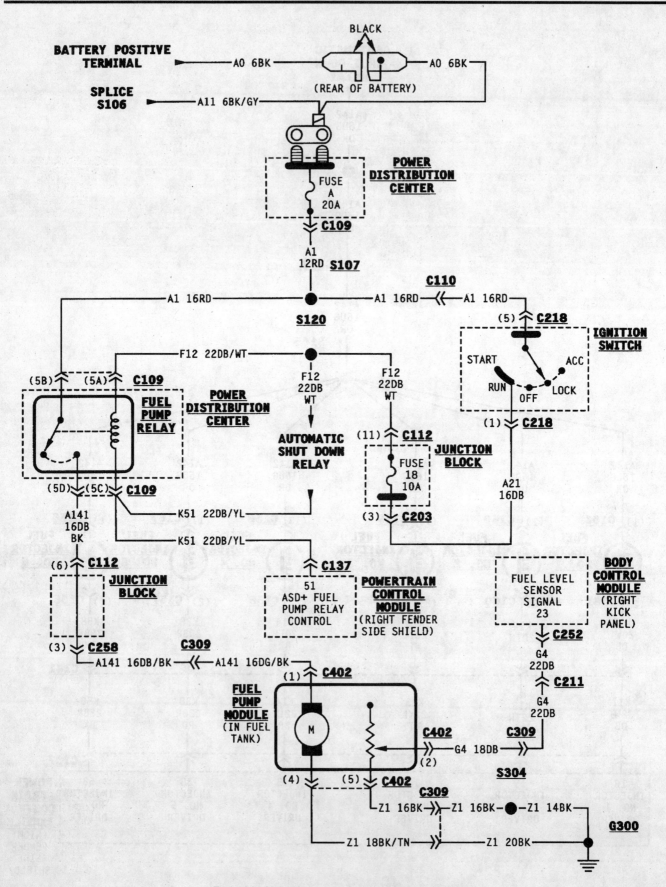

Typical fuel injection system wiring diagram (4 of 9)

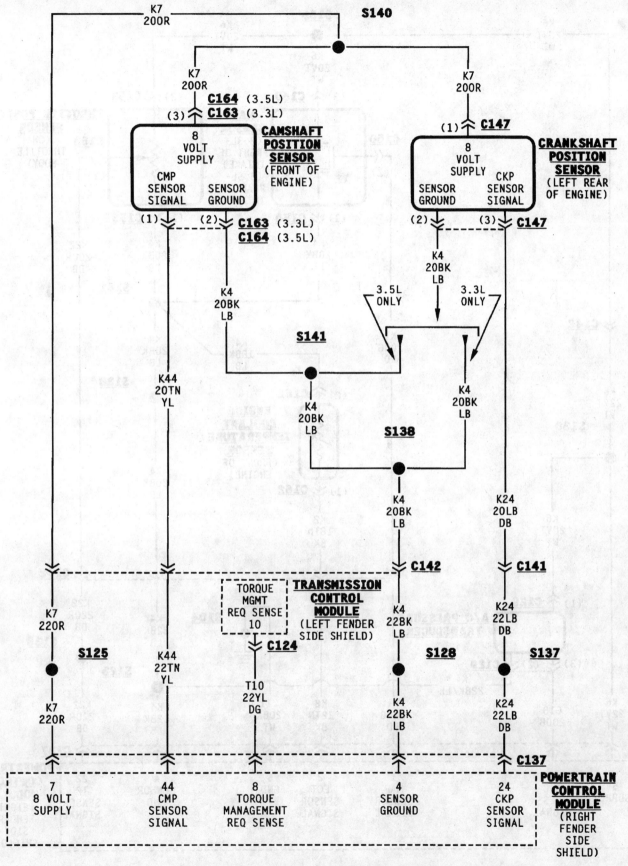

Typical fuel injection system wiring diagram (5 of 9)

12

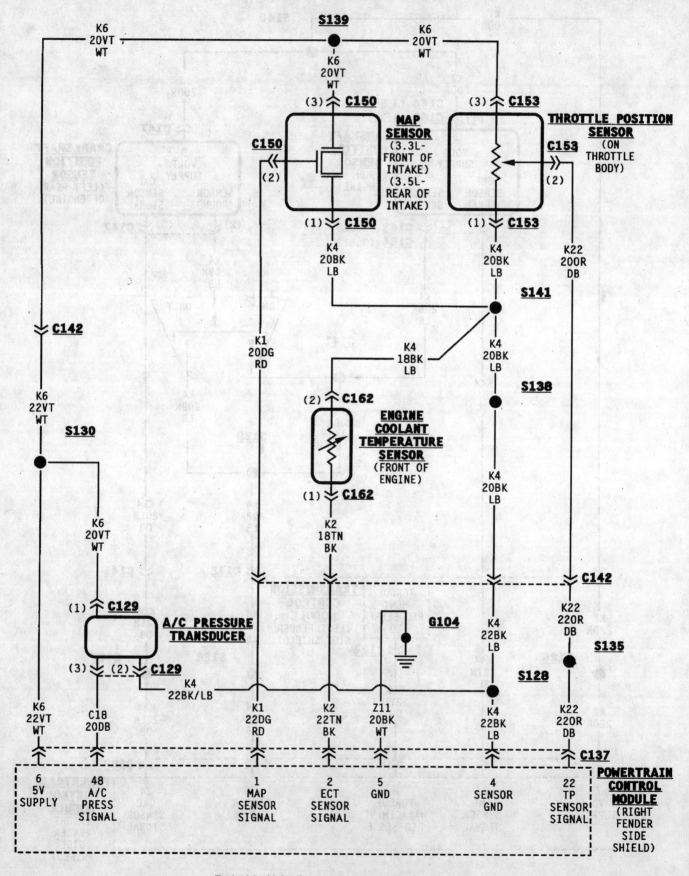

Typical fuel injection system wiring diagram (6 of 9)

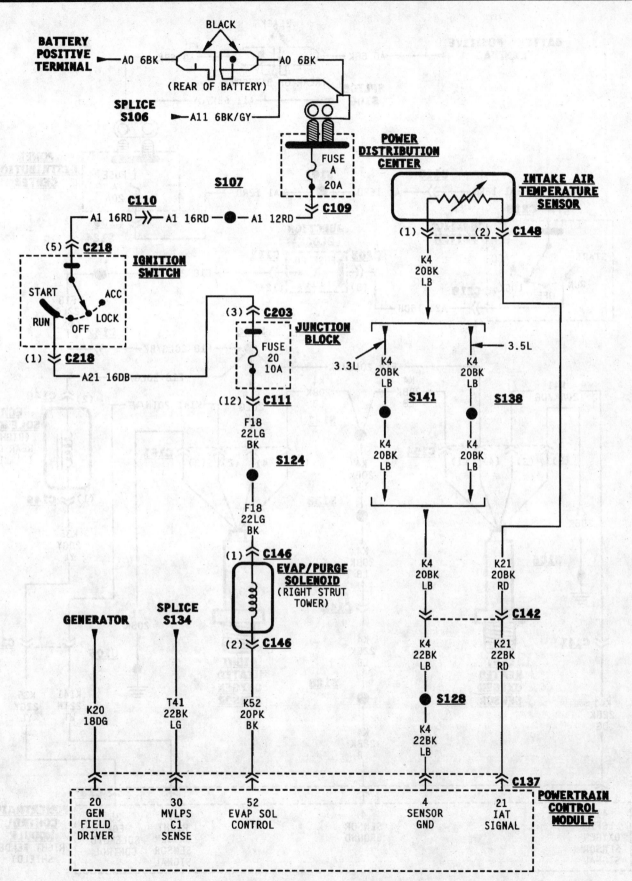

Typical fuel injection system wiring diagram (7 of 9)

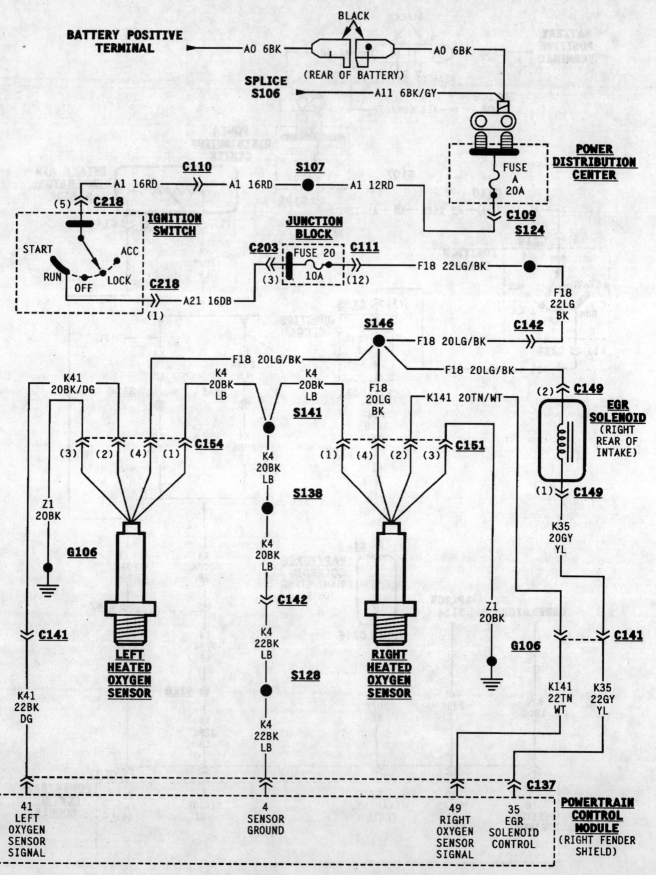

Typical fuel injection system wiring diagram (8 of 9)

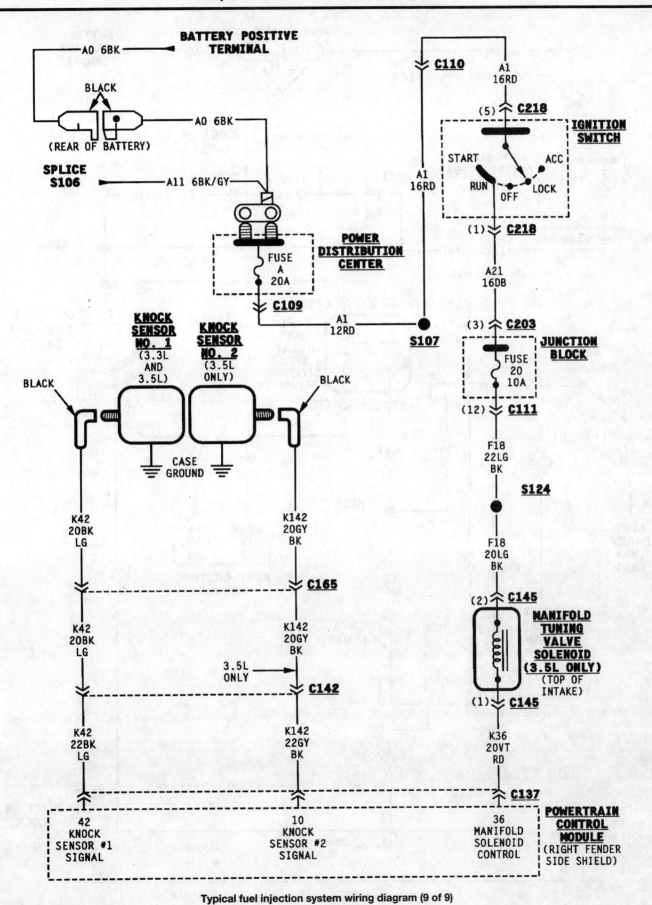

Typical fuel injection system wiring diagram (9 of 9)

12

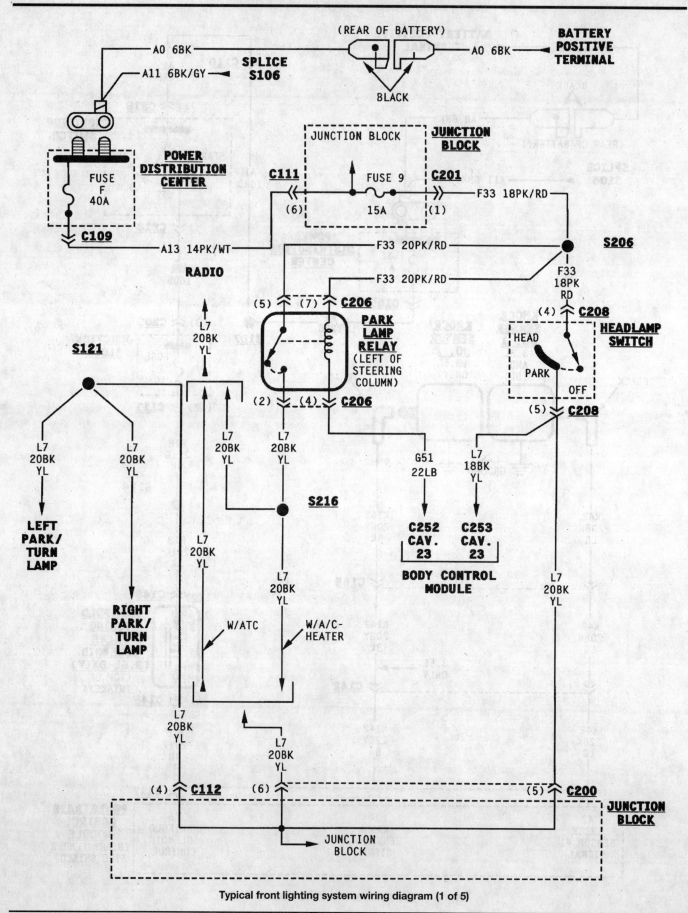

Typical front lighting system wiring diagram (1 of 5)

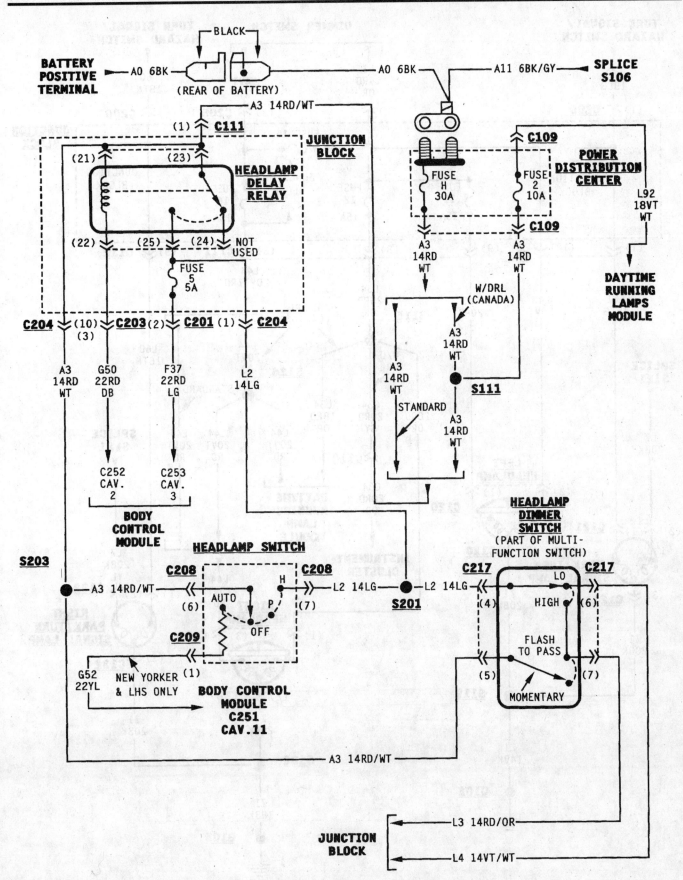

Typical front lighting system wiring diagram (2 of 5)

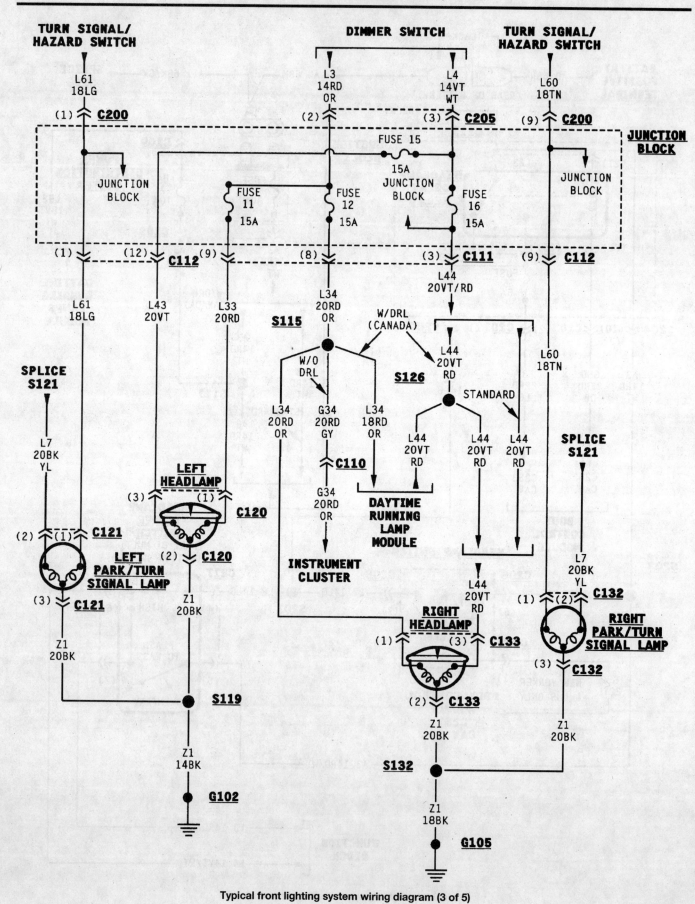

Typical front lighting system wiring diagram (3 of 5)

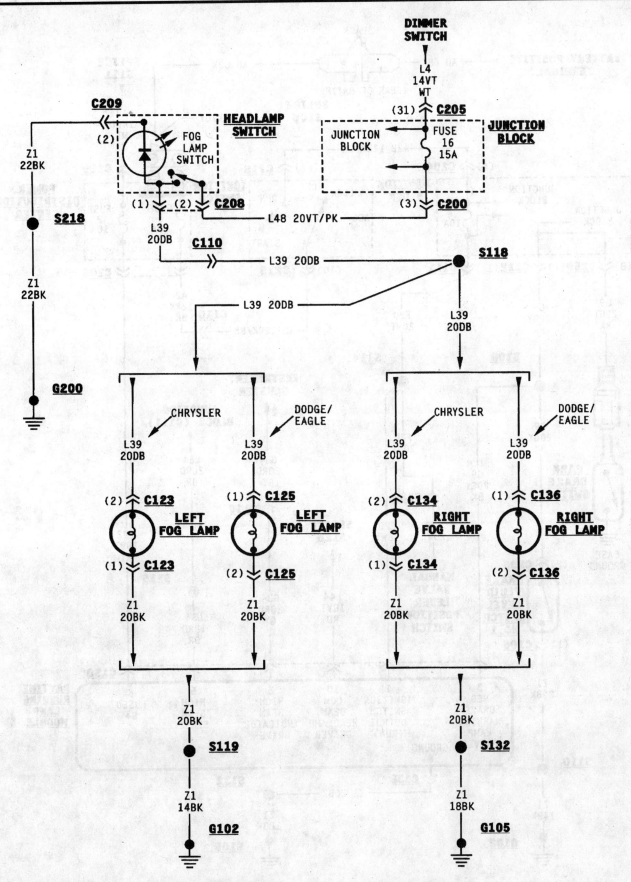

Typical front lighting system wiring diagram (4 of 5)

12

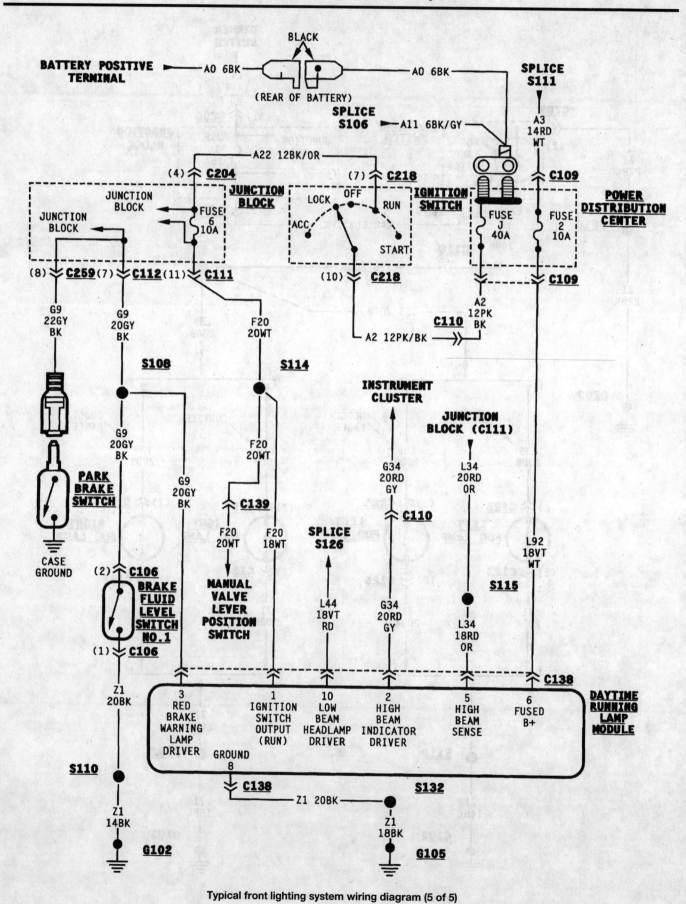

Typical front lighting system wiring diagram (5 of 5)

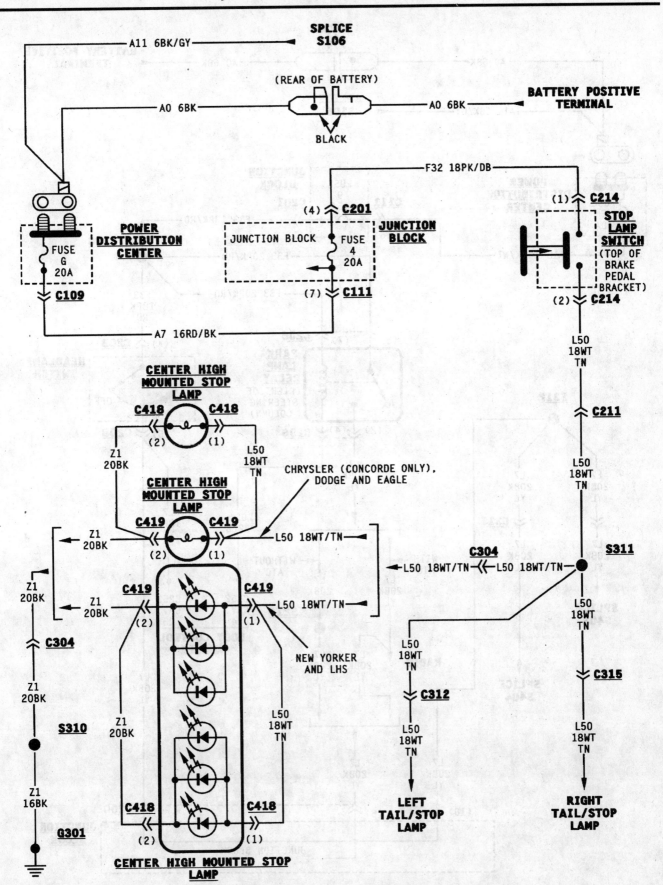

Typical rear lighting system wiring diagram (1 of 5)

12

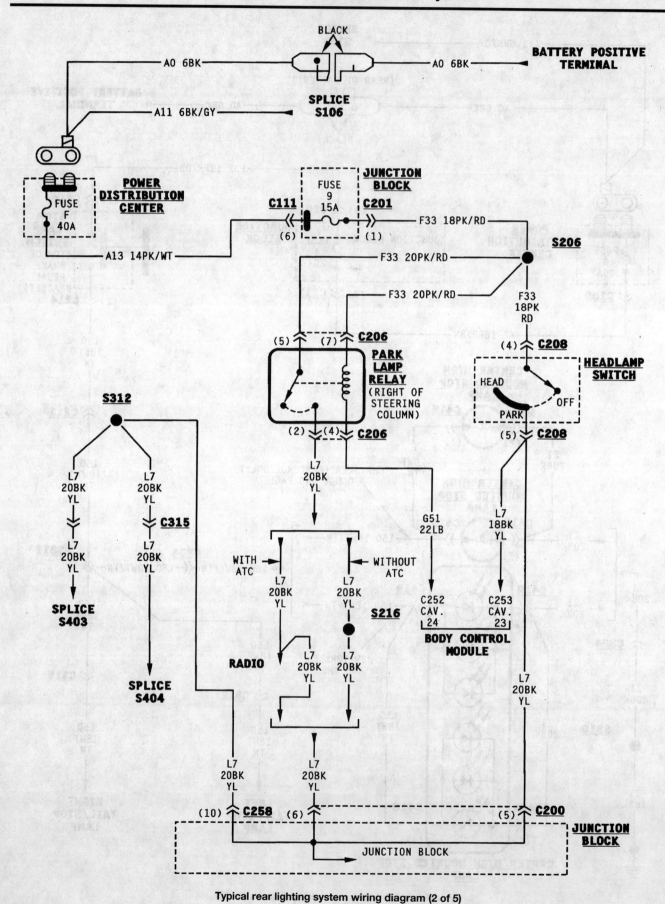

Typical rear lighting system wiring diagram (2 of 5)

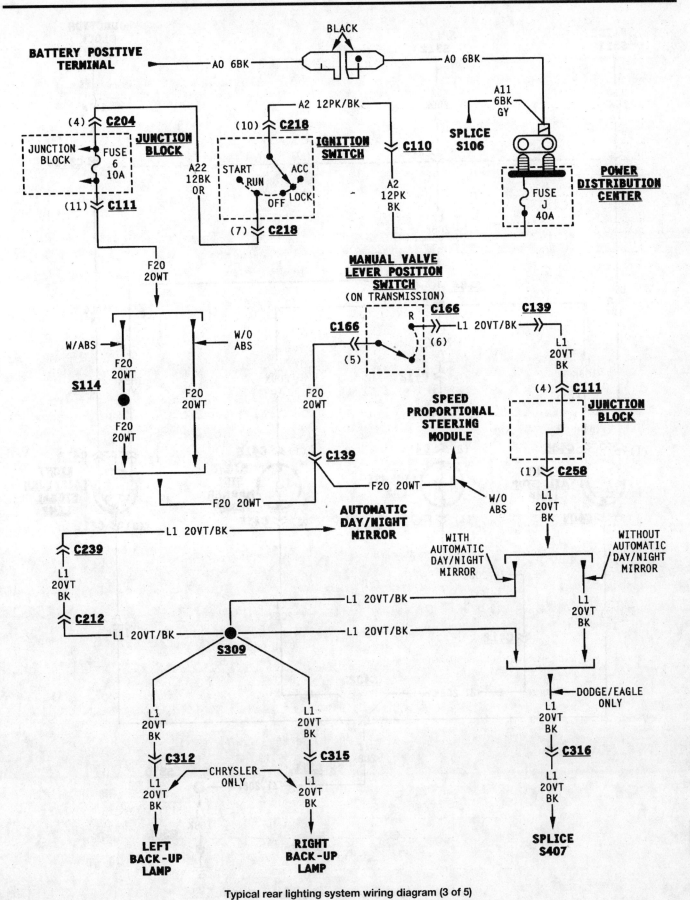

Typical rear lighting system wiring diagram (3 of 5)

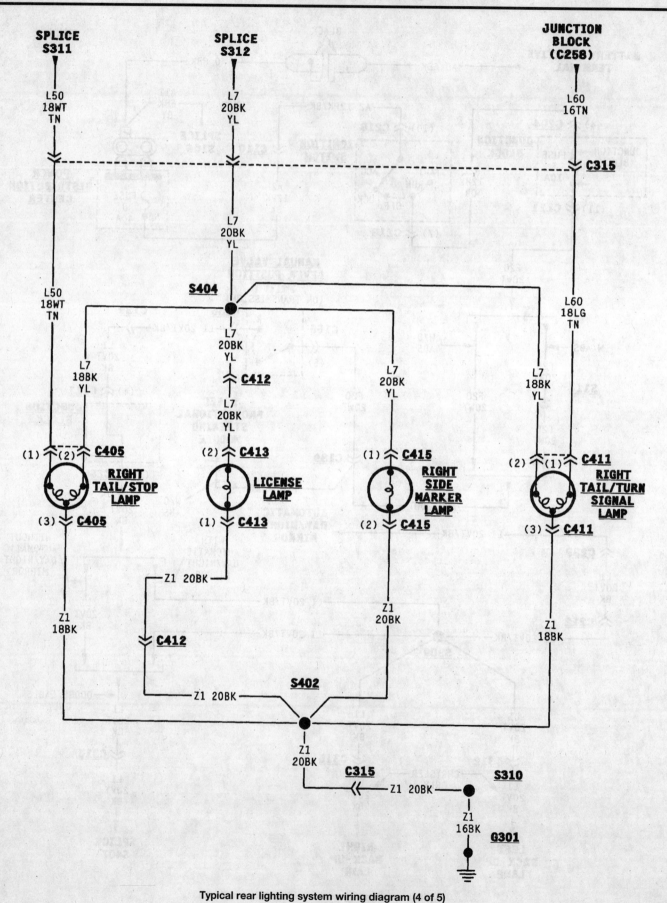

Typical rear lighting system wiring diagram (4 of 5)

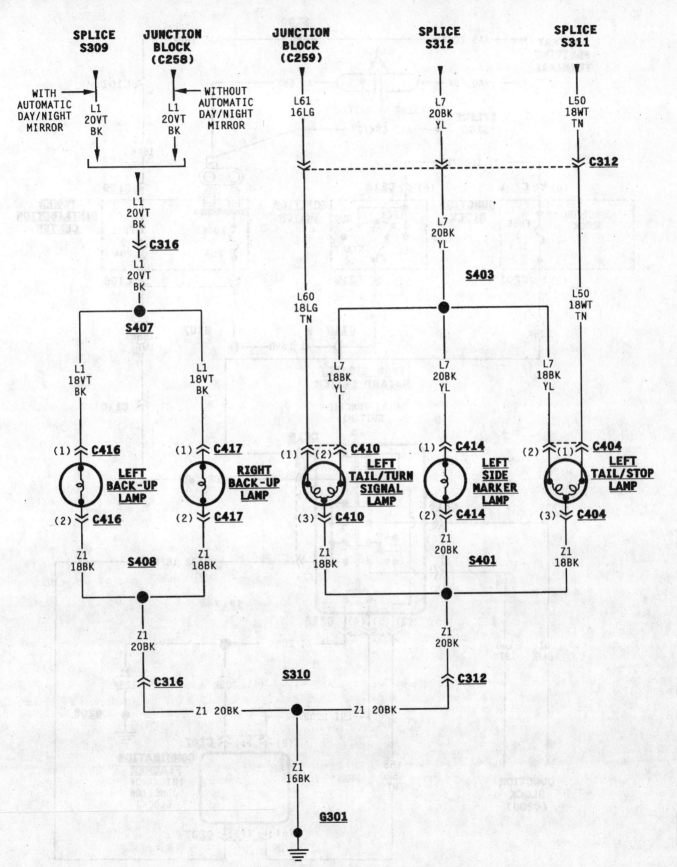

Typical rear lighting system wiring diagram (5 of 5)

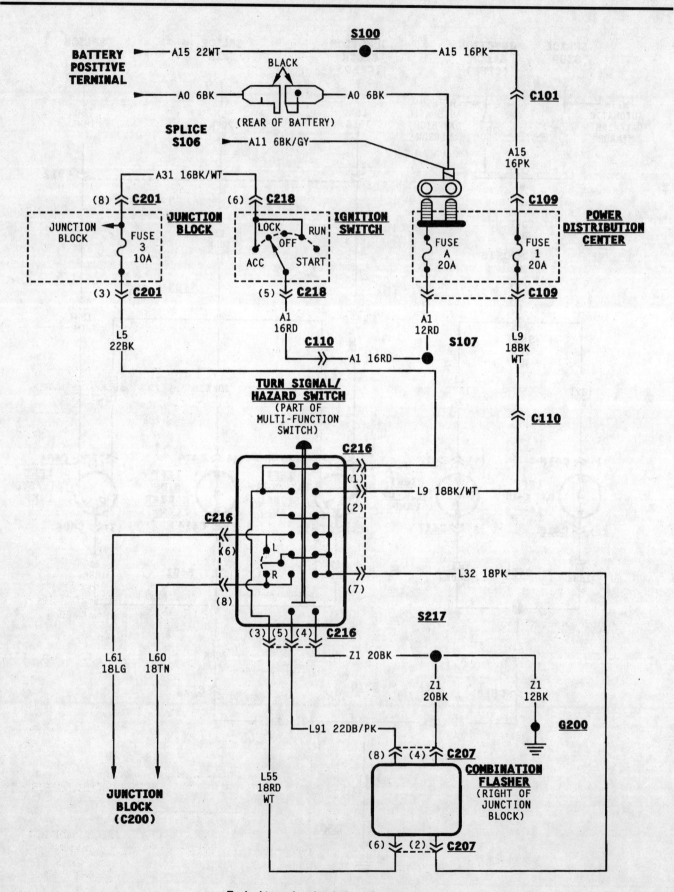

Typical turn signal switch wiring diagram

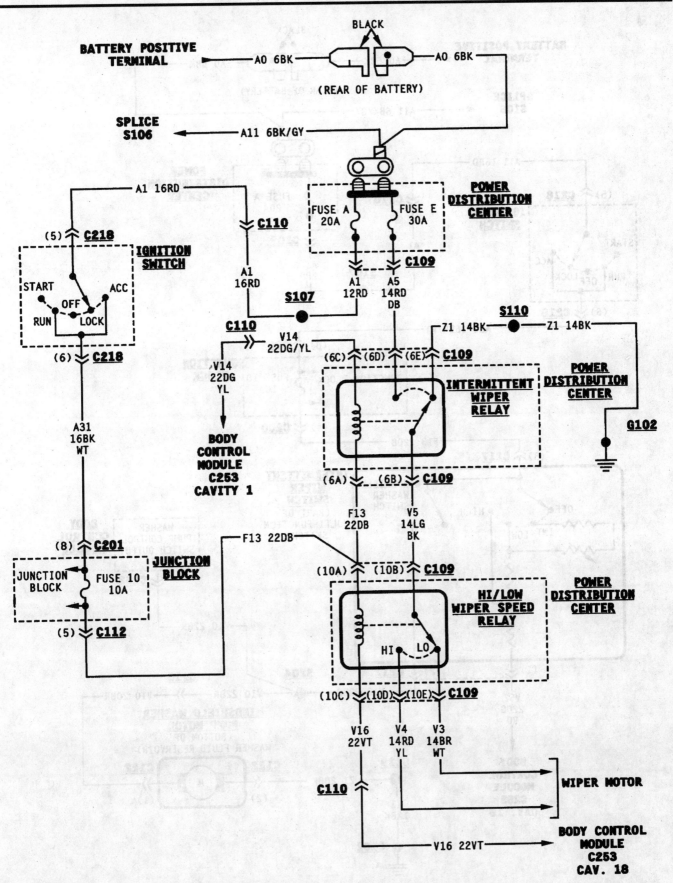

Typical windshield wiper system wiring diagram (1 of 3)

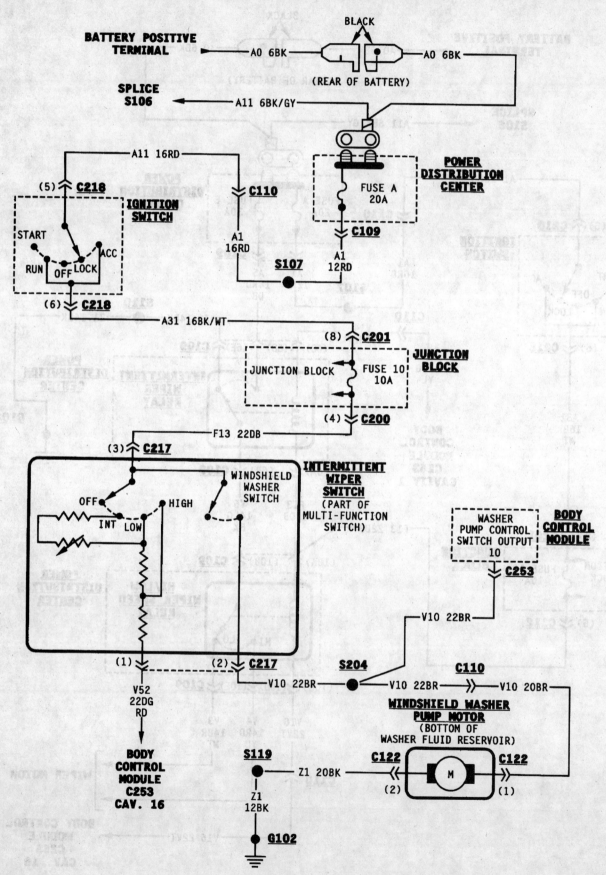

Typical windshield wiper system wiring diagram (2 of 3)

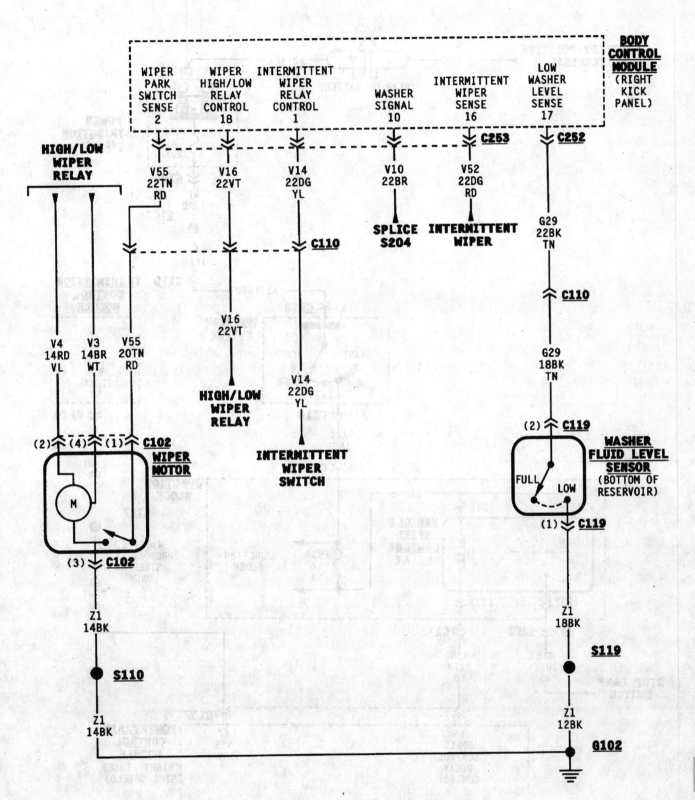

Typical windshield wiper system wiring diagram (3 of 3)

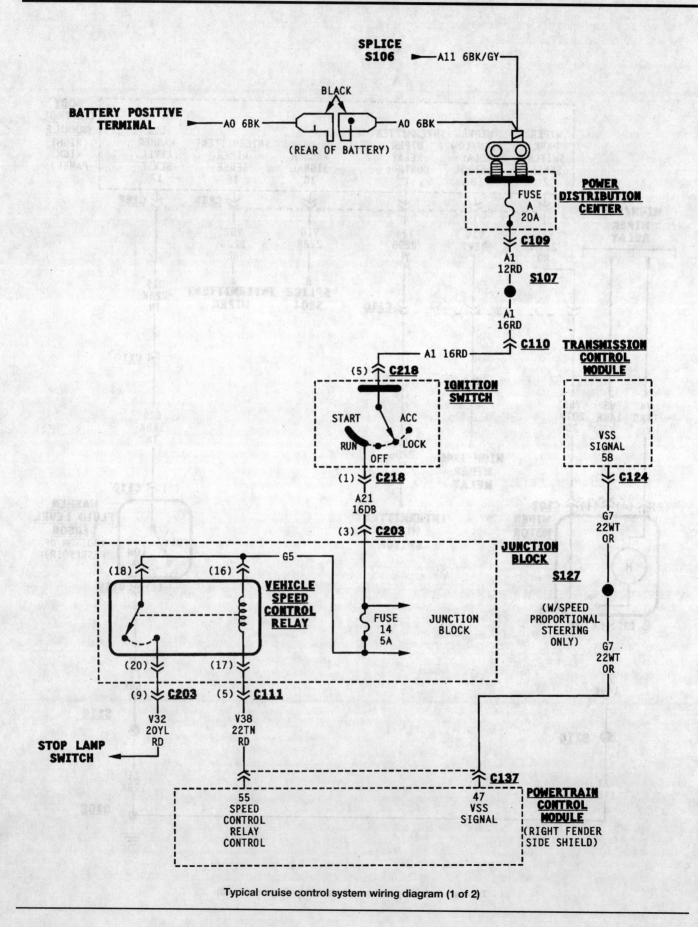

Typical cruise control system wiring diagram (1 of 2)

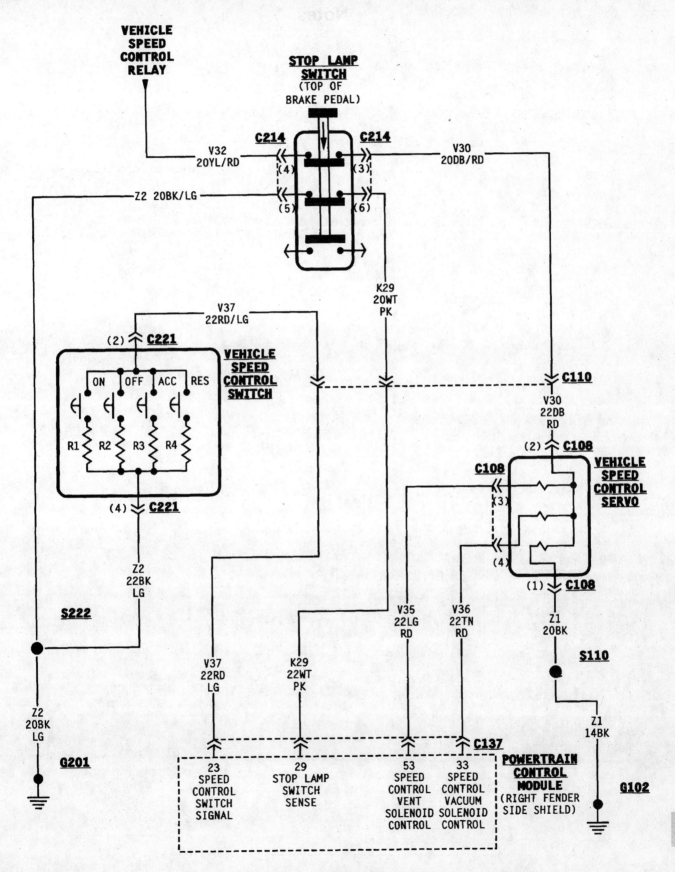

Typical cruise control system wiring diagram (2 of 2)

Notes

Index

Haynes Automotive Manuals

NOTE: New manuals are added to this list on a periodic basis. If you do not see a listing for your vehicle,
consult your local Haynes dealer for the latest product information.

ACURA
*1776 **Integra** '86 thru '89 **& Legend** '86 thru '90

AMC
Jeep CJ - see JEEP (412)
694 **Mid-size models,** Concord,
Hornet, Gremlin & Spirit '70 thru '83
934 **(Renault) Alliance & Encore** '83 thru '87

AUDI
615 **4000** all models '80 thru '87
428 **5000** all models '77 thru '83
1117 **5000** all models '84 thru '88

AUSTIN-HEALEY
Sprite - see MG Midget (265)

BMW
*2020 **3/5 Series** not including diesel or
all-wheel drive models '82 thru '92
276 **320i** all 4 cyl models '75 thru '83
632 **528i & 530i** all models '75 thru '80
240 **1500 thru 2002** except Turbo '59 thru '77

BUICK
Century (front wheel drive) - see GM (829)
*1627 **Buick, Oldsmobile & Pontiac Full-size
(Front wheel drive)** all models '85 thru '95
Buick Electra, LeSabre and Park Avenue;
Oldsmobile Delta 88 Royale, Ninety Eight
and Regency; **Pontiac** Bonneville
1551 **Buick Oldsmobile & Pontiac Full-size
(Rear wheel drive)**
Buick Estate '70 thru '90, Electra '70 thru '84,
LeSabre '70 thru '85, Limited '74 thru '79
Oldsmobile Custom Cruiser '70 thru '90,
Delta 88 '70 thru '85,Ninety-eight '70 thru '84
Pontiac Bonneville '70 thru '81,
Catalina '70 thru '81, Grandville '70 thru '75,
Parisienne '83 thru '86
627 **Mid-size Regal & Century** all rear-drive
models with V6, V8 and Turbo '74 thru '87
Regal - see GENERAL MOTORS (1671)
Riviera - see GENERAL MOTORS (38030)
Skyhawk - see GENERAL MOTORS (766)
Skylark '80 thru '85 - see GM (38020)
Skylark '86 on - see GM (1420)
Somerset - see GENERAL MOTORS (1420)

CADILLAC
*751 **Cadillac Rear Wheel Drive**
all gasoline models '70 thru '93
Cimarron - see GENERAL MOTORS (766)
Eldorado - see GENERAL MOTORS (38030)
Seville '80 thru '85 - see GM (38030)

CHEVROLET
*1477 **Astro & GMC Safari Mini-vans** '85 thru '93
554 **Camaro V8** all models '70 thru '81
866 **Camaro** all models '82 thru '92
Cavalier - see GENERAL MOTORS (766)
Celebrity - see GENERAL MOTORS (829)
24017 **Camaro & Firebird** '93 thru '96
625 **Chevelle, Malibu & El Camino** all V6 &
V8 models '69 thru '87
449 **Chevette & Pontiac T1000** '76 thru '87
550 **Citation** all models '80 thru '85
*1628 **Corsica/Beretta** all models '87 thru '96
274 **Corvette** all V8 models '68 thru '82
*1336 **Corvette** all models '84 thru '91
1762 **Chevrolet Engine Overhaul Manual**
704 **Full-size Sedans** Caprice, Impala, Biscayne,
Bel Air & Wagons '69 thru '90
Lumina - see GENERAL MOTORS (1671)
Lumina APV - see GENERAL MOTORS (2035)
319 **Luv Pick-up** all 2WD & 4WD '72 thru '82
626 **Monte Carlo** all models '70 thru '88

241 **Nova** all V8 models '69 thru '79
*1642 **Nova and Geo Prizm** all front wheel drive
models, '85 thru '92
420 **Pick-ups '67 thru '87** - Chevrolet & GMC,
all V8 & in-line 6 cyl, 2WD & 4WD '67 thru '87;
Suburbans, Blazers & Jimmys '67 thru '91
*1664 **Pick-ups '88 thru '95** - Chevrolet & GMC,
all full-size pick-ups, '88 thru '95; Blazer &
Jimmy '92 thru '94; Suburban '92 thru '95;
Tahoe & Yukon '95
831 **S-10 & GMC S-15 Pick-ups** '82 thru '93
*24071 **S-10 & GMC S-15 Pick-ups** '94 thru '96
*1727 **Sprint & Geo Metro** '85 thru '94
*345 **Vans - Chevrolet & GMC,** V8 & in-line
6 cylinder models '68 thru '96

CHRYSLER
25025 **Chrysler Concorde, New Yorker & LHS,
Dodge** Intrepid, **Eagle** Vision, '93 thru '96
2114 **Chrysler Engine Overhaul Manual**
*2058 **Full-size Front-Wheel Drive** '88 thru '93
K-Cars - see DODGE Aries (723)
Laser - see DODGE Daytona (1140)
*1337 **Chrysler & Plymouth Mid-size**
front wheel drive '82 thru '95
Rear-wheel Drive - see Dodge (2098)

DATSUN
647 **200SX** all models '80 thru '83
228 **B - 210** all models '73 thru '78
525 **210** all models '79 thru '82
206 **240Z, 260Z & 280Z** Coupe '70 thru '78
563 **280ZX** Coupe & 2+2 '79 thru '83
300ZX - see NISSAN (1137)
679 **310** all models '78 thru '82
123 **510 & PL521 Pick-up** '68 thru '73
430 **510** all models '78 thru '81
372 **610** all models '72 thru '76
277 **620 Series Pick-up** all models '73 thru '79
720 Series Pick-up - see NISSAN (771)
376 **810/Maxima** all gasoline models, '77 thru '84
Pulsar - see NISSAN (876)
Sentra - see NISSAN (982)
Stanza - see NISSAN (981)

DODGE
400 & 600 - see CHRYSLER Mid-size (1337)
*723 **Aries & Plymouth Reliant** '81 thru '89
1231 **Caravan & Plymouth Voyager Mini-Vans**
all models '84 thru '95
699 **Challenger/Plymouth Saporro** '78 thru '83
Challenger '67-'76 - see DODGE Dart (234)
610 **Colt & Plymouth Champ** (front wheel drive)
all models '78 thru '87
*1668 **Dakota Pick-ups** all models '87 thru '96
234 **Dart, Challenger/Plymouth Barracuda &
Valiant** 6 cyl models '67 thru '76
*1140 **Daytona & Chrysler Laser** '84 thru '89
Intrepid - see CHRYSLER (25025)
*30034 **Neon** all models '94 thru '97
*545 **Omni & Plymouth Horizon** '78 thru '90
*912 **Pick-ups** all full-size models '74 thru '93
*30041 **Pick-ups** all full-size models '94 thru '96
*556 **Ram 50/D50 Pick-ups & Raider and
Plymouth Arrow Pick-ups** '79 thru '93
2098 **Dodge/Plymouth/Chrysler** rear wheel
drive '71 thru '89
*1726 **Shadow & Plymouth Sundance** '87 thru '94
*1779 **Spirit & Plymouth Acclaim** '89 thru '95
*349 **Vans - Dodge & Plymouth**
V8 & 6 cyl models '71 thru '96

EAGLE
Talon - see Mitsubishi Eclipse (2097)
Vision - see CHRYSLER (25025)

FIAT
094 **124 Sport Coupe & Spider** '68 thru '78
273 **X1/9** all models '74 thru '80

FORD
10355 **Ford Automatic Trans. Overhaul**
*1476 **Aerostar Mini-vans** all models '86 thru '96

268 **Courier Pick-up** all models '72 thru '82
2105 **Crown Victoria & Mercury Grand
Marquis** '88 thru '96
1763 **Ford Engine Overhaul Manual**
789 **Escort/Mercury Lynx** all models '81 thru '90
*2046 **Escort/Mercury Tracer** '91 thru '96
*2021 **Explorer & Mazda Navajo** '91 thru '95
560 **Fairmont & Mercury Zephyr** '78 thru '83
334 **Fiesta** all models '77 thru '80
754 **Ford & Mercury Full-size,**
Ford LTD & Mercury Marquis ('75 thru '82);
Ford Custom 500,Country Squire, Crown
Victoria & Mercury Colony Park ('75 thru '87);
Ford LTD Crown Victoria &
Mercury Gran Marquis ('83 thru '87)
359 **Granada & Mercury Monarch** all in-line,
6 cyl & V8 models '75 thru '80
773 **Ford & Mercury Mid-size,**
Ford Thunderbird & Mercury
Cougar ('75 thru '82);
Ford LTD & Mercury Marquis ('83 thru '86);
Ford Torino,Gran Torino, Elite, Ranchero
pick-up, LTD II, Mercury Montego, Comet,
XR-7 & Lincoln Versailles ('75 thru '86)
231 **Mustang II** 4 cyl, V6 & V8 models '74 thru '78
357 **Mustang V8** all models '64-1/2 thru '73
*654 **Mustang & Mercury Capri** all models
Mustang, '79 thru '93; Capri, '79 thru '86
*36051 **Mustang** all models '94 thru '97
788 **Pick-ups & Bronco** '73 thru '79
*880 **Pick-ups & Bronco** '80 thru '96
649 **Pinto & Mercury Bobcat** '75 thru '80
1670 **Probe** all models '89 thru '92
*1026 **Ranger/Bronco II** gasoline models '83 thru '92
*36071 **Ranger** '93 thru '96 &
Mazda Pick-ups '94 thru '96
*1421 **Taurus & Mercury Sable** '86 thru '95
*1418 **Tempo & Mercury Topaz** all gasoline
models '84 thru '94
1338 **Thunderbird/Mercury Cougar** '83 thru '88
*1725 **Thunderbird/Mercury Cougar** '89 and '96
344 **Vans** all V8 Econoline models '69 thru '91
*2119 **Vans** full size '92-'95

GENERAL MOTORS
*10360 **GM Automatic Transmission Overhaul**
*829 **Buick Century, Chevrolet Celebrity,
Oldsmobile Cutlass Ciera & Pontiac 6000**
all models '82 thru '96
*1671 **Buick Regal, Chevrolet Lumina,
Oldsmobile Cutlass Supreme &
Pontiac Grand Prix** front wheel drive
models '88 thru '95
*766 **Buick Skyhawk, Cadillac Cimarron,
Chevrolet Cavalier, Oldsmobile Firenza &
Pontiac J-2000 & Sunbird** '82 thru '94
38020 **Buick Skylark, Chevrolet Citation,
Olds Omega, Pontiac Phoenix** '80 thru '85
1420 **Buick Skylark & Somerset,
Oldsmobile Achieva & Calais and
Pontiac Grand Am** all models '85 thru '95
38030 **Cadillac Eldorado** '71 thru '85,
Seville '80 thru '85,
Oldsmobile Toronado '71 thru '85
& Buick Riviera '79 thru '85
*2035 **Chevrolet Lumina APV, Olds Silhouette
& Pontiac Trans Sport** all models '90 thru '95
**General Motors Full-size
Rear-wheel Drive** - see BUICK (1551)

GEO
Metro - see CHEVROLET Sprint (1727)
Prizm - '85 thru '92 see CHEVY NOVA (1642),
'93 thru '96 see TOYOTA Corolla (1642)
*2039 **Storm** all models '90 thru '93
Tracker - see SUZUKI Samurai (1626)

GMC
Safari - see CHEVROLET ASTRO (1477)
Vans & Pick-ups - see CHEVROLET
(420, 831, 345, 1664 & 24071)

(Continued on other side)

---

*Listings shown with an asterisk (*) indicate model coverage as of this printing. These titles will be periodically updated to include later model years - consult your
Haynes dealer for more information.*

Haynes North America, Inc., 861 Lawrence Drive, Newbury Park, CA 91320 • (805) 498-6703

Haynes Automotive Manuals (continued)

NOTE: New manuals are added to this list on a periodic basis. If you do not see a listing for your vehicle, consult your local Haynes dealer for the latest product information.

HONDA

351	**Accord CVCC** all models '76 thru '83	
1221	**Accord** all models '84 thru '89	
2067	**Accord** all models '90 thru '93	
42013	**Accord** all models '94 thru '95	
160	**Civic 1200** all models '73 thru '79	
633	**Civic 1300 & 1500 CVCC** '80 thru '83	
297	**Civic 1500 CVCC** all models '75 thru '79	
1227	**Civic** all models '84 thru '91	
*2118	**Civic & del Sol** '92 thru '95	
*601	**Prelude CVCC** all models '79 thru '89	

HYUNDAI

*1552	**Excel** all models '86 thru '94	

ISUZU

*1641	**Trooper & Pick-up,** all gasoline models Pick-up, '81 thru '93; Trooper, '84 thru '91	
	Hombre - see CHEVROLET S-10 (24071)	

JAGUAR

*242	**XJ6** all 6 cyl models '68 thru '86	
*49011	**XJ6** all models '88 thru '94	
*478	**XJ12 & XJS** all 12 cyl models '72 thru '85	

JEEP

*1553	**Cherokee, Comanche & Wagoneer Limited** all models '84 thru '96	
412	**CJ** all models '49 thru '86	
50025	**Grand Cherokee** all models '93 thru '95	
50029	**Grand Wagoneer & Pick-up** '72 thru '91 Grand Wagoneer '84 thru '91, Cherokee & Wagoneer '72 thru '83, Pick-up '72 thru '88	
*1777	**Wrangler** all models '87 thru '95	

LINCOLN

2117	**Rear Wheel Drive** all models '70 thru '96	

MAZDA

648	**626** (rear wheel drive) all models '79 thru '82	
*1082	**626/MX-6** (front wheel drive) '83 thru '91	
370	**GLC Hatchback** (rear wheel drive) '77 thru '83	
757	**GLC** (front wheel drive) '81 thru '85	
*2047	**MPV** all models '89 thru '94	
	Navajo - see Ford Explorer (2021)	
267	**Pick-ups** '72 thru '93	
	Pick-ups '94 thru '96 - see Ford Ranger (36071)	
460	**RX-7** all models '79 thru '85	
*1419	**RX-7** all models '86 thru '91	

MERCEDES-BENZ

*1643	**190 Series** four-cyl gas models, '84 thru '88	
346	**230/250/280** 6 cyl sohc models '68 thru '72	
983	**280 123 Series** gasoline models '77 thru '81	
698	**350 & 450** all models '71 thru '80	
697	**Diesel 123 Series** '76 thru '85	

MERCURY

See FORD Listing

MG

111	**MGB** Roadster & GT Coupe '62 thru '80	
265	**MG Midget, Austin Healey Sprite** '58 thru '80	

MITSUBISHI

*1669	**Cordia, Tredia, Galant, Precis & Mirage** '83 thru '93	
*2097	**Eclipse, Eagle Talon & Plymouth Laser** '90 thru '94	
*2022	**Pick-up** '83 thru '96 & **Montero** '83 thru '93	

NISSAN

1137	**300ZX** all models including Turbo '84 thru '89	
*72015	**Altima** all models '93 thru '97	
*1341	**Maxima** all models '85 thru '91	
*771	**Pick-ups** '80 thru '96 **Pathfinder** '87 thru '95	
876	**Pulsar** all models '83 thru '86	
*982	**Sentra** all models '82 thru '94	
*981	**Stanza** all models '82 thru '90	

OLDSMOBILE

	Achieva - see GENERAL MOTORS (1420)	
	Bravada - see CHEVROLET S-10 (831)	
	Calais - see GENERAL MOTORS (1420)	
	Custom Cruiser - see BUICK RWD (1551)	
*658	**Cutlass** V6 & V8 gas models '74 thru '88	
	Cutlass Ciera - see GENERAL MOTORS (829)	
	Cutlass Supreme - see GM (1671)	
	Delta 88 - see BUICK Full-size RWD (1551)	
	Delta 88 Brougham - see BUICK Full-size FWD (1551), RWD (1627)	
	Delta 88 Royale - see BUICK RWD (1551)	
	Firenza - see GENERAL MOTORS (766)	
	Ninety-eight Regency - see BUICK Full-size RWD (1551), FWD (1627)	
	Ninety-eight Regency Brougham - see BUICK Full-size RWD (1551)	
	Omega - see GENERAL MOTORS (38020)	
	Silhouette - see GENERAL MOTORS (2035)	
	Toronado - see GENERAL MOTORS (38030)	

PEUGEOT

663	**504** all diesel models '74 thru '83	

PLYMOUTH

Laser - see MITSUBISHI Eclipse (2097)
For other PLYMOUTH titles, see DODGE.

PONTIAC

	T1000 - see CHEVROLET Chevette (449)	
	J-2000 - see GENERAL MOTORS (766)	
	6000 - see GENERAL MOTORS (829)	
	Bonneville - see Buick FWD (1627), RWD (1551)	
	Bonneville Brougham - see Buick (1551)	
	Catalina - see Buick Full-size (1551)	
1232	**Fiero** all models '84 thru '88	
555	**Firebird** V8 models except Turbo '70 thru '81	
867	**Firebird** all models '82 thru '92	
	Firebird '93 thru '96 - see CHEVY Camaro (24017)	
	Full-size Front Wheel Drive - see BUICK, Oldsmobile, Pontiac Full-size FWD (1627)	
	Full-size Rear Wheel Drive - see BUICK, Oldsmobile, Pontiac Full-size RWD (1551)	
	Grand Am - see GENERAL MOTORS (1420)	
	Grand Prix - see GENERAL MOTORS (1671)	
	Grandville - see BUICK Full-size (1551)	
	Parisienne - see BUICK Full-size (1551)	
	Phoenix - see GENERAL MOTORS (38020)	
	Sunbird - see GENERAL MOTORS (766)	
	Trans Sport - see GENERAL MOTORS (2035)	

PORSCHE

*264	**911** except Turbo & Carrera 4 '65 thru '89	
239	**914** all 4 cyl models '69 thru '76	
397	**924** all models including Turbo '76 thru '82	
*1027	**944** all models including Turbo '83 thru '89	

RENAULT

141	**5 Le Car** all models '76 thru '83	
	Alliance & Encore - see AMC (934)	

SAAB

247	**99** all models including Turbo '69 thru '80	
*980	**900** all models including Turbo '79 thru '88	

SATURN

2083	**Saturn** all models '91 thru '96	

SUBARU

237	**1100, 1300, 1400 & 1600** '71 thru '79	
*681	**1600 & 1800** 2WD & 4WD '80 thru '89	

SUZUKI

*1626	**Samurai/Sidekick & Geo Tracker** '86 thru '96	

TOYOTA

1023	**Camry** all models '83 thru '91	
92006	**Camry** all models '92 thru '95	
935	**Celica Rear Wheel Drive** '71 thru '85	
*2038	**Celica Front Wheel Drive** '86 thru '93	
1139	**Celica Supra** all models '79 thru '92	
361	**Corolla** all models '75 thru '79	
961	**Corolla** all rear wheel drive models '80 thru '87	
1025	**Corolla** all front wheel drive models '84 thru '92	
*92036	**Corolla & Geo Prizm** '93 thru '96	
636	**Corolla Tercel** all models '80 thru '82	
360	**Corona** all models '74 thru '82	
532	**Cressida** all models '78 thru '82	
313	**Land Cruiser** all models '68 thru '82	
*1339	**MR2** all models '85 thru '87	
304	**Pick-up** all models '69 thru '78	
*656	**Pick-up** all models '79 thru '95	
*2048	**Previa** all models '91 thru '95	
2106	**Tercel** all models '87 thru '94	

TRIUMPH

113	**Spitfire** all models '62 thru '81	
322	**TR7** all models '75 thru '81	

VW

159	**Beetle & Karmann Ghia** '54 thru '79	
238	**Dasher** all gasoline models '74 thru '81	
96017	**Golf & Jetta** all models '93 thru '97	
*884	**Rabbit, Jetta, Scirocco, & Pick-up** gas models '74 thru '91 & Convertible '80 thru '92	
451	**Rabbit, Jetta & Pick-up** diesel '77 thru '84	
082	**Transporter 1600** all models '68 thru '79	
226	**Transporter 1700, 1800 & 2000** '72 thru '79	
084	**Type 3 1500 & 1600** all models '63 thru '73	
1029	**Vanagon** all air-cooled models '80 thru '83	

VOLVO

203	**120, 130 Series & 1800 Sports** '61 thru '73	
129	**140 Series** all models '66 thru '74	
*270	**240 Series** all models '76 thru '93	
400	**260 Series** all models '75 thru '82	
*1550	**740 & 760 Series** all models '82 thru '88	

TECHBOOK MANUALS

2108	**Automotive Computer Codes**	
1667	**Automotive Emissions Control Manual**	
482	**Fuel Injection Manual, 1978 thru 1985**	
2111	**Fuel Injection Manual, 1986 thru 1996**	
2069	**Holley Carburetor Manual**	
2068	**Rochester Carburetor Manual**	
10240	**Weber/Zenith/Stromberg/SU Carburetors**	
1762	**Chevrolet Engine Overhaul Manual**	
2114	**Chrysler Engine Overhaul Manual**	
1763	**Ford Engine Overhaul Manual**	
1736	**GM and Ford Diesel Engine Repair Manual**	
1666	**Small Engine Repair Manual**	
10355	**Ford Automatic Transmission Overhaul**	
10360	**GM Automatic Transmission Overhaul**	
1479	**Automotive Body Repair & Painting**	
2112	**Automotive Brake Manual**	
2113	**Automotive Detailing Manual**	
1654	**Automotive Eelectrical Manual**	
1480	**Automotive Heating & Air Conditioning**	
2109	**Automotive Reference Manual & Dictionary**	
2107	**Automotive Tools Manual**	
10440	**Used Car Buying Guide**	
2110	**Welding Manual**	
10450	**ATV Basics**	

SPANISH MANUALS

98903	**Reparación de Carrocería & Pintura**	
98905	**Códigos Automotrices de la Computadora**	
98910	**Frenos Automotriz**	
98915	**Inyección de Combustible 1986 al 1994**	
99040	**Chevrolet & GMC Camionetas** '67 al '87 Incluye Suburban, Blazer & Jimmy '67 al '91	
99041	**Chevrolet & GMC Camionetas** '88 al '95 Incluye Suburban '92 al '95, Blazer & Jimmy '92 al '94, Tahoe y Yukon '95	
99042	**Chevrolet & GMC Camionetas Cerradas** '68 al '95	
99055	**Dodge Caravan & Plymouth Voyager** '84 al '95	
99075	**Ford Camionetas y Bronco** '80 al '94	
99077	**Ford Camionetas Cerradas** '69 al '91	
99083	**Ford Modelos de Tamaño Grande** '75 al '87	
99088	**Ford Modelos de Tamaño Mediano** '75 al '86	
99095	**GM Modelos de Tamaño Grande** '70 al '90	
99118	**Nissan Sentra** '82 al '94	
99125	**Toyota Camionetas y 4-Runner** '79 al '95	

Over 100 Haynes motorcycle manuals also available

5-97

* Listings shown with an asterisk (*) indicate model coverage as of this printing. These titles will be periodically updated to include later model years - consult your Haynes dealer for more information.

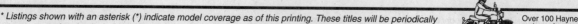

Haynes North America, Inc., 861 Lawrence Drive, Newbury Park, CA 91320 • (805) 498-6703